Outside

MAGAZINE'S

Adventure Guide to the
Pacific Northwest

BY KARL SAMSON

Macmillan • USA

Reader Alert!

Just as we went to press with this book, the National Forest Service announced that it was instituting a fee system for parking at trailheads on Forest Service lands throughout the Northwest and within the Columbia Gorge National Scenic Area. Contact any ranger station in Washington or Oregon for information on permit fees and to find out where you can buy your permit.

MACMILLAN TRAVEL

A Simon & Schuster Macmillan Company
1633 Broadway
New York, NY 10019

Find us online at **http://www.mgr.com/travel** or on America Online at Keyword: **Frommer's**

Find Outside Online at **http://outside. starwave.com**

ISBN 0-02-861160-8
ISSN 1092-2946

Series Editor: Ian Wilker
Cover by Mike Bain, *Outside* Magazine
Design by Amy Peppler Adams, designLab
Digital Cartography by Ortelius Design

Special Sales
Bulk purchases (10+ copies) of Frommer's and selected Macmillan travel guides are available to corporations, organizations, mail-order catalogs, institutions, and charities at special discounts, and can be customized to suit individual needs. For more information write to: Special Sales, Macmillan General Reference, 1633 Broadway, New York, NY 10019.

Manufactured in the United States of America

Karl Samson, who now lives in Oregon, first started backpacking at age 12, canoeing at 14, surfing at 15, sailboarding at 24, and snowboarding at age 34 (you *can* teach an old dog new tricks). He got his start in travel-book writing more than a decade ago when he wrote about Nepal for a guidebook to India and Nepal. Since then he has authored *Frommer's Nepal* and numerous other guidebooks and travel articles that have taken him all over the world. Being chased by a sea snake in the Andaman Sea, struck at by a fer-de-lance in Costa Rica, stalking stinking corpse lilies in Sumatra, riding a camel across India's Thar Desert, and being eyeballed by sharks in Belize are past adventures that sometimes make Northwest outings seem tame by comparison. However, it is still the Northwest, his own backyard, that he finds offers the greatest variety of adventures in the smallest space.

Contents

1 The Basics 1

How to Use This Book 2

Getting Underway 2

Beaches 2
Bird Watching 2
Boardsailing 3
Cross-Country Skiing 3
Downhill Skiing &
  Snowboarding 4
Fishing 5
Hiking &
  Backpacking 5
Horseback Riding 7
Hot Springs 8

Mountain Biking 8
Mountaineering 9
Packstock Trips 9
Road Biking 9
Rock/Ice Climbing 10
Scuba Diving 10
Sea Kayaking & Flat-
  Water Canoeing 11
Snowshoeing 11
Spelunking 12
Surfing 12

Swimming &
  Tubing 12
Walks & Natural
  Roadside
  Attractions 13
Whale Watching 13
Whitewater Kayaking
  & Canoeing 14
Whitewater Rafting 15
Wildlife Viewing 15

Northwest Weather 16

Maps 18

On Camping in the Northwest 19

Schools & Educational Outings 19

Other Useful Addresses & Phone Numbers 20

Features:

◆ *The Ten Essentials 4*
◆ *The Pacific Crest Trail 6*
◆ *The Outdoors on the Wire: Internet Resources 17*

2 The San Juan Islands & Washington's Northwest Coast 21

The Lay of the Land 24

Parks & Other Hot Spots 26

5 The North Cascades 133

The Lay of the Land 134

Parks & Other Hot Spots 136

What to Do & Where to Do It 401

Campgrounds & Other Accommodations 426

Features:

13 The Oregon Coast & Coast Range 430

The Lay of the Land 431

Parks & Other Hot Spots 433

The North Coast (Astoria to Cape Perpetua) ◆ What to Do & Where to Do It 435

The South Coast (Cape Perpetua to the California Line) ◆ What to Do & Where to Do It 451

List of Maps

Map Legend

≡35≡	Interstate highway	▨ Metropolitan area
≡53≡	Primary road	○ ○ City
⊸27⊢A16⊢	Secondary road	↗ Beach
= =A25= =	Unimproved road	⤙ Dam
≡╪≡	Interchange	⅂ Picnic area
·········	Specialized trail	▲ Camping
········	Trail	▲ Peak
�–╁–╁–	Railroad	■ Point of interest
– · – · –	State boundary	▭ ♣ National/State/County park
– – – – – –	County boundary	▭ National/State forest
——————	Park/wilderness area boundary	▭ Indian/military reservation
– – – – – –	Ferry route	✕ ✈ Airstrip/Airport
ⓘ	Information	)(Pass
		⚐ Ski area

Special Thanks

THE CREATION OF THIS BOOK HAS BEEN AN IMMENSE TASK. I FIRST FELL IN LOVE WITH THE Northwest in 1984 and thought I knew a thing or two about outdoor recreation here. I mean, I was out there as much as possible so it seemed that I must know a bit about getting outside in the region. However, in researching this book I found there was a lot I didn't know. I'd like to thank all the people who helped me fill in those gaps in my knowledge. From forest rangers to strangers on trails, I couldn't have done this without lots of help. Among the people deserving of very special thanks are my wife Jane, my brother Eric, Dave Coryell, David Ellis, Sara Intrilligator, Robert Killen, Rebecca Laszlo, Tom Lowry, Mike Juenke, Steve and Claire Deremer, Graham MacLean, Pat Patterson, Robin Phillips, Pat and Ana Quinn, and Bob Roth.

Invitation to the Reader
In researching this book, I criss-crossed Washington and Oregon in search of the very best places to get outside. I'm sure you have your own favorite spots, or at least will find new ones as you explore. Please share your secrets with me, so I can pass them on in upcoming editions. If you were disappointed with a recommendation, I'd love to know that, too. Please write to:

Karl Samson
Outside Magazine's
Adventure Guide to the Pacific Northwest
Macmillan Travel
1633 Broadway
New York, NY 10019

An Additional Note
Please be advised that travel information is subject to change at any time. Every effort has been made to ensure the accuracy of the information provided in this book, but we suggest that you write or call ahead for confirmation when making your travel plans. The authors, editors, and publisher cannot be held responsible for the experiences of readers while traveling. Outdoor adventure sports are, by their very nature, potentially hazardous activities. In doing any of the activities described herein, readers assume all risk of injury or loss that may accompany such activities. The Publisher disavows all responsibility for injury, death, loss, or property damage which may arise from a reader's participation in any of the activities described herein, and the Publisher makes no warranties regarding the competence, safety, and reliability of outfitters, tour companies, or training centers described in this book.

Introduction

OVER THE YEARS I'VE NOTICED THAT MY FRIENDS' GARAGES ARE crammed full of outdoor sports gear. One has two sea kayaks, a sailboard, cross-country skis, and a pair of road bikes; another is cluttered with a raft, two road bikes, a ton of fishing gear, and several pairs of downhill skis. In a third, there are two backpacks, a snowboard, downhill skis, cross-country skis, a surfboard, and two mountain bikes.

This abundance and variety of gear points up how important getting outside is to Northwesterners. It's more fun to be a generalist here, and like my friends, I too pursue far more outdoor sports than I can ever hope to master. Sure, we probably all harbor secret desires to ski like we belong in a Warren Miller film, paddle Class V drops, do 360s on our sailboard, and scale big-wall rock like Spiderman. But the fact is, to look that good doing any one of these sports you'd need to work at it with single-minded, year-round dedication.

The rest of us get jobs, play on the weekends, and help support the sports-medicine industry. And the way I look at it, who wants to spend the winter riding a bike around in the rain when there's snow in the mountains? Who wants to spend the summer poling down the street on roller skis when mountain trails are waiting to be hiked? If it's too windy to paddle a canoe, why not do a little boardsailing? Not enough wind to sail? Great day for some mountain biking!

If you, too, have a roomful of gear, then maybe you can relate to what happened to me when I first moved to the Northwest. As soon as I had settled in, I wanted to know where to get outdoors. I wanted to know what the best hikes in the region were—trails with views and meadows and wildlife. I asked friends and acquaintances for suggestions. I gleaned ideas from magazines and newspapers. I went out and bought an Oregon hiking guide, and then I bought another book about trails in the southern part of that state. That first summer I found myself hiking on the Oregon Coast, in the northern Oregon Cascades, on Mount Rainier, on the Olympic Peninsula, and in the central Oregon Cascades.

As my library of hiking guides expanded, my wallet kept getting thinner. With more than $60 invested in books, I hadn't even started exploring the region's mountain-bike trails. Then came winter and another round of guidebooks showing me where to ski. Then I bought a sea kayak. I took it with me to the Puget Sound and onto rivers and lakes in both states. I turned to other books to find the best places to paddle. I had to get a new bookshelf to hold all the books I was amassing.

Soon enough I had books detailing more than 1,000 hikes, maybe 250 mountain-bike rides, and equally staggering numbers of river runs, cross-country ski trails, fishing holes, hot springs, and on and on. And clearly I'd never need all of this information—if I did one hike a weekend 52 weeks a year, it would take me almost 20 years just to do those 1,000 hikes. And I'd have no time to go snowboarding or kayaking or boardsailing or mountain biking. Each time I bought a new book for a new sport or a new region, I kept wishing there was just one book that would tell me only the very best places to do the things I love to do. There ought to have been such a book, but there wasn't—until now.

Whether you've never been to the Northwest before, are new to the area, or just want to expand your field of play, you won't find a more concise and useful year-round guide to the outdoors than this book. I only wish I'd written it years ago—have you checked the price of bookshelves lately?

—Karl Samson, February 15, 1997

Also available:

Outside Magazine's Adventure Guide to Northern California
Outside Magazine's Adventure Guide to New England
Outside Magazine's Guide to Family Vacations

1

THE BASICS

THE STATES OF WASHINGTON AND OREGON ARE AN OUTDOOR recreationist's nirvana. About the only things missing from the area covered in these pages—everything in these two states from the eastern edge of the Cascade Range to the coast fronting the Pacific—are a warm ocean and reliable powder skiing. From the rain forests of the Olympic Peninsula to the high desert of central Oregon, this region boasts amazing geographical and climatic diversity. Four national parks, dozens of state parks, wild and scenic rivers, an inland sea with its own archipelago, the longest wilderness coastline in the U.S. south of Alaska, the biggest salmon outside Alaska, volcanoes both young and old—these are just some of the attractions of this region.

With so much to offer, it comes as no surprise that the western halves of Washington and Oregon are the most populous parts of both states. It's also no surprise that numerous outdoor equipment and sportswear manufacturers call this region home. Seattle is headquarters for outdoor equipment giant REI. Vashon Island, Washington, is home to ski manufacturer K2. Beaverton, Oregon, is Nike world headquarters. Portland is home to Columbia Sportswear. Numerous small companies manufacture snowboarding, sea kayaking, and sailboarding equipment.

Subaru wagons—long thought of as the mountain goats of the auto world—seem to be the vehicle of choice for a goodly portion of the region's population, and at times it seems that every third or fourth car has a ski rack, bike rack, or kayak rack on the roof. The outdoors are in the blood of most Northwesterners, whether they are lifetime residents or recent transplants, and whether you're a fifth-generation Oregonian or just someone spending your summer vacation in the Northwest, you'll find countless adventures out there just waiting to be experienced. This book will guide you to those adventures.

More than two dozen different outdoor activities—from cross-country skiing to wildlife viewing and just about everything in between—are covered between the covers of this book. While wildlife viewing can be a pretty mild activity as adventure goes, there are plenty of other adventures listed here that more than live up to the name. Rock climbing at Smith Rock, rafting the Rogue River, sea kayaking the San Juan Islands, hiking the Pacific Crest Trail, cross-country skiing the Methow Valley, boardsailing the Columbia Gorge—these are the Pacific Northwest's marquee outdoor adventures, but you'll also find many low-key forays into the outdoors, adventures that don't require washboard abs and thighs of steel. A leisurely pedal through bucolic countryside, a walk on the beach, a visit to a beautiful waterfall, a quiet paddle on a mountain lake, adding a few more birds to your life list—these kinds of soft adventures are covered here, too. So, no matter what your definition of outdoor adventure happens to be, you'll find plenty of great information within these pages.

How to Use This Book

This book divides western Washington and Oregon into 12 regions, each of which gets its own chapter. Most of these areas are big enough to have more than one town—or mountain pass or other geographic feature—serving as a natural gateway to the outdoors; I've often broken the main section of each chapter, the "What to Do & Where to Do It" section, into two and even three subsections built around these gateways. Within each "What to Do & Where to Do It" section, all the sports and activities are listed alphabetically; within a sport category, say "Cross-Country Skiing," individual listings are organized geographically (say from north to south or west to east). I have tried to include enough specific hikes, rides, paddles, and other activities under each individual category so that a person could spend a weekend enjoying several good outings wearing the same togs (be they for mountain biking, or hiking, or skiing, and so on) right around one of those gateways, or an entire vacation sampling the activities of a single chapter.

If you're a single-sport person, this guide may not at first seem of much value. But when the conditions aren't always right for you to do your particular thing—when, for example, boardheads hellbent for the Columbia Gorge find the waters becalmed on their arrival—you may find it useful to know just where to go mountain biking, or hiking. And if you don't live here, you just might find that this book has more than enough information for you to pay a visit to the Northwest in pursuit of new adventures in your sport. Likewise, if you're just getting started in a sport, this book may prove an appropriate introduction, a way to test the waters before committing to that new sport.

Getting Underway

BEACHES

Forget about swimming at Washington or Oregon beaches. Although there are some where the water won't turn you blue immediately, beaches in the Northwest are mostly for looking (and hiking, tide-pool exploring, and kite flying). From tiny coves to miles-long swaths of sand and dunes, the coasts of Washington and Oregon are incredibly diverse. Within the coastal chapters of this book, you'll find recommendations of the best beaches and what there is to do on them.

FAVORITE BEACHES

◆ **Cape Alava to Sand Point, The Olympic Peninsula** (page 98).

◆ **Second and Third Beach, The Olympic Peninsula** (page 109).

◆ **Cannon Beach, The Oregon Coast** (page 435).

◆ **Short Sands Beach, The Oregon Coast** (page 436).

◆ **Samuel Boardman State Park beaches, The Oregon Coast** (page 434).

BIRD WATCHING

From coastal mud flats to high desert lakes, western Washington and Oregon have a surprising diversity of bird habitats. Most of the best bird watching in the region centers around places where migratory waterfowl and shorebirds gather briefly during spring and fall migrations. Other good birding spots are wintering grounds for species that spend their summers in the Arctic. Coastal regions of the state, home to such seabird species as marbled murrelets, tufted puffins, pigeon guillemots, and common murres, are among the region's favorite birding spots. Offshore islands are nesting grounds for many of these species.

The National Audubon Society sponsors expeditions and field seminars in both Washington and Oregon. For more information, contact the **National Audubon Society,** Washington State Office (tel. 360/786-8020) or the **Audubon Society of Portland** (tel. 503/292-6855).

Crucial information for the serious birder: the **rare-bird hotlines** for the area are 206/933-1831 (Washington) and 503/292-0661 (Oregon).

> **"Life is either a daring adventure or nothing."**
> **—Helen Keller**

FAVORITE BIRDING HOT SPOTS

◆ **San Juan Islands** (page 28).
◆ **Bowerman Basin, The Olympic Peninsula** (page 110).
◆ **Skagit River, The North Cascades** (page 138).
◆ **Klamath Basin Wildlife Refuges, Southern Oregon** (page 401).
◆ **Bayocean Spit, The Oregon Coast** (page 438).

BOARDSAILING

The Columbia Gorge is probably the Lower 48's most famous boardsailing spot and people come from all over the world to ride the strong winds and big waves that blast through this gap in the Cascades. While there are days and places within the gorge where novices and intermediate sailors can have some fun, the gorge is mostly the turf of expert sailors. There are, however, plenty of other good sailing spots around the region where you can keep practicing until you're ready for the gorge. There are also plenty of places where you can take a class and learn anything from the very basics to how to get serious air time.

FAVORITE BOARDSAILING SPOTS

◆ **Magnusson Park, Puget Sound** (page 66).
◆ **Columbia Gorge** (page 268).
◆ **Waldo Lake, West Central Oregon Cascades** (page 343).
◆ **Manzanita, The Oregon Coast** (page 439).
◆ **Floras Lake, The Oregon Coast** (page 454).

CROSS-COUNTRY SKIING

While cross-country skiing was once a sort of personal rebellion against the crowds and fashion consciousness of the downhill slopes, it has grown far away from those roots in recent years. Cross-country skiing has broken down into numerous styles, with each style—track, skate, backcountry, telemark, *randonee*—requiring its own specially designed skis, boots, bindings, and even clothes. Which type of cross-country skiing to pursue depends on what you

want out of your experience. If speed and aerobic exercise are your goal, opt for skate skiing. If backcountry explorations are your goal and you've previously been a downhill skier, then **randonee** skiing (a sort of Nordic/Alpine hybrid system in which boot heels are locked down for descents) may be for you. Within this book, you'll find routes described that fall into most of the above categories.

Now, I don't want to preach, but if I were you and I had never cross-country skied before, I'd make damn sure my first outing was on groomed trails. Too often I've seen first-time skiers head out for a day of fun on skis only to spend frustrating hours wobbling over icy ruts, taking frequent falls in deep, untracked powder, or struggling unsuccessfully to deal with the ascents and descents of rolling topography (I've even been the one who got these skiers into this fine mess). Too often a bad first experience translates into a lack of enthusiasm toward giving skiing a second chance. This can all be avoided by skiing a groomed trail system your first time out.

In both Oregon and Washington, you'll need to buy a sno-park permit in order to park in plowed parking lots in the mountains. In Washington, sno-park permits cost $7 for one day, $10 for three days, and $20 for the season. In Washington, sno-park permits are not required in downhill ski area parking lots. In Oregon, sno-park permits are $2 for one day, $3 for three days, and $10 for the season (a 50¢ surcharge is also possible). In Oregon, you *will* need a sno-park permit when you park at most downhill ski areas, as well as at cross-country trailheads.

In Washington, your sno-park permit gets you more than just a place to park—it gets you nearly two dozen groomed ski trail systems for which you don't need to pay a penny more in trail-use fees. For a directory of these and other groomed trails, get a copy of *Washington State Groomed Cross-Country Ski Trails,* from Washington State Parks Winter Recreation Office, P.O. Box 42662, Olympia, WA 98504-2662 (tel. 360/902-8552). The booklet has simple maps and general information on all the groomed ski trails in the state and costs $4. You can also check on cross-country skiing conditions in Washington by calling the **Cross-Country Ski Report** (tel. 206/632-2021).

FAVORITE GROOMED TRAILS

◆ Methow Valley, The North Cascades (page 157).

◆ Ski Acres/Hyak Nordic Center, The Central Washington Cascades (page 192).

◆ Teacup Lake, The Columbia Gorge (page 281).

◆ Mount Bachelor Nordic Center, Central Oregon (page 373-4).

FAVORITE UNGROOMED TRAILS

◆ Artist Point and Herman Saddle, The North Cascades (page 140).

◆ Reflection Lakes, Mount Rainier and Mount St. Helens Areas (page 220-1).

◆ Mount Adams, The Columbia Gorge (page 270).

◆ McKenzie Pass Lava Fields, Central Oregon (page 363).

◆ Maxwell and Big Springs Sno-Parks, The West Central Oregon Cascades (page 332).

◆ Crater Lake West Rim Trail, Southern Oregon (page 404).

DOWNHILL SKIING & SNOWBOARDING

Cascade concrete—those are the watchwords of Northwest skiing. With those wet winds blowing in off the Pacific, the snows of the western Cascades are nearly legendary for their heaviness. Regardless of snow quality, however, the ski areas of western Washington and Oregon are extremely popular. This is mostly because they are very convenient to large metropolitan areas such as Seattle and Portland. From congested downtown streets to congested lift lines is but an hour's drive for Seattleites and Portlanders. However, there are alternatives. Both Mount Bachelor outside Bend and Mission Ridge outside Wenatchee are far enough east of the Cascade divide that they tend to have lighter, fluffier snow. Some even dare call it powder skiing.

By most standards, the ski areas of the Northwest are very reasonably priced. It's still possible to ski some very respectable

The Ten Essentials

Whether you're heading out for a quick day hike, an overnight backpacking trip, a mountain-bike ride, or a paddle down a lazy river, there are a few things that you should always bring with you. These items have come to be known as the Ten Essentials. Don't leave home without them.

1. A topographic map of the area
2. A compass
3. Extra food and clothing (preferably rain gear)
4. A whistle
5. A first-aid kit
6. A flashlight, with extra bulb and extra batteries
7. A fire starter
8. Waterproof matches (regular matches in a waterproof case will do)
9. Sun protection (sunglasses and sunscreen)
10. A pocket knife

areas for under $20 if you can come on a weekday or after work. You'll never pay more than $36 or $38, unless, of course, you want to do some snowcat skiing or heli-skiing. Snowcat skiing is available in southern Oregon on Mount Bailey (and occasionally at Mount Hood Meadows). Heli-skiing can be done out of the Methow Valley in the North Cascades.

All the ski areas in this book are open to snowboarders, and Mount Baker Ski Area is known primarily for its fabulous snowboarding. All the ski areas in this book also rent skis and snowboards and offer classes. However, if you are renting skis, you will probably save time by renting somewhere other than at the slopes themselves.

For a downhill ski report for Washington ski areas, call the **Cascade Ski Report** (tel. 206/634-0200).

FAVORITE SKI HILLS

◆ **Mount Bachelor, Central Oregon** (page 375-6).

◆ **Crystal Mountain, Mount Rainier and Mount St. Helens** (page 223).

◆ **Mount Baker, The North Cascades** (page 142-3).

◆ **Stevens Pass, The Central Washington Cascades** (page 179).

◆ **Mount Hood Meadows, The Columbia Gorge** (page 284).

FISHING

The fishing of Oregon and Washington enjoys near legendary status, and while there may be few streams in the region of national importance among anglers, there are still plenty of great rivers. Salmon of half a dozen species and steelhead are the favored game fish of the region among dedicated anglers. However, wild cutthroat and redside rainbow trout also have their fans. If your idea of a great fishing trip is a skillet full of frying rainbow trout, the many stocked streams and mountain lakes of the region will keep you content. Scattered throughout the two states are also the odd fisheries that become the obsessions of some anglers—Mackinaw trout, Kokanee salmon, Atlantic salmon, and sturgeon. Even bass anglers have plenty of places to fish for both smallmouth and largemouth.

The most important thing to know about fishing in Washington and Oregon is that the rules are complicated and they're always changing. It is absolutely essential that you know all the regulations for whatever body of water you happen to be fishing in. To find out what the current regulations are, you'll need to pick up a copy of *Fishing in Washington (Sport Fishing Rules)* or *Oregon Sport Fishing Regulations.* These publications are free and are available at sporting goods stores and bait-and-tackle shops. Alternatively you can order copies by contacting the **Washington Department of Fish and Wildlife,** 600 Capitol Way N, Olympia, WA 98501-1091 (tel. 360/902-2200), or the **Oregon Department of Fish & Wildlife,** 2501 SW First Ave. (P.O. Box 59), Portland, OR 97207 (tel. 503/229-5403).

For information on freshwater fishing in Washington, contact the **Department of Fish and Wildlife Sport Fishing Hotline** (tel. 206/976-3200). For information on freshwater fishing in Oregon, contact the **Oregon Department of Fish and Wildlife** (tel. 503/229-5222) or the **Oregon Sport Fishing Info Line** (tel. 800/ASK-FISH).

FAVORITE FISHING SPOTS

◆ **Strait of Juan de Fuca, The Olympic Peninsula** (page 97-8).

◆ **Skagit River, The North Cascades** (page 143).

◆ **Alpine Lakes Wilderness, The Central Washington Cascades** (page 176).

◆ **Olympic Peninsula Rivers, The Olympic Peninsula** (page 93).

◆ **Deschutes River, Central Oregon** (page 376).

◆ **Hosmer Lake, Central Oregon** (page 377).

◆ **North Umpqua River, Southern Oregon** (page 406).

◆ **Rogue River, Southern Oregon** (page 406-7).

HIKING & BACKPACKING

While hiking in western Washington and Oregon is primarily a three-season pursuit, it is not restricted to the months of spring, summer, and fall. Because elevation is the primary determinant of the severity of the winter in the Northwest, if you stick to low elevations, you can hike right through the winter. The only problem is, trails tend to be very muddy during the winter and often are not maintained, which means that you might find yourself climbing over a lot of downed trees. Besides, if you want to hike in winter, why not strap on snowshoes and do it in the snow?

Throughout this book you will find both day hikes and overnight backpacking routes. Actually, many of the day hikes could just as easily be overnight trips, but they are short enough that they don't have to be. Hikes of roughly 3 miles or less are listed under "Walks & Natural Roadside Attractions." I've tried to make route descriptions fairly thorough, but a good topographic map should always be part of your pack when you head into the backcountry, whether for a few hours or a few days.

Although the most interesting trails can be quite crowded on sunny summer weekends, there are still few trails in

The Pacific Crest Trail

The Pacific Crest Trail (PCT), which stretches for 2,600 miles from Canada to Mexico, is perhaps most celebrated for its segments in California's High Sierra, where the national scenic trail reaches its highest elevations. However, while keeping to much lower elevations throughout Washington and Oregon (the trail reaches its lowest elevation at the Columbia River crossing between the two states), it still passes through some of the finest scenery these two states have to offer. However, there seem to be fewer people compelled to hike long segments of this trail in the Northwest than there are those who find it a life's calling in California.

In the Northwest, which is actually where the idea for the trail originated and its first segments were built, the PCT is perhaps most noteworthy for where it doesn't go. It bypasses two of the most breathtaking and famous locales in the region—the rim of Crater Lake and Mount Rainier National Park. However, it manages to compensate for these two shortcomings by taking in plenty of other worthy landscapes.

The trail actually begins in Canada at Manning Provincial Park, and between here and Rainy Pass, on Wash. 20, it passes through the remote Pasayten Wilderness, where deep, U-shaped valleys remind hikers of the massive sheet of glacial ice that once covered this land. This segment lacks the rugged topography of segments to the south, and consequently is lightly traveled. Segment length: 69 miles.

Between Rainy Pass and Stevens Pass, on U.S. 2, the trail passes through the Glacier Peak and Henry M. Jackson wildernesses. This is the most rugged and challenging stretch of the PCT outside of California. Glacier Peak, due to the long hikes in to its slopes, is one of the least visited of the major Cascade peaks. Segment length: 117 miles.

The segment of trail between Stevens Pass and Snoqualmie Pass, on I-90, is the most spectacular and most frequently hiked long segment in the Northwest. Passing through the Alpine Lakes Wilderness, the trail takes in vistas of granite peaks, the likes of which are not seen again until the High Sierra. However, though these peaks have been scoured by glaciers, they never even reach 10,000 feet in elevation here. Segment length: 74 miles.

South of Snoqualmie Pass, the PCT crosses a land of clear-cuts, a segment of trail that is rarely hiked except by those seeking to do the entire trail. However, continuing south, the trail passes through the Norse Peak and William O. Douglas wildernesses, skirting the edge of Mount Rainier National Park before reaching White Pass, on U.S. 12. Most hikers with time to hike 100 miles choose the national park's Wonderland Trail over this segment of the PCT. Segment length: 99 miles.

South of White Pass, the trail enters its longest stretch in Washington without a major road crossing. This segment passes through the Goat Rocks Wilderness, where the Northwest where you'll need a reservation for a backcountry campsite or a special permit for a day hike. However, in upcoming years such trails are likely to become more common. To avoid disappointment, it's a good idea to call the nearest ranger station to find out about current permit requirements before heading for the hills.

FAVORITE DAY HIKES

◆ **Railroad Grade–Scott Paul Loop, The North Cascades** (page 145-6).

◆ **Maple Pass Loop Trail, The North Cascades** (page 160).

◆ **Snow Lake/Gem Lake, Snoqualmie Pass** (page 196-7).

◆ **Bird Creek Meadows, The Columbia Gorge** (page 272).

it climbs above 7,000 feet to the highest point on the PCT in Washington. The trail then traverses the flanks of Mount Adams in the Mount Adams Wilderness. However, between here and Indian Heaven Wilderness, there are lots of clear-cuts, as there are also south from Indian Heaven to the Columbia River. Segment length: 147 miles.

After crossing the Columbia River on the Bridge of the Gods, the trail climbs 4,000 feet up the south wall of the Columbia Gorge to enter the densely forested Columbia Wilderness. South of here, the trail enters the Mount Hood Wilderness, as it traverses the flanks of Oregon's highest peak. At Barlow Pass, the trail crosses Ore. 35. Segment length: 54 miles.

Between Barlow Pass and Santiam Pass, on U.S. 20, the PCT passes through roughly 40 miles of unremarkable scenery before reaching first the Ollalie Lakes Basin and then the Mount Jefferson Wilderness, which holds one of the most popular backpacking destinations in all of Oregon—Jefferson Park. Segment length: 95 miles.

A short but very interesting stretch of trail lies between Santiam Pass and McKenzie Pass, on Ore. 242. Here the trail crosses the Mount Washington Wilderness, much of which is blanketed with raw, black lava flows. Segment length: 17 miles.

South from McKenzie Pass to Willamette Pass, on Ore. 58, the trail passes through the Three Sisters Wilderness for roughly 50 miles. This is one of the most scenic stretches of the trail in the state and is another of the state's most popular backpacking areas. Expect crowds. South of the wilderness, the trail passes close to Waldo Lake, one of the purest lakes in the world. Segment length: 76 miles.

The segment of trail from Willamette Pass to Ore. 138 north of Crater Lake National Park is one of the less frequented stretches of trail in the state, even though it passes through both the Diamond Peak Wilderness and the Mount Thielsen Wilderness. Segment length: 61 miles.

South of Ore. 138, the trail enters Crater Lake National Park but for some strange reason stays completely clear of any lake views. Consequently this stretch of trail is little used.

South of Ore. 62, on the south side of the national park, the trail spends roughly 50 miles in the Sky Lakes Wilderness, which is the most scenic and most popular wilderness area in southern Oregon. The next road crossed is Ore. 140, near Fish Lake. Segment length: 76 miles.

The segment of the PCT between Ore. 140 and I-5 near Ashland is one of the least interesting in the entire length of the trail. Four major roads are crossed and clear-cuts abound. Segment length: 54 miles.

Between I-5 and the Oregon–California state line, the PCT climbs into the Siskiyou Mountains. There are good views, but the trail is paralleled by a road. Segment length: 28 miles.

◆ **Grand Ridge (Obstruction Point to Green Mountain), The Olympic Peninsula** (page 97).

FAVORITE MULTIDAY HIKES
◆ **Cape Alava to Rialto Beach, The Olympic Peninsula** (page 98-9).
◆ **Hoh River Trail to Glacier Meadows, The Olympic Peninsula** (page 112).
◆ **Hannegan Pass–Ross Lake Route, The North Cascades** (page 146).

◆ **Enchantment Lakes, Central Washington Cascades** (page 181).
◆ **Wonderland Trail, Mount Rainier and Mount St. Helens Areas** (page 225-6).

HORSEBACK RIDING

If you happen to have your own horse, you'll find hundreds of miles of excellent trails throughout Washington and Oregon. The most popular equestrian trails tend to be on the east slopes of the Cascades, where the landscape is drier, more open, and less steep. If you don't have your own horse, you'll find lots of stables that offer rides of varying lengths. Many stables operate only during the summer months.

FAVORITE RENTAL STABLES
◆ **Early Winters Outfitting, The North Cascades** (page 162).
◆ **Cascade Corrals, The North Cascades** (page 162).
◆ **Indian Creek Corral, Mount Rainier and Mount St. Helens Areas** (page 230).
◆ **Black Butte Ranch Stables, Central Oregon** (page 367).
◆ **Sea Ranch RV Park, Cannon Beach** (page 442).

HOT SPRINGS

There is something exceedingly pleasurable about getting up to your neck in hot water in the woods. Hot springs are among Mother Nature's greatest wonders. The Cascades, which run the length of both Washington and Oregon, are volcanic peaks, and along this backbone there are plenty of hot springs. I prefer hike-in hot springs to those you can reach by car, and at such remote springs, nudity is the norm. At hot springs visible to roads you risk a fine if the local authorities catch you *au naturelle.*

FAVORITE HOT SPRINGS
◆ **Olympic Hot Springs, The Olympic Peninsula** (page 99).
◆ **Sol Duc Hot Springs, The Olympic Peninsula** (page 99).
◆ **Bagby Hot Springs, The Columbia Gorge** (page 288).
◆ **Cougar Hot Springs, West Central Oregon Cascades** (page 337).
◆ **Umpqua Hot Springs, Southern Oregon** (page 411).

MOUNTAIN BIKING

While there are thousands of miles of logging roads throughout the national forests of the Northwest, many of these lack the sort of scenic qualities one hopes to find when heading outdoors. Consequently, you'll find that most rides listed in this book are single-track routes. However, since cyclists seem to like loop rides, stretches of single-track are often linked with logging roads to create loops. Some trails could just as easily and just as enjoyably be ridden as out-and-backs.

Just as elsewhere in the country, mountain bikers in the Northwest have been losing ground over the years. Each year trails get closed to mountain bikes (and occasionally reopened). To help keep them open, it pays to be courteous to other trail users, specifically hikers and horseback riders. On trails where all three uses are permitted, mountain bikers are required to yield to both hikers and horses. Some mountain-bike trails are open only certain months of the year, while others are open only in an uphill direction.

Perhaps it's because I live in Oregon, but there seems to be a decidedly more accommodating attitude toward mountain bikes in Oregon's national forests than there is in Washington's national forests. In Washington, the majority of trails open to mountain bikes are designated motorcycle and ORV trails. Many of these trails are absolutely overwhelmed by screaming two-strokers every weekend, and that is hardly my idea of pleasant company in the forest. The same attitude prevails on Washington Department of Natural Resources lands. If you can do your riding on a weekday, you can generally avoid the crowds, but spinning motor-driven knobbies tend to trash trails so badly that they become little but trenches carved into the ground. Such trenches hardly make for enjoyable mountain biking.

In Oregon, on the other hand, several national forests have trails that are open to hikers, equestrians, and mountain bikers, but not motorcycles, which in my opinion is a much better division of use—although some people may not agree. These trails tend to be in areas off the main hiking/horseback riding routes and away from wilderness areas where hikers tend to congregate. Mount Hood National Forest, Willamette National Forest, and Deschutes National Forest all have many excellent mountain-biking trails.

FAVORITE RIDES

◆ **Moran State Park Trails, The San Juan Islands** (page 29-31).

◆ **Cutthroat Pass, The North Cascades** (page 163).

◆ **Surveyor's Ridge, The Columbia Gorge** (page 288).

◆ **Youngs Rock–Moon Point Loop, The West Central Oregon Cascades** (page 349-50).

◆ **Waldo Lake, The West Central Oregon Cascades** (page 350).

◆ **370 Road Ride, Central Oregon** (page 382).

◆ **High Lakes Trail, Southern Oregon** (page 412).

MOUNTAINEERING

From Mount Baker and Mount Shuksan in the north to the Three Sisters and Mount Thielsen in the south, the high peaks of the Cascades offer a wide variety of mountaineering challenges. However, it is **Mount Rainier** and **Mount Hood** that are the region's two most sought-after summits. On both of these mountains you'll find mountaineering companies that offer classes and guide services.

Of the other major peaks, Washington's **Mount Adams** is the easiest to climb. Central Oregon's **South Sister** also can be summited without technical equipment or training. **Mount Baker, Mount Shuksan, Glacier Peak,** and **Mount Olympus** (on the Olympic Peninsula) are all much more challenging technical climbs that require familiarity with glacier crossings. In central Oregon, **Mount Jefferson, Mount Washington, North and Middle Sister** all offer challenging ascents for experienced climbers. Although it hardly counts as a mountaineering conquest, the ascent of **Mount St. Helens** is one of the most popular climbs in the Northwest.

If you want to take a mountaineering class, you have two options in this region. **Rainier Mountaineering,** 535 Dock St. Suite 209, Tacoma, WA 98402 (May–Sept, tel. 206/627-6242 or 360/569-2227; fax 206/627-1280), which operates out of Paradise inside Mount Rainier National Park, offers one-day classes for $85, three-day summit climbs for $460, and five-day

mountaineering seminars for $695. **Timberline Mountain Guides,** P.O. Box 340, Government Camp, OR 97028 (tel. 800/464-7704; fax 503/272-3677), leads summit climbs on Mount Hood. They also offer snow, ice, and rock-climbing courses. A two-day Mount Hood mountaineering course with summit climb costs $245. Rates for other courses range from $95 for a day-long rock-climbing class at Smith Rock to $750 for a five-day mountaineering seminar.

If you already have some mountaineering experience and are looking for a company to guide you on a climb, contact either of the two companies above or **Valhalla Adventures,** P.O. Box 17360, Seattle, WA 98107 (tel. 206/782-3767). This company leads trips across some of the most rugged terrain in the North Cascades and Olympic Mountains, and also does a Mount Baker climb. Costs range from $230 for a two-day Mount Baker climb to $930 for a nine-day traverse of the Olympic Mountains' Bailey Range.

PACKSTOCK TRIPS

While this is more the Northwest than the Wild West, the region does have its fair share of outfitters that can take you into the mountains on horseback. There are also plenty of llama-packing outfitters, and even at least one burro-packing company. While quite a few of these companies are mentioned in this book, you can get directories of outfitters from the **Washington State Outfitters and Guides Association,** 22845 NE Eighth Ave., Suite 331, Redmond, WA 98053 (tel. 206/392-6107). For a directory of Oregon outfitters and guides, contact the **Oregon Outdoors Association,** P.O. Box 10841, Eugene, OR 97440 (tel. 800/747-9552 or 541/683-9552).

ROAD BIKING

Covered in these pages are two of the most popular bicycle touring locales in the country—the San Juan Islands and the Oregon coast. However, there are also lots of other great rides around the region. While the Cascades are for the most part not very popular with cyclists due to the steep climbs and lack of easy loop rides, the low-lands of the Puget Sound area and the Willamette Valley abound in great cycling routes. Rural pedals are the focus of the rides I've listed in this book, but there are also listings of urban bike paths and even a few good mountain routes.

For information on bicycle routes in Washington, contact the **Bicycle Hotline,** Washington State Department of Transportation, P.O. Box 47393, Olympia, WA 98504-7393 (tel. 360/705-7277). You can get a free Oregon coast bicycle map, as well as other bicycle maps for the state of Oregon, by contacting the **Oregon Bicycle/Pedestrian Program,** Oregon Department of Transportation, 210 Transportation Building, Salem, OR 97310 (tel. 503/986-3556).

If you're interested in a guided bicycle tour in the Northwest, there are a couple of tour companies to try. **Backroads,** 801 Cedar St., Berkeley, CA 94710-1740 (tel. 800/462-2848 or 510/527-1555; fax 510/527-1444), offers guided trips in the San Juans, the North Cascades, and on the Oregon coast and Olympic Peninsula with tour prices ranging from $749 to $1,498. **Bicycle Adventures,** P.O. Box 11219, Olympia, WA 98508 (tel. 800/443-6060 or 360/786-0989; fax 360/786-9661), offers road-bike trips in the San Juan Islands, the Oregon Cascades, the Columbia Gorge, and on the Oregon coast and Olympic Peninsula, with tour prices ranging from $700 to $1,600. They also offer an off-road bike trip through the Washington Cascades.

FAVORITE RIDES

◆ **Lopez Island, The San Juan Islands** (page 33).
◆ **Burke–Gilman/Sammamish Bike Path, Puget Sound** (page 71).
◆ **McKenzie Pass, Central Oregon** (page 369).
◆ **Crater Lake Rim Road, Southern Oregon** (page 415).

ROCK/ICE CLIMBING

While at first it might seem that the Northwest would be a fabulous rock-climbing area, the reality is a little bit different. The Cascade Range, volcanic in nature, abounds in basalt rock, which, unfortunately for climbers, tends to be rather rotten. This said, there are some excellent basalt climbing areas scattered around the region, just not as many as you might expect. However, as sport climbing gains popularity, more and more good climbing spots are being discovered.

While much of the rock in the region isn't very good for climbing, there are those exceptions to the rule. Chief among these is Oregon's Smith Rock, which though no Yosemite Valley, offers an amazing variety of climbs in a spectacular high desert setting. While summer is the primary climbing season in most of Washington and Oregon, summer at Smith Rock can fry your brain. Better to come in spring or fall.

There is even a bit of ice climbing scattered around the region. While most of this is high on the slopes of glaciated peaks such as Mount Hood and Mount Rainier, there is occasionally sea-level ice climbing in the Columbia Gorge when particularly nasty cold fronts descend on the area.

FAVORITE CLIMBING SPOTS

◆ **Seattle REI's climbing spire, Puget Sound** (page 74).
◆ **Peshastin Pinnacles State Park, Central Washington Cascades** (page 188).
◆ **Beacon Rock, The Columbia Gorge** (page 277).
◆ **Skinner Butte Columns, The Willamette Valley** (page 320).
◆ **Smith Rock State Park, Central Oregon** (page 369-70).

SCUBA DIVING

While it is sometimes possible to dive in the Pacific Ocean along the coasts of Washington and Oregon, for the most part, the open ocean is too rough for diving. Add to this the lack of good shore dives, and you're faced with the cost of chartering a boat if you want to dive offshore. For this reason, the best and most popular dive sites in the region are in Puget Sound and the waters surrounding the San Juan Islands.

These waters never get much above about 55°F, which means a full wetsuit or dry suit is a necessity for diving here, especially when you consider that these waters are at their clearest during the winter months.

For more information on diving in Washington, contact the **Washington Scuba Alliance,** 120 State Ave. NE, #18, Olympia, WA 98501-8212.

FAVORITE DIVE SITES

◆ **San Juan Islands** (page 34).
◆ **Deception Pass State Park, The San Juan Islands** (page 48).
◆ **Keystone Spit State Park, The San Juan Islands** (page 48).
◆ **Edmonds Underwater Park, Puget Sound** (page 75).
◆ **Clallam Bay, The Olympic Peninsula** (page 103).

SEA KAYAKING & FLAT-WATER CANOEING

Seattle and Puget Sound may as well have invented sea kayaking, as popular as it is in the region. All up and down this inland sea, from Olympia to Bellingham, there are dozens of great places to paddle. Canoeists and inland paddlers will, however, find far fewer interesting quiet waters to explore. Most lakes in Washington and Oregon are open to, and dominated by, powerboats, with ski boats and personal watercraft particularly popular.

With sea kayaking continuing to gain popularity in the Puget Sound area, and with dozens of parks scattered up and down the many miles of coastline here, the region's paddlers have developed a plan for a sea kayaking route, known as the **Cascadia Marine Trail,** that stretches from Olympia in the south to the San Juan Islands in the north. Along this route are more than two dozen parks with campsites for paddlers. Waterfront bed-and-breakfast inns have also been joining the program to promote inn-to-inn paddling. For more information on the Cascadia Marine Trail, contact the **Washington Water Trails Association,** c/o Good Shepherd Center, 4649 Sunnyside Ave. N, Suite 345, Seattle, WA 98103-6900 (tel. 206/545-9161).

Before striking out on your own in the greater Puget Sound area, you'll need to familiarize yourself with current tables. These tables are an essential tool for predicting what direction and speed currents will be traveling at any given time and location. Misjudging currents can be both bothersome and fatal. Pick up current tables and charts at Puget Sound kayaking shops.

While the coasts of Washington and Oregon are beautiful, coastal waters tend to be rough and unpredictable, which keeps the Pacific off-limits to all but the most competent and experienced of paddlers. If you fall into this category, you may want to take a drive down the coast during the summer and check out some of the more interesting stretches of coastline.

FAVORITE SALTWATER PADDLE ROUTES

◆ **Patos, Sucia, and Matia Islands, The San Juans** (page 37-8).
◆ **Cypress Island, The San Juans** (page 50).
◆ **Blake Island, Puget Sound** (page 77).
◆ **Crescent Bay, The Olympic Peninsula** (page 104).

FAVORITE FRESHWATER PADDLE ROUTES

◆ **Lake Ozette, The Olympic Peninsula** (page 104).
◆ **Ross Lake, The North Cascades** (page 150).
◆ **Cooper Lake, The Central Washington Cascades** (page 202-3).
◆ **Sparks Lake, Central Oregon** (page 377).
◆ **Clear Lake, The West Central Oregon Cascades** (page 339).
◆ **Spring Creek, Southern Oregon** (page 416).

SNOWSHOEING

While some people think it shows a lack of sense to slog up a hill in the middle of winter only to slog back down instead of letting gravity do its thing, there are others who think snowshoeing is a blast.

Snowshoeing is hot right now and each year more and more people are showing up on the snow wearing tubes and webbing instead of boards. However, as yet there are no designated snowshoe trails, and for access to the outdoors, snowshoers use the same sno-parks that cross-country skiers use. This has led to some conflicts as snowshoers stomp along nice, neat ski tracks. In several places, including Snoqualmie Pass, Mount Rainier National Park, Mount Bachelor, and Crater Lake National Park, there are regularly scheduled ranger- or volunteer-led snowshoe hikes most weekends of the winter.

FAVORITE SNOWSHOEING TRAILS

◆ **Stehekin Valley, The North Cascades** (page 166).

◆ **Mount St. Helens, Mount Rainier and Mount St. Helens Areas** (page 246).

◆ **Tumalo Mountain, Central Oregon** (page 386).

◆ **Crater Lake's West Rim Trail, Southern Oregon** (page 417).

SPELUNKING

While the Northwest isn't a spelunking hotbed, it does have a fair number of caves. However, most of these are lava tubes, which lack the dramatic subterranean rock gardens that are found in limestone caverns. Lava tubes, formed when molten lava developed a crust beneath which hot lava continued to flow, can be found throughout the Cascade Range, where volcanic peaks dominate the horizons. However, the greatest concentration of lava tubes and lava caves (formed when lava tubes collapse in places) is to be found in **central Oregon** just south of Bend. Here there are several caves open for exploration. **Ape Cave,** the longest lava cave in the Northwest, is on the south side of Mount St. Helens. **Oregon Caves National Monument,** near Cave Junction in southern Oregon, preserves an extensive network of marble-walled caverns high in the Siskiyou Mountains.

SURFING

Cold water and no large cities along the Washington and Oregon coasts keep these waters uncrowded for the most part. A wetsuit is necessary year-round here, with booties, gloves, and a hood mandatory in winter. While winter storms generate waves of 10 to 20 feet, summers bring swells in the 4- to 8-foot range. Just as in northern California, the occasional surfer gets attacked by a great white shark that mistakes the wetsuited surfer for a sea lion.

FAVORITE SURFING BEACHES

◆ **Fort Ebey State Park, The San Juan Islands** (page 51).

◆ **Salt Creek County Park, The Olympic Peninsula** (page 105).

◆ **Westhaven State Park, The Olympic Peninsula** (page 127).

◆ **Seaside Cove, The Oregon Coast** (page 446).

◆ **Short Sands Beach, The Oregon Coast** (page 446).

SWIMMING & TUBING

There's really only one thing to say about swimming in the Northwest: The water's cold! Forget about the ocean. The Puget Sound? Maybe in the south sound or someplace where the water doesn't circulate very well. The way my brother—who lives on Puget Sound—tells it, you can go swimming in a few places in the sound as long as you don't let any part of your body drop below the upper 1 foot of relatively warm water. Below the thermocline, it's the instant hypothermia zone. The warmest Northwest waters are generally going to be in shallow lakes. Unfortunately an inordinate number of such lakes, especially in Washington, are posted as being home to a skin parasite that causes swimmers' itch. In other lakes, the density of children in shallow waters has caused closures to all children who are not toilet trained (outbreaks of gastrointestinal illnesses on Portland's popular Blue Lake were traced to too many dirty diapers in the swimming area). Of course, there are some lakes that are clean, parasite-free, and get warm enough for swimming. These are rare jewels that should not be missed.

Rivers are the ticket for swimming—rivers at low elevation to be specific—and preferably rivers somewhere in southern Oregon. Now *those* are good swimming rivers. Other rivers are considered swimmable as long as your definition of swimming doesn't include being in the water for more than five minutes at a time.

I look on tubing as a subset of swimming rather than a subset of kayaking or canoeing. It takes no skill other than the ability to open a can of beer. However, it does require the ability to recognize a good tubing stream. Class III and up waters are definitely out. So are 10-mile runs with lots of flat water between rapids. All it takes is a good upriver breeze, and a quick float can turn into an all-day affair. No, the best tubing runs are those that offer short trips of a mile or two with lots of Class I and II water. Oh yeah, and the water can't be too cold. Now this may sound like I'm ruling out all Northwest rivers, but actually there are some rivers that are just perfect for tubing.

FAVORITE SWIMMING HOLES
◆ **Whistle Lake, The San Juan Islands** (page 51).
◆ **Flaming Geyser State Park, Puget Sound** (page 77-8).
◆ **Lake Wenatchee State Park, The Central Washington Cascades** (page 188-9).
◆ **Fall Creek, The Willamette Valley** (page 321).
◆ **North Fork Middle Fork Willamette River, The West-Central Oregon Cascades** (page 352).
◆ **Crescent Lake, The West-Central Oregon Cascades** (page 352).
◆ **Cleawox Lake, The Oregon Coast** (page 461).

WALKS & NATURAL ROADSIDE ATTRACTIONS

This is the easy stuff, the stuff you do with your kids, the stuff you do when you've only got a few minutes to get out of your car, and the stuff that you shouldn't miss if you want to be able to tell people you've done the Northwest. Walks through parks make up a large portion of the listings under this category. Also under this heading you'll find waterfalls, ice caves, big trees, scenic viewpoints, nature trails, and the like. I consider a walk anything under 3 miles that doesn't involve a lot of elevation gain.

FAVORITE WALKS
◆ **Hurricane Hill Trail, The Olympic Peninsula** (page 106).
◆ **Hall of Mosses/Spruce Nature Trail, The Olympic Peninsula** (page 119).
◆ **Table Mountain Trail, The North Cascades** (page 151-2).
◆ **Nisqually Vista, Mount Rainier and Mount St. Helens Areas** (page 235-6).
◆ **Beacon Rock, The Columbia Gorge** (page 278-9).

FAVORITE NATURAL ROADSIDE ATTRACTIONS
◆ **Snoqualmie Falls, Central Washington Cascades** (page 204).
◆ **Multnomah Falls, The Columbia Gorge** (page 256).
◆ **Oux-Kanee Overlook, Southern Oregon** (page 421).
◆ **Hellgate Canyon, Southern Oregon** (page 421).
◆ **Devil's Punch Bowl, The Oregon Coast** (page 448).

WHALE WATCHING

Whether you want to keep both feet on shore or would rather get up close and personal, there are dozens of places to see whales in the Northwest. The two species common to Northwest waters are gray whales, which migrate along the coast as they travel back and forth between Alaska and Baja California (what a life), and killer whales (properly known as orcas), which are resident during the summer months in the San Juan Islands. Tour boats leave from various ports along the coast on gray whale spotting trips and from the San Juan Islands on orca tours. For the past few years quite a few gray whales have been spending all year off the Oregon coast, so there is now no month of the year when you don't stand a good chance of spotting one of these leviathans.

FAVORITE WHALE-WATCHING SPOTS

◆ **Lime Kiln State Park, The San Juan Islands** (page 40).

◆ **Cape Flattery, The Olympic Peninsula** (page 106).

◆ **Cape Lookout, The Oregon Coast** (page 448).

◆ **Devil's Punch Bowl State Park, The Oregon Coast** (page 448).

◆ **Depoe Bay Charter Boats, The Oregon Coast** (page 448).

WHITEWATER KAYAKING & CANOEING

Abundant rains and lots of mountains mean the Northwest is whitewater country. However, for the most part, kayaking in the Northwest is not a summertime activity. A few rivers, whether because they're spring-fed or dam-controlled, are runnable year-round. But most of the region's rivers carry enough water for good paddling conditions only during the rainy months from October or November through April. Other rivers are really runnable only during the snowmelt season of May and June (sometimes into early July). Consequently, about the single most important piece of equipment you can have for paddling in the Northwest is a good wetsuit.

The best advice I can give regarding paddling in the Northwest is, "Find a paddling buddy." The information in this book, while it will tell you where a river is and what class of water you'll find, won't tell at what level to run a river or exactly how to run individual rapids. For this sort of information, you're best off relying on locals, whether in the form of a kayaking shop, a club, or a local individual. Running a river the first time with someone familiar with that particular stretch can mean the difference between having a blast and accidentally missing that crucial little eddy above the Class V waterfall just downstream.

Good manners are another plus in the Northwest, where paddling season and steelhead fishing season overlap. Narrow rivers can be crowded with anglers, and there's no quicker way to give paddlers a bad name than to cause someone to lose the steelhead he or she has been fighting for an hour. Stay clear of anglers' lines and give them a chance to motion you through their fishing spot. Each summer, one section of Oregon's North Umpqua River is completely closed to boats and other sections are only open during the midday hours when the fish aren't usually biting.

In this book, you'll find rivers organized by class of water from Class I to Class V (which I have often lumped in with Class IV waters). I think you'll find this organization helpful in finding rivers to suit your paddling skills.

Two winters of the worst flooding in decades have been rearranging Northwest rivers, and with all the downed timber littering the mountainsides, some rivers are getting pretty clogged with debris. Logjams, sweepers, and strainers have always been a big problem on most Northwest rivers (especially smaller ones), and with the recent floods things have gotten worse in many places. Always scout your river and find out beforehand if it has been run recently and what new obstacles you might encounter.

Before heading out to do some paddling, you can check on river levels by calling the National Oceanic and Atmospheric Administration's **Washington Whitewater and Steelhead Hotline** (tel. 206/526-8530) or, in Oregon, NOAA's **River Level Info Line** (tel. 503/261-9246).

If you're interested in joining a paddling club, there are several good ones in the region. These include the following:

Lower Columbia Canoe Club, 22800 Unger Rd., Colton, OR 97017.

Oregon Kayak and Canoe Club, P.O. Box 692, Portland, OR 97207.

Paddle Trail Canoe Club, P.O. Box 24932, Seattle, WA 98124.

Washington Kayak Club, P.O. Box 24264, Seattle, WA 98124 (tel. 206/433-1983).

FAVORITE RIVERS

◆ **Skykomish River, Central Washington Cascades** (page 189-91).

◆ **Deschutes River, Central Oregon** (page 388-9).

◆ **White Salmon River, The Columbia Gorge** (page 279).

◆ **North Umpqua, Southern Oregon** (page 422).
◆ **Rogue River, Southern Oregon** (page 422).

WHITEWATER RAFTING

Whitewater rafting is a decidedly seasonal activity in the Northwest, and unfortunately, summer, when most people's minds turn to thoughts of spending a day on a raging river, isn't always the best season. Most Washington and Oregon rivers, with a few exceptions, are run by commercial rafting companies during the late spring and early summer snowmelt season. A few rivers can, however, be run throughout the summer months.

If you happen to be heading out in your own raft, call the National Oceanic and Atmospheric Administration's **Washington Whitewater and Steelhead Hotline** (tel. 206/526-8530) to check river levels. In Oregon, call NOAA's **River Level Info Line** (tel. 503/261-9246).

FAVORITE WHITEWATER RAFTING TRIPS
◆ **Wenatchee River, Central Washington Cascades** (page 191).
◆ **Skykomish River, Central Washington Cascades** (page 191).
◆ **Deschutes River, Central Oregon** (page 372-3).
◆ **Rogue River, Southern Oregon** (page 424-5).
◆ **North Umpqua River, Southern Oregon** (page 425).

WILDLIFE VIEWING

I have always felt that the chance to see wildlife is one of the primary reasons to be outdoors. I'm not talking about squirrels and chipmunks here (or birds, which are a sport unto themselves); I'm talking charismatic macrofauna: deer, elk, mountain goats, sea lions, sea otters, river otters, marmots, beavers, porcupines, coyotes, cougars, bobcats, black bears, and salmon. These are the animals that instill in viewers a sense of wildness, a sense that as long as these animals still roam the woods, nature is still holding its own against the inroads of development.

While some of these large animals are rarely seen, others are quite commonplace, at least if you're in the right neighborhood at the right time. Unfortunately, the right neighborhoods are getting smaller and smaller. For the most part, if you want to be sure of seeing terrestrial wildlife, head for a national park. Outside these preserves, hunters and hikers with dogs make sure that the rest of us won't see much of anything in the way of wildlife.

Marine wildlife, on the other hand, is a different story. Protected everywhere they're found in the Northwest, sea lion and seal populations have been on the increase for many years now. Today these pinnipeds can be seen up and down the coast, in Puget Sound, and the San Juan Islands. Sea otters, on the other hand, can be seen only off the most remote sections of the Olympic Peninsula.

Although rapidly disappearing from Northwest rivers for a wide number of reasons, from overfishing to dams to silting of spawning-ground gravels, salmon are still a symbol of the region. There is something thrilling and primordial in the sight of 2-foot-long salmon struggling up a stream only inches deep. Spawned in that same creek, these adult salmon expend their last reserves of energy to return from saltwater to spawn in the streams and rivers of the Northwest. The sudden, explosive bursts of speed and power necessary to ascend a rapid or leap a waterfall instill in all who witness such power a sense of respect and awe. From shallow streams to fish ladders to powerful rivers, there are many places around the Northwest where you can see salmon (and steelhead) and witness their primeval drive to spawn in the stream where they were born.

FAVORITE WILDLIFE VIEWING SPOTS
◆ **Mount Rainier National Park, Mount Rainier and Mount St. Helens Areas** (page 237).
◆ **Olympic National Park, The Olympic Peninsula** (page 107-9).
◆ **Deadline Falls, Southern Oregon** (page 426).
◆ **Jewell Meadows, The Oregon Coast** (page 450).

◆ **Sea Lion Caves, The Oregon Coast** (page 464).

Northwest Weather

Whenever the subject of the Northwest comes up, the topic of the weather is sure to follow. The region's rainfall is infamous (and hasn't been helped by all the national news coverage of the floods of 1996). However, contrary to popular belief, the sun does sometimes shine. Just don't count on it.

Generally speaking, the lowlands west of the Cascades have a mild climate with rainfall coming primarily between October and June. Summers in the Puget Sound area rarely see temperatures above 90° F, though in the Willamette Valley and southern Oregon, summer temperatures frequently top 100°. Winter temperatures rarely drop below 10 or 15° F in the lowlands and then only on one or two week-long cold spells each year. While lowlands in October through June are, for the most part, gray and wet, July through September can be glorious, with clear blue skies and little rainfall. However, recent years have seen what many longtime Northwesterners are calling a shift back to the climate patterns that dominated the region 15 to 20 years ago, when rain was common throughout the summer. In 1995 and 1996, there were long periods of rainy weather scattered throughout the summer months. The long-term climate forecast is for similar weather.

However, as new Northwest residents soon learn, what's true for the west side of the Cascades is not necessarily true for the east side, where colder winters, hotter summers, and clearer skies year-round prevail. Especially during the late spring and early fall, the eastern slopes of the Cascades offer shelter from the storms of the western slopes. Autumn is also the best time to visit the coast. During the summer, the coast is subject to fogs, but by autumn, seawater and air temperatures are about the same, the fogs dissipate, and days can be beautiful.

The Northwest is very different from the rest of the United States in that temperatures and rainfall are amazingly variable within only a few miles. These striking contrasts are due to the region's varied topography, which creates its own weather. My two favorite examples of the Northwest's peculiar climate are the Olympic Peninsula and the Columbia Gorge.

The Olympic Peninsula is well known for its temperate rain forests, some of the only such forests in the world. In an average year the peninsula's lowland rain-forest valleys receive in excess of 150 inches of rain. That's more than 12 feet of rain annually! Up at the top of Mount Olympus, more than 200 inches fall, though mostly in the form of snow. However, barely 40 miles away in the town of Sequim, in the rain shadow of the Olympic Mountains, it rains less than 20 inches per year.

The single most striking contrast of climates in the Northwest occurs in the Columbia Gorge, the only sea-level gap in the Cascades. This massive gorge forms a sort of wind tunnel and creates its own weather. The winds are well known to the boardsailing community, but what's less well known are the ice storms that regularly paralyze the gorge in winter as cold inland air mixes with wet coastal air. While the gorge is only about 50 miles long, its west end lies in the lush western slopes of the Cascades, where Douglas firs grow more than 200 feet tall, and its east end lies in the high desert, the sort of sagebrush country usually associated with Wyoming and Colorado. The climate within the gorge varies so much from end to end that weather forecasts split it into two sections.

For planning hikes in the spring, summer, and fall, snow level is the crucial factor, and this hinges on how deep the snowpack was the previous winter. In an average winter, the subalpine meadow regions favored for summer hiking aren't usually free of snow until sometime in mid- to late July. Until the snow melts off, it can be difficult to follow trails; it can also be dangerous to cross snowfields. In a heavy snow year, some trails never melt out. Hikers need to check with ranger stations to find out if trails are clear of snow (though even this information is not always reliable). And anyone heading to high elevations must be aware that snow can fall any month of the year in the mountains.

The Outdoors on the Wire: Internet Resources

Anyone who's explored the pathways of the Internet knows that, for now anyway, it's more like a logging road gone to seed than an "Information Superhighway." You can grow old searching for a specific piece of information, what with slow connection and data transmission speeds, sites that promise the world and deliver almost nothing, outdated links, and so on. And there's no guarantee that what you do find will be accurate—many sites reflect personal or commercial biases.

Still, with patience and a little perspective on all this, the Internet can be a great tool for finding out things about getting outdoors.

Outside magazine's very own **Outside Online** (http://outside.starwave.com) is an excellent all-around outdoor site. In addition to many features and articles from the magazine, you'll find content that's hard to find elsewhere: loads of advice on outdoor gear and outdoor travel, plus interactive features that allow you to enlist Outside's help on questions you can't find the answer to.

The **Northwest Recreation Page** (http://www.halcyon.com/richardc/) is so comprehensive and well annotated a collection of links that it eliminates—to my great relief—any need to list the scores of good sites that zero in on the Northwest and all the things you can do outside here. Virtually every good Northwest page I've found is listed here. It also includes a listing of recreation-oriented Usenet newsgroups, which are the loci of all the "virtual communities" that the cyber-pundits like to refer to. If you have a specific question about getting outside in the Northwest, post it to one of the newsgroups and you'll soon have more knowledgeable answers than you can shake a stick at.

Happy surfing—and remember that you'd rather be outside than getting cross-eyed in front of a computer!

With spring skiing often lasting through April and into May, many Northwesterners don't bother putting away their skis until well after gardens are in full bloom in the lowlands (and some ski all summer on Mount Hood and Mount Rainier). However, you can generally count on being able to hike at elevations lower than 2,500 feet almost any month of the year (unless a nasty weather system has dropped in). Between 3,000 and 4,500 feet, the hiking season usually lasts from May or June to November. Above 4,500 feet the hiking season generally lasts from about mid-July until late September or early October, when the snows once again begin falling. Keep in mind that these are rough dates that vary from year to year. Also, in the Olympic Mountains and North Cascades, the high-elevation hiking season starts a little later and ends a little earlier.

May, June, and October then become the most unpredictable months for hikers. During these months you might get good weather and be able to hike as high as 4,000 feet or so, but then again, you might encounter snow. Check with a ranger station in the spring and watch the weather forecast in the fall. Anyone hiking at altitude after mid-September should be prepared for a sudden snowstorm. In fact, you should always carry plenty of warm clothes and rain gear whenever hiking at altitude in the Northwest, whether you are on a day hike or a backpacking trip.

The key to pursuing winter sports in Washington and Oregon is keeping an eye on the snow level. In any given week, the snow level can range from sea level (snow in Seattle and Portland) to 6,000 feet or more (which sometimes causes floods like those of February 1996). With most ski area base elevations between 4,000 and 5,000 feet, you want to be sure that the snow is at least that low before heading for the ski slopes or cross-country trails. Otherwise, you're going to be skiing in the rain.

Just about the hardest aspect of skiing in the Northwest is growing accustomed to the fact that while it may be pouring rain in Seattle and Portland, it can be snowing in the mountains. The region's best skiing usually takes place on gray days just after it has snowed. If the sun comes out in the Northwest, it usually means the snow will melt and then ice over. Clear spells are also usually cold spells. Either way, skiing on sunny days in the Northwest usually isn't that great, unless you happen to be on the east side of the Cascades (say at Mount Bachelor or Mission Ridge) where the air is almost always colder and the snow just a little bit fluffier. One of the oddest twists of the Northwest's winter climate is that while Mount Bachelor is the best ski area in the region, the nearby town of Bend, the closest town to Bachelor's slopes, is often completely snow-free.

Whitewater kayakers have an entirely different perspective on Northwest weather. For them the rainy season (from October through April) is the prime paddling season on many rivers. Snowmelt season in May and June, as the snowpack level begins to rise, is prime season on other rivers.

Mountain bikers also have a different set of parameters with which to contend. While some mountain bikers relish a good muddy ride, muddy trails in the Northwest tend not to recover well from tire tracks. Some trails are closed to riding until they are completely dry and others would benefit from such closures. Responsible riders stay off easily damaged trails until summer.

The single best piece of advice I can give you is, "Get a weather radio." With one of these dedicated little receivers, you'll always know the predictions for the next few days. A weather radio is particularly handy in the winter for determining whether a ski area is going to get snow or rain.

As crazy as the weather has been in the Northwest the past few years, there are some road-condition phone numbers that can come in handy if you're planning a trip in the winter:

◆ **Northwest Avalanche Center,** tel. 503/326-2400 or 206/526-6677

◆ **I-90 Sno-Park Report,** tel. 509/656-2230

◆ **Mountain Pass Road Report,** tel. 900/407-7277 (35¢ per minute)

◆ **Washington Highway and Pass Conditions Information,** tel. 206/434-7277

◆ **Washington Avalanche Report,** tel. 206/526-6677

◆ **Oregon Road Conditions Hotline,** tel. 503/889-3999

Maps

While the best maps money can buy are the USGS 7.5-foot quads, these maps are not really designed as reference materials for recreationists. Although it isn't a frequent problem, it is sometimes necessary to use several USGS maps just to do a short hike. This shortcoming has been addressed by a couple of companies that have taken USGS maps and altered them so as to make them more useful to hikers, cross-country skiers, snowshoers, and mountain bikers.

For the Washington Cascades and the northernmost of the Oregon Cascades, the Green Trails series of maps is superior to USGS maps. These maps show trail mileages and campsites, two bits of information that prove very useful when planning an extended hike. Custom Correct maps do the same thing for Washington's Olympic Peninsula. These maps are available at outdoor-recreation equipment stores and at ranger stations throughout the region.

The U.S. Forest Service also publishes quite a few maps that cover popular wilderness areas. I have found that most of the time these maps are all that are really necessary to stay unlost in the wilderness. Wildernesses covered by these maps include, among others, the Mount Adams Wilderness, the Indian Heaven Wilderness, the Kalmiopsis and Wild Rogue wildernesses, and the Sky Lakes Wilderness. The Geo-Graphics company also does wilderness maps, including maps for the Mount Hood Wilderness, the Mount Jefferson Wilderness, and the Three Sisters Wilderness.

A few other maps worth knowing about are the Alpine Lakes Protection Society's

Alpine Lakes Wilderness map, the USGS Mount Rainier National Park and North Cascades National Park maps, and the Imus Geographics maps of Diamond Peak Wilderness and Willamette Pass Oregon Cross-Country Ski Trails.

For getting into the woods and finding trailheads, USFS national forest maps are useful. These maps cover entire national forests as well as individual districts, and though they are usually not topographic, they show the numbers of Forest Service Roads (FS is used as an abbreviation for these roads throughout this book). These maps also show the location of forest service campgrounds, which can be very useful when trying to find a place to stay for the night.

However, the best solution to the problem of finding your way to trailheads is to get copies of the DeLorme Mapping Company's *Washington Atlas & Gazetteer* and *Oregon Atlas & Gazetteer*. These topographic atlases are incredibly thorough and in almost all cases will get you to your destination, no matter how remote. You'll find these atlases at bookstores and outdoor recreation stores throughout the Northwest.

On Camping in the Northwest

As in most places, campgrounds in Washington and Oregon are really hit-or-miss propositions. They can be peaceful places in attractive settings, but they can also be hellholes full of rowdy partyers. Personally, I prefer remote national forest campgrounds. I've found that large state park campgrounds with lots of amenities tend to attract noisy crowds. These campgrounds usually also stay full throughout the summer and getting a site can be difficult (reservations are taken at many state parks in both states). However, if you want a hot shower, a state park campground is the place to be. Campgrounds on large lakes also tend to be noisy and attract the water-ski and personal-watercraft crowd.

The most popular campgrounds in Washington and Oregon are those in the region's national parks, those just outside the national parks, and those in coastal areas. Washington and Oregon national park campgrounds do not accept

reservations and tend to fill up early on weekends. Your best bet is to arrive as early as possible and to come on a weekday.

Virtually all mountain campgrounds are operated seasonally and generally are open only between May or June and September or October. Many lowland campgrounds are also open only from late spring to early fall. If you want to go camping in the mountains in September or October, your best bet will be in a more remote national forest campground. On the other hand, many state parks along the shores of Puget Sound and the Oregon coast stay open year-round. In Oregon some of these campgrounds also have rental yurts (large circular tent cabins) that make camping in the rainy season a drier affair.

A certain percentage of campsites at many U.S. Forest Service campgrounds can be reserved at least five days in advance by calling the **National Forest Reservation Service** (tel. 800/280-CAMP). The reservation fee is $7.50. National forest campground reservations can be made up to 240 days (eight months) in advance.

State park campground reservations for both Oregon and Washington parks that take reservations (not all do) can be made by calling **Reservations Northwest** (tel. 800/452-5687). The reservation fee is $6. To make a reservation you'll need to know the name of the campground you want to stay at and the dates you plan to visit. Have some alternatives, too. State park campground reservations can be made up to 11 months in advance.

I have made it a practice to always keep at least a gallon of water in the car if I plan to be staying in a public campground. While most campgrounds with more than five campsites have piped drinking water, I have been to larger campgrounds where the water has been turned off for one reason or another. Small, remote national forest campgrounds are not likely to have piped water, so be sure to bring your own.

Schools & Educational Outings

The **Nature Conservancy** is a nonprofit organization dedicated to the global preservation of natural diversity, and to this end it operates educational field trips and work parties to its own nature preserves and those of other agencies. For information about field trips in both Oregon and Washington, contact the Nature Conservancy, 821 SE 14th Ave., Portland, OR 97214 (tel. 503/230-1221).

The **Sierra Club Outings Department,** 85 Second St., Second Floor, San Francisco, CA 94105 (tel. 415/977-5630; fax 415/977-5795), offers a variety of trips in the Northwest each year. For information on outings by local chapters, you can call, in Oregon, the Portland chapter (tel. 503/238-0442) or, in Washington, the Cascade chapter (tel. 206/523-2147), which is in Seattle.

Earth Watch, P.O Box 9104, Watertown, MA 02172 (tel. 617/926-8200), sends volunteers on scientific research projects. Contact them for a catalog listing trips and costs. Current projects include studies of orcas, chimpanzee communication, and Oregon caves.

Island Institute, P.O. Box 661, Vashon, WA 98070 (tel. 800/956-6722 or 206/463-6722), located on Spieden Island in Puget Sound, offers multiday programs focusing on snorkeling, kayaking, whale watching, and the natural history of the San Juan Islands. Accommodations are in wood-floored tents or cottages. Rates are all-inclusive and range from $399 for three days to $895 for a week's stay.

The **North Cascades Institute,** 2105 S.R. 20, Sedro-Woolley, WA 98284-9394 (tel. 360/856-5700, ext. 209), is a nonprofit organization that offers field seminars focusing on natural and cultural history in the North Cascades.

The **Northwest School of Survival,** P.O. Box 1465, Sandy, OR 97055 (tel. 503/668-8264), can teach you everything from how to start a fire with a stick to how to build a snow cave to how to evaluate avalanche hazard.

The **Olympic Park Institute,** 111 Barnes Point Rd., Port Angeles, WA 98363 (tel. 360/928-3720), offers a wide array of trips and educational programs each year between May and October. In the past there have been overnight canoe trips on Lake Ozette, a class on mosses, a birding trip to Protection Island, and various backpacking trips, including one specifically for women.

Sea Quest Expeditions/Zoetic Research, P.O. Box 2424, Friday Harbor, WA 98250 (tel. 360/378-5767), is a nonprofit organization that sponsors educational sea kayaking trips through the San Juans. Biologists and naturalists lead the trips.

Other Useful Addresses & Phone Numbers

One of the all-around best places to know about is the **Outdoor Recreation Information Center,** 915 Second Ave., Suite 442, Seattle, WA 98174 (tel. 206/220-7450). This office, which is a joint venture of the U.S. Forest Service and the National Park Service, has a wealth of information for anyone interested in getting outdoors.

Other useful offices you might want to contact include the following:

GOVERNMENT AGENCIES

Bureau of Land Management (OR/WA Office), 1515 SW Fifth Ave. (P.O. Box 2965), Portland, OR 97208 (tel. 503/952-6024).

Oregon Parks and Recreation Department, 1115 Commercial St. NE, Salem, OR 97310-1001 (tel. 503/378-6305).

National Park Service, Pacific Northwest Region, 909 First Ave., Suite 546, Seattle, WA 98104-1060 (tel. 206/220-4013).

Washington Parks & Recreation Commission, 7150 Cleanwater Lane (P.O. Box 42650), Olympia, WA 98504-2650 (tel. 800/233-0321).

Washington Department of Natural Resources, 111 Washington St. SE (P.O. Box 47000), Olympia, WA 98504-7000 (tel. 360/902-1000).

OUTDOORS ORGANIZATIONS

The Mazamas, 909 NW 19th Ave., Portland, OR 97209 (tel. 503/227-2345); a hiking and climbing club.

The Mountaineers, Club Headquarters, 300 Third Ave. W, Seattle, WA 98119 (tel. 206/284-6310); the Northwest's biggest outdoors organization.

Trails Club of Oregon, P.O. Box 1243, Portland, OR 97207 (tel. 503/233-2740); a hiking, skiing, snowshoeing, and bicycling club.

THE SAN JUAN ISLANDS &
WASHINGTON'S NORTHWEST COAST

A LITTLE MORE THAN 200 YEARS AGO THE SPANISH, ANXIOUS ABOUT Russian, American, and British expansion on the west coast of North America, sailed north from San Francisco to stake their own claims on the Pacific Northwest. They named a few islands and waterways, but one Northwest rainy season had them headed back to southern California to work on their tans and tend their vineyards.

Had they stuck around the islands they named long enough to do some atmospheric studies, they might have decided to stay. Washington's San Juan Islands and northwest coast lie within what is known as the Blue Hole, a rain-shadow vortex. While Seattle, 60 miles south, sips its lattés to the constant *drip, drip, drip* of 40 annual inches of rain, and while the Hoh Valley, 60 miles to the west, drowns under its deluge of more than 150 inches of rain each year, rainfall within the Blue Hole averages less than 30 inches per year. There are as many as 250 days of sunshine each year within the Blue Hole, which swirls over all of the northern Olympic Peninsula, southern Vancouver Island, and the San Juans.

What the Spanish failed to notice has become one of the San Juan Islands' greatest attractions. Waterlogged Seattleites and other human sponges of the soggy Northwest flock to the San Juans throughout the year. It may not be Aruba, but it sure beats mildew land.

Sunshine (or at least a lack of rain) may be what sets the San Juans apart from their neighbors, but it is unrivaled beauty that has made these islands famous. The tops of mountains that were mostly submerged by floods at the end of the last ice age, these islands are draped in the emerald green of coniferous forests and surrounded by sapphire blue waters. More than 100 pairs of bald eagles live in the San Juans, thriving on the fish and waterfowl that frequent these waters. There are also more than 90 killer whales (orcas) plying these same waters feeding on the abundant salmon. Together these natives of the San Juans lend the area a wild, untrammeled feel, belied somewhat by the countless vacation homes that now sprout from the islands like chanterelles after the first autumn rains.

Despite the ever-increasing development of these islands, to the casual observer the San Juans remain elusive, inscrutable, and beautifully pristine. Only four of the 170 or so islands within this archipelago are accessible by ferry, and only three of these islands have anything in the way of commercial development. To visit any of the other islands, you'll need a boat. Some of these smaller islands are populated, some are privately owned, and still others are publicly owned. These latter are broken down into islands that are state marine parks and those that are part of the San Juan Islands National Wildlife Refuge.

The latter islands tend to be small, rocky islets favored by birds and sea lions. The marine parks, on the other hand, are the destinations of choice for gunkholing sailors, powerboaters, and island-hopping sea kayakers. Marine parks often offer the same sort of amenities any other state park might have, but without the road access. For many Washingtonians, these marine parks are reason enough to own a boat. Many a Washington sea kayaker has taken up the sport simply for the chance to paddle among these fabled islands, camping on remote beaches, eating clams and crabs for dinner, and communing with the orca whales.

With killer whales cruising offshore, the San Juans do a brisk business in whale-watching cruises. On San Juan Island there is even a park dedicated solely to whale watching. Bird watching is equally productive in the islands, with the ferryboats that ply these islands providing the best observation platforms for adding to life lists.

Even landlubbers who have never skippered a skiff can find, on the four ferry-accessible islands of San Juan, Orcas, Lopez, and Shaw, an escape from the fast pace of mainland life. Chief among the land-based island activities of the San Juans is probably bicycling. Perhaps nowhere outside the back roads of Vermont have cyclists made a stronger claim to the roadways (often to the anger of island residents who hate being stuck behind slow-moving cycles on winding roads). Tours of the San Juans are offered by cycle touring companies both large and small, and on San Juan, Orcas, and Lopez, bicycles can be rented. Hiking and walking are the next most popular activities of terra firma visitors to the islands.

San Juan Island, the largest and most populous of the islands, is also among the most geographically diverse, with farmland, coniferous forests, and dry windswept pasturelands. Bicycling is among the most popular island activities, though distances here are a bit greater than those on Orcas Island and, for the most part, a bit less interesting. However, the west side of the island, with a handful of parks, offers plenty of diversions for cyclists, walkers, and whale watchers. San Juan Island also offers several good launch sites for sea

kayaking forays through the surrounding islands, and Friday Harbor, the largest town in the San Juans, is now the only place where you can unload and launch your sea kayak if you ferried over with no car.

Orcas Island, distinctively horseshoe shaped, has long been preferred as a summer vacation spot by holidaying Puget Sounders, and consequently, the island offers a lot of outdoors activities. Though popular with cyclists, the roads here are narrow, very hilly, and relatively heavily traveled (all those tourists). At Moran State Park, once a private estate, you'll also find the only mountain-biking trails on the islands (actually some of the very best in the state). This large park also has miles of hiking trails, lakes for fishing and swimming, and, as its centerpiece, Mount Constitution, the highest point in the San Juans. The view from the top of this mountain is one of the most bliss-inducing in the state. Try riding up to the 2,407-foot summit on your bike, either by road or trail, to fully appreciate—wheeze, wheeze, wheeze—the view. Other popular Orcas activities include sea kayaking and whale watching. All in all, this island is the best choice for active vacationers.

Though neither the largest nor the smallest of the San Juan Islands, **Lopez Island** is the most popular with bicyclists. With less traffic than Orcas or San Juan and fewer steep hills, too, Lopez makes for easy pedaling. Accommodations and campgrounds are limited, as are public parks. What attracts people is the idyllic rural atmosphere of the island. One of my favorite spots in all the San Juans, Shark Reef Park is at the south end of the island and overlooks the churning waters of San Juan Channel. Spencer Spit State Park is the largest park on the island and offers camping, beach walking, and bird watching.

Shaw Island is the fourth, and least developed, of the ferry-accessible islands. You'll find a general store and a campground but no restaurants or lodgings of any sort on this island. Ferry travelers' first impressions of Shaw are of Franciscan nuns guiding the ferry into the dock and directing the loading and unloading of the ferry's passengers and vehicles. Although

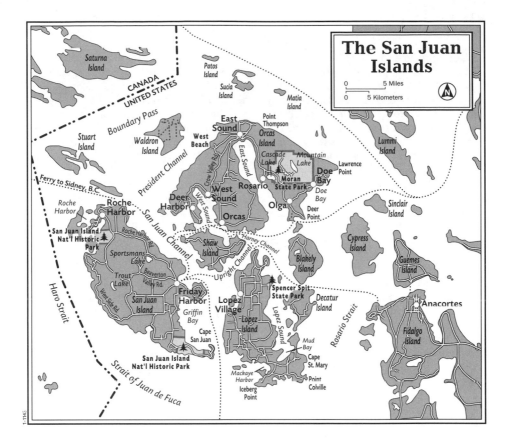

the entire island is not run by nuns, the people who do live here guard their privacy fiercely. Those few people who do come here for a visit mostly do so on a day trip from another island. If you bring your own food and water, the island makes for a good day's bike ride. Just don't miss the last ferry of the day!

Those same ferries that provide first glimpses of the San Juans are also these islands' single greatest caveat. Dealing with the ferries, especially in the summer, can be a real pain. Expect hours-long waits to get on a ferry, both coming and going, and plan accordingly. Long lines at the ferry landings also mean big crowds on the islands. Campgrounds stay full throughout the summer, as do most lodgings. Make reservations as far in advance as possible and have alternate dates ready.

Over on the mainland, the northwest coast of Washington offers many of the same attributes as the San Juans, but not in such a compact form. However, the mainland coast, which actually includes several bridge-accessible islands, is, for the most part, without the waits for ferries, and sometimes even without the crowds. Agriculture, not tourism, dominates this region, but there are still areas of interest to outdoor sports enthusiasts. **Whidbey Island,** which at 45 miles in length is the longest island in the continental U.S., offers the greatest variety of outdoors options and is a popular weekend getaway for Seattleites. **Fidalgo Island,** which lies just north of Whidbey Island across the Deception Pass Bridge, is considered by some to be part of the San Juan Islands, and though best known as the site of the ferry dock for San Juan Islands ferries, also offers good bicycling, hiking, fishing, and sea kayaking. From atop Mount Erie, this island's highest point, there is a view to rival that from atop Orcas Island's Mount Constitution. The Bellingham area farther to the north comes in a close second to the Whidbey/Fidalgo area for variety of outdoors activities, with Larrabee State Park and the Chuckanut Drive area being the Bellingham area's biggest recreational playground.

Convoluted shorelines up and down this coast provide plenty of opportunities for exploration by sea kayak, and with the easternmost of the San Juan Islands lying just offshore from Anacortes, paddling from the mainland can be easier and just as rewarding as heading out by ferry to start your paddle tour. **Cypress Island,** in fact, is one of the most popular overnight sea kayak destinations in the state. The waters of Deception Pass State Park also attract paddlers of all skill levels, despite the reputation the pass has for strong currents (the park also includes plenty of protected water).

Both the hilly roads of Whidbey Island and the flat farmlands of the **Skagit River valley** attract numerous cyclists as well. Farmlands and marshes also combine to provide some of the very best bird watching in the state, especially during the winter months when shorebirds and waterfowl congregate along **Padilla Bay** and the **Skagit Flats.** For more leisurely pursuits, the beaches of this region are far more extensive and accessible than those of the San Juans. Sailboarding and surfing are even possible at a few spots, and there are numerous excellent dive sites scattered up and down this coast.

Together the San Juan Islands and the northwest coast of Washington provide the greatest variety of water-oriented activities in the state. Yet with their diverse landscapes, these areas also provide a wealth of land-based recreational activities.

The Lay of the Land

Although Washington state borders the Pacific Ocean, the San Juan Islands and the state's northwest coast lie 80 to 100 miles from the open ocean. A coast without an ocean seems strange only until you take a look at a map and recognize that this shore lies on an inland sea formed behind the buttress of the Olympic Peninsula and the southern tip of massive Vancouver Island. Many people (and I once counted myself among these) mistakenly think that the San Juan Islands lie within Puget Sound. The sound, however, lies to the south of these islands due east of the Olympic Peninsula. The waters of

the state's northwest coastal region do not go by a single name, as does the Puget Sound. They are, instead, a maze of channels, straits, and passes.

This complex network of waterways is the result of glacial activity 12,000 years ago. During the last ice age, the Vashon Glacier blanketed this region with a thick sheet of ice, gouging out deep valleys and scouring mountainsides down to bare rock. At the time, sea level was far below what it is today. The San Juan Islands and nearby Whidbey Island were land-bound mountains surrounded by ice. As the ice melted and the sea level rose, the bases of these mountains were submerged and seawater penetrated deep into the glacial valleys of western Washington, forming the watery maze of the Puget Sound and leaving the San Juan Islands adrift in an inland sea. Today the tops of more than 200 submerged mountains comprise the San Juan Islands and their environs, in an area roughly 25 miles by 30 miles. About 170 of the San Juan Islands are large enough to have names, while others are merely unnamed rocks on navigational charts.

Rocky, glacial soils, a drier, rain-shadow climate, and strong winds have combined to give this region some of its distinctive flora and habitats. The madrona tree, with its flaking, coppery bark and dark green, waxy leaves, is an icon of the San Juan Islands. Growing from bare rock and clinging to cliffs, these trees capture the thin light of this northerly region and reflect it back with a warm glow. Madrona prefer a dry climate, yet on the same islands that support these trees, moisture-loving western red cedars and Douglas firs are also to be found. In some places, such as Whidbey Island's South Whidbey State Park, remnant groves of ancient trees can still be seen. Such huge trees once covered the islands and mainland uplands of this region. However, their easy accessibility from the water and to ports made these the first of the region's trees to be cut for lumber when white settlers first arrived in the area.

While tree cutting was among the earliest livelihoods of settlers in this region, farming soon followed. Part of the reason that the British and Americans were willing to fight over San Juan Island was because it was such good agricultural land. Natural prairies there, as well as on Whidbey Island, attracted farmers in the mid-19th century. These pockets of grasslands made farming so much easier (no old-growth trees to chop down before you could plow) that they were among the first lands in the region to be tilled. Today, Ebey's Prairie on Whidbey Island has been preserved as a National Historical Reserve, the first of its kind in the nation. Within this reserve, 19th-century farms have been preserved intact to capture the look and feel of Whidbey Island's agricultural heritage. A similar natural prairie has been preserved at the San Juan Island National Historical Park, at its American Camp unit.

This latter prairie is today home to thousands of rabbits, which along with deer are probably the most-sighted wildlife species in the San Juan Islands. The deer are native to the islands, but the rabbits are not. They are descendants of rabbits that escaped years ago from a commercial rabbit farm on San Juan Island. With few natural predators, the rabbit population has skyrocketed over the years, and though a disease swept across the island some years back and reduced the population considerably, since then the rabbit population has rebounded. Likewise, the islands' deer have no natural predators, and because the islands are so densely populated, hunting is restricted here. Consequently, the deer population is large. The deer tend to be quite tame and are a major pest to island gardeners.

Sea kayakers and other people camping on any of the small islands that are designated marine state parks are more likely to be bothered by raccoons. These pesky animals raid campsites for food and can quickly ruin a paddling trip by making off with all the food. James Island is infamous for its marauding raccoons.

Less likely to be a problem are the orca whales that frequent the waters off the west coast of San Juan Island during the summer months. Boaters, including kayakers, who encounter whales should always stay at least 100 feet away.

Any time of year, the islands are home to harbor seals and sea lions, which can often be seen lounging on rocky islets and the more remote and rocky shores of larger islands. Minke whales, gray whales, and porpoises are also sighted occasionally in waters throughout this region. What attracts these sea mammals to the islands is the wealth of fish life, and this in turn is due to the unusual underwater topography of the region.

As the tides ebb and flow within this inland sea, they generate strong currents. When these currents encounter the many submerged mountains and islands of these waters, they are deflected, often welling up from the deep seafloor. These cold seafloor waters carry heavy loads of plankton and constantly replenish the food supply in the surface waters. The now-nutrient-rich surface waters attract large numbers of fish that feed on plankton. These fish in turn attract feeders higher on the food chain, such as killer whales, sea lions, and humans.

Just as the region's waters are among the most productive in the state, so too are the agricultural lands of the mainland. The flatlands near the mouth of the Skagit River produce not only large vegetable and berry crops but are also well known for their tulip fields. Farms here specialize in growing tulip and daffodil bulbs, and each year in late March and early April the countryside between Mount Vernon and La Conner is awash in acres of red and yellow. At this time the roadways are also awash in traffic as flower gazers descend on the area in much the same way as leaf peepers descend on New England in the autumn.

Other river mouths, including those of the Stillaguamish, Samish, and Nooksack, are also flanked by wide agricultural flatlands. However, this coastline does have its more mountainous shores as well. In the south, Whidbey Island and Fidalgo Island, both of which are accessed by bridges, as well as ferries, are dominated by hilly, forested terrain. At 1,270 feet, Fidalgo Island's Mount Erie is one of the highest points in the region. South of Bellingham, Chuckanut Mountain rises nearly 2,000 feet straight from the waters of Bellingham and Samish bays. Chuckanut Drive, one of the most scenic and famous roads in the state, parallels the water along this stretch of coastline, providing access to the shore at Larrabee State

Park and a few other sites. North of Bellingham, agriculture once again dominates the landscape all the way to the Canadian border, not far north of which begin the suburbs of sprawling Vancouver, British Columbia. However, just before reaching the Canadian border, Washington's northwest coast features two long, sandy beaches—one at Birch Bay State Park and the other at Semiahmoo Spit—that together solidify the coast's position as a recreational shoreline.

Small farm communities predominate throughout this region, although along the I-5 corridor many of these farm towns have now grown to larger proportions. The largest city in the area is Bellingham, which is 90 miles north of Seattle. With a major port facility that includes the Alaska ferry terminal and Western Washington University, Bellingham has a decidedly urban character that sets it at odds with the more conservative farm communities of the region.

Parks & Other Hot Spots

One important telephone number you'll probably need is for the **Washington State Ferries** (tel. 800/84-FERRY or 206/464-6400); their World Wide Web address is http://www.wsdot.wa.gov/ferries/.

THE SAN JUAN ISLANDS

Moran State Park

On Orcas Island 12.5 miles from the ferry landing on Horseshoe Hwy. Tel. 360/376-2326. Camping, hiking, mountain biking, swimming, flatwater canoeing.

As the largest and most popular state park in the San Juan Islands, Moran has a lot to offer. Throughout the summer, the campgrounds stay packed, but visitors can find a touch of solitude on the 32 miles of trails that lead through dense forest and past five lakes. These trails are open to hikers and bikers alike. There is also fishing, canoeing, and swimming to be done on the park's Cascade and Mountain lakes. The park, which takes up a large part of the

island's eastern arm, has at its center 2,409-foot Mount Constitution, the highest peak in the San Juans. Both trails and a road lead to the summit of this mountain, and from the top there is one of the most splendid views imaginable. In every direction, emerald-green islands rise from the cobalt-blue waters, while in the distance rise the Olympic Mountains, Mount Baker and the North Cascades, and even Mount Rainier.

San Juan Island National Historical Park

On San Juan Island with units at the north end of the island off West Valley Rd. and at the south end of the island off Cattle Point Rd. Tel. 360/378-2240. Sea kayaking, hiking, whale watching, bird watching, swimming, picnic areas.

This historical park on San Juan Island is divided into two units, one at the north end of the island and one at the south end. The park preserves two army camps—one English and one American—from the middle of the 19th century. The camps were established during a military confrontation that arose after an American settler on the island shot and killed a pig belonging to the Hudson's Bay Company. At the time, the United States and Great Britain were both laying claim to San Juan Island due to vague wording in the agreement that had set the 49th parallel as the boundary between the United States and Canada. Eventually, it took third-party mediation in the form of Kaiser Wilhelm I of Germany to settle the dispute over the ownership of San Juan. The kaiser ruled in favor of the United States and brought an end to the Pig War of San Juan Island.

Today reconstructed buildings at each of the two camps are the main focus of the park. However, each section also has a few miles of walking trails. American Camp, at the south end of the island, has the more extensive and varied trails, and also has the longest public beach on the island. Bird watching is also good at this unit of the park, and during the summer, you may also see orca whales just offshore. English Camp, at the north end of the island, makes a good launch site for sea kayaks and has a trail that leads to one of the highest points on the island.

Marine State Parks

Accessible only by boat. Tel. 360/378-2044. Sea kayaking, sailing, scuba diving, swimming, fishing, hiking.

Scattered among the larger San Juan Islands are dozens of smaller islands. Some of these are privately owned, some (those that provide critical wildlife habitat) are part of the San Juan Islands National Wildlife Refuge, and still others are state parks. Many of these latter have designated campsites and are very popular with boaters, including sea kayakers. Among the more popular marine state parks are Stuart Island, Jones Island, Matia Island, Sucia Island, Patos Island, Clark Island, and James Island.

THE NORTHWEST WASHINGTON COAST

Deception Pass State Park

Located at the north end of Whidbey Island and the south end of Fidalgo Island on Wash. 20. Tel. 360/675-2417. Camping, sea kayaking, scuba diving, swimming, fishing, hiking.

Lying on either side of Deception Pass, a narrow, cliff-edged channel between Whidbey Island and Fidalgo Island, this is the most popular state park in Washington and annually attracts millions of visitors. Most come simply to gaze down into the pass at the churning, eddying waters that sometimes flow through here at speeds of up to 7 knots, which is fast enough to form whirlpools and flip sea kayaks. The park, however, has far more to offer than a roadside glimpse of a hydraulic phenomenon. The park also contains many miles of walking trails, a long beach, two lakes that offer good swimming and fishing, scuba diving, and camping. Despite the strong currents through the pass, the area is popular with sea kayakers also.

Larrabee State Park

6 miles south of Bellingham on Chuckanut Dr. Tel. 360/676-2093. Camping, hiking, mountain biking, scuba diving, fishing, swimming.

Chuckanut Drive, south of Bellingham, is a popular scenic drive along a steep mountainside overlooking the San Juan Islands. Sunsets here are stunning, and the forested setting makes the entire drive a local favorite. About midway through the scenic drive is Larrabee State Park, which was Washington's first state park and remains the site of the prettiest beach in the region. The beach is the main attraction here and is tucked into a small cove surrounded by steep, forested mountain slopes and sea cliffs. Tide pools offer onshore diversions, while offshore, scuba divers explore the park's underwater flora and fauna. Although some people actually go swimming here, it is more popular with divers. Inland there are hiking trails that lead up Chuckanut Mountain. This is also the southern terminus of the Interurban Trail, a multiuse trail that was once a railroad grade and is now popular with mountain bikers. Needless to say, this park stays packed on summer weekends.

Birch Bay State Park

8 miles west of I-5 off Grandview Rd. Tel. 360/371-2800. Beach, picnic areas, camping, bird watching, swimming.

Located only a few miles south of the Canadian border, this state park provides access to a long, sandy beach with water that warms up enough in the summer to make swimming a feasibility. The surrounding community of Birch Bay is a classic beach town complete with water slides and minigolf, which detracts considerably from the natural setting of this park. However, the park is a bird sanctuary and birding here can be quite good.

The San Juan Islands ◆ What to Do & Where to Do It

BEACHES

Because most of the shoreline in the San Juan Islands is either rocky, privately owned, or both, beaches are in surprisingly short supply here. There are, however, quite a few parks that provide access to both large and small beaches. The longest stretches of public sand are at **Spencer Spit State Park** on Lopez Island and the **American Camp** unit of San Juan Island National Historical Park, which includes South Beach. Small coves offering narrow strips of beach include **Obstruction Pass Recreation Area** on Orcas Island, **Odlin County Park** on Lopez, and **South Beach County Park** at Shaw Island's Indian Cove.

BIRD WATCHING

Of all the birds to be seen in the **San Juan Islands,** none command greater attention from the masses than the area's resident bald eagles. These islands support the largest year-round population in the U.S. south of Alaska, and it is almost impossible to take a ferry through the islands without seeing several. The best way to spot bald eagles is to scan the trees along the shores of passing islands as you wend your way through the San Juans on the ferry. Watch for a bright patch of white amid the walls of green. During February, you might even be lucky enough to catch a glimpse of bald eagles going through their courtship rituals and displays.

Pelagic birding trips have been all the rage with serious birders over the past few years. (How else are you going to see birds that almost never come ashore?) These trips, usually on chartered boats, are generally rather expensive (but then serious birders rarely balk at spending cash to add a few more birds to the old life list, right?). Not so in the San Juan Islands, where an inexpensive ferry trip as a passenger from Anacortes to Sidney, B.C., can easily add a dozen new birds to your list. Along the winding route expect to see lots of bald eagles, golden eagles, tufted puffins, rhinoceros auklets, three species of scoters, three species of cormorants, pigeon guillemots, common murres, ancient and marbled murrelets, and old-squaws, among others.

There are also some onshore opportunities for bird watching at various spots around the islands. On San Juan Island, visit **Jackle's Lagoon,** which is near American Camp at the south end of the island and is a good place to spot bald eagles. In the open fields surrounding American Camp, you might also spot a few European skylarks, descendants of birds released on nearby Vancouver Island years ago. On Orcas Island, head to the south end of the east arm of the island to **Obstruction Pass Recreation Area,** where you also are likely to see bald eagles.

FISHING

You'd think that on islands surrounded by salt water, trout fishing wouldn't be a high priority, but anglers just don't seem able to give up trying their luck at these wily piscine torpedoes. In Orcas Island's **Killebrew Lake,** if you can avoid snagging on all the water lilies, you might hook into a stocked cutthroat trout. Trout fishing is far more popular, however, in **Moran State Park's Cascade Lake** and **Mountain Lake,** both of which are stocked with rainbows and cutthroats. The much smaller Twin Lakes are also stocked with rainbow and cutthroat trout and are popular fly-fishing spots. On San Juan Island, **Sportsman Lake** is popular for its largemouth bass.

However, it is charter fishing for salmon and bottom fish that is the most popular type of fishing on these islands, and there are several charter companies willing to take you out. Keep in mind, though, that due to the plummeting salmon population in the Northwest, charter fishing for salmon is no longer as good as it once was. However, you can still try your luck. These days, bottom fishing for halibut and rockfish seems to be more productive. On San Juan Island, try **Buffalo Works Fishing** (tel. 360/378-4612) or **Trophy Charters** (tel. 360/378-2110); on Orcas Island, try **Eclipse Charters** (tel. 800/376-6566 or 360/376-4663). Expect to pay around $65 for a half day of fishing.

HIKING

SAN JUAN ISLAND

The only walking trails on San Juan Island are within the San Juan Island National Historic Park, which has units at the north and south ends of the island. You'll find information about these trails in the "Walks & Natural Roadside Attractions" section, below.

ORCAS ISLAND

Mountain Lake-Mount Constitution Loop

7 miles. Moderate–strenuous. 1,300-foot elevation gain. Access: In Moran State Park, 12.5
miles from the ferry landing on Horseshoe Hwy.
Map: Hiking and Biking Trails of Moran (available at the park).

If you have time for only one hike while
visiting Orcas Island, this is the one to do.
Taking in forest paths, lakeside trails, and
mountaintop vistas, this route has it all.
From the Mountain Lake Campground,
head north along the west shore of the
lake. At the north end, a trail branches off
to the left to follow a creek gradually uphill to the two Twin Lakes. You can hike
around these two lakes, or take the left fork
when you reach Big Twin Lake (the first
lake you come to) and begin the steep
climb up to the summit of Mount Constitution. Before reaching the summit, you
will come to a spur trail that leads out to a
grassy knoll overlooking Mountain Lake
and the east face of Mount Constitution.
Continue up from here to the tower at the
summit of Mount Constitution for the best
views anywhere in the San Juans and one
of the finest views in the whole state. At
the back of the television station here at
the summit, find the Little Summit Trail
and start downhill. For 0.5 miles, this trail
follows an open ridgeline with excellent
eastward views before entering the forest
again. Eventually, the trail reaches Little
Summit, which has outstanding views to
the west and south, with the snowcapped
Olympic Mountains visible far to the
south. From here it is just over a mile down
an often-steep trail to Mountain Lake.

Cascade Lake-Cascade Falls Loop

5.3 miles. Easy. 130-foot elevation gain. Access:
In Moran State Park, 12.5 miles from the ferry
landing on Horseshoe Hwy. Map: Hiking and Biking Trails of Moran (available at the park).

If the hike described above seems a bit
more strenuous than you are up for, try this
easy hike around Cascade Lake and up to
Cascade Falls. Cascade Lake is the lowest and most readily accessible of the

park's five lakes and is the site of three
campgrounds, which means that this trail
sees a lot of use. Heading counterclockwise around the lake from the Cascade
Lake picnic area, the trail hugs the
lakeshore. Midway down the shore of the
lake, the trail crosses Rosario Lagoon on a
footbridge that provides a good vantage for
bird watching and wildlife viewing (deer,
muskrats, river otters, and raccoons all frequent these shores). At the south end of
the lake, you enter the South End Campground. Walk to campsite 17 and head up
the Cascade Creek Trail, which leads in
1 mile to Cascade Falls. The falls are most
impressive in spring and early summer
when rainfall feeds the creek. From here,
hike up to the road to pick up the trail to
the Midway Campground. Along this
1.3-mile stretch of trail, you'll pass through
several clearings that provide good views
of Cascade Lake. From the campground,
continue north to your starting point.

MOUNTAIN BIKING

See the "Road Biking" section, below, for
advice on avoiding the ferry system's
overheight fees for cars with rooftop bike
racks.

ORCAS ISLAND

Aside from the occasional stretch of gravel
road, all of the mountain biking in the San
Juans takes place in Moran State Park on
Orcas Island. Here mountain bikers will
find many miles of trails, some of which,
however, are closed from May 15 to September 15, when hikers become the dominant trail users. Because Moran State Park
is hilly, it makes for some strenuous
climbing, with plenty of fast downhills for
payoff. In fact, this is some of the best
single-track riding in the state.

Mount Constitution Hill Climb

10.3 miles. Strenuous. 1,850-foot elevation gain.
Access: In Moran State Park, 12.5 miles from
the ferry landing on Horseshoe Hwy. Map: Hiking and Biking Trails of Moran (available at the
park).

For mountain-bike masochists who aren't
happy unless their thighs ache and their

fingers cramp, this is the perfect trail (well, almost). The only drawback is that much of the uphill climb is on the paved Mount Constitution Road. Oh well, you can't have everything. Start this ride at the North End day-use area and begin climbing immediately on the trail to Cascade Falls. This trail parallels the paved road through the park and has some short but very steep climbs. In 1.3 miles, reach the Mount Constitution Road and begin the serious business of uphill slogging. Though you will have to contend with a bit of traffic on this road, the views make it all worthwhile. As you climb, vistas of the islands to the south open up, and there are a few places to stop and soak up these views. At one point the road passes through rocky meadows where I have seen deer grazing.

After switchbacking up to 2,200-foot Little Summit, the road levels off for more than 1 mile before making the final short climb to the top of Mount Constitution, where there is a stone tower and views, views, views! Soak them in for as long as it takes to feel rested, then head down the trail on the south side of the tower. This is the Little Summit Trail, and it cruises along an open ridgeline with fabulous views to the east for 0.5 miles. About 1 mile from the tower, a trail leads down to Summit Lake, which is well worth a visit. South of here, take a trail to the right and cross over the Mount Constitution Road onto the Cold Springs Trail. In 0.5 miles of riding through the forest, turn left at a trail junction to stay on the Cold Springs Trail. At this point you might want to stop and stretch your fingers. They're about to get a killer workout.

For the next 1.5 miles, the trail switchbacks down the steepest stretch in the park. Luckily, along the way you can rest your fingers at various clearings that afford views as good as any you had on the way up. This trail has every conceivable technical challenge a good mountain-bike trail should have, so be prepared for some fancy pedal work before you finally bottom out at Cascade Lake.

Keep in mind that this loop can be done only in months that the trail sections are open to bikes. During the summer, you may have to content yourself with an out-and-back on the paved Mount

Constitution Road, or try the variation on the next ride.

Pickett Road–Twin Lakes–Mountain Lake Loop

10.5 miles. Moderate–strenuous. 1,400-foot elevation gain. Access: The trailhead is at the North End day-use area in Moran State Park, 12.5 miles from the ferry landing on Horseshoe Hwy. Map: Hiking and Biking Trails of Moran (available at the park).

There are five lakes in Moran State Park, and this ride takes in all but one of them. The ride starts at the north end of Cascade Lake and parallels the paved road through the park for a ways. After passing the Midway Campground, take the left fork in the trail to climb to Cascade Falls Trail parking area on the road up to the summit of Mount Constitution. From this parking area, head down double-track Pickett Road, the abandoned road to the summit of Mount Pickett. This wide trail leads steadily uphill through the forest to reach Mount Pickett in just over 5 miles from the trailhead. From here, the trail drops to Twin Lakes, shortly before which the double track ends and you pick up single track. Trails loop around both these lakes, either of which makes a good place to get off your bike and rest for a while.

After pedaling around these pretty little lakes, look for the trail junction at the south end of Big Twin Lake. This is the upper end of the Twin Lakes Trail, from which you begin your return route. After cruising south along a flat section of trail for a little bit, the trail begins a long descent as it parallels the creek that feeds into Mountain Lake. Once you reach this lower lake, which is the longest in the park, take the left fork to follow the east shore of the lake on the Mountain Lake Loop trail (the west shore section of trail is closed to bicycles throughout the year). The trail rolls along with lots of ups and downs following the many curves of the lakeshore. Across the lake you can see Mount Constitution and Little Summit. This is the most scenic stretch of the trail and should be savored. At the south end of the lake, cross the outflow creek and descend to the Pickett Road just east of the Cascade Falls parking area. From here, backtrack to the trailhead. If you are looking for an easier ride, you can do an out-and-back up the east shore of Mountain Lake.

During the summer, the Pickett Road leg of this ride stays open to bicycles and can be linked with the Southeast Boundary Trail for a challenging loop. These two trails are the only ones open to mountain bikes during the summer.

Little Summit–Mount Constitution Loop

8 miles. Easy–moderate. 375-foot elevation gain. Access: In Moran State Park, 12.5 miles from the ferry landing on Horseshoe Hwy., start at the Little Summit parking area on Mount Constitution Road. Map: Hiking and Biking Trails of Moran (available at the park).

If you aren't up for the sort of climbing involved in the first two rides mentioned previously, but you still want to get out on the trails here in Moran, this makes a good, easy loop with all the best views in the park. Start at the Little Summit parking area, and after taking in the views from here, head up the fairly flat section of paved Mount Constitution Road that leads north. If you happen to be up here in the late spring, watch for newts migrating across the road. There is very little elevation gain along this road until the last short, steep climb to the summit.

After spending some time gazing at the superb island scenery from atop the stone summit tower, the real fun begins. Head down the Little Summit Trail on the south side of the tower, steep at first, but quickly becoming more gradual. For more than 0.5 miles, this trail runs along an open ridge with unobstructed views to the east. After this scenic section of the trail, you'll come to a side trail that leads west to Summit Lake. After a visit to this lake, continue along the forest trail all the way back to Little Summit.

ROAD BIKING

The San Juan Islands, with their bucolic scenery and winding country roads, are the most popular road-biking destination in Washington. People come from all over the country, often on organized bicycle tours, to pedal these roads. **Lopez Island,** the flattest, is the most popular with cyclists. **Orcas,** the hilliest, is the most scenic but most difficult island to ride. **San Juan Island** is somewhere in between Lopez and Orcas and lends itself well to multiday rides. So bicycle-oriented are these islands that on San Juan Island there is a private campground just for cyclists.

You can save a considerable amount of money on ferry tickets by leaving your car in Anacortes and just visiting the islands with your bike. This, however, requires advance planning and reservations at campgrounds and lodgings. Although summer is the best time of year to ride here, it is also the busiest season. Try late spring and early fall if you want to avoid the largest crowds. If you do come out here in the summer, don't even think about coming without reservations, unless, of course, you intend to make your visit a one-day trip. Campgrounds and B&Bs start filling up months ahead of time. Reserve early.

If you are heading out this way with bikes, you can avoid the substantial overheight fee if you carry your bikes anywhere other than the roof of your car. Anything over 7 feet, 6 inches gets slapped with this ridiculous and largely unnecessary charge. Two solutions: don't use a roof rack or put as many bikes as you can inside the car before getting on the ferry. Any bikes left over can be ridden on by their owners for only slightly more than you would pay for a passenger inside the car.

If you didn't bring your own bike, there are plenty of places on the islands where you can rent one. On San Juan Island, try **Island Bicycles,** 380 Argyle St., Friday Harbor (tel. 360/378-4941), which charges from $3 to $10 per hour and $15 to $50 per day. On Orcas Island, both mountain bikes and road bikes can be rented at **Dolphin Bay Bicycles** (tel. 360/376-4157), which is located just to the right as you get off the ferry. Rates are between $5 and $8 per hour or $20 per day. On Lopez Island, you can rent bicycles from **Lopez Bicycle Works,** Fisherman Bay Road (tel. 360/468-2847).

If you aren't already here on a bike tour, but you'd like to have a guide show you Lopez, Orcas, or San Juan Island, contact **Cycle San Juans,** Route 1, Box 1744, Lopez Island, WA 98261 (tel. 360/468-3251), which offers tours starting at $35.

San Juan Island

39 miles. Strenuous. 3,500-foot elevation gain.
Access: This ride starts at the San Juan Island
ferry landing in Friday Harbor.

San Juan Island, site of the county seat
(Friday Harbor), is the busiest and most
developed of the San Juan Islands, yet it
still makes a great place for bicycle touring. The two units of San Juan Island
National Historical Park make pleasant
off-bike diversions, and the old Hotel de
Haro at Roche Harbor Resort is well worth
a visit (and a stop for lunch) as well. There
are three campgrounds spaced roughly
equally around the island, so you could
turn a trip here into a leisurely three-day
camping trip (or you could rush through it
all in a day). If you're hungry when you
arrive, be sure to eat before leaving Friday Harbor. Outside of town there are few
restaurants. Also, you should know before
you start that this tour includes 7.4 miles
of riding on gravel roads, which makes this
a good ride for a mountain bike or hybrid.

Starting in Friday Harbor at the ferry
landing, head uphill on Spring Street, turn
right onto Second Street, left onto Guard
Street, and then right onto Tucker Street
to head out of town (all this happens in
about 0.5 miles). Tucker soon changes
names to become Roche Harbor Road and
after 8 meandering miles reaches the turnoff for the Roche Harbor Resort. About
halfway along this stretch of road, you'll
pass the private Lakedale Campground,
which is the island's best choice if you're
here in the summer and plan to camp
(they've got a swimming lake). From the
Roche Harbor turnoff, it is 1.5 miles down
to the resort, where you'll find the historic
Hotel de Haro, a white clapboard building with a beautiful garden in front. Beside the hotel is a good restaurant with a
waterfront deck that is the most scenic
lunch spot on the island. After hanging out
here for a while, head back up to the turnoff, and turn right onto English Camp
Road, which soon passes through the
English Camp unit of San Juan Island
National Historical Park.

From English Camp Road, it is only 0.3
miles down to the reconstructed buildings
at English Camp, where soldiers posted
here during the 19th-century Pig War even
constructed a formal garden. There are
also several miles of walking trails here.

Back on the main road, continue south
for 1.5 miles and turn right onto Mitchell
Bay Road, which winds around a bit and
becomes West Side Road. In 3.2 miles,
come to San Juan County Park, which has
a campground overlooking the Haro Strait.
Beyond this park, you reach the first
stretch of gravel road (4 miles). In 2.6 miles
you will come to Lime Kiln State Park,
which has been set aside as a whale-
watching park. During the summer
months, orcas are often spotted from the
park.

After the pavement resumes, you'll
climb the longest and highest hill on this
route (on appropriately named Bailer Hill
Road). After 3.2 miles of pavement, turn
right onto False Bay Road, the second
stretch of gravel road on this route. This
road winds through wide-open farmland
for 3.4 miles, passing the Pedal Inn Bicycle
Campground along the way. At the end of
this road, turn right onto Cattle Point Road
and head 2 miles down to the American
Camp unit of San Juan Island National
Historical Park.

Here, grasslands reminiscent of the
prairies are all that can survive on the windswept bluffs above the water. Rabbits,
descendants of rabbits that were raised for
meat years ago, have claimed this area as
their very own and are seemingly everywhere. You're also likely to see bald eagles
in this area. You can walk around the trails
here, stroll along South Beach, or continue
all the way to the southern tip of the island at Cattle Point (another 2.75 miles),
where there is a picnic area. After exploring this area, head back north on Cattle
Point Road. From False Bay Road, it is 5
miles back to the ferry landing.

If you want to split this trip up into two
or three days, you have a couple of options.
You can utilize one or more of the campgrounds, mentioned above, stay at a hotel
or B&B along the route, or do a north loop
and a south loop by cutting back across the
island on West Valley and Beaverton Valley roads or any of the other roads that cut
through the middle of the island.

Orcas Island

50–60 miles. Strenuous. 4,900–6,900-foot elevation gain. Access: This ride starts at the Orcas Island ferry terminal.

Orcas Island is the most mountainous of the San Juan Islands, and its many long, steep hills present a real challenge to cyclists. However, if you are in good shape, this island also offers the most spectacular scenery. The single most difficult climb on the island is the road to the top of Mount Constitution, which climbs 2,000 feet in a little more than 5 miles but also happens to be the most scenic stretch of road on the island. Because of the distance of this ride, and the fact that there are so many places to stop along the way, it is best done as an overnight ride. I suggest staying at one of the lodgings listed under "Inns & Lodges" later in this chapter, both of which are at the far end of the island, making either one a suitable place to end the day's ride. Moran State Park, also on the far side of the island from the ferry landing, offers camping.

From the ferry landing, you have two choices depending on what kind of bike you are riding. If you are on a road bike, head north 2.6 miles to a left turn that leads to the community of Westsound. From here, turn right onto Crow Valley Road and ride 4 miles north to a left turn that leads, in 1.3 miles, to West Beach, site of a rustic resort. From here it is 3 miles to the town of Eastsound, where there are several restaurants and a grocery store. Along the way, you should be sure to stop at the pottery studios. If you are on a mountain bike, you can ride the gravel Dolphin Bay Road for 8 miles before linking up with the busy Horseshoe Highway. Continue north on this road for 3 miles to Eastsound.

From Eastsound, it is 4.4 miles to Moran State Park, and less than 1 mile farther to Cascade Lake, a great place to get off your bike and rest for a while. If it's hot out, you can even go for a swim here. At the far end of the lake, the Mount Constitution Road forks off the main road and makes its grueling climb to the highest point in the San Juan Islands. The view from the summit is stunning. If you're feeling beat already, consider saving this climb until the next day. In 2 miles from the Mount Constitution turnoff, you'll come to the village of Olga and the Olga Cafe, a combination artists' cooperative and restaurant. From here it is only 0.5 miles to the turnoff for Obstruction Pass Recreation Area, which has a walk-in campground on a small, wooded cove. From this turnoff, it is another 2.9 miles to Doe Bay, both a place to stay, with cabins and campsites, and a good place to turn around. The hot tubs here (clothing optional) make a fitting end to a day's ride.

For the return journey, head back the way you came, perhaps making any side trips you passed on the first leg of the ride. If you have the energy on your return ride, be sure to ride to Deer Harbor from Westsound. This out-and-back ride adds 8.2 miles and takes you to beautiful fjord-like Deer Harbor, where there is a lodge and cafe.

Lopez Island Loop

33.5 miles. Moderate. 1,600-foot elevation gain. Access: This ride starts at the Lopez Island ferry landing.

As the least hilly of the major San Juan Islands, Lopez is the most popular with cyclists, and a tour of the entire island makes for a pleasant day's ride. There are six waterfront parks on the island (two of which have campgrounds) that make pleasant distractions from pedaling, and in Lopez Village, you'll find several good restaurants. Starting from the ferry landing, head south on Ferry Road (wait until all the automobile traffic from the ferry has passed and you'll have the road to yourself). In 1.2 miles, come to Odlin County Park, where there is a beach and campground. From here, head east on Port Stanley Road, which leads along the shore of Swifts Bay, and then, at 3.8 miles from the ferry landing, passes the road leading to Spencer Spit State Park, the island's other campground and a great place to walk along the beach (add 2.4 miles to your total if you ride to the park). At the end of Port Stanley Road in 1.9 miles from the Spencer Spit turnoff, turn left onto Lopez Sound Road and follow this road for 1.5

miles to a right turn onto School Road. In 1 mile, at Lopez School, turn left onto Center Road. In 1.5 miles, at the end of Center Road, turn left onto Mud Bay Road, which twists and turns for 4.4 miles to Aleck Bay Road, which heads south and then west along the south end of the island. In 2 miles, at the end of this road, turn left onto McKaye Harbor Road and ride to Agate Beach Park at the end of the road. This is the turnaround point of the ride and a good place for a picnic if you have brought one.

From here, head back up McKaye Harbor Road for 2.7 miles to Mud Bay Road. Turn left here and ride 0.9 miles to a left onto Vista Road. In 1.3 miles you'll come to the turnoff for Richardson and Jones Bay, which are only 0.5 miles away and worth the side trip. From the Vista Road intersection, ride north on Richardson Road for 1 mile and turn left onto Davis Bay Road. Follow this road for 1.7 miles (it will become Burt Road) to the trailhead for Shark Reef Wildlife Sanctuary, a rocky, windswept stretch of shoreline that is the prettiest piece of public land on the island. From here, ride north on Shark Reef Road for 0.8 miles and turn right onto Airport Road. In 0.4 miles, turn left onto Fisherman Bay Road. From here it is 2.6 miles to Lopez Road, the turnoff for Lopez Village. Along this stretch of road, you can make a 0.5-mile detour out to Otis Perkins Park on the far side of Fisherman Bay. Lopez Village is the island's commercial center and the site of several excellent restaurants. From Lopez Village, continue north on Lopez Road (it becomes Ferry Road) for 2.4 miles to a left turn onto Ferry Road. If you'd like another side trip, turn left onto Military Road and ride less than 0.5 miles to the entrance to Upright Channel Park. From the turnoff onto Ferry Road, it is 2.1 miles to the ferry terminal.

SCUBA DIVING

Despite the cold water, scuba diving is popular in the San Juans. In fact, the best time to dive here, and throughout the Puget Sound, is during the winter, which is when the water is at its clearest. This happens to coincide with the quietest time of year on the islands and the easiest time

of year to get a weekend reservation. Most of the best dive sites in the islands are off the many small marine state park islands in the archipelago. Among these many islands, the south tip of **Henry Island,** the north side and Ewing's Cove areas of **Sucia Island** (near Ewing's Cove three ships have been sunk to form an artificial reef), the north side of **James Island,** and the underwater cliffs of **Clark Island** are some of the best dive sites. These can be reached only by boat, so you'll need to bring your own, charter a boat, or go on a guided dive trip. **Point Doughty,** on the north shore of Orcas Island, is another good dive site that, again, is accessible only by boat. **Davidson Rock,** off the southern tip of Lopez Island, is another good dive site that is also accessible only by boat. Just about anywhere you dive in the San Juans, you need to be aware of the currents, which can be quite strong in places.

If you're a diver and want to rent equipment or go on a guided dive, or if you want to take a diving class while you're here, contact **Emerald Seas Dive Center,** 2-A Spring St. (P.O. Box 476), Spring Street Landing, Friday Harbor, WA 98250 (tel. 800/342-1570 or 360/378-2772).

SEA KAYAKING

Among sea kayakers, the San Juan Islands enjoy a legendary status. Dozens of forested islands (both large and small), fjordlike settings, tiny rocky islets, numerous state parks and recreation areas (many with paddle-in campgrounds), orca whales, bald eagles, seals, and sea lions all add up to the stuff of dreams. From brief paddles on protected coves, to multiday excursions across often rough seas, these islands offer routes for paddlers of all abilities. However, paddling the San Juans is not something to be done without planning. These are tidal waters, despite the often placid appearance, and because the islands rise up from deep water, currents flowing around the islands as tides change can be as strong as 5 knots (comparable to a swift whitewater river). Add high winds that can blow even during clear weather, tide rips (rough water where two currents meet), large Pacific Ocean swells that can penetrate through the Strait of Juan de Fuca,

The Truth About Killer Whales

Killer whales, once maligned as the wolves of the deep and dreaded as ruthless marauders of the sea, have been going through a change of image over the past few years. Even before the release of the popular children's movie *Free Willy*, an unofficial public-relations campaign was being waged to convince people that these are not ferocious killer whales but gentle orca whales. The more one learns about these intelligent, family-oriented animals, the more evident it becomes that this whale has been unfairly maligned.

Orcas can be found in every ocean, but one of their highest concentrations is in the waters stretching north from Puget Sound along the coast of British Columbia. This population has become one of the most studied and most publicized populations of orcas in the world.

Orcas, which can grow to be 30 feet long and weigh almost 9,000 pounds, are the largest member of the porpoise family. In the wild, they can live for up to 80 years, with female orcas commonly living 20 to 30 years longer than males. Orcas are among the most family-oriented animals on earth, and related whales will often live together for their entire lives, sometimes with three generations present at the same time.

These family groups frequently band together with other closely related groups into extended families known as pods.

A community of orcas consists of several pods, and in this area, these communities number around 100 individuals. There are three populations of orcas living in the waters off Vancouver Island. These are known as the northern and southern resident communities and the transient community. It is the southern resident community that whale-watchers in the San Juan Islands are most likely to encounter.

As predators, orcas do live up to the name "killer," and have been known to attack other whales much larger themselves. Some orcas off the coast of Argentina even swim onto the shore to attack resting seals. However, not all orcas feed on other marine mammals. Of the three communities in this area, only the transients feed on mammals. The two resident communities feed primarily on salmon, which are abundant in these waters.

If you haven't already heard, Keiko, the star of the movie *Free Willy*, who was once a sickly resident of a Mexico City marine park, now lives in a huge new tank at the Oregon Coast Aquarium in Newport, Oregon. Keiko was brought to this aquarium through donations of people who wished to see the whale released back to the wild, as in the movie. There are still plans to do just that once Keiko can be nursed back to health and taught how to survive in the real world.

and sudden weather changes that can bring high winds or fog, and you have the potential for very dangerous conditions, even for experienced paddlers. Fatalities have occurred in these waters. This said, there are still many routes that stay in protected waters. However, it is always a good idea to check the Canadian *Current Atlas: Juan de Fuca Strait to Strait of Georgia* (Canadian Hydrographic Service Department of Fisheries and Oceans) or *Washburne's Tables* (Weatherly Press)—two

guides that can be used in conjunction with each other and that map out current strengths and directions of flow. Using these books, you can determine what sort of conditions to expect in any given area on any given date and at any specific hour of the day. You'll find these books at kayaking supply shops around the greater Puget Sound area.

Although a knowledge of currents and tides is the single most important consideration when planning any paddle trip in the San Juan Islands, there are some other things to be aware of. These islands are very popular, especially during the summer months. Expect long waits to get on ferries and plan accordingly. Although there are many state parks accessible only by water, these parks are popular both with individual sea kayakers, kayak tour companies, and the powerboat and yachting crowds. Campsites will fill up on summer weekends, so arrive early. Some state parks provide water whereas others don't, so it is always a good idea to carry enough drinking and cooking water for your trip, say one gallon per person per day.

One of the greatest dangers of kayaking in the San Juans is hypothermia (cooling of the body's core temperature). The waters here stay cold year-round, and should you capsize, hypothermia sets in very quickly. Be prepared; pack warm, dry clothes in waterproof bags and in winter wear a wetsuit or dry suit. Other times of year, a paddle jacket and thermal underwear are a good idea.

Although it was once possible to board a ferry in Anacortes with just your kayak and gear, and then launch from any of the four islands served by the ferry sytem, kayaks can no longer launch from the ferry docks on Lopez, Orcas, or Shaw Island. So, if you want to save time and money by leaving your car in Anacortes and walking onto a ferry with your kayak in tow, you'll have to settle for launching from Friday Harbor. For the most part, this does not make a great launch site, unless you are planning a circumnavigation of Shaw Island.

If you don't have your own kayak, or would simply prefer to have your first San Juan Islands excursion be with a guide, you have plenty of options. Guided tours around the shores of Orcas Island are offered by **Shearwater Adventures,** P.O. Box 787, Eastsound, WA 98245 (tel. 360/376-4699), which offers three-hour tours for $35, and **Island Kayak Guides** (tel. 360/376-4755), which operates out of Doe Bay Village and offers a variety of trips, including moonlight trips at prices ranging from $25 to $125. If you want to explore Lopez Island's coastline by kayak, contact **Lopez Kayaks,** Lopez Island, WA 98261 (tel. 360/468-2847), which charges $37.25 for a half-day trip. You can take multiday kayak tours with **San Juan Kayak Expeditions,** P.O. Box 2041, Friday Harbor, WA 98250 (tel. 360/378-4436); **Shearwater Adventures,** P.O. Box 787, Eastsound, WA 98245 (tel. 360/376-4699); or **Pacific Water Sports** (tel. in Seattle 206/246-9385). Trips are generally offered between April and October and last from two to five days. Tour prices range from $195 to $595.

San Juan Island

The west coast of San Juan Island has numerous launch sites and offers some of the islands' most interesting paddling. However, what makes these waters among the most popular in the islands are the orca whales that feed here during the summer months. From May to September, you are just about guaranteed to see orcas when you paddle these waters. The whales come to feed on the many salmon that pass through the Haro Strait on their way back to the rivers and streams where they were spawned. With good launch points at both the north and south ends of the island, you can easily spend a couple of days paddling around just in this one area, see most of the west coast of the island, and probably see plenty of orcas.

If your main goal is to see orcas, launch from **San Juan Island County Park** on Smallpox Bay and paddle south 2 miles to the waters off **Lime Kiln State Park.** Although you're likely to see orcas anywhere in these waters, Lime Kiln State Park is dedicated to whale watching and makes a good destination and turnaround point. If you want to go ashore here, there is a beach south of the point. Round-trip distance for this paddle is around 4 miles. Keep in mind that these waters are quite exposed and are subject to strong winds and high seas. Early morning paddles are best.

On the other hand, if you are more interested in doing some exploring, head to Roche Harbor at the north end of the island. Here the waters are more protected and you can spend time poking around several bays and islands, including **Posey Island State Park.** You can also go ashore at the English Camp unit of **San Juan Island National Historical Park** and do a little hiking.

The southern end of the island is the most exposed and windswept and requires the most caution and experience. This area is characterized by grassy bluffs and is the site of the American Camp unit of San Juan Island State Park. This end of the island is a narrow arm culminating in Cattle Point. Most of the land is part of the national park, though at the very tip of the island the only public land is a small picnic area. If the weather is good, and your skills are such that you can handle tide rips, strong currents (up to 5 knots), and unexpected weather changes, you can put in on the west shore at either Eagle Cove or South Beach. If you'd rather launch and paddle in more protected waters, put in at the Cattle Point picnic area or Fourth of July Beach. North of Fourth of July Beach, at **Griffin Bay Recreation Area,** you'll find three lagoons that can be explored at high tide.

Off the east side of San Juan, **Turn Island,** a marine state park, makes a good destination for a short, easy paddle. From Friday Harbor, it is about a 5-mile round-trip paddle to Turn Island. Camping is allowed at the west end of the island. Alternatively, you can launch your boat at Jackson Beach, which is south of Friday Harbor. Take Argyle Street to Pear Point Road to Jackson Beach Road. This route makes for a 6-mile round-trip paddle.

Orcas Island

The **Obstruction Pass** area, at the south end of Orcas Island's eastern arm, offers quintessential San Juan Islands paddling. Dense forests, steep shores, rocky islands, and an almost certain chance of spotting bald eagles all make this a good place to explore for half a day. However, be aware that there can be strong currents around Obstruction Island, with Peavine Pass having the stronger currents. Check current charts before starting out. Launch sites are at Obstruction Pass boat launch and at Doe Bay (where there are rental cabins and a private campground favored by sea kayakers and counterculture types). From Doe Bay it is an 8-mile round-trip paddle to the Obstruction Pass area. Otherwise you launch right into the pass and can simply explore at a leisurely pace in the immediate vicinity. West of the Obstruction Pass boat launch, you'll find a wonderful little beach on a tiny cove at **Obstruction Pass Recreation Area.** This makes a great picnic spot and camping is also allowed.

One of my favorite paddling areas on Orcas Island is the fjord-like **Deer Harbor.** High cliffs here rise straight out of the water and a marina and resort provide an easy launch, a possible place to stay, and a good place for a postpaddle meal. From Deer Harbor, it is less than 2 miles to **Jones Island State Park,** which is around to the northwest as you leave the protection of the harbor. There are numerous campsites on this island, but they fill up on summer weekends. If you aren't planning on overnighting, it is still worth going ashore and exploring the island on foot as well as from the water. En route to Jones Island, you can paddle through the picturesque **Wasp Islands,** and visit the Nature Conservancy's **Yellow Island Preserve.** All of these waters are moderately well protected.

On Orcas's north shore, **Point Doughty** is another favorite destination for sea kayakers. This point is a Department of Natural Resources recreation site and is accessible only from the water. The rocky point has some small, protected beaches and makes a great picnic spot. From the North Beach launch site, due north of the town of Eastsound, it is a 6-mile round-trip paddle to the point. The waters of **East Sound** are also worth exploring and are popular with local sea kayaking companies.

If for some strange reason you have come out to these islands with a canoe rather than a sea kayak (or if you want really, truly protected waters to paddle on), you'll want to head to **Moran State Park,** where you can paddle around on Cascade and Mountain lakes.

Orcas Island is also the starting point for one of the most scenic overnight or multiday paddle routes in the San Juan Islands. Lying off the north shore of Orcas are three large islands—**Patos, Sucia,** and **Matia**—and several smaller ones, most of which are protected as state parks (some are part of the San Juan Islands National

Wildlife Refuge). Separated from Orcas by 2 miles of open water that is subject to strong currents and tide rips (especially around Parker Reef), this paddle route is recommended only for the most experienced of sea kayakers. If you have the skills to deal with these waters, you will find a maze of beautiful shorelines. Horseshoe-shaped Sucia Island, with its several bays, is the most fascinating of these islands to explore. It is also here that you will find the most campsites (and people). Both Matia and Patos islands are eagle refuges, and consequently, access to these islands is limited. However, because they are maintained in as wild a state as possible, they are fascinating to paddle around. Despite the refuge status, both islands do have campsites (at Rolfe Cove on Matia Island and at Active Cove on Patos Island). Although both of these latter islands can be reached directly from Orcas, it is often safer and easier to first paddle to Sucia Island and then head for the other two. Because Matia and Patos are in opposite directions from Sucia, they make good day-trip destinations for a multiday trip using a Sucia Island campsite as your base.

Lopez Island

On Lopez Island, there are good kayak launch sites at both **Odlin County Park** and **Spencer Spit State Park.** The former, about 1 mile south of the ferry landing, offers the easier and more protected paddling, with the crossing of Upright Channel, past privately owned Canoe Island, to the shore of Shaw Island, a favorite route with sea kayakers. The crossing involves only 0.25 miles of open water, and currents are rarely a problem. From Odlin Park, follow the shore southwest, passing the DNR's Upright Channel Recreation Site in about 1 mile. The tip of Flat Point marks the narrowest crossing of Upright Channel. Once along the shore of Shaw, you can explore Squaw Bay and Indian Cove, which is the site of **South Beach County Park,** where there is a campground and picnic area. Just keep in mind that the park is on a shallow cove that is across a mudflat from the water at low tide.

Spencer Spit is on the opposite side of the island from Odlin Park. The long, triangular spit points straight at **Frost Island,** which is worth a quick circumnavigation. However, the most popular paddle from Spencer Spit is out to **James Island State Park,** which is on the far side of Decatur and Blakely islands. Although this paddle can be done as a long day trip, it is better as an overnight. This will give you time to explore both James Island and the several islands along the west shore of Decatur Island. From Spencer Spit, head straight east through Thatcher Pass if you want to make the trip as quickly as possible. Out and back this way makes for an 8-mile round-trip. If you plan to spend the night or feel up to an 11-mile day trip, head southeast from Spencer Spit across Lopez Sound to the west shore of Decatur Island. This route passes Trump Island, Center Island, and a few smaller islands before rounding the southern tip of Decatur Island. After visiting James Island, continue around the north end of Blakely Island and paddle west through Thatcher Pass to return to Spencer Spit. If you spend the night on James Island, be aware that raccoons are notorious for raiding camps. Good luck trying to keep food out of their hands.

SWIMMING

Despite all the water, there isn't a whole lot of swimming to be done in the San Juans. The waters surrounding the islands stay unbearably cold throughout the year except in the shallowest coves where the sun has a chance to warm the water sufficiently. Try the beach at **Spencer Spit State Park** on Lopez Island or **Odlin County Park,** also on Lopez on the hottest summer day.

There are, however, a couple of lakes where you can go for a swim. In Moran State Park on Orcas Island, there is good swimming in **Cascade Lake.** It is also possible to swim in **Mountain Lake,** also in this park, but this lake has no designated swimming area. On San Juan Island, the private **Lakedale Campground** is set on a lake with good swimming for guests of the campground only.

WALKS & NATURAL ROADSIDE ATTRACTIONS

SAN JUAN ISLAND

British Camp Trails

2–5 miles. Easy–moderate. 0–650-foot elevation gain. Access: Take Beaverton Valley Rd. or Roche Harbor Rd. northwest from Friday Harbor. Map: San Juan Island National Historical Park Official Map and Guide.

Here in the northern unit of the San Juan Island National Historic Park, you'll find two short trails. One leads up to the top of 650-foot-high Mount Young, and one leads out to Bell Point and an overlook onto Westcott Bay. The former trail leads to the island's highest viewpoint, from which there is a good view westward across the Haro Strait to Vancouver Island. Along the way to the summit of Mount Young, the trail passes by the old British cemetery. The easier of the two trails follows level ground northward along the shore of Garrison Bay. The nicest view of the buildings at British Camp is from the Officers' Quarters Trail, which leads up the hill to the south of the buildings.

American Camp Trails

1–6 miles. Easy. 0–290-foot elevation gain. Access: Head south out of Friday Harbor and continue to the south end of the island on Cattle Point Rd. Map: San Juan Island National Historical Park Official Map and Guide.

Located at the southern end of the island, the American Camp unit of the San Juan Island National Historical Park is a barren, windswept landscape on a bluff above Haro Strait. Here natural grasslands create a miniature prairie by the sea. A 1-mile interpretive trail loops through the reconstructed buildings of the American Camp and out to a blufftop viewpoint above Grandma's Cove. From here you can access the park's other trail system by way of a 0.75-mile gravel road. Just beyond the far end of this road is another parking area that serves as the trailhead for the Jackle's Lagoon Trail. This trail, which leads through a forest of Douglas firs, and others in the vicinity can be linked together for a 3-mile walk that takes in not only the forest and lagoon, where there is good bird watching, but also the summit of 290-foot Mount Finlayson from which you can see, on a clear day, the Olympic Mountains, Mount Baker, and Mount Rainier. A mile of beach (the longest public beach on the island) lies on the south side of this point and can be reached by crossing Cattle Point Road from the Jackle's Lagoon parking area and driving to the end of Pickett's Lane.

ORCAS ISLAND

Sunrise Rock Trail

1 mile round-trip. Moderate. Access: The trailhead is in Moran State Park, 12.5 miles from the ferry landing on Horseshoe Hwy., in the South End Campground by campsite 17. Map: Hiking and Biking Trails of Moran (available at park).

This 300-foot-tall rock outcropping gained its name from the beauty of sunrises as seen from the top of the rock. Even if you can't get up early enough to be up here for sunrise, you can still get a nice view over Cascade Lake any time of day.

Obstruction Pass Trail

1 mile round-trip. Easy. 100-foot elevation gain. Access: Take Horseshoe Hwy. 17 miles to signed turnoff for Obstruction Pass Park. Map: Not necessary.

This 0.5-mile trail leads steeply down through the forest to a tiny sliver of a beach overlooking Obstruction Pass, a narrow channel between Orcas Island and Obstruction Island. The secluded spot is a tranquil place to while away a few hours, especially if the tide is out and has exposed the tidepools at either end of the beach.

LOPEZ ISLAND

Spencer Spit State Park

1 mile. Easy. 50-foot elevation gain. Access: From the ferry landing, drive south 1.3 miles, turn left on Port Stanley Rd., continue 2.5 miles, turn

left onto Baker View Rd., and continue 1.2 miles to the park. Map: Not necessary.

Although this park has trails through its forests, it is the spit that offers the greatest appeal. The spit, forming a triangle with the landward shore as its third side, encloses a marsh that is home to a wide variety of birdlife. Off the seaward point of the spit lies Frost Island, looming high and forested but seemingly out of scale with its surroundings. A stroll along the spit, either on the trail or, at low tide, along the beach, is one of the highlights of any visit to Lopez.

Shark Reef Sanctuary

1 mile round-trip. Easy. 50-foot elevation gain. Access: From the ferry landing, drive 2.1 miles south, turn right on Fisherman Bay Rd. and continue 4.5 miles south, turn right on Airport Rd. and then left in 0.4 miles on Shark Reef Rd., continuing 1.8 miles south on this road. Map: Not necessary.

Down at the south end of the island, you'll find the tiny Shark Reef Sanctuary, where a short trail leads through the forest to a rocky stretch of coast. Small islands offshore create strong currents that swirl past the rocks here. Seals and occasionally whales can be seen just offshore. This is my favorite picnic spot on the island.

WHALE WATCHING

The San Juan Islands are well known for their populations of orca whales, or killer whales as they have long been known. The best months to see orcas are June through September, but it's possible to see them throughout the year.

There are several different ways to do some whale watching here in the San Juans. Cheapest and easiest is to drive to San Juan Island's **Lime Kiln State Park** (tel. 360/378-2044), a park dedicated exclusively to whale watching. Within the park, a short trail leads down to a rocky coastline from which orca whales, minke whales, Dall's porpoises, and sea lions can sometimes be seen. To reach this park, take any of the roads leading to the west side of the island. If coming from the

south, drive north on Hannah Road; if coming from the north, take West Side Road.

You can also take a whale-watching cruise. Whale-watching cruises are offered in the summer by **Western Prince Cruises** (tel. 800/757-6722 or 360/378-5315), **Bon Accord Charters** (tel. 360/378-5921), and **San Juan Boat Tours** (tel. 800/232-6722 or 360/378-3499), all of which are on San Juan Island; and **Eclipse Charters** (tel. 800/376-6566 or 360/376-4663) and **Deer Harbor Charters** (tel. 800/544-5758 or 360/376-5989) on Orcas Island. Expect to pay around $45 for a four-hour whale-watching cruise.

The third possibility, and the most exciting, is to take a sea kayak trip through the islands. Few island experiences are as exciting as finding yourself side by side and eye level with a 30-foot-long orca. See the "Sea Kayaking" section, above, for a list of island companies offering kayak tours. Should you happen to see a whale on your travels through the San Juans, report the sighting to the **Whale Sighting Hotline** (tel. 800/562-8832).

The Northwest Washington Coast ◆ What to Do & Where to Do It

BEACHES

Whidbey Island, with its numerous state parks, has the best beaches in the region. Whether you're looking for classically Northwest beaches backed by steep, forested slopes or bluff-rimmed beaches or sand dunes, you'll find something to fit your image of the perfect beach (that is, unless for some strange reason your idea of the perfect beach includes warm water). My favorite beach on the island is North Beach in **Deception Pass State Park.** This beach overlooks the Deception Pass Bridge and is set at the foot of dense forest. This same park's West Beach has an entirely different character and is backed by low sand dunes. Farther south on Whidbey Island, there is a long, wide sand-and-gravel beach at **Joseph Whidbey**

State Park. At **Ebey's Landing State Park** there is a 1.5-mile cobblestone beach that is backed by Perego Lagoon for more than 0.5 miles of its length. A high bluff, with a trail atop it, backs the beach. At **Keystone Spit State Park,** the mile-long beach is popular with strollers and birders.

On **Camano Island,** due east of Whidbey Island across Saratoga Passage, **Camano Island State Park** has a wide pebble beach. To reach this park, which is on the west coast of the island, take exit 212 off I-5. The beach at **Washington Park,** west of the Anacortes ferry landing off Sunset Avenue, has a good view across Rosario Strait to the San Juan Islands. This park also has a very scenic loop drive around Fidalgo Head. Along this drive there are numerous great picnic spots above the water.

South of Bellingham, along scenic Chuckanut Drive, are a couple of my favorite area beaches. First along the road as you drive south from Bellingham is **Teddy Bear Cove,** a secluded spot with a 300-yard-long beach surrounded by forests. A steep trail leads down to the beach itself. Down at the south end of Chuckanut Drive is **Larrabee State Park,** which was the first state park in Washington and is the site of a 0.75-mile–long beach. Dramatic sandstone cliffs and tide pools make this the most beautiful and interesting beach in the area. Swimming and scuba diving are both popular here.

If you're looking for a long, sandy beach with plenty of wind for kite flying, try **Semiahmoo Park** on Semiahmoo Spit just south of Blaine. This low, windswept sand spit is also a good place to do some birding. On the other hand, if you grew up on the Jersey shore and long for beaches like those back home, head to **Birch Bay State Park,** a few miles south of Sehmiahmoo Spit. To reach the park, take exit 266 off I-5, drive 8 miles west on Grandview Road, and turn right on Point Whitehorn Road.

BIRD WATCHING

The flatlands ringing the waterways of this region provide some of the best bird habitat in the state. Between Birch Bay State

Park, near the Canadian border, and the south end of Whidbey Island there are half a dozen good birding spots. At **Birch Bay State Park,** which is a designated bird sanctuary, there are 2 miles of beach, including a large area of eelgrass that attracts large numbers of waterfowl and wading birds, including great blue herons from a nearby rookery that is one of the largest in the state. Adjacent to the salt water here at Birch Bay, there is also a freshwater marsh. In April black brants stop here during their migration. However, winter is the busiest time of year with numerous species of waterfowl, including harlequin ducks, in residence. Bald eagles and peregrines are also frequently spotted. To reach the park, take exit 266 off I-5 north of Ferndale and drive west on Grandview Road, and then turn north on Jackson Road. The park is at the south end of Birch Bay.

At **Tennant Lake Interpretive Center,** just outside the town of Ferndale, shorebirds, wading birds, and several species of ducks are frequently sighted, as are several species of raptors, including rough-legged and Cooper's hawks. An observation tower here provides an excellent vantage point. The best season is fall through spring. To reach this site, take exit 262 off I-5 and turn south on Neilson Road on the outskirts of Ferndale.

The region's very best birding takes place at the **Padilla Bay National Estuarine Research Reserve,** a vast expanse of tide flats and eelgrass beds that attracts an amazing number of waterfowl, marine birds, shorebirds, and raptors. This is another good place to see black brants and harlequin ducks. You're also likely to see black-bellied plovers and dunlins here. Trails lead through different habitats within the reserve, including along a dike with good views. An observation deck and viewing blind provide other good birding spots within the reserve. You'll find the reserve north of Bayview off Wash. 20 (take Bayview–Edison Road between Burlington and Anacortes).

A similar setting is to be found at the **Skagit Wildife Area,** which sprawls across the Skagit River Delta southwest of Conway. This large estuary serves as a wintering ground for well over 100,000 ducks, but is best known for its large wintering population of lesser snow geese and small population of tundra swans. With so many waterfowl around, it is no surprise that bald eagles and peregrines are frequently sighted, as are several other species of raptors. The best viewing area is from the dike trail near the headquarters, which is reached by driving west from Conway on Fir Island Road and then turning south on Mann Road. Keep in mind, however, that this area is managed not for bird watchers but for hunters. Throughout most of the winter, there is a great deal of hunting activity here.

A little bit farther south, **Kayak Point Regional Park,** overlooking Port Susan Bay northeast of Marysville, is a good spot for sighting marine birds. Here you'll find a fishing pier that provides a good viewing spot. Expect to see both snow geese and black brants, as well as loons and grebes. Fall through spring are the best seasons. To reach the park, take exit 206 off I-5, drive west for 8 miles, and turn north on Marine Drive.

Over on Whidbey Island, there are several good birding spots. At the north end of the island, **Deception Pass State Park** contains a wide variety of habitats. Expect to see loons on Cranberry Lake and marbled murrelets in the offshore waters. Not far south of here, at the end of Swantown Road west of Oak Harbor, **Joseph Whidbey State Park** is a good summer birding spot with marine birds plentiful in the offshore waters. You stand a good chance of seeing pelagic cormorants, tufted puffins, rhinoceros auklets, black brants, and pigeon guillemots. A freshwater marsh also attracts a good variety of wading birds. The marshes around **Crocket Lake,** which is beside the Keystone ferry landing, often provide good birding. A stroll along the road south of the ferry landing, with binoculars in hand, is a good way to kill time until your ferry leaves. Once on the ferry headed to Port Townsend, don't put the binoculars away. There is always a good chance of spotting rhinoceros auklets and pigeon guillemots on these waters. Down at the south end of the island, in the town of Langley, bald eagles can often be seen in the fall from **Seawall Park.**

BOARDSAILING

BOARDSAILING

On Whidbey Island, **Keystone Spit State Park** frequently offers excellent sailing. Located on the elbow of Whidbey Island and backed by a wide, flat wetland, this beach gets winds from just about every direction. Easy beach access and strong winds make it a regional favorite.

There are several good places to windsurf in the immediate Bellingham vicinity. **Lake Padden,** off Samish Way (take exit 252 off I-5 and drive south), offers protected waters and sailboard rentals. Winds are usually fairly light here, making this a good spot for beginners. **Samish Park,** 673 N. Lake Samish Dr., on Lake Samish, is another good novice windsurfing area, though this lake is quite deep and at 4 miles in length is long enough to get some good winds. Sailboard rentals are available here. More experienced sailors can launch into the waters of Bellingham Bay at Bellingham's **Marine Park,** which is located at the foot of Harris Street in the Fairhaven district, or at **Boulevard Park,** at the corner of South State Street and Bayview Drive in Bellingham. Up near the Canadian border, you'll find more good saltwater sailing from the beaches at **Birch Bay State Park** and **Semiahmoo Park** on Semiahmoo Spit. To reach the Birch Bay State Park, take exit 266 off I-5 north of Ferndale and drive west on Grandview Road, and then turn north on Jackson Road. To reach Semiahmoo Spit, take exit 270 off I-5, drive west 3 miles on Birch Bay–Linden Road, turn right, and continue 1 mile north on Blaine Road. Turn left onto Lincoln Road and go 1.75 miles. Turn right onto Shintaffer Road and drive north to Drayton Road, continuing west on Drayton to a right turn on Semiahmoo Drive.

FISHING

In the Bellingham area, **Samish Lake** and **Lake Padden** are both popular spots. The former is mostly a warm-water fishing lake and is best known for its kokanee, which start biting in late spring. There are also rainbows and cutthroats of good size in this lake. Lake Padden, a much smaller lake that is popular with families, holds

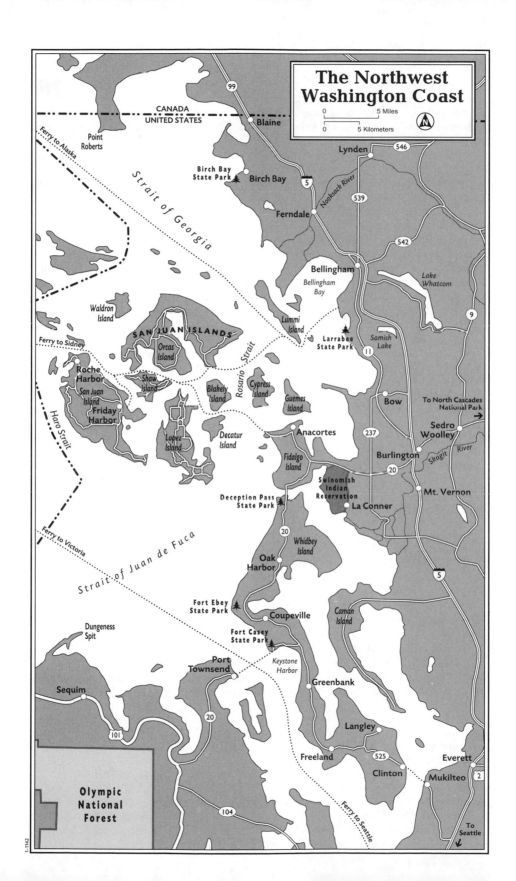

The Northwest Washington Coast

0   5 Miles

0   5 Kilometers

CANADA
UNITED STATES

Ferry to Alaska

Point Roberts

Blaine

99

Lynden

546

Birch Bay State Park

Birch Bay

5

Nooksack River

539

Ferndale

Strait of Georgia

542

Bellingham

Bellingham Bay

Lake Whatcom

Waldron Island

SAN JUAN ISLANDS

Orcas Island

Lummi Island

Larrabee State Park

Samish Lake

9

Ferry to Sidney

Roche Harbor

Shaw Island

Rosario Strait

11

San Juan Island

Blakely Island

Cypress Island

Bow

To North Cascades National Park

Friday Harbor

Guemes Island

Haro Strait

Decatur Island

Anacortes

237

Sedro Woolley

Lopez Island

Fidalgo Island

Burlington

Skagit River

20

Deception Pass State Park

Swinomish Indian Reservation

Mt. Vernon

La Conner

20

Whidbey Island

Ferry to Victoria

Strait of Juan de Fuca

Oak Harbor

Dungeness Spit

Fort Ebey State Park

Coupeville

Camano Island

Fort Casey State Park

Port Townsend

Keystone Harbor

Greenbank

Sequim

Langley

5

20

101

Freeland

525

Everett

Clinton

Mukilteo

2

Olympic National Forest

104

Ferry to Seattle

To Seattle

1-1142

rainbows and cutthroats as well. The deep waters of **Lake Whatcom** hold kokanee, big cutthroats, and a few mackinaw, as well as bass and rainbows. Summer is the best season on this lake.

Whatcom Creek, which drains Lake Whatcom and flows through Bellingham, holds trout, steelhead, and salmon. Regulations for this creek are complex; be absolutely certain you know what regulations apply before dropping a line in this water. The **Samish River,** which flows into Samish Bay south of Bellingham, has some good winter steelheading waters in its lower reaches (below Friday Creek and the Old Highway 99 bridge). Wild steelhead, however, must be released. There is also a good run of sea-run cutthroats in this river. Again, regulations are complex. Study them carefully. Near the mouth of the **Skagit River,** where the river runs slowly through the flats of its delta, there is often good fishing for dolly varden (this is one of the few places in the state where they can be kept), sea-run cutthroat, and chum salmon. The main-stem **Stillaguamish River,** which starts just in Arlington at the confluence of the north and south forks, offers good summer and winter steelheading, as well as sea-run cutthroats. There are also coho, chum, Chinook, and pink (humpie) salmon. Due to their spawning cycle, the pinks are in the river only during odd-numbered years.

There is good fishing in the lakes in Deception Pass State Park. **Cranberry Lake** yields rainbow and brown trout as well as yellow perch and largemouth bass. **Pass Lake,** the park's other large lake, is open to fly fishing only and is best fished from a float. Down at the south end of Whidbey Island, **Goss Lake, Lone Lake,** and **Deer Lake** all are good rainbow lakes, while Goss Lake and Deer Lake also have cutthroats.

The salt water of this region also offers plenty of good salmon fishing, but for the most part, you need a boat to get to where the salmon are. If you want to do some saltwater salmon fishing, there are charter boats operating out of Bellingham and Anacortes. In Bellingham, try **Jim's Salmon Charter** (tel. 360/332-6724) or **Bellingham Salmon Charters** (tel. 360/650-9584). In Anacortes, try **Island Adventures Charters**

and Tours (tel. 800/465-4604 or 360/293-2428).

HIKING

Perego's Bluff-Ebey's Prairie Trail

5 miles. Easy. 300-foot elevation gain. Access: From Wash. 20 in Coupeville, drive west on Terry Rd., which curves around to become Ebey Rd. Map: Not necessary.

Located in both Ebey's Landing State Park and the Ebey's Landing National Historical Reserve, this is one of the most enjoyable walks on Whidbey Island and captures much of this island's appeal in its easy 5 miles. Starting from the beach in Ebey's Landing State Park, the trail climbs up a stairway to the top of the bluff overlooking the beach and then parallels the water for 1.5 miles. Along the way there are views not only of the water below but of Ebey's Prairie inland. On a clear day you can also see the Olympic Mountains and Mount Rainier.

After about 0.5 miles, you will come to a spur trail that leads to a historic cemetery in 1 mile. This ridgeline trail leads through the heart of the Ebey's Landing National Historical Reserve, which was created to preserve the historic rural heritage of this portion of central Whidbey Island. The trail follows a fence line between Isaac and Jacob Ebey's two original land claims from the 1850s. There are far-reaching views across the grasslands that came to be known as Ebey's Prairie. Such prairies by the sea are characteristic of the San Juan Islands. After visiting the cemetery, walk back the way you came to continue the bluff trail. In another mile this trail drops down to the water. From this point, you can return along the beach. For roughly 0.5 miles you walk between the waters of the Strait of Juan de Fuca and the waters of Perego Lagoon, across which the bluff rises.

Deception Pass Trails

Up to 10 miles. Easy. 300-foot elevation gain. Access: Deception Pass State Park is on Wash. 20 approximately 7 miles south of Anacortes. Map: Available at the park.

Within this park, which spans both sides of Deception Pass, there are nearly 10 miles of short, easy trails, plus more miles of beaches that can be walked. String together a bunch of these trails and you can manage a respectable day's hike. Pack a lunch and you can picnic on a beach or some other equally scenic setting. Just don't expect solitude. This is one of the most visited state parks in Washington. The trails are about equally split between those on the north side of Deception Pass and those on the south side. The northern trails are the more scenic and rugged. These trails link three rocky headlands by way of Bowman Bay and wander along the 100-foot high cliffs above the west end of the pass.

On the south side of the park, which is on Whidbey Island, most of the trails lead through forests on the Skagit Bay side of the park. For an overview of the area, hike up the Goose Rock Summit Trail, which is the highest in the park at 300 feet. Trails also lead along North Beach and West Beach; this latter trail is paved and leads into sand dunes on the west side of Cranberry Lake.

Fragrance Lake

4 miles round-trip. Easy–moderate. 900-foot elevation gain. Access: The trailhead is across Chuckanut Dr. (south of Bellingham) from the main entrance to Larrabee State Park. Map: Larrabee State Park.

Although Larrabee State Park is better known for its beach and as the southern terminus of the Interurban Trail, it also contains several miles of hiking trails. The hike from just above the beach onto the flanks of Chuckanut Mountain to diminutive Fragrance Lake is a longtime favorite. The trail passes through an old-growth forest of western red cedars and Douglas firs as it climbs the mountainside, and there are occasional views of the water far below and the San Juan Islands to the west. Once you reach the quiet waters of Fragrance Lake, be sure to follow the trail around the lake before heading back down the hill.

HORSEBACK RIDING

If you'd like to do some horseback riding in the area, contact **Scimitar Ridge Ranch** (tel. 360/293-5355), which has its stables just south of Anacortes adjacent to Mount Erie, the highest point on Fidalgo Island. Horses are $25 per hour.

MOUNTAIN BIKING

Interurban Trail

12 miles round-trip. Easy. 150-foot elevation gain. Access: Start this ride in Bellingham on Old Fairhaven Parkway 0.5 miles west of I-5 or at Larrabee State Park south of Bellingham on Chuckanut Dr. Map: Chuckanut Mountain Roads and Trails, available at local bike shops.

Located south of Bellingham, this trail follows the grade of the old trolley line that once ran from Fairhaven to Mount Vernon. Today the old railroad grade has become a popular multiuse trail that parallels the ever-popular Chuckanut Drive, which is a favorite road-bike ride for area cyclists. The trail meanders through the forest with occasional views across the waters to the San Juan Islands. Because it is fairly level, this trail is fun for novices. The only difficult section of the whole trail is where it passes through aptly named Arroyo Park. Here, an old trestle is long gone and riders must switchback into the arroyo and then back up the other side (usually on foot).

More experienced riders will enjoy this trail simply for its setting, but can also link this to the Fragrance Lake ride described below for more of a challenge. The southern terminus of the trail is at Larrabee State Park, which has the area's best beach, as well as a campground. Part of the great appeal of this ride is that there is so much to do at either end of it that the ride is only part of the pleasure here. Explore the tide pools or wade in the water at Larrabee; duck into a Fairhaven cafe for a latté or bowl of soup. No matter how you look at it, this is a fun ride for those of any skill level.

Chuckanut Mountain

Distance varies. Moderate–strenuous. 1,600-foot elevation gain. Access: Cleator Rd., a favored access route to this area, is 1.5 miles up the Interurban Trail from Larrabee State Park. Map: Chuckanut Mountain Roads and Trails, available at local bike shops.

Chuckanut Mountain, which lies to the south of Bellingham and serves as the uphill backdrop for both the Interurban Trail and Chuckanut Drive, is laced with logging roads and is a great place for gravel-road riding. Parts of the mountain are within Larrabee State Park and there are even some stretches of single track that are open to mountain bikes. A favorite route is to ride up Cleator Road from the Interurban to the summit of Chuckanut Mountain, where there are fabulous views of the San Juans and Mount Baker. From here you can backtrack a little less than a mile and ride down the Fragrance Lake Trail, though you won't actually go past the lake; that section of the trail is for hikers only (but it's worth getting off your bike to walk down to the lake). Pick up the gravel Fragrance Lake Road here and continue downhill. On the left is an abandoned road that leads around the mountain to Lost Lake. If you continue downhill, you will quickly reach Chuckanut Drive just south of the Larrabee State Park entrance.

ROAD BIKING

If you are here on Whidbey and decide you'd like to do some cycling, you can rent a bike from **All Island Bicycle,** 302 Main St., Coupeville (tel. 360/678-3351), which charges $8 per hour and $19 per day.

South Whidbey Loop

37 miles. Moderate–strenuous. 3,000-foot elevation gain. Access: Start this ride by boarding the Mukilteo–Clinton ferry.

Because you can start a South Whidbey ride with a ferry trip from Mukilteo *without* your car, rides at this end of the island are particularly popular. This ride takes in the quaint old fishing village of Langley

as well as a couple of parks. The route passes through both forests and farmlands and manages to avoid busy Wash. 525 for all but about 1 mile of the trail. As you can see from the elevation gain above, there are a lot of hills on this route.

After coming off the ferry, start uphill, and in 0.6 miles, turn right onto Bob Galbreath Road. At 1.4 miles turn right on Wilkenson Road and follow this road through many twists and turns and a couple of name changes to reach Langley at about 6 miles. In Langley, you can stop for an espresso and a snack, do a little window-shopping, or walk to the beach. From Langley, continue north along the shore following Saratoga Road, which has several hills. This road eventually becomes Baby Island Road and drops down a very steep road to the northernmost point on this ride at about 13 miles from the ferry. From here the road loops around to the south and becomes East Harbor Road, following the shore of Holmes Harbor.

Continue south to Freeland Park at 19.5 miles from the ferry (take a right on Vinton and a right on Stewart to reach the park). This park, overlooking the water, is a good spot for a picnic. After resting at the park, follow Stewart Road back east, then south, and turn left onto Main Street and left onto Newman Road. At the end of Newman Road, pick up that 1 mile of Wash. 525. At a wide curve to the right, go straight on a smaller road that ends at a T-intersection with Bayview Road. You'll find the Pedaler Bike Shop on this corner. Turn right and follow Bayview Road 2.5 miles, and turn right on Sills Road. At Maxwelton Road, turn right and ride 1 mile down to Dave Mackie Memorial County Park. To avoid a steep hill on Swede Hill Road, ride back north to French Road, turn right, and then take a right onto Bailey Road in less than 0.5 miles. Follow this road until it ends at Jewett Road and turn left up a steep hill. At the end of Jewett, turn right onto Glendale Road and descend to Holst Road. Turn left here and climb again. After cresting this hill, drop down past Deer Lake (Holst Road becomes Deer Lake Road) and follow this road to Wash. 520 about 0.5 miles from the ferry. Turn right and ride down to the ferry.

Fidalgo Island Loop

30 miles. Strenuous. 2,220-foot elevation gain. Access: Start this ride in Deception Pass State Park at the West Beach parking area.

There are a lot of hills on this ride, so you'll need to be in good shape. However, the crossing of the Deception Pass Bridge, the views across the water to the San Juan Islands, and the rough but wonderfully scenic loop through Washington Park outside Anacortes are suitable rewards for all the sweat. In addition to the route described here, you can add on a few more miles by visiting some of the beaches in Deception Pass State Park. These beaches provide access to several miles of hiking trails. Better yet, camp out in the park and start your ride from the campground.

Begin the ride by riding away from the beach along the north shore of Cranberry Lake. At the park entrance, turn left on Wash. 20 and begin one of the few busy stretches of road on this ride. In just over 0.5 miles, reach Deception Pass Bridge. When crossing the bridge be very wary of cars—drivers are likely to be distracted by the view into the swirling waters of this famous channel, which flows between high cliff walls. Currents in Deception Pass sometimes exceed 9 miles per hour and can form whirlpools. There are parking areas on the south side of the pass and on Canoe Island, which is the midway point of the bridge. Be sure to get off your bike and have a closer look.

From here, continue north on Hwy. 20 for 2 miles and turn right onto Deception Road. Continue 0.8 miles and turn right onto Gibraltar Road. In 2.2 miles, turn right and back onto Wash. 20. From here it is 0.6 miles downhill on a wide shoulder to a left turn onto a rough road just before the Wash. 20 stoplight. Follow this road as it parallels the highway for 0.4 miles. At the stop sign, cross the highway, and follow Fidalgo Bay Road, which runs between the highway and the waters of Fidalgo Bay. Across the water you will see the oil refineries and storage tanks of March's Point. This road has a surprisingly rural feel to it despite the highway and oil refineries.

After 2.2 miles, turn right, and then left onto 34th Street in another 0.2 miles. Turn right on Q Avenue and follow this road through the port area of Anacortes. You can switch over to the parallel R Avenue up near the marina, or switch over to Commercial Avenue, where there are stores and restaurants where you can fuel up. At the north end of R Avenue or Commercial Avenue, turn left just before reaching the water and wind your way westward through a residential neighborhood, keeping close to the water for the best views. Eventually you will be forced onto Oakes Avenue, the road to the San Juan Islands ferry terminal. Follow this road almost to the ferry landing and take the left fork onto Sunset Avenue, which leads into Washington Park in 0.8 miles.

Once inside the park, follow the signs for the loop drive, a narrow, winding, one-way road (with speed bumps) that wanders around Fidalgo Head with many views of the water and lots of great picnic spots. Windswept fir trees and copper-barked madrone trees line the twisting road. About halfway through the loop, the road breaks into a clearing with a breathtaking view of Burrows Island. After 2.1 miles on this loop, you return to Sunset Avenue.

Head back toward Anacortes, but in 0.9 miles from the end of the loop, turn right onto Skyline Way to continue this loop ride. In 0.2 miles, turn left on Kings Way West, and then in another 1 mile turn right onto Anaco Beach Road, passing a large marina and dropping down a steep hill. From the bottom of the hill, you have a long, steep climb ahead and the road becomes Marine Drive. Follow this road through its many twists and turns, up hills and down, with frequent glimpses of the water for 1.7 miles to Rosario Road, keeping right at the Havekost Road junction along the way.

Turn right onto Rosario Road and climb a steep hill in less than 1 mile. Continue past the Rosario Beach and Bowman Bay entrances to Deception Pass State Park (both of which are worth a stop, though they both include steep descents to the water). After 3.5 miles on Rosario Road, reach Wash. 20 again and turn right to cross the Deception Pass Bridge and return to your starting point.

Skagit River Delta

23.7 miles (additional side trips possible). Easy. 100-foot elevation gain. Access: Take exit 226 off I-5, drive west through Mount Vernon toward La Conner, and, after crossing the Skagit River bridge, turn left on Baker St. to reach the parking lot at Edgewater Park.

Although flat countryside, rural scenery, and a chance to wander around historic La Conner (now a boutique-filled berg just oozing charm) would make this ride commendable any time of year, you should really save this one for late March or early April. It is at this time of year that the valley's acres and acres of tulip fields burst into primary colors, painting the landscape with bold swaths of red and yellow. It's almost like cycling through an Impressionist painting.

From Mount Vernon's Edgewater Park, ride back to West Division Road and head west a few blocks. Turn left on South Wall Street, which curves around to become McLean Road, a 7-mile-long stretch of straight, flat pedaling through the heart of the flower fields. As you pass Bradshaw Road, after 3.5 miles on McLean Road, consider a detour to the right to see some spectacular fields. Continue west on McLean Road, which becomes Downey Road and comes to an end at West Shore Acres Bulb Farm. This farm always has some of the best flower fields. After admiring the flowers here, turn around and backtrack 1.25 miles to La Conner–Whitney Road. Turn right and ride 2.5 miles south to the La Conner waterfront historic district, which, if it is a weekend, will be packed with people. Be glad you don't have to try to park a car. Shop, eat, sip a latté, look at the boats, whatever.

Head back the way you came for 1.1 miles and turn right onto Dodge Valley Road, which winds around for 3.2 miles to meet up with Chilberg Road. Turn right, continue 0.3 miles, and turn left onto Summers Fork Drive. Follow this about 0.4 miles and turn left on Bradshaw Road. Ride north on Bradshaw, passing more flower fields for 2.4 miles, and turn right

onto Calhoun Road. Go 2.5 miles on Calhoun and turn left onto Penn Road. This road winds along the dike of the North Fork Skagit River and in 1.6 miles reaches a junction with McLean Road. Turn right here and continue 1.2 miles back to Edgewater Park.

SCUBA DIVING

Divers will find some of the finest diving in the region off Rosario Bay on the Fidalgo Island side of **Deception Pass State Park** south of Anacortes. Northwest Island and Urchin Rocks offshore from Rosario Bay are the favorite destinations here. Experienced divers also sometimes dive the walls of **Pass Island** in the middle of Deception Pass, but only at slack currents.

Keystone Spit State Park, just east of the Keystone ferry landing on Whidbey Island, has a designated underwater park and is one of the finest dive sites anyplace in the greater Puget Sound region. The dive is along the jetty built to protect the ferry landing. One of the best aspects of this dive is that it is a shore dive, so you won't need a boat. Currents here are strong, so schedule your dive for the slack current.

North of Anacortes by boat, there are a couple of excellent wall-diving sites. The **Cone Islands** are between Guemes Island and Cypress Island. In addition to the interesting walls here, there are also kelp beds. Off the southeastern tip of Guemes Island, **Huckleberry Island** has good walls on three sides of the small island.

Farther north, **Larrabee State Park,** on Chuckanut Drive south of Bellingham, offers interesting explorations in a sheltered cove. East of Whidbey Island, on Camano Island, divers frequent the waters off **Camano Island State Park.** This park is on the west coast of the island, which is reached by taking exit 212 off I-5.

SEA KAYAKING & FLAT-WATER CANOEING

Listed below are some of the more interesting sea kayaking routes in the region. However, if you'd rather stay on the more protected waters of freshwater lakes, you also have plenty of options. At **Deception Pass State Park, Pass Lake** and **Cranberry Lake** both provide pleasant paddling on waters restricted to electric motors. In the Bellingham area, you can rent canoes during the summer months at **Samish Park,** 673 N Lake Samish Dr., on Samish Lake, and at Sudden Valley resort community on **Lake Whatcom. Lake Padden,** which is accessible at Lake Padden Park, 4882 Samish Way, is another Bellingham-area lake that is quiet enough to be enjoyable for paddling.

When sea kayaking in this area, be sure you check the tides before heading out. Strong currents that develop depending on the tide level and direction can turn an otherwise easy paddle into a very challenging and sometimes dangerous trip. The cold waters of this area make capsizing especially dangerous due to the possibility of developing hypothermia. Always wear layers of warm clothing when paddling these waters. In winter a wetsuit or dry suit is imperative. Also, remember to carry enough water for your trip. Although there are many developed campgrounds on islands throughout the region, few have available drinking water.

If you don't have a sea kayak of your own but would like to get out on the waters of this region, you have a few options. **Penn's Cove Kayak Adventures** (tel. 360/678-3545) is located on the Coupeville Wharf on Whidbey Island and offers kayak rentals for those who'd like to explore Penn Cove on their own. Kayaks can also be rented from **Eddyline Watersports Center,** 1019 Q Ave., Anacortes (tel. 360/299-2300). On the waterfront in the Fairhaven District of Bellingham, you'll find sea kayaks for rent at Fairhaven Boatworks, 501 Harris St. (tel. 360/676-1146).

Deception Pass and Hope and Skagit Islands

2–12 miles. Easy–very difficult. Access: From I-5, drive west on Wash. 20 and follow signs for the park. To reach Bowman Bay, turn right 0.5 miles before the Deception Pass Bridge. To reach Cornet Bay, turn left 1 mile south of the bridge and continue 1.25 miles east to the bay.

Deception Pass is legendary for its powerful currents, which sometimes form whirlpools amid the rocks along the cliff-ringed channel. Although experienced paddlers sometimes head into the pass specifically to work on their current-handling skills, other paddlers will want to stay clear of the pass except at slack tide. However, there are nearby paddle destinations that are fun and don't include the sort of challenging currents found directly in the pass. Because there are several possible launch sites within Deception Pass State Park, you can choose a route that meets your skill levels and available time.

For novice paddlers, a trip around the protected waters of Bowman Bay, on the north side of the pass, is highly rewarding. The next best choice is Cornet Bay, on the south side of the pass and east of the highway. Because the waters off Reservation Head and Lighthouse Point are more exposed and lead close to the currents through the pass, this area is best left to paddlers of intermediate skills. The trip through the pass itself is for intermediate and expert paddlers only, depending on the currents. On the east side of the pass, Hope and Skagit islands make ideal destinations for longer paddles. Both islands are state parks and both have campsites. Skagit Island is characterized by rocks, meadows, and madronas, while Hope Island is more forested. There are strong currents around Hope Island. Launch from Cornet Bay.

Saddlebag Island

5 miles round-trip. Easy. Access: From I-5, take Wash. 20 west, cross the Swinomish Channel Bridge, turn right onto S March Point Rd., go north 1 mile, turn right onto March Point Rd., and continue 2.5 miles to a boat ramp.

This small island barely 2 miles east of Anacortes is a state marine park and takes its name from its resemblance to that cowboy carryall. Formed by two low, rocky hills connected by a narrow isthmus, the island has meadows and forests, as well as campsites that make it an ideal choice for a first overnight sea kayak trip. However, the island is popular, and securing one of the few campsites can be difficult. From the launch site amid the oil refineries and storage tanks on March Point, paddle due north toward Hat Island, keeping an eye out for fast-moving boats and wakes. Near Hat Island, you may encounter tide rips, but don't let this stop you from enjoying the interesting shoreline of this private island. Continuing north, you pass tiny Dot Island, which is a nesting ground for several species of birds, including bald eagles, and is part of the San Juan Islands National Wildlife Refuge. You are asked to stay at least 200 yards away from this island. Finally you reach Saddlebag Island, where you will find beaches on both the north and south sides of the island. Keep your eyes open for harbor seals in these waters.

Cypress Island

20–23 miles round-trip. Moderate. Access: Launch sites are at the Guemes Island ferry terminal at the north end of I St. and in Washington Park, which is at the end of Oakes Ave. beyond the San Juan Islands ferry terminal.

This is a favorite destination of experienced Puget Sound paddlers. The island, which is reached from Anacortes, is more than 4 miles long, is almost entirely owned by the Washington Department of Natural Resources, and has a remote feeling. With three campgrounds around the island, it lends itself perfectly to an overnight or two-night paddle. A circumnavigation of the island is the standard excursion here, and the Pelican Beach campground on the north end of the island is the preferred campsite due in large part to its proximity to Eagle Cliff, which rises more than 800 feet above the water on the northwest shore of the island. When seen from the water, this cliff is one of the most impressive sights in the San Juan Islands. There are also trails that lead to the top of the cliff, though the trail to the summit is closed for the first six months of the year due to the presence of nesting falcons.

There are also other trails on the island, some of which lead to small lakes. With the great paddling and good campsites, this all adds up to a superb sea kayak destination. Also keep in mind that you don't

have to take a ferry to the launch point, yet you get a true San Juan Islands paddling experience.

The Guemes ferry launch site provides the easier crossing to Cypress Island. If launching from Washington Park, you will have a 2.5-mile open-water crossing and will have to contend with sometimes tricky currents off the tip of Shannon Point, which is just northeast of Washington Park. This latter launch site is best on a flood tide, whereas the former is marginally better on an ebb tide. Off Cypress Island's east shore, be careful around Cypress Head, which is the site of one of the island's campsites. Currents off this headland can be strong and dangerous. Along the west side of the island, you will be paddling in the Rosario Strait, where currents are reliably strong. Consult a chart and utilize these currents as much as possible. The island's third campsite is actually on another island—Strawberry Island—which lies just off the west side of Cypress.

Chuckanut Bay

4–5 miles. Easy–moderate. Access: Take exit 250 off I-5, drive west on Fairhaven Parkway, then turn south on Chuckanut Dr. At 21st St., turn right and reach Chuckanut Park in less than 0.5 miles.

Chuckanut Bay, just south of Bellingham, is rimmed with steep cliffs and forests that rise up to the top of Chuckanut Mountain. This is the same stretch of land that drivers and cyclists enjoy along Chuckanut Drive. As seen from the water, the area is just as dramatic, though in an entirely different sort of way. From the water, it is the cliffs and green mountain that are the focus of attention rather than the distant views across the water. Paddling along close to shore, you can explore the fascinating life along these rocky tidelands and even examine the fossil remains of ancient palm trees. To launch at Chuckanut Park the tide has to be in sufficiently to cover the extensive mudflats that fill this end of the bay. Before heading out on the water, make sure that you won't be trying to get back to shore at low tide. It's no fun dragging a boat across the mud.

From the park, paddle across this shallow end of the bay, past many interesting rock formations, and under the railroad bridge. If you keep to the west shore of the bay here, you will soon round Clarks Point, where you'll find the fossilized-palms rock walls that rise straight from the water in a small bay. From here you can paddle across the mouth of the bay to Chuckanut Island, a Nature Conservancy Preserve where you can go ashore and hike the trail around the island. Back in your boat, head down to the south end of Chuckanut Bay and begin a shoreline paddle back north. Near the north end of the bay, you'll come to Teddy Bear Cove, a county beach. Should you want a longer paddle, you can explore around Gobernors Point south to Larrabee State Park or north to Bellingham's Fairhaven Historic District and the Alaska Ferry Terminal.

SURFING

This is the Puget Sound, right? Protected waters, safe harbors, and all that. So, how can there be surfing in this shredder's backwater? Get a map, preferably a big one that includes everything from Washington to Alaska. Now, look at the Strait of Juan de Fuca. They don't call it straight for nothing. It's a straight shot from the Pacific Ocean to **Fort Ebey State Park** on the westernmost point of Whidbey Island and nearby **Joseph Whidbey State Park.** Now look at what a line taken northwest of here does. It takes you straight into the middle of the Gulf of Alaska with nothing in between, and as we all know, the Gulf of Alaska is well known for kicking up killer winter storms.

Now all you have to do is tune in to the NOAA weather station nearest you and wait until you hear a report of swells out of the west–northwest. When you hear that report, call in sick, throw your dry suit in the Subaru (leaving the snowboard at home), and make tracks to Whidbey Island.

SWIMMING & TUBING

Although there is plenty of water in Deception Pass State Park, most of it is far too cold and too dangerous for swimming. However, there is a designated swimming area at the north end of **Cranberry Lake.** On adjacent Fidalgo Island, you'll find **Whistle Lake,** one of the very best swimming holes in the region, in the Anacortes Community Forest lands south of Anacortes. This idyllic lake is rimmed by cliffs and has a picturesque island toward its south end. Jumping into the lake is a favorite pastime of teenagers, who flock to this lake in the summer months. To reach the lake, drive to the south end of Commercial Avenue in Anacortes. At the end of Commercial Avenue, turn left, then immediately right onto Hillcrest Road. Turn right again onto Whistle Lake Road and continue down this road; turn left when the road becomes gravel and follow signs to the lake.

There are numerous small lakes around Bellingham that are perfect for cooling off on hot summer days. Located on the north shore of **Lake Whatcom,** Washington's fifth-largest lake, **Bloedel Donovan Park** is popular with families because of the lifeguards at the swimming area. This park is the area's most convenient swimming area and is reached from I-5 by taking exit 253 and driving east on Lakeway Drive. **Lake Padden Park,** 4882 Samish Way, just southeast of downtown Bellingham off I-5 (take exit 252 and head south), is another convenient swimming lake and is at the heart of an extensive city park. A little bit farther south, **Samish Park,** 673 N Lake Samish Dr., on the northwest shore of **Samish Lake** in a large cove, is a small county park with a good guarded swimming area popular with families. The park was formerly a log-rafting site. If you can stand the cold waters of Chuckanut Bay, it's also possible to swim at **Larrabee State Park** at the south end of Chuckanut Drive. The waters here are actually more popular with scuba divers than with casual swimmers.

Although the rivers of this region drain glaciers and tend to be far too cold for swimming, one exception is the **South Fork Nooksack River** east of Lake Whatcom. Beginning just east of Saxon and continuing downstream to a gravel beach at the end of Strand Road (between Acme and Van Zandt), this river is a favorite tubing river. Sure the water is cold, but on a hot day, it feels great, and there are lots of swift sections to keep the float interesting. This entire run covers about 8 miles.

WALKS & NATURAL ROADSIDE ATTRACTIONS

South Whidbey State Park

3.5 miles round-trip. Easy. 100-foot elevation gain. Access: From Wash. 525 at Freeland on Whidbey Island, go west on Bush Point Rd., and then north on Smugglers Cove Rd. Map: Trailhead maps.

This park toward the south end of Whidbey Island preserves some of the island's last remaining old-growth trees, including a cedar that is 40 feet in circumference. There are numerous short trails within the park, but it is the Harry Wilbert Trail that has the park's largest trees, including the big cedar. The Beach Trail and Hobbit Trail both lead down through the forest to the beach, which is almost nonexistent at high tide.

Mount Erie/Sugarloaf Mountain

Up to 2 miles round-trip. Easy. 200-foot elevation gain. Access: From downtown Anacortes, drive south on Commercial Ave., turn right onto 29th St., left onto Heart Lake Rd., continue south 1 mile, and turn left onto Auld Rd., and then left again onto Erie Mountain Dr.

At 1,270 feet high, Mount Erie is the highest point on Fidalgo Island and offers an excellent vantage point from which to gaze across the San Juan Islands. Also visible from this summit are Mount Baker, Mount Rainier, and the Olympic Mountains. Much of Mount Erie is a city park, and though there are trails leading to the summit from below, most people simply drive up. If you'd like to hike to a similar viewpoint, try the 1-mile trail that leads from a trailhead near the base of Erie Mountain Drive to the summit of Sugarloaf Mountain. The trail is an easy 200-foot climb to the rocky, meadowed summit of the 750-foot-high "mountain."

Lake Padden Park

3 miles. Easy. No elevation gain. Access: Take exit 252 off I-5 and drive south on Samish Way. Map: Not necessary.

A flat, unpaved, 3-mile trail surrounds this pretty little lake, and this, coupled with the park's convenient in-town location, makes it a favorite of strollers, joggers, dog-walkers, and bicyclists. As you walk around the park, the views reach across the lake to low, forested hills. At the south end of the lake, there are trails that climb into the woods above the lake. These are most popular with mountain bikers but can add a bit more of a workout to a walk around the lake.

WHALE WATCHING

Although the region's best whale watching is off San Juan Island, it is also possible to spot orcas from Whidbey Island. Pods of orca whales can often be seen from **Seawall Park** in Langley during the early months of autumn.

WHITEWATER KAYAKING & CANOEING

Because this region lies in the lowlands, there is little in the way of whitewater paddling. There are, however, a few Class I runs that can be fun for canoeists.

CLASS I

The **South Fork Nooksack River** offers the very best run in this region. On summer weekends, this river is a favorite of tubers and can be just as fun if you are paddling a canoe. The water in summer is usually clear and there are plenty of riffles to keep things moving. Sandy beaches and gravel bars make great places for a picnic or a quick dip in the water. Just be sure to keep an eye out for logjams and sweepers, which often clog this narrow river. The 8-mile run starts west of the community of Saxon off Wash. 9 north of Sedro Woolley. Be sure you're on the right river before you launch; the Saxon Road crosses the Samish River twice before reaching the Nooksack. The take-out is at the end of Strand Road, which goes west from Wash. 9 about 2 miles south of Van Zandt.

If you're looking for more challenging waters, head to the main-stem **Nooksack River** downstream from Everson. The river flows fast and swift through this section and the 18-mile run down to Ferndale makes for an exhilarating day's paddle. This is agricultural land but there are good views of Mount Baker in the distance. This isn't a run for novices though, since the river is dangerously cold should you capsize, and the constant flow can make swimming to shore and retrieving your canoe a problem. If this run is too tame for you, try putting in at the Wash. 542 bridge in Cedarville. The river between here and Everson is characterized by braided channels and islands that require lots of decision making. The water also occasionally kicks up into Class II rapids in this upper 8-mile stretch. Throughout this entire run, you need to stay alert for logjams and sweepers.

For the Everson-to-Ferndale run, put in at the Wash. 544 bridge south of Everson. To reach the take-out, take exit 262 off I-5 and drive toward Ferndale. Turn left onto Hovander Road before crossing the bridge into town. The boat ramp is on the right. To get to the Everson put-in, drive back across I-5 and continue 4 miles east to Wash. 539. Turn left, drive 3 miles north to Wash. 544, and turn right to reach the bridge just south of Everson. To reach the Cedarville put-in, continue east on Wash. 544 to Nooksack, turn right on Wash. 9, drive south to Wash. 542, and turn right to reach the bridge.

Campgrounds & Other Accommodations

CAMPING

Campground reservations for **Birch Bay, Moran,** and **Spencer Spit state parks** can (and should) be made by calling Reservations Northwest (tel. 800/452-5687). To make a reservation you'll need to know the name of the campground you want to stay at and the dates you plan to visit. The reservation fee is $6. Reservations are taken beginning in January, and Moran State Park fills up fast for the summer months. Don't procrastinate.

THE SAN JUAN ISLANDS

San Juan Island. There is only one public campground on San Juan Island, but there are some good private campgrounds as well. My personal favorite on the island is San Juan County Park, 380 Westside Rd. N, Friday Harbor, WA 98250 (tel. 360/378-2992), which is set on the site of an old waterfront farm on the island's west coast and has 25 campsites. The views are unbeatable, and this is a great spot for bicyclists. If you are heading up here in the summer, however, make reservations months in advance (as early as January). Snug Harbor Marina Resort, 2371 Mitchell Bay Rd., Friday Harbor, WA 98250 (tel. 360/378-4762), is your other waterfront option on San Juan's west coast. This private campground has 12 tent sites and 4 RV sites and is popular with scuba divers (air is available) and anglers (boat rentals are available). Lakedale Campground, 2627 Roche Harbor Rd., Friday Harbor, WA 98250 (tel. 800/617-CAMP or 360/378-2350), is the largest of the island's private campgrounds (100 sites) and is located 4 miles north of Friday Harbor. With 82 acres, campsites for tents as well as RVs, and several lakes, Lakedale makes an ideal spot for a family vacation. Cyclists should consider the small Pedal Inn, 1300 False Bay Dr., Friday Harbor, WA 98250 (tel. 360/378-3049), which is at the south end of the island and has 25 campsites.

Orcas Island. Moran State Park (166 sites, including 15 primitive sites) is the most popular camping spot on the island. Reservations are recommended April through September and are accepted beginning on January 1. Three of the park's four campgrounds are on Cascade Lake and the fourth is on Mountain Lake, which is on the road to the summit of Mount Constitution. If you're a counterculture type (drive a Volkswagen van, like to get naked in hot springs, that sort of thing), then you'll want to head for **Doe Bay Village Resort,** Star Route Box 86, Olga, WA 98279 (tel. 360/376-2291), a private campground with 50 campsites. There are hot springs here and guided kayak tours are offered. If you enjoy roughing it, there are a few hike-in or paddle-in campsites at **Obstruction Pass State Park** (9 sites) at the south end of the east arm of the island. Keep in mind that there is no water available at this isolated and beautifully situated park.

Lopez Island. The first park off the ferry is **Odlin County Park,** Route 2, Box 3216, Lopez, WA 98261 (tel. 360/468-2496), which has 30 campsites along the water and also provides boating access and picnic tables. Athletic fields make this more of a community sports center than a natural area. A little farther south and on the east side of the island you'll find **Spencer Spit State Park,** Route 2, Box 3600, Lopez, WA 98261 (tel. 360/468-2251), which has 35 campsites set amid tall fir trees.

Shaw Island. South Beach County Park (12 sites) at the south end of the island is the only campground on this little-visited, though ferry-accessible, island. Some of the campsites are right on the water. If you want to get away from it all and have a San Juans experience the way it used to be, this is the place. Bring your kayaks and bikes and have a great time.

THE NORTHWEST COAST

By far the most popular campsites in the region, and not without just cause, are those at **Deception Pass State Park** (251 sites), which flanks the notoriously fast waters that churn through Deception Pass between Whidbey Island and Fidalgo Island. There are five hiker/biker campsites here if you happen to be pedaling through the area. Farther south on Whidbey Island there are more campsites at three other state parks. At **Fort Ebey State Park** (56 sites), campsites are tucked into the forests a bit away from the beach, while at **Fort Casey State Park** (38 sites), the campsites are right on the water at the Keystone

Ferry Landing. At the south end of the island, **South Whidbey State Park** (60 sites) is set amid majestic old-growth forest. All of these parks are along the west coast of the island and are well signed on Wash. 20.

Just north of Deception Pass on Fidalgo Island, there is camping at **Washington Park** (75 sites) on the west side of Anacortes. This city park is on Fidalgo Head and has a scenic loop drive with some of the nicest picnic sites in the region. East of Whidbey Island across Saratoga Passage, there is camping in the blufftop forests at **Camano Island State Park** (87 sites), which is very popular with boaters.

South of Bellingham, **Larrabee State Park** (87 sites) provides a quintessentially Northwestern setting amid big trees and steep mountains wrapping around a small cove. North of Bellingham and less than 10 miles south of the Canadian border, **Birch Bay State Park** (167 sites) offers oceanside camping in a setting reminiscent of east-coast beaches. The long sandy beach here is the main attraction.

INNS & LODGES

SAN JUAN ISLAND

Olympic Lights Bed & Breakfast

4531-A Cattle Point Rd., Friday Harbor, WA 98250. Tel. 360/378-3186. 5 rms (1 with private bath). $70–$105 double. All rates include full breakfast. No credit cards.

Located at San Juan's dry southwest tip, Olympic Lights is a yellow Victorian farmhouse surrounded by windswept meadows. The ocean breezes, nearby beach, and friendliness of innkeepers Christian and Lea Andrade lend a special feel to this American classic. This inn makes a good bicycling base.

ORCAS ISLAND

Spring Bay Inn

P.O. Box 97, Olga, WA 98279. Tel. 360/376-5531. Fax 360/376-2193. 4 rms. $150–$175 double. All rates include continental breakfast, brunch, and daily kayak tour. MC, V.

As one of the only waterfront B&Bs in the San Juans this inn would deserve recommendation. However, innkeepers Sandy Playa and Carl Burger, both retired park rangers, make a stay here fun and educational. You can soak in the hot tub on the beach and watch the sunset, spot bald eagles from just outside the inn's front door, and best of all, go for a guided sea kayak tour each morning. The four guest rooms all have fireplaces.

Doe Bay Village Resort

Star Rte., Box 86, Olga, WA 98279. Tel. 360/ 376-2291. 24 cottages, hostel. $14.50 hostel; $12–$16 camping; $45–$92 double. AE, DISC, MC, V.

This funky collection of cottages and tiny cabins is now a sort of counterculture resort. The cottages are furnished in early Salvation Army and are generally clean. The folks who stay here tend to have similar interests—healthy foods, the outdoors, relaxation. You can't help but absorb a bit of the laid-back attitude when you check in here, especially after you check out the spring-fed hot tubs and sauna, which are available for an additional $3 per person. They're set on a big deck overlooking a picturesque little cove with a pebble beach. The tubs, sauna, and beach are clothing optional. For those on a really tight budget, there are campsites and even a hostel. Kayak tours operate from the resort. If you'd just like to drop by for a few hours and soak in the tubs or sauna, you can do so for only $6.

LOPEZ ISLAND

Islander Lopez Resort

Fisherman Bay Rd. (P.O. Box 197), Lopez Island, WA 98261. Tel. 800/736-3434 or 360/468-2233. 36 rms, all with TVs. June 1–Sept 30, $80–$120 double; Oct 1–May 30, $55–$80 double. AE, MC, V.

Located about a mile from Lopez Village, the Islander Lopez may not look too impressive from the outside, but it is a very comfortable lodging. All the rooms have great views of Fisherman Bay. The Islander offers such amenities as a full-service marina with kayak rentals, seasonal restaurant, lounge, an outdoor pool, whirlpool, and adjacent bike-rental shop.

Inn at Swifts Bay

Rte. 2, Box 3402, Lopez Island, WA 98261. Tel. 360/468-3636. Fax 360/468-3637. 2 rms (both with shared bath), 3 suites (all with private bath), 1 luxury cabin. $75–$85 double room; $125–$155 double suite. All rates include full breakfast. AE, DISC, MC, V.

You'll find the Inn at Swifts Bay on the north end of Lopez Island, and though you can't actually see the bay from the inn, it is just a short walk to the private beach. Innkeepers Robert Herrmann and Christopher Brandmeir do all they can to assure that guests enjoy an idyllic stay on the island. A gourmet breakfast in a cafe-like setting starts the day, and after long hours of pedaling or paddling around the island, you can soak in the hot tub.

THE NORTHWEST COAST

Log Castle

3273 E Saratoga Rd., Langley, WA 98260. Tel. 360/221 5483. 4 rms. $90–$115 double. All rates include full breakfast. MC, V.

A mile and a half outside of the Whidbey Island town of Langley, overlooking Saratoga Passage and distant Mount Baker, stands a sprawling log home. Everywhere one looks inside this fascinating home there are logs. The walls, the beams, the tables, the shelves, the door handles. Of the four rooms, the two turret rooms are the most popular, and everyone's favorite is the third-story octagonal turret room.

Captain Whidbey Inn

2072 W Captain Whidbey Inn Rd., Coupeville, WA 98239. Tel. 800/366-4097 or 360/678-4097. 25 rms (13 with bath), 4 cottages, 3 houses, 2 suites. $85–$95 double with shared bath, $125 double with private bath; $145 suite; $150 cottage; $175–$195 house. All rates include continental breakfast. AE, DC, DISC, MC, V.

Three miles west of Coupeville off Madrona Way stands one of the Northwest's most unique inns. Built in 1907 of small madrona logs, the historic inn is architecturally fascinating, a bit of American folk art. The rooms in the main building are small and lack private bathrooms, but they manage to capture the feel of the island's seafaring past. Larger rooms, cottages, and even a few houses are available for those who need more room. The inn's dining room overlooks Penn Cove and serves creative Northwest cuisine that often features the inn's own mussels.

THE PUGET SOUND

WATER, WATER, EVERYWHERE. THAT'S THE PUGET SOUND. Around seemingly every corner, over every hill, behind every tree, there is a view of the water. No wonder then that the sound is now home to millions of people and is by

far the most populous region in all of Washington State. Water is always a powerful attractant, especially to those who enjoy the outdoors.

Although the waters of the Puget Sound rarely get above 50°F, that hasn't stopped people from enjoying the region's abundant aquatic offerings. Wetsuits, dry suits, paddle jackets, and mitts—these are the adaptations that have allowed scuba divers to explore the fascinating underwater environment of Puget Sound, boardsailors to ride the winds on lake and bays, and sea kayakers to paddle area waters even in the dead of winter.

There are more sea kayaks in the Puget Sound area than in any other single spot in the country, and for good reason. The winding waterways of this region are perfect for exploration by sea kayak. There are waterfront parks and boat ramps, as well as numerous campgrounds, scattered up and down the maze of waterways. Some of these parks are even on islands inaccessible to automobiles, although there is not the abundance of these marine state parks as there is in the San Juan Islands to the north. Currently a sea kayak trail known as the Cascadia Marine Trail is being developed to link the sound's many public access areas so that paddlers will be able to journey from Olympia north to the San Juan Islands, spending many days on the waters of Puget Sound.

There are also plenty of land-based activities possible for the terra-firma crowd. One of the things that has made Seattle such a popular place to live is its abundance of parks, many of which are on the water, so that even those people who prefer to keep both feet on the ground can keep an eye on the water as they wander. Throughout the Seattle metropolitan area, there are dozens of large city and county parks that range from neatly manicured gardens and arboretums to muddy marshlands to rocky mountaintops. There is also a surprising number of state parks. Within these parks there are many miles of hiking and walking trails that provide area residents with quick escapes to the woods. These trails often come into their own when the Cascade and Olympic mountains are snowed in.

More than a few of these parks have beaches within their borders, and for most of these parks, these beaches are the main attraction. Beach access is relatively hard to come by in the Puget Sound region, where waterfront homes seem to line every last one of the hundreds of miles of shoreline. Consequently, beach parks are among the most popular in the region. From rocky tide pools to eroding bluffs to sandy beaches, the shores of Puget Sound and area lakes are rich in variety and provide options for all beach tastes.

Although Seattle has been described as a mountain biker's hell for its lack of off-road riding, it is heaven for road biking. An extensive network of paved bike paths has become the focus of in-city riding, with the linked Burke–Gilman and Sammamish River trails providing enough miles of trail to do an exhaust-free half-century. However, because the trails see heavy use, many cyclists prefer to head for the country, which is often only a ferry ride away. Kingston–Edmonds, Seattle–Bainbridge Island, Fauntleroy–Vashon, Point Defiance–Tahlequah—these are the ferries that carry cyclists from city streets to country lanes.

The mild climate of the Puget Sound lowlands makes year-round outdoor activity a way of life here (that is, if you have good rain gear). However, you really have to enjoying biking or walking in the rain, and with the mountains so close by, why not take up skiing instead of staying down in the drizzle? No, the Puget Sound, like all good bodies of water, comes into its own during the months of summer.

The Lay of the Land

An inland sea lying to the south of Whidbey Island, Puget Sound is a convoluted maze of waterways winding among forested mountains and hills. Twisting, turning, doubling back on itself, the sound is flanked by more than 2,000 miles of coastline. This entire landscape of blue water and green forests, deep channels and steep hills, is of ice-age origin. Around 12,000 to 15,000 years ago the Vashon Glacier blanketed this region. As it ground slowly over the land, it gouged out deep valleys and dumped mountainloads of rocky debris in its wake. Today those valleys are deep, narrow inlets, channels, lakes, and occasionally fertile valley floors. The rubble that was deposited by the glaciers formed long hills called drumlins. It is such hills that comprise much of the uplands of the region. However, less than 20 miles to the east of the sound rise real mountains. Known as the Issaquah Alps, the peaks of Tiger Mountain and Cougar Mountain at the south end of Lake Sammamish are a spur range of the Cascades.

The deep, flooded valleys have dictated the development of the region for a century and a half. The first Euro-American communities in the sound were all port towns, and they were scattered around the sound on islands, spits, bays, and mudflats. However, when the railroads arrived and chose to stop at Seattle and Tacoma, those two cities became the most important on the sound. Too wide and too deep for bridging in most places, the sound became a natural barrier to development for islands such as Bainbridge and Vashon and for communities on the western shores. Although ferries connected, and still connect these places to the population centers on the sound's eastern shores, they have never developed into major cities, with the possible exception of Bremerton, which staked its fortune as a naval shipyard.

Puget Sound is today the population center of Washington State. From north of Seattle down through Tacoma to south of Olympia, the east side of the sound has become almost an unbroken sprawl of 60 miles or more. Traffic congestion has come to rival that of southern California (much to the chagrin of the thousands of Californians who moved here to escape urban sprawl and jammed freeways). It is easy to think that there couldn't possibly be anywhere to get outdoors amid this concrete jungle, but that is far from the truth. Tucked amid the asphalt are countless pockets of greenery, manicured and otherwise, and it is to these green spaces that area residents flock whenever the sun shines, and frequently when it doesn't.

On the west side of the sound lies the **Kitsap Peninsula,** covered with thick forests but rapidly becoming suburbanized. This peninsula, comprised of countless smaller peninsulas, is a sort of negative image of Puget Sound. All the bodies of water that comprise the sound shape the Kitsap Peninsula into what at times seems to be only coastline. Tucked within the folds of this peninsula are not only forested shorelines but also nuclear submarines at Bangor Navy Base on the shores of Hood Canal. In Bremerton, mothballed battleships and aircraft carriers crowd the naval shipyards. However, for the most part this is tree country, and includes large tracts of

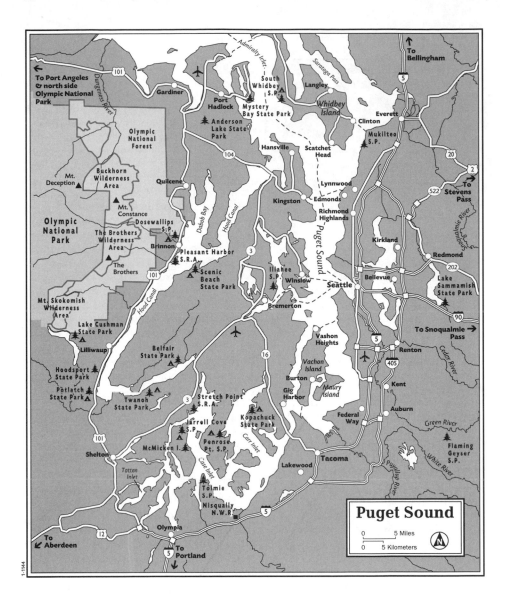

Puget Sound

| 0 | 5 Miles |
| 0 | 5 Kilometers |

state forests. **Tahuya State Forest** and **Capitol State Forest,** though both managed primarily for timber, also have become the region's favorite riding areas for hard-core mountain bikers.

Like the giant octopus that lives in its depths, the Puget Sound in its southern reaches stretches out its many arms in every direction, poking and prying deep into the landscape. Where you least expect to see the waters of the ocean, there they suddenly are, lurking behind the Douglas firs. The far shore may be less than half a mile away, but to get there by car, you may have to drive 80 or 90 miles. Such

convolutions have stymied development in the south sound since the arrival of the first settlers. Along these remote shores are numerous small state parks, which for the most part are the domain of locals—a place to picnic by the water or launch the fishing boat.

Most dramatic of the Puget Sound arms shaping the Kitsap Peninsula is **Hood Canal.** Not a canal at all, this is actually a long, narrow, fjord-like bay that stretches 50 miles southwest from its mouth and then hooks around to the northeast another 20 miles before coming to an inglorious end in unremarkable marshland.

> "There is no country in the world that possesses waters equal to these."
>
> —Capt. George Vancouver, who charted the waters of Puget Sound in 1792

Throughout its entire length, Hood Canal is rarely more than 2.5 miles wide.

Cradled within the tentacles of Puget Sound are half a dozen large islands and easily twice that many smaller ones. **Bainbridge** and **Vashon,** connected to Seattle by ferry, to the most populous, yet both retain their rural flavor and are favored by road cyclists who flee congested city streets by ferry and escape to the quiet countryside. In the south sound, **Fox Island** and **Hartsene Island** are connected to the mainland by bridges, while a tiny ferry services residential **Anderson Island.** The sixth of the sound's large islands, **McNeil,** serves as a federal penitentiary. Among the smaller islands, there are several that are state marine parks. These include **McMicken Island, Cutts Island,** and **Eagle Island,** this latter uncomfortably close to McNeil Island Penitentiary. These parks, which can be reached only by private boat, are popular with kayakers as well as sailors and powerboaters.

Although salt water is ubiquitous in this region, the glaciers that scoured out this landscape also scoured out valleys that seawater has not been able to reach. In the very heart of Seattle lies **Lake Union,** a small lake ringed with marinas, office buildings, condominiums, and houseboats. However, this urban lake, with the famous Space Needle rising near its south shore and a city park with a rusted and abandoned refinery in the middle of it, is where a large percentage of Puget Sound sea kayakers have taken their first tentative strokes. To the east of Seattle, and connected to Lake Union by the narrow channel known as the Montlake Cut, lies **Lake Washington,** stretching nearly 18 miles from north to south. Encircled by expensive waterfront homes, this lake is a favorite playground of powerboaters and sailors, but also has numerous parks and natural areas along its shores, which are actually 10 feet below what they were 100 years ago. In 1916, when the Lake Washington ship canal was built connecting this lake with Lake Union and westward to salt water at Shilshole Bay, the lake drained considerably to attain an equilibrium with Lake Union. Still farther east lies the smaller **Lake Sammamish,** which is now ringed with suburbs. At the southern end of this lake lies Lake Sammamish State Park and one of the region's busiest little beaches.

Flowing into the sound are numerous rivers, and with mountains crowding the margin of the sound, some of these rivers are surprisingly rambunctious. Less than 20 miles as the raven flies from Puget Sound, the **Green River** carves its way through a 300-foot-deep gorge, kicking up Class IV rapids as it roars over and around massive boulders. To the north, 270-foot **Snoqualmie Falls** on the Snoqualmie River mark for many Seattleites the eastern edge of the lowlands. The Snoqualmie below the falls is a relatively gentle river, however, with a penchant for overflowing its banks during the rainy winter months.

Although it may seem at times that the megalopolis of the Puget Sound has paved over every inch of wildlife habitat, the truth is not quite so extreme. Just as people are drawn to the waters of the region, so too is wildlife. Salmon, sea lions, otters, bald eagles—all of these and more are often spotted around the shorelines of this region. Ferry riders are often treated to the sight of Dall porpoises rocketing through the water beside the ferry, and even orca whales are occasionally spotted in these waters.

Signs announcing "Salmon Stream" are common sights at roadway bridges throughout the region, and though salmon runs are severely depleted, the fish still return to rivers and streams flowing into Puget Sound.

The waters of the sound also serve as home or wintering grounds for a wide variety of waterfowl. Buffleheads, goldeneyes, wigeons, teals, and harlequin ducks are all to be seen floating on these waters.

Likewise, those 2,000 miles of shoreline attract a good many shorebirds.

Both the salmon and the waterfowl attract two of the region's most noteworthy wild residents. While bald eagles are more numerous in the San Juan Islands, they are also frequently seen throughout Puget Sound, especially in the autumn months when area streams are filled with dying salmon. Sea lions, on the other hand, don't bother waiting for salmon and steelhead to die; they take them in the prime of their lives before they can head up from salt water into fresh.

Water is the focus of life in the Puget Sound region, but what makes this inland sea truly unique are the backgrounds to the watery foregrounds. Rising to the west are the craggy Olympic Mountains, to the southeast rises Mount Rainier (or, as Seattleites think of it, "The Mountain"), and to the northeast stand Mount Baker and Glacier Peak. Filling the middle ground are the hills that ring the lowlands, sometimes rising directly from the water, sometimes set back across wide, flat valleys.

And everywhere over this land is the color green. Watered by more than 40 inches of rain each year, the forests of the Puget Sound grow with botanical abandon. At times it seems that the only reason for the cities is to open up a little sky overhead, to keep the darkness of the forests at arm's length. But then the sun comes out, and everyone heads for the woods, to wander beneath the boughs of Douglas firs and western red cedars, to watch the eagles and salmon, to glimpse the shimmering snowclad peaks in the distance, as people have done in the Puget Sound for thousands of years.

Parks & Other Hot Spots

Discovery Park

From downtown Seattle, drive north on Elliot Ave. W, which becomes 15th Ave. W. Turn left onto West Dravus St. and then right on 20th Ave. W, which changes names a couple of times as it curves around to the west to reach the park's main gate. Tel. 206/386-4236. Beach, picnicking, walking.

At 535 acres, Discovery Park is Seattle's largest city park. Within the borders of this park northwest of downtown on what was once a military base, there are several miles of hiking trails, more than 4 miles of beaches, high bluffs, forests, and meadows. Views across the sound to the Olympic Mountains are always uplifting, and even Mount Baker can be seen to the north. Walking and beachcombing are favorite activities here.

Washington Park Arboretum

From I-5 north of downtown Seattle, take Wash. 520 east to Montlake Blvd., continue straight on E Lake Washington Dr., turn left on Park Dr., and park in the Museum of History and Industry parking lot. Tel. 206/543-8800. Picnicking, walking, bird watching, canoeing, sea kayaking.

Lying just north of the Capitol Hill neighborhood on the shore of Lake Washington's Union Bay, the Washington Park Arboretum is one of the best reasons to call Seattle home. Containing not only an outstanding collection of trees, it is home to the Japanese Garden and a wetland that is home to swans and great blue herons. Trails wander among the arboretum's interesting plantings of exotic trees providing gardeners with inspiration. However, my favorite trail is the Waterfront Trail, which leads past marshes and over bridges. The bird watching here is always good. The shoreline of the arboretum is also a favorite spot with sea kayakers and canoeists (canoes can be rented across Union Bay at the University of Washington).

Seward Park

The park is off Lake Washington Blvd. S. From I-5 south of downtown Seattle, take exit 161 and drive east on S Graham St., north on Rainier Ave. S, and then east again on S Orcas St. Picnicking, walking, bird watching, road cycling, swimming.

Encompassing the entire Bailey Peninsula, which juts into Lake Washington due east of Mercer Island, this pleasant park offers views across the lake and a pocket of forest that includes Douglas firs more than 6 feet in diameter. Strolling and biking on the park's waterside perimeter road (closed to traffic) are the most popular pursuits here, but there are also picnic and swimming areas. The park's real jewel, however, is the forest that occupies the center of the peninsula. Numerous short trails wind through these woods. For the past few years, the park has been home to a nesting pair of bald eagles. Also in the park are a small Japanese garden and a fish hatchery.

Saint Edward State Park

North of Kirkland. From I-405, take exit 23, drive west on Wash. 522, turn left on 68th Ave. NE, which becomes Juanita Dr. NE, and continue 1.5 miles south. Tel. 206/823-2992. Picnicking, walking, mountain biking, swimming.

Formerly a Catholic seminary, this park lies on the eastern shore of Lake Washington just outside of Kirkland. Forests, fields, and shoreline are partly wild and partly manicured, and trails wind throughout the 316-acre day-use park. This is one of the few parks in the Seattle area that allows mountain biking on any of its trails; there's a 3-mile loop open to bikes. There are also equestrian trails here, but the walking trails are the main attraction. Add up all the short trails, one of which runs along the shore of the lake, and you have more than 3 miles of paths.

Lake Sammamish State Park

North of Issaquah. From I-90 take exit 15 and follow signs north to the park entrance. Tel. 206/455-7010. Picnicking, boardsailing, canoeing, sea kayaking, swimming.

This large park in Issaquah at the south end of Lake Sammamish is most popular for its beach, wide lawns, and picnic areas. Together these facilities make this a favorite beach hangout during the summer months. The park's boat ramps are most popular with water-skiers and people launching personal watercraft. Consequently the waters off the beach here are always noisy on weekends. The beach itself often resembles nothing more than a giant ashtray. Unless you like crowds and noise, stay away.

Cougar Mountain Regional Wildland Park

South of Issaquah. Take exit 13 off I-90, drive west on SE Newport Way, and turn left onto 164th Ave. SE. In 1.7 miles turn right onto Lakemont Blvd. SE and continue 1.4 miles to the Red Town Trailhead; or take exit 15 off I-5 and drive south 4.2 miles on Wash. 900 to the Wilderness Creek Trailhead. Tel. 206/296-4171. Hiking.

Once upon a time there were coal mines and logging railroads on these hills. Today, luxury homes cling to steep hillsides and forests are regenerating. Part of the Issaquah Alps, a spur of low mountains extending westward from the main body of the Cascades, this area was once known as the Newcastle Hills, an obvious reference to its coal-mining history. Today, Cougar Mountain is the name known to area hikers who come here for quick access to wild lands at elevations low enough to provide year-round hiking. There is an extensive network of trails here leading out from various trailheads. These trails are included on the Tiger Mountain Map, which is sold at REIs in the Seattle area.

Tiger Mountain State Forest

Take exit 20 off I-90, turn right and then right again to reach the High Point Trailhead (hikers only); or take exit 25, turn south onto Wash. 18, and continue 4.2 miles to a parking area on the right (mountain biking). Tel. 206/800/527-3305. Paragliding/hang gliding, hiking, mountain biking, horseback riding.

Although managed by the state as much for timber as for recreation, this large forest southeast of Issaquah is extremely popular with a wide range of recreational users. It is perhaps best known now as the best, and only, extensive network of mountain-biking trails and roads in the Seattle area. However, cyclists share the roads with 4×4s and motorcycles. Horseback riding is also popular with rentals available just outside the forest. From the summit of Poo Poo Point, hang gliders and paragliders launch into the skies over the

Puget Sound. There are also hiking trails here that include surprisingly steep climbs. To find your way around the trails and gravel roads of this forest, pick up a copy of the Tiger Mountain Map, which is sold at REIs in the Seattle area.

Saltwater State Park

Take exit 149 off I-5, drive west on Wash. 516, and turn south on Wash. 509. Tel. 206/764-4128. Beach, picnicking, camping, hiking, swimming, scuba diving, fishing.

The most amazing thing about this little park (only 88 acres) is that it exists at all. Completely surrounded by suburbia, the park is a tiny pocket of wild land on the shore of Puget Sound. Within the park is not only a beach that attracts throngs during the summer months, but also, most surprisingly, a campground. There are also 2 miles of hiking trails through the woods here.

Dash Point State Park

Northeast of Tacoma. Take exit 143 off I-5, drive west on SW 320th St., turn right on 21st Ave. SW, and then left onto Wash. 509. Tel. 206/593-2206. Beach, picnicking, camping, scuba diving, swimming, fishing.

Very similar in setting and facilities to Saltwater State Park, this park is much larger (almost 400 acres). Amid the park's forests are 6 miles of hiking trails, a campground, and two-thirds of a mile of beach. Campsites, though almost within hearing distance of the crowds cheering in the Tacoma Dome, have a sense of being miles away from the city.

Point Defiance Park

From Wash. 16 west of I-5, take Pearl St. north to the park, or take I-705 into Tacoma from I-5 and continue north on Ruston Way. Tel. 206/591-3690. Beach, picnicking, walking, hiking, road biking, sea kayaking, fishing.

With many miles of hiking trails winding through its wooded acres, Point Defiance Park is Tacoma's favorite spot for a quick commune with nature. Any time of year the trails here offer respite from urban life. However, on summer weekends, crowds in the park are so large that it becomes difficult to forget you are still in the city. Trails are generally well marked, so you can strike out on almost any path and simply watch for a return route when you are ready to head back to your starting point. The park's meandering one-way roads are favorites of area cyclists. Sea kayakers sometimes paddle along the shore of the park, and anglers sometimes fish from the waterside walkways near the park's boathouse (now a restaurant). The park also has a zoo, a logging museum, a reconstruction of an old fort, and a fairy-tale land for children, which together all add up to lots of business for this large, forested area.

Flaming Geyser State Park

East of Auburn. From I-5 drive east on Wash. 18 through Auburn to Auburn–Black Diamond Rd., turn right, and then right again onto SE Green Valley Rd. Tel. 206/931-3930. Swimming, tubing, whitewater kayaking and canoeing, fishing.

With a name straight out of *Dungeons & Dragons*, this park is the region's favorite swimming hole and tubing river. The park stretches along the banks of the Green River, with most of the riverfront cleared to wide, sunny lawns. The crowds here on sunny summer afternoons can be daunting, but everyone has fun bouncing down the river on anything that floats. The Green River is one of the state's premier steelhead rivers, and there is plenty of access for anglers within the park.

Kanaskat-Palmer State Park

East of Auburn. From I-5 take Wash. 516 east, continuing on Kent–Kangley Rd. to Lake Retreat–Kanaskat Rd. Tel. 206/886-0148. Picnicking, camping, swimming, whitewater kayaking, whitewater rafting.

Located farther up the river than Flaming Geyser, this park is a much more natural and less crowded setting. Set in a loop of the river, the park is bordered on three sides by noisy waters tumbling over boulders and small waterfalls. Anglers know the park as one of the best steelheading areas around, and kayakers come here to challenge Class IV whitewater. However, in places, the waters here are tame enough for swimming, with lots of deep holes and rocks for jumping points. Although not far from the city, the campground has the feel of a remote mountain camp.

Fay-Bainbridge State Park

From the Bainbridge Island ferry landing, drive north on Wash. 305, and turn right on Phelps Rd. NE. Tel. 206/842-3931. Beach, picnicking, camping, sea kayaking.

Located at the north end of Bainbridge Island, this park has a good view of the Seattle skyline on the far side of the sound, but people come here more for the forest setting and beach access than they do for the view. The campground, the only one on the island, is convenient to Seattle yet well removed from the city's bustle. Sea kayakers often put in here and paddle north and west around Point Monroe to explore, at high tide, the lagoon formed inside the point's curving sand spit.

Blake Island State Park

Accessible only by boat. Nearest boat launches are in towns of Harper and Manchester on the Kitsap Peninsula northwest of the Southworth ferry terminal. Tillicum Village Tours (tel. 206/443-1244) operates boat/dinner tours to the park from Pier 56 in Seattle. Tel. 206/731-0770. Camping, hiking, fishing, swimming, scuba diving.

Located in the middle of Puget Sound between West Seattle and the Kitsap Peninsula, Blake Island is accessible only by boat. Sea kayakers and powerboaters frequent the island's campsites during the summer, and any time of year people come out here to hike the island's forest trails. During the summer, the sandy beaches here are particularly popular. Many people come here on boat tours that include a salmon barbecue and a performance of Native American dancing in a reconstructed Indian longhouse on the island. The island's small, tame deer suffer from overpopulation and are always begging for food. Don't oblige them.

Outdoor Resources

INFORMATION
Issaquah Alps Trail Club
Tel. 206/328-0480
King County Parks and Recreation
Tel. 206/296-4232
Washington State Parks
Tel. 800/233-0321

EQUIPMENT STORES
Backpacker's Supply
5206 S Tacoma Way, Tacoma
Tel. 206/472-4402

Marmot Mountain Works
827 Bellevue Way NE, Bellevue
Tel. 206/453-1515

The North Face
1023 First Ave., Seattle
Tel. 206/622-4111

REI
222 Yale Ave. N, Seattle
Tel. 206/223-1944

Wilderness Sports
14340 NE 20th St., Bellevue
Tel. 206/746-0500

Kopachuck State Park

Take Wash. 16 west from I-5 in Tacoma and follow signs to the park from the Gig Harbor/Kopachuck State Park exit. Tel. 206/265-3606. Beach, camping, sea kayaking, scuba diving.

Popular with both sea kayakers and scuba divers, both of whom head out from Kopachuck to Cutts Island Marine State Park to do their exploring, this wooded park lies on the shore of Carr Inlet southwest of Gig Harbor. There is also a campground here.

What to Do & Where to Do It

BEACHES

Alki Beach, in West Seattle, is Seattle's most popular beach, and is as close as you'll come to a southern California beach scene in the Northwest. A paved biking/walking path runs the entire length of the beach and is very popular with in-line skaters. Views take in the Olympic Mountains as well as the downtown Seattle skyline.

For a much more natural setting, try the beaches at **Discovery Park.** Accessible only on foot, the two beaches here are backed by high bluffs and provide a sense of seclusion and wildness that is missing from other beaches in the immediate Seattle area. **Golden Gardens Park,** northwest of the Ballard neighborhood along Shilshole Bay, is another pretty beach. High, wooded bluffs back the park, but right behind the beach, there are wide lawns. Walk north from the large parking lot for a more secluded setting.

South of Seattle, there are several small state and regional park beaches on the shore of Puget Sound. About 3 miles south of the West Seattle ferry dock, there is **Ed Munro Seahurst County Park,** where a manmade beach provides enough sand for sunbathing. Much more popular are **Saltwater State Park,** on Wash. 509 north of Federal Way, and **Dash Point State Park,** which is on Wash. 509 just north of the port of Tacoma. Saltwater State Park is the most popular beach in the region. The beach itself is not that large, but there is also a long, narrow strip of land along a rock seawall. The small beach at Dash Point grows to nearly 2,000 feet in width on low tides, and at high tides, the water over this shallow beach is warm enough that some people actually go swimming.

On Bainbridge Island, there are beaches at both the north and south ends of the island. At the north end, there is **Fay–Bainbridge State Park,** which has campsites right on a beach that overlooks Seattle across the sound. At the south end of the island, **Fort Ward State Park** has a long stretch of beach good for beachcombing and bird watching.

On Vashon Island, there are a couple of nice little beaches at county parks on Quartermaster Harbor, the bay on the southeast side of the island. **Burton Acres County Park** (take 99th Avenue SW to SW 240th Street) sits on a headland jutting out into the harbor. Across the bay is **Dockton County Park** (take 99th Avenue SW to SW Portage–Dockton Road), which has a longer stretch of beach than Burton Acres.

If you have your own boat (a sea kayak will do), the beaches of **Blake Island** are a great place to spend a day. Although only tour boats and private boaters can reach the island, it still gets a lot of visitors on weekends. However, wander the trails through the forests and find a beach away from the tour-boat dock and you'll likely have plenty of peace and quiet.

BIRD WATCHING

In Bellevue on a backwater of Lake Washington north of I-90, **Mercer Slough Nature Park** provides habitat for ruddy ducks and goldeneyes during the winter and pied-billed grebes in the spring. A well-built trail provides access to the slough from SE 118th Avenue. Another good way to observe birdlife here is from a canoe or sea kayak.

If you want a close-up view of nesting great blue herons, head south of Seattle 20 miles or so to **Great Blue Heron Marsh,** which is located between Federal Way and Auburn (take exit 143 off I-5 and go east on South 320th Street for about 3 miles, then turn right on West Valley Highway). Surprisingly, herons only began nesting here in 1968 after an abandoned gravel pit had developed into a healthy little pond.

Midway between Tacoma and Olympia, just off I-5, is the region's most noteworthy and extensive birding area. The **Nisqually Delta,** a wide, flat wetland, is the largest undeveloped estuary on Puget Sound and is a National Wildlife Refuge. Fall and winter, when tens of thousands of waterfowl take up residence here, is the best birding season. Wigeons, teals, and several other species of ducks can be seen. Throughout the year, bald eagles and other raptors can be seen here, and along the forest trails, various songbirds are common. There are several miles of trails leading from the headquarters parking area, but parts of the refuge can also be explored by sea kayak or canoe. To reach the refuge, take exit 114 off I-5.

On the west side of the sound, you'll find a couple of viewing blinds on the water in **Fort Ward State Park** on the south end of Bainbridge Island. Waterfowl, shorebirds, and marine birds are all regular visitors here.

BOARDSAILING

With water all around, it is not surprising that boardsailing is very popular in the Puget Sound region. In Seattle, **Lake Union** is a favorite area with beginners, who benefit from the light winds, flat waters, and easy access at Gasworks Park on the north end of the lake. North Seattle's **Green Lake,** which is surrounded by park, is another popular beginners' spot.

Lake Washington has some of the most popular sailing spots in the Seattle area. When strong winds blow up from the south, **Magnusson Park** at Sand Point on the northwest shore of Lake Washington is a good place to sail. **Juanita Beach,** tucked into a cove in Kirkland, on the east side of Lake Washington, is good when the winds are out of the west and will blow you back into the cove. Down at the south end of the lake, there is also good sailing from **Newcastle Beach.**

On the waters of Puget Sound, where a wetsuit or dry suit is even more necessary than on Lake Washington, winds from the north, south, and west all provide good sailing. **Alki Beach** in West Seattle, and **Golden Gardens Park,** northwest of Ballard, are both popular sailing spots.

Urban Surf, 2100 N Northlake Way (tel. 206/545-WIND), rents boards and will give you lessons if you need them.

FISHING

Lots of water means lots of fishing in and around Puget Sound. Salmon fishing in the sound itself is just about the favorite sport of area anglers, but there are also plenty of options for lake and stream fishing for trout, steelhead, and salmon.

The **Green River,** which empties into Puget Sound at the port facility as the industrial Duwamish River, is Puget Sound's top steelheading river. With good access at, and just downstream of,

Flaming Geyser State Park (south of Black Diamond off Wash. 169), and at Kanaskat Palmer State Park (east of Wash. 169 off Wash. 516), this is primarily a winter steelhead river. So healthy are the wild runs on this river that in 1996 it was still possible to keep wild steelhead at certain times of year. In the lower reaches of this river there are also some salmon, and in the upper reaches there is good trout fishing. However, steelheaders rule here. A summer steelhead run is not as lively as the winter run.

The **Snoqualmie River** is the area's other good steelheading river, with the big silver fighters being confined to the waters below 270-foot Snoqualmie Falls. Once again it is the winter run that brings most of the action. This river is liberally supplied with hatchery fish. Only barbless artificial flies and lures are allowed. There is good access along much of the river, with the stretch directly below the falls being some of the most popular water. There are also plenty of trout, including sea-run cutthroats.

The **Tolt River,** which flows into the Snoqualmie River at the town of Carnation, is yet another good steelheading river. Tolt River–John McDonald Park at the mouth of the river just off Wash. 203 is a good spot to try. There is also a road that parallels the river for several miles upstream from here. Once again, only barbless artificial flies and lures can be used.

Capitol Lake, in downtown Olympia, is one of the most unusual fishing spots in the region. This manmade lake was created in 1949 to give the city a nice focal point and is now a popular spot to fish for trout and salmon, which pass through the lake on the way up the Deschutes River. What makes the lake unusual is the company you'll be keeping when you fish here—I-5 crosses the lake on a high bridge and on a bluff above the lake rises the state capitol building, from which the lake takes its name. A hiking trail follows one side of the lake, but a canoe or other small boat opens up more fishing holes around the lake.

Although most of the saltwater fishing in the Puget Sound is done from boats,

There Is a Free Lunch

Those pesky sea lions. They've tried scaring them away with firecrackers and air horns. They've tried shooting them with rubber bullets. They've tried relocating them. But still they just won't go away. Hey, a sea lion knows a good thing. In Seattle there is a free lunch, and it's to be had at the Ballard Locks fish ladder at the mouth of the Lake Washington ship canal.

In 1917, a shipping canal was built to link Lake Washington to Puget Sound by way of Lake Union. This canal caused the water level of Lake Washington to drop by 10 feet to the level of now interconnected Lake Union. When this happened, lake Washington's natural outflow—the Black River—was left high and dry, and all the waters of Lake Washington and Lake Union began draining through the new ship canal, which meant that the salmon and steelhead from all the creek and river drainages of Lake Washington now had to to use the narrow ship canal as their route back to the streams where they were born. To get over the locks, a fish ladder was built. Eventually, the sea lions figured out that this fish ladder was a seafood buffet.

Climbing the fish ladder is a slow process, and the fish gather at its base preparing to make the climb. As they mill about at the foot of the fish ladder, they become easy game for hungry sea lions, which have been gathering here since the 1980s. In recent years, as many as 120 sea lions have gathered in this area. It wasn't a problem when fish runs were large, but the steelhead run has dwindled to almost nothing. Responsibility for the reduced runs is not entirely in the fins of the sea lions, but these efficient predators have been exacerbating an already bad situation. In order to protect the steelhead run, fish-and-wildlife managers decided some of the most voracious sea lions had to go.

Some of the sea lions were trapped and then released miles away, but within days they returned. They were relocated farther away, and took a little bit longer to get back. Killing them was out of the question. Sea mammals are protected by law, and besides, the public outcry was too great. Eventually three of the most gluttonous sea lions—known as Hondo, Big Frank, and Bob—were captured and sent to Sea World of Florida. Shortly thereafter, Hondo, the largest known California sea lion at more than 1,000 pounds, died of some sort of infection. Big Frank and Bob remain under custody.

However, other sea lions remain, and a new ploy is currently being used to save the steelhead. A dummy killer whale (orca) named Fake Willy has been installed in the sea lions' favorite feeding area. While some orcas feed on salmon, others prefer seals and sea lions. Not knowing which type of feeder the fake orca is, the area's freeloading sea lions have been giving it a wide berth. Let's just hope this orca doesn't end up attracting some of the area's salmon-eating whales.

---

there are some places where an angler standing on shore (or a dock or pier) stands a good chance of hooking a fish. You'll find a fishing pier at **Dash Point County Park** northeast of Tacoma and another not far north of here at **Redondo County Park.** At **Illahee State Park,** just outside Bremerton, a boat dock is popular with anglers. Another good dock-fishing spot is from the boathouse in Tacoma's **Point Defiance Park.**

When residents of Puget Sound decide they want to go for a day hike, they generally head for the hills. From either side of the sound it is possible to be hiking in the mountains within an hour of the flatlands. Add to this the fact that there are few wild areas large enough to include trails of sufficient length for a day hike here in the lowlands, and you'll understand why the lowlands are a great place for short, easy strolls, but not so good for longer hikes. There are, however, a couple of exceptions that I have listed below. Additionally, if it's the middle of winter, but you really want to walk (rather than cross-country ski), a few of the region's parks have networks of trails long enough to provide a good workout. Such parks include **Discovery Park** in Seattle and **Point Defiance Park** in Tacoma. The **Burke–Gilman Trail** and the **Sammamish River Trail,** which are most popular with cyclists, are also good places for long walks.

Wilderness Peak Loop, Cougar Mountain Regional Wildland Park

4 miles. Moderate. 1,250-foot elevation gain. Access: Take exit 15 off I-5 and drive south 4.2 miles on Wash. 900 to the Wilderness Creek Trailhead. Map: DNR Tiger Mountain Map (available by calling the Department of Natural Resources [tel. 800/527-3305 or 360/577-2025]).

With nearly 2,000 acres of forests to explore, this park is the largest of its kind in the Seattle metropolitan area. Within the large park, there is a maze of hiking trails that meander through the various habitats here. You might hike to Claypit Peak or Nike Peak, or watch for wildlife at Klondike Swamp. A few of the names to be found in this area—Coal Creek, Coalfield, Newcastle—should give you an idea of what it was known for before it became a park. There are few signs left today to remind hikers of the intensive mining and logging that took place on this mountain earlier in this century. Of all the hikes in the park, the walk up Wilderness Creek to Wilderness Peak is perhaps the finest.

From the trailhead begin climbing immediately up the steep, rocky valley of Wilderness Creek. In just under 1 mile, reach a trail junction and turn left into the area known as The Boulders, which is named for the moss-and-fern–draped boulders that litter the stream valley at this point. Continuing upward from The Boulders, reach a major trail junction in 1.6 miles. The trail to the left leads to Long View Peak in 0.4 miles if you want to

add a bit more distance to this hike. To continue the loop, go right on the Wilderness Peak Trail and climb the last 0.5 miles to Wilderness Peak. Unfortunately there are no views from here. Never fear, though—you'll have your views soon enough. Continuing down through old-growth forest from the summit on what is now Wilderness Cliffs Trail, pass Wild View Cliff and Big View Cliff—your viewpoints—before dropping steeply to the trail junction at The Boulders. Continue back down alongside the creek to return to your car.

West Tiger Mountain Trail, Tiger Mountain State Forest

8 miles round-trip. Moderate–strenuous. 2,100-foot elevation gain. Access: Take exit 20 off I-5, turn right, and then right again to reach the High Point Trailhead. Map: DNR Tiger Mountain Map (available by calling the Department of Natural Resources [tel. 800/527-3305 or 360/577-2025]).

This state forest south of I-90 between Issaquah and North Bend is managed primarily for timber and not for recreation but is a magnet for outdoor recreationists. Not only are there trails for hikers, but horseback riding, mountain biking, and paragliding are also popular activities here. The north side of the forest, which has been set aside as the Tiger Mountain Natural Resources Conservation Area, is the domain of hikers. A maze of hiker-only trails winds through the steep hills here, climbing to the summits of West Tiger Mountain. Although two of these summits, West Tiger 1 and West Tiger 2, are topped with radio towers, West Tiger 3 remains a relatively natural viewpoint that looks out on seemingly all of western Washington— from Mount Baker in the north to Mount St. Helens in the south, eastward to the Cascades and westward across Puget Sound to the Olympics. There isn't a better view anywhere in the region.

The hike to these views starts by following an old dirt road (as do many of the trails in this forest) toward Tradition Lake. Before reaching the lake, come to a junction and turn left. Keep left at the next two forks, and then at the third fork, go right and begin the 2,000-foot climb to the summit of West Tiger 3. After almost 2 miles of climbing, go right on the West Tiger Railroad Grade and then left again to continue to the summit.

After enjoying the views from on high, drop back down to this last trail junction, turn left, and contour around for 0.5 miles to a junction with the Nook Trail. Turn right here and drop down off the mountain almost to Tradition Lake. When the Nook Trail ends, turn left on the Bus Trail, and in a quarter-mile, turn right to drop down to the Round the Lake Trail. Turn right onto this trail and follow it around to the dirt road that brought you in from the High Point Trailhead.

Nisqually Delta National Wildlife Refuge

7 miles. Easy. No elevation gain. Access: Off I-5 at exit 114 between Tacoma and Olympia. Map: Trailhead maps.

The Nisqually Delta is the largest undeveloped estuary on Puget Sound and has been preserved as a National Wildlife Refuge. Within the refuge, there are three loop trails that can be combined for a total hike of 7 miles. However, the largest single loop covers 5.5 miles. The trails pass through all the various habitats within the refuge from streamside deciduous forest to freshwater marshes to salt marshes. Much of the trail system is on a dike that surrounded the farm that once comprised much of this land. There are nearly constant views of the refuge's many waterways along the trails, and from the flat open spaces of the marshlands, you can see the Olympics and Mt. Rainier. This is a favorite area with bird watchers (and duck hunters), but other wildlife you might see includes several species of raptors (including bald eagles) and beavers. During the fall and winter duck-hunting season, parts of the refuge are closed.

HORSEBACK RIDING

At the south end of Lake Washington near the airport, you can rent horses at **Aqua Barn Ranch,** 15227 SE Renton–Maple Valley Hwy., Renton, WA (tel. 206/

255-4618). Reservations are required. **Tiger Mountain Outfitters,** 24508 SE 133rd St., Issaquah (tel. 206/392-5090), leads guided rides into Tiger Mountain State Forest. Down in the Olympia area, **The Horse Ranch** (tel. 206/458-7074) on 336th Street South off Wash. 507, offers guided rides on its 120-acre property.

MOUNTAIN BIKING

In addition to the rides listed here, you'll also find a 3-mile-long trail in **Saint Edward State Park** near Kirkland. See "Parks & Other Hot Spots," above, for details. Also, the rather disjointed **Tolt Pipeline Trail,** which is maintained by King County Parks Division and runs in sections from Bothel to the Tolt River, is worth exploring—especially the 7-mile-long section between the paved Sammamish River Trail and the Snoqualmie Valley. This trail can be accessed just north of Sammamish River Park, which is located adjacent to the Wash. 202 bridge over the Sammamish River.

Snoqualmie Valley Trail

13.5–35 miles round-trip. Easy. 75-foot elevation gain. Access: Take exit 22 off I-90 and drive north through Preston to Fall City, and turn left on Wash. 203 to reach Carnation. In Carnation, turn right on Entwhistle St. and continue to Nick Loutsis Park. Map: Not necessary.

The Seattle area abounds with old railroad grades that have been converted to hiker/ biker trails, and this is one such trail. Although still a work in progress, the Snoqualmie Valley Trail will one day run through the most scenic, rural sections of the valley from Duvall to Snoqualmie Falls. This nearly flat gravel trail is perfect for the beginning mountain biker who wants a taste of what off-road riding is all about. There's nothing difficult about this trail. From the east side of the park in Carnation, simply head south for just over 6.5 miles to a deep ravine once crossed by a railroad trestle. By the time you read this, there may be a new bridge here; if so, you can continue another 4 miles to the town of Snoqualmie and visit the falls. The first 2.5 miles is through farmland and the rest is through tree farms. If after riding back to your car you still feel like riding, you can head north about the same distance through more farmland.

Tiger Mountain

12–20 miles. Moderate–strenuous. 1,100–1,900-foot elevation gain. Access: From I-90 east of Issaquah, turn south onto Wash. 18 and continue 4.2 miles to a parking area on the right. Map: DNR Tiger Mountain Map.

With dozens of miles of logging roads and roughly 8 miles of single-track trails, Tiger Mountain is Seattle's main mountain-biking area. This large forest is owned by the Washington Department of Natural Resources and is popular with horseback riders, hikers, and motorcyclists, as well as mountain bikers. The miles of roads provide long, steady climbs to views from the summits of the various Tiger Mountains, of which there are five. Although Tiger Mountain is open year-round, the two stretches of single track are closed from mid-October to mid-May to prevent damage to the muddy trails.

Any ride here is going to be a workout, so be prepared. If your goal is the single-track trails, you can ride a loop by heading up Tiger Mountain Road for just over 3 miles and watch for the Preston Railroad Grade Trail, which rolls up and down through the forest for 3.5 miles to connect with East Side Road. Continue downhill on this road and turn right onto the East Side Road. In another 2 miles, turn right onto the NW Timber Trail, which will lead you back to your car in another 2.5 miles. Unfortunately neither of these trails is very challenging. However, this is the best you can do in this area. If you aren't after single-track or are out here during the trail closure season, you can ride to the summit of East or West Tiger and put together a loop route with Tiger Mountain Road and the East Side Road.

Capitol Forest Trails

Up to 21 miles. Strenuous. 1,900-foot elevation gain. Access: Take exit 95 off I-5 and drive east through the town of Little Rock (the Little Rock Grocery sometimes has copies of the Capitol Forest Map), keeping right and following signs toward Capitol Forest and Mima Mounds. Turn right on Wadell Creek Rd. and continue 4.3 miles to Sherman Valley Rd. Turn left and continue 1.25 miles to Noschka Rd., turn right again, and continue 1 mile to Bordeaux Camp. Map: DNR Capitol Forest Map.

Located southwest of Olympia, this large state forest is laced with logging roads and motorcycle trails and has become a favorite mountain-biking area with Puget Sound pedalers. There is one big problem, however, with riding here—you will get lost. Even people who have ridden here repeatedly sometimes get lost. Making riding here even more difficult is the clear-cutting that is taking place, destroying trails midway through a ride and otherwise uglifying the landscape. Your best bet is to arm yourself with a compass and the DNR map of the forest and head out in any direction. Just leave plenty of time for getting unlost. One of the best bases for starting your explorations of this forest is the Bordeaux Campground. From here there are lots of roads and trails leading in all directions, but the most popular destination is the top of Rock Candy Mountain. Alternatively, you can make the grueling climb to the top of Capitol Peak. Again, for this ride you can head up on gravel roads and descend on single-track.

Howell Lake Loop, Tahuya State Forest

8.5 miles. Easy–moderate. 300-foot elevation gain. Access: From Tacoma, take Wash. 16 west past Port Orchard and turn south on Wash. 3 toward Belfair. Drive 8 miles to Belfair and turn right (marked Tahuya) onto Wash. 300. Continue south, passing Belfair State Park, and turn right on NE Belfair–Tahuya Rd. In 4.1 miles, turn left to stay on Belfair–Tahuya Rd., and in 1.7 miles, reach the turnoff on the left for Howell Lake Campground. The trail can be accessed just past the gate on this road. Map: Tahuya State Forest Maps (available from DNR) and trail-head maps.

Just as in the Capital Forest, there is a mind-boggling maze of logging roads and motorcycle trails in Tahuya State Forest. The scenery isn't much to talk about, but the riding is superb—that is, if you like challenging trails with lots of roots and rocks. The rolling hills that comprise this extensively clear-cut area are perfect for mountain biking. You get plenty of uphills and downhills without any gruelingly long climbs. The Howell Lake Loop is a favorite, and in the summer you can even go for a swim in the lake after a hard ride. The well-marked Howell Lake Loop is mostly on single-track, crossing through forests and clear-cuts. There is even a brief glimpse of the Olympic Mountains. You won't actually see Howell Lake from the trail, but it isn't far away. You'll know you're near the lake when you pass through the campground.

If you want a longer ride, you can start in the same place and use the Tahuya River Trail and Howell Lake Trail to ride a larger loop (roughly 12 miles). For a 20-mile ride, start at the Mission Creek trailhead, which is located 1.1 miles up Belfair–Tahuya Road from Wash. 300. Starting here, you can ride an additional 4 miles of single-track on the Tahuya River Trail. Check the roadside maps in the area for ideas for other rides in the vicinity. None include more than a few hundred feet of climbing and all are loads of fun.

ROAD BIKING

Bicycles can be rented at several shops around Seattle including **Gregg's Green Lake Cycle,** 7007 Woodlawn Ave. NE (tel. 206/523-1822), the **Bicycle Center,** 4529 Sand Point Way NE (tel. 206/523-8300), and **Sammamish Valley Cycle,** 8451 164th Ave. NE, Redmond (tel. 206/881-8442)— all rent bikes by the hour, day, or week. Rates range from $4 to $7 per hour and $15 to $32 per day.

Burke–Gilman Trail

25 miles round-trip. Easy. 300-foot elevation gain. Access: To reach Gasworks Park, take N 45th St. west from I-5 and turn left on Wallingford Ave N.

This 12.5-mile trail created from an old railway bed is Seattle's premier bike trail and on summer weekends is absolutely packed with leisure cyclists, racers in training, in-line skaters, dog walkers, and strollers. Although the crowds can be daunting and aren't at all conducive to a high-speed workout, the trail provides an outstanding ride away from traffic. The trail starts at Gasworks Park at the north end of Lake Union and continues to Kenmore Logboom Park at the north end of Lake Washington by way of the University of Washington. Along the way, there are views of Lake Washington, and even a beach at Mathews Beach Park, 7 miles north of Gasworks Park. At its northern end, the Burke–Gilman connects to the 12-mile Sammamish River Trail, which opens up the possibility of doing a half-century ride without having to worry about automotive traffic (except at road crossings and a couple of short stretches on roads).

Sammamish River Trail

24 miles round-trip. Easy. 200-foot elevation gain. Access: Take I-405 north to Wash. 522 (Bothel Way) and drive west to the trailhead parking area at Bothel Landing Park.

Following the bank of the Sammamish River from Lake Washington to Marymoor Park on Sammamish Lake, this trail provides a slightly more rural (growing ever more suburban) experience compared to the Burke–Gilman. The trail clings to the bank of the slow-moving river the entire way, and along the trail, you can bird watch or have a picnic. The trail also passes within a short side trip of several wineries and a brew pub, any or all of which could provide a bit of distraction along this ride. If you happen to be on a mountain bike, you can access the gravel Tolt Pipeline Trail south of Woodinville and head east to the Snoqualmie River and another superb road-riding area. This trail connects to the Burke–Gilman Trail. Combine the two trails and you have a 50-mile ride without cars. If this isn't reason enough to move to the Seattle area, I don't know what is. Just be prepared for crowds. This trail is extremely popular.

Bainbridge Island Loop (The Chilly Hilly)

33 miles. Strenuous. 3,000-foot elevation gain. Access: Take the Bainbridge Island ferry from the downtown Seattle ferry terminal.

There is always something special about starting a bike ride with a trip by ferry, and that is exactly what makes this ride a favorite of Seattle pedalers. This grand loop around Bainbridge Island, Seattle's favorite bedroom community, follows much of the route of the February Chilly Hilly ride, the first race/ride of the Seattle cycling season. Along the route, there is plenty of rural scenery, as well as two state parks—Fay–Bainbridge and Fort Ward—that are ideal spots for a picnic. As you've probably guessed, both by the elevation gain listed above and the name of the race, there are a lot of hills on this ride.

From the ferry terminal on Bainbridge Island, ride uphill for 0.2 miles and turn right on Winslow Way. Then in 0.2 miles, turn left onto Ferncliff Avenue. In 2.1 miles, turn right onto Moran Road, and in 0.3 miles, turn right again onto Manitou Beach Drive, which passes Manitou Beach on Murden Cove. This road becomes Valley Road. In 1.7 miles, turn right onto Sunrise Drive and begin a long, straight ride to Fay–Bainbridge State Park, which is reached in 2.8 miles. Turn into the park if you feel like a walk on the beach or are ready for a picnic.

From the park, continue north and turn left onto Lafayette Avenue. In 0.6 miles, turn left onto Euclid Avenue, which becomes Phelps Road. After 0.8 miles, turn right onto Hidden Cove Road, which winds around for 2 miles, crossing Wash. 305, to reach Manzanita Road. Turn left here. In 1.3 miles, turn right on Peterson Hill Road, and in 0.5 miles, merge into southbound Miller Road. In 0.5 miles, turn right onto Arrow Point Drive and head toward Battle Point Park, a former military installation. Follow this road for 1.2 miles to a left turn onto Frey Avenue. Turn left again onto Battle Point Drive and ride south 2.1 miles to return to Miller Road. Turn right and ride 4.6 miles south, through Lynwood and changes in the name of the road (first Fletcher Bay Road, then Lynwood Center Road, and finally Pleasant Beach Road), to Fort Ward State Park. This park is popular with bird-watchers and has a great view of narrow Rich Passage, through which ferries bound for Bremerton pass. Continue 0.7 miles through the park,

stopping for a picnic, a rest, or to walk on the beach.

Leave the park on South Beach Road, ride 1.1 miles to Toejam Hill Road (no fooling), and turn left. Ride up and over the hill 1.2 miles and turn left onto Country Club Road. In 0.8 miles, turn right onto Blakely Avenue and follow this road as it changes names to become Halls Hill Road, then Rockaway Beach Drive, and finally Eagle Harbor Drive. After 4.6 miles on these roads, turn right on Wyatt Street. In just under 1 mile, turn right on Grow Avenue, then left on Winslow Way, and then right onto Olympic Drive to coast down to the ferry. Before you reach the ferry, be sure to stop for a latté to celebrate completing this ride.

Point Defiance–Vashon Island Ride

36 miles. Strenuous. 2,200-foot elevation gain. Access: Start this ride from the main parking lot at Point Defiance Park in northern Tacoma. To reach the park, follow Pearl Street north from Wash. 16 west of I-5, or take I-705 into Tacoma and continue north on Ruston Way.

Riding on Vashon Island is as popular as riding on Bainbridge Island for all the same reasons—views of the water, quiet rural roads, parks. It's also a bit of a challenge for the same reason—lots of hills. Although Seattle cyclists ride a loop around the island from the northern ferry terminal, I prefer the roads at the southern end of the island. With views of Quartermaster Harbor and two waterfront parks for possible picnic spots, this is the more enjoyable end of the island. Combine this area, by way of the Tahlequah ferry, with 5 miles of pedaling on the quiet one-way roads of Point Defiance Park in Tacoma and you have the ingredients for a very enjoyable ride.

The Five-Mile Loop around Point Defiance Park makes a good, relatively flat warm-up for this ride. After looping through the park, passing the zoo, Fort Nisqually, Camp Six, and Never-Never-Land, follow signs to the ferry dock and make the 15-minute cruise to Vashon Island. Once on the island, the riding gets serious.

From the ferry landing, head uphill on 131st Avenue for 2 miles and angle right onto the Vashon Island Highway. In

0.8 miles, you can add a short side trip to Inspiration Point, where there are good views of Quartermaster Harbor, which you will be riding around on this leg of the trip. Continuing north 2.1 miles on Vashon Island Highway, turn right on 240th Street, which leads in 0.4 miles to Bayview Road, a 1.9-mile loop around the Burton Peninsula. This road provides access to the water at Burton County Park and makes a good rest or picnic stop. Ride back to the Vashon Island Highway on 240th Street and turn right. In 1 mile, turn right onto 225th Street, which becomes Quartermaster Drive, and ride 1.4 miles to Dockton Road. Turn right here and cross the isthmus that connects Vashon Island to Maury Island. This isthmus is known as Portage, and that is exactly what sea kayakers paddling around Maury Island do at this point.

In 1.6 miles, turn right to stay on Dockton Road and continue 2 miles south along the shore of Quartermaster Harbor to Dockton County Park, another option for a picnic spot. South of the park 0.4 miles is the Dockton store, where you can get snacks and drinks if you need them. From the park, ride east on 260th Street for 1 mile. Turn left on 70th Avenue, right on 256th Street, left on 75th Avenue, and right on 248th Street to reach 240th Street in 3.5 miles. Turn right on 240th Street and coast downhill to Point Robinson County Park in 1.4 miles. There is a lighthouse beside this forested park on the shore of Puget Sound.

From the park, turn right onto Luana Beach Road and follow this winding road along the north shore of Maury Island for 2.5 miles. Turn right onto 228th Street and continue 1.3 miles to return to Quartermaster Drive. Turn left and retrace your route back to the ferry landing. From the Point Defiance ferry landing, it is 0.5 miles to the park's main parking lot, if that is where you left your car.

Fall City-Carnation-Snoqualmie Falls Loop

27 miles. Moderate. 900-foot elevation gain. Access: Take I-90 to exit 22 and drive north through Preston to Fall City. Park at Olive Taylor Quigley Park on the bank of the Snoqualmie River in downtown Fall City.

Bucolic farm country on the banks of the Snoqualmie River has the feel of a Vermont valley—orchards, grazing cows and horses, forests and mountains in the distance, a lazy river, farm stands, quaint little towns. However, add to this rural ride the climb up to 270-foot Snoqualmie Falls, and you have a quintessentially Northwestern ride. The section of this ride from Fall City to Carnation lies in the flat floodplain of the Snoqualmie River. This area frequently floods in winter, so if you're planning a rainy season ride, first make sure the roads up here aren't underwater. The best times to ride this route are in spring when snowmelt turns Snoqualmie Falls into a thundering torrent, and in late summer when area farm stands are laden with local produce.

From Quigley Park ride west out of town on Wash. 202 for 0.7 miles and turn right onto 324th Avenue, which winds along through farm country roughly following the meanders of the river, which is usually out of view. After 1.8 miles on this road, turn right onto West Snoqualmie River Road. This road continues the meandering, but soon passes a golf course that is in sharp contrast to the surrounding farmland. Pass Jubilee Farms, an organic farm with a produce stand in the summer. Along this stretch of road, note how houses are raised on 8-foot foundation walls to keep them above flood waters. After 4.1 miles of almost completely flat pedaling through this idyllic countryside, turn right onto Tolt Hill Road and cross the Snoqualmie River. In 0.7 miles reach Wash. 203. If you go straight, you will reach Remlinger Farms, with a restaurant and produce stand, in 0.5 miles. This is a great spot for lunch or to pick up some fruit for a picnic later in the day. If you opt not to ride to Remlinger Farms, turn left on Wash. 203 and cross the Tolt River to reach the town of Carnation. Turn left on 40th Street to reach Tolt River–John McDonald Park, a good spot for a picnic.

From this park, head back south on Wash. 203, which is a 55-mph highway with wide shoulders. In 3.8 miles turn right onto Neal Road, which parallels the river and has a public fishing access in case you happen to have your fishing rod with you.

Follow this road for 2.9 miles before rejoining Wash. 203.

In 0.2 miles, turn left onto Wash. 202, an unfortunately busy stretch of road, to begin the leg of the ride that leads to Snoqualmie Falls. Turn off the highway onto Fish Hatchery Road in 0.8 miles. This winding road leads down to a boat launch at Plum's Landing. Here, the river takes on a very different character from the sluggish waters downstream. Upstream of the boat launch the river is fast, filled with rocks, and popular with kayakers. Continue up Fish Hatchery Road, turning right at the stop sign to continue on a rough road to a powerhouse at the base of Snoqualmie Falls. Lock up your bike and walk down the trail for a view of the falls.

Here you have two options. If you want to avoid the biggest hill of the ride (nearly 400 feet) but still want a look at the falls from up top, you can hike the 0.5-mile trail up to the park near the lip of the falls. After enjoying the view and fighting the crowds, hike back down to your bike and ride back the way you came to Fall City. This will shorten the ride by 3.5 miles.

If you want to do the whole ride to the falls, ride back down to the stop sign and turn right on Fish Hatchery Road. In 0.4 miles, turn right onto Wash. 202 and climb the hill to the Snoqualmie Falls Park in 1.3 miles. Return to Fall City by backtracking the way you just came as far as the bridge over the Snoqualmie. Turn left here and then right onto Redmond–Fall City Road to return to your car.

ROCK CLIMBING

As sport rock climbing has taken off in popularity, city parks around the sound have begun to cater to this new sport by constructing outdoor climbing walls. The largest and most impressive of these is **Marymoor Alps,** which is located in Redmond at Marymoor Park. This 45-foot-tall outdoor climbing wall provides seemingly infinite climbing routes. The direct route is a 5.6, but if you're looking for a challenge, there is a 5.13 route also. When built a few years ago, this was the largest freestanding climbing wall in the U.S.

There are also some less impressive walls around. **Schurmann Rock,** which is located in West Seattle's Camp Long (5200 block of 35th Street SW), dates back to 1939. The **University of Washington's Climbing Rock,** located near the waterfront activities center and Husky Stadium, is 32 feet tall but is open only to students, faculty, and alumni.

In addition to the outdoor climbing areas mentioned above, there are numerous indoor rock gyms and climbing walls around the area. By far the most impressive of these is the wall at the new **REI,** 222 Yale Ave. N, Seattle (tel. 206/223-1944). This 65-foot-tall, 110-ton spire enclosed in a glass-walled tower rises beside I-5 like some huge religious relic or shrine to rock. I keep expecting it to cause massive rush-hour pile-ups. Other area rock gyms include **Stone Gardens Indoor Climbing Facility,** 2839 NW Market St., Seattle (tel. 206/781-9828); **Vertical Club,** 1111 Elliott Ave. W, Seattle (tel. 206/283-8056); **Vertical Club,** 15036B 95th St., Redmond (tel. 206/881-8826); and **Olympia Rock Gym,** 215 Seventh Ave. SW, Olympia (tel. 206/705-1585).

SCUBA DIVING

While most people associate coral reefs and balmy tropical waters with scuba diving, there are those hardy (some say crazy) souls who find the frigid waters of Puget Sound to offer some of the finest diving in the country. The sound's protected waters are indeed a fascinating place for underwater exploring. From colorful starfish to giant octopi, the sound harbors an amazing variety of sea life, and much of it in fairly shallow waters. Because scuba diving has grown so popular in recent years, the state has accommodated divers by creating artificial reefs and underwater parks that are perfect places to dive.

Dive classes, equipment, and advice are available at numerous shops around the sound. One of the oldest dive shops in the Puget Sound area is **Underwater Sports Inc.,** which now has stores all over the region: 264 Railroad Ave., Edmonds (tel. 206/771-6322); 9608 40th Avenue SW,

Tacoma (tel. 206/588-6634); 10545 Aurora Ave. N, Seattle (tel. 206/362-3310); 9020 Martin Way E, Olympia (tel. 206/493-0322).

One of the most popular dive sites in Puget Sound is the **Edmonds Underwater Park.** The heart of the park is a dry dock that was sunk here in 1935. Today this "wreck" is covered with an amazing variety of anemones, tube worms, starfish, and other sea life. The dry dock is about 450 feet offshore in 35 feet of water. Because this area is protected from fishing, many large cabezons and lingcod seek refuge here. To get to this underwater park, take exit 177 off of I-5 and follow signs for the Edmonds–Kingston ferry. The parking area is on Main Street right beside the ferry dock at Sunset Beach.

At **Ed Munro Seahurst County Park** in Burien (northwest of Sea-Tac Airport) a barge has been sunk just offshore to form an artificial reef. This sunken wreck provides a home for a great variety of sea life and makes this beach an interesting place to dive. To reach the park, take exit 154B off I-5 and drive west on Wash. 518. Turn right onto Ambaum Boulevard, left onto 144th Street, and then right onto 13th Avenue.

A bit farther south, **Saltwater State Park** also has an artificial reef, comprised of a sunken barge and old tires, that attracts a lot of sea life. To reach this park, take exit 149 off I-5, drive west on Wash. 516, and turn south on Wash. 509.

Down in the south sound, southwest of Gig Harbor, **Kopachuck State Park** has an underwater park, complete with a sunken barge. To reach this park, take Wash. 16 west from I-5 in Tacoma and follow signs to the park from the Gig Harbor/Kopachuck State Park exit.

SEA KAYAKING & FLAT-WATER CANOEING

There are several places around the city where sea kayaks or canoes can be rented. **Northwest Outdoor Center,** 2100 Westlake Ave. N (tel. 206/281-9694), is located on Lake Union and will rent you a sea kayak for $8 to $12 per hour. You can also opt for guided paddles lasting from a few hours to several days, and there are plenty of classes available for those who are interested. The **University of Washington Waterfront Activities Center,** on the university campus behind Husky Stadium (tel. 206/543-9433), is open to the public and rents canoes and rowboats for $4 per hour. Rentals are available February to October daily from 10am to about an hour before sunset. Over in Bellevue, canoes and kayaks can be rented (from June to Labor Day) for $5 an hour at **Enatai Beach City Park,** 108th Ave. SE and SE 34th St. (tel. 206/455-6855). On Vashon Island, you can rent kayaks at **Vashon Island Kayak** (tel. 206/463-YAKS).

If you'd like to do a guided paddle in the south sound area, contact **Northwest Passages,** 8811 N Harborview Dr., Gig Harbor, WA 98335 (tel. 206/851-7987), which offers everything from quick and cheap paddles on Gig Harbor ($20) to overnight kayak camping trips ($135 per person per night).

In addition to the routes described below, the waters off **Kopachuck State Park,** southwest of Gig Harbor, and **Fay–Bainbridge State Park,** at the north end of Bainbridge Island, both offer several hours of leisurely exploring. Off Kopachuck, the tiny Cutts Island makes an interesting destination, and near Fay–Bainbridge, there is a lagoon to explore.

Lake Union and Washington Park Arboretum

6 miles. Easy–moderate. Access: Gas Works Park at the north end of the lake off NE Northlake Way, and Chandler's Cove (beside the Burger King) at the south end of the lake off Fairview Ave. N, are two of the most convenient launch sites.

Lake Union, with its convenient downtown Seattle location, protected water, paddle-up restaurants, and interesting shoreline and views is sort of the equivalent of a bicycle with training wheels for Puget Sound paddlers. Almost everyone gets started here (myself included). This is due not only to the reasons listed above but to the fact that sea kayak sales and rentals are available right here on the water. Whether paddling your own boat or a rental, be sure to paddle east through the Montlake Cut, a narrow channel that connects Lake Union to Union Bay on Lake Washington. The south shore of this little bay is the Washington Park Arboretum, where narrow waterways wind through a wetland area. After exploring the arboretum, you can head back to Lake Union and get a bowl of clam chowder at Ivar's Salmon House.

Mercer Slough Nature Park

4 miles round-trip. Easy. Access: Boats can be launched at Enatai Beach City Park, 108th Ave. SE and SE 34th St., or at Sweyolochen boat launch, 3000 Bellevue Way.

This is a very different sort of a paddle compared to the other routes listed here. Mercer Slough, which lies just north of I-90 in Bellevue, is a backwater canal that feeds into Lake Washington. However, before the Chittenden Locks and Lake Washington ship canal were opened in 1917, Lake Washington was 9 feet higher than it is today and Mercer Slough was a marshy cove. Today the slough curves its way quietly through a deciduous forest that is home to many species of birds, as well as beavers, muskrats, and otters, all of which are frequently sighted during the summer months. Although this is a little pocket of nature, the skyscrapers of downtown Bellevue can be seen rising beyond the forest. Because the slough is bounded by deciduous forests, autumn is a particularly good time to go for a paddle here.

Nisqually River Delta

2–14 miles. Access: From I-5, take the Nisqually National Wildlife exit (exit 114) and drive east away from the delta to Martin Rd. Turn right and drive 1 mile south, turn right on Meridian Rd., and continue 2.6 miles to a right on 46th Ave. NE. After 0.2 miles more, turn left onto D'Milluhr Dr. and continue 0.5 miles to the boat launch.

The Nisqually River Delta is the last large, undeveloped estuary on the Puget Sound. Though parts of it have been diked and drained, today it is a wildlife refuge cut by meandering tidal waterways that

> "The rivers are our brothers, they quench our thirst. The rivers carry our canoes and feed our children. If we sell you our land, you must remember and teach your children that the rivers are our brothers and yours, and you must henceforth give the rivers the kindness you would owe any brother."
>
> —Chief Sealth, Suquamish tribe, for whom Seattle was named

make for interesting exploring and great bird watching. The one most important thing to remember when paddling these waters is that these are shallow tidelands. Time your trip for the few hours on either side of high tide unless you like dragging your boat through the mud. And remember, in the fall and winter this area is popular with duck hunters.

From the boat launch, you can paddle due east up McAlister Creek for 3 miles or so; however, this route takes you back toward the noise of the freeway. More preferable is to head north across the delta, exploring nooks and crannies as you go, to the mouth of the Nisqually River. This river can also be paddled upstream a ways if the tide is with you. However, most enjoyable for many is to simply take a leisurely paddle around the marshlands that form the west shores of the delta. Keep your binoculars handy for observing the birdlife.

Vashon Island's Quartermaster Harbor

2–10 miles round-trip. Easy–strenuous. Access: Take the Vashon ferry from West Seattle. Once on Vashon, drive south on 99th Ave. SW. There are possible launch sites at Burton Acres County Park off S 240th St., at Portage (the narrow causeway between Vashon and Maury), and at Dockton County Park on Portage–Dockton Rd.

Vashon Island, connected to Seattle by ferry, has in recent years become something of a bedroom community for the city. However, the island still retains a very rural flavor. Lying off the southeast coast of Vashon, and connected by a narrow causeway, is Maury Island. Quartermaster Harbor, the bay that lies between the two islands, is a fun place to explore in a sea kayak. The shores of the harbor have enough twists and turns that you'll want to paddle just a little bit longer to see what's around the next point. The shores of the harbor are residential in character, there is still plenty of forest, and many of the houses are hidden among the trees. The southern portions of Quartermaster Harbor are exposed to southern winds, but the upper bay is protected.

Blake Island

8 miles. Moderate–strenuous. Access: Take the Fauntleroy–Southworth ferry with only your kayak and launch from the ferry landing, or drive your car on and continue north from the ferry landing to the boat launch a mile away at Harper.

Few paddle destinations in the Puget Sound have as much to offer as the paddle out to Blake Island State Park. The island, which lies almost due west of the Fauntleroy ferry terminal in West Seattle, has hiking trails, campsites, and a reconstructed Indian longhouse that is the site of regularly scheduled salmon barbecue dinners that are followed by Native American dancing. There are also hiking trails through the island's forest. From the water, the island offers both sandy beaches and cobblestone shores, as well as high bluffs. Depending on your paddling skills, you can launch from West Seattle's Alki Point and paddle 3 miles across the sound to the island; from Vashon Island's ferry landing and paddle 1.5 miles through more protected waters; or from the Southworth ferry landing on Kitsap Peninsula and paddle 1 mile through well-protected waters. Once here, it is a 5-mile paddle around the island. The best plan is to paddle to the island and then go partly around to one of the campgrounds and pitch camp for the night. The next day,

continue around the island back to your launch site. The most developed campground is at Tillicum Village (site of the longhouse) on the northeast corner of the island.

SWIMMING & TUBING

Although some people go swimming in Puget Sound, for most it is far too cold. Much more bearable are the waters of nearby lakes and, occasionally, rivers. This said, there are a few places where shallow, protected waters of the south sound can get, if not warm enough for long swims, at least not so cold that you can't dive in for a quick dip. The waters of the south sound tend to be warmer than those in the north, and shallow bays, where the water has a chance to be warmed by the sun, are best. Some places to try include **Dash Point State Park,** north of Tacoma, and **Burton** and **Dockton county parks** on Vashon Island's Quartermaster Harbor, which is toward the south end of the island.

Lake Washington, which to Seattleites serves primarily as a barrier between the city proper and the disparaged east side suburbs of Bellevue, Issaquah, Kirkland, et al., also happens to provide plenty of places to swim during the summer months. Luckily, the waters are quite a bit warmer than those of Puget Sound, and despite the density of the population surrounding the lake, the waters are still surprisingly clean. On the south side of the city, there is a beach at **Seward Park,** while all along this western shore of the lake there are also greenways and parks that provide numerous swimming areas. Over on Mercer Island, there is **Luther Burbank State Park** (at the north end of the island). In Bellevue, there is a beach at **Enatai Beach City Park,** at 108th Ave. SE and SE 34th St. North of Kirkland, there is swimming in Juanita Bay at **Juanita Beach.**

Perhaps no other park in the region is more fun than **Flaming Geyser State Park** on a hot summer day. Stretching for a mile or so along the banks of the Green River, this park has deep swimming holes, shallows for the kids, and best of all, perfect conditions for tubing. People float through the park on everything from inflated waterbeds to air mattresses to old truck inner tubes. Nearby, and also on the Green River, is **Kanaskat Palmer State Park,** which is better known as a challenging kayaking river. This park does, however, also have several excellent swimming holes and rocks that serve as jumping points. You'll find Flaming Geyser off Wash. 169 between Enumclaw and Black Diamond. Kanaskat–Palmer is also north of Enumclaw (follow the signs). The **Green River,** between Auburn and Kent, is another stretch of river that is popular for tubing.

WALKS & NATURAL ROADSIDE ATTRACTIONS

In addition to the walks listed here, many of the parks listed previously under "Parks & Other Hot Spots" have walking trails. Any of these parks can provide an hour or two of leisurely strolling.

Discovery Park

3–5 miles. Easy. 0–350-foot elevation gain. Access: From downtown Seattle, drive north on Elliot Ave. W, which becomes 15th Ave. W. Turn left onto W Dravus St. and then right on 20th Ave. W, which changes names a couple of times as it curves around to the west to reach the park's main gate. Map: Trailhead maps.

Discovery Park, northwest of downtown Seattle past Queen Anne Hill and Magnolia Bluff, is the city's biggest park. Set on bluffs above West Point, the park, like so many others around Puget Sound, was once a military installation. A 3-mile loop trail circles through the park's highlands, and takes in almost all of the best the park has to offer. The trail leads through second-growth forests to views both north and south across the sound to such landmarks as Mount Baker and the Olympic Mountains. In fact, this park has the best Sound views in the city.

Along the park's southern bluffs, the trail passes through a large meadow. For a longer walk, drop down to the beaches, which offer several miles of leisurely strolling beneath the bluffs. At the tip of West Point, which separates the park's North Beach from its South Beach, is a lighthouse.

O. O. Denny Park

1–4 miles. Easy. 100–600-foot elevation gain. Access: From Bellevue, take I-405 north to exit 20A, drive west to Kirkland on NE 116th St. and 98th Ave. NE, continue on Juanita Dr., turn left on 76th Place NE, and then right onto Holmes Point Rd. Map: Trailhead maps.

This little park claims the largest Douglas fir in the Seattle metro area, and surrounding this aged giant are many other old-growth trees that together make a walk here a quick glimpse into the heart of the Northwest's greatest controversy—whether to allow the continued cutting of such majestic trees. The park has two trails, a beach, and views across Lake Washington to Seattle. If you hike both trails, plus spurs, and then stroll along the beach, you can easily get in more than 3 miles of walking. If you just want a quick walk, head up the trail on the north side of the creek straight to the big Douglas fir.

West Hylebos Wetlands State Park

1 mile. Easy. No elevation gain. Access: From I-5 south of Federal Way, take exit 147B, drive west on S 348th St. for 1.1 miles, and turn left on Fourth Ave. S. Map: Trailhead maps.

This tiny (58 acres) pocket of wetlands may be small on acreage but it is big on information. The trail that meanders through the wooded wetlands has lots of interesting interpretive signs along its route, much of which is on a raised wooden walkway. The trail leads to two small lakes, and in one part of the park species of trees that might have grown here millions of years ago have been planted. Within the park are also many signs left by the glaciers that covered this area as recently as 12,000 years ago.

Mima Mounds Natural Area Preserve

2 miles. Easy. No elevation gain. Access: Take exit 95 off I-5, drive west through the town of Little Rock, and continue straight through town following signs for Capitol Forest. At the T intersection, turn right and continue 1 mile to the Mima Mounds entrance on the left. Map: Trailhead maps.

Gopher mounds? Glacial deposits? Undeciphered ancient messages to passing alien spaceships? No one is quite sure what caused the Mima mounds, but one thing is for sure: these thousands of 6-foot-high, 30-foot-diameter mounds make for an unusual landscape. In 1847, an employee of the Hudson's Bay Company reported walking 22 miles through such mounds, which formed a strange prairie at the south end of Puget Sound. Today, only 445 acres are preserved, and though you can see more mounds on private lands surrounding the preserve, much of this unique landscape was long ago bulldozed or plowed. Spring and fall, when the wildflowers bloom, the meadows that cover the mounds are awash in colors. A walk among the mounds is a truly unique sort of stroll.

WHITEWATER KAYAKING & CANOEING

CLASS I

Below Snoqualmie Falls, the **Snoqualmie River** winds through wide, flat farm country. However, on the upper portion of this stretch of river, the water still moves pretty quickly. The 15-mile run from Plum Landing, a mile below the falls, to Tolt River–John McDonald Park in Carnation makes for a very pleasant day's outing. Between the put-in and Fall City, 4 miles downstream, there are several riffles that make this the funnest stretch of this run. Below Fall City, the river meanders back and forth across its floodplain, first flowing north, then east or west, and at one point looping almost all the way back on itself to flow due south for a ways. This is farm country, but much of the way the river is lined with trees. To reach the take-out, take exit 22 off I-90, drive north through Preston to Fall City, and turn left on Wash. 203 to reach Carnation. In Carnation, turn left on NE 40th Street into Tolt River–John McDonald Park. To reach the put-in, drive back south on Wash. 203 to Fall City, turn left on Wash. 202, and in 0.8 miles, turn right onto Fish Hatchery Road to reach the Plum's Landing boat launch.

The lower 14.5-mile section of the **Cedar River,** which parallels Wash. 169 between Maple Valley and Renton, lies on the fringes of suburbia. However, with its gravel bottom and riverside trail (once a railroad bed), the river has a pleasant rural feel, despite the intruding sound of traffic from the nearby highway. The water keeps moving fairly quickly for most of this route, with a few small rapids and riverside bluffs for visual interest. As it approaches Renton, the river slows down and becomes more urban, though with parks along its banks. The river then flows *under* the Renton Library before reaching the take-out at the edge of Lake Washington. Keep your eyes out for salmon and steelhead on this river. Although the river can be run all year, it gets pretty shallow in late summer. To reach the take-out, take exit 5 off I-405 in Renton, drive north on NE Park Drive, and turn left on Logan Avenue North. The boat launch is at the Cedar River Trail and Park complex. To reach the put-in, drive Wash. 169 (Renton–Maple Valley Highway) southeast to Maple Valley. Turn left off the highway after crossing the Cedar River Bridge, and then turn left again into a gravel parking area beside the river.

Although the **Green River** is best known for its wild Green River Gorge run, this river also offers some of the nicest Class I paddling in the region. From the boat launch at Big Soos Creek, the river meanders along the edge of suburbia to the town of Kent. Along the way there are opportunities to bird watch, and paddlers might also spot a few beaver. The Green is one of Washington's top steelheading rivers and has salmon runs as well. Keep your eyes out and you might spot some, or bring your rod and do a little fishing yourself. The first mile of this 15.5-mile run has the liveliest water. After that, the river calms down but remains fairly swift. This river can be run all year and is particularly popular in summer. To reach the take-out, take exit 1 off I-405 and drive south on Wash. 181 for 4 miles, turn right on South 212th Street, and drive to the Green River bridge, where there are access points left off South 212th Street on either side of the bridge. To reach the put-in, drive Wash. 181, or the larger, parallel Wash. 167, south to Auburn, and turn east on Wash. 18. In 3 miles, turn right onto Auburn–Black Diamond Road and then right again onto

SE Green Valley Road to reach a fishing access.

CLASS II

The Puget Sound area seems to be custom-made for novice to intermediate paddlers. The region abounds in Class II waters. The same rivers mentioned above that provide easy Class I paddling also have Class II stretches. In addition to the runs listed here, there are several runs not far east of Seattle on the Snoqualmie River. These runs are listed in chapter 6.

The **Cedar River** upstream from Maple Valley has a challenging 7.5-mile Class II run. Downed trees are often a problem on this run, so stay alert. In places, this river gets narrow and quick maneuvering is required. In particular, the rapid at the second railroad bridge requires care. The river gets shallow in the summer, so this run is best done in the rainy season. The take-out is the put-in for the Class I Cedar River run listed above. To reach the put-in for this run, drive east out of Maple Valley on SE 216th Street, turn right on 276th Avenue SE, and continue 2.5 miles south to the Cedar River Bridge. Be sure to put in below the dam!

Known as the Yo Yo Stretch, the 3-mile **Green River** run through Flaming Geyser State Park to the Whitney Bridge is short but loads of fun for novice paddlers just working their way into Class II water. Most of this run passes through the park, but it isn't until you leave the park that you hit the first Class II water, which is just upstream from the take-out. Although this run can be done all year, the river gets low in summer, which is also when sunseekers float through the park on inner tubes, air mattresses, tiny rubber rafts, and anything else that will float. Because the run is so short, many paddlers just do it again, and again—thus the name. This run is perfect for a bicycle shuttle. To reach the take-out, drive east from I-5 on Wash. 18 through Auburn to Auburn–Black Diamond Road. Turn right and then right again onto SE Green Valley Road, which leads to Flaming Geyser. Just before reaching the park, turn right on 212th Avenue SE and park or leave a bike at the bridge boat launch. Continue to the park and drive to the last parking area.

The **Puyallup River** upstream from the town of McMillan has a nearly constant gradient and nonstop Class II waters. The 9-mile run from the gauging station south of Orting down to McMillan is a fast one, with braided channels, gravel bars, and lots of small waves. Keep an eye out for downed trees. Snowmelt season is the best time to do this run. The take-out is the put-in of the Class I Puyallup River run listed above. To reach the put-in from McMillan, drive south on Wash. 162 to Orting, and just south of town, turn right on Orville Road East. The gauging station is 3 miles south down a dirt road on the right.

CLASS III & ABOVE

The **Green River Gorge** run from just above Kanaskat–Palmer State Park to Flaming Geyser State Park on the Green River is one of Washington's most scenic, challenging, and frequently run stretches of whitewater. Huge boulders, ledge drops, steep cliff walls (300 feet high in places) dripping with greenery, and a warm spring are the main attractions of this 14-mile run. It starts with a bang right in Kanaskat–Palmer State Park where there are a couple of Class IV ledge drops and boulder gardens. Below the park is where the gorge really begins, and more big rapids await. This is a dam-controlled river but is best run during the rainy season when there is sure to be enough water. The take-out is the put-in for the Class II Green River run listed above. To reach the put-in, drive east from Flaming Geyser State Park on SE Green Valley Road, turn left onto Wash. 169 toward Black Diamond, turn right on Green River Gorge Road in less than 2 miles, follow this road (crossing the Green River Gorge at Franklin Bridge) to Cumberland–Kanaskat Road SE, and turn left. At Kanaskat, turn right at the sign for Green River (Tacoma) Headworks and drive just over 1 mile up this road to a side road that leads down to the river.

WILDLIFE VIEWING

At the **Hiram M. Chittenden (Ballard) Locks** in the Ballard neighborhood of Seattle, salmon and steelhead can be seen both in the fish ladders and through an underwater viewing window. You can see some species of migrating fish (sockeye, coho, or steelhead) just about any time from June through February. Because all these fish are forced into the narrow channel of the locks, they are easy prey to sea lions that for several years now have taken up residence here to enjoy the easy pickins (see "There Is a Free Lunch" earlier in this chapter). To reach the locks, take North 45th Street west from I-5 just north of Lake Union and continue west to the locks on NW Market Street.

Just outside Olympia, at **Tumwater Falls Park** on the Deschutes River, you can see migrating coho and Chinook salmon from mid-September to early November. These falls are in a very urban setting, wedged between I-5 and the Olympia Brewery; however, the setting detracts little from the sight of salmon struggling to fulfill their goal of returning upstream to spawn. Many of the fish are captured by a hatchery for egg production. A trail leads along the river at the falls.

On the west side of the sound, on the Kitsap Peninsula, there are some other places to see migrating and spawning salmon.

Campgrounds & Other Accommodations

CAMPING

Two of the most convenient campgrounds to Seattle are in state parks on the shore of Puget Sound north of Tacoma. **Saltwater State Park** (52 campsites; year-round), 2 miles south of Des Moines on Wash. 509, is the more popular of the two parks even though **Dash Point State Park** (109 regular campsites, 29 utility sites; year-round), 5 miles northeast of Tacoma on this same road, is the larger of the parks. Both parks have trails through forest settings but are more popular for their beaches. Reservations can be made for Dash Point campsites by calling Reservations Northwest (tel. 800/452-5687).

Today Bainbridge Island is little more than a suburb of Seattle, but it is still home to the most convenient public campground in the Seattle area. **Fay–Bainbridge State Park** (36 campsites; year-round), located at the north end of the island, has good views across the sound to downtown Seattle and is only a few minutes' drive from the ferry terminal. Equally close to Seattle but far less convenient is **Blake Island State Park** (54 campsites; year-round), which is located on an island in the middle of Puget Sound and is accessible only by boat. Still, this campground is very popular due in large part to the feeling of isolation you get so close to the city.

The south sound area, less developed than the north sound, has far more campgrounds. Throughout these southern waters are numerous state parks. Just outside the town of Bremerton, **Illahee State Park** (33 campsites; year-round) is a small park (only 75 acres) on the shore of Port Orchard. To reach this park, drive north from downtown Bremerton on Wash. 303 and follow signs. **Manchester State Park** (50 campsites; seasonal), across Rich Passage from the south end of Bainbridge Island, is a former military installation overlooking the water. To reach the park, follow signs north from Wash. 16 between Gig Harbor and Port Orchard. **Belfair State Park** (134 regular campsites, 47 utility sites; year-round), 3 miles west of Belfair on Wash. 300, is a big, wooded campground popular throughout the year. Although it is most popular for its location on Hood Canal, it makes a good base for mountain bikers riding in the nearby Tahuya State Forest, and it has a swimming pond. On the opposite side of Hood Canal, 8 miles southwest of Belfair on Wash. 106, is **Twanoh State Park** (38 regular campsites, 9 utility sites; seasonal), which is also set amid dense forest. **Kopachuck State Park** (41 campsites; year-round), set in dense forest on the shore of Carr Inlet 5 miles southwest of Gig Harbor, is favored by sea kayakers and scuba divers, although they make up a tiny minority of the people who camp here.

INNS & LODGES

M. V. Challenger

1001 Fairview Ave. N, Seattle, WA 98109. Tel. 206/340-1201. Fax 206/621-9208. 8 rms (5 with private bath). TEL. $75–$165 double. All rates include full breakfast. AE, CB, DC, MC, V. Free parking. Yale Street Landing, on Chandler's Cove at the south end of Lake Union.

If you love ships and the sea and don't mind cramped quarters, don't pass up this opportunity to spend the night on board a restored and fully operational 45-year-old tugboat. This is a great place to stay if you're in town with your sea kayak.

Seattle International AYH Hostel

84 Union St., Seattle, WA 98101-2084. Tel. 206/622-5443. Fax 206/682-2179. 126 beds. $16.25 for members. JCB, MC, V.

This conveniently located hostel is housed in the former Longshoreman's Hall, which was built in 1915. To find it, walk down Post Alley, which runs through and under Pike Place Market, to the corner of Union Street.

Salish Lodge

37807 SE Fall City–Snoqualmie Rd. (P.O. Box 1109), Snoqualmie, WA 98065. Tel. 800/826-6124 or 206/888-2556. 91 rms, 4 suites. $165–$295 double; $500–$575 suite. AE, CB, DC, DISC, MC, V.

Set at the top of 270-foot Snoqualmie Falls and only 35 minutes east of Seattle on I-90, Salish Lodge is a popular weekend getaway spot for folks from Seattle. With its country lodge atmosphere, the Salish aims for casual comfort and hits the mark. With fireplaces and whirlpool baths in every room, this lodge is made for romantic weekend getaways but does nicely as a base for hikes and bike rides in the area.

4

THE OLYMPIC PENINSULA & SOUTHWEST WASHINGTON COAST

IN MOST PLACES A FORECAST OF RAIN IS ENOUGH TO CAUSE PEOPLE TO cancel plans for that backpacking trip or weekend at the beach. Sure, if it was just an afternoon's outing you might put on the rain gear and hope that your expensive, breathable high-tech fibers do their job at keeping the wet, and the sweat, out. But what if the forecast calls for a foot of rain? Would you still go? That's the dilemma that faces everyone planning a visit to the Olympic Peninsula.

Here, in valleys on the west side of the peninsula, in the only temperate rain forests in the contiguous U.S., rainfall is measured in feet rather than inches—more than 12 feet of rain, in fact, in an average year. And while most regions of the Northwest can count on drying out during the summer months, the Olympic Peninsula, at least on the west side facing the Pacific Ocean, rarely goes long without a good dousing. Be forewarned. Sure, you can hit a week of sunshine in July or August, but I wouldn't count on it.

Yet people are drawn to this peninsula, much of which is preserved as Olympic National Park; they come in spite of the rain, or perhaps specifically to see for themselves what a landscape this wet could possibly look like. Herein can be found the wettest spot in the Lower 48, the longest stretch of uninterrupted wilderness coastline south of Alaska, a landlocked fjord 900 feet deep, deer as tame as puppies, and views that encompass not only glacier-clad peaks but also three distinct bodies of water—the Pacific Ocean, the Strait of Juan de Fuca, and Puget Sound. Just as during the Klondike gold rush Seattle was known as the southernmost city in Alaska, so too could the Olympic Peninsula be considered the southernmost Alaskan wilderness.

Today, no road crosses through the heart of the rugged Olympic Mountains, and only a handful of roads, all dead ends, penetrate Olympic National Park at all. For most visitors, the bulk of the peninsula is still terra incognita, a land that can only be glimpsed from afar as tiny snapshots that don't even begin to capture the grand beauty of this complex landscape. However, for those willing to expend the energy required to penetrate deep into the Olympics' heart of darkness, there are untold riches to be discovered: moss-draped rain forests where trees grow more than 200 feet tall and 15 feet thick at the base, hidden lakes surrounded by glacier-carved peaks, high meadows that are home to deer and mountain goats unafraid of humans, and hot springs surrounded by lush forests.

And while other national parks have craggy peaks and hot springs and "tame" wildlife, no other south of Alaska has a coastline to equal that of Olympic National Park. The wild Olympic coastline of beaches framed by rocky headlands is punctuated by hundreds of offshore rocks and islands that are home to more than a million birds. Sea otters and harbor seals frolic in the cold waters. Beaches strewn with massive driftwood logs, some more than a hundred feet long, are guarded by bald eagles that perch on seaside snags, the driftwood of tomorrow. In nearly 60 miles only one road touches this coast. Today this coast is preserved as part of the national park, while offshore waters and islands are preserved both as national wildlife refuges and as the controversial Olympic Coast National Marine Sanctuary. This latter preserve was created to protect offshore waters from overfishing, oil exploration, and oil spills, any one of which could wreak havoc on the delicate balance of life here on the coast.

South of the Olympic Peninsula, along Washington's southern coast, tamer sports—kite flying, clamming, bird watching—prevail where vacation homes crowd the shore and timber companies have buzz-cut the inland hills. However, despite the development, this coast still has its pockets of wildness. The Willapa National Wildlife Refuge and the Long Beach Peninsula's Leadbetter Point together host a vast number of bird species each year. These areas, when combined with the Gray's Harbor National Wildlife Refuge to the north, offer the best bird watching in the entire Northwest. Sea kayakers also are attracted to Willapa Bay, where the paddle around Long Island is as rewarding as any paddle in the Puget Sound or San Juan Islands.

The Lay of the Land

The Olympic Peninsula is the end of the road, the edge of the nation. It is here, at Cape Alava, that the contiguous United States reach their westernmost point (although this claim is also made by Cape Blanco in Oregon). It is also here, at Cape Flattery, that the Lower 48 reach their northwesternmost point.

Formed of folded upthrust sandstone and pillow basalts that once rested on the seafloor, the Olympic Peninsula was created when oceanic crust collided with continental crust. As the oceanic crust buckled and folded some 35 million years ago, it was forced upward to form the Olympic Mountains. This landmass has only just arrived, geologically speaking.

However, despite this "recent" heritage, the Olympic Peninsula is rapidly being washed away by the powerful waves that constantly gnaw away at its bedrock. The massive rocks that lend such drama to the peninsula's Pacific Ocean coastline are remnants of the former edge of the continent—the softer shoreline washed away to leave only the more resistant rock. This more resistant rock becomes headlands, but as the sea continues its ceaseless, unrelenting attack on the shore, even the hardest of rock succumbs. Sea caves, arches, and tunnels, such as those at Hole in the Wall, are formed. Eventually the shoreline will move eastward, and these wave-cut headlands, too, will be cut off from the land by the erosive forces of wind and water to add another jagged sea stack off the shore of the Olympic Peninsula. So quickly is this coast eroding that photographs from the early 20th century show an almost unrecognizable coastline. On the north shore of Willapa Bay, the land is eroding so quickly that abandoned roads lead straight into the bay at a place called Washaway Beach.

However, it is not just the ocean that is carving away at the Olympic Peninsula. Beginning about 2 million years ago, ice-age glaciers began carving this mountain range into the rugged landscape encountered by today's visitors. As recently as 12,000 years ago, these glaciers extended down from the peaks of the Olympics to meet the massive sheets of ice that at the time filled the Puget Sound and Strait of Juan de Fuca. Today, though the 60 glaciers of the Olympic Mountains are much smaller than they were during the last ice age, they are holding their own, neither advancing nor receding. Although the climate here is mild and the highest Olympic peak, Mount Olympus, is not quite 8,000 feet, heavy snowfalls ensure that the glaciers on these mountains are well supplied with ice and snow.

The same storms that bring heavy snowfalls at high elevations produce the peninsula's well-known rain forests. A combination of geography, ocean currents, and arctic weather are responsible for these rain forests, which annually receive more than 150 inches of rain. Along the west slope of the Olympic Mountains are four major valleys—the Bogachiel, the Hoh, the Queets, and the Quinault—that open directly to the west, the direction from which moisture-laden arctic storms arrive. Because the mountains rise so abruptly from the coast, moisture-laden air is forced rapidly upward by the prevailing winds. As this air rises, it cools and can no longer hold the water it has been carrying. Down from the clouds come the deluges that turn these valleys into verdant wonderlands of botanical excess. Conifers grow to sizes surpassed only by the coast redwoods of northern California, epiphytic mosses and ferns form dense mats on the branches of bigleaf maples, and terrestrial ferns grow head high.

So efficient are these valleys at wringing moisture from the clouds that while 150 inches fall each year in the Hoh Valley, 60 miles away on the other side of the mountains at Sequim (rhymes with *swim*), less than 20 inches fall each year. Consequently, Sequim, which was once a natural prairie where even cactus grew, was among the first places on the peninsula to be settled by pioneers.

While to the casual observer the Olympic Peninsula appears to be a playground for outdoor-sports enthusiasts, anyone bothering to peer a little more closely at that forest beside the road is likely to learn differently. More than likely those trees are but a curtain to deceive speeding motorists into believing that all is well on this northwest-ernmost tip of the continent. Looks are deceiving. Glance in your rearview mirror and you're likely to see the other side of the Olympic story—a logging truck loaded with freshly cut trees. The Olympic Peninsula has been at the heart of the Northwest's battle over old-growth

forests. It is here that northern spotted owls have been nailed to road signs, that cars sport bumper stickers proclaiming, "I like spotted owls—in stew." Unless you enjoy a good conflict now and then, I suggest you hide your Sierra Club sticker before venturing into this battleground.

Outside the boundaries of the Olympic National Park, the forests have been decimated. Only a fraction of the mature, old-growth forest that once covered this peninsula still remains. When the heart of the Olympic Peninsula was first set aside (originally as a Roosevelt elk reserve), preserving forests—which at that time seemed unlimited—was not the park's priority. Consequently, the largest trees, those growing in the lowland valleys, were left out. These eventually became part of the Olympic National Forest or private timber holdings and have since been logged off with the exception of a few small areas dedicated to showing the public how beautiful this forest once was. Today, with few trees left to cut, unemployment runs high in this neck of the clear-cuts.

While no roads cross through the center of the peninsula, one does wrap around three sides of it. **U.S. 101** is the peninsula's most important highway, and connects all the major towns of the region, as well as those on the southern Washington coast. **Port Townsend,** with its Victorian architecture, is the most important tourist community on the peninsula. However, its location makes it a poor choice for anyone planning to explore the national park.

To the west of Port Townsend lies sunny **Sequim,** now a popular retirement community. To the west of this is **Port Angeles,** site of Olympic National Park headquarters. Lying at the foot of the Hurricane Ridge Road, Port Angeles has numerous motels and is a popular base for park visitors who are not camping. From here it is possible to day-trip to Hurricane Ridge, Sol Duc Hot Springs, Lake Crescent, Lake Ozette, and the Rialto Beach/La Push area. However, for exploring the coastal regions, the timber town of **Forks,** 60 miles west of Port Angeles, may be a better choice.

While U.S. 101 encircles the peninsula on three sides, it actually lies within

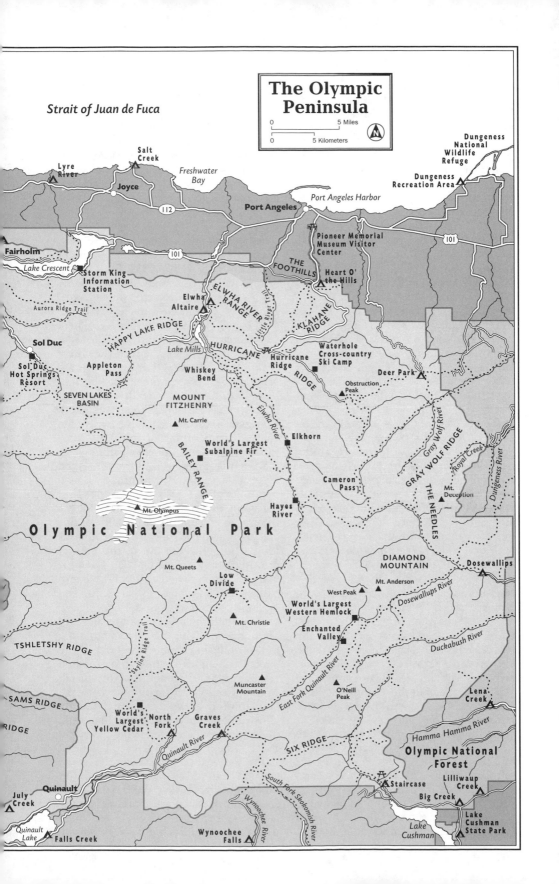

Olympic National Park in only two places— in the vicinity of Lake Crescent, west of Port Angeles, and for 12 coastal miles between the mouths of the Hoh and Queets rivers.

Although it is difficult to say exactly where the Olympic Peninsula begins on its southern, landward side, the logical choice (if not the geographically accurate choice) is the U.S. 12/Wash. 8 corridor, which stretches from Olympia to Gray's Harbor. While **Olympia,** the state capital, is solidly a Puget Sound city, it is also the start (or finish) of U.S. 101, which from here makes its loop around the peninsula and then continues south through Oregon and into California. Across the pinched neck of the peninsula lies **Gray's Harbor** and its blue-collar sister towns of **Aberdeen** and **Hoquiam,** which together comprise the largest port on the Washington coast. This little corner of industrialization puts a distinct end to the wilds of the Olympic Peninsula.

To the south of Gray's Harbor lie the far more developed shores of the southern Washington coast. Aside from two last rocky headlands at the mouth of the Columbia River, this coastline is a tame strip of sandy beaches and windswept dunes. Gray's Harbor and **Willapa Bay** divide this stretch of coast into two distinct strips of sand, but these two strands have far more in common with one another than they do with the wild, rock-strewn beaches to the north.

To give you some idea of how this region sees itself, consider that **Long Beach,** a beach resort town for more than 100 years, sees itself as the kite-flying capital of America and boasts of having the longest drivable beach in the world. While vacationing families drive the local economy, oysters still reign supreme in Willapa Bay, one of the cleanest estuaries on the west coast. However, glance up from the bay and your eyes fall on clearcuts. Trained eyes can also now spot the spartina grass, a nonnative species of marsh plant that is slowly crowding out native saltmarsh plants and turning this bay into unproductive mudflats. With the trees gone and the days of the oyster numbered, the south coast turns more and more to tourism and retirees for salvation.

Parks & Other Hot Spots

Olympic National Park

Numerous access points around the Olympic Peninsula. Tel. 360/452-4501. Camping, hiking, backpacking, mountain biking, sea kayaking, flat-water canoeing, whitewater kayaking and rafting, fishing, bird watching, wildlife watching, cross-country skiing, snowshoeing.

The heart and soul of the Olympic Peninsula, this park was created by President Franklin Roosevelt in 1938. Prior to this time, much of the peninsula had already been set aside as protected public lands. In 1897 President Grover Cleveland created the Olympic Forest Reserve. Then, 12 years later in 1909, President Theodore Roosevelt designated part of the forest reserve as Mount Olympus National Monument to protect the peninsula's rapidly dwindling herds of Roosevelt elk (guess who these animals were named for). Roosevelt elk are a larger subspecies of the Rocky Mountain elk and were being ruthlessly pursued by commercial hunters primarily interested in their teeth, which were sold as watch-fob ornaments to members of the Elks Club. Washington legislators and the timber industry fought bitterly to prevent the designation of this area as a national park, which would effectively lock them out of the natural resources they coveted. When Olympic National Park was finally signed into existence, it encompassed far less than had originally been envisioned.

Though primarily created to preserve the majestic Olympic Mountains and the forests of the mountains' lower slopes, the park also includes a narrow strip of coastal land stretching 57 miles from the Makah Indian Reservation in the north to the Quinault Indian Reservation in the south. This land was not part of the original park, but was instead acquired in the 1950s and 1970s. The last coastal tract to be added to the national park was acquired at the end of a divisive battle that pitted Supreme Court Justice William O. Douglas, a staunch environmentalist, against the land exploiters and developers who wanted to build a highway along the northern Olympic coast and open the coast up to rampant housing developments. Luckily, the developers lost and this coastline was preserved.

Unlike many other national parks, this one makes you work for your rewards. Sure you can drive to Hurricane Ridge, Ruby Beach, and the Hoh Rain Forest, but if you want to see such gems as Enchanted Valley, Cape Alava, or Olympic Hot Springs, you'll have to stretch your legs. What this means is that much of the park remains untrammeled, the domain of elk and bald eagles and backpackers.

On the east side of the park, two roads penetrate into the park from U.S. 101. One road follows the Dosewallips River and the other follows the North Fork Skokomish River, past popular Lake Cushman. Both of these roads are used exclusively by hikers and anglers.

Hurricane Ridge, at 5,200 feet, is one of only two places in Olympic National Park where you can drive to alpine meadows, and only Hurricane Ridge has a paved road. Consequently, it is one of the most visited spots in the park. Summer or winter, the crowds descend (ascend?) on this superb viewpoint for the unequaled views of peaks, glaciers, and deep, forested valleys. In summer there are some short hiking trails here, and in winter cross-country ski trails head out along the ridge. In winter there is also a rope tow that provides downhill skiers with a bit of slope. For the best area hikes, you'll need to continue on from Hurricane Ridge to Obstruction Point, which is at the end of a side road that begins just before you reach the Hurricane Ridge parking area. Just one very important piece of advice: If it isn't clear, don't bother. It's a long drive up here just to look at clouds. On the road up to Hurricane Ridge is Heart O' the Hills Campground, which is one of the most popular campgrounds in the park.

The only other place where you can drive to subalpine meadows is at **Deer Park,** elevation 5,250 feet, which is east of Hurricane Ridge at the end of a precipitous gravel road. With a campground and trailhead and little else, Deer Park is infrequently visited, yet quite beautiful.

To the west of Deer Park, another road leads into the park along the Elwha River. This road is perhaps best known as the route to **Olympic Hot Springs.** These springs can be reached only by hiking 2.2 miles up an abandoned road. More popular is the developed resort at **Sol Duc Hot Springs,** which are up the Soleduck Road west of Lake Crescent.

Situated on the north side of the park, **Lake Crescent** is among the most popular spots, not only for its fabulous fjordlike setting and fishing for elusive Beardslee and Crescenti trout, but also because of its lakeshore lodges and campground. When the winds aren't blowing, it's pleasant to paddle a canoe around the lake, and roads and a trail along the shore provide a bit of cycling. However, it is the proximity to both Hurricane Ridge and Sol Duc Hot Springs that make this a popular base for people exploring the park.

Of the park's three large lakes, **Lake Ozette** is the most remote and undeveloped. While Lake Crescent and Lake Quinault have historic lodges and buildings along their shores, Lake Ozette has only a campground and a few old cabins. The lake, which is separated from the Pacific by only a mile of land, offers good canoeing and fishing. The lake is also known for its unusual boardwalk hiking trails, which lead to Sand Point and Cape Alava. From here backpackers can head either north or south and have miles of remote beaches almost to themselves. It is here at Cape Alava that a Native American village was inundated by a massive mudslide 500 years ago. The excavation of this well-preserved village has produced a wealth of artifacts, many of which are now on display at the Makah Museum in nearby Neah Bay. The village site is currently off-limits to visitors and has been reburied to preserve it.

West of the town of Forks lie some of the national park's most beautiful easily accessible beaches. These beaches lie on either side of the Quillayute River and the Quileute Indian Reservation. To the north is **Rialto Beach,** at the north end of which is Hole in the Wall, a rocky headland with a wave-carved tunnel through it. To the south are **Second and Third beaches,** which are both accessed by short hiking trails.

If you want to see what a temperate rain forest is all about, the **Hoh Valley,** southeast of Forks, is the place. Just be sure you bring your umbrella and a snorkle (just kidding). This is the most easily accessible of the park's rain-forest valleys and is the site of the wettest campground in the contiguous states as well as a couple of short rain-forest interpretive trails and an information center. This is also the trailhead for the classic backpacking trip to Glacier Meadows, a trip that begins in moss-draped rain forest and ends in alpine meadows beside a glacier.

South of the mouth of the Hoh River is the only long stretch of Olympic National Park coastline that is paralleled by U.S. 101. From **Ruby Beach to South Beach,** there is easy access from the highway. It is toward the south end of this 12-mile stretch of beach that you will find the national park's oceanfront Kalaloch Lodge.

Though it is, in my opinion, the least impressive of the park's three major lakes, **Lake Quinault** is still an impressive sight, especially on a clear day with the Olympic Mountains shimmering above the northeast end of the lake. With several lodges, motels, and campgrounds on the shores of the lake, it makes a good base of operations for exploring the west side of the peninsula. There are also a couple of short rain-forest interpretive trails on the shore.

Buckhorn Wilderness

Accessed from Big Quilcene Rd. west of Quilcene and Palo Alto Rd. east of Sequim. Tel. 360/765-2200. Hiking, backpacking, fishing.

Located on the east side of Olympic National Park, this wilderness area has several of the best and most popular short mountain hikes in the Olympic Mountains. Within the wilderness are lowland forests, deep river valleys, craggy peaks, and flower-filled subalpine meadows. From the summits of many of the wilderness's peaks, there are views not only of the Olympic Mountains, but of much of Puget Sound and the Cascade Range as well.

Fort Flagler State Park

On Wash. 116 south of Port Townsend off Wash. 20. Tel. 360/385-1259. Camping, sea kayaking, scuba diving, wildlife watching.

This former military installation has lent itself quite nicely to the role of state park. Originally built to protect the waters of Puget Sound from enemy attack, the fort has an enviable location at the tip of Marrowstone Island just south of Port Townsend. One side of the park fronts on the exposed waters of Puget Sound while the other side is on the more protected waters of Kilisut Harbor. The beach is a nice spot for picnicking and walking.

Dungeness National Wildlife Refuge/ Dungeness Recreation Area

North of U.S. 101 on the west side of Sequim. Tel. 360/683-7040. Camping, hiking, boardsailing, sea kayaking, bird watching, wildlife watching.

Together these two areas have turned the Dungeness Spit, one of the longest natural sandspits in the world, into a refuge for wildlife and a recreation area for humans. This is the north Olympic Peninsula's premier coastal recreation area, with the protected waters of Dungeness Bay providing ideal conditions for both sea kayakers and boardsailors (though not on the same days). Birdlife abounds here and harbor seals also call the Dungeness Spit home. The flat walk out Dungeness Spit to the lighthouse is long but easy; pack a picnic lunch.

Fort Canby State Park

On Wash. 100 south of Long Beach off U.S. 101. Tel. 360/642-3078. Camping, road biking, whale watching, fishing.

Set at the mouth of the Columbia River, this park is the most interesting of the state parks on the south Washington coast. Here, rocky headlands once again make an appearance after many miles of flat, sandy beaches. Several trails wind through the large park, and the two headlands provide opportunities to whale watch. The park's roads are popular with bicyclists and are the starting and ending points for a cycle tour of the Long Beach Peninsula.

The Eastern & Northern Olympic Peninsula ◆ What to Do & Where to Do It

BIRD WATCHING

If you happen to be driving up the west side of Hood Canal on U.S. 101, you might want to stop at **Potlatch State Park** or nearby at the mouth of the Skokomish River and scan the water for yellow-billed loons, which, though rare, are sometimes seen here.

In the Port Townsend area, **Kah Tai Lagoon Park,** covering only about 100 acres, is a surprisingly productive birding spot. Shorebirds and various species of ducks are common. You'll find this park at the end of Haines Place off East Sims Way shortly before reaching the Port Townsend Visitor Information Center. If you're looking to add pigeon guillemots or tufted puffins to your life list, a ferry ride across Admiralty Inlet to Keystone on Whidbey Island should be rewarding on a calm day. Once on Whidbey Island, there is also good birding in the marshland beside the ferry dock.

Formed by the currents that sweep through the straight of Juan de Fuca, the 5.5-mile-long **Dungeness Spit** is one of the longest sand spits in the world. Today the spit and its environs are protected as the **Dungeness National Wildlife Refuge** (tel. 360/457-8451) and provide some of the best birding in the state. During spring and fall migrations, there are always many species of shorebirds around, and during the winter, harlequin ducks and black brants frequent the protected waters inside the spit. Bald eagles also winter here and feed on the ducks. Pelagic birds, as well as tufted puffins and rhinoceros auklets, are frequently seen. There is a viewing area on the bluff above the spit, but there is also good viewing along the first mile or so of the spit. To reach the spit, drive west from Sequim on U.S. 101, turn right onto Kitchen–Dick Road, and then right again onto Lotzgesell Road.

Salt Creek Recreation Area, west of Port Angeles off Wash. 112 at the end of Camp Hayden Road, is another good place to look for puffins and rhinoceros auklets. Black oystercatchers also nest here during the summer months. If you don't mind a 6.6-mile round-trip hike to do your bird watching, head out the **Cape Alava Trail** from Lake Ozette. Along the way, you're likely to see bald eagles and ospreys, and out at the cape there is usually a good variety of waterfowl, shorebirds, and marine birds.

BOARDSAILING

At the south end of **Indian Island,** which is south of Port Townsend, there is a small beach that is a popular boardsailing spot when winds are out of the south. To reach this site, take Wash. 19 south from Port Townsend, turn east on Wash. 116, and continue onto Indian Island (a naval base). Watch for a small parking area on the right after the county park but before reaching the marshland separating Indian Island from Marrowstone Island. Up at the north end of this latter island, which is connected to Indian Island by a causeway, there is also boardsailing at **Fort Flagler State Park,** which has lots of good beach for board launching.

Just north of Dungeness, **Cline Spit,** which tucks under the much larger Dungeness Spit, is a popular sailing spot, especially when winds are from the east. The area is out of the shipping channels, is protected by the spit (so waves are small), and if winds are out of the east, you won't be blown into the strait. You'll find Cline Spit off Marine Drive, which can be reached by following Sequim–Dungeness Way north from U.S. 101 across the Dungeness River. Farther west, on the north side of Port Angeles, **Ediz Hook** is another good sailboarding spot that is exposed both to the winds and waves that blow through the Strait of Juan de Fuca.

Boardsailing equipment is available in Port Angeles from **Scuba Supplies,** 1717 W Seventh St. (tel. 360/457-3190).

Outdoor Resources

Hoh Ranger Station
HC 80, Box 650
Forks, WA 98331
Tel. 360/374-6925

Hood Canal Ranger Station
150 N Lake Cushman Rd.
(P.O. Box 68)
Hoodsport, WA 98548
Tel. 360/877-5254

Kalaloch Ranger Station
HC 80, Box 10
Forks, WA 98331
Tel. 360/962-2283

Lake Crescent Ranger Station
HC 62, Box 10
Port Angeles, WA 98362
Tel. 360/928-3380

Mora Ranger Station
HC 79, Box 170
Forks, WA 98331
Tel. 360/374-5460

Olympic National Park
600 E Park Ave.
Port Angeles, WA 98362
Tel. 360/452-4501

Quilcene Ranger Station
20482 Hwy. 101 S
(P.O. Box 280)

Quilcene, WA 98376
Tel. 360/765-2200

Quinault Ranger Station
353 South Shore Rd.
(P.O. Box 9)
Quinault, WA 98575
Tel. 360/288-2525

Quinault River Ranger Station
908 North Shore Rd.
Amanda Park, WA 98526
Tel. 360/288-2444

Sol Duc Ranger Station
196281 Hwy. 101
Forks, WA 98331
Tel. 360/374-6522

EQUIPMENT SHOPS

Brown's Outdoor Store
112 W Front St., Port Angeles
Tel. 360/457-4150

Olympic Mountaineering
221 S Peabody St., Port Angeles
Tel. 360/452-0240

Sport Townsend
1044 Water St., Port Townsend
Tel. 360/379-9711

CROSS-COUNTRY SKIING

Although there is snow in the Olympics and it is possible to cross-country ski here, with the exception of Hurricane Ridge, the conditions generally aren't very good and access is lousy.

Hurricane Ridge Trails

3–6 miles round-trip. More difficult–most difficult. 200–750-foot elevation gain. Access: From U.S. 101 in Port Angeles, drive 17 miles south on Mount Angeles Rd. to the Hurricane Ridge Lodge and parking area. Map: Green Trails Mount Angeles, Custom Correct Hurricane Ridge.

Though perhaps a bit more popular with families of downhill skiers, Hurricane Ridge also serves as the starting point for a few cross-country ski trails. These trails are worth skiing if for no other reason than that, on a clear day, they offer the most drop-dead views of any ski trails in the Northwest. However, if the weather is cloudy, a ski along these trails is no different than a ski through any forest, and if the winds are blowing, as they often do, a ski here can be absolute misery. Be sure to call Olympic National Park (tel. 360/452-0330) first before heading up here; the road is often closed by big dumps of snow and usually is only plowed on weekends.

The most popular trail here is the road route that leads 1.5 miles west to the base of Hurricane Hill. Although the route is along an unplowed road and is fairly wide, icy conditions, corniches, and steep drop-offs can make this road nerve-wracking for novice skiers (which was the case the first time I skied here). Beyond the base of Hurricane Hill, steep slopes demand advanced skills and are popular with telemarkers. However, anyone willing to brave the ascent of this hill, across a narrow ridge, will find glorious open slopes to ski.

The other Hurricane Ridge ski tour heads southeast from below the main parking area and follows the road to Obstruction Point. It is a 16-mile round-trip to Obstruction Point, a trip that is usually done only as an overnight trip by the well prepared. Getting caught out here at night when the weather turns bad is a fate I wouldn't wish on even my worst enemy. A much easier plan is to do a day ski about halfway along this road to Waterhole Camp, a camping area frequently used by skiers. Although this route follows the road along the crest of the ridge, the start is a steep, though short, descent that is very intimidating when the slopes are icy. Views to the south abound along the first half of the route, which makes this a superb choice on a clear day when conditions are just right. If they are, consider skiing a ways past Waterhole Camp for more views from open slopes.

DOWNHILL SKIING & SNOWBOARDING

The only downhill skiing is a tiny little family hill at **Hurricane Ridge** (tel. 360/452-0329), 17 miles south of Port Angeles. This ski area is open on weekends and has only one poma and two rope tows. However, with the next nearest ski slopes hours away on the far side of Puget Sound, Hurricane Ridge stays busy with families. The majority of skiers seem to be children just learning the ropes (so to speak). So, if

> "If the exploiters are permitted to have their way with the Olympic Peninsula, all that will be left will be the outraged squeal of future generations over the loss of another national treasure."
>
> —Harold Ickes, Secretary of the Interior under President Franklin Delano Roosevelt, who was responsible for creating Olympic National Park

you happen to be out this way with your skis, you just might want to strap them on up here so you can tell people that you've skied in the Olympics.

FISHING

The rivers of the Olympic Peninsula are well known for their fighting salmon, steelhead, and trout, and the fishing season runs just about year-round. In Lakes Crescent and Ozette, the northern peninsula's large natural lakes, you can fish for such elusive and legendary species as Beardslee rainbows and Crescenti cutthroats. Offshore waters yield salmon and bottom fish, with plenty of charter companies operating out of various coastal communities.

The Hood Canal has long been known for its good sea-run cutthroat fishing, and though the catch has been limited for several years now, there is still some good fishing in the area for these native trout. Way down at the south end of Hood Canal, on the Great Bend, there is good spring and fall fly-fishing for cutthroats near the mouth of the **Skokomish River.** (The waters near the mouth of the Skokomish lie on the Skokomish Indian Reservation, for which you'll need to pick up an inexpensive fishing permit.) The **Hamma Hamma River,** a short distance north of Hoodsport on U.S. 101, also has a cutthroat run just upstream from the mouth, as do the **Duckabush, Dosewallips,** and **Big Quilcene rivers.** The best cutthroat fishing is from early July to late fall.

The Skokomish River has a good winter steelhead run and fishing for chum salmon in November and early December. In the waters of Hood Canal itself, October and November bring good fishing for chum salmon near the Hoodsport Salmon Hatchery in Hoodsport. Casting with small, green fly patterns or tufts of green nylon yarn seems to work best.

The **Elwha River,** which once produced what were considered the finest salmon on the peninsula, has been blocked by two hydroelectric dams since early in this century. However, there is still good fishing for trout on sections of this river, which is designated for artificial flies and lures with barbless hooks only. The river is increasingly popular with fly anglers. The stretch of river between Lake Aldwell and Lake Mills lies alongside the Olympic Hot Springs Road and is the most easily accessible. Upstream from Lake Mills, a trail parallels the river and provides access to 20 miles of less heavily fished waters that are perfect for a backpacking and trout-fishing weekend.

For lake trout fishing, no other Olympic Peninsula lake can compare with **Lake Crescent,** which is home to monster rainbow trout ranging up to 20 pounds. These Beardslee rainbows are descended from steelhead that were cut off from saltwater when a mudslide 10,000 years ago blocked the lake's outlet. The lake's other legendary fish are its slightly smaller Crescenti cutthroats, which were cut off from the sea by the same mudslide. Both types of fish are very elusive and run deep. Try trolling for them between 50 and 150 feet deep with a salmon plug. Check national park fishing regulations first.

If you prefer fishing for lake trout in a remote setting, consider hiking into the **Seven Lakes Basin** from Sol Duc Hot Springs. It's 8 miles each way to these lakes, but once here, you'll find the big brookies and rainbows are worth the effort.

If you don't want to leave your catch to chance, there are plenty of guides in the area who will take you to their favorite fishing holes. **Four Seasons Guide Service** (tel. 360/327-3380) will take you fishing for steelhead, salmon, and trout on the region's rivers (rates $180 per day for one person, $225 for two people).

If you're interested in heading out on open water to do a bit of salmon or bottom fishing, there are several ports from which to start. In Port Townsend, contact **Sea Sport Charters** (tel. 360/385-3575). In Sequim, contact **Admiralty Charters** (tel. 360/683-1097) or **Dungeness Charters** (tel. 360/683-8873). In Port Angeles, contact **Captain Tuna** (tel. 360/457-8972), **Lucky Strike** (tel. 360/683-2416), **Port Angeles Charters** (tel. 360/457-7629), or **The Whaler** (tel. 360/457-0648). In the Sekiu-Clallam Bay area, contact **Herb's Charters** (tel. 360/963-2346) or **Olson's Charters** (tel. 360/963-2311). In Neah Bay, contact **Big Salmon Fishing Resort** (tel. 800/959-2374 or 360/645-2374) or **Far West Fishing Resort** (tel. 360/645-2270).

Fly anglers in need of supplies or gear can stop in at the **Greywolf Angler,** 275953 U.S. 101 (tel. 360/797-7177), which is in Gardiner (between Discovery Bay and Sequim Bay).

HIKING & BACKPACKING

INLAND HIKES

Mount Ellinor

4.5 miles round-trip. Moderate. 2,100-foot elevation gain. Access: From U.S. 101 in Hoodsport (near the Great Bend of Hood Canal), turn west on Lake Cushman Rd. (Wash. 119). In 9 miles, turn right onto FS 25, continue 1.5 miles, and turn left onto FS 2419. Follow this road 6.5 miles and turn left onto FS 014 to reach the trailhead. Map: Green Trails Mount Steel and The Brothers, Custom Correct Mount Skokomish–Lake Cushman.

Unlike most other summit hikes in the Olympics, on which you end up on a broad, meadowed mountaintop, this trail brings you to the tip of a rocky peak with barely enough room for two people and a mountain goat to sit and admire the view. The trail starts near the timberline and follows a rocky chute skyward. This hike is best done in the summer or fall when the trail is well defined and cairns are visible to get you through a few boulder fields and scree slopes. In the spring (conditions permitting), an ice axe and faith in the footsteps of those who went before you are necessary. Personally, I prefer the snow trip, with its rapid glissading descent. It's a fairly short hike either way, but the view at the summit is always stupendous. Below you is the shimmering expanse of Lake Cushman. To the east lie Hood Canal, the Kitsap Pennisula, and the Cascades. To the north and west you are surrounded by a seemingly endless sea of craggy mountain peaks with Mount Olympus rising in the distance. Avoid the temptation to scout out a route to the adjacent peak of Mount Washington. There is no safe nontechnical route connecting the two.

Big Quilcene Trail/Marmot Pass

10.5 miles round-trip. Strenuous. 3,500-foot elevation gain. Access: From U.S. 101 about 2 miles south of Quilcene, turn west onto Penny Creek/Big Quilcene River Rd. In 1.5 miles, turn left onto FS 27 (Big Quilcene River Rd.) and follow signs for 15 miles to the Big Quilcene trailhead on FS 2750. Map: Green Trails Tyler Peak, Custom Correct Buckhorn Wilderness.

This long, straight trail climbs steadily along the upper reaches of the Big Quilcene River, and like so many trails in the Olympics, it starts low in old-growth forest and climbs to alpine meadows. The views begin after 2.5 miles of uphill trudging when the trail crosses a large scree field. Here the valley seems quite narrow, with the rock face opposite you almost within touching distance. Looking down the valley you can see Hood Canal, Puget Sound, and the Cascade Range, including Glacier Peak. A little more climbing brings you into the realm of the marmots, and yes, this place is just thick with the cute, fuzzy whistlers.

The pass itself is a wide, treeless saddle with wildflowers everywhere and a killer view of The Needles and Gray Wolf Ridge. Look for campsites along the ridgeline that runs uphill to the left, or find others by dropping down the far side of the saddle and turning north. There is also a good campsite 0.75 miles before you reach the pass at a spot called Camp Mystery. A great exploration destination from your campsite is the way trail up to the summit of 6,998-foot Buckhorn Mountain on the north side of the pass.

Mount Townsend

11 miles round-trip. Strenuous. 3,430-foot elevation gain. Access: From U.S. 101 about 2 miles south of Quilcene, turn west onto Penny Creek/Big Quilcene River Rd. In 1.5 miles, turn left onto FS 27 (Big Quilcene River Rd.), follow this road 14 miles, and turn left onto FS 2760 to reach the trailhead in 0.75 miles. Map: Green Trails Tyler Peak, Custom Correct Buckhorn Wilderness.

June is rhododendron season in the high country, and nowhere are there more superlative displays than on the Mount Townsend Trail. Keep in mind, however, that the path to the summit is not always clear of snow at this time of year, so it's a good idea to call the Quilcene Ranger District (tel. 360/765-2200) before you head out. Take a close look at your *Washington Atlas & Gazetteer* or trail map, and you'll see that there are two places to start this trail. The lower section has great rhodies and skirts the small Sink Lake before reaching the second trailhead in about 1 mile. From here the trail continues more steeply uphill, breaking into meadows and views in another half-mile. Another 2 miles of hiking brings you to Windy Lake and Windy Camp, where it is easy to lose the trail. However, as the track is well worn (it's the most popular summit hike on the peninsula), a little scouting will help you find it again. There are several good campsites here.

The trail now switchbacks up through open meadows with the view to the east getting bigger and better with each step. From the broad summit you can see Hood Canal, Bangor Submarine Base, the entire Kitsap Peninsula, the Cascades from Canada to Rainier, ferryboats on Puget Sound, and the tiny skyscrapers of Seattle. Look west and you'll see the solid rock wall of Gray Wolf Ridge rising more than 3,000 feet above the ancient forest of the Dungeness River valley. Close at hand are bizarrely shaped spires of pillow basalt extruded on the seafloor millions of years ago. From Mount Townsend's summit you can wander the ridgeline south toward campsites around Silver Lake, which is

It's Not Nice to Fool
with Mother Nature

Attempts to reengineer fragile eco systems often yield unintended results, as a grand scheme gone awry in Olympic National Park shows. Back in the 1920s, 11 mountain goats from Alaska and Canada were introduced to the higher elevations of the park. It was thought that these goats would make a great addition to the annual hunting season. Good idea; too bad it backfired. When this area became a national park, hunting was prohibited. The goats, with few predators to keep their numbers in check, have reproduced with admirable speed. However, the billies, as they battle for the privilege of mating with herds of nannies, have been destroying the mountains' fragile alpine meadows. These meadows are now deeply rutted with tracks dug by the sharp hooves of the goats. With the area's plentiful rains, erosion has become a serious problem in the high country. The National Park Service has for nearly two decades been struggling with various remedies to the goat problem. Capture and relocation has proven expensive and ineffective, and killing the goats has proven highly unpopular, especially with animal rights activists.

nestled in a cirque. Alternatively, you can drop down to Silver Creek and then head up Copper Creek toward Tubal Cain Mine for an extra day or two of wandering.

Royal Basin

14.5 miles round-trip. Moderate–strenuous. 2,750-foot elevation gain. Access: From U.S. 101 almost opposite Sequim Bay State Park, turn south on Louella Rd. In 1 mile, turn left on Palo Alto Rd. (FS 28), follow this road 6.5 miles, turn right on FS 2860, and continue 11.5 miles to the trailhead. Map: Green Trails Tyler Peak, Custom Correct Gray Wolf–Dosewallips.

This is a classic Olympic Mountains trail, starting in lush moss-covered low-country forest and climbing steadily to the lakes and spires above. From the parking lot the trail follows the Dungeness River through open old-growth forest that at times appears to be covered with green shag carpeting due to the unbelievably thick moss growing over absolutely everything, from boulders to nurse logs. At about 1 mile, where the trail reaches a junction with the trail to Camp Handy, stay right and begin the long walk up Royal Creek. As you climb you progress into fragrant subalpine forest that is crossed in several places by rather impressive avalanche tracks. Further on you reach a lovely meadow area where the creek has the most beautiful milky-blue glacial coloring I've ever seen. There are several campsites here, but keep your pack on—you're almost there.

As the trail climbs a glacial moraine out of the meadow, you are treated to views of Tyler Peak, Old Baldy, Gray Wolf Ridge, and The Needles, soon to be followed by the lovely Royal Lake. There are many excellent campsites around the lake, but you may wish to climb farther still, passing around a large (mosquito-filled) wetland that was once a lake, and picking a spot among the rocks at the base of glacier-clad Mount Deception.

Grand Valley

10 miles round-trip (to Gladys Lake). Moderate. 1,850-foot elevation gain (on the way out). Access: From U.S. 101 in Port Angeles, drive south 17 miles to Hurricane Ridge on Mount Angeles Rd. At Hurricane Ridge, turn left onto the dirt road to Obstruction Point and continue 8.5 miles to the end of the road. Map: Green Trails Mount Angeles, Custom Correct Gray Wolf–Dosewallips.

After the scenic and nauseating drive along the single-lane road that leads from Hurricane Ridge to the trailhead at Obstruction Point, you will likely have made peace with your god and be glad to leave your car behind. Glorious wilderness awaits you! Unlike most trails in the park, this one starts in the high country (6,200 feet) and then drops (and I mean drops!) into a lovely valley filled with lakes, meadows, and wildlife.

From the parking lot the trail crosses late summer snow fields as it makes its way along Lillian Ridge where marmots whistle and ptarmigans whoop. To your left looms the massive Elk Mountain and Grand Ridge, while below you lie the green flower fields and glittering blue lakes of the aptly named Grand Valley. Enjoy the moment, for you are about to make a Dante-like quad-burning descent down the side of Lillian Ridge. But it's paradise, not hell, that you are dropping into.

Come here in July for a floral show that rivals any in the Northwest. There are three lakes to choose from, strung like pearls along Grand Creek, in a classic glacial pattern, with each sitting behind its own morainal dam. Grand Lake is the biggest, lowest, and most visited of the three. It has many nice campsites. Moose Lake also has many campsites, is smaller, sits in a higher meadowed area, and is utterly devoid of its namesake. There is, however, a sizable and bold population of deer in the area. Wonderful wandering opportunities lie further up the valley, where the trail leads you to Gladys Lake, Grand Pass, and the oddly named 6701 Peak.

As an alternative route back, you can continue down the valley past Grand Lake and then turn west up the Badger Valley to reach Obstruction Point in only 1.3 miles more than on the more direct route back.

A national park backcountry camping permit is necessary if you plan to spend the night here.

Grand Ridge (Obstruction Point to Green Mountain)

11 miles round-trip. Moderate. 1,700-foot elevation gain. Access: From U.S. 101 in Port Angeles, drive south 17 miles to Hurricane Ridge on Mount Angeles Rd. At Hurricane Ridge, turn left onto the dirt road to Obstruction Point, and continue 8.5 miles to the end of the road. Map: Green Trails Mount Angeles, Custom Correct Hurricane Ridge.

There are few places in the world where you feel more poised between sea and sky than you do along this 6,000-foot-high trail. This is the highest section of trail in the park, above tree line for almost its entirety. Can you say *views?* Balanced on a knife-edge ridge for much of the hike, you look off to the north and see Victoria, the Canadian Cascades, and Mount Baker. At your feet lie the Straight of Juan de Fuca, the towns of Port Angeles and Sequim, and the lovely Dungeness Spit. Look the other way and you are treated to views of Grand Valley with its string of lakes, and the numerous snowclad peaks of the Olympic interior, including the glacier-laden volcanic Mount Olympus. Bring plenty to drink as there is no water or shade to be had on this hike. There are two ways to approach this hike: from the Deer Park trailhead or the Obstruction Peak trailhead. Go with Obstruction Peak.

From the parking lot follow the trail to the left (right takes you to Grand Valley) where it is carved into the south side of Obstruction Peak. Wind your way higher and higher, reaching Elk Mountain in two breathtaking miles. Drop into Roaring Winds Camp and then back up to Maiden Peak and, at 5.5 miles, Green Mountain. In late June the air here is filled with the fragrance of Lyle's lupine, which grows amid the loose scree and is a small, ground-hugging variety of that wildflower staple. This is a good turnaround point since the trail drops steeply from here, out of the views and into the fire-damaged forest surrounding Deer Park.

If you have two cars and just love driving miles of steep, one-lane gravel roads, you can park one car at Deer Park and make this a one-way hike. Either way, plan this as a day hike, since Roaring Winds has no water other than snowmelt and lives up to its name.

COASTAL HIKES

Dungeness Spit

Up to 12 miles round-trip. Easy–moderate. 100-foot elevation gain. Access: From U.S. 101 on the east side of Sequim, drive north on Kitchen–Dick Rd., turn right on Lotzgesell Rd., and then left into the recreation area. Map: Not necessary.

This is a lovely place to stroll for miles along the shore of the Strait of Juan de Fuca, with its slow-moving traffic of ships (and sometimes Trident submarines) arriving from and departing to points all across the globe. Across the water is British Columbia's Vancouver Island and the town of Victoria. To the south and closer at hand are the snowy peaks of the Olympic Range, and the glacial mass of Mount Baker. This is a prime spot for bird watching, so don't come without your binoculars. From the parking area, where campsites are located along the bluffs to the left, take the trail at the east end of the lot into the forest. A short, canopied half-mile brings you to the start of the spit. Don't be discouraged by the abundance of families and exuberant kids—these will virtually vanish by the end of the first mile. Soon the only sound you will hear is the rattle of wave-tossed gravel and the calls of seabirds.

As you continue down the impossibly long sandbar, you will pass all manner of marine debris, from net floats and beach logs, to the boats of last season's unfortunates who went when they should have stayed. The farther you go the more likely you will be to encounter the spit's rather shy population of harbor seals. If you have the energy, definitely go all the way to the end (about 6 miles) to the lighthouse. When I was there, the wife of the Coast Guard officer who manned the station took us on a tour of the facility. She gave me a piece of advice I should share with you: Avoid the temptation to make a "round-trip" out of it by walking back along the landward side of the spit. A protrusion of the spit on this side will add an extra 6 miles to your trip.

Cape Alava-Sand Point-Yellow Banks Loop

6–13.3 miles. Easy–moderate. 200-foot elevation gain. Access: From U.S. 101, drive north on Wash. 113 for 10 miles and continue toward Neah Bay on Wash. 112 for another 11 miles. Turn left on Hoko–Ozette Rd. and continue to the end of the road. Map: Green Trails Ozette, Custom Correct Ozette Beach Loop.

There are several options hiking from the Lake Ozette parking lot, and each has

plenty to recommend it. Two boardwalk trails start here, each of them about 3 miles long and ending at the beach. For a day hike I recommend taking the less-used northern boardwalk trail and turning south once you reach the shore. This will take you around Cape Alava with its many deer and bald eagles. This cape is the westernmost point in the continental United States. There are plenty of tide pools to explore and sea stacks to look at all along the walk, but most interesting are the petroglyphs carved into a rocky headland about 1.5 miles from where the trail reached the beach. Another 1.5 miles beyond the petroglyphs brings you to the raccoon-infested campground at Sand Point, where the other boardwalk takes you back to the parking lot.

If you prefer to backpack, I would suggest taking the southern boardwalk and heading south once you reach the Sand Point campground. A lovely stretch of beach called Yellow Banks lies just 2 miles south on the far side of several small headlands. Several wonderful tent sites lie nestled in the forest just behind the high-tide jumble of drift logs. This is a top choice for Olympic coastal camping, with deer, seals, eagles, and even sea otters to keep you company. Sunsets, sea stacks, bioluminescence, fires on the beach—what more could you ask for? Just be sure to use a tide table when crossing the headlands, some of which are a little tricky to negotiate with a pack on your back.

North Wilderness Coast Hike (Lake Ozette to Rialto Beach)

20.8–24.1 miles. Moderate–strenuous. 400-foot elevation gain. Access: From U.S. 101, drive north on Wash. 113 for 10 miles and continue toward Neah Bay on Wash. 112 for another 11 miles. Turn left on Hoko–Ozette Rd. and continue to the end of the road. Map: Green Trails Ozette, Custom Correct North Olympic Coast.

The 20.8-mile stretch of coast from Cape Alava to Rialto Beach is the longest uninterrupted stretch of the Olympic National Park's coastal strip. It is also the easiest of this coastal strip's three hikes. Starting at Lake Ozette, it is possible to hike to Cape Alava and follow the beach all the way to the mouth of the Quillayute River at Rialto Beach. Plan on three to four days to complete this hike. You'll need to set up a car shuttle, so be sure to factor this into the time you allot for the hike. It is more than 60 miles by car between the trailhead at Ozette Lake and the trailhead at Rialto Beach.

All but one of the headlands on this stretch of coast can be rounded at low tide, and for the most part, these headlands do not have alternate over-the-top trails. This means that to hike this stretch of coast, you must be especially aware of the tides. Be sure to carry a tide table for the dates of your hike. You may be able to avoid hours-long waits for the tide to go out, and it might be possible to round this or the other headland. There are also no major streams to ford. Along the entire route there are many good campsites either on the beach or tucked back in the trees.

HORSEBACK RIDING

The Olympic Peninsula may not exactly feel like the Wild West, but there are several places where you can saddle up and hit the trail. **R. D. N. Ranch,** 258053 U.S. 101 (tel. 360/457-3923 or 360/452-9656), located outside of Port Angeles, offers rides of varying lengths in the foothills of the Olympic Mountains.

Out in the town of Neah Bay, on the Makah Indian Reservation, there are a couple of stables that offer guided beach rides. **Ray's Horseback Rides** (tel. 360/6435-2391) offers inexpensive one-hour rides, while **Tsoo–Yess River Ranch** (tel. 360/645-2391) offers one- and two-hour rides on beaches about 6 miles west of Neah Bay.

HOT SPRINGS

There are two readily accessible hot springs in Olympic National Forest. One is developed, and the other used to be but has long since reverted to a somewhat natural state.

Sol Duc Hot Springs (tel. 360/327-3583) is the one *everybody* goes to. With cabins, a restaurant, and a campground, Sol Duc is certainly not for solitude seekers or lovers of hot springs *au naturelle*. But if the thought of a swim in a hot springs–fed pool surrounded by verdant forests of evergreens or a soak in a private tub followed by a massage is appealing, this place will probably have you sighing with contentment. Just be prepared for the sort of scene you remember from a hot day at the public pool when you were a kid. To reach these hot springs, drive 4 miles west from Fairholm Store at the west end of Lake Crescent, turn left onto Soleduck River Road, and continue 14 miles to the springs.

Olympic Hot Springs, on the other hand, is in a natural setting a 2.2-mile walk from the trailhead on an abandoned road. Unfortunately, despite the fact that there are numerous soaking pools scattered throughout the woods, they still get crowded, especially on summer weekends. The best advice I can give is get an early start. If you're up here just after dawn, you beat the majority of the crowds and may even get a nice quiet soak by yourself. Nude bathing is the norm here, although it is officially prohibited. To reach these springs, drive south on the Olympic Hot Springs Road, which begins at the southern end of Lake Aldwell about 8 miles west of Port Angeles. Follow this road almost to Lake Mills and cross over to the west side of the Elwha River and continue to the end of this road. The trail/abandoned road to the springs can also be ridden on a mountain bike.

MOUNTAIN BIKING

The first and most important thing to know about mountain biking on the Olympic Peninsula is that almost all trails in Olympic National Park are closed to bikes (the exceptions to this rule are mentioned below). Bikes can be rented at **Pedal 'n' Paddle,** 120 E Front St., Port Angeles (tel. 360/457-1240), which can recommend good rides and also offers bicycle tours, and at **Rainforest Rentals,** 6540 E Beach Rd. (tel. 360/928-2269), at Lake Crescent's Log Cabin Resort (close to the Spruce Railroad Trail).

Foothills Trail

8 miles. Strenuous. 900-foot elevation gain.
Access: From Port Angeles, go south on Pine

St., which becomes Old Black Diamond Rd., for 4.8 miles; turn left on Little River Rd. Go 1.1 miles, turn left on Foothills Trail Rd., and drive 0.2 miles to the trailhead. Map: Green Trails Port Angeles, Custom Correct Hurricane Ridge.

Lying just to the south of Port Angeles, between U.S. 101 and the Olympic National Park boundary, is a low range of hills known as The Foothills. The land belongs to the Washington Department of Natural Resources (DNR), and is crossed by a maze of ORV trails. Although not very extensive, these trails offer some great, and challenging, riding. A modified figure-eight loop through this forest is a good introduction to these trails.

From the trailhead, head east on single-track and climb for a mile to a trail junction. Go left here and continue climbing for more than a mile as the trail contours around one of the area's biggest hills. When this trail reaches the end of a road, ride down this road for 0.25 miles to a spur road on the right. Up this side road is an excellent view across the Strait of Juan de Fuca to Vancouver Island. Head back up these roads to where you left the trail and take the other trail from the road's end. From here it is 2 miles of great up-and-down riding to the next major trail junction. Take a right here on a connector trail and quickly reach another trail junction. Turn left to circle around another of those Foothills. In 1 mile, keep left at a trail junction, and in another mile, close the loop at the junction with the connector trail you took to start this loop. If you liked the loop, do it again; otherwise, ride the connector to the next trail junction, and instead of going left, turn right. From here it is 1 mile to the trail that started you on this figure eight and 2 miles to the trailhead.

Gold Creek Loop

18.5 miles. Strenuous. 3,100-foot elevation gain. Access: Map: USGS Mount Zion and Tyler Peak, Green Trails Tyler Peak.

This is likely the most popular mountain-biking trail on the entire Olympic Peninsula, and justly so. There are views of both snow-covered peaks and the Strait of Juan de Fuca, good gravel road (with some

high-speed descents), and best of all, 6.5 miles of very challenging, roller-coaster single-track complete with creek crossings, switchbacks, cliffside riding, and lots of mud most of the year (for the sake of the trail, however, it is wise to ride only when the mud has dried).

The ride starts with a grueling 2,000-foot climb in the first 3 miles, and once you top out, you should be sure to take time to enjoy the views—the strait of Juan de Fuca to the north and the snowcapped peaks of the Buckhorn Wilderness to the south. To the east stands Dirty Face Ridge, along the lower slopes of which you will be riding when you hit the single-track. About 0.75 miles from this viewpoint, the road tilts downward and, in the next 5 miles, you lose half of the elevation you just gained. I know it hurts to lose all that elevation, but at least the descent is fast and fun. The road then climbs for 3.75 miles to regain that lost 1,000 feet and reach the Gold Creek Trail on the left. Take a breather, then let the fun begin.

The trail winds through clear-cuts and rhododendron groves (June is flowering season), and across steep cliffs where the trail tread is dangerously narrow. In about 3.5 miles, reach a clear-cut with a trail junction and keep left to stay on the Gold Creek Trail. As the trail passes through dense stands of second-growth trees, pay attention to the many roots across the trail. To let the attention stray is to beg an endo. Although the trail is mostly downhill, there is some climbing to be done before you finally bottom back at your car.

As you ride up FS 2860, you will twice pass the **Lower Dungeness Trail**—once at less than a half-mile and the second time at 8.5 miles. If you're interested in a shorter (15 miles) though no less challenging ride, peel off FS 2860 at this upper crossing of the Lower Dungeness Trail and hold on tight. Switchbacks abound on this grueling trail. Looking for the ultimate challenge? Try riding up the Gold Creek Trail and down the Lower Dungeness Trail or vice versa.

Spruce Railroad Trail

11 miles round-trip. Easy. 150-foot elevation gain. Access: Drive 25 miles west from Port Angeles

on U.S. 101 to the west end of Lake Crescent, turn right onto North Shore Rd., and continue 3.5 miles to the North Shore Picnic Area. Map: USGS Lake Crescent, Custom Correct Lake Crescent–Happy Lake Ridge.

This trail, which as its name implies was once a railroad grade, is the only Olympic National Park trail of any length that is open to bicycles. Though flat and quite easy for its 4-mile length, it stays close to the shore of the lake and provides outstanding views. Should it be hot enough, there are even places where you can get down to the water for a swim. Just keep an eye out for poison oak. The highlight of the trail is a much-photographed arched bridge across a rocky cove. Although you can start this ride at the end of North Shore Road, which is the trailhead for the Spruce Railroad Trail, the last 1.5 miles of road from the North Shore Picnic Area see little traffic and are very scenic, well worth the extra 3 miles on this out-and-back route.

PACKSTOCK TRIPS

R. D. N. Ranch, 258053 U.S. 101 (tel. 360/457-3923 or 360/452-9656), located outside of Port Angeles, offers overnight rides into the foothills of the Olympic Mountains. However, if you'd rather have a llama carry your gear, you've got several options in this area. **Wooley Packer Llama Co.,** 5763 Upper Hoh Rd., Forks, WA 98331 (tel. 360/374-9288), offers trips of up to seven days within Olympic National Park. **Kit's Llamas,** P.O. Box 116, Olalla, WA 98359 (tel. 360/857-5274), offers day hikes as well as overnight trips. **Olympak Llamas,** 3175 Old Olympic Hwy., Port Angeles, WA 98362 (tel. 360/452-4475), specializes in trips up the Elwha Valley and within the national park.

ROAD BIKING

If you don't mind heavy traffic (including lots of logging trucks) on narrow winding roads with lots of long hills, why not consider the ride around the Olympic Peninsula? Surprisingly, many people do. Actually, if you start at Port Angeles, you can do quite a bit of riding on Wash. 112,

which goes all the way to Neah Bay on the Makah Indian Reservation. From this road you can also ride out to Ozette Lake on the Hoko–Ozette Road, and if you're so inclined, connect to U.S. 101 by way of Wash. 113 for a total of nearly 150 miles of riding off U.S. 101. If you continue south from the crossroads of Sappho, taking in such Olympic National Park sites as the beaches north and south of La Push and the Hoh Rain Forest, and continue onward to Lake Quinault, you can put together a ride of almost 300 miles. A very respectable road trip.

The main drawback to this ride, other than those already mentioned, is weather. Although July and August are considerably sunnier than the other months of the year out here, the likelihood of getting a week without rain (long enough to do this ride) is very small. Plan to get wet. Luckily, an abundance of campgrounds along the route makes short days a possibility, and with public buses running all along La Push, if you decide to give it up, you can catch a bus back to your starting point from much of the route.

For leisurely cycling, it's hard to beat the historic neighborhoods of Port Townsend. You won't put on a lot of miles here, but, if you're interested in Victorian architecture, you'll have a lot of fun. Pedal up and down these streets admiring the Victorian homes, and when you've worked up an appetite, coast down the bluff on Washington Street to reach the restaurants and shops of downtown.

Sequim Loop

33 miles. Moderate. 850-foot elevation gain. Access: Start this ride at Sequim Bay State Park on U.S. 101 east of the town of Sequim.

Because it lies within the rain shadow created by the Olympic Mountains, Sequim receives less than 20 inches of rain per year, which makes it a great place to ride year-round. The farms and pastures of Sequim Prairie provide a rural setting unique on the Olympic Peninsula, and quiet country roads are perfect for pedaling. Along the way, you can stop at a winery and visit a wild-animal park where many of the residents are former film and TV stars. Only the first and last 0.6 miles of the ride are on busy U.S. 101.

From Sequim Bay State Park, which has picnic areas and a campground, ride north on U.S. 101 for 0.6 miles. Turn right onto West Sequim Bay Road and ride close to the bay, passing John Wayne Marina, land donated by "the Duke." After 3.3 miles on this road, turn right onto Washington Harbor Road. In 0.7 miles, turn left onto Schmuck Road. In 1.5 miles, turn left onto Port Williams Road, and in another 1.5 miles pass the old cooling tower that was once used to keep milk fresh before it could be shipped to Seattle. In another 0.7 miles, reach the Sequim–Dungeness Road and turn right. Pedal north for 1.5 miles and turn left onto Woodcock Road. Ride west for 2.3 miles, crossing the Dungeness River, and turn right onto Ward Road. You will soon be riding past fields where the buffalo roam and the deer and the antelope play. These are some of the animals of the Olympic Game Farm, which is reached in 1.5 miles. The farm was started in the 1940s to provide animal footage for Walt Disney movies but today is more concerned with breeding endangered animals. Guided tours are offered throughout the summer.

Beyond the farm, turn right on Lotzgesell Road and go a half-mile to Marine Drive. Turn left here and follow this road along a bluff overlooking the Dungeness Spit, which is a national wildlife refuge frequented by many species of birds, as well as harbor seals. This is about the most scenic stretch of road on the whole ride. In 2.7 miles, turn left back onto Lotzgesell Road and continue 1.5 miles to Voice of America Road. Turn right on this road to enter the Dungeness Spit Recreation Area, which has a picnic area and campground and is adjacent to the wildlife refuge. This is a good place for lunch and some bird watching or a walk on the beach.

From the recreation area, ride back to Lotzgesell Road, turn right, and follow this road as it curves around to the south and becomes Kitchen–Dick Road. In 1.2 miles, reach Woodcock Road, turn left, and pedal 1.5 miles to Cays Road. Turn right and go a half-mile to the Old Olympic Highway and turn left. In 2.4 miles, go left to stay on Old Olympic Highway, which soon becomes Port Williams Road. In 1.5 miles, turn right onto Brown Road and pedal 1 mile south to U.S. 101, cross the highway, and continue as this road curves around to the left to reach U.S. 101 again. Make a sharp right turn here on Still Road to reach the Neuharth Olympic Cellars winery in 0.25 miles. After tasting a few wines, head back north to U.S. 101 and turn right, crossing the highway, onto West Sequim Bay Road. Follow this road first east and then south as it reaches Sequim Bay. Pass the John Wayne Marina again and continue south to pick up that last stretch of U.S. 101 before returning to Sequim Bay State Park.

SCUBA DIVING

Novice divers who haven't yet mastered the skill of drift diving or predicting slack currents will appreciate the waters off **Potlatch State Park,** south of Hoodsport on the Great Bend of Hood Canal. Although the waters are somewhat clouded by the nearby outflow of the Skokomish River, it is still clear enough to be a good dive site. The park is located between Shelton and Hoodsport on U.S. 101.

In Port Townsend, divers will find an underwater park at **Fort Worden State Park,** a former military base. Near the wharf, on the park's east shore, there are pilings to explore, while on the north shore, off Point Wilson, there are submerged rocks that house an amazing variety of sea life. Currents can be quite strong here, so time your dive for slack current. To reach the park, follow the signs from downtown Port Townsend. Also in the area, **Fort Flagler State Park** on Marrowstone Island has an underwater park off the wharf on the park's east beach. To reach this park, take Wash. 116 east from Wash. 19, south of Port Townsend, and follow signs to the park. If you have a boat, **Klas and Colvos rocks,** about a half-mile off the mouth of Mats Mats Bay, between Port Townsend and Port Ludlow, is another good dive site, but only if the winds are calm and the tide is slack. For equipment, air, rentals, and advice in the Port Townsend area, contact **Orca Divers,** 1761 Irondale Rd. (tel. 360/385-5688) in

Port Hadlock. The protected waters of Clallam Bay, out toward the northwest tip of the peninsula, are a favorite diving area. In the the town of Sekiu, you can get air, equipment, rentals, and advice at **Sekiu Dive Shop** (tel. 360/963-2281), which is on the main road through the town.

SEA KAYAKING & FLAT-WATER CANOEING

In Port Townsend, **Kayak Port Townsend,** 1044 Water St. (P.O. Box 1387), Port Townsend, WA 98368 (tel. 360/385-6240), offers both guided kayak tours and kayak rentals. **Olympic Outdoor Center,** P.O. Box 2247, Poulsbo, WA 98370 (tel. 800/659-6095 or 360/697-6095), offers guided kayak trips and kayaking lessons at Dungeness Spit. Kayak tours in this area are also offered by **Pedal 'n' Paddle,** 120 E Front St., Port Angeles (tel. 360/457-1240), and **Olympic Raft & Guide Service,** 239521 U.S. 101 W, Port Angeles (tel. 360/452-1443).

Mystery Bay and Indian Island

2–12 miles. Easy–moderate. Access: From Wash. 19 south of Port Townsend, follow signs to Port Hadlock and follow Wash. 116 across Port Townsend Canal to Indian Island, where you will pass a county park and an unsigned pull-off, both of which provide water access. Continuing up Wash. 116 on Marrowstone Island, you will come to Mystery Bay State Park, which has a boat ramp. At the north end of Marrowstone Island, there is another boat ramp at Fort Flagler State Park.

Because most of Indian Island is a naval base, the island's shores still have a wild, undeveloped look about them. These wild shores act like a magnet for area paddlers. Although it isn't possible to go ashore except at the southern end of the island, the longshore paddling is very scenic, especially at the island's south end. One of the most interesting stretches of this island's shoreline is along its southwest corner in the Port Townsend Canal. Here, low cliffs topped with madrona trees are reminiscent of some of the wilder shores of the San Juan Islands. A couple of launch spots at the south end of the island

provide easy access to this part of the island, but paddlers need to be familiar with currents and paddle with the tides to enjoy this area. This southern end is also open to the strong southerly winds that blow up the Puget Sound, especially in the winter months.

More protected paddling is in and around Mystery Bay, which is on the west shore of Marrowstone Island. From here it is possible to explore this little bay and then cross Kilisut Harbor to the middle of the east shore of Indian Island. Exploring southward is your best bet if you're looking for scenic shoreline. However, if you head north to the mouth of Kilisut Harbor at Fort Flagler State Park, you might encounter the area's resident harbor seals. Strong paddlers often paddle all the way around Indian Island, either portaging across the causeway between Indian and Marrowstone islands or, when the tide is right, paddling through the culvert that connects Kilisut Harbor from Oak Bay.

Dungeness Spit National Wildlife Refuge

Distance varies up to 10 miles. Easy–moderate. Access: From U.S. 101, drive north on Sequim–Dungeness Way, turn onto Marine Dr., and continue to Cline Spit County Park.

The Dungeness Spit is well known as a great bird-watching spot where waterfowl and shorebirds of many species can be seen. A paddle around the protected waters within the bay formed by the spit provides ample opportunities for observing these many bird species. However, likely to be of even greater interest to paddlers are the harbor seals that frequent these waters. Any paddle around these waters, especially if you head out toward the end of the spit, is likely to bring you close to harbor seals (or is it they who come close to you?). If the weather is calm enough, you can also paddle along the outer edge of the spit on the waters of the Strait of Juan de Fuca. These waters can be reached by paddling around the end of the spit or by portaging across the flat, narrow sand spit. The campground in the adjacent Dungeness Spit Recreation Area makes this a great spot for an overnight kayaking trip. However, the campground is a short drive from the best launch site, which is located off Marine Drive at Cline Spit County Park.

Lake Crescent

Distance varies. Easy–moderate. Access: Boat ramps can be found on U.S. 101 at Rosemary (near the middle of the lake) and at Fairholm (at the west end of the lake). On E Beach Rd., on the lake's northeast shore, there is a private boat ramp at the Log Cabin Resort.

Although large and often windy, glacier-carved Lake Crescent is a beautiful place to do a little paddling. Lush, green forests rise straight up from the shores of this 900-foot-deep lake, giving these waters a fjord-like quality unmatched anywhere on the peninsula. If you launch at Rosemary, you can explore around Barnes Point, away from U.S. 101 traffic noise (but in view of the Lake Crescent Lodge). From Fairholm, you can paddle along the north shore, and from the Log Cabin Resort, you can explore the narrow bay that feeds the Lyre River, the lake's outlet stream. When winds blow down this lake, as they often do, the waters can become very danger-ous for small boats. Keep an eye on the weather. Capsizing in these cold waters can very quickly lead to hypothermia.

If you haven't got your own boat, you can rent a canoe at **Fairholm General Store** (tel. 360/928-3020), at the west end of the lake, or at the **Log Cabin Resort,** 3183 E Beach Rd. (tel. 360/928-3325), on the lake's northeast shore.

Crescent Bay

2–6 miles. Easy–difficult. Access: From Port Angeles, go west on U.S. 101 and turn onto Wash. 112. Follow this road 7 miles west and turn right onto Camp Hayden Rd.

Although this shallow bay west of Port Angeles is exposed to large swells that roll down the Strait of Juan de Fuca, the wild-lands along the shore make this one of the most interesting paddling areas on the north side of the Olympic Peninsula. Pick a day when the winds are calm, and, if you can, listen to a weather radio to make sure the swells are small. If you can find

just the right conditions, you'll be treated to a beautiful stretch of rocky shoreline, much of which is preserved as Clallam County's Salt Creek County Park and the Washington Department of Natural Resource's land. At low tide, the county park's Tongue Point area shelters numer-ous tide pools, and at higher tides, you may be able to paddle over these same pools, observing starfish and anemones as you go. Paddle west across the bay and around a rocky headland to Agate Bay or east around Tongue Point for 3 miles to the more protected waters of Freshwater Bay. You won't find a more beautiful stretch of shoreline anywhere on the northern peninsula.

Lake Ozette

5–25 miles. Easy–difficult. Access: Lake Ozette is located at the end of the Hoko–Ozette Rd., which goes south from Wash. 112 west of Clallam Bay. There are three boat launches on the lake: at Swan Bay; on the Hoko–Ozette Rd. where it first reaches the lake; and at the end of the Hoko–Ozette Rd. near the Ozette Ranger Sta-tion.

Lake Ozette, 300 feet deep, nearly 10 miles long, and the third largest natural lake in Washington, is a fascinating place to explore by sea kayak or canoe. Situated only a mile from the Pacific Ocean, the lake is indented by numerous coves and bays, both large and small, and three small islands dot its waters. There are campsites along the shore of the lake (including the boat-in Ericksons Bay Campground), and a trail leads from the lake to the ocean.

The Swan Bay boat launch is probably the best choice for paddlers heading out on this large lake. For a leisurely half-day paddle, just explore the shores of this con-voluted bay, in the middle of which is Garden Island. For a day-long paddle, try heading down the lake to Tivoli Island. For an overnighter, head to the lake's west shore and the Ericksons Bay Campground. From here, you can explore up and down the west shore.

Because this lake is so large, it can get very rough if the wind picks up. Check the weather forecast before heading out and always keep an eye on the sky.

SNOWSHOEING

If the Olympic Mountains aren't very good for cross-country skiing, they're at least good for snowshoeing. Any snow-covered road leading into the mountains will offer some sort of winter walking. However, if it's views you seek (and don't we all), then head to **Hurricane Ridge** with all t he rest of the winter crowd and set out on any of the area's trails. Snowshoe rentals are available at the Hurricane Ridge Lodge.

SURFING

Tucked under Vancouver Island as it is, the north side of the Olympic Peninsula does not offer a lot of surfing options. However, when the storms roll in from just the right direction, the waves roll down the Strait of Juan de Fuca and are picked off by a few points of land that create good conditions. **North Beach County Park,** in Port Townsend, is a long way from the open waters of the Pacific, but sometimes the waves are good enough to make it worthwhile to pull on the wetsuit and wax the board.

For the best waves on the north Olympic coast, head to the **mouth of the Elwha River** when the swell is running 4 to 6 feet (usually in the middle of winter). At this height, the waves are perfectly shaped! For the very best waves, plan to be here when the tide is out. To reach this primo surf spot, drive west from Port Angeles on Wash. 112, and, 1.5 miles after crossing the Elwha River, turn right on Place Road, follow the road to its end, and turn right onto Elwha Dike Road.

About 11 miles west of the Elwha mouth, you can also find good waves on Crescent Bay at **Salt Creek County Park,** which must be the prettiest surfing spot in the whole Northwest—sand beach, rocky cliffs, a tiny forest-topped island. To reach this beach, turn north off of Wash. 112 on Camp Hayden Road and follow it to the park.

Neah Bay, way out at the northwestern corner of the peninsula, is just about the most exposed spot on the entire north shore and consequently gets the most frequent rideable waves. To reach Neah Bay,

> **"If that not be the home wherein dwell the Gods, it is beautiful enough to be, and I therefore call it Mount Olympus."**
>
> **—Capt. John Meares, 1788**

follow Wash. 112 west from Port Angeles, or take U.S. 101 west to Wash. 113 and then on to Wash. 112.

SWIMMING & TUBING

It doesn't often get warm enough and sunny enough on the Olympic Peninsula to make swimming a high priority with most people, but there are those occasional days.

Down the east side of the peninsula, along Hood Canal, there are a few places worth checking out. However, by far the most popular is **Lake Cushman State Park.** The large lake for which this park is named is a favorite of water skiers, but in the park itself, there is also a designated swimming beach with a little island just offshore. To reach the park, drive U.S. 101 to Hoodsport and follow the Lake Cushman Road (Wash. 119) to the park.

West of Port Angeles, there are a couple of lake's that are shallow enough that their waters warm sufficiently for swimming to be almost enjoyable. **Lake Sutherland,** just east of Lake Crescent, is perhaps the most popular of these. However, this lake is highly developed, with houses all along its shore. There is public access on the south shore of the lake. **Lake Crescent** is so deep that it stays cold throughout the year, but along the Spruce Railroad Trail on the lake's north shore, there is a little cove, crossed by an arched wooden bridge, that is a very tempting spot to jump in if you have been hiking or biking on a hot summer day. East Beach County Park, in the northeast corner of the Lake Crescent on East Beach Road, is the most popular swimming spot on the lake. Farther west, just past Sappho where U.S. 101 turns south, there is a swimming beach on **Lake Pleasant.** At the north end of **Lake Ozette,** there is a designated swimming beach at the Ozette Campground.

If you aren't a member of the polar bear club, but do like to swim, you'll find the peninsula's warmest water in the big swimming pool at **Sol Duc Hot Springs.** It doesn't get much better than this! To reach these hot springs, drive 4 miles west from Fairholm Store at the west end of Lake Crescent, turn left onto Soleduck River Road, and continue 14 miles to the springs.

WALKS & NATURAL ROADSIDE ATTRACTIONS

Hurricane Hill Trail

3 miles round-trip. Easy. 550-foot elevation gain. Access: From U.S. 101 in Port Angeles, drive 17 miles south on Mount Angeles/Hurricane Ridge Rd. to the Hurricane Ridge Lodge and parking area. Map: Green Trails Port Angeles, Custom Correct Hurricane Ridge.

Short but spectacular is the best way to describe this trail atop Hurricane Ridge. Starting from the end of the road, the trail climbs through gorgeous meadows of wildflowers, where black-tailed deer are often seen grazing. From the summit of 5,757-foot Hurricane Hill, the view to the south takes in the heart of the Olympic Mountains and to the north can be seen the Strait of Juan de Fuca and the town of Port Angeles. Because it offers the most stunning scenery with the least amount of effort, this trail is always busy during the summer months.

Marymere Falls

2 miles round-trip. Easy. 200-foot elevation gain. Access: The trailhead is just off U.S. 101 beside the Storm King Ranger Station on Lake Crescent. Map: Not necessary.

Set at the end of a short trail through lush old-growth forest, 90-foot-tall Marymere Falls plummet through a crack in the rock of a high cliff. The trail to the falls, which follows Barnes Creek, is mostly flat, but after crossing a bridge over the creek, it switchbacks a bit to a viewpoint. Barnes Creek below the falls is a spawning ground

for Lake Crescent's unique Crescenti cutthroat trout.

Sol Duc Falls

1.4 miles. Easy. 50-foot elevation gain. Access: Drive 4 miles west from Fairholm Store at the west end of Lake Crescent, turn left onto Soleduck River Rd., and continue 15 miles to the end of the road. Map: Not necessary.

Although at only 40 feet tall these falls are not as imposing as Marymere Falls, they lie in a beautiful little gorge. An old wooden footbridge crosses the gorge below the falls, providing a head-on view of the cascades. It is possible to turn this into a 4.5-mile level-loop hike by starting at Sol Duc Hot Springs and hiking up one side of the Sol Duc River and down the other.

WHALE WATCHING

Between October and May, gray whales migrate past the coast of the Olympic Peninsula. From the waterfront park in the town of **Clallam Bay** (on Wash. 112 west of Port Angeles), it is often possible to see migrating whales as they feed in kelp beds that are just offshore. Late October is the best time to see whales here. Farther west, **Cape Flattery,** the peninsula's northwestern tip and the most northwesterly point in the contiguous United States, is another good place from which to spot migrating gray whales. **Cape Alava,** which is accessible via a 3.3-mile trail from Lake Ozette, is yet another good whale-watching spot if you don't mind a 6.6-mile round-trip hike.

WHITEWATER KAYAKING & CANOEING

Although the Olympic Mountains generate an astounding number of runnable rivers, the best of these are on the west side of the peninsula and along the southern slopes of the Olympic Mountains. However, the east and north sides of the peninsula do offer some good runs. As elsewhere in the Northwest, sweepers, strainers, and logjams are always a problem on the Olympic Peninsula's steep, narrow rivers.

If you're interested in taking a whitewater kayaking class, contact **Olympic Outdoor Center,** P.O. Box 2247, Poulsbo, WA 98370 (tel. 800/659-6095 or 360/697-6095), which offers five-day kayaking classes on the Elwha River.

CLASS II

The **Elwha River** is one of the few rivers on the Olympic Peninsula that is run by commercial rafting companies. The run, which starts at Altaire Campground on Olympic Hot Springs Road, is also popular with kayakers, even though it is only between 3 and 4.5 miles long. Lots of Class II+ rapids (some say Class III) keep paddlers entertained, and the shuttle is short enough that you can do the run several times in a day if you're so inclined. The take-out is just downstream from the national park boundary alongside the road. Two dams on this river many soon be removed to restore salmon runs, and if this happens, the entire character of this river could change.

CLASS III

On the **Dosewallips River,** west of Brinnon and U.S. 101, there is a put-in off Dosewallips Road that provides access to a fun 6.5-mile run that ends at Dosewallips State Park. The last half mile of this scenic run is through the state park. Take out at the U.S. 101 bridge.

West of Port Angeles, the **Sol Duc River** offers up an astounding 23 miles of Class III whitewater, with numerous access points. The first of these is about 5.5 miles west of Fairholm Store (west end of Lake Crescent) on FS 2918. The next is at Klahowya Campground. A third is about 5.5 miles west of Klahowya at Bear Creek Campground on the south side of U.S. 101, 2 miles east of Sappho. A fourth access is at the Sol Duc Salmon Hatchery, and a fifth is nearby at the Tumbling Rapids Campground.

CLASS IV & V

If you're searching for some Class IV water to get the adrenaline really pumping, there are several peninsula rivers to accommodate you. The upper reaches of the **Dosewallips River** border on unrunnable, but the Class IV and V waters here do attract a few dedicated maniacs. On the **Elwha River,** you can put in above Altaire Campground to add a Class IV drop to that run.

WHITEWATER RAFTING

The steep mountains and plentiful rains of the Olympic Peninsula are the source of some great whitewater rafting on the Elwha River. If you'd like to dig in a paddle, contact **Olympic Raft & Guide Service,** 239521 U.S. 101 W, Port Angeles, WA 98363 (tel. 360/452-1443). Rates start at $35.

WILDLIFE VIEWING

In autumn, after the season's first heavy rains, the salmon still return to the Olympic Peninsula despite the decimation of runs throughout the region. Places to watch adult **salmon** make their fateful trips back upriver to spawn can be found all around the peninsula. Off of U.S. 101, 9 miles up the Dosewallips Road from Brinnon, which is on Hood Canal, there are several ponds where salmon can be seen. The Salmon Cascades Interpretive Area on Sol Duc Hot Springs Road is just about the most convenient place to view salmon. The Hoko River west of Clallam Bay on Hoko–Ozette Road is another good spot to see leaping salmon. Stop at the bridge that is 5 miles south of Wash. 112 on the Hoko–Ozette Road. The Sooes River, on the Makah Indian Reservation south of Cape Flattery, is another good place to watch salmon as they journey up this river to a salmon hatchery.

Harbor seals are fairly common in the waters around the Olympic Peninsula, but even so, it's always fun to watch the antics of these lithe pinnipeds. If you happen to be down at the south end of the Hood Canal on U.S. 101, look for harbor seals off the mouth of the Skokomish River. The mouth of the Duckabush River, at Pleasant Harbor State Park, is another good place to scan the waters for harbor seals. Farther north along U.S. 101, which parallels Hood Canal, at Dosewallips State Park, harbor seals have become so common that they are considered pests by some people. They frequently are seen lounging on the beach here or feeding just off the mouth of the Dosewallips River. Walk the park's beach access trail to reach the best viewing area. In Fort Flagler State Park on Marrowstone Island (south of Port Townsend), you can often see seals hauled out on the sand spit at the far west side of the park. This spit curves around the entrance to Kilisut Harbor, which lies between Marrowstone and Indian islands. Harbor seals can also be seen at Dungeness Spit National Wildlife Refuge, where they tend to stay toward the far end of the spit.

At Cape Flattery, the northwesternmost point in the contiguous states, you may spot some of the region's few **sea otters** bobbing in the kelp beds just offshore. Before the arrival of whites in the Northwest, sea otters were plentiful in these waters, but it was the fur of these animals, highly prized in China, that brought traders into the region. The population was soon almost completely wiped out. To reach Cape Flattery, drive Wash. 112 to Neah Bay and continue through town, following signs onto gravel roads that lead out to the cape. Car break-ins are common at the Cape Flattery parking area, so be sure to take all your valuables with you. Sea otters can also be seen off Cape Alava, which is reached by a 3-mile trail from Lake Ozette.

Olympic marmots are among the most frequently sighted animals within Olympic National Park. These furry cousins of the squirrel are similar to the hoary marmot of the Cascade Range, but are a separate species. They live in subalpine meadows where they fatten themselves on wildflowers and sun themselves on rocks in the meadows. When frightened, they emit an ear-piercing whistle. Hurricane Ridge is one of the only places in the park where you can drive into marmot country. If it's sunny, you'll see them in the meadows. However, if it is raining, they stay in their burrows to avoid getting their fur wet. Unlike the fur of otters, marmot fur does not shed water.

If you're unlucky, you may also encounter **raccoons** during a visit to Olympic National Park. These aggressive little pests have staked turf at some of the back-country campsites along the coast and will torment you throughout the night if you don't hang your food out of their reach and deny them the pleasure of ransacking your larder. They are particularly problematic at Sand Point, on the Lake Ozette–Cape Alava hike.

Roosevelt elk are the largest of the area's wild residents and it was for the preservation of these majestic creatures that Olympic National Park was originally created. These animals migrate up and down the Olympic Mountains following the seasons and can be seen throughout the region. South of Quilcene and Brinnon, a herd of elk winters in Dosewallips State Park on U.S. 101.

Because no hunting is allowed in Olympic National Park, **black-tailed deer** have become so tame and so common that they are almost unremarkable. The best places to observe these sloe-eyed, gentle grazers are in the meadows of Hurricane Ridge and, not surprisingly, at Deer Park, which is reached on a nerve-wracking single-lane gravel road that goes south from U.S. 101 just east of Port Angeles. There is a population of albino deer that live near Ozette Lake and can sometimes be seen along the trail to Cape Alava.

Anyone venturing into the national park's high country stands a good chance of seeing **mountain goats.** Not native to these mountains, these relatives of antelopes live amid the high crags and alpine meadows. In search of salt, they often visit backcountry campsites to sniff out places where people have urinated. If this happens to be in a meadow, they will paw up the ground to get at the salt. To minimize such damage, try to urinate on rocks or bare ground (such as the middle of a trail). Mount Ellinor is one good place to look for mountain goats (see "Hiking & Backpacking," above, for details). For more about the park's mountain goats, see "It's Not Nice to Fool with Mother Nature," above."

Although relatively plentiful in the backcountry of Olympic National Park, **black bears** are rarely seen by most of the millions of people who visit the park each year. They are occasionally seen in the Hurricane Ridge area. However, if you hike back into the park's more remote areas, you stand a much greater chance of encountering bears. The likelihood of seeing bears increases dramatically during huckleberry season, when the bears fatten up on these delectable little morsels. The bears will usually sit in one spot amid the huckleberry bushes and systematically strip every bush within reach before moving on to another spot.

Cougars also live in these forests, but for the most part are rarely seen. You will, however, see many signs warning you that you are in cougar country. These signs explain precautions to be taken to avoid encountering a cougar and actions to take should you happen upon one. Basically it boils down to this: Make noise as you hike, and if you meet a cougar, try to make yourself look as big as possible and don't run away (slowly back away).

The Western & Southern Olympic Peninsula ✦ What to Do & Where to Do It

BEACHES

The Pacific shore of the Olympic Peninsula is the wildest stretch of coastline in the state, and 57 miles of this shoreline are part of Olympic National Park. Although you can drive right to the beach at Rialto, La Push, and Kalaloch, the rest of this coast is accessible only to hikers and the occasional sea kayaker. South of the national park, however, there is more access to beaches, some of which are almost as beautiful as those within the park.

Most people driving to the Olympic Peninsula for the first time are surprised and disappointed by how long it takes to get here and how inaccessible are the peninsula's beaches. Unless you make the long side trip to Cape Flattery and Shi Shi Beach, the most northerly road-accessible beaches are west of the town of Forks on either side of the mouth of the Quillayute River. On the north side of the river is **Rialto Beach,** which lies at the south end of the national park's northern wilderness strip. From here it is almost 29 miles north to the next road. Stretching for 1 mile

south to the tip of the sand spit at the mouth of the Quillayute and 1 mile north to Hole in the Wall, a massive monolith through which the sea has bored a tunnel, this sandy beach is a favorite of strollers.

On the south side of the river lies the Quileute Indian Reservation and the small community of La Push. The beach here, backed by rental cabins and known as **First Beach,** is a favorite of surfers and beach walkers. However, it is a pair of trail-accessed beaches just south of here that are the area's most beautiful stretches of sand. **Second Beach,** just outside La Push off Wash. 110, is reached by a half-mile trail cut into a cliff. The beach at low tide has tide pools to explore, and offshore are some of the most impressive sea stacks (steep-sided rocky islets) on this coast. Collectively known as the Quillayute Needles, these rocks lend their name to the national wildlife refuge that protects the bird-nesting grounds along this stretch of coast. Camping is allowed on this beach.

A little farther out from La Push on Wash. 110 (and the first beach you'll come to as you approach from Forks) is **Third Beach,** which is reached by a 1.5-mile trail through the forest. Ringed by forests and cliffs, this mile-long beach is popular with campers and is a common starting point for the coastal hike south to the Hoh River. High headlands guard the beach at both ends (with tide pools at their bases), and offshore there are a few sea stacks. Huge driftwood logs litter the beach.

From La Push, it is more than 30 miles, via Wash. 110 and U.S. 101, to the next beach. After continuing its inland route, U.S. 101 finally swings southwest toward the beach along the valley of the Hoh River. A side road on the north bank of the Hoh leads to the river's mouth at **Oil City,** the southern end of the coastal hike from Third Beach. Look for harbor seals feeding in the river mouth.

By far the busiest beaches of this coast begin where U.S. 101 reaches the shore at **Ruby Beach,** which takes its name from the garnet that colors its sands. Here you'll find a few tide pools and the last of the big sea stacks for a while. The beaches that stretch southward from here are not nearly so dramatic as those to the north near La Push, but because they lie right beside the highway, they see a lot of visitors. If you're going to encounter crowds anywhere out this way, this is it. Stretching south from here is a string of numbered beaches, all gentle strips of sand and all with views of Destruction Island, which lies 3 miles offshore and is a bird sanctuary. Near the south end of this string of beaches is Kalaloch Lodge (pronounced Kuh-*lay*-lock), the only oceanfront hotel in the park, and a very popular spot throughout the year. In winter, people come here to watch the massive waves from winter storms crash against the Kalaloch Rocks just offshore. South of the lodge, there are a few more beaches before U.S. 101 turns inland again.

South of here, three roads lead westward from U.S. 101 to connect with Wash. 109. Along this road, between Pacific Beach and Copalis Beach, are the last stretches of rugged shoreline in Washington. However, there is very little public access along this stretch of coast. There are several small communities along the coastline, and several lodges provide waterfront accommodations. Although beachcombing and kite flying are popular on these beaches, the rare chance to dig for razor clams is what brings most people out here. **Pacific Beach State Park** is a tiny patch of sand crowded with RVs and popular with clammers. However, it is otherwise unappealing. **Griffiths–Priday State Park** in Copalis Beach, though larger, is a day-use-only beach, and during the summer months all of the park except the beach is off-limits to protect the nests of endangered snowy plovers. A little bit farther south, **Ocean City State Park** also provides beach access and camping. South of this park, there are several public accesses to the long sandy beaches of the **Ocean Shores** resort community, which is about as close as the Northwest comes to the beach communities of the Mid-Atlantic states.

<hr>

BIRD WATCHING

Any beach along the Olympic Peninsula's Pacific coast will provide opportunities for spotting an incredibly wide variety of birds from common murres and tufted puffins to bald eagles and ospreys. The reasons for the abundance of birdlife along these shores are the 870 islands and rocks that serve as nesting grounds for numerous species of seabirds. These nesting grounds are now protected as both national wildlife refuges and as the Olympic Coast National Marine Sanctuary. Gulls, murres, tufted puffins, rhinoceros auklets, and pigeon guillemots all nest on these offshore outcroppings, safe from four-legged predators, though not from gulls and eagles. By some estimates, more than 250,000 birds nest off this shoreline. Many other bird species also frequent these shores at different times of year.

Federally threatened marbled murrelets fish these waters and nest in inland old-growth forests. Black brants spend winters here. Cormorants are abundant, often seen drying their wings on rocks near the beach. Even brown pelicans occasionally stray up this way from the south. Loons, grebes, and scoters are common. Other birds to look for include black oystercatchers, snowy plovers, greater yellowlegs, spotted sandpipers, Wilson's phalaropes, long-billed dowitchers, turnstones, surfbirds, dunlins, jaegars, gulls, black-legged kittiwakes, fulmars, and shearwaters.

The easiest coastal bird-watching access is on either side of the mouth of the Quillayute River west of Forks, at nearby Second and Third beaches, along the national park's coastal strip from Ruby Beach to South Beach, and between Moclips and Ocean Shores.

The beaches of the **Ocean Shores area,** on the north side of Gray's Harbor, are home to both semipalmated plovers and endangered snowy plovers. The semipalmated plovers here reach their normal southern limit, while the snowy plovers reach their northern limit in this area. Snowy plovers nest in the dunes at Griffiths–Priday State Park between March and August. In winter, this area abounds with shorebirds.

Each year between late April and early May, **Bowerman Basin** in the Gray's Harbor National Wildlife Refuge (tel. 360/532-6237), which is located adjacent to the Aberdeen/Hoquiam Airport, becomes a magnet for migrating shorebirds, as well as bird watchers. For these few weeks of spring, this area becomes a staging area (resting and feeding area) for more than a million arctic-bound shorebirds coming from as far south as Argentina. This is one of only four such staging areas in North America. Attracted by mudflats that abound in shrimplike invertebrates on which these shorebirds feed, the Bowerman Basin is the last stop in the spring migration. From here the birds fly nonstop to their breeding grounds in the arctic.

Although western sandpipers make up 85% of the shorebirds that gather here in the spring, also to be seen are dunlins, short-billed and long-billed dowitchers, semipalmated plovers, red knots, and pectoral sandpipers. About 25 shorebird species gather here, which means birders have an absolute field day. Many other species of birds are found here, including great blue herons, various species of ducks, terns, and gulls. Also lured to this avian gathering are merlins and peregrine falcons, which come to feed on the gathered flocks.

The best viewing times are from two hours before to two hours after the high tide. The trail to the viewing area is frequently muddy and rubber boots are recommended. For more information, contact the refuge headquarters.

BOARDSAILING

For the most part, when the wind is up on this coast, the surf is pounding, and it isn't usually a clean break. Consequently, this coast isn't particularly popular with boardsailors. One exception, however, is **Damon Point,** a state beach access at the south end of Ocean Shores on Point Brown Road. Set on a spit of land jutting into Gray's Harbor on the east side of Ocean Shores, Damon Point provides just the right combination of winds and protected waters. To reach the point, drive to the south end of Ocean Shores, head southeast on Marine View Drive, and then, in less than a half-mile, take a dirt road out to the point.

FISHING

Aside from the usually complicated fishing regulations aimed at preserving wild fish populations, there are two important things to know about fishing on the west side of the Olympic Peninsula. You don't need a Washington State fishing license to fish inside Olympic National Park. However, you do need a salmon and steelhead punchcard. Such waters include the trail-accessible upper reaches of the Bogachiel River, the upper reaches of both the Hoh and South Fork Hoh rivers, the Queets River all the way to the Quinault Indian Reservation boundary, and the Quinault River above where North Shore and South Shore roads come together. The other important thing to remember is that Quinault Lake is within the Quinault Indian Reservation, so you'll need to get a special permit (available at lakeside resorts) to fish this lake, which holds steelhead, salmon, cutthroat trout, and Dolly Vardens.

The rivers of the Olympic Peninsula's west side, including the **Hoh, Queets, Quinault, Chehalis,** and **Humptulips,** are among the best steelheading rivers in the state, and there are runs of both summer and winter steelhead to keep the action up year-round. Fishing from drift boats in the winter is about the most popular way to get these silver fighters, but there are also plenty of opportunities for bank fishing. The winter steelheads run from December through April and the summer fish hit between late June and September or October. To protect wild steelhead runs, regulations for many peninsula rivers either limit the number of wild fish you can catch or require that you release all wild fish. Check the regs before keeping any fish. The Quillayute River system, which includes the 5-mile-long **Quillayute** (which has almost no bank access), the **Dickey,** the **Bogachiel,** the **Sol Duc,** and the **Calawah,** offers excellent steelheading with plenty of good access both from the banks and by boat (numerous boat ramps). Try the deep pool at the confluence of the Sol Duc and the Bogachiel. This pool marks the start of the Quillayute River and has a boat ramp. The best Bogachiel access is west of U.S. 101. The **North Fork Calawah** also has good road access. The Sol Duc is paralleled by U.S. 101 for much of its length with several good access points, including several campgrounds.

The Bogachiel and Humptulips rivers are both heavily stocked, which means though they're heavily fished, they still produce well.

All of the region's rivers also have good trout fishing. The Humptulips, the **Satsop,** and the Chehalis below the mouth of the Satsop are all known for their sea-run cutthroats. Cutthroat season traditionally starts on the Fourth of July and runs into early fall. Currently all wild cutthroats caught on the Chehalis and Satsop must be released.

October and November are salmon season on area rivers. The Chinook salmon sometimes reach 50 pounds and are considered the best eating, while the smaller coho are known for the fight they put up. The Hoh River also has a good run of spring Chinook starting in May and extending to August.

Surf fishing is not a very popular sport along the Washington coast, but this is not because there isn't anything to catch. There is—red-tailed surf perch to be precise. These fish average around a foot long and are good eating. Beaches to try include those at **Kalaloch,** at **Griffiths–Priday State Park** in Copalis, and at **Ocean Shores.**

For fishing gear and advice, stop in at **Olympic Sporting Goods** (tel. 360/374-6330) in Forks. If you're looking for a fishing guide for local waters, try **Skookum Outfitter** (tel. 360/683-9867), **Uncle Dave's Guide Service** (tel. 360/374-2577), **Fish Hawk Guide Service** (tel. 360/374-5488), **George Rose Guide Service** (tel. 360/374-2566 or 360/288-2840), **Jake's Guide Service** (tel. 360/374-6019 or 360/648-2408), **Three Rivers Resort and Guide Service** (tel. 360/374-5300), or **Z's Guide Service** (tel. 360/962-2140).

HIKING & BACKPACKING

The west side of the Olympic Peninsula is the rainiest part of the peninsula, and the wettest region in the continental United States. Good rain gear is important for hiking out here. If you don't like hiking in the rain, you may want to do your hiking elsewhere. However, if you don't mind being damp while you hike, there are some very rewarding routes in the area.

INLAND HIKES

Hoh River Trail to Glacier Meadows

35 miles round-trip. Moderate–strenuous. 3,750-foot elevation gain. Access: From U.S. 101, drive 19 miles up the Hoh River Rd. to the Hoh Rain Forest Visitor Center. Map: Green Trails Mount Tom and Mount Olympus, Custom Correct Seven Lakes Basin–Hoh.

The Hoh Valley is the most easily accessible of the region's several rain-forest valleys, and as such it sees a lot of hikers. However, the hike up the valley is the west peninsula's classic hike, the very essence of the Olympic Peninsula. Starting on the valley floor, the trail leads through riotous rain forest and then climbs up onto the flank of Mount Olympus at the snout of the Blue Glacier. On the verdant valley floor, infinite permutations on the color green are plastered over every solid surface.

The trail starts from the same parking lot that serves the Hoh Visitor Center. It's here that Olympic tourists come for a quick glimpse of the rain forest. Short interpretive trails loop out from the visitor center and are often as crowded as a city sidewalk. However, once beyond the interpretive signs, on the Hoh River Trail, the crowds thin out, but the trees certainly don't. Massive Douglas firs, Sitka spruces, and western red cedars, reaching hundreds of feet skyward, line the trail. Sounds within this forest seem to be eaten up by the dense mats of mosses that hang from the big-leaf maples and by the sponging forest floor that is more decomposing logs and leaves than it is solid ground. At times the trail is right beside the braided channels of the glacier-fed Hoh River, and at other times, the river is but a distant murmur. Quiet hikers may well spot some of the valley's resident Roosevelt elk, and will most certainly see signs that these massive herd animals are in the area.

The trail is almost completely flat for the first 9.25 miles to the Olympus Guard Station (campsites), and passes campsites at about 2.5 and 6 miles from the trailhead. It isn't until about the 13-mile point, where the trail crosses the Hoh River on a bridge, that the trail begins to climb in earnest. From this point, the route gains nearly 3,000 feet in the next 4 miles. After 2 miles of steady climbing, pretty little Elk Lake (campsites) is passed. Beyond this lake, the trail becomes even steeper as it climbs to Glacier Meadows (campsites) below the Blue Glacier. Above the wildflowers of these meadows rise the ramparts of 7,965-foot Mount Olympus, the park's highest peak.

Enchanted Valley Trail

26–35 miles round-trip. Strenuous. 1,500–4,000-foot elevation gain. Access: From U.S. 101, drive 18.5 miles up the South Shore Lake Quinault Rd. Map: Green Trails Mount Christe and Mount Steel, Custom Correct Enchanted Valley–Skokomish.

With a name like Enchanted Valley, how can a hiker resist? This hike starts out in the dripping rain forest of the Quinault Valley and slowly climbs up to a meadow encircled by 3,000-foot cliffs. Waterfalls stream from the slopes and high above hangs the Anderson Glacier. If that ain't enchantment, I don't know what is.

To fully enjoy this hike requires at least three days and an acceptance of being damp for those three days. The trail is entirely in rain forest for the 13 miles to Enchanted Valley, with only occasional glimpses of 7,321-foot Mount Anderson and Anderson Glacier through the trees. The rumble of the Quinault River keeps you company most of the time, and if you're quiet and lucky, you're likely to encounter a herd of elk.

Once you reach Enchanted Valley, the trees give way to a wide meadow bursting with colorful wildflowers in the spring. Encircling this meadow are cliffs that rise up to West Peak and Mount Anderson. High above shimmers the Anderson Glacier, from which streams of meltwater cascade. In the middle of the meadow stands a three-story chalet that was once a hotel, but that is now government property. From the valley, the trail climbs steadily for 4.5 miles to 4,500-foot Anderson Pass, from which views to the east open up. Two miles past the Enchanted Valley Chalet,

watch below the trail for one of the world's largest western hemlock trees, which is more than 28 feet in circumference at its base. At just over 5 miles from Enchanted Valley, a side trail heads uphill toward the Anderson Glacier.

If you have lots of time, a 24-mile loop can be done over White Mountain to the Duckabush River and then back up and over to the West Fork Dosewallips River. By arranging a pickup or shuttle, you could also make this a one-way, transpeninsula trek by hiking eastward from Anderson Pass down the West Fork Dosewallips. Other one-way alternatives would be to hike out the Duckabush River or south down the Skokomish River.

Queets River Trail to Spruce Bottom

10.5 miles round-trip. Easy. 150-foot elevation gain. Access: From U.S. 101, drive 13.5 miles to the end of the Queets River Rd. Map: Green Trails Kloochman Rock, Custom Correct Queets.

The Queets River valley is home to the largest Douglas fir in Olympic National Park and surrounding this lone monster are thousands of other equally impressive trees. Because this hike starts with a fording of the Queets River, which is safe to do really only in the late summer, it is not a very popular trail. The fact that this trail does not connect to any other park trails also limits its appeal to some hikers; you'll have the beauty of this shadowy rain forest mostly to yourself.

Find a wide, shallow spot to ford the river, and once across, head upstream on a wide, flat trail. In 2.4 miles, watch for the old Kloochman Rock Trail on the left. This trail once led to a fire lookout atop 3,356-foot Kloochman Rock, which can be seen rising above the forest to the north. In 0.2 miles, this trail leads to the park's largest Douglas fir, which is an amazing 45 feet around at its base and 212 feet tall. Continuing up the Queets from this side trail, the trees are draped with a thick mat of mosses. Spruce Bottom, roughly 5 miles from the trailhead, is a good campsite or turnaround point for a day hike. If you're so inclined, you can follow this trail for more than 10 miles farther upstream.

Watch Your Step–Banana Slugs Crossing

If you happen to be a gardener who lives where summers are humid, you probably curse slugs, which can do immense damage to a vegetable patch. Now, imagine that those slimy little slugs chomping on your tomatoes are not an inch long but rather a foot long! Sound like a late-night monster movie? Think again. And if you go out in the woods today, be sure to watch your step.

The banana slug (*Ariolimax columbianus*), which can grow to be a foot in length and live for up to five years, is the only slug native to the Pacific Northwest. Taking its name from its yellowish color and elongated shape, this slug makes its way through the region's lowland forests dining on plants, mushrooms, and decaying vegetable matter. Though slugs may seem to wander aimlessly, they have two eyes on the ends of long stalks and two olfactory organs on short stalks. The eyes detect light and dark and help them find cool, dark places to sleep away the day, while the olfactory organs are used to locate food. A slug eats by shredding organic matter with its tongue, which is covered with thousands of tiny teeth and is known as a radula.

Aside from their disgusting appearance and annoying habit of devouring gardens, slugs get a bad rap for sliming anyone unlucky enough to grab one accidentally. Slug slime, if you take the time to study it instead of just rubbing your fingers furiously to remove it, is amazing stuff. It is at once both slippery as soap and sticky as glue. It is this unusual combination of properties that allows slugs to use their slime as a sort of instant highway on which to travel. Secreting the slime from their chin like so much drool, they stick the slime to the surface of whatever they are crawling on and then just slide along on this instant road. Slugs lack the protective shell of their close relatives, the snails, but they can defend themselves by secreting copious amounts of slime, which renders them unpalatable to predators such as shrews, beetles, crows, and garter snakes.

Where *do* baby slugs come from? The cabbage patch, of course! Just kidding. In fact, slugs come from wherever they want. You see, slugs are hermaphroditic. That's right—it takes only one to tango. However, if two slugs should chance to meet on a dark night, well, sometimes the chemistry is just right. Let this last bit of information sink in, and you'll soon realize that every slug in your garden is going to lay eggs! Now that's a nightmare.

Slugs are so much a part of Northwest culture and humor that they have been the subject of cartoons, humorous books, even a tongue-in-cheek cookbook. In Eugene, Oregon, there is even an annual festival held each September that crowns a slug queen. In gift shops all over the region, you'll find slug refrigerator magnets, so you can take a little bit of the Northwest home with you when you leave. Don't say I didn't warn you if your one slug magnet turns into dozens all over your refrigerator. Remember, it takes only one.

Colonel Bob Mountain

8.5 miles. Strenuous. 3,500-foot elevation gain. Access: From U.S. 101 north of Humptulips, go east on Donkey Creek Rd. (FS 22) for 8 miles and turn left (north) onto FS 2204. Continue another 11 miles north to the trailhead (if you reach Campbell Tree Grove Campground you've gone too far). Map: Green Trails Quinault Lake and Grisdale, Custom Correct Colonel Bob.

Most of the hikes on the Olympic Peninsula's west side spend miles and miles on valley floors deep in the rain forest. There are few places where trails climb up to the heights for views of both the Olympic Mountains and the Pacific Ocean, and fewer still that can be done as a day hike. If you have time for only a short hike and views are what you seek (not a drippy rain-forest experience), then the

Pete's Creek Trail to the top of Colonel Bob Mountain is the trail you're looking for. Lying outside the national park boundaries east of Quinault Lake, Colonel Bob rises to 4,492 feet and lends its name to the surrounding wilderness area. There are two trails to the summit of this peak. However, this trail is half as long as the other and works better as a day hike.

The trail ascends alongside the creek and is steep and rocky. Almost the entire 4.25 miles to the summit is through the forest, but when you finally do step into the meadows at the craggy summit, the views (on a clear day, of course) are just that much more surprising. To the west lies the vast expanse of the Pacific Ocean and seemingly at the very foot of the mountain is Quinault Lake. Due north is Mount Olympus and to the northwest are many more of the Olympic peaks. To the east rise the Cascades, with Mount Rainier, Mount Adams, and Mount St. Helens all visible. Not surprisingly there used to be a fire lookout atop this peak. Should you want to camp (the sunrise and sunset views are superb!), there are numerous campsites along both this route and the 7.25-mile trail up the north side of the mountain. This latter trail starts 2.5 miles east of the Quinault Ranger Station on Quinault Lake's South Shore Road.

COASTAL HIKES

Third Beach to Oil City Hike

17.3 miles. Strenuous. 500-foot elevation gain. Access: From U.S. 101 just north of Forks, drive 12 miles west on La Push Rd. and park at the Third Beach trailhead. Map: Green Trails La Push, Custom Correct South Olympic Coast.

Although slightly shorter than the coastal route from Lake Ozette to Rialto Beach, this stretch of coast presents more challenges. Not only are there headlands to be rounded at low tide and headlands to be scrambled up and over, but there are also five creeks to be forded, three of which can be crossed only in months when the water level is low. However, these challenges only serve to keep out hikers who aren't serious about solitude, and anyone

seeking blissfully remote stretches of sand will find them on this hike. In misty weather, the sea stacks that rise from the surf along this shore take on the look of the mountains in old Chinese scroll paintings. Some are bare rock while others are topped with tiny natural bonsai forests. Bald eagles can often be seen perched atop these and other trees along the coast, and the bird watching in general is superb on this hike. Sea lions and gray whales are also frequently spotted along this stretch of coast.

Do not start this hike without acquiring a copy of the tide tables for the days you will be hiking. These are available at ranger stations and are also usually posted at the trailhead. Also pick up a copy of the national park's *Olympic Coastal Strip* brochure, which includes a map that marks which headlands can be rounded at low tide and which cannot. Camping is allowed on beaches and there are also numerous campsites set back in the trees at regular intervals. Allow about three days to do the one-way hike.

The hike starts with the easy 1.5-mile forest walk to Third Beach, which is lined with huge driftwood logs, crossed by a stream, and flanked on either end by high headlands. Tcahwhit Head to the north cannot be crossed, and Taylor Point to the south can be crossed only on a 1.2-mile-long inland trail. Third Beach is a popular day hike, but once you are over Taylor Point, you leave the crowds behind.

Across 0.7 miles of beach, you come to Scott's Bluff, which can be rounded at low tide or hiked over at high tide. Once on the other side of this bluff, there are 4.2 miles of easy hiking along the beach and over low headlands and bluffs. At this point, the trail heads inland for 1.5 miles to fords on both Falls Creek and Goodman Creek. Neither of these creeks is crossable in the winter months, so if you are hiking at this time, this will have to be your turnaround point. Once you regain the beach, it is 2.25 miles south to Mosquito Creek, which also cannot be forded in winter. If you were hiking from the south, this would be your winter turnaround point.

Although it is possible to continue south along the shore during periods of extremely low tides, you must be certain of conditions. A mistake could prove fatal. Even when the tide is out, the waterside route requires that you scramble over several small points of land. A safer, high-tide route lies inland through the forest and returns to the beach south of Hoh Head in 3.5 miles. From this point you have 2 miles more of beach walking before turning inland along the Hoh River to the Oil City trailhead (where you will find neither oil nor a city, but where there was once an oil prospectors' camp).

HORSEBACK RIDING

Although the dank, dark rain forests of the Hoh River valley don't generally instill in people a desire to go horseback riding, if the urge should strike you, try contacting **De Blary Trail Rides,** Hoh River Road (tel. 360/374-5015), which has its stables 6 miles east of U.S. 101. Down at Ocean Shores, on the north side of Gray's Harbor, **Nan–Sea Stables** (tel. 360/289-0194) offers both sunset beach rides and forest rides.

MOUNTAIN BIKING

If you're out on the west side of the peninsula and need bicycle gear or want to rent a bike, check with **Olympic Mountains Bike Shop** (tel. 360/374-9777) in Forks. This shop also offers guided rides and shuttles.

Wynoochee Lake Trail

12 miles round-trip. Moderate. 1,500-foot elevation gain. Access: From Montesano on U.S. 12, drive 35 miles north, turn onto FS 2294, cross a bridge below the Wynoochee Dam, and pull into the Wynoochee Lake Picnic Area adjacent to the Coho Campground. Map: USGS Wynoochee Lake.

With Wynoochee Lake right beside the trail much of the time, views northward to the Olympic Mountains, a few stately old-growth trees, and the Wynoochee River to be forded, this is an entertaining ride. It is also quite challenging and technical in places where exposed roots and rocks in the trail require tight maneuvering. Also

on this trail are a few steep pitches and switchbacks that may necessitate a bit of walking. However, the ascents and descents are generally short, making this something of a roller-coaster ride. The hardest part of the whole ride can be the crossing of the river. Don't even think about it until about June, when the water level has begun to subside as the rains slow down for the summer. The trail is best done in a clockwise direction.

ROAD BIKING

U.S. 101, as it crosses the west side of the Olympic Peninsula, does a lot of meandering back and forth, but manages to spend only 11 miles right by the ocean. Inland it is mostly bordered by thin strips of trees that hide the clear-cuts beyond, and at times there are not even these curtains of greenery to hide the denuded hills. Combine this with the heavy traffic of tourists and logging trucks and this becomes a rather unappealing stretch of road to ride.

Quillayute-La Push Loop

22 miles. Easy. 200-foot elevation gain. Access: From Forks, go north on U.S. 101, turn left on La Push Rd., drive 10 miles west, turn right onto Mora Rd., and park your car at Leyendecker County Park.

If riding to two different, equally beautiful beaches on either side of the mouth of the Quillayute River sounds like fun, then this ride may appeal to you. Along the way, you'll ride through a corridor of big trees that flank these narrow roads. At the beaches, you can do some hiking if you're so inclined, and there are a couple of other beaches—Second Beach and Third Beach—that are also well worth checking out. Second Beach is a 1-mile round-trip, and Third Beach is a 3-mile round-trip. Rialto Beach is a wild stretch inside Olympic National Park, while First Beach and the adjacent community of La Push (which has a couple of old cabin resorts) lie within the Quileute Indian Reservation.

From the Leyendecker Park, pedal 4 miles west to the entrance to Olympic

National Park. Once inside the park, continue another 1.25 miles to the end of the road at the Rialto Beach parking area. After a walk on the beach (Hole in the Wall, 2 miles north is a favorite destination), head back the way you came, ride past Leyendecker Park to the road fork, and turn right onto La Push Road. From here it is about 6 miles to the old resorts at La Push, which has a rather run-down feel. First Beach is to the south. As you ride west along La Push Road, you'll pass first the trailhead for Third Beach and then the trailhead for Second Beach. Both beaches are spectacularly beautiful and well worth getting off your bike for a bit of hiking.

Ocean City State Park to Pacific Beach State Park

29.5 miles. Easy. 700-foot elevation gain. Access: From U.S. 101 in Hoquiam, drive west on Wash. 109, and turn left onto Wash. 115 toward Ocean Shores to reach Ocean City State Park.

If you think the Olympic Peninsula must have at least a little bit of good coastal cycling, you're right. Wash. 109, which parallels the shore from near Ocean City north to the Quinault Indian village of Taholah, has good views, three state parks with beach access, and far less traffic than U.S. 101. I like cycling with the roar of the waves close at hand, and consequently, I think it's fun to ride this stretch of road out and back. If you prefer to do loop rides, you can head inland at Pacific Beach and follow Ocean Beach Road southeast all the way to Wash. 109 east of Ocean City State Park.

From Ocean City State Park, ride north on Wash. 115 and turn left onto Wash. 109; if you want to ride an even smaller road, turn left immediately and ride over to a road that parallels the highway. This side road passes through residential neighborhoods of the town of Ocean City. Eventually the parallel road dead-ends and you have to get back on Wash. 109. In just over 6 miles from the start, reach the town of Copalis Beach, which is the site of Griffiths–Priday State Park. This park encompasses a long sand spit at the mouth of the Copalis River and is a nesting

ground for the endangered snowy plover. Do some bird watching or walk the long sandy beach.

Continuing north, the river parallels the Copalis River for a mile. In about 3.5 miles from Copalis Beach, you'll pass Iron Springs, where there is a rustic old resort with cabins set back in the trees. North of here, the road winds around a lot, rising and falling, sometimes overlooking the ocean and sometimes as much as half a mile inland, before dropping down to the tiny patch of sand at Pacific Beach State Park. This makes a good picnic spot and is the turnaround point. If the thought of dining in a restaurant overlooking the ocean is enough to get you to pedal another 2 miles north, then by all means, head up to the Ocean Crest Resort in Moclips.

SEA KAYAKING & FLAT-WATER CANOEING

Despite the name, sea kayaks are far more popular on the protected inland waterways of Washington State than they are out here on the open sea. The Pacific Ocean is temperamental, and this fickleness keeps most sea kayakers away. The big surf that pounds these shores makes sea kayaking in the ocean less fun than fanatical. Most feared of all are not the storm waves, which can be easily predicted and avoided, but the rogue waves that sometimes rear up from a gentle swell. Such waves can break much farther out than other waves have been breaking and often catch sea kayakers off their guard. The least one of these waves might do is dump you, but if you happen to be paddling near shore to look at some interesting rocks, such waves can be deadly. For this reason, only a few experienced kayakers paddle these ocean waters. There are, however, a few more protected places to do some paddling.

La Push

8 miles round-trip to Third Beach; 4 miles round-trip to Hole in the Wall, 40 miles one way to Neah Bay. Moderate–strenuous (for experienced paddlers only). Access: From U.S. 101 north of Forks, take La Push Rd. (Wash. 110) 13.5 miles west to La Push.

In the summer months, when the Pacific finally begins to live up to its name, experienced sea kayakers familiar with paddling on open-ocean swells often put in at La Push, west of Forks, and explore the fascinating shoreline that stretches north and south from here. A knowledge of waves and a wetsuit are essentials for paddling these waters. Both north and south from La Push lies Olympic National Park, and because camping is permitted on most beaches here, this coast is popular for overnight paddle trips. Just remember that the weather can change very quickly along this coast, and what was a glassy smooth ocean yesterday could be a raging maelstrom tomorrow. Know the weather forecast before paddling.

Just offshore lies James Island, which always beckons paddlers to do a circumnavigation. A mile or so south of La Push lie the Quillayute Needles, a dramatic grouping of towering sea stacks (offshore rocks) that lie just offshore from the Olympic National Park's Second Beach. The sea stacks are part of the Quillayute Needles National Wildlife Refuge. To protect nesting birds, landing on any of these rugged rocks (even if it were possible) is prohibited. At the south end of Second Beach rises Teahwhit Head, a rugged promontory that is fascinating to explore. Around this headland is Third Beach, less than 4 miles from La Push. Camping is permitted on both Second and Third beaches, and, weather permitting, these make ideal destinations for an easy overnight trip.

North from La Push is Rialto Beach, a 2-mile-long swath of sand that ends at Hole in the Wall, a rock with a tunnel carved through it by waves. North of Hole in the Wall, the shoreline is breathtakingly rugged, though with few places to go ashore should you need to land. There are also several islands along this stretch of coast. Heading in this direction, you'll have to paddle quite a ways before you can find a place to safely go ashore and pitch a tent. This northern shore is favored by expert kayakers making the 40-mile, multiday trip around Cape Flattery to Neah Bay. This trip takes at least three days if the weather stays good, longer if it turns bad and you have to wait for the seas to calm down.

Copalis River

2–4 miles. Easy. Access: From U.S. 101 west of Hoquiam, drive west on Wash. 109, which curves north when it reaches the shore, and follow the road north to Copalis Beach and Griffiths–Priday State Park.

For its last 1.5 miles or so, the Copalis widens into a narrow estuary that is bordered on its west side by Griffiths–Priday State Park. This park is home to a nesting ground for endangered snowy plovers, which can often be seen feeding along the shores here. Many other species of birds can also be seen on this stretch of river.

Lake Sylvia

2–3 miles. Easy. Access: From U.S. 12, drive into Montesano and go north out of town for 1 mile on N Third St.

Located in the state park of the same name, Lake Sylvia is barely a mile long, yet because it is closed to gasoline engines, it is a tranquil place for a paddle. To the north end of the lake, which is actually a dammed reservoir, there is a maze of marshes and narrow channels that are perfect for exploring in a canoe or sea kayak. Lots of waterfowl call these wetlands home, so binoculars and a bird book are a good idea for this paddle. Near the middle of the lake there is a small island to be paddled around and a narrow cove to be explored. A campground here has lots of lakeshore campsites.

SURFING

The waves that break at **First Beach** in **La Push,** a small Quileute Indian community at the mouth of the Quillayute River, are fabled to be among the biggest and baddest in the state. On a good south swell, they wrap around Quateata, a headland at the south end of the beach. Farther south, there are sometimes good waves at **Ocean City State Park** and **Pacific Beach State Park,** both of which are reached by following Wash. 109 west from U.S. 101 west of Hoquiam. Down at the south end of the town of Ocean Shores, there is also occasionally good surfing at **Damon Point,** a state beach access on the east side of the Ocean Shore peninsula. To reach this spot, go south through Ocean Shores (off Wash. 109 and Wash. 115), turn left onto Marine View Drive, and then follow a dirt road out to the point. See the "Surfing" section under "Washington's South Coast—What to Do & Where to Do It," below, for a listing of area surf shops.

SWIMMING & TUBING

The waters of the Pacific Ocean rarely reach 60°F, even in the middle of summer. Consequently, ocean swimming is not a popular activity along this coast (or anywhere in the Northwest, for that matter). Powerful surf and huge log driftwood add further elements of risk to a dip in the ocean around here. Rivers and lakes are generally slightly warmer and safer than the ocean.

Near the town of Forks, you'll find some good swimming holes in the pools along the Bogachiel River in **Bogachiel State Park,** which is south of town on U.S. 101. At the confluence of the Bogachiel and the Sol Duc River, you'll find another wide, deep pool at **Leyendecker County Park.** To reach this park, drive north from Forks, turn west on La Push Road (Wash. 110), drive about 10 miles, and turn right onto Mora Road. On the Hoh River at **Hoh Oxbow Park** just off U.S. 101, there is a good swimming hole.

Inland, you'll find a nice little swimming beach in **Lake Sylvia State Park** north of Montesano. To reach this park, follow North Third Street north out of Montesano. **Schafer State Park,** north of the towns of Satsop and Brady on the East Fork Satsop River, is a great place to do a little tubing. Within the park there is almost a mile of shallow, rocky, fast-flowing river. To reach this park, drive U.S. 12 to Satsop, drive west on the road that parallels the highway, turn north on East Satsop Road, and continue 8.5 miles north.

WALKS & NATURAL ROADSIDE ATTRACTIONS

Along this coast, in addition to the walks and short excursions listed here, there are also several good beaches that are accessed by short trails. These include **Rialto, Second,** and **Third beaches** near La Push, the beach near **Oil City** on the north side of the Hoh River mouth (this is one of the least visited beaches in the national park), **Ruby Beach,** and all the numbered beaches south of Ruby Beach.

Hall of Mosses/Spruce Nature Trail

2 miles round-trip. Easy. 100-foot elevation gain. Access: From U.S. 101, drive 19 miles east on Hoh River Rd. to the Hoh Rain Forest Visitor Center. Map: Not necessary.

More than 140 inches of rain fall in the Hoh River valley in an average year. That's almost 12 feet of rain! On these two short trails—the 0.75-mile Hall of Mosses Trail and the 1.25-mile Spruce Nature Trail—park visitors marvel at the effect of that much water on the plant kingdom. Sitka spruces grow 300 feet tall; branches of big-leaf maples are covered with foot-thick mats of club moss and licorice ferns; downed trees and rotting stumps serve as nurseries for the next generation; Douglas firs grow to girths of nearly 50 feet. But there are more than just plants to marvel at in these dark, dank woods. Banana slugs almost a foot long patrol the trail, elk weighing half a ton graze the greenery on the forest floor, and crystal-clear water seeps from earth that becomes like a sponge in the constant rainfall. Together these two trails introduce people to all these facets of rain-forest life and more.

Rain Forest Nature Trail

0.5 miles. Easy. 50-foot elevation gain. Access: 1.5 miles east of U.S. 101 on Lake Quinault's South Shore Rd. Map: Not necessary.

Although the interpretive trails in the Hoh Valley are the best known of the area's short nature trails, they are by no means the only brief introductions to life in the drip zone. This short trail is located almost across the road from Lake Quinault Road, and connects to more than 6 miles of other trails through this patch of rain forest just outside the boundaries of the national park.

There is another half-mile rain-forest trail, the **Maple Glade Nature Trail,** nearby at the national park's Quinault Visitor Center on Quinault North Shore Road, which is also reached from U.S. 101.

WHALE WATCHING

Although you can never predict when or where you might spot a gray whale or two, these migratory cetaceans are frequently spotted along this coast. The biggest difficulty in whale watching from shore is always finding a spot with enough elevation to provide a good vantage point. The **Destruction Island overlook** north of Kalaloch Lodge is just such a vantage point. Another good spot for observing gray whales is at **Griffiths–Priday State Park** near the town of Copalis Beach on Wash. 115. Whales can usually be seen between October and May.

WHITEWATER KAYAKING & CANOEING

With rainfall that is measured in feet instead of inches, it should come as no surprise that there are a lot of rivers on the west side of the Olympic Peninsula, and these rivers offer an amazing amount of whitewater kayaking. However, while rivers on the north and east sides of the Olympic Peninsula tend to be short and steep, the west and south sides of the peninsula are a completely different story. Here the rivers wind their way down long valleys before reaching the Pacific Ocean. In their lower reaches, these rivers provide plenty of Class I and Class II paddling.

For a thorough look at Olympic Peninsula whitewater, get a copy of Gary Korb's book *A Paddler's Guide to the Olympic Peninsula* (1992, Gary Korb).

CLASS I

For a fun 10.5-mile Class I run in the Forks area, put in on the **Bogachiel River** at the boat ramp off La Push Road about 3.5 miles west of U.S. 101. From here paddle past huge old trees for 6.5 miles to the confluence with the Sol Duc River. At this confluence, these two rivers merge to become the **Quillayute River,** one of the shortest rivers in the state. From here it is only 4 miles downstream to the Dickey

River boat ramp in Olympic National Park near the Mora Ranger Station. To reach this boat ramp from the river, turn right up the Dickey River 1.5 miles before the Quillayute reaches the Pacific. To reach the boat ramp by road, take the Mora Road fork off Wash. 110 (La Push Road) about 7 miles west of U.S. 101. The flow of the Quillayute will depend on the tides. If you're short on time, there is a boat ramp at Leyendecker County Park at the Bogachiel–Sol Duc confluence, which is on the Mora Road just past the Mora–La Push fork. Although this run can be done year-round, it is best in the rainy season when there is plenty of water in the river. Stay alert for downed trees across the river.

Lying to the east of the only section of U.S. 101 that actually runs alongside the Pacific Ocean is the **Clearwater River,** which empties into the Queets River barely 6 miles before the latter empties into the ocean. For its entire length, the Clearwater, which lives up to its name most of the time, is paralleled by Clearwater Road. Many maps list numerous named rapids on this river, but they are all merely riffles that hardly warrant the names given to them. However, they do add a bit of excitement and will be the main reason for doing this run for many paddlers. Of concern are the many overhanging tree limbs beneath which the main current of this river often flows. This 11.5-mile run starts about 9 miles up the Clearwater Road from U.S. 101 at a bridge over the river and ends at a Department of Natural Resources (DNR) picnic area less than 2 miles up this same road. Although runnable all year, this river is best run in the rainy season.

The **West Fork Humptulips River,** although it lies outside the national park, is a good river to paddle if you want to get a feel for the luxuriance of a rain-forest valley. In places the river flows past low bluff walls that drip with water and plants and give this run a very wild feel. From the put-in on Fishtrap Road (FS 2263) off Donkey Creek Road (north of the town of Humptulips off U.S. 101), a 20-mile run is possible, though this could be shortened to less than 7 miles if you were pressed for time and just wanted to take in the most scenic upper section of the run. However, if you're looking to spend an enjoyable day on the river, the entire run is pleasant. Take out downstream of U.S. 101 and the town of Humptulips at a fishing access off Copalis Crossing Road. This river is best run in the rainy season but can be run in the summer as well.

For all intents and purposes, the **Chehalis River** forms the southern boundary of the Olympic Peninsula. This long river and its tributaries—the Wynoochee and the Satsop—drain the southern slopes of the Olympic Mountains. The east–west run of the Chehalis between Gray's Harbor and I-5 south of Olympia is paralleled the entire way by U.S. 12. The river flows through a broad agricultural valley, and though the character of this river is quite different from that of other peninsula rivers mentioned above, it still makes for pleasant paddling. The water is usually clear and flows past farm fields and forests. For nearly 50 miles, from the confluence of the Black River to its mouth at Aberdeen on Gray's Harbor, this river offers leisurely paddling and numerous boat launches. A favorite stretch is the 20-mile run from Porter, where there is a boat ramp just off U.S. 12, down to Montesano, where there is a boat ramp at the Wash. 107 bridge over the Chehalis south of town. Because of its size, this river can be run year-round.

With meadows and grand old trees lining its banks, the **West Fork Satsop River** is one of the most scenic runs on this side of the peninsula. The only drawback is that by late summer, when it's hot enough that you really feel like getting on the river, there isn't enough water left in this stream to float a kayak. The rainy season and on, into early summer, are the best times to paddle this river. The 7-mile run down the West Fork passes through a narrow, forested gorge in its first few miles, and then in its lower stretch meanders through peaceful meadows, before passing through yet another small gorge. *Gorgeous* is the word, for sure. To reach the put-in, drive 3.5 miles north from the town of Brady (west of the town of Satsop off U.S. 12), turn onto West Satsop Road, and continue 6 miles to Swinging Bridge Park. The take-out lies on the West Fork just upstream from the confluence with the East Fork.

CLASS II

For an easy Class II run in the forks area, try the **Bogachiel River.** From the put-in at Bogachiel State Park, it is roughly 9 miles downstream through forests and farmland to the boat ramp 3.5 miles off U.S. 101 by way of Wash. 110 (La Push Road).

Occasionally floated by commercial rafting companies, the **Queets River** lies within a long arm of Olympic National Park. Despite the fact that there are only a couple of decent rapids on this river, its location alone makes it the most recommendable river on the peninsula. However, there are other good reasons as well. There are superb views up the river valley to the snow-clad Olympic Mountains, massive trees cast up on gravel bars by winter floods, and best of all, lots of wildlife. Because this is part of the national park, hunting is prohibited, and the animals know it. Expect to see deer, elk, river otters, and beaver. If you're lucky, you might even see a bear. Put in at the Queets Campground, 13.5 miles up the Queets River Road. For a 16-mile run, take out at the Clearwater Road bridge, which is reached by continuing 2.5 miles west from Queets River Road on U.S. 101. There are also three other take-outs above this point if you want to do a shorter run.

The 20-mile **Hoh River** run from the Hoh Rain Forest Visitor Center down to Hoh Oxbow Campground is one of the quintessential Olympic Peninsula runs. Although this run has a lot of Class I water in its middle section, the first 6 miles, all within the park, are filled with sweepers, logjams, and braided channels that keep things exciting. If you'd rather avoid the potential portages in this stretch, you can put in near the confluence with the South Fork Hoh River. In the last bit of this run, the river drops through a small gorge. The take-out is on U.S. 101 on the north side of the Hoh River. To reach the put-in, continue north on U.S. 101 and drive 19 miles up the Upper Hoh Road. Fed by more than 150 inches of rain per year (and by glacial melt waters in summer), this run can be done all year, but is best in the rainy season.

Canoeists looking for a long run with the potential for overnighting should check out the **Wynoochee River,** which has a 19-mile run that is easy and enjoyable. Most of the river is Class I but there are a few Class II rapids to teach the novice paddler a few new skills.

CLASS III

The **Calawah River,** a tributary of the Bogachiel River, has a great 14.5-mile Class II–III run that starts at Klahanie Campground east of Forks and ends with a couple miles of paddling on the Bogachiel River. This run has lots of play spots and fun waves but is perhaps best known for the fact that it has been free of logjams for many years. This is a very important factor in enjoying an Olympic Peninsula run. To reach the put-in, drive FS 29 east from the U.S. 101–La Push Road intersection to Klahanie Campground. To reach the take-out, drive the La Push Road 5.2 miles and turn left onto a gravel road that leads to a footbridge over the Bogachiel River. You can also shorten this run by putting in at the U.S. 101 bridge or at the North Fork–South Fork confluence. This run is best done during the rainy season.

The **Wynoochee River** abounds in good paddling water from Class I up to Class III, but by far the river's finest stretch of water is the 10-mile Class II–III run from the Wynoochee Dam down through the Wynoochee Gorge. This run actually takes in two gorges, the first one easy and the second one much more difficult. Two miles into the run there is a low dam that must be portaged, and then, in the middle of the second gorge, there is a Class V rapid that also must be portaged. To reach this run, drive north from U.S. 12 just west of Montesano on Wynoochee Road (follow signs for Wynoochee Lake/Dam). The take-out is down a dirt road on the left in about 30 miles (keep left at the first fork in this road). The put-in is at the bridge on FS 2294 at the foot of the Wynoochee Dam. Because this river is dam-controlled, it is runnable year-round.

CLASS IV & V

Steep, narrow gorges crammed full of big boulders are a specialty of Olympic Peninsula rivers, and if this sort of river is what you seek, you'll find runs all over the place. However, for the most part they tend to be short runs that are best done in the middle of winter. Also, the narrower the river, the more likely it is to have trees blocking it. This makes paddling the steeper creeks and rivers of this region particularly challenging. From year to year the logs on these runs can get rearranged; landslides sometimes bury rapids or create new ones. Your best bet for paddling the Class IV and V rivers out here is to find a local paddler to go out with.

WHITEWATER RAFTING

Olympic Raft & Guide Service, 239521 U.S. 101 W, Port Angeles, WA 98363 (tel. 360/452-1443), offers scenic Class I floats on both the Hoh River and the Queets River. The Hoh River trips last only a couple of hours, but trips on the Queets are overnight excursions. Hoh River trip rates start at $35; call for rates for Queets River trips.

WILDLIFE VIEWING

Although winter isn't the best time to visit the Olympic Peninsula (it's a bit rainy), it is the best time to see the herd of **Roosevelt elk** that lives in the Hoh River valley near the Hoh Rain Forest Visitor Center. In summer these elk move to higher elevations. **Black-tailed deer** are also frequently sighted in this area throughout the year. If you're lucky, you might spot **river otters** on the Hoh River. They tend to be active early and late in the day. At the mouth of the Hoh River, accessible by a half-mile trail from the end of the Oil City Road, **harbor seals** can often be seen.

Washington's South Coast ✦ What to Do & Where to Do It

BEACHES

The beaches of the southern Washington coast south, from Gray's Harbor to the Columbia River, are for the most part long

The Southwest Washington Coast

0   15 Miles
0   15 Kilometers

strands of sand backed by low dunes. Between the mouth of Gray's Harbor at Westport and the mouth of Willapa Bay at Tokeland are 18 miles of sand known as South Beach (North Beach being the strand on the north side of Gray's Harbor). South of Willapa Bay is the Long Beach Peninsula, the most built-up piece of oceanfront real estate in the state. These two stretches of beach are lined with vacation homes and small beach towns, but are also punctuated by several state parks. Although summer is still the most popular time of year out here, other months of the year see plenty of people on the beach digging for razor clams.

On South Beach, there are four state parks that provide beach access and facilities. Just outside the marina area of Westport is **Westhaven State Park,** which is known for having the best surfing waves on the Washington coast. Just south of this park is **Westport Light State Park,** popular with beachcombers and named for the adjacent lighthouse, which at 107 feet is the tallest on the West Coast. **Twin Harbors State Park** is 2 miles south of Westport

and is the largest of the four, with more than 3 miles of beach. **Grayland Beach State Park** is just south of the town of Grayland and has almost a mile of beach. The latter two parks have nature trails, picnic areas, and campgrounds. In addition to these state parks, there are several beach access points up and down South Beach. Vehicles are allowed on much of this beach, with some restrictions.

The longest stretch of uninterrupted sand in the state of Washington is on the **Long Beach Peninsula.** For more than a century, this beach has been attracting vacationers, and some of the original Victorian-era cottages are still standing. However, the beaches at the south end of this peninsula also wear the attire of late-20th–century family beaches—Go-Kart tracks, minigolf, kite shops, saltwater taffy stores, and gift shops galore. The beach here at the south end is also extremely wide, and instead of fronting on the beach, the town of Long Beach now looks out onto a wide expanse of sand dunes. This is all the work of the Columbia River jetty, which, by protecting the shipping channels, has caused sand to be deposited to its north. Despite the vast expanses of sand, everyone tends to crowd into the same small areas of beach just off downtown Long Beach. Kite flying and horseback riding are the most popular activities here, although beach driving is also popular. More and more kite buggies (kite-pulled tricycles) are also being seen on this beach. About halfway up the Long Beach Peninsula there is public access at **Loomis Lake State Park,** which is mostly just a huge parking lot providing beach access.

If you're looking to ditch the crowds, head up to the north end of the Long Beach Peninsula, where you'll find **Leadbetter Point State Park,** which has trails that lead through forests and sand dunes to the beach. The dunes here, and to the north in Willapa National Wildlife Refuge, are nesting grounds for the endangered snowy plover and are closed to the public during the spring and summer nesting season. Between the state park and the wildlife refuge, there are more than 4 miles of nearly deserted beaches to be walked. The big drawbacks of this beach are mosquitoes and the closure of the northern section of beach during plover nesting season.

Down at the south end of the peninsula, the rocks make one last appearance near the mouth of the Columbia River. Here, at **Fort Canby State Park,** a former coast artillery site built during the Civil War, there are two beaches with decidedly different characters. **Benson Beach,** a vast expanse of sand directly north of the Columbia River jetty, is 2 miles long and bounded on the north by North Head, atop which is a lighthouse. At the base of the jetty, below the bluffs of Cape Disappointment, is the tiny cove of **Waikiki Beach,** which though small, is the most dramatic beach on this stretch of coast. Some people even go swimming here.

BIRD WATCHING

If you're in Westport in the summer, keep an eye out for brown pelicans, which sometimes come this far north from their nesting grounds in California. If you

happen to be driving between Westport and Raymond on Wash. 105, watch for eagles on the bluff between the North Cove Pioneer Cemetery and the Shoalwater Bay Indian Reservation. The bluff is north of the highway, away from the water. This stretch of highway runs right along the shore and provides good opportunities for spotting Caspian terns, black brants, sandpipers, and other migratory birds during April and May.

Up at the northern tip of the Long Beach Peninsula is the region's premier birding area. Here you'll find both **Leadbetter Point State Park** and a portion of the **Willapa National Wildlife Refuge,** where together more than 100 species of birds have been spotted. Among these is the endangered snowy plover, which nests at the point. Because the plovers nest on the sand, a portion of the point is closed to all visitors from April to September. During these months you can still hike the trails, use the beach, and explore the marshes.

The spring migratory season—April and May—is the best birding season at Leadbetter Point. At this time thousands of black brants, the smallest species of goose, stop here to rest and feed. White-fronted geese also congregate here. Shorebirds known to stop here during spring migration include red knots, pectoral sandpipers, and western sandpipers. Caspian terns may also be sighted during this time. During the fall and winter, trumpeter and tundra swans both frequent the point, as do numerous species of ducks, including pintails, buffleheads, canvasbacks, and shovelers. Winter is also a good time to look for dunlins, sanderlings, American pipits, and Lapland longspurs. During the summer, you can observe nesting snowy plovers from a distance and may also see a few stray brown pelicans. Any time of year you might spot a horned lark here.

South of Leadbetter Point State Park, between Oysterville and Ocean Park, at **Skating Lake State Park** (which is primarily a golf course), a lake and marshes are the winter home to many species of waterfowl, including trumpeter swans. South of Ocean Park, there is also good bird watching at **Loomis Lake State Park,** which, though better known for its beach access, does border 2-mile-long Loomis Lake, another wintering area for trumpeter swans.

FISHING

Gray's Harbor is the charter boat capital of Washington, with boats heading out daily in summer from Westport marina in search of salmon, tuna, and bottom fish. If you'd like to try your luck at reeling in a big one, try **Bran Lee Charters** (tel. 800/562-0163 or 360/268-9177), **Cachalot Charters** (tel. 800/356-0323 or 360/268-0323), **Deep Sea Charters** (tel. 800/562-0151 or 360/268-9300), **Neptune Charters** (tel. 800/422-0425 or 360/268-0124), or **Travis Charters** (tel. 800/648-1520 or 360/268-9140). Rates are between $55 and $65 for a day of fishing.

You don't have to go out on a boat to catch fish around here, though. You can also catch rockfish, perch, and lingcod from both the north and south jetties of Gray's Harbor. You can also try your hand at surf fishing along South Beach. Farther south, the North Jetty of the Columbia River, located in Fort Canby State Park, is another popular fishing spot where anglers even hook into salmon on occasion. **Ed's Bait and Tackle,** 207 SW Second St., Ilwaco (tel. 360/642-2248), has everything you could need to fish this area.

At Ilwaco, at the south end of the Long Beach Peninsula, you'll find more charter boats that will take you out fishing for salmon, halibut, sturgeon, or bottom fish. Try **CoHo Charters** (tel. 800/339-COHO or 360/642-3333), **Land's End Charters** (tel. 360/642-3837), **Pacific Salmon Charters** (tel. 800/831-2695 or 360/642-3466), or **Sea Breeze Charters** (tel. 360/642-2300).

Most of the rivers that empty into Willapa Bay, as well as the Johns River, which empties into the south side of Gray's Harbor, have good winter steelheading. Many of these rivers are also good for sea-run cutthroat in their lower reaches.

HORSEBACK RIDING

If you've ever dreamed about riding a horse down the beach, you can make your dream come true in Long Beach. You'll find several rental stables by the boardwalk at 10th Street. If you want to make a reservation, call **Back Country Horse Rentals** (tel. 360/642-2576) or **Skipper's Horse & Pony Rental** (tel. 360/642-3676).

ROAD BIKING

Long Beach Peninsula Loop

Up to 50 miles. Moderate–strenuous. 600-foot elevation gain. Access: From U.S. 101 in Ilwaco (south end of Long Beach Peninsula), follow Robert Gray Rd. (Wash. 100) south to Fort Canby State Park. Park at the Lewis and Clark Interpretive Center parking lot.

Stretching for nearly 26 miles, the Long Beach Peninsula is a great place to ride if you like flat roads. The route takes in Fort Canby State Park, which has an extensive network of quiet roads, then heads north through the peninsula's many small towns, eventually turning around at the quaintest historic village in the state. Along the way there are excellent restaurants, hotels, and B&Bs where you can stay for the night, cranberry bogs, oyster-packing companies, art galleries, and small state parks where you can do a bit of bird watching.

By starting at the Lewis and Clark Interpretive Center, you can learn about the history of this area before beginning your ride with a downhill coast. At the bottom of the hill, turn left to head out along the North Jetty for views of crashing surf at the mouth of the Columbia River. Turn around at the end of the road, and ride back the way you came with a view of Cape Disappointment, atop which stands the interpretive center and the oldest lighthouse in the state. Back at the main intersection, turn left. In 0.6 miles, take a left fork, and in another half-mile, turn left on the road up to North Head, site of the peninsula's other historic lighthouse. Here you encounter the longest hill of the ride as you climb up to the top of North Head.

After visiting the lighthouse and taking in the views of the ocean, ride back down the hill and turn left onto the road that leads north out of the park. In about 1 mile, turn left onto Willows Road, which will take you into Seaview, the most historic of the southern peninsula towns and home to the Shelburne Inn and its excellent Shoalwater Restaurant. Continue north on L Street (which becomes California Street), and in 1.5 miles, turn left on Tenth Street and then immediately right onto Boulevard North. Pass through the heart of Long Beach town, where there are lots of places to get snacks, and continue north for 2 miles to 95th Street. Turn right here and pedal 1.5 miles east across the peninsula (95th becomes Pioneer Road), passing several cranberry bogs along the way (October is harvest season).

At the end of Pioneer Road, turn left onto Sand Ridge Road. This side of the peninsula is much less developed and still has forests to shade you on a sunny day. It is 9 miles north to the community of Nahcotta, which is home to The Ark, one of the two most highly acclaimed restaurants on the peninsula, and an oyster-processing facility, both of which are on the shore of Willapa Bay. Continue north from Nahcotta for another 3.5 miles to the historic village of Oysterville, which was founded in 1854 on the site of productive oyster beds. Ride around the village admiring the historical buildings.

From Oysterville, cross back to the west side of the peninsula on Oysterville Road, and in 1.25 miles, turn left onto I Street and then right onto G Street. Ride through the community of Surfside, and at the end of G Street, turn left onto 295th Street. In five blocks, turn right onto N Street and then left onto Joe Johns Road. Turn right onto Vernon Avenue and ride 0.75 miles south to 274th Place. Turn right here and visit Pacific Pines State Park if you feel like a walk on the beach. Turn south off of 274th Place onto Park Avenue/L Place. In about 1.4 miles, this road dead-ends and you must continue south on North Pacific Highway (Wash. 103), the peninsula's main north–south route. In 2.8 miles, pass a road on your left that provides access to Loomis Lake, and in another 0.6 miles, reach the entrance (on the right) to the oceanfront portion of Loomis Lake State Park. From this park it is 4.3 miles south on the highway to 95th Street/Pioneer Road. Ride across the peninsula again on

this island, but this time turn right. Follow Sand Ridge Road 4.3 miles south (it eventually merges with U.S. 101) into the town of Ilwaco.

In Ilwaco, continue straight through town almost to the water and take the last road to the right. Take your next left onto Second Street, which becomes Robert Gray Drive and leads back to Fort Canby State Park and your car.

This ride can be shortened at many points along the way simply by crossing the peninsula and turning south. If you make Pioneer Road your northern limit, you'll end up doing a nice 25-mile loop.

SEA KAYAKING & FLAT-WATER CANOEING

In Gray's Harbor, kayak rentals and guided sea kayak trips are available from **Northwest Experiences** (tel. 360/533-0154). Many of these trips are on the Chehalis River.

Willapa Bay and Long Island

Up to 20 miles. Moderate–strenuous. Access: The boat launch for Long Island is at the Willapa National Wildlife Headquarters on U.S. 101 about 11 miles north of Seaview/Long Beach.

Willapa Bay is perhaps best known for its tasty oysters, but among sea kayakers it is also well known as the best place to paddle on the southern Washington coast. Long Island, which is more than 6 miles long and is part of the Willapa National Wildlife Refuge, is the main destination of paddlers. The island has five boat-in campsites, which makes this a popular overnight trip. The island's main attraction is its 274-acre grove of old-growth western red cedars, the last such grove anywhere in the region. These trees are humongous, some reaching 11 feet in diameter at the base. Unfortunately, much of the rest of the island was logged off by Weyerhaeuser in 1993. A logging road runs 2.5 miles across the island and serves as a hiking trail for island visitors.

Several sloughs cut into the shoreline of this island, and it is to these sloughs that sea kayakers invariably gravitate. Just be sure to pay attention to the tides when paddling here. Tides fluctuate several feet, can create strong currents, and leave Long Island surrounded by mudflats at low tide. High tide is definitely the time to paddle here. These waters can also be quite dangerous when sudden squalls sweep across. Choppy seas and cold water are no place to capsize. A sea kayaker drowned under just such conditions a few years ago.

SURFING

The Westport area, on the south side of Gray's Harbor, is home to the best and most reliable surfing on the Washington coast. At **Westhaven State Park,** the jetty at the mouth of Gray's Harbor creates excellent waves. These waves hold their shape up to about 6 or 7 feet, but over that they tend to break up. The best waves are at low tide. In addition to the surf at Westhaven, there are often good waves down the beach at **Westport State Park.** There are also sometimes rideable waves east of the Westhaven jetty on **Halfmoon Bay** and off the **finger jetties** at the end of Neddie Rose Drive on the north side of the Westport Marina. For an area surf report, equipment, or board and wetsuit rentals, contact **The Surf Shop,** 207 N Montesano St., Westport (tel. 360/268-0992), the **North Coast Surf Co.,** 321 Dock St., Westport (tel. 800/648-1520), or **Free Fall Surf Shop,** 2172 Wash. 105, Grayland (tel. 360/267-0705).

WALKS & NATURAL ROADSIDE ATTRACTIONS

Leadbetter Point Trails

3.5 miles. Easy. 20-foot elevation gain. Access: From U.S. 101 in Seaview, drive north on Wash. 103, and follow signs for Oysterville and Leadbetter Point State Park at the northern tip of the peninsula. Map: Not necessary.

Leadbetter Point State Park, at the north end of the Long Beach Peninsula, may be well known to bird watchers for its wintering and migratory birds, but for most visitors it is best known as a great place to go for a walk. The park, which adjoins a unit of Willapa National Wildlife Refuge,

has a surprising diversity of landscape, from sandy beach to grassy dunes to shady pine forests to salt marshes. A loop trail between the park's two parking lots takes in several of these areas. At low tide this loop can be closed by hiking along the shore of Willapa Bay on the park's east side. Add to this walk the half-mile walk out to the beach and you get a fascinating look at what this peninsula was like before all the development. If you come out here anytime other than winter, be sure to bring lots of mosquito repellent. From April through August, parts of the north end of Leadbetter Point are closed to protect the snowy plover nests, which are nothing more than scraped-out areas in the sand.

Cape Disappointment

2 miles round-trip. Easy. 200-foot elevation gain. Access: From U.S. 101 in Ilwaco (south end of Long Beach Peninsula), follow Robert Gray Rd. (Wash. 100) south to Fort Canby State Park. The trailhead is at the Waikiki Beach parking lot on the road to the North Jetty. Map: Not necessary.

Perched atop Cape Disappointment are two of Fort Canby State Park's most popular attractions—the Lewis and Clark Interpretive Center and the Cape Disappointment lighthouse. These two buildings can both be visited by way of a 2-mile–long trail starting at Waikiki Beach, and though there are easier accesses to the two buildings, none are as scenic as this walk, which climbs steeply through forest to the top of the cape. From the top, views out over the mouth of the Columbia River frequently make it evident why this river mouth has sunk so many ships and taken so many sailors' lives. An alternate route back to Waikiki Beach goes past the nearby Coast Guard Station.

North Head Trail

3.5 miles round-trip. Easy. 200-foot elevation gain. Access: From U.S. 101 in Ilwaco (south end of Long Beach Peninsula), follow Robert Gray Rd. (Wash. 100) south to Fort Canby State Park. The trailhead is 0.25 miles west of the campground on Lake O'Neil. Map: Not necessary.

The longest hike in Fort Canby State Park takes in two headlands, only one of which is on the water. From the parking lot, first head up to the top of 150-foot McKenzie Head. Atop this headland is a bunker that was used as a gun battery during World War II. Today McKenzie Head is more than half a mile from the ocean, but before the construction of the North Jetty, the waves crashed at the foot of this bluff. Head back down this trail to the parking lot, cross the road, and strike out on the trail to North Head. This trail winds its way past marshes and bluffs and then climbs the 200-foot-high wooded bluff of North Head. The trail ends at the North Head Lighthouse, which is perched on cliffs above the ocean. This is a good place to watch for gray whales. Return the way you came.

Coastal Forest Trail

1.5 miles round-trip. Easy. 50-foot elevation gain. Access: From U.S. 101 in Ilwaco (south end of Long Beach Peninsula), follow Robert Gray Rd. (Wash. 100) south to Fort Canby State Park. The trailhead is adjacent to the general store. Map: Not necessary.

Located on the east side of the park overlooking Baker Bay and the Ilwaco boat channel, this trail loops through a magnificent forest of old-growth Sitka spruce trees.

WHALE WATCHING

Each year between February and May, gray whales migrating to and from the calving grounds off Baja California pass by the Washington coast. The whales sometimes come so close to the mouth of Gray's Harbor that they can be seen from the observation tower at the marina in Westport. However, for a closer look, you might want to head out on a whale-watching boat trip. These trips usually run between March and May. Contact **Neptune Whale Watch Cruises** (tel. 800/422-0425 or 206/268-0124) or **Westport Charters** (tel. 800/562-0157 or 206/268-9144) if you're interested. Rates are around $20 for adults and $13 for children.

Down in the Long Beach area, whales, as well as seals, can sometimes be seen

from the North Jetty in Fort Canby State Park. Nearby North Head is an even better vantage point from which to scan the seas for the distinctive spout of the gray whale.

WILDLIFE VIEWING

At the John's River Wildlife Area on Wash. 105 between Aberdeen and Westport, **Roosevelt elk** can often be seen from a trail that leads along the top of a dike. **Black-tailed deer** are often spotted here. You might also be able to spot some elk near the mouth of the Bear River in, or adjacent to, Willapa National Wildlife Refuge on U.S. 101 northeast of Seaview/Long Beach. From the harbor jetties in Westport, you might spot both **harbor seals** and **California sea lions.**

Campgrounds & Other Accommodations

CAMPING

If you plan to camp, you can find out about the region's numerous campgrounds by contacting **Olympic National Park** (tel. 360/452-4501 or 360/452-0330) or **Olympic National Forest** (tel. 360/956-2300). There are 16 campgrounds within the national park. Campground fees range from $8 to $10 per night.

Reservations for some national forest campgrounds can be made by calling **National Forest Reservation Service** (tel. 800/280-CAMP). Olympic Peninsula and Washington coast state parks that accept campsite reservations through **Reservations Northwest** (tel. 800/452-5687) include Lake Cushman, Dosewallips, Fort Flagler, Sequim Bay, Pacific Beach, Ocean City, Twin Harbors, Grayland Beach, and Fort Canby.

THE EAST & NORTH SIDES OF THE PENINSULA

On the east side of the Olympic Peninsula, the several state park campgrounds are among your best choices. **Potlatch State Park** (35 campsites, 18 with hookups; year-round), on U.S. 101 near the

Great Bend of Hood Canal, is popular with anglers. Inland on Lake Cushman Road (Wash. 119) from U.S. 101, **Lake Cushman State Park** (81 campsites, 30 with hookups; year-round) is favored by water skiers, so don't expect quiet. North of here, **Dosewallips State Park** (87 campsites, 40 with hookups; year-round), on U.S. 101 at the mouth of the Dosewallips River, is a good choice both for anglers and for whitewater kayakers.

Inland from Hood Canal, there are several more remote campgrounds that are good bases for day hikes or as starting points for backpacking trips. Up the Skokomish River from Lake Cushman on FS 24 is the national park's **Staircase Campground** (59 campsites; year-round), which is the trailhead for the Six Ridge, Flapjack Lakes, and Anderson Pass trails. Up FS 25 from U.S. 101, along the Hamma Hamma River, the **Lena Creek Campground** (13 campsites; seasonal) provides access to the Lena Lakes Trail, part of which is open to mountain bikes. On FS 2610, which parallels the Dosewallips River and provides access to Hayden Pass, Anderson Pass, and Lake Constance trails, you'll find the national forest's **Elkhorn Campground** (16 campsites; seasonal) and, at the end of the road, the national park's **Dosewallips Campground** (30 campsites; seasonal). Both of these are in forested settings on the river's banks.

In the Port Townsend area, there are also several state park campgrounds that are former military bases. These campgrounds tend to attract mostly RVers. At the north end of Marrowstone Island on Wash. 116 is **Fort Flagler State Park** (116 campsites; seasonal), where the campsites (some on a forested bluff and some in an open field) are close to a protected beach on Kilisut Harbor. Fishing is what attracts most people, but this campground is a good base for road-bike rides and sea kayak explorations of Indian Island. **Fort Worden State Park** (83 campsites, 80 with hookups; year-round), on the west side of Port Townsend, has the distinct feel of a 19th-century military base and, with a restaurant and conference facility, is not for campers seeking solitude. The beach is the big draw here, and the campsites are in a field close to the sand. About midway

between these two campgrounds is **Old Fort Townsend State Park** (40 campsites; seasonal), which is smaller and quieter than either of the other two old-fort campgrounds. Some of the campsites are in the forest and some are on the edge of a field.

In the Sequim area, there are two campgrounds, both of which are on the water. **Sequim Bay State Park** (86 campsites, 26 with hookups; year-round) is right on U.S. 101 and gets a lot of traffic noise. The **Dungeness Recreation Area** (65 campsites; seasonal), at the foot of Dungeness Spit, is by far the better choice in this area. Sea kayakers, boardsailors, bicyclists, hikers, and bird watchers will all find that this is a good base camp. You'll find this campground 4 miles north of U.S. 101 off Kitchen–Dick Road on the west side of Sequim.

The six national park campgrounds on the northern edge of the park are some of the busiest in the park due to their proximity to U.S. 101. **Deer Park Campground** (18 campsites; seasonal) is the easternmost of these campgrounds (take Deer Park Road from U.S. 101 east of Port Angeles) and the only high-elevation (5,400 feet) campground in Olympic National Park. Deer Park is reached by a winding one-lane gravel road that will have you wondering how you're ever going to get back down the mountain. Deer frequent the campground and hiking trails head out across the ridges and valleys. Because of its proximity to Hurricane Ridge, the national park's **Heart O' the Hills Campground** (105 campsites; year-round), on Hurricane Ridge Road 5 miles south of the Olympic National Park Visitor Center, is very popular. Several trails start at or near the campground, which makes this a good choice if you want to do lots of day hikes. On Olympic Hot Springs Road up the Elwha River, which is popular with kayakers and fly anglers, there are a couple of national park campgrounds almost side by side. **Elwha Campground** (41 campsites; year-round) is the trailhead for a trail leading up to Hurricane Ridge. **Altaire Campground** (30 campsites; seasonal) has a boat ramp used by rafters and kayakers. Yes, there are hot springs up this road (see "Hot Springs," above).

West of Port Angeles along Wash. 112, there are three campgrounds on the shore of the Strait of Juan de Fuca. **Salt Creek County Park** (80 campsites; year-round), 13 miles west of Port Angeles, is a great choice for sea kayakers and surfers and is among the most scenic spots on this whole coast. About 20 miles west of Port Angeles, where the Lyre River empties into the strait, is the private **Lyre River Park** (75 campsites, 65 with hookups; year-round; tel. 360/928-3436 for reservations), which is one of the best private campgrounds around. Also in the same area is the DNR's **Lyre River Campground** (11 campsites; seasonal). About 40 miles west of Port Angeles is **Pillar Point County Park** (37 campsites; seasonal), which perches atop a bluff overlooking the strait.

The only campground on Crescent Lake is at **Fairholm** (87 campsites; seasonal) at the west end of the lake. This campground is very popular with power-boaters and consequently tends to be rather noisy. The nearby **Sol Duc Campground** (80 campsites; year-round), set amid impressive stands of old-growth trees, is adjacent to the Sol Duc Hot Springs, and is, not surprisingly, one of the most popular campgrounds in the national park.

Heading west from Lake Crescent on U.S. 101, there are several campgrounds along the banks of the Sol Duc River. The national forest's **Klahowya Campground** (55 campsites; seasonal) is 9 miles west of Lake Crescent. Continuing west, other riverside campgrounds popular with anglers and kayakers include the DNR's **Bear Creek Campground** (10 campsites; seasonal) and **Tumbling Rapids Campground** (20 campsites; year-round) on Rayonier timberlands.

The national park's remote **Ozette Campground** (14 campsites; year-round), on the north shore of Lake Ozette, is a good choice for sea kayakers/canoeists and people wanting to day hike to the beaches on either side of Cape Alava. There is a designated swimming beach on the lake. Also on Lake Ozette is the boat-in **Erickson's Bay Campground** (15 campsites; year-round).

THE WEST & SOUTH SIDES OF THE PENINSULA

If you want to say you've camped at the wettest campground in the contiguous U.S., head for the national park's **Hoh Campground** (95 campsites; year-round) in the Hoh River valley. Despite the damp, this is a very popular campground. The national park's **Queets Campground** (20 campsites; year-round), which is more off the beaten track, has good hiking and whitewater kayaking nearby. This campground is 14 miles up the Queets Road from U.S. 101. Other rain-forest camping options include the three campgrounds on Quinault Lake. On the north shore, in the national park, is the walk-in **July Creek Campground** (29 campsites; year-round). On the south shore are two national forest campgrounds—**Willaby** (22 campsites; seasonal) and **Falls Creek** (31 campsites; seasonal), both of which are most popular with boaters and anglers. East of Lake Quinault, up the Quinault River valley, are two more national park rain-forest campgrounds—**North Fork** (7 campsites; year-round) and **Graves Creek** (30 campsites; year-round)—that provide access to a couple of the park's long-distance hiking trails.

Paddlers and anglers will find that **Bogachiel State Park** (41 campsites; year-round), on the Bogachiel River, 6 miles south of Forks on U.S. 101, is a convenient choice. Campsites are set under huge old spruce trees. From here, canoeists and kayakers can paddle 20 miles down almost to the mouth of the Quillayute River. Farther south, on the banks of the Hoh River, the Washington Department of Natural Resources operates four primitive campgrounds for tenters. **Hoh Oxbow Campground** (8 campsites; year-round) is right on U.S. 101 and is the most convenient and most popular. Heading upriver on the Hoh Rain Forest Road are **Willoughby Creek** (3 campsites; year-round) and **Minnie Peterson** (8 campsites; year-round). Downriver on Oil City Road is **Cottonwood Campground** (9 campsites; year-round; no water), which is a good place to camp if you want to explore the national park coast north of the Hoh River. An alternative here is to hike a half-mile to the beach and camp there.

Along the peninsula's west side, there are also several beach campgrounds. These include the national park's **Mora Campground** (91 campsites; year-round) on the beautiful Rialto Beach at the mouth of the Quillayute River west of Forks. If you're prepared to hike in with your gear, you can also camp on Second Beach (half-mile hike) and Third Beach (1.5-mile hike). South of the Hoh River, along the only stretch of U.S. 101 that is right on the beach, you'll find **Kalaloch Campground** (177 campsites; year-round), which is the national park's largest campground. On Wash. 109 north of Ocean Shores are two state park campgrounds. **Pacific Beach State Park** (138 campsites, including 20 hookup sites; year-round) is a small, ex-posed, and crowded patch of sand with little to recommend it other than good ra-zor clamming nearby. More appealing is **Ocean City State Park** (178 campsites, in-cluding 29 with hookups; year-round), which at least has trees for protection against the wind. This is a good choice if you plan to bicycle along this stretch of coast.

Inland from Aberdeen, off of U.S. 12, there are several out-of-the-way camp-grounds that are good choices for canoeists and mountain bikers. **Schafer State Park** (53 campsites, 6 with hookups; year-round) is on the East Fork Satsop River, which has good Class I paddling and tubing. More challenging whitewater pad-dling is available nearby. **Lake Sylvia State Park** (35 campsites; year-round) is on a small lake that is fun to explore in a canoe or sea kayak. Farther north, on Lake Wynoochee off Wynoochee Road (FS 22) north of Montesano, is **Coho Campground** (56 campsites, including 10 walk-in sites; seasonal), which is right on the mountain-bike trail that circles the lake and has a good view of the Olympic Mountains. This campground is, however, primarily a fishermen's hangout.

THE SOUTH COAST

Washington's south coast is more a vaca-tion home/beach cottage kind of coast, and consequently, campgrounds are in short supply. South of Westport, you'll find two beach campgrounds—**Twin Harbors State Park** (326 campsites, including 49 hookup sites; year-round) and **Grayland Beach State Park** (65 campsites, including 60 with hookups; year-round). The only other rec-ommendable area campground is **Fort Canby State Park** (254 campsites, includ-ing 60 with hookups; year-round), down at the mouth of the Columbia River at the southern end of the Long Beach Penin-sula. This park has campsites on a small lake, as well as campsites at the foot of North Head. Some of the sites in the lat-ter area are tucked in amid massive boul-ders, which gives these campsites a unique feel. These are by far the best campsites on the south coast.

INNS & LODGES

NORTH SIDE

Lake Crescent Lodge

416 Lake Crescent Rd., Port Angeles, WA 98363-8672. Tel. 360/928-3211. 52 rms and cabins (48 with bath). $67 double with shared bath; $88–$99 double with private bath; $99–$130 cottage. AE, CB, DC, MC, V.

Located 20 miles west of Port Angeles on the south shore of picturesque Lake Crescent stands this historic lodge. Wood paneling, hardwood floors, a stone fire-place, and a sunroom make the lobby a popular spot for just sitting and relaxing with friends. The guest rooms in this main lodge building are the oldest and all have shared bathrooms. I like these rooms the best, even though they are a bit small. Rowboat rentals are available.

Log Cabin Resort

3183 E Beach Rd., Port Angeles, WA 98362. Tel. 360/928-3325. Fax 360/928-3245. 4 rms, 24 cabins (8 with bath). $42 double cabin with shared bath; $67–$80 double cabin with private bath; $95 double room; $109 chalet. MC, V. Closed Oct–May.

This log-cabin resort on the sunny north shore of Lake Crescent first opened in

1895 and still has buildings that date back to the 1920s. The least expensive accommodations here are rustic one-room log cabins in which you provide the bedding and share a bathroom a short walk away (basically this is camping without the tent). More comfortable are the 1928 cabins with private bathrooms, some of which also have kitchenettes (you provide the cooking-and-eating utensils). The lodge rooms and a chalet offer the greatest comfort and best views.

Sol Duc Hot Springs Resort

P.O. Box 2169, Soleduck Rd., Hwy. 101, Port Angeles, WA 98362. Tel. 360/327-3583. 32 cabins. $78–$88 double. AE, DISC, MC, V. Closed Oct to mid-May.

Sol Duc Hot Springs has for years been a popular family vacation spot. Campers, day-trippers, and resort guests all spend the day soaking and playing in the hot-water swimming pools. Cabins are done in modern motel style and are comfortable, if not spacious. Three hot-springs–fed swimming pools are the focal point at Sol Duc, and the pools are open to the public for a small fee. Massages are available.

WEST SIDE

Manitou Lodge

P.O. Box 600, Forks, WA 98331. Tel. 360/374-6295. 7 rms. $60–$75 double. MC, V.

This secluded B&B is set on 10 private acres and is only minutes from some of the most beautiful and remote beaches in the Northwest. The best room in the house is the Sacajawea, which has a marble fireplace and king bed. A separate cabin houses two of the rooms.

Kalaloch Lodge

157151 Hwy. 101, Forks, WA 98331. Tel. 360/962-2271. Fax 360/962-2271. 18 rms, 40 cabins. June–Oct $56–$80 double, $99–$150 double in cabins (lower weekday rates in off season). AE, MC, V.

When you arrive at Kalaloch Lodge (pronounced Kah-*lay*-loch) you have an immediate sense of having arrived at the edge of the continent. The rustic, cedar-shingled lodge and its cluster of cabins perch on a grassy bluff. Below, the Pacific Ocean thunders against a sandy beach where huge driftwood logs are scattered like so many twigs. The breathtaking setting makes this one of the most popular lodges on the coast, and it is advisable to book rooms at least four months in advance.

Lake Quinault Lodge

P.O. Box 7, Quinault, WA 98575. Tel. 800/562-6672 (in Washington and Oregon) or 360/288-2900. 92 rms. June–Oct $92–$125 double, $170–$220 suite; Oct–June $52–$110 double, $100–$180 suite. AE, MC, V.

Located on the shore of Lake Quinault in the southwest corner of the park, this imposing grande dame of the Olympic Peninsula wears an ageless tranquility. Huge old firs and cedars shade the rustic lodge, and Adirondack chairs on the deck command a view of the lawn. There's a wide range of room styles, from small rooms in the main lodge to larger, modern rooms with wicker furniture and little balconies, to rooms with fireplaces. Canoes and paddleboats can be rented. Other facilities include an indoor pool, whirlpool, croquet lawn, and badminton court.

THE NORTH CASCADES

VAST AND INACCESSIBLE ARE NOT WORDS THAT ARE OFTEN USED TO describe the Cascade Range, but here in the northern reaches of the range, they are the only words that seem appropriate for a landscape that contains the largest wilderness areas in the state.

The North Cascades, though lying only 120 miles northeast of Seattle by road, are the least visited and most inaccessible mountains in Washington. Here, and nowhere else in the state, gray wolves and grizzly bears still roam, and human encroachment on their dominion is limited for the most part to the edges of the wilderness. So rugged are the North Cascades that although the first attempt to build a road across these mountains was begun in 1893, it was not until 1972 that a road was finally completed through the steep-walled valleys and over the high passes. However, each winter, with the coming of heavy snows, avalanches and landslides make keeping the road open to traffic an impossible task. Consequently, from November to May, the North Cascades Highway is closed and the region sinks back into its isolated natural state.

The North Cascades National Park Complex is at the heart of this region. Note the name; this is not just a park but a complex. The complex includes not only the park itself but also Ross Lake and Lake Chelan national recreation areas. (For those not familiar with the semantics of government land use, a national park is a preserve where the ecosystem is maintained in as natural a state as possible—a sort of museum of the way it used to be out there. In contrast, a national recreation area is a vast playground, often somewhat

impacted by humans, where people and recreational uses of the outdoors receive equal priority with nature.) Although the two national recreation areas are not wilderness areas in the strictest sense of the word, they are wild and remote nonetheless, with minimal development or signs of human habitation outside of a few areas. The park complex is in effect a massive wilderness area—and beyond the boundaries of the park complex, the wilderness does not end. To the west lie the Mount Baker Wilderness, Mount Baker National Recreation Area, and Noisy–Diobsud Wilderness. To the south, the park complex is bordered by the Glacier Peak Wilderness, and it in turn borders the Henry M. Jackson Wilderness. On the east, the park complex is bordered by the Lake Chelan–Sawtooth Wilderness and the Pasayten Wilderness.

Mount Terror, Mount Despair, Mount Fury, Damnation Peak, Forbidden Peak, Phantom Pass, Jagged Ridge, Icy Peak, Rainy Pass. With names like these, is it any wonder that North Cascades National Park Complex is one of the nation's least visited national parks? It's obvious that this park was not created by the PR department or the tourism board. If you had the choice between a visit to such places as Paradise and Sunrise in Mount Rainier National Park and Diablo Lake or Rainy Pass, which would you choose? It also doesn't help that there is only one paved road through the park and even the trails tend to be long one-way routes that don't lend themselves at all to weekend trips or loop hikes. A hike in these mountains requires planning and a good chunk of time if you want to really get into the heart of the park, but for anyone with time to explore, there are incomparable outdoors adventures and experiences to be had here. If you're looking for someplace to really get away from it all, there is no better place than these mountains.

The Lay of the Land

Geologically speaking, the North Cascades are some of the most complex and least understood mountains in North America. Though as elsewhere in the Cascade Range there are volcanic peaks here—Mount Baker and Glacier Peak—the vast majority of the region's peaks are metamorphic in origin and display a bafflingly wide range of ages and origins. These peaks were formed over millions of years as a tectonic plate drifting northward from the South Pacific slammed into the North American coast, causing the area's sedimentary rocks to buckle, fold, and metamorphose. In some areas, the rock in the North Cascades is obviously the result of this collision and subsequent metamorphosis. However, in other areas, there is rock that predates the tectonic collision. Nowhere is this complexity more readily observable than from Heather Meadows on the northern slopes of Mount Baker.

At 10,778 feet, **Mount Baker** is the most northerly of the Cascades's volcanic peaks. The mountain, which dates back roughly 1 million years, is comprised of layers of ash and lava. As with other Cascade volcanoes, Mount Baker has been formed by the upwelling of molten lava as the oceanic plate has slid under the continental plate. Although the last lava flows poured off this mountain 9,000 years ago, there have been more recent signs that Mount Baker is still an active volcano. In the 1800s there were ash eruptions, and in 1975 steam melted ice fields and formed a lake in Sherman Crater near the summit of the mountain.

Though the volcanic bulk of Mount Baker dominates the region, the peaks surrounding Baker are not of volcanic origin. Rugged **Mount Shuksan** (9,127 feet), which is among the most photographed mountains in the country, is an upthrust plug of igneous rock that dates back 10 million years. **Mount Herman** (6,285 feet), which rises above the Mount Baker Ski Area on its northwest corner, is far older than either Shuksan or Baker. Geologists currently believe this mountain rose as an island in the South Pacific some 300 million years ago and then rafted atop moving tectonic plates to eventually slam into this region.

Geologic complexity has been further augmented in the North Cascades by glaciation both past and present. In past ice ages both alpine glaciers and the continental ice sheet covered this region. The visual legacy of this intensive glaciation today can be seen in the wide U-shaped valleys carved out by the ice sheet. The single most fascinating legacy of this region's ice-age glaciation is **Lake Chelan.** At 1,500 feet deep and only 2 miles wide at its widest, this 55-mile-long lake is the third deepest lake in the United States. The bottom of the lake is actually 400 feet below sea level, due to the fact that during the ice ages, sea level was considerably lower than it is today. The lake was formed by the interaction between the continental ice sheet, which spread down the valley of the Columbia River, and an alpine glacier that flowed down the Stehekin Valley from the North Cascades. As the alpine glacier reached the Columbia River and the continental ice sheet, a large terminal moraine was formed, eventually blocking the entire valley mouth to a depth of nearly 1,500 feet.

Glacial activity continues to this day due to the large amounts of snow that fall each winter in the North Cascades. Almost 600 inches of the white stuff fall on Mount Baker each winter. That's 50 feet of snow! No wonder the North Cascades lay claim to more than half the glaciers in the lower 48 states. Among these is Mount Baker's **Coleman Glacier,** which is the only advancing U.S. glacier south of Alaska. The massive amounts of snow that fall on Mount Baker have also become the major claim to fame of the Mount Baker Ski Area, which is a major snowboarding mecca famous for its deep snow, steep chutes, and radical cliff drops.

While snow dumps by the foot on the west side of the North Cascades, on the east side a drier snow is falling in lesser quantities. Draining the eastern slopes of the North Cascades, the Methow River carves a narrow, steep-walled valley as it makes its way southeastward to the Columbia River at Pateros. Due to its northerly setting and the height of the mountains to the south, the air in the **Methow Valley** stays cold longer than it does in other parts of the Cascades. In the Methow Valley, it's cross-country skiers (and snowmobilers) rather than downhillers who have taken advantage of this dry powder snow and the plentiful east-side sunshine. Within this narrow valley is the second most extensive network of cross-country ski trails in the country.

The Methow Valley is rapidly gaining national recognition for its cross-country skiing, but not too many years ago developers were hoping to construct a massive downhill ski resort, complete with thousands of condominiums. The battle over what was to be known as the Early Winters ski resort was a harsh one here in the valley. Those valley residents who saw a chance for the valley to overcome its economic straits were all for the resort. Other valley residents saw the construction of such a resort as the end of the quiet life they most valued in the Methow Valley. Eventually, through the development of the Methow Valley Sport Trails Association and the construction of the valley's 175-kilometer network of ski trails (now also used in summer by mountain bikers), the forces fighting the downhill resort won the valley over to their point of view.

Today, though the valley is rapidly being subdivided even without the presence of a ski resort, the development is on a far more manageable, sustainable, and responsible level. The small town of **Winthrop**—which long before ski resorts became a topic of conversation in this valley—gave itself a makeover as a Wild West town, complete with wooden sidewalks and rustic false fronts, and has become the commercial center of the valley. Ski shops, hotels, and even a tiny brew pub hint at the town's changing character. Strangely enough, this development is coming despite the fact that in winter Winthrop cannot be reached by way of the North Cascades Highway and is roughly 250 miles from Seattle.

During the summer months, when Winthrop serves as the eastern terminus of the scenic highway, many of the valley's ski trails become popular with mountain bikers, which is increasingly turning this into a summer destination as well as a winter destination. The Methow River is run by several whitewater rafting companies and is also popular with kayakers. This valley is home base for numerous outfitters that lead horse, llama, and even burro trips into the remote Pasayten Wilderness.

Inaccessibility is the watchword on the region's two largest lakes. Lake Chelan, which lies to the south of the Methow Valley on the east side of the Cascades, is the third deepest lake in the country and stretches for 55 miles from the town of **Chelan** deep into the North Cascades. The community of **Stehekin,** at the lake's northern end, is accessible only by foot, boat, or plane. The name Stehekin is derived from a Native American word meaning roughly "the way through," a reference to the fact that for centuries the route up the Stehekin River to Cascade Pass was a Native American trading route and one of the only ways across the rugged North Cascades. Today there is a road that follows this ancient trading route up the Stehekin Valley for another 23 miles deeper into the North Cascades. During the summer months, shuttle buses carry campers and backpackers up and down this road.

North of Wash. 20 (the North Cascades Highway), **Ross Lake** is even more inaccessible. This lake, a reservoir formed by the Ross Dam, extends 25 miles north to just over the border into Canada and has no regularly scheduled boat service and no communities on its shores. There is, however, the rustic Ross Lake Resort at the lake's south end. This resort rents floating cabins and offers water taxi service up and down the lake. At the northern end, a wolf pack has taken up residence in recent years, and grizzly bears have occasionally been seen. Together the presence of these two species of predators indicates how remote and untrammeled is the wilderness of this region.

Draining the North Cascades are numerous rivers, the largest of which is the **Skagit River.** This river still supports strong salmon runs, and during January and February as many as 500 bald eagles descend on the river to feast on dying salmon. In its upper regions, the Skagit River is dammed in three places. The **Gorge Dam** is the first of these dams and is the upper limit of salmon runs today. Above this dam, in rapid succession, is the **Diablo Dam,** which forms **Diablo Lake.** This lake is fed by 10% of the glaciers in the lower 48 states, and due to suspended sediment in these glacial meltwaters, the lake takes on an amazing shade of turquoise. Above this lake lies **Ross Dam** and **Ross Lake.**

In addition to the **North Cascades Highway (Wash. 20),** several other roads provide access to the North Cascades. **Wash. 542** leads east from Bellingham to the Mount Baker Ski Area and Heather Meadows scenic area. After the North Cascades Highway, this is probably the busiest road in the region, and is busier in the summer than it is in the winter. **Wash. 530** heads east from Arlington to connect with **Wash. 20** at Rockport. This highway also connects to the Mountain Loop Highway, a narrow winding road that is unpaved between Barlow Pass and the White Chuck River. The **Mountain Loop Highway** starts north of Snohomish off Wash. 9 and ends at the small town of Darrington. This road provides access to the Glacier Peak Wilderness and the Boulder River Wilderness.

Parks & Other Hot Spots

THE NORTH CASCADES WEST

Mount Baker Wilderness Area/Mount Baker National Recreation Area

Accessible from Wash. 542 in the north and the Baker Lake Rd. in the south. Tel. 800/627-0062, 360/856-5700, or 360/599-2714. Camping, hiking, backpacking, cross-country skiing, downhill skiing, fishing.

Mount Baker is the northernmost of the U.S. volcanic Cascade peaks and sits alone on the western edge of the North Cascades. Visible from all over the north end of Puget Sound and the San Juan Islands, the mountain stays cloaked in snow throughout the year, and on its glacier-clad slopes can be found the only advancing glacier in the contiguous United States. This phenomenon is due to the almost constant winter storms that dump nearly 600 inches of snow each winter on this and other area peaks. It is this immense load of snow that annually makes the Mount Baker Ski Area the first Washington ski area to open and the last to close. This ski area is one of the nation's snowboarding meccas, and despite the name, it is actually many miles from Mount Baker, which lies within the wilderness area and is off-limits to such intrusions as ski lifts and parking lots.

Heather Meadows, at the end of Wash. 542, is the site of the Mount Baker Ski Area, and in the summer is the most visited spot in the area. The panoramic views, numerous short hiking trails, and beautiful meadows have earned the Heather Meadows area a reputation to rival that of Paradise or Sunrise in Mount Rainier National Park. The scene of Mount Shuksan reflected in Picture Lake is one of the most photographed in the country, and the road up from Heather Meadows to Artist Point is equally breathtaking.

North Cascades National Park

Accessible from Wash. 20 (the North Cascades Hwy.). Tel. 360/873-4500 (ext. 37 or 39), 360/386-4495, or 360/856-5703 (ext. 14). Hiking, backpacking, fishing.

One of the least visited and most overlooked national parks in the West, North Cascades National Park preserves the Northwest's most rugged mountains. The park is very unusual in that there isn't a single road within the park. Although the North Cascades Highway (Wash. 20) passes between the two units of the park, it is actually within the Ross Lake National Recreation Area as it passes through the North Cascades. Making the park even more inaccessible is the fact that the North

Cascades Highway is closed by snow for half of the year. Though there are a few short trails suitable for day hikes or overnight backpacking trips, most trails here require multiple nights backpacking in the wilderness to be fully appreciated. So remote is this park that, in its northernmost section along the Canadian border, there are wolves in residence. This same section of the park is also home to a few grizzly bears, among the only ones in Washington State. A trip into this region is a true wilderness experience. The flip side of long hiking trails is that the shorter trails are extremely crowded. Don't head someplace like Cascade Pass seeking solitude!

Ross Lake National Recreation Area

Accessible from Wash. 20. Tel. 360/873-4500 (ext. 37 or 39) or 360/386-4495. Camping, hiking, backpacking, flat-water canoeing, fishing.

Stretching for 25 miles north from Wash. 20 into Canada, Ross Lake, a vast reservoir formed by the Ross Dam, is something of an inland fjord. Long and narrow, the lake is flanked on either side by steep forested mountains as it slices through the snow-clad peaks of the North Cascades. Inaccessible by road, except through Canada to Hozomeen at the far north end of the lake, this recreation area is remote and little visited. Consequently, it is still home to both wolves and grizzly bears in its northernmost reaches. Backcountry campsites line the eastern shore of the lake, which is paralleled by a hiking trail. These campsites are popular both with boaters and hikers. The former either rent boats at the Ross Lake Resort, a collection of floating cabins at the south end of the lake, or pay to have their own boat or boats shuttled around Ross Dam on a truck operated by the resort. The recreation area also includes the North Cascades Highway corridor, as well as turquoise Diablo Lake.

Glacier Peak Wilderness

Accessible from the Mountain Loop Hwy. east of Granite Falls. Tel. 360/436-1155 or 360/691-7791. Hiking, backpacking, fishing.

The trails of the Glacier Peak wilderness are some of the most difficult in the state. Many are old miners' trails, while others can be reached only by first hiking miles of abandoned roads. These two factors have conspired to keep the crowds away from much of this wilderness. Sure, there are the popular trails that are packed on weekends, but there are also long-distance hikes for people with plenty of time. One of the more popular long hikes here is the route around Glacier Peak.

THE NORTH CASCADES EAST

Lake Chelan National Recreation Area

Accessible by boat, plane, or hiking trail only; no road access. Tel. 360/856-5703 (ext. 14). Camping, hiking, backpacking, whitewater kayaking and rafting, fishing, cross-country skiing, snowshoeing.

Lake Chelan, at 1,486 feet deep, is the third deepest lake in the U.S. It is a long, narrow glacial lake (only a quarter-mile wide at one point), stretching for 55 miles from the lake resort town of Chelan deep into the heart of the North Cascades. There are no roads to the upper half of the lake, yet at its upper end there is the community of Stehekin, which is comprised of vacation homes, a few lodges, and the homes of a handful of stalwart year-round residents. Leading into the wilds from Stehekin and a few other spots along the lake are trails heading off into two wilderness areas and North Cascades National Park. Together these areas comprise the Lake Chelan National Recreation Area, which is accessible by boat or float plane from Chelan and the lower end of the lake. The Stehekin area is primarily a summer destination and serves as a staging point for hikers headed into the backcountry. However, rafting on the Stehekin River, which feeds Lake Chelan, is also popular. In winter, when far fewer visitors descend on Stehekin, there are cross-country ski trails to keep visitors active.

To arrange boat transport to Stehekin, contact the Lake Chelan Boat Company (tel. 509/682-4584 or 509/682-2224), which operates both the *Lady of the Lake* and *Lady Express*. Advance ticket reservations are highly recommended during the summer. For floatplane transport to Stehekin, contact Chelan Airways (tel. 509/682-5555 or 509/682-5065).

Lake Chelan-Sawtooth Wilderness

Accessible from Twisp River Rd. west of Twisp. Tel. 509/997-2131. Hiking, backpacking, fishing.

This wilderness lies to the east of the Lake Chelan National Recreation Area, stretching from the north shore of Lake Chelan to the mountains between the Methow and Twisp valleys. Characterized by dry east-side vegetation, the high ridges of this wilderness offer many miles of uncrowded wandering for anyone seeking solitude over stunning vistas (although this area does have plenty of the latter as well).

Pasayten Wilderness

Accessible from Chewuch River Rd. north of Winthrop and Harts Pass Rd. northwest of Mazama. Tel. 509/996-2266. Hiking, backpacking, fishing.

Lying to the east of Ross Lake and the north of the Methow Valley, this huge wilderness stretches to the Canadian border and contains the northernmost stretch of the Pacific Crest Trail. Its remoteness has made the Pasayten one of the least visited wildernesses in the state. Long, U-shaped valleys, carved out during the ice ages by the continental ice sheet, separate the region's many rugged peaks, few of which are higher than 9,000 feet. This wilderness is a favorite with horsepackers.

The North Cascades West ◆ What to Do & Where to Do It

BIRD WATCHING

One of the largest gatherings of eagles in the contiguous states takes place each January on the **Skagit River** between Rockport and Marblemount, where dying, spawned-out chum salmon attract hundreds of bald eagles. Because Wash. 20 parallels the river quite closely, eagle watching is quite easy. Many of the best viewing spots now have parking areas, interpretive signs, and, from Friday through Sunday during the season, volunteers with spotting scopes. Milepost 100 at the Sutter Creek rest area has one of the best viewing areas. Other good spots for eagle watching include Howard Miller Steelhead Park in Rockport and the Washington Eddy lookout. Although eagles are in the area from November through March, the largest concentration usually occurs in mid- to late January. Contact the Mount Baker Ranger District (tel. 360/856-5700) for status reports beginning in early January.

If you'd rather do your eagle viewing from water level, contact one of the rafting companies that offer float trips down this relatively flat section of the river during eagle season. Companies offering eagle-watching float trips include **Alpine Whitewater** (tel. 800/926-RAFT), **Downstream River Runners** (tel. 800/234-4644), and **River Riders** (tel. 800/448-RAFT or 206/448-RAFT). Just remember to dress warmly.

The Mountain Loop Highway, which loops around from Darrington to Granite Falls, also offers several good birding spots. West of Darrington 6 miles on Wash. 530, you'll find **Fortson Ponds,** where you can see waterfowl, kingfishers, and other birds on the ponds and in the surrounding wetlands. On the first section of the trail to **Big Four Ice Caves,** an elevated boardwalk through a marsh provides some good birding in the summer. At **Gold Basin Pond** east of Verlot on Wash. 92, expect to see waterfowl, wading birds, and if you're up here in the late fall or winter, bald eagles.

CROSS-COUNTRY SKIING

GROOMED TRAILS

Salmon Ridge Sno-Park

18.6 miles. Easy–more difficult. 200-foot elevation gain. Access: 46 miles east of I-5 on Wash. 542 (Mount Baker Hwy.). Map: Trailhead map.

Outdoor Resources

INFORMATION

**North Cascades National Park Complex/
Mount Baker Ranger District**
2105 Wash. 20
Sedro Woolley, WA 98284
Tel. 360/856-5700

Darrington Ranger District
Darrington, WA 98241
Tel. 360/436-1155

Verlot Public Service Center
Granite Falls, WA 98252
Tel. 360/691-7791

Glacier Public Service Center
P.O. Box C
Glacier, WA 98244
Tel. 360/599-2714

Winthrop Ranger District
P.O. Box 579
Winthrop, WA 98862
Tel. 509/996-2266

Chelan Ranger District
P.O. Box 189
Chelan, WA 98816
Tel. 509/682-2576

Wilderness Center
728 Ranger Station Rd.
Marblemount, WA 98267
Tel. 360/873-4500, ext. 37 or 39

North Cascades Visitor Center
501 Newhalem St. (mailing address;
   actually located in Newhalem)
Rockport, WA 98283
Tel. 206/386-4495

Golden West Visitor Center
P.O. Box 7
Stehekin, WA 98852
Tel. 509/856-5703, ext. 14

**Early Winters Visitor Information
Center**
P.O. Box 579 (16 miles west of
   Winthrop on Wash. 20)
Winthrop, WA 98862
Tel. 509/996-2534

Twisp Ranger Station
502 Glover St. (P.O. Box 188)
Twisp, WA 98856
Tel. 509/997-2131

EQUIPMENT SHOPS

Winthrop Mountain Sports
Riverside Avenue, Winthrop
Tel. 509/996-2886

Chelan Sporting Goods
205 E Woodin Ave., Chelan
Tel. 509/682-4303

Lake Chelan Sports
132 E Woodin Ave., Chelan
Tel. 509/682-2629

Maintained by the Nooksack Nordic Ski Club for both traditional and skate skiing and located on the bank of the Nooksack River, these trails are one of your few options on the west side of the North Cascades if you want groomed tracks. Consequently, the trails are very popular with Bellingham skate skiers. Bring your Lycra. The trails are mostly flat and meander along the bank of the Nooksack River with a few views of the water. A series of loop trails provides variety at the start of the trail system. For distance skiing, head down Razorhone Road, from which you can ski up a spur for a view of Mount Shuksan, or continue a little farther to Bear Flats Trail, this area's only trail with a "Most Difficult" rating.

Mount Baker Ski Area Nordic Trail

1.25 miles. Moderate. 200-foot elevation gain. Access: 56 miles east of Bellingham on Wash. 542. The trail starts at west end of the parking area near the main lodge. Fee: $1. Map: Not necessary.

Mount Baker Ski Area is one of a handful of ski areas in the Northwest that is decidely cross-country unfriendly. Although the area has the potential for a superb system of Nordic trails that would be the most scenic in the state, there is currently a single short loop. This trail starts from the parking area west of the main downhill lodge and shares a short section of trail with downhill skiers. The trail then heads out along the road that leads up to Artist Point and loops north on undulating terrain to return to the parking area.

UNGROOMED TRAILS

Artist Point

5 miles round-trip. More difficult. 1,100-foot elevation gain. Access: 56 miles east of Bellingham on Wash. 542. The trail starts at the west end of the parking area near the Mount Baker Ski Area main lodge. Map: USGS Shuksan Arm, Green Trails Mount Shuksan.

It would be difficult to imagine more spectacular views than those to be had from this moderately difficult route that starts at the Mount Baker Ski Area and leads up to Artist Point, a viewpoint that stays absolutely mobbed during the summer, but that in winter sees very few visitors. The route starts out on the ski area's meager groomed ski trail, for which you are requested to make a donation. You then climb up a cat track used by downhill skiers, so keep to the side of the track and stay alert. All along here you have a splendid view, with Mount Herman rising on the north side of the bowl-shaped valley that holds the Bagley Lakes. On the west side of this bowl rise the cliffs (and avalanche slopes) of Table Mountain. This is a steep and steady climb that is made much easier with climbing skins. Once you reach Austin Pass, you can either continue to follow the road's gradual ascent to Artist Point, or head straight uphill to cut a long switchback on the road. A short distance above lie incomparable views of Mount Baker and Mount Shuksan. This

is a tour that should be made only under the best conditions. Avoid cloudy days when there are no views and it would be easy to accidentally ski off some of the steeper slopes in the area. Also, avoid coming up here when the slopes are icy, for the same reason.

Herman Saddle

5 miles round-trip. Most difficult. 1,050-foot elevation gain. Access: 56 miles east of Bellingham on Wash. 542. The trail starts at the west end of the parking area near the Mount Baker Ski Area main lodge. Map: USGS Shuksan Arm, Green Trails Mount Shuksan.

For telemark skiers (and snowboarders in search of free snow), the vast bowl west of the Mount Baker Ski Area west parking lot is a vision of beauty. Lying below the cliffs of Table Mountain, Herman Saddle, and Mount Herman, this valley offers excellent telemark skiing. However, it is also subject to avalanches, so be sure to check on the avalanche probability before attempting to ski. From the parking area, the route leads west along the ski area's short groomed Nordic trail and then drops to the floor of the valley, crossing the frozen and snow-covered Bagley Lakes. Once across the valley, you must regain all the elevation you just lost, plus more, to reach the 5,300-foot Herman Saddle, which is the obvious low point on the ridge west of the parking area. Keep to the north side of the valley as you make this ascent. Once you have topped out, rested, and enjoyed the views east and west from the saddle, it's time to carve your S-turns to the bottom. If you've got plenty of energy, you might do this two or three times for a truly memorable day of teleskiing.

Pilchuck Mountain Road

14 miles round-trip. More difficult. 2,100-foot elevation gain. Access: Drive Wash. 92 east from Granite Falls, and 1 mile past the Verlot Public Service Center, turn right onto FS 42. Map: Green Trails Granite Falls.

The Pilchuck Mountain Trail is one of the most popular hiking trails in the region,

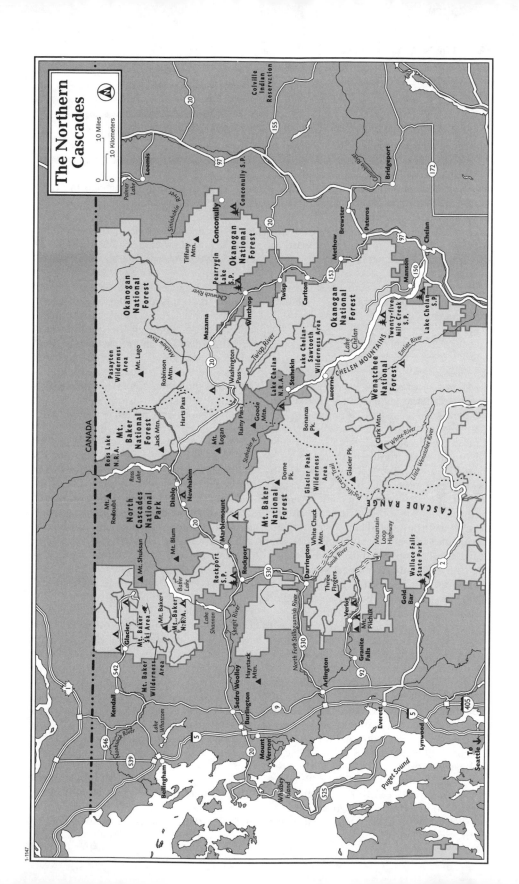

The Northern Cascades

0 10 Miles
0 10 Kilometers

and likewise, Pilchuck Road, which is closed to snowmobiles, is one of the most popular cross-country ski routes in the area. Start this route as far up FS 42 as you can drive (the road is gated all winter at 1.5 miles from Wash. 92). From here, it is a steady climb along the closed road, with occasional clear-cuts providing views. This road once led to a downhill ski area that has long been out of business. However, the view and the steep ski slopes remain. Anyone can enjoy the view northward to the impressively jagged Three Fingers, across the valley of the South Fork Stillaguamish River. Telemark skiers will likely find the old ski hill more fascinating than the view.

Deer Creek Road

8.5 miles round-trip. More difficult. 1,500-foot elevation gain. Access: Drive Wash. 92 east from Verlot 12 miles to the end of the plowed road and park. Map: Green Trails Silverton.

This out-and-back road tour is one of only a handful of ski routes in this whole region that are closed to snowmobiles, and as such is a magnet for skiers. However, it's better to deal with other skiers on the trail than snowmobiles. The route climbs steadily with better and better views opening up the higher you climb. Before you reach the end of this trail, Big Four and the rugged Monte Cristo peaks come into view. At about the 1-mile point, pass FS 4054 (Double Eagle Road) on your right. If you still have energy left after skiing to the end of Deer Creek Road, this road makes an excellent addition to a ski tour in the area. Alternatively, you could make this road the destination of your day's outing. This alternate route offers a ski of roughly the same distance, same elevation gain, and same sort of views. If you are confident in your ability to negotiate trees, you can continue on from the end of the Deer Creek Road to Kelcema Lake, which is barely 0.5 miles beyond the end of the road up Deer Creek. Because these trails start at only 1,600 feet, snow cover is unreliable. Check to make sure there is snow up here before committing to the drive.

DOWNHILL SKIING & SNOWBOARDING

Mount Baker

Location: 56 miles east of Bellingham on Wash. 542. Tel. 360/734-6771 (Snow reports: tel. 360/671-0211 in Bellingham; tel. 604/688-1595 in Vancouver, B.C.; tel. 206/634-0200 in Seattle). 38 trails; 1,500 feet of vertical; 8 lifts (6 double, 2 quad). Lift hours: Weekends and holidays 8:30am–3:30pm. Adult lift tickets $28 weekends and holidays, $18.50 midweek.

Mount Baker is one of the top three snowboarding areas in the country and is home base to some of the country's top snowboarders, so anyone who has done much snowboarding will already know of this shredhead Nirvana. More than 500 inches of snow annually make this the first Washington ski area to open each year. Mount Baker is as popular with Canadians as it is with Americans, and all comers are here for the regular fresh snows and the many extreme runs that keep boarders in the air almost as often as they're in the snow.

There aren't many wide-open slopes here, which means beginners might want to pick another ski area. For the quickest route to the slopes, head to the new White Salmon day lodge and the lifts at the east end of the ski area (C-4, C-5, C-7, and C-8). However, if you're here for some legendary extreme boarding down cliffs, through chutes, and are into steep tree skiing, head straight to the main Heather Meadows day lodge and the C-1 lift, which will take you to the top of Panorama Dome and more than a dozen diamond and double-diamond runs.

Ski and snowboard lessons for all levels of ability are available. Day care is available for toilet-trained children 2 years and older. **Mount Baker Shuttle & Limo Service** (tel. 360/599-1180) operates from the community of Glacier at the base of the mountain. Glacier is also where you'll find the **Mount Baker Snowboard Shop,** 9996 Forest St. (tel. 360/599-2008), which offers sales, rentals, and repairs of snowboards. Here in Glacier you'll also find numerous cabins and chalets for rent through **Mount Baker Lodging** (tel. 360/ 599-2453).

FISHING

The **Skagit River,** the second largest river in the state after the Columbia River, is one of the finest steelheading and salmon-fishing rivers in Washington. Because of the size of the river, drift-boat fishing is very popular. However, there is good bank fishing at Howard Miller Steelhead Park in Rockport, which as the name implies is very popular with anglers. Winter steelheads run from early December through mid-April, and there is also a summer steelhead run. Several salmon runs also add to the popularity of this river. There are spring and fall Chinook runs as well as a run of silvers in the fall. During odd-numbered years, the Skagit also gets a run of humpies. There is good fishing in the Skagit for rainbows. Upstream from Marblemount, there is often good fishing for sea-run cutthroat trout.

South of the Skagit, the **Stillaguamish River** is another popular steelheading river, and though both the north and south forks of this river offer good chances to hook one of these silver rockets, the South Fork gets the nod as the more productive stream. North of the Skagit River, the **North Fork Nooksack River,** which is followed for almost its entire length by Wash. 542, has fairly good trout fishing in its upper reaches. Wait until the river clears in late summer before trying to catch anything.

Baker and Shannon lakes, both off Wash. 20 near Concrete, are well known for their kokanee, though you'll need a boat to fish these deep lakes. On Shannon Lake, chumming with corn is permitted and almost always brings the kokanee up to the surface to feed.

Ross Lake is rather unusual among Washington in that it is not stocked. Its remote and inaccessible location and the fact that the stream valleys that feed the lake are protected from logging and mining have assured plenty of healthy spawning streams around the lake. Consequently, the lake contains naturally reproducing populations of both native rainbow and cutthroat trout, as well as eastern brook trout. There are also bull trout in the lake, but any caught must be released. Only barbless flies and artificial lures are allowed. Fishing boats can be rented at the **Ross Lake Resort** (tel. 360/ 386-4437).

Many of the high-altitude lakes of the North Cascades are also stocked with trout. Up in the Heather Meadows area near the Mount Baker Ski Area, **Lake Ann** is stocked with cutthroats, and the four small **Chain Lakes** are stocked with rainbows and brook trout. All of these are hike-in lakes, but they are heavily fished nonetheless.

Fly anglers may want to try **Granite Creek,** which is paralleled by the North Cascades Highway between Ross Lake and Rainy Pass. In late summer and early fall, the stream's rainbows and cutthroats are usually biting.

HIKING & BACKPACKING

This section of the chapter covers some of the finest hiking areas in the state of Washington, but represents only a small fraction of the good hikes in the North Cascades. A dedicated hiker could probably spend a lifetime exploring the trails just within this one small corner of Washington and never grow tired of them.

Although the **North Cascades National Park Complex** covers 634,614 acres and has 360 miles of trails, there are only 206 designated campsites within the entire complex. Consequently, when backpacking here, you must have a backcountry permit issued for a specific date and camp. Permits are issued on a first-come, first-served basis only on the first day of a trip and are available at the North Cascades National Park Complex headquarters in Sedro Woolley, the Wilderness Center in Marblemount, the North Cascades Visitor Center in Newhalem, the Glacier Public Service Center in Glacier, the Hozomeen Ranger Station, the Golden West Visitor Center in Stehekin, and Forest Service ranger stations in Winthrop, Early Winters, Chelan, and Twisp. After-hours self-registration is available, but not for such heavily used areas as Cascade Pass and Copper Ridge. Keep in mind that if the

> "Nowhere do the mountain masses and peaks present such strange, fantastic dauntless and startling outlies as here."
>
> —Henry Custer, assistant of reconnaissances for International Boundary Commission 1859

camp you had hoped to stay at is full, there may be easily accessible cross-country camping (at least 0.25 miles off the trail) nearby. Any camp that lends itself to a weekend backpacking trip will likely be full on a weekend in July or August. Plan accordingly by coming on a weekday, arriving early on Friday, or by having alternative choices.

The North Cascades also mark the northern end of the **Pacific Crest Trail.** In these mountains, the trail is at its most lonesome, and north of Hart Pass, its most remote. Between Allison Pass, the start of the trail in Canada (on the Trans-Canada Highway), there are 40 miles of trail to the next road crossing, which is at Harts Pass. Much of this route is through beautiful meadowlands. From Harts Pass to Rainy Pass (on Wash. 20) is a distance of 31 miles and the scenery is even better, though there are a lot of ups and downs. Because this stretch of trail is so easily accessible, it is the best choice for anyone looking to hike just a portion of the PCT in this area. South from Rainy Pass, the trail leads through the North Cascades National Park and reaches High Bridge, on the Stehekin Valley Road, in 16 downhill miles. You can catch a shuttle bus from here to Stehekin, and then take a boat or plane to the town of Chelan at the far end of Lake Chelan. South of High Bridge, the PCT does not cross another road until it reaches U.S. 2 at Stevens Pass almost 100 miles away. This stretch of trail loops around the west side of Glacier Peak. There are, however, several side trails leading down from the PCT that would allow you to make a shorter trip through this remote area.

Pilchuck Mountain Trail

4 miles round-trip. Moderate. 2,400-foot elevation gain. Access: From the Verlot Public Information Center on Wash. 92 (Mountain Loop Hwy.), drive east 1 mile, turn right onto FS 42 (Mount Pilchuck Rd.), and drive 7 miles to the trailhead. Map: Green Trails Granite Falls.

Like Mount Index southeast of here off U.S. 2 and Mount Si south of here off I-90, Mount Pilchuck jumps out at you. It's only 20 miles as the raven flies from the waters of Puget Sound to the summit of this peak, with hardly a hill between the water and the base of the mountain. Because of this in-your-face placement, Mount Pilchuck is one of the most popular hikes in the region. The trail starts in an old-growth forest and immediately begins climbing, passing an abandoned ski area (the snow wasn't reliable enough). By the time you reach the summit, forest has given way to subalpine heather meadows and glacier-scarred rocks. At the top, an old lookout has been restored and converted into a museum. However, it is the views that really command attention here. To the west, Puget Sound is spread out below you, and in every other direction you see Cascade Peaks, including Mount Baker, Glacier Peak, and Mount Rainier. For proximity and outstanding views, few trails can compare with this one.

For the past couple of years work has been progressing on new sections of trail and restoration of some of the existing trail, so it is open only on weekends. Be sure to call the Darrington Ranger Station to make sure the trail is open when you want to hike it.

Skyline Divide Trail

10.5 miles. Moderate. 2,263-foot elevation gain. Access: From Glacier, on Wash. 542, drive 1 mile east, turn right onto FS 39 (Glacier Creek Rd.), then left onto FS 37 (Deadhorse Rd.), and continue 13 miles to the trailhead. Map: USGS Mount Baker and Bearpaw Mountain, Green Trails Mount Baker.

This trail, which climbs 1,500 feet in 2 miles to a long meadowed ridge, is one of the most rewarding hikes in the Mount

Baker area, and because it serves up great views in a short distance, it tends to see a lot of traffic. However, don't let the presence of many other hikers on the trail dissuade you from hiking this route. Once the trail breaks out of the forest of silver firs at 5,800 feet, the views begin. To the west you can see as far as the Strait of Georgia and Vancouver Island, to the east lies Mount Shuksan, to the north rise the Border Peaks, and to the south, of course, lies the imposing, snowy bulk of Mount Glacier. The trail heads south along the ridge with nearly constant views of Mount Baker that just get better and better with each step. At the 4-mile point, you reach a 6,215-foot knoll, with the best view on the hike. Continue past here, dropping to a saddle and then climbing to a second knoll at 6,563 feet. Come in mid-summer when the snow has melted and the wildflowers are in bloom. Stay the night and you'll be treated to twinkling stars above and twinkling city lights below. By late summer and early fall, water is scarce, so carry plenty.

Heliotrope Ridge

6 miles round-trip. Moderate. 2,100-foot elevation gain. Access: From Glacier, on Wash. 542, drive 1 mile east, turn right onto FS 39 (Glacier Creek Rd.), and continue 8 miles to the trailhead. Map: Green Trails Mount Baker.

If you are fascinated by glaciers, then a hike up Heliotrope Ridge to get a close-up look at massive Coleman Glacier is in order. This huge glacier rumbles down the north face of Mount Baker with thousands of crevasses striping its bulk. The trail up to the glacial moraine, from which there are excellent views down onto the glacier, begins in forest and remains in the trees for slightly more than 2 miles as it climbs up to timberline. The trail passes the site of a climbers' shelter shortly before leaving the forest for meadow country. The trail eventually ends at the foot of the glacier (where properly equipped climbers continue onward). Spread out before you will be not only the glacier, but also the Nooksack Valley, far below. This is the most popular climbing route to the summit of Mount Baker, so expect to see lots of mountain climbers.

Lake Ann

8 miles round-trip. Moderate. 1,100-foot elevation gain in, 950 feet out. Access: Drive to the Mount Baker Ski Area at the end of Wash. 542 and continue 1.5 miles to the trailhead at Austin Pass. Map: USGS Shuksan Arm, Green Trails Mount Shuksan.

A Canadian woman I once met picking huckleberries along the Lake Ann Trail said she liked Lake Ann so much she'd been there three times over the years. Any trail worth hiking repeatedly must have something going for it, and this trail does indeed have a lot to offer. From the trailhead on the road up to Artist Point, you can look down into the Swift Creek Valley and see the trail you will be hiking. From the parking lot, the trail drops almost 1,000 feet through forest, with occasional views, and then crosses Swift Creek on the meadowed valley floor below gray and red cliffs and talus slopes of Shuksan Arm (red from 3-million-year-old underground hot water seeps that dissolved iron and stained the cliffs). To reach the lake, you then climb back up all the elevation you just lost. This beautiful little lake hangs on the mountainside facing Mount Shuksan, while at the lake's outlet, the mountain drops steeply away and the water goes cascading down the mountainside. The Lower Curtis Glacier is about an hour's hike above the lake and makes a great destination for a bit of exploring. There are lots of campsites around the lake, the best being those at the far end. However, they all fill up early on weekends.

Railroad Grade–Scott Paul Loop

13 miles. Moderate–strenuous. 4,500-foot elevation gain. Access: From Sedro Wooley, drive east 14.5 miles on Wash. 20, turn left at signs for Baker Lake, and continue 12.5 miles to the FS 12 turnoff just past Rocky Creek Bridge. Turn left here onto a gravel road. In 3.5 miles turn right onto FS 13 and continue 5.2 miles to the Mount Baker National Recreation Area parking lot. Map: USGS Baker Pass, Green Trails Hamilton.

Don't be fooled by the name. This trail is *not* on a former railroad grade; it is along the narrow lip of a lateral moraine high up in the meadow country on the south side of Mount Baker. Sublimely beautiful but very popular, the Railroad Grade and nearby Park Butte (atop which there is a fire lookout) are glorious areas to wander among meadows and marmots. The trail up to the Railroad Grade starts in a huckleberry meadow and then crosses Rocky Creek on a bouncy suspension bridge. Expect to get your feet wet crossing this creek, which has a tendency to meander all over the mountainside. After the bridge, the trail switchbacks through the forest for 1 mile before passing the Paul Scott Trail junction (the return route) and breaking into Morovitz Meadows. In the meadows the trail branches, with the left branch climbing to Park Butte, a rocky plug of a crag, and the lookout. The right fork climbs a stone stairway to reach the edge of the moraine formed long ago by Easton Glacier. This is the Railroad Grade, and the in-your-face view of Mount Baker is astonishing. However, the view at your feet is equally astonishing.

On one side of the trail, meadows swoop away, but on the other, a steep, barren slope of gravel and rock drops sharply down to the wide valley of aptly named Rocky Creek. Friendly marmots lounge on the precipice of this knife-edge moraine trail, seeming to enjoy the views as much as human hikers. Several campsites are strung along the Railroad Grade (though they are set a little too close together for backpackers to get away from each other). The entire area invites off-trail exploring and uphill scrambling. And wherever you wander up here, you are never far from views of Glacier Peak, Mount Rainier, and the North Cascades. To return, take the Scott Paul Trail from just below Morovitz Meadows and descend to cross Rocky Creek between the lateral moraines (you can see this trail and its bridge from the Railroad Grade). The trail then climbs the Metcalf Moraine for new views and continues around the mountain to the east, making several stream crossings and taking in more views. Eventually, you are far enough around Mount Baker to gain views of Mount Shuksan. The trail then drops down to the trailhead. This area easily makes for a day of wandering or a weekend of exploring.

Hannegan Pass-Ross Lake-North Cascades Highway

46 miles. Strenuous. 7,500-foot elevation gain. Access: From the town of Glacier, drive east 13 miles on Wash. 542 and turn left onto FS 32 (Nooksack River Rd.) just before crossing a bridge over the river. In 1.3 miles, keep left to stay on FS 32 and continue 5.4 miles to Hannegan Campground. To leave a car at the other end, drive Wash. 20, 8 miles east of Diablo Dam to the Ross Lake trailhead. Map: USGS Mount Seftrit, Copper Mountain, Mount Redoubt; Green Trails Mount Shuksan and Mount Challenger.

This long trek across the North Cascades is the region's ultimate hike. Starting in the meadows below Hannegan Pass north of Mount Shuksan, the trail leads up over this pass, down into the Chilliwack Valley, up and over Whatcom Pass, and down Big Beaver Creek to Ross Lake. Along the way are the most stupendous mountain views to be had in North Cascades National Park. This is the most remote wilderness area in the state and may still be home to both wolves and grizzly bears. From virgin forests in glacial valleys to high meadows with head-on views of the park's jagged Picket Range, this hike has everything. If you want, you can even start or end your hike from Big Beaver Landing with a water taxi ride on Ross Lake. This ride will cost you $20 and must be arranged in advance.

The trail starts out by climbing 2,000 feet through nearly constant views to Hannegan Pass. From here drop down 1 mile to the Copper Ridge junction. Turn left to head out this long and amazingly scenic ridge and regain the elevation you just lost. This trail soon crosses the narrow Hell's Gorge. Camp at either Egg or Silesia Lake.

The second day, continue along the ridge and then drop down to the Chilliwack River, ford the river at an often-difficult crossing, and head south (upriver). Indian Creek Camp is about 1 mile up the trail and makes a good second night's stop.

On the third day, climb up and over Whatcom Pass, gaining another 2,600 feet in the process. This pass boasts one of the finest vistas in the park, with glacier-clad peaks both north and south. This is about as remote a spot as you'll find anywhere in the state. After lingering here and perhaps doing some off-trail exploring, drop down the east side of the pass into the drainage of Little Beaver Creek. Twin Rocks Camp, below the pass, should not be missed as a night's resting spot if you have the time for a very short day. Set in a cirque with waterfalls cascading down the walls and Challenger Glacier at the head of the bowl, this is an amazing spot.

The fourth day, drop down into the forest and continue down the Little Beaver Valley. Roughly 4.5 miles from the pass, cross the creek and head up to low, forested Beaver Pass. If you crave some more views, head cross-country 0.5 miles east from this pass to climb high enough for a view of the Pickets and the impressive Luna Cirque rising to the west. From Beaver Pass, drop into the valley of Big Beaver Creek, where there are many beaver ponds, and continue to 39 Mile Camp.

The fifth day, continue down the Big Beaver on a level trail through groves of old-growth western red cedars to the Big Beaver Campground. This is where you could be picked up by water taxi (or start a hike in the reverse direction). If you want to keep hiking, cross the creek, climb above the lake, and contour around Sourdough Mountain. The trail then drops down to the lake and crosses Ross Dam. From here, hike up the gravel road to Wash. 20.

Cascade Pass/Sahale Arm Trail

11 miles. 3,000-foot elevation gain. Strenuous. Access: From Marblemount on Wash. 20, cross the bridge and drive east for 23.5 miles on the Cascade River Rd. to the trailhead. Map: USGS North Cascades National Park, USGS Cascade Pass, Green Trails Cascade Pass.

My brother is a glacier fanatic. Every summer we schedule at least one backpacking trip together and when it's his turn to choose, he invariably picks a trail to a glacier. This trail is one of his choices (and is

also one of the most popular hikes in North Cascades National Park). Starting high above the valley of the North Fork Cascade River, this trail follows an ancient Indian trading route over the Cascades to Lake Chelan. Today the trail is popular as a day trip, as an overnight trip, as a climbers' route to some challenging North Cascades rock, and as a through trail to Stehekin. What I'm trying to say here is that you won't be alone, but you'll probably be so busy ogling the views of the surrounding peaks that you won't even notice when you pass people.

The trail climbs steeply up the north side of the valley with an astounding view of Johannesburg Mountain, Cascade Peak, and The Triplets directly across the valley to the south. Shortly before reaching the pass, you cross a talus slope and leave the forest behind. At the pass itself, views to the east open up, with Boston Peak and the Sahale Glacier rising to the north and the Stehekin Valley stretching far off to the east. If you have a permit for an overnight stay up here, then you're headed up Sahale Arm to the foot of Sahale Glacier, where there are several campsites amid the jumble of rocks at the foot of the glacier. The trail up Sahale Arm is hardly deserving of the title of trail in its upper stretch, where it is mostly just a scramble across the rocks. However, lower down, it passes through beautiful meadows where marmots bask in the sun. Once up at the foot of the glacier, you can explore a bit. The source of the Stehekin River is here and is so small that you can step across it. Just drinking in the views is enough to keep most people busy for hours. Be forewarned that a freestanding tent is almost a necessity up here and it is almost always windy and cold (witness the rock walls people have erected as windbreaks around the campsites).

If you can't get a campsite permit for the Cascade Pass area or you just can't get enough of the local scenery, there are a couple of other trails in the area that you might want to hike. However, fewer people on these alternate trails still doesn't mean you'll be able to get a camping permit on a sunny summer weekend. Arrive early or come on a weekday to avoid disappointment.

The Boston Basin Trail starts just 0.5 miles back down the road from the Cascade Pass trailhead. The hike up to Boston Basin gains 3,000 feet in only 3.5 miles, so be prepared for some huffing and puffing. The view of Mount Johannesburg is as good as it is on the Cascade Pass Trail, and the meadows are equally colorful.

The trail up to Hidden Lake and its namesake peak and lookout is accessed from the rough FS 1540 off the Cascade River road only 10 miles out of Marblemount. This trail gains 3,700 feet if you go all the way to the top of Hidden Lake Peak, but there are good views after far fewer feet of climbing. There are no glaciers on this 6- to 10-mile route, but there is plenty of snow to be crossed most of the summer, so bring an ice axe and maybe some crampons just in case. There are campsites near Hidden Lake.

MOUNTAIN BIKING

For whatever reason, this area has almost nothing in the way of single-track trail riding. However, there are some rewarding rides on gravel roads in the area.

Monte Cristo Road

8 miles round-trip. Easy. 500-foot elevation gain. Access: The ride starts at the gated road at Barlow Pass, 31 miles east of Granite Falls on Wash. 92 (Mountain Loop Hwy.). Map: USGS Monte Cristo, Green Trails Monte Cristo, or Darrington Ranger District Map.

At the turn of the 20th century, Monte Cristo was a booming silver-mining town, complete with hotels, aerial tramways to haul ore down from the steep mountainsides, and a railway to haul the ore out of the valley. Today, nothing remains of Monte Cristo but a handful of old cabins that have been preserved by the Monte Cristo Preservation Association (MCPA). However, the old railroad grade is now a rough dirt road that is closed to most traffic (MCPA members have keys to the gate at the start of the road) and is popular with both mountain bikers and hikers. The ghost-town setting is enough to recommend this ride, but, if you are willing to get off your bike and do some hiking, there

is spectacular scenery to be found in the hanging valleys above Monte Cristo. The floods of February 1996 did considerable damage to the Monte Cristo Road, but it was still passable by the summer. There are, however, some sections of the road that are just about unrideable due to the rocks left in the tread by the floodwaters. Because this is a railroad, you hardly notice that you're even climbing on the way into Monte Cristo. Then, on the way out, the downhill cruising is a joy.

North Mountain

13.5 miles. Strenuous. 1,865-foot elevation gain. Access: From Darrington, drive north on Wash. 530, turn left onto FS 28 after crossing the second set of railroad tracks, and continue 3 miles to a right fork onto FS 2810. Follow this road another 3.8 miles and park where FS 2811 forks to the left. Map: Darrington Ranger District Map.

Lying just southwest of the town of Darrington is a breathtakingly beautiful grouping of rugged, glaciated mountains that stands off by itself amid a sea of green forest. These peaks—Whitehorse Ridge, Three Fingers, and Mount Bullon—are all within the Boulder River Wilderness, so forget about riding any of the trails that lead up to them. However, there is a gravel-road ride just outside Darrington that will give you a view even better than the one to be had from town. Lying due north of Darrington, North Mountain has a fire lookout on its summit and a gravel road that leads to that lookout. The ride is straightforward enough. Just start pedaling uphill and don't stop until you reach the top (well, okay, you can stop to rest along the way). The view is the thing here, so pick a clear day to do this ride. Watch out for traffic on the way down; it's easy to get carried away with the great downhill riding and forget that this is an active road.

Schweitzer Creek Loop

10.8 miles. Moderate. 1,600-foot elevation gain. Access: Drive Wash. 92 east from the Verlot Public Service Center for 4.7 miles and turn right onto FS 4020. Drive 0.3 miles up this road to a pull-off that makes a good starting point for the ride. Map: USGS Mallardy Ridge, Green Trails Silverton.

Although all but a very short stretch of this route is on logging roads, it is still one of the most popular rides in the area. Start your ride by heading up FS 4020 (Schweitzer Creek Road), which is already climbing at a steady incline at the start of the ride. In 2.4 miles, take the left fork to stay on FS 4020 (the right fork is FS 4021, the return route on this loop). In another 2.4 miles, reach the Boardman Lake trailhead. Only 100 yards up this trail is Evans Lake, which makes a good resting spot after all the climbing. If you feel like a longer walk, continue 0.75 miles up the trail to slightly larger Boardman Lake. From the trailhead, the road continues climbing for a ways and then begins to descend. In 1.3 miles, watch for a ski trail on the left. This trail leads through a stand of old-growth cedars for 0.3 miles to connect to an abandoned logging road that is now crossed by numerous ditches. Ride this road down past the Ashland Lakes Trail sign (the lakes are 2 miles up this hiker-only trail) and turn left. This road will then connect you to FS 4021, where a right turn will have you headed back down the mountain. (If you want to add another 3.2 miles of riding, turn left onto FS 4021 and ride to the Bear Lake trailhead. It is a 0.25-mile walk to this lake.) At the junction with FS 4020, turn left to return to your car.

ROAD BIKING

The North Cascades Highway (Rockport to Winthrop)

94 miles. Strenuous. Approximately 6,500-foot elevation gain. Access: Start this ride at Howard Miller Steelhead Park in Rockport.

One of the classic Northwest rides, the tour over the North Cascades is demanding, but incredibly scenic. The best time to ride this route is in late July or August, but even during those months, bad weather can descend and eliminate all views of the mountains. Try to hold off until a stretch of good weather if you can.

The road has a wide shoulder most of the way, and there are campgrounds spaced at good intervals. At 33 miles from Rockport, the Colonial Creek Campground makes a good first day's destination. Along the way you can take time to explore the power-company towns of Newhalem and Diablo, stop in at the North Cascades Visitor Center in Newhalem, and walk some of the short trails in Newhalem. This will also put you at the foot of the first killer hill of this ride, so you can take it on the next morning when you've got plenty of energy.

Be sure to load up on carbohydrates at breakfast. This second day is a killer. The hill from Colonial Creek Campground climbs a little more than 1,000 feet from the turquoise waters of Diablo Lake to the Ross Lake overlook and then loses about a third of that gain to drop down almost to the shore of the Ruby Arm of Ross Lake. A hiking trail leads down to the lake. From this point, the road climbs slightly more than 3,000 feet in the 20-mile trip up Ruby Creek and then Granite Creek to 4,855-foot Rainy Pass, which hopefully won't be living up to its name. At Rainy Pass there are two very scenic hiking trails—one to Rainy Lake and one to Maple Pass—that should tempt you off your bike if you have any extra energy. There are also picnic tables where you can collapse if need be. From here it is only 5 miles to Washington Pass, the route's high point. However, between the two passes, the road drops about 400 feet before climbing back up to the second pass.

The view from Washington Pass is phenomenal and takes in some of the most rugged rock of the North Cascades including Liberty Bell, Early Winters Spires, and Kangaroo Ridge. Breathe a big sigh of relief at this point. Ahead of you lies only downhill riding, starting with the delicious swoosh below the cliffs of Liberty Bell and around the massive switchback that proved the most difficult stretch of this road to construct. About 6 miles down the hill is the Lone Fir Campground.

On the third day, continue down the Methow Valley 24 miles to Winthrop. Don't miss the chance to stop in Mazama at the Mazama Store, which sells all manner of gourmet goodies and fixes great sandwiches and espresso as well. The ride is quite flat and passes through valley-bottom pastures. In Winthrop, you can toast your tour with a pint of ale at the Winthrop Brewery.

Because this is a one-way route, you'll need to arrange some sort of shuttle or have someone come get you at the end of the ride.

Eagle Watch Loop

20 miles. Easy. 500-foot elevation gain. Access: Start this ride at the Howard Miller Steelhead Park in Rockport on Wash. 20.

Frequently, Northwest winters toss out a few warm days, even some warm *clear* days (though clear days are more frequently cold days around these parts). If such a day is bestowed upon you and you feel like a bike ride, I can think of no better ride in the area than this loop up one bank of the Skagit River and down the other. If you do the ride on a weekend you'll have plenty of company. The roadsides along Wash. 20 between Rockport and Marblemount will be jammed with bird watchers observing the hundreds of bald eagles that gather here each winter to feed on dying salmon. Start the ride by heading east from Rockport on Wash. 20. In the next 8 miles, you will pass numerous good spots to stop and watch the eagles. The birds are generally most active early in the day. During the middle of the day, expect to see them roosting in the trees along the river.

At Marblemount, cross the bridge and head up the Cascade River Road 0.5 miles and then turn right over another bridge. This will put you on the Rockport Cascade Road, continuing straight at the junction on the far side of this second bridge. From here it is 9 miles downriver to Wash. 530 (Sauk Valley Road). Turn right on this road to head back into Rockport in another 1.5 miles.

ROCK CLIMBING

The North Cascades abound in rock-climbing opportunities, but they are for the most part relatively remote. For information on climbing the region's many spires, crags, and pinnacles, consult Fred Beckey's *Cascade Alpine Guide: Climbing and High Routes* (The Mountaineers, 1987), which is a three-volume series.

SEA KAYAKING & FLAT-WATER CANOEING

Diablo Lake and **Ross Lake** both offer excellent flat-water paddling and are among the few inland waters in the Northwest with extensive boat-in campsites. However, there are two major drawbacks to paddling on Ross Lake: There is no road access to the lake and strong winds often blow down the lake in the afternoon, making paddling against the wind almost futile. The former difficulty can be surmounted by calling the Ross Lake Resort (tel. 360/386-4437), which offers a canoe and kayak shuttle service to transport boats from Diablo Lake (which is accessible by car) around Ross Dam to Ross Lake. The resort charges from $15 to $25 per canoe or kayak for this service and reservations must be made in advance for the shuttle at both the beginning and end of your trip. You'll also need a backcountry permit to overnight on Ross Lake. These permits are available at the North Cascades National Park Complex headquarters in Sedro Woolley, at the Marblemount Wilderness Center, or at the North Cascades Visitor Center in Newhalem. The permits allow you to stay at the many campsites along the shores of Ross Lake and do indeed specify at what campsite you will be staying on what night, so you must have a set itinerary before you start your trip.

Because of the length of the lake and the difficulties of dealing with the wind, many paddlers stick to the lower end of the lake. Here you can explore up the narrow Ruby Arm using **Green Point Campground** (1 mile above the dam, seven campsites) as a base camp. Farther north are the **Cougar Island** (2 miles above the dam, two campsites), **Roland Point** (4 miles above the dam, one campsite), **Big Beaver** (4 miles above the dam, seven campsites), **McMillan** (5.5 miles above the dam, three campsites), and **Spencer's** (6 miles above the lake, two campsites).

If you aren't inclined to spend the money for the shuttle, you can have a similar experience paddling on Diablo Lake, which is an amazing turquoise color.

Diablo Lake is fed by 10% of all the glaciers in the lower 48 states, and the color is due to the amounts of glacial flour suspended in the water. Diablo also has three boat-in campsites (**Thunder Point, Hidden Cove,** and **Buster Brown**) as well as a couple of small islands to explore. Alternatively, you can explore the lake from the drive-in Colonial Creek Campground on the Thunder Arm of the lake.

If you're looking for a quicker and easier place to do a little paddling, try **Silver Lake Park** 4 miles north of Maple Falls off Wash. 542. This county park has picnic areas, a campground and rental cabins, and also offers canoe and pedalboat rentals. Although there are summer cabins around much of the lake, it still has a peaceful feeling, especially early in the morning.

SNOWSHOEING

The **Mountain Loop Highway** (Wash. 92) east of Granite Falls provides access in winter to numerous logging roads and ski trails, some of which are popular with snowshoers. The **Schweitzer Creek** area along FS 4020 (4 miles east of Verlot), the **Red Bridge** area along FS 4037 (7 miles east of Verlot), and the unplowed stretches of the Mountain Loop Highway beyond the **Deer Creek Road** (12 miles east of Verlot) are particularly popular snowshoeing areas. However, all of these areas are also open to snowmobiles.

On winter weekends, when there is sufficient snow, the **North Cascades National Park Visitor Center** in Newhalem offers guided snowshoe nature walks. These walks focus on the winter wildlife of the area and are suitably short and easy for families.

SWIMMING & TUBING

Sure, if you're a member of the Polar Bear Club you might enjoy a quick dip in the **Skagit River** on the hottest day of the year, but for the most part, this river, fed by snowmelt and glacier runoff, is a look-but-don't-touch kind of river. On the other hand, **Baker Lake,** with its long sandy beaches and large campgrounds, is a favorite place to head on a hot summer day. The best and most popular beaches are at **Horseshoe Cove** and **Panorama Point.**

Located just off the Mount Baker Highway (Wash. 542) north of the town of Maple Falls, **Silver Lake Park** is a popular summer getaway for people who want to cool off in the water. Unfortunately, this is one of many lakes in Northwest Washington that contains the parasite that causes "swimmer's itch." Be sure to shower and wash out your bathing suit as soon after swimming as possible.

WALKS & NATURAL ROADSIDE ATTRACTIONS

Artist Ridge Trail

1 mile round-trip. Easy. 150-foot elevation gain. Access: The trailhead is above the Mount Baker Ski Area at the end of Wash. 542.

This short gravel interpretive trail is the most popular trail of the many short trails on Artist Ridge. Starting from the southeast corner of the larger parking lot, the trail meanders across the rocky landscape of an ancient lava flow. The views of Mount Shuksan and Mount Baker are superb, and interpretive signs explain much of the unusual history of these two peaks. To the north, you can see as far as the aptly named American Border Peak, which lies on the border with Canada. To avoid the crowds, visit in the autumn and stick around until sunset, when Mount Shuksan is bathed in beautiful shades of pink and orange. The many ponds that dot this rocky ridge serve as reflecting pools for the alpenglow show.

Table Mountain Trail

2 miles round-trip. Moderate. 650-foot elevation gain. Access: The trailhead is above the Mount Baker Ski Area at the Artist Ridge parking lot.

If you aren't afraid of heights and are up to a steep but short trail, the Table Mountain Trail is even more rewarding than the Artist Ridge Trail. Though almost as crowded, 5,742-foot Table Mountain, a small plateau, is still large enough that you can get away from the crowds. Formed by a lava flow approximately 50,000 years ago, Table Mountain is an impressive block of rock rising above Artist Ridge. The trail has been cut right into the cliff face in some places and stairsteps steeply up to the top of the mountain. From the summit, the views are even better than those at Artist Ridge.

Big Four Ice Caves

2 miles round-trip. 100-foot elevation gain. Easy. Access: The trailhead is at milepost 25 on the Mountain Loop Hwy. east of Verlot.

Although very crowded on summer weekends, these large ice caves take on a very different aspect when visited on a foggy weekday in autumn. On such a day, the caves, though much reduced in size by years of drought and summer melting, take on a Pleistocene appearance. The cliffs above them are shrouded in mists and a barren, rock-strewn valley hints at the recent retreat of the ice. Just get here early to beat the crowds. The caves are formed by compacted snow at the base of an avalanche slope. Through the snow flows a waterfall and stream that cascades off the cliffs of Big Fout Mountain, which rises directly above. The caves vary in size from year to year and depending on when in the year you visit. When I was there one September, they were smaller than usual, but at 20 feet deep and 20 feet high were still impressive. Because the snow is subject to collapse, visitors are encouraged not to go inside. People have in the past been trapped by falling ice.

WHITEWATER KAYAKING & CANOEING

This area probably offers the greatest variety of whitewater in the smallest area anywhere in the state. From winter eagle-watching floats to late summer Class III runs to some of the gnarliest Class V drops you'll ever want to run, the many rivers flowing off the North Cascades offer a little of everything. There are, however, two constants on these rivers—change and logjams. Every few winters floods seem to rearrange everything, turning once familiar rivers into total strangers. These same floods drop huge tree trunks, and occasionally boulders, where you least expect them. Stay alert for logjams, scouting downstream far enough to be able to get ashore safely.

CLASS I

The 10-mile stretch of the **Skagit River** between Marblemount and Rockport is the region's most popular Class I/Class II run, and it is most often run during the winter months. Between January and February, hundreds of bald eagles congregate along this stretch of river to feed on dying salmon that spawn. Because the eagles tend to feed in the morning and roost in the trees during the afternoon, boaters are requested to launch between 10am and noon and be off the river by 3pm. Another good Class I run covers the 6 miles between Copper Creek and Marblemount. This run is best done in the autumn, when the river is often thick with spawning salmon.

CLASS II

If you're looking for Class II waters, your best bets are on the North Fork and South Fork Stillaguamish River. Each of these rivers has at least two good Class II runs. On the **South Fork Stillaguamish River,** try the 9-mile run from Granite Falls down to Jordan. If you put in at the base of the falls, which are east of the town of Granite Falls, you'll catch some good Class II+ paddling. If you want to stick to slightly easier water, put in north of town at the bridge over the river. You can take out either at the pedestrian suspension bridge in the town of Jordan (north on Jordan Road from Granite Falls) or 5 miles farther downstream at River Meadows County Park (continue north on Jordan Road), which involves less carrying than the Jordan take-out.

On the **North Fork Stillaguamish River,** two back-to-back runs can fill an entire weekend with scenic paddling on fun Class II waters. The upper run starts at the end of a dirt road 0.7 miles east of milepost 46 on Wash. 530 (if you reach Darrington, you've gone too far). The river here is narrow, shallow, and winding, with frequent views of the snow-clad slopes of Whitehorse Ridge. From this put-in, it is

14 miles downstream to a take-out at the Evergreen Fly Fishing Club's boat ramp, which is off Whitman Road, roughly 11 miles by road west of the put-in turn-off. This take-out also serves as the put-in for the next run, which covers 8 miles to a Department of Wildlife boat ramp just over the Wash. 530 bridge in Cicero. Take Monty Road to reach this boat ramp. This is the most popular run on the North Fork and provides fun water and good views.

The **Sauk River,** between Darrington and the Skagit River, also has two good Class II runs. The upper run covers 15 miles between Darrington and Sauk County Park, while the lower run covers the remaining 6 miles to the Skagit plus 6 miles on the Skagit. The upper run gets the nod as the better of the two. This stretch is on designated Wild and Scenic River waters and has the better views of surrounding peaks. Put in at the Sauk Prairie Road bridge east of Wash. 530 just north of downtown Darrington. The take-out is at Sauk County Park, which is on the Concrete–Sauk Valley Road north of Darrington. The lower run starts at this same park and ends at a public fishing access area 5 miles southeast of Concrete. It passes through wide, flat areas where the Sauk forms a delta at its confluence with the Skagit. The water below the delta can be some of the most difficult on this run, so pay attention. However, also keep your eyes open for bald eagles if you're doing this run during the winter. The delta area is part of the Skagit River Bald Eagle Natural Area. On both of these runs, stay alert for logjams.

CLASS III

One of the region's most popular kayak runs is the 10-mile stretch of the **North Fork Nooksack River** between Douglas Fir Campground (east of the town of Glacier) and the town of Maple Falls. Each year in the fall, the water just upstream from the Douglas Fir Campground is the site of a slalom event that utilizes a good Class III rapid. This run consists of lots of Class II and III rapids, with the bigger rapids confined to the narrow gorge at the start of the run. This river is fed by glacial runoff from Mount Baker and other area peaks and is best run during the warm summer

months when the sun keeps the water running off the glaciers. Great scenery.

Above the popular eagle-watching stretch of the **Skagit River** is a run that offers more challenging waters. Starting at the Goodell Creek Campground just west of Newhalem and continuing for 9 miles to the Copper Creek boat launch, this run is mostly easy Class I and II water, but pushes up into the Class III range at the S turns, which can be scouted from the highway a couple miles upriver from the take-out point. This run can be done year-round, but at flood levels the S turns push up to Class IV.

South of Darrington, on the **Sauk River,** there is another popular Class III run. Covering the 8.5 miles from Bedal Campground to White Chuck Campground, this run is at its best during the snowmelt season. Keep alert for logjams.

The **Suiattle River,** which flows into the Sauk River between Darrington and Rockport, is another good Class III river with a couple of possible runs. The more popular is the 13-mile lower run, which starts at the FS 25 bridge, 10 miles up FS 26 from Wash. 530. This run is mostly Class II but has a bit of Class III water, and is popular with rafting companies. The upper run is strictly Class III and III+ and starts at Sulphur Creek Campground, 12 miles upriver from the FS 25 bridge take-out. The run starts with 2 miles of uninterrupted whitewater, so take a deep breath when you push off from shore. This river can be run year-round. Logjams can be a problem on the upper run—be prepared for some portaging.

CLASS IV & ABOVE

If you're a Class V boater in search of some challenge in this area, consider the Horseshoe Bend rapid, upstream from the Douglas Fir Campground on the **North Fork Nooksack River.** Another noteworthy Class V run is the 8-mile stretch of the **Cascade River** below Marble Creek Campground. This run has several Class V rapids. However, the most legendary stretch of Class V water in this region is Robe Canyon on the **South Fork Stillaguamish River.** Located downstream from the community of Verlot, this 3-mile-long gorge is a nonstop adrenaline rush topping out with Class V+ waters. Robe Canyon sits in the middle of a 12-mile run that ends at the bridge above unrunnable Granite Falls with a steep climb up from the river. From beginning to end this run is a mind-numbing challenge.

WHITEWATER RAFTING

With numerous excellent whitewater rivers pouring out of the North Cascades, it is not surprising that several are run by commercial rafting companies. These runs range from the wintertime bald-eagle-viewing floats on the Class I **Skagit River** to the Class IV waters in the gorge on the **Nooksack River** near the town of Glacier. In between these two extremes is the **Suiattle River,** which has a nice, easy Class II and III run that is popular with families. Both of these latter runs are summer runs, which also helps make them popular. Rafting companies running these rivers include **Alpine Adventures** (tel. 206/838-2505 or 509/782-7042), **Cascade Adventures** (tel. 800/723-8386), **Osprey River Adventures** (tel. 509/997-4116), **River Riders** (tel. 800/448-RAFT or 206/448-RAFT), and **River Recreation Inc.** (tel. 800/464-5899 or 206/831-1880).

WILDLIFE VIEWING

The **Granite Falls Fishway** on the South Fork Stillaguamish River is a good place to watch coho, Chinook, and pink salmon making their way up a fish ladder to spawning areas above the falls. Farther upstream, at **Gold Basin,** you can also see coho salmon as they make their way through an old millpond. Salmon runs on the Stillaguamish last from October through February. During roughly this same period, you can also see coho and chum salmon spawning around **Fortson Ponds,** which are just north of Wash. 530 about 6 miles west of Darrington. Near **Newhalem,** on Wash. 20, you can see summer Chinook and pink salmon spawning from late August through October in both the Skagit River and Goodell Creek. From August through December, Chinook, coho, chum, and pink salmon can all be seen in the Park Slough Spawning Channel, which is also in Newhalem.

The North Cascades East ◆ What to Do & Where to Do It

BIRD WATCHING

In the **Methow Wildlife Area,** which includes part of Pearrygin Lake, you may catch glimpses of blue grouse. During the April mating season, listen for the blue grouse's booming vocalizations that sound a bit like the hooting of a great horned owl. Low elevation trails such as the Monument Creek Trail and the West Fork Methow River Trail, both off of FS 54 (the Harts Pass Road) west of Mazama, provide riparian habitat that attracts a good variety of birds during the summer months. To reach the head of the West Fork Trail, turn left at the River Bend Campground and continue another 0.2 miles.

Osprey, bald, and golden eagles are all fairly common along the shores of **Lake Chelan,** as are several species of waterfowl, including harlequin ducks, which can often be seen in Stehekin. A trip up the lake on the *Lady of the Lake* or *Lady Express* is a good way to do a day's bird watching. Along the way you may also see deer and mountain goats, and even black bears and cougars are sometimes spotted. **Coon Lake,** which is a popular day hike out of Stehekin, is another good location for watching waterfowl.

CROSS-COUNTRY SKIING

Although the Lake Chelan area has some groomed ski trails, as well as plenty of backcountry exploring possibilities, the Methow Valley is this region's premier cross-country skiing destination. In fact, with 175 kilometers of ski trails groomed for both classic and skate skiing, the Methow Valley is one of the nation's premier cross-country ski areas. The dry eastside snow and abundant sunshine have helped to make this valley the ski destination it is. The one big drawback is that the Methow Valley is so far from Seattle. With the North Cascades Highway closed in the winter, it is necessary to first drive over Stevens Pass on U.S. 2 , north on U.S. 97, and then back west on Wash. 153 and Wash. 20 for a total distance from Seattle of around 230 miles, and Stevens Pass can be slow goin' in the winter. People who come up here to ski usually stay for longer than just the weekend.

Needless to say, there are plenty of places in the area to buy or rent equipment and also plenty of opportunities to take a ski class and improve your skills. Equipment rentals, sales, and ski instruction are all available at **Sun Mountain Lodge** (tel. 800/572-0493 or 509/996-2211), **Winthrop Mountain Sports,** 257 Riverside Ave., Winthrop (tel. 509/996-2886), and **Mazama Country Inn,** 42 Lost River Rd., Mazama (tel. 800/843-7951 or 509/996-2681).

If you need to rent skis in the Lake Chelan area, they're available at **Lake Chelan Sports,** 132 E Wooden Ave. (tel. 509/682-2629). There are no skis for rent in Stehekin, but Lake Chelan Sports will send you up a pair on the ferry if you get there and then decide you need them.

METHOW VALLEY: GROOMED TRAILS

The trails of the Methow Valley Sport Trails Association are all immaculately groomed and wind from one end of the valley to the other. A daily fee of $10 on weekdays and $12 on weekends is charged for the use of these trails. Three-day passes are also available for $25. Trail passes and trail maps are available at Sun Mountain Lodge, Winthrop Mountain Sports, and the Mazama Country Inn.

Sun Mountain Ski Trails

70 kilometers. Easy–most difficult. 50–1,200-foot elevation gain. Access: The parking area for these trails is between Patterson Lake and Sun Mountain Lodge, 9.5 miles outside Winthrop. From downtown Winthrop, drive east on Wash. 20 and turn right onto Twin Lakes Rd. immediately after crossing the bridge. In 3.3 miles, turn right onto Patterson Lake Rd. and continue to the parking area. Map: MVSTA Sun Mountain Ski Trails.

Located just below Sun Mountain Lodge and high above the valley floor, this is the finest and funnest trail system in the Methow Valley. Not only are there enough loops of different lengths to put together

as many or as few miles of skiing as you can handle, but the terrain is varied, which keeps things interesting. There are also views, and if you're so inclined, you can ski up to Sun Mountain Lodge for a lunch or more phenomenal views. This system breaks down into roughly two distinct skiing areas. The relatively flat trails to the west of the Chikadee trailhead parking area are favored by beginning skiers. However, the Yellow Jacket Trail features rolling terrain that is a lot of fun for intermediate skiers, and the Rodeo Trail includes some short steep pitches and tight turns to challenge experienced skiers. The Beaver Pond Trail, which passes by the pond and through a beautiful aspen grove, is the most scenic of the trails in this area. If, on the other hand, you are looking for distance and plenty of intermediate skiing, head up the Thompson Ridge Road and ski some of the blue trails. This area provides the best views, but to reach these views, you'll have to cover some distance. The basic loop up Thompson Ridge Road around Meadowlark and back covers roughly 16 kilometers. If you want views without the distance, ski up Sunnyside to Sun Mountain Lodge and continue up above the lodge on View Ridge.

From this trail system you can ski down to Winthrop on the Winthrop Trail, which is rated "Most Difficult" at the upper end and "More Difficult" in its lower stretches. Alternatively, you can take the "Most Difficult" Power's Plunge to connect to the Methow Valley Community Trail into Winthrop or anywhere upvalley.

Rendezvous Ski Trails

48 kilometers. More difficult–most difficult. 2,000-foot elevation gain. Access: From downtown Winthrop, drive west on Wash. 20, cross the river, and turn right onto W Chewuch Rd. Continue up this road 6 miles and turn left on Cub Creek Rd. and continue 2.5 miles to the parking area. These trails are also accessible from a parking area east of Mazama on the Goat Creek County Rd. Map: MVSTA Rendezvous Ski Trails.

These are the most challenging trails in the MVSTA system and are also where you'll find the valley's hut-to-hut ski

The Pika and the Marmot—Two Solutions to the Same Problem

As Cascade hikers well know, the summer hiking season is all too brief. Many areas are free of snow for only two or three months of the year. These high-altitude areas, often meadows and talus slopes near or above timberline, would seem a most inhospitable location in which to take up year-round residence, but at least two mammals do just that. Pikas and marmots both call these short-summer regions home, and the two animals have developed very different ways of dealing with the long, snowbound winters.

Pikas, tiny relatives of rabbits, live in talus slopes where they seem to be forever on the move. Their high-pitched squeaks, which act as warnings to other pikas, are a familiar sound to hikers. However, though the sound of the pika is familiar, they are rarely seen as they scuttle about beneath the rocks. Like rabbits, pikas are herbivores. They spend their summers frantically gathering plants, which they set out on rocks to dry. After these plants have dried, becoming a sort of miniature hay, the pikas store them in rock crevices. A single pika can store up to 50 pounds of hay in a single summer. The reason for this food storage is that pikas do not hibernate. They stay awake throughout the entire 9 to 10 months that they are trapped beneath the snow in their rocky chambers. Consequently they need all that hay in order to survive until the next summer.

Marmots, the largest member of the squirrel family, have an entirely different way of dealing with the long winters and short summers of the high altitudes. Living in flower-filled meadows, marmots are often seen sunning themselves on rocks, spending their summers much the way many humans wish they could. Marmots eschew the fast-paced life of the pika in favor of a much more laid-back lifestyle. During the summer, marmots fatten themselves up on all manner of wildflowers and grasses, adding as much as half their body weight in fat. When winter sets in, they snuggle up together in their burrows and go into hibernation for the next seven months or so. During hibernation, a marmot's body temperature drops to just above freezing and its heart rate slows to between 8 and 10 beats per minute.

Now which would you rather be, a pika or a marmot?

---

system. All the trails in this area do a lot of climbing (and descending), so you need to have very good downhill skills to ski here. Many people do overnight tours and stay at one or more of the five huts along the trail system. Although there are plenty of miles of very challenging "Most Difficult" trails, you don't have to be an expert skier to tackle these trails. Intermediates will be able to get around most of the system, and three of the huts (Heifer, Rendezvous, and Fawn) are accessible from blue trails. This system of trails gets you onto the most remote groomed trails in the valley and provides the feel of a backcountry trip without the dangers or difficulties of backcountry travel. A multiday hut-to-hut here is a memorable experience. If you just want to do a day ski, try the 16-kilometer Little Cub Creek–Cow Creek Loop or the 13-kilometer Cow Creek–Cedar Creek Loop.

To stay in the Rendezvous huts, contact **Rendezvous Outfitters,** P.O. Box 728, Winthrop, WA 98862 (tel. 800/422-3048 or 509/996-2148). The huts sleep up to eight people and can be rented by the bed or by the hut. Rates are $30 per bed or $160 per hut.

Mazama Ski Trails

35 kilometers. Easy. 700-foot elevation gain. Access: 13 miles west of Winthrop in Mazama at the corral parking near the Mazama Store, at Wilson Ranch Nordic Center, or at the Wash. 20 parking lot just before the highway gate. Map: MVSTA Mazama Ski Trails.

These are the uppermost trails in the valley and are almost all rated "Easy." This system spends a lot of miles in the forest but also has impressive views of Goat Wall, which rises on the north side of the valley just west of Mazama. If you're looking for sunshine and wide-open flats for working on your skate-ski stride, head down the valley from the corral parking lot on either the Lower River Run or the Inn Run/Flag Mountain Loop. For a more remote feel, head up the valley from the last parking lot (by the highway gate). Here you can do some long loops through the forests on the south side of the Methow River and stop for a while at the Cow Beach warming hut. The Doe Canyon Spur Trail, a "More Difficult" route, gains 600 feet as it climbs to a view, but otherwise is not too remarkable. However, the return downhill ski is a lot of fun. The Goat Creek Trail, also rated "More Difficult," is a more interesting route for intermediate skiers and leads to the finest view in the whole valley at Flagg Mountain overlook. The biggest benefit of this area is that it has several places to stay and has a country feel (as opposed to the town feel in Winthrop).

Methow Valley Community Trail

28 kilometers. Easy–more difficult. 330-foot elevation gain. Access: This trail can be accessed in Winthrop near Spring Creek Ranch B&B, at Wolfridge Resort, at Brown's Farm B&B, and at Mazama. Map: Any MVSTA Ski Trails map.

This trail is the grand link that makes the Methow Valley such an incredible cross-country ski area. Beginning in Winthrop near the Spring Creek Ranch B&B, it winds its way upvalley for 28 kilometers to the community of Mazama. All but about 5 kilometers of this trail is rated "Easy," which means if you're looking to do some distance skiing, this trail makes a good workout. Along the way there are plenty of views as you pass through forests and farms. However, the real beauty is that the trail passes by several lodgings, allowing skiers to forsake their cars for the entire time they are in the valley. Lodges and B&Bs include Spring Creek Ranch, Wolfridge Resort, Brown's Farm B&B, and

Fosters Ranch. If you include a few more kilometers of skiing on the Mazama ski trails, you'll also take in Mazama Ranch House, Mazama Country Inn, Wilson Ranch, and North Cascades Basecamp.

METHOW VALLEY: UNGROOMED TRAILS

Sure there are places to ski in the Methow Valley that aren't groomed, but with 175 kilometers of groomed trails, you have to really want to break trail yourself. If you happen to be a telemark skier, don't despair—there are several places to carve some S turns. Most accessible is **Sandy Butte,** which rises to the south of Wilson Ranch in Mazama. Stop at the Mazama Inn or Mazama Store to pick up a map of this butte before heading uphill. It's easy to get lost. There is also a moderate danger of avalanches here, so you need to be familiar with avalanche safety procedures. It's 4,000 feet to the top of this mountain, but don't feel obligated to reach the summit (you do want to get down before dark, don't you?).

LAKE CHELAN AREA: GROOMED TRAILS

Echo Ridge Sno-Park

23 kilometers. Easy–most difficult. 400-foot elevation gain. Access: 7 miles northwest of Chelan off Wash. 150 (Manson Hwy.). Follow the signs to Echo Valley downhill area and continue another 2 miles to this sno-park. Fee: $6 donation. Map: Available at Chelan Ranger Station or at trailhead.

Set on the outskirts of apple-orchard country, this network of ski trails provides more views per mile than any ski trail in the state. The lack of forest almost guarantees that any trail will yield superb views of snow-covered hills, apple orchards, mountains, and Lake Chelan. With a half-dozen loop trails, skiers can string together as few or as many miles as they want. Advanced skiers will want to head for Telly Hill, or for challenging track skiing, Zoom or Outer Rim. You'll find this sno-park 2 miles past the Echo Valley downhill ski area, which has in the past also had several groomed cross-country trails. There have also been groomed trails at Echo Valley.

Stehekin Ski Trails

16 kilometers. Easy. 50-foot elevation gain. Access: These trails start in Stehekin, which can be reached by ferry on the *Lady of the Lake* or *Lady Express.* There is also floatplane service. Map: Snow Trails of Stehekin (available at North Cascades Lodge), USGS Stehekin, Green Trails Stehekin.

If you're looking for someplace to do some skiing away from the crowds, consider Stehekin, which is accessible only by boat or floatplane. Here you'll find several groomed trails around the lower section of the Stehekin Valley. The 5- to 7-kilometer Buckner Orchard Loop, which begins at the Rainbow Falls Road 3.5 miles from Stehekin Landing, is probably the most popular route in the valley. The chance to ski past 312-foot-tall Rainbow Falls should also not be missed. The area around the airstrip, just off the ungroomed River Trail, is another good place to ski. This area has 4 to 5 kilometers of groomed trails and good views of McGregor Mountain. The High Bridge Trail is an 8-kilometer round-trip trail that starts at the end of the plowed road. The trail follows the summer road uphill to High Bridge. Trailhead shuttles can be arranged through the North Cascades Lodge for $7.50 per person per day.

LAKE CHELAN AREA: UNGROOMED TRAILS

Stehekin Ski Trails

16 kilometers. Easy. 50-foot elevation gain. Access: These trails start in Stehekin, which can be reached by ferry on the *Lady of the Lake* or *Lady Express.* There is also floatplane service. Map: Snow Trails of Stehekin (available at North Cascades Lodge), USGS Stehekin, Green Trails Stehekin.

In addition to the groomed trails, the Stehekin Valley also has many miles of ungroomed trails. The River Trail (8 miles round-trip), which starts upvalley at Harlequin Campground, is a scenic route that follows the bank of the Stehekin River down to Weaver Point, which is across the bay from the boat dock. More experienced skiers may want to ski from the end of the plowed road up to Coon Lake and from there up the Old Wagon Road to Bridge Creek (12.4 miles round-trip). It is also possible to ski all the way to Cottonwood Campground, but be sure to check on the avalanche danger before heading up this route.

DOWNHILL SKIING & SNOWBOARDING

North Cascade Heli-Skiing

In Mazama, 13 miles west of Winthrop on Wash. 20. Tel. 800/494-HELI; fax 509/996-3660. 4,000 vertical feet. Packages: $510 for one day, $1,705–$1,755 for three days (rates include room and board and are based on double occupancy of a room).

Sure it's expensive, but if you've got the money, there's nothing like the excitement of heli-skiing. Untracked powder is the goal here, and with 300,000 acres of mountain slopes available for skiing, you can be assured that you will find plenty of steep and deep powder. Runs range in vertical feet from 1,500 to 4,000 and start as high as 9,000 feet. A typical day includes six to eight hours of skiing, five runs, and 10,000 feet of total vertical skiing. It's hard to beat numbers like these, so if you've already done the Bugaboos, maybe its time to try the North Cascades. There is, however, one drawback to heli-skiing in this area. Cloudy weather occasionally prevents the choppers from going up, and in such an event, trips are made by snowcat.

Loup Loup Ski Bowl

On Wash. 20, between Omak and Twisp. Tel. 509/826-2720. 10 trails; 1,240 vertical feet; 2 Pomas, 1 rope tow. Lift hours: Wed, Fri–Sun 9:30am–4pm. Adult lift tickets: Wed $16 (9:30am–4pm), $11 (9:30am–1pm or 1–4pm); Fri $10 (9:30am–4pm); Sat–Sun $18 (9:30am–4pm), $12 (9:30am–1pm or 1–4pm).

Although the Methow Valley is best known for its amazing network of cross-country ski trails, downhill skiers and snowboarders also have someplace to go when the snow falls. Loup Loup, though small, is a very respectable little ski hill that offers good long runs and plenty of variety. In fact, this ski area has almost as much vertical as some of the much larger ski areas in the region. It may not be worth going out of the way for, but if you're in the neighborhood and have your downhill skis or snowboard equipment with you, this place is pretty fun.

Echo Valley

7 miles northwest of Chelan, on Boyd District Rd. Tel. 509/682-4002. 8 trails; 500 vertical feet; 1 Poma, 3 rope tows. Lift hours: Sat–Sun 9am–4pm. Adult lift tickets $10.

Sure it's small, but families in Chelan love it. With this little hill tucked behind the apple orchards, no one has to make the drive to Mission Ridge when they want to get in a bit of skiing. This is a good place to learn or maybe practice your telemark turns. The ski area is totally run by volunteers and is a nonprofit endeavor.

FISHING

Although there is good fishing along the entire length of the **Methow River** for steelhead, rainbow, cutthroat, and Dolly Varden (bull) trout, most of the lower river is bordered by private lands. If you head upriver to the West Fork, you'll find both good fishing and good public access along Methow River Trail and along Harts Pass Road. Fly fishing is particularly popular on these upper waters, as well as on the adjacent **Lost River.** Many area lakes are also popular with fly anglers using floats. The Methow is stocked with rainbows and steelheads.

The **Chewuch River,** which enters the Methow at Winthrop, is another good trout stream that is stocked throughout the summer. Likewise, the **Twisp River,** which enters the Methow at the town of Twisp, is also stocked with rainbows and has numerous campgrounds and good public access. This is a good fly-fishing river. Many of the lakes in the Methow Valley are stocked with rainbow trout. In **Pearrygin Lake,** many of these trout

survive the winter and some hefty fish can sometimes be caught. Nearby **Cougar** and **Campbell** lakes also are productive rainbow waters.

Across the valley near Sun Mountain Lodge, **Twin Lakes** and **Patterson Lake** are stocked with rainbows, and Patterson also holds brookies. Many of the high-altitude lakes of the North Cascades are also stocked with trout. **Rainy Lake,** at Rainy Pass, is one such lake that is easily accessible by way of a 1-mile paved trail.

For gear and fishing reports on Methow Valley waters, contact **Mazama Troutfitters,** 50 Lost River Rd. (tel. 509/996-3674), which is next door to the Mazama Store in the community of Mazama west of Winthrop. This shop also rents fly-fishing equipment and offers a fly-fishing guide service.

Lake Chelan, although it looks like an awesome fishing hole, is so large, so deep, and so cold that it doesn't support a large fish population. However, it does have quite a variety, including kokanee, landlocked Chinook salmon, cutthroat, rainbow, Mackinaw trout, and freshwater ling cod (burbot). Each year more than 100,000 keeper-size rainbow trout are stocked in the lower basin of the lake, so if you keep at it, you're bound to hook a few of these. At the upper end of the lake, near stream mouths and the mouth of the Stehekin, 20-inch rainbows are not unusual. If larger fish are your quarry, try trolling between 50 and 150 feet for monster Mackinaw that can approach 30 pounds. The Chinook also run to about 30 pounds. Good luck!

In the vicinity of Manson, 8 miles northwest of Chelan, are three small lakes that provide very different fishing conditions from those found in Lake Chelan. **Wapato Lake** is stocked with rainbow trout and is consistently productive whether you are using a spinning reel or a fly rod. Nearby **Roses Lake** is open only in winter and then only when the ice is thick enough. This lake also yields good-size rainbow trout. **Dry Lake,** in the same area, is warmer than these other two lakes and is home to bass, crappie, perch, and bluegill.

In the **Stehekin River,** which feeds Lake Chelan, the rainbows and cutthroat trout are so hungry they'll take just about any small fly you toss their way. Only artificial lures and flies are allowed on this river. Tributary streams of the Stehekin, such as the Boulder, Rainbow, Company, Devore, and Bridge creeks, also offer excellent fly fishing.

Down in the **Columbia River,** in the dammed waters of Entiat Lake, there is fishing for steelhead, walleye, smallmouth bass, whitefish, and rainbows. Some of the best fishing is in side channels. South of Chelan, you can try the **Entiat River,** but you'll have to head 30 miles upriver before the fishing for rainbows and steelheads gets good. North of the Methow River, the **Okanogan River** offers year-round fishing, a rarity on the region's rivers. Steelhead, smallmouth bass, walleye, and rainbows can all be pulled out of this river.

HIKING & BACKPACKING

METHOW VALLEY AREA

Maple Pass Loop Trail

7.5-mile loop. Moderate. 1,950-foot elevation gain. Access: The trailhead is at Rainy Pass on the North Cascades Hwy. (Wash. 20) 30 miles west of Winthrop. Map: USGS Washington Pass, Green Trails Washington Pass and Mount Logan.

The view from Maple Pass just might be the most astounding 360° view in the Northwest, which alone would make this one of the best hikes covered in this book. However, add two sublime little cirque lakes and you have the most gratifying, soul-satisfying day hike I can think of. The trail starts with switchbacks through the forest but soon lessens its gradient as it crosses an open slope with views to the north. At 1 mile the trail forks, with the Lake Ann trail leading 1 flat mile to this perfect little cirque lake with an island at the far end. Sloping to the lake's shores are subalpine forest, talus slopes, and meadows. The view of the lake is actually much better from the Maple Pass Trail, so you can save yourself 2 miles of hiking to the lake and back by simply heading up this trail to begin with. The trail climbs steadily through meadows and talus slopes

to Heather Pass in another mile. But Maple Pass can be seen above, beckoning with the promise of southerly views (Heather has a superb westerly view that includes Lewis Lake). Crossing some cliffs where the trail has been carved out of rock, it climbs to the undulating meadows at the pass and an astonishing view of Glacier Peak and the Stuart Range to the south.

From here, continue along the ridgeline to the east (after first exploring the area), climbing a bit from the pass, to find a trail leading down the ridge between Lake Ann and Rainy Lake. From this ridge, you'll have views of both lakes before dropping into the forest as you descend to meet the paved Rainy Lake Trail. From this trail junction, it is about 0.5 miles to Rainy Lake and then 1 mile back to the parking lot.

Blue Lake Trail

4 miles round-trip. Moderate. 1,100-foot elevation gain. Access: 31 miles west of Winthrop on Wash. 20 (0.8 miles west of Washington Pass). Map: USGS Washington Pass, Green Trails Washington Pass.

This moderately easy trail passes through some of the most spectacular scenery in the North Cascades as it winds its way more than 1,000 feet up to the turquoise waters of Blue Lake, at 7,807 feet. The trail climbs steadily through forest for much of the way, passing a small pond at the very start of the trail. Unfortunately, the first mile of the trail is so close to the highway that you'll be listening to the roar of cars and trucks as they grind their way up to Washington Pass. At 1 mile there's a brief opening with a view, and then at 1.5 miles the trail leaves the forest for good with excellent views across the valley to Cutthroat Peak and a neck-straining view of Liberty Bell.

As you reach the lake, you walk beside and then cross a small stream, beside which stand the remains of a log cabin. Hike up to the west for great views of Liberty Bell and the Early Winter Spires. The lake's far end is all talus slopes with summer-long snows and rugged cliffs rising above. The scenic beauty and easy access make this one of the busiest trails in the national park—the sort of place where people light up a cigarette when they reach the top.

Cutthroat Pass Trail

11 miles round-trip. Moderate. 2,300-foot elevation gain. Access: Drive Wash. 20 west from Mazama for 12 miles, turn right onto signed Cutthroat Creek Rd. (FS 400), and continue 1 mile to the parking area. Map: USGS Washington Pass, Green Trails Washington Pass.

The chance to see mountain goats up close is perhaps the best reason to hike this trail. However, even if no goats are to be seen, the alpine vistas at the pass are certainly reward enough. Along the way, you can stop to rest on the shores of Cutthroat Lake, which is ringed by steep walls and forest and is just a short distance off the main trail. Most of the trail is through open forests of lodgepole pines interspersed with clumps of spruce trees. As you near the pass, the forest gives way to rocky slopes. In summer, water is scarce beyond the lake (which, of course, is where the trail gets steep). A knoll just south of the pass provides even more breathtaking views, and if you have the energy to hike another 3 miles round-trip from the pass, be sure to continue to Granite Pass, where a completely different view to the northwest presents itself.

LAKE CHELAN/ STEHEKIN AREA

The community of Stehekin, at the north end of Lake Chelan, has a split personality. On the one hand, it is a popular summer getaway and as such has numerous easy day hikes in the vicinity. On the other hand, it is the starting (or ending) point for several long multiday hikes through North Cascades National Park and Glacier Peak Wilderness. The shuttle bus that runs from Stehekin to Cottonwood Campground (barring road washouts caused by floods) provides access to several trailheads, any one of which can provide hours of hiking before it's time to catch the bus back downvalley. Stehekin is not accessible by car. The favored way to get here is by ferry on the *Lady of the Lake* or the *Lady Express*.

Chelan Lakeshore Trail (Prince Creek to Stehekin)

17.2 miles. Moderate. 1,900-foot elevation gain. Access: The *Lady of the Lake* will drop you at Prince Creek if you make arrangements in advance. Map: USGS Stehekin, Sun Mountain, Lucerne, Prince Creek; Green Trails Stehekin, Lucerne, Prince Creek.

There is something enchanting about hiking for miles along the deep blue waters of Lake Chelan. With mountains all around, the lake seems oddly out of place, as if it shouldn't be there, but there it is and there it has been since the ice age. Because of its low elevation and south-facing location, this trail is the first in the area to be free of snow in the spring and can usually be hiked by May 1. Shortly after the trail is clear of snow, the wildflowers put on a brilliant display, making early summer the best time to hike. As the name implies, the trail follows the lakeshore, though not always right at the water. Due to the topography, the trail is sometimes as much as 500 feet above the water. Along the way you may see deer, mountain goats, or black bears, and as you approach Stehekin, you'll pass a few vacation cabins. About 10.2 miles from Prince Creek, you'll reach Moore Point, site of a popular boat-in campsite. From Moore Point, continue to Stehekin. An alternative is to start this hike in Stehekin and arrange to be picked up at either Prince Creek or Moore Point.

Rainbow Loop Trail

6 miles. Moderate. 1,450-foot elevation gain. Access: This hike starts at the Rainbow Creek trailhead, 5.5 miles from Stehekin, and is a stop on the shuttle bus route. Map: USGS Stehekin, Green Trails Stehekin.

While trails in the Stehekin area tend to be flat valley-bottom hikes or grueling climbs straight up the steep walls of the valley, this hike makes a good in-between choice. Not too easy, not too difficult. Views of the Stehekin Valley and Lake Chelan are the payoff. Start the hike from the Rainbow Creek trailhead, which can be reached on the shuttle bus. From here climb 1,000 feet in 2.5 miles, along the way passing a bluff with a view of the valley, to a bridge over Rainbow Creek. Just before reaching the creek there is a trail junction. If you turn left here and hike up this trail 0.5 miles, you'll find views even more stunning than the ones along the main trail. The creek marks the midpoint of the trail, from which it is 2.5 miles down to the lower trailhead, which is at the bottom of a steep trail with more great views. Once back down on the Stehekin Valley road, you can wait for a bus or hike back to where you started.

Horseshoe Basin

8 miles round-trip. Moderate. 2,000-foot elevation gain. Access: The trailhead is at Cottonwood Camp, 23 miles from Stehekin (in the past a bus has traveled between Stehekin and Cottonwood Camp). Map: USGS Cascade Pass, Green Trails Cascade Pass.

This hike starts out on the trail to Cascade Pass, which is one of the most popular trails in North Cascades National Park and consequently sees a lot of use, especially on weekends. The trail follows a route first used by Native Americans and then by pioneers. The trail begins along the Stehekin River, and after less than 1.5 miles begins the long, steady climb to the pass. At 2.2 miles, the trail up to Horseshoe Basin cuts off from the main trail. It is 1.5 miles up to Horseshoe Basin, which is surrounded by cliffs from which cascade as many as 15 waterfalls. These cascades are tumbling off the slopes of Buckner, Booker, and Sahale mountains, which are all connected by the appropriately named Ripsaw Ridge. If you are day hiking, you can spend time exploring the basin and, if you have a flashlight with you, the abandoned Black Warrior Mine, which has been stabilized so that it is safe to enter. This basin also makes an excellent destination for an overnight trip.

If you have the stamina to do Horseshoe Basin and the 5,400-foot Cascade Pass in one day, the two make for an exhilarating and exhausting 14-mile hike. You could also camp one night in Horseshoe Basin and one night at Sahale Arm,

1,200 feet above Cascade Pass at the foot of Sahale Glacier. Horseshoe Basin can be an 18-mile, one- or two-night trip from the Cascade River trailhead on the west side of Cascade Pass. See the "Hiking & Backpacking" section, above, in "The North Cascades West—What to Do & Where to Do It" for details on this hike.

This alternate routing is especially worth considering if the shuttle bus is not running all the way to Cottonwood. In the winter of 1995–96, a section of the road to Cottonwood Camp was washed out and it was uncertain when repairs would take place. Consequently there may no longer be bus service from Stehekin to Cottonwood Camp. Check with the national park or National Forest Service before heading out on this hike.

HORSEBACK RIDING

The Methow Valley claims to be the inspiration for the famous Western novel and film *The Virginian,* so it is no surprise that folks around here take horseback riding very seriously. Consequently there are several places where visitors to the valley can saddle up and ride the purple sage or yellow-belly pines. **Chewack River Guest Ranch & Riding Stables** (tel. 509/996-2497), 6 miles north of Winthrop on East Chewuch River Road; **Early Winters Outfitting** (tel. 509/996-2659) in Mazama; and **North Cascades Outfitters** (tel. 509/997-1015) in Twisp all offer guided rides ranging in length from one or two hours to overnight. Expect to pay between $25 and $30 for a two-hour ride. In Stehekin, at the north end of Lake Chelan, you can ride out of **Cascade Corrals** (tel. 509/682-4677), which charges similar prices.

MOUNTAIN BIKING

Although the rides listed below represent some of the best the area has to offer, they are hardly the tip of the iceberg. At the Winthrop Ranger Station, Sun Mountain Lodge, or Winthrop Mountain Sports, you can pick up various maps, flyers, and booklets outlining many other rides in the Winthrop area.

METHOW VALLEY

Cutthroat Pass Trail

12 miles round-trip. Strenuous. 2,300-foot elevation gain. Access: Drive Wash. 20 west from Mazama for 12 miles, turn right onto signed Cutthroat Creek Rd. (FS 400), and continue 1 mile to the parking area. Map: USGS Washington Pass, Green Trails Washington Pass.

I can think of no other trail in the Northwest that allows you to ride into such an incredible alpine environment. Topping out at a 6,800-foot pass, this is a grueling climb, but the views are to die for. Keep in mind that this trail is open both to bikers and hikers (who make up the majority of trail users)—control your speed on the downhills, stay alert, slow down on corners, and otherwise be as polite as possible so that this trail continues to be open to mountain bikes. The first 2 miles are on a gentle grade on an excellent trail, and at about 1.75 miles a 0.25-mile spur trail leads to shallow little Cutthroat Lake with Cutthroat Peak rising high above. From the 2-mile point, however, the trail starts to climb with a vengeance on a hot, south slope with no water. However, every step of the way has a view, and as you switchback up you also switch back and forth between east views and west views. Even if you're in good shape you may find yourself stopping every tenth of a mile to catch your breath (blame it on the elevation). At roughly 4 miles there's a flat area with campsites, and at about 5 miles the trail breaks into open meadows amid boulders and glacier-smoothed bedrock for an astounding 1-mile traverse across steep meadows to the pass.

At the pass, the views are even better, and still better from the little knoll to the south. Beyond the pass, in any direction, trails are closed to bicycles, but this shouldn't stop you from exploring on foot. From here it is 1.5 miles on a gentle uphill grade beneath high cliffs and across steep talus slopes to Granite Pass, where there are new views to the northwest. Be sure to continue 100 yards past this pass for the best views, which take in slopes of an almost uniform beige scree, including Golden Horn.

Buck Mountain Loop

14.3 miles. Moderate–strenuous. 1,500-foot elevation gain. Access: From downtown Winthrop, drive west on Wash. 20, cross the river, and turn right onto W Chewuch Rd. Continue up this road 6 miles, turn left on Cub Creek Rd., and continue 2.5 miles to a gravel pullout on the left. Map: Green Trails Mazama and Doe Mountain.

This is a real bonanza of a ride with all the scenery of a classic western movie. Before the ride is through, you may even be calling your bike Trigger and wishing you knew a Roy Rogers song or two. There are hillsides of sagebrush, cinnamon-barked ponderosa pines dripping with fluorescent green lichen, views of forests and snowy mountains, aspen groves, even cows to herd (and flops to avoid). You might even stumble upon a herd of deer, in case you remembered to strap your trusty Winchester across your handlebars. Ride hard, pardner. Oh, yeah, and don't forget to fill the canteen.

The whole way is ridiculously well marked with brown-and-yellow bicycle signs. From the starting point, head up FS 52, which starts out paved but soon turns to gravel, and then take a right fork onto FS 100. At 3.75 miles from the start, watch for an interpretive "Deer Country" sign and turn right onto rough FS 140. Just up this road is the start of the trail riding, which begins on some double-track. From here on out the trail just goes up and down, often with fast mile-long descents. Cross through forests and then open hillsides of sagebrush with spectacular views down the valley. Watch out for twisted sagebrush trunks—they're worse than tree roots. The last 2 miles or so are a fast, smooth, look-Ma-no-brakes double-track (some occasional traffic, so pay attention on those corners).

Sun Mountain Trail System

Up to 30 miles. Easy–strenuous. Up to 1,000-foot elevation gain. Access: Take Wash. 20 south from Winthrop across the bridge and turn right, following signs for Sun Mountain Lodge. After 8 miles watch for a left turn onto Thompson Ridge Rd. The trailhead is on the left. Map: MVSTA Ski Trails Map, Green Trails Buttermilk Butte and Twisp.

During the winter, this system of loop trails is the most popular and varied of the Methow Valley's cross-country ski trail systems, and by summer these same trails provide the best riding in the valley. Whatever your level of riding ability, you'll find miles of trails to suit you. The trails near the beaver pond northwest of the parking area are the easiest, while those to the south (Thompson Ridge Road, Meadowlark, and Inside Passage) are both longer and more demanding. It is these latter trails that offer the best views in the area.

However, my single favorite is the Yellowjacket Trail, which is a roller-coaster ride on exquisitely smooth trail. It's so much fun I sometimes catch myself just going round and round in circles, using the Rodeo Trail to get me back to the start. You could easily spend an entire day just exploring all the trails here, and to add more elevation to your day, you can pedal all the way from Winthrop on the Winthrop Trail (which begins at Wash. 20 across from the Marigot Hotel and reaches these trails in 5 miles, climbing 900 feet from the valley floor) or add the climb to Sun Mountain Lodge (perhaps for a gourmet lunch).

LAKE CHELAN

Stehekin River Road

23 miles. Moderate–strenuous. 1,700-foot elevation gain. Access: To reach Stehekin with your bike, take the *Lady of the Lake* or the *Lady Express* from either Chelan or Field's Point. Map: USGS Stehekin, Goode Mountain, Cascade Pass; Green Trails Stehekin, McGregor Mountain, Cascade Pass.

Stretching for 23 miles from Stehekin to Cottonwood Camp, this road is paved for only the first stretch through the community of Stehekin. The road parallels the glacier-fed Stehekin River for its entire length and provides plenty of great views of North Cascades peaks. This whole valley was carved by the same glacier that formed Lake Chelan, and among the valley's most spectacular glacial reminders are the 312-foot-high Rainbow Falls, which is a required stop along this road.

If pedaling isn't enough for you, you also have your pick of several hiking trails along the way. Just remember that riding off the road is not allowed in North Cascades National Park. This ride makes an excellent overnight ride and provides access to lots of good day hiking. You can pack your gear into one of the campgrounds and set up a base camp. You can then ride the road to various trailheads, do some hiking, and then ride back to camp. If you aren't set up to bike camp, you can stay at a lodge in Stehekin. If you get tired on this ride, you can always catch the shuttle bus.

Echo Ridge Trails

18 miles. Easy–moderate. Up to 1,000-foot elevation gain. Access: 7 miles northwest of Chelan, off Wash. 150 (Manson Hwy.). Follow the signs to Echo Valley downhill area and continue another 2 miles to the sno-park. Map: Trailhead maps or stop by the Chelan Ranger Station.

In winter, these trails are the terrain of cross-country skiers, but once the snow melts, mountain bikers take over. The many loops here can be combined to create a ride of almost any length without ever getting boring. If you've done every trail once, try them all in reverse. It will all look completely different. The great views across the hills eastward to the Columbia River basin and westward to the North Cascades are the main attraction here, but there is also plenty of good riding through open hillsides that are a fascinating change from the westside landscape. If you're out for a real workout, head for the Outer Rim Trail, which offers the most climbing.

PACKSTOCK TRIPS

Several outfitters lead trips into the nearby Pasayten Wilderness in the North Cascades. If you're an aspiring cowpoke, check out **Early Winters Outfitting,** HCR 74, Box B6, Mazama, WA 98833 (tel. 800/737-8750 or 509/996-2659), **Rendezvous Outfitters** (tel. 800/422-3048 or 509/996-2148), or **Rocking Horse Ranch** (tel. 509/996-2768) in Winthrop. If, on the other hand, you're curious about hiking with a llama to carry your gear, contact **Pasayten**

Llama Packing, Route 1, Box 223, Winthrop, WA 98862 (tel. 509/996-2326). One other alternative that lacks the glamor of either of the above packing styles is burro packing, which is particularly popular with families. **Back Country Burro Treks,** Box 246, Winthrop, WA 98862 (tel. 509/996-3369), has been leading such trips since 1983. Their burros are gentle enough to carry small children.

Horse-packing trips into the high country above the Stehekin Valley are available through **Cascade Corrals,** P.O. Box 36, Stehekin, WA 98852 (tel. 509/682-4677), which is located at Stehekin Valley Ranch, one of the valley's only lodges.

PARAGLIDING & HANG GLIDING

High, treeless buttes and sunshine team up in the Lake Chelan area to produce excellent thermals that have earned Lake Chelan the reputation of being the best hang gliding and paragliding area in this state. Chelan is even claiming to be the hang gliding capital of the world, and with pilots regularly flying for more than 100 miles from **Chelan Butte** just south of the town of Chelan, it is hard to dispute this claim. In recent years Chelan has been the site of numerous national hang gliding and paragliding competitions. The emphasis here is on long-distance flights, which are achieved by utilizing powerful thermals rising off the wheat fields on the east side of the Columbia River. To reach these thermals, glider pilots must first catch a thermal off Chelan Butte and ride this initial column of rising air up to 6,000 feet higher to make the flight across the Columbia to the next area of thermals.

Throughout the summer, paragliders and hang gliders descend on Chelan to ride the thermals, launching from the Sky Park atop Chelan Butte. This launch site is reached by driving west from downtown Chelan on the south shore of the lake and turning left onto Chelan Butte Road, which is one block west of the Calico Cow Restaurant. The road to the top of the butte is graveled, narrow, and winding.

To arrange a paragliding class, contact **Chelan Paragliding** (tel. 509/682-7777 or 206/432-9800).

ROAD BIKING

METHOW VALLEY

Although the Winthrop Valley is solidly mountain-bike territory, there is still some good road riding to be done.

Sun Mountain Climb

20 miles. Moderate. 900-foot elevation gain. Access: Start this ride at the Red Barn, Winthrop's community center and best public parking area, on the west side of town just across the bridge.

The climb up to Sun Mountain Lodge from downtown Winthrop is the area's most rewarding ride. Along the way, you pass Twin Lakes and then Patterson Lake before finally reaching the resort at the top of the mountain. Here you can have a gourmet lunch, sip a drink on the patio, or simply soak in the view of Winthrop far below. From here it is a fast coast back down to the valley floor.

Chewuch River Loop

18 miles. Easy. 500-foot elevation gain. Access: Start this ride at the Red Barn, Winthrop's community center and best public parking area, on the west side of town just across the bridge.

The loop up West Chewuch Road and back down East Chewuch Road is another good ride in the area. This ride doesn't climb quite as much as the ride up to Sun Mountain, but still offers plenty of scenery as it passes through rolling ranchland with views of all the surrounding mountains. From Winthrop's Red Barn, cross Wash. 20 and head uphill on West Chewuch Loop past the baseball field. This road climbs steeply at first, then becomes a slow, steady uphill pedal for 7 miles, at which point you reach the bridge over the Chewuch River. This bridge connects you to the East Chewuch Road and the route back to downtown Winthrop.

If you want to make the ride longer, you can continue up West Chewuch Road, leaving ranchland behind and entering the forest. Turn around when you decide it's time to head back. About 5 miles below the bridge, turn left onto the Pearrygin Lake road and ride up to Pearrygin Lake State Park for a picnic and maybe a swim in the lake. After resting by the lake, head back the way you came and turn left onto East Chewuch Road to continue back into Winthrop.

LAKE CHELAN

Manson Loop

20 miles. Easy. 300-foot elevation gain. Access: Take Wash. 150 west from Chelan to Mill Bay Park on the east side of Manson.

The quiet apple orchard and resort community of Manson is 8 miles up the north shore of Lake Chelan from the town of Chelan and offers a pleasant ride through orchards, along the shore of Lake Chelan, and past a couple of smaller lakes. Start at Old Mill Bay Park and ride west on Wash. 150. In Manson, this becomes Wapato Way, and just after passing Manson Bay Park, becomes Manson Boulevard. Turn left onto Lakeshore Drive, which leads to Willow Point Park. From this park, continue along the lakeshore, turning left onto Summit Boulevard and then left again onto Loop Avenue. Another left onto Green's Landing Road, a right onto Lower Joe Road, and another right onto Wapato Lake Road will bring you past both Wapato Lake (which is well known for its trout fishing) and Roses Lake. You can then follow this road back to Wash. 150 and turn left, or turn left on Swartout Road and then right onto Klate Road to return to Old Mill Bay Park.

ROCK CLIMBING

The North Cascades are some of the most rugged mountains in the Northwest and offer the most adventurous climbing in the state. The countless peaks, pinnacles, and crags offer innumerable opportunities for skilled climbers willing to hike many miles to do their climbing. The premier climbing guide to the region is Fred Beckey's *Cascade Alpine Guide: Climbing and High Routes* (The Mountaineers, 1987), of which there are three volumes covering all of Washington's Cascades. Beckey, a Northwest climbing legend, has made hundreds of first ascents throughout the region over his many decades of climbing, and today's climbers still follow his routes. In the Methow Valley area, **Liberty Bell** is the most popular climb.

SEA KAYAKING & FLAT-WATER CANOEING

Pearrygin Lake is about the only lake in the area large enough to be interesting to paddle around. The lake is very popular with anglers and consequently they motor around the lake in large numbers searching for holes where the fish might be biting. The rolling hills surrounding the lake are blanketed with golden grasses in summer, which gives this lake a very different feel from lakes on the west side of the Cascades.

Patterson Lake, on the road to Sun Mountain Lodge, is also a popular place to paddle, but this is primarily because the lodge offers canoe rentals on the lake. Unfortunately, traffic driving by on the road that parallels the lake's east shore eliminates any wilderness feelings you might have hoped to encounter here.

SNOWSHOEING

Perhaps the most important thing to know about snowshoeing in this area is that snowshoes are not welcome on the many miles of groomed ski trails in the Methow Valley. These trails are maintained strictly for skiing. The **Stehekin Valley,** on the other hand, makes an ideal snowshoeing destination. Not only are there quite a few miles signed for cross-country skiing, but many hiking trails also offer opportunities for exploring the slopes of the mountains surrounding the valley. High Bridge is a good place from which to start your snowshoe explorations. From here you can hike 1.2 miles up to Coon Lake for a view of Agnes Mountain, and then continue as far as you want up the Old Wagon Trail. From High Bridge, you can also follow the 4-mile Bullion Trail, a loop on the valley floor, or explore 2.5 miles up the Agnes Gorge Trail, which begins on the oposite side of the road from the Coon Lake Trail.

SWIMMING & TUBING

Although its waters are cold, **Lake Chelan** is one of the most popular lakes in Washington. All summer long people crowd the lakeshore's parks and beaches. You'll find swimming areas right in town at Don Morse Park, as well as in Manson at Manson Bay Park. On the south shore, there are swimming areas at Lakeside Park on the outskirts of Chelan and at Lake Chelan State Park and 25-mile Creek State Park.

Though the Methow River is too cold for swimming, Pearrygin Lake, just outside Winthrop, is not. Within the **Pearrygin Lake State Park,** which is a popular destination with campers, boaters, anglers, and anyone wishing to cool off a bit, there is a designated swimming area.

WALKS & NATURAL ROADSIDE ATTRACTIONS

ALONG THE NORTH CASCADES HIGHWAY

Rainy Lake Trail

2 miles round-trip. Easy. Access: At Rainy Pass, 50 miles east of Marblemount on Wash. 20. Map: USGS Washington Pass, Green Trails Washington Pass.

Rainy Lake is a glacier-fed cirque lake on Rainy Pass and is accessed by a flat, paved trail. Because of the trail's short length, it is popular with people on a scenic drive over the North Cascades Highway. The trail passes through dense forests before reaching the lake, which is surrounded by high cliffs from which cascade two long waterfalls. High above, you can see a sliver of glacier. This lake is even more picturesque than nearby Lake Ann and is a much easier hike.

Washington Pass Scenic Overlook

200 yards. Easy. 50-foot elevation gain. Access: At Washington Pass, 55 miles east of Marblemount (30 miles west of Winthrop) on Wash. 20.

Although the trail here is hardly long enough to warrant being called a trail, the scenic overlook should not be missed. The view from here is fascinating and takes in the huge road switchback up to Washington Pass. This stretch of road was the hardest part of the North Cascades Highway to build, and it is this section of road that produces the big avalanches that close the road every winter. However, the views take in far more than just a road. Rising above are the bare-rock crags of Early Winters Spires and the 7,720-foot Liberty Bell, while across the valley of Early Winters Creek rises the equally rugged Kangaroo Ridge.

LAKE CHELAN/ STEHEKIN AREA

Rainbow Falls

Easy. No elevation gain. Access: From Stehekin, take the shuttle bus to Rainbow Falls.

At 312 feet high, Rainbow Falls are among the most impressive falls in Washington and are a popular destination for day-trippers who visit Stehekin on the *Lady of the Lake* or *Lady Express.* The falls were created when a glacier scraped out the walls of the Stehekin Valley, leaving Rainbow Creek hanging high above the valley floor in much the same way that the famous waterfalls of the Yosemite Valley were formed. The falls are 3.5 miles from Stehekin landing and make a good day-hike destination if you are staying at the North Cascades Lodge. Alternatively, you can ride the bus to and from the falls or just one way.

Coon Lake Trail

2.4 miles round-trip. Moderate. 600-foot elevation gain. Access: The trailhead is at High Bridge, which is a stop on the shuttle bus route up the valley. Map: USGS Goode Mountain, Green Trails McGregor Mountain.

This short trail leads to a pretty little lake that was created by beavers. Wildlife, especially waterfowl, is plentiful on and around the 15-acre lake, and on the far side a waterfall on Coon Creek can be seen. Though forests surround the lake, there are views southwest to Agnes Mountain.

If you have energy left for a longer hike, you can head up the McGregor Mountain Trail or the Old Wagon Road until you get tired.

WHITEWATER KAYAKING & CANOEING

CLASS II

If you aren't up to the Black Canyon run on the **Methow River,** you can do the easier Gold Creek run and still claim to have paddled this most popular of east-side rivers. The first half of this 9.5-mile run is fairly straightforward with lively waters that push the limits of Class I boating. Throughout this section, you should be able to enjoy the dry, brown hillsides above the river. However, at the confluence with Gold Creek, the river turns to a steady Class II for the rest of the run and your attention must turn to the water. Much of this meandering stretch of river can be seen from the highway. The put-in is at the fishing access site in the town of Carlton and the take-out is at the McFarland Creek fishing access site 3 miles upstream from the town of Methow.

If you have cash to spare and plenty of time on your hands, you could also run the Stehekin River at the north end of Lake Chelan. This river is run in summer by commercial rafting companies and has plenty of good Class II waters plus some Class III and IV rapids. However, the trip to this river is an adventure in itself. First you must take one of the ferries 55 miles up the lake, then you must take a shuttle bus up the river to the put-in. All this costs money, requires reservations, and takes time. To do this one 10-mile run will cost you at least $25 in transportation alone and take at least two days and possibly three (one to get there, one to do the run, and one to get back). You have to really want to run this river!

CLASS III

The 19-mile Black Canyon run on the lower **Methow River** is the most popular run in this region and attracts plenty of commercial rafting companies as well as individual paddlers in both kayaks and rafts. What draws everyone is not just the whitewater but the summer sunshine and dry east-side scenery. The run starts out fairly easy with some Class II water for warming up; then at about 6 miles into the run, you are hit with nonstop action as you negotiate the waves and holes in Black Canyon. The put-in is at a fishing access area 3 miles up Wash. 153 from the town of Methow and the take-out is just before the town of Pateros on this same highway.

If the crowds put you off or you've already run the Methow and want to try something different, it may be time for you to try the **Chewuch River,** which flows south into the town of Winthrop. The 13-mile run from Camp 4 Campground to Five-Mile Bridge on FS 51 about 6.5 miles north of Wash. 20 includes several challenging rapids (including a weir at the lower end of the run). Both this run and the Methow River run are best during the snowmelt season from May to July.

CLASS IV & ABOVE

If the aforementioned stretch of the **Chewuch River** just wasn't challenging enough for you and you crave some really outrageous Class IV water, head upstream from Big 4 Campground for another 5 miles to the Andrews Creek trailhead and put in here. Lots of boulders and occasional logs across the river mean you have to stay constantly alert on this run.

WHITEWATER RAFTING

Two rivers on the east side of the Cascades—the **Methow** and the **Stehekin**—are run by commercial rafting companies. The Methow is the more popular of these two rivers simply because of its accessibility. The Stehekin River is at the north end of Lake Chelan and is accessible only by boat, plane, or hiking trail. On the Methow, there are two sections of the river that are regularly run. One is a wild Class IV that is run from May to July, while the other is tamer Class II and III water that can be run from April to August.

Companies running the Methow River include **All Rivers Adventures** (tel. 800/74-FLOAT or 509/782-2254), **Alpine Adventures** (tel. 206/838-2505 or 509/782-7042), **Osprey Rafting Co.** (tel. 800/743-6269 or 509/548-6800), **Osprey River Adventures** (tel. 509/997-4116), **River Recreation** (tel. 800/464-5899 or 206/831-1880), and **River Riders** (tel. 800/448-RAFT or 206/448-RAFT). Raft trips on the Stehekin River are offered by the **Stehekin Valley Ranch**, P.O. Box 36, Stehekin, WA 98852 (tel. 509/682-4677).

Campgrounds & Other Accommodations

CAMPING

A certain percentage of campsites at many National Forest Service campgrounds can be reserved at least five days in advance by calling the **National Forest Reservation Service** (tel. 800/280-CAMP). State park campground reservations can be made by calling **Reservations Northwest** (tel. 800/452-5687). To make a reservation you'll need to know the name of the campground you want to stay at and the dates you plan to visit. The reservation fee for NFS campgrounds is $7.50, and for state parks it's $6.

THE NORTH CASCADES WEST

If you're heading up to the Heather Meadows area, there are several campgrounds in the forests along the banks of the Nooksack River. **Silver Fir Campground** (30 campsites), 13 miles east of Glacier, is the closest campground to the Heather Meadows area. **Douglas Fir Campground** (50 campsites), 2 miles east of Glacier, is the next best choice in the area and is open year-round. The most developed (and expensive) campground in the area is at **Silver Lake County Park** (78 campsites), north of Maple Falls.

On the south side of Mount Baker, there are several campgrounds on the shore of Baker Lake. These campgrounds are most popular with anglers and other powerboaters. **Panorama Point** (16 campsites) and **Horseshoe Cove** (34 campsites) are the busiest of the campgrounds here.

For a quieter stay, try **Boulder Creek** (10 campsites) or **Park Creek** (12 campsites), neither of which are right on the lake, but the water isn't far. All of these campgrounds are located along the Baker Lake Road. If you are headed onto the trails of the Mount Baker National Recreation Area, you may find it helpful to know that there are a few campsites at the NRA parking area. However, campers can use these sites for only one night.

Heading over the North Cascades Highway from the west side, you'll find a very nice campground, with walk-in sites, at **Rockport State Park** (62 campsites) just west of Rockport. This campground is set amid large old-growth trees. Right in Rockport itself, there are campsites in a large open field at **Howard Miller Steelhead Park** (59 campsites). The **Goodell Creek Campground** (21 campsites) is just west of Newhalem and is popular with paddlers and anglers. There is a good view of the Picket Range of the North Cascades from just across the highway. **Newhalem Creek Campground** (111 campsites), the area's busiest campground and a good base for exploring the North Cascades Highway, is also just outside the town of Newhalem and is the site of the North Cascades Visitor Center. There are many short hiking trails in the immediate vicinity. Continuing east, the next campground is at **Colonial Creek** (162 campsites) on the bank of the Thunder Arm of Diablo Lake. This is the largest campground on the North Cascades Highway and has some very nice campsites right on the water. Beyond here, there are no more campgrounds until you reach the east side of the mountains.

East of Marblemount, there are a couple of small campgrounds on the Cascade River Road, which leads to the trailhead for the popular hike to Cascade Pass. **Marble Creek** (24 campsites) is the first of these two campgrounds and is located 8 miles east of Marblemount. **Mineral Park Campground** (4 campsites) is 15 miles east of Marblemount and is that much more convenient to the Cascade Pass Trail.

Along the Mountain Loop Highway, there are 15 Forest Service campgrounds between the Verlot Public Service Center and Barlow Pass, where the road turns to gravel. These are (from west to east) **Turlo, Verlot, Hempel Creek, Gold Basin, Wiley Creek, Esswine, Boardman Creek, River Bar, Red Bridge, Tulalip Mill Site, Marten Creek, Coal Creek Bar, Beaver Creek, Big Four,** and **Perry Creek.** Almost all of these are along the banks of the South Fork Stillaguamish River and are popular with anglers, paddlers, and hikers headed into the Boulder River Wilderness and the Monte Cristo area. Farther north along the Mountain Loop Highway, there are several more campgrounds.

THE NORTH CASCADES EAST

Lone Fir (27 campsites) is the first real campground below Washington Pass, but there are a few campsites at the **Cutthroat Pass trailhead** that can used for a single night. Continuing eastward on Wash. 20, you come to **Klipchuck** (46 campsites) and **Early Winters** (13 campsites) campgrounds. There are also several campgrounds west of Early Winters on the Harts Pass Road. **Harts Pass** (5 campsites) and **Meadows** (14 campsites), a little bit farther on this rough road, are both at high elevations and provide access to the Pacific Crest Trail and other good hiking in the area. These are my two favorite campgrounds in the region.

In the Winthrop area, **Pearrygin State Park** (113 campsites) is a good choice if you are in need of a hot shower. This park is popular with families and anglers, and offers swimming and canoeing. There are also more than half a dozen Forest Service campgrounds north of here on the Chewuch River and Eightmile Creek. Of these, **Falls Creek** (7 campsites), beside a 75-foot waterfall, and **Buck Lake** (9 campsites), which provides access to some excellent mountain-bike riding, are two favorites. There are also five campgrounds up the Twisp River Road from Twisp. These campgrounds make good bases for mountain bikers and hikers heading into the Lake Chelan–Sawtooth Wilderness. **Road's End Campground** (4 campsites) is the last of these campgrounds and is almost 25 miles from Twisp.

On Lake Chelan, there are two state park campgrounds at the southern end of the lake. **Lake Chelan State Park** (46 campsites) and **Twenty-Five Mile Creek State Park** (85 campsites) both tend to be very crowded and noisy. At the north end of the lake, there are also campgrounds that are served by the shuttle bus from Stehekin. **Purple Point Campground** is right in Stehekin and is the most convenient to the boat landing. Next up the valley is **Harlequin,** which is a very popular base for exploring the lower valley. Many short trails are easily accessible from this campground. Between here and **Cottonwood,** at the end of the 23-mile Stehekin Valley Road, there are seven more campgrounds.

INNS & LODGES

THE WEST SIDE OF THE NORTH CASCADES HIGHWAY

Ross Lake Resort

Rockport, WA 98283. Tel. 360/386-4437. 13 cabins. $54–$104 double. MC, V.

There may not be another lodging of this sort anywhere in the United States. All 13 of the resort's cabins are built on logs that are floating on Ross Lake. If you're looking to get away from it all, this place comes pretty close. There is no road to the resort. To reach it, you first drive to Diablo Dam on Wash. 20, and then take a tugboat to the end of Diablo Lake, where a truck carries you around the Ross Dam to the lodge. Alternatively you can hike in on a 2-mile trail from milepost 134 on Wash. 20. There is no grocery store or restaurant here, so be sure to bring enough food for your stay. What do you do once you get here? Rent a boat and go fishing, rent a kayak or canoe, do some hiking, or simply sit and relax.

Clark's Skagit River Cabins

5675 Hwy. 20, Rockport, WA 98283. Tel. 360/ 873-2250. 23 cabins. TV. $47–$97 double. DISC, MC, V.

The first thing you notice when you turn into the driveway to Clark's Skagit River Cabins is the rabbits. They're everywhere, hundreds of them in all shapes and sizes, contentedly munching the lawns or just sitting quietly. Today the bunnies are one of the main attractions at Clark's, but it's the theme cabins that keep people coming back. Western, nautical, Victorian, Native American, Adirondack, hacienda, and mill are the current choices of interior decor.

THE METHOW VALLEY

Sun Mountain Lodge

P.O. Box 1000, Winthrop, WA 98862. Tel. 800/572-0493 or 509/996-2211. 87 rms. Summer $125–$185 double; winter $89–$155 double; spring/fall $49–$100 double. AE, MC, V.

If you're looking for resort luxuries and proximity to hiking, cross-country skiing, and mountain biking trails, the Sun Mountain Lodge should be your first choice in the region. Most guest rooms feature rustic western furnishings and views of the surrounding mountains. If seclusion is what you're after, opt for one of the less luxurious cabins down on Patterson Lake.

The lodge offers cross-country ski rentals and a cross-country ski school, horseback and sleigh rides, guided hikes, boat rentals, mountain-bike rentals, and ice-skate rentals. Facilities include an outdoor heated pool, two whirlpools, tennis courts, an exercise room, a ski shop, and an ice-skating pond.

Mazama Country Inn

42 Lost River Rd. (P.O. Box B9), Mazama, WA 98833. Tel. 509/996-2681, or 800/843-7951 in Washington. Fax 509/996-2646. 14 rms. Summer $70–$80 double; winter (including three meals) $165–$175 double. MC, V.

Set on the flat valley floor but surrounded by rugged towering peaks and tall pine trees, this modern mountain lodge is secluded and peaceful and offers an escape from the crowds in Winthrop. If you're out here to get some exercise, be it hiking, mountain biking, cross-country skiing, or horseback riding, the Mazama Country Inn makes an excellent base of operations. Guest rooms are of medium size, simply furnished, but modern and clean.

STEHEKIN

Stehekin Valley Ranch

P.O. Box 36, Stehekin, WA 98852. Tel. 509/682-4677. 12 cabins. Including all meals and transportation in lower valley: $55 per person; $45 per child ages 7–12; $30 per child 4–6; $15 per child 3 or under. $5 off if you bring a sleeping bag or sheets. No credit cards.

If you're a camper at heart, then the "cabins" at the Stehekin Valley Ranch should be just fine. With canvas roofs, screen windows, and no electricity or plumbing, the cabins are little more than permanent tents. Bathroom facilities are in the nearby main building. Activities available at additional cost include horseback riding, river rafting, and mountain biking.

North Cascades Lodge

P.O. Box 457, Chelan, WA 98816. Tel. 509/682-4494. 28 rms. $69–$85 double. MC, V.

Located right at Stehekin Landing, the North Cascades Lodge is shaded by tall conifers and overlooks the lake. There are a variety of room types ranging from basic rooms with no lake view to spacious apartments. The studio apartments, which have kitchens, are the best deal and all have lake views. Boat and bicycle rentals are available, and after a long day of pedaling, paddling, hiking, or riding, you'll appreciate the hot tub.

6

THE CENTRAL WASHINGTON CASCADES

I F REI COULD BUILD A NATURAL ALPINE THEME PARK TO MATCH ITS new flagship megastore in Seattle, it would probably look a lot like the compact slice of wilderness between Snoqualmie Pass and Stevens Pass. There's hiking in the summer, skiing in the winter, rafting in the spring, and mountain biking in the fall. Rock climbing, boardsailing, road biking, rafting, fishing, canoeing—you name it, it's here. In fact, there's always something to do in these mountains, and not one of these activities requires a substantial commitment of time. Who has time anymore for long hikes in the wilderness or weeklong ski vacations, right? The central Washington Cascades are wilderness within reach—mountains for the '90s (just don't count on your cell phone working if you're two days into the Alpine Lakes Wilderness).

So convenient are these mountains that overworked lowland residents can squeeze a quick bit of outdoor adventure into their lives any day of the week. In summer, when sunsets linger until 10pm, it's not unusual to find people hiking Mount Si after work just to catch the evening light show. In winter, both Stevens and Snoqualmie passes are lit up as bright as day, allowing alpine skiers to ignore the fact that the sun goes down at 4pm in December. Need a quick adrenaline buzz? Get your paddle wet in churning whitewater only 30 minutes from the concrete jungle. Want to lose yourself on granite mountainsides the equal of anything in the Sierras? An hour from the Space Needle, you're on the trail.

For an overview of what makes this corner of the Cascades so important to hikers, paddlers, skiers, and other outdoor adventurers, it is necessary to drive only as far as the town of North Bend, which is quickly becoming the easternmost suburb of Seattle. Just outside this town rises 4,167-foot Mount Si, which though barely a hill in height, has the grandeur of much taller mountains. One of the most climbed peaks in the state, Mount Si rises abruptly from the floor of the Snoqualmie Valley, its flanks long ago scoured down to bare rock by ice-age glaciers. Each summer weekend, and just about any other weekend that the trail isn't covered with snow and ice, hordes of hikers sweat their way to the top of this peak. They come not just because it's there, but because the view from the summit is unlike any other in the Northwest. To the west lies the sprawl of Seattle. To the east lies the Alpine Lakes Wilderness. Separating the two are barely 40 miles. This proximity of city and wilderness has made the land between the passes a veritable mountain playground.

The Lay of the Land

Only two roads—**I-90** and **U.S. 2**—cross the central Washington Cascades to the east of Seattle. These two roads, known by the passes they cross—Snoqualmie and Stevens, respectively—have decidedly different characters despite the fact that they form the northern and southern boundaries of one of the most astounding wilderness areas in the Northwest.

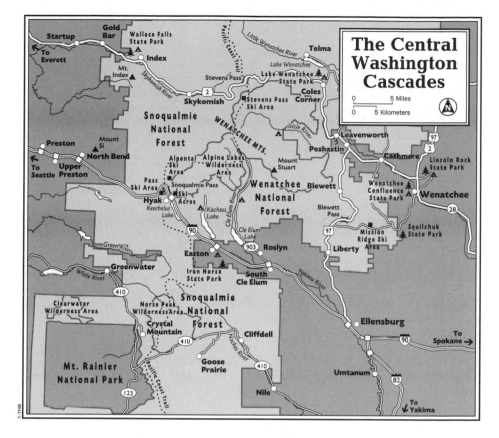

The Central Washington Cascades

Together U.S. 2 and I-90 serve as bridges between civilization and the wilderness.

On U.S. 2, the 4,061-foot **Stevens Pass** is a rugged, narrow gap in the Cascades. Although U.S. 2 is today an important highway link between Washington's east and west sides, Stevens Pass is best known for its ski area, which is a favorite of Puget Sound downhill skiers who like steep, fast runs. However, so vertical are the slopes of the Stevens Pass area that there is very little in the way of cross-country skiing here.

From either side of Stevens Pass, U.S. 2 rises quickly, and both east and west of the pass, the highway parallels raging waters that offer some of the most challenging whitewater paddling in the state. On the west side, the **Skykomish River** between Index and Gold Bar tempts Class III paddlers to push the envelope at the infamous Class IV Boulder Drop rapid. On the east side, the Tumwater Canyon stretch of the **Wenatchee River** is attempted by only the most skilled paddlers (I've seen paddlers standing beside the highway in the middle of Tumwater

Canyon apparently wondering how they were going to get out of this mess). However, below the town of Leavenworth, relatively tamer Class III waters are a magnet in early summer for kayakers and rafters alike.

Snoqualmie Pass, with its four-lane interstate highway (I-90), is today the state's most important pass. At only 3,022 feet, it is also the lowest pass in the state. Snoqualmie Pass is as different from rugged Stevens Pass as Washington's west side is from its east side. While Stevens is rugged and vertical, Snoqualmie is wide and flanked by low, rounded mountains. Those on the south side of the pass are now the site of an extensive downhill ski area—The Pass—which is the closest ski area to Seattle. Although The Pass is far from the best ski area in the state, the easy access makes it extremely popular. These same low hills and the width of Snoqualmie Pass make this one of the best places in the state for cross-country skiing.

Snoqualmie Pass can also boast of being the ugliest pass in the state. Whether because of proximity to good roads or because of lack of foresight on the part of the Forest Service, this busiest of passes, gateway to the Puget Sound, is also the most butchered. The clear-cut mountainsides look as though some cosmic barber went berserk with the electric clippers. In seemingly every direction clearcuts dominate the vistas to such an extent that it is less painful to stare at the freeway pavement than at the surrounding landscape.

However, the decimation of the visible mountainsides at Snoqualmie Pass hides the presence to the north just over these mountains of the untouched forests and meadows of the Alpine Lakes Wilderness. Several trails lead north from the Snoqualmie Pass area into this wilderness, making the Alpine Lakes area one of the most easily accessible wildernesses in the country. Few other metropolitan areas the size of Seattle can claim wilderness hiking within an hour of downtown skyscrapers.

On either side of Snoqualmie Pass, I-90 is paralleled by a river. On the west side, it is the **South Fork Snoqualmie River,** which has its source in a small lake above the Alpental Ski Area. This and the other two forks of the Snoqualmie River provide a wide range of whitewater to challenge paddlers of all skill levels. Not far west of where the three forks of the Snoqualmie River come together, the waters of this river plunge over the 270-foot **Snoqualmie Falls,** one of the biggest tourist attractions in the region. On the east side of the pass, I-90 parallels the **Yakima River,** which is fed by three large dammed lakes—**Keechelus, Kachess,** and **Cle Elum**—all of which are popular with powerboaters. Although the stretch of the Yakima between Cle Elum and Ellensburg is popular with kayakers, it is the stretch of this river that runs through the **Yakima River Canyon** that gets the most clotted with paddlers. Situated south of Ellensburg in a landscape of brown, grasscovered hills, this basalt-walled canyon is rugged yet accessible, perfect for leisurely summer float trips. Other rivers in the area, including the **Cle Elum** and the **Cooper,** are far more challenging.

While U.S. 2 and I-90 define the northern and southern limits of this region, the western border is less distinct and is comprised of the lower slopes of the mountains. This west side of the Cascades between the highways is a region of clearcuts, logging roads, and the watershed for Tolt Reservoir, which is the source of Seattle's drinking water. The nearest north–south road is **Wash. 203,** which follows the banks of the Snoqualmie River from Fall City to Monroe. The wide, flat valley of the Snoqualmie is prone to flooding and is still primarily an agricultural region. Defining the east side of the region are **U.S. 97** and the two Blewett passes—**old Blewett Pass** and **new Blewett Pass.** Officially the new Blewett Pass, on a new section of highway that is far less steep and winding than the old highway, is known as Swauk Pass. However, all those years of traveling the twisting route over Blewett Pass have left that name ingrained in the psyches of the region's drivers.

While I-90 and U.S. 2 are bridges between urban life and the wilderness, the lands these two highways embrace are a bridge between fire and ice. To the south, the volcanic peaks of Mount Rainier, Mount St. Helens, and Mount Adams dominate the horizons. To the north, Glacier Peak and Mount Baker hide their rock beneath expansive glaciers and the North Cascades rise rugged and remote from a landscape that owes its sculpting to intensive ice-age glaciation. And as you'd expect from an area where fire and ice meet, the central Washington Cascades are a land of lakes. The bulk of the area between Snoqualmie Pass and Stevens Pass is comprised of the **Alpine Lakes Wilderness,** 400,000 acres of rugged granitic peaks dotted with 800 azure lakes. Though the peaks here average only 6,000 to 7,000 feet high, the jumble of jagged granite peaks has the countenance of a mountain range far larger. Deep, steepwalled valleys, often with the distinctive U shape caused by geologically recent glaciation, further enhance the rugged topography of this region.

Through the middle of the Alpine Lakes Wilderness runs the **Cascade Crest,**

Outdoor Resources

RANGER STATIONS

Skykomish Ranger Station
P.O. Box 305
Skykomish, WA 98288
Tel. 360/677-2414

Lake Wenatchee Ranger Station
22976 Wash. 207
Leavenworth, WA 98826
Tel. 509/763-3103

Leavenworth Ranger Station
600 Sherbourne St.
Leavenworth, WA 98826
Tel. 509/782-1413

EQUIPMENT SHOPS

The Mountain Company
617 Croft St., Gold Bar
Tel. 360/793-0221
hiking & climbing equipment sales,
rentals

Leavenworth Ski & Sports
U.S. 2, next to the Icicle Inn,
Leavenworth
Tel. 509/548-7864

Wenatchee Cycle & Fitness
228 S Wenatchee Ave., Wenatchee
Tel. 509/663-5206

a system of ridgelines that form the roughly north–south backbone of these mountains. The crest forms the boundary between the Mount Baker–Snoqualmie National Forest to the west and the Wenatchee National Forest to the east. It is also along this crest that the Pacific Crest Trail passes on its journey through the Alpine Lakes Wilderness. However, though this is the most scenic segment of the PCT in Washington, it is the **Stuart Range,** farther to the east, that is the geological focal point of this wilderness. Bare granite weathered into serrated ridges characterizes the mountains of this small range. On the north side of the Stuarts lie the basins of the **Enchantment Lakes,** the most visited area in this wilderness.

Though barely 40 miles across from west to east, the Alpine Lakes Wilderness takes in an amazing variety of life zones. In the lowland valleys of the west side, where rainfall exceeds 50 inches per year, dense forests of Douglas fir, western red cedar, and western hemlock predominate. These are the trees and valleys coveted by logging companies, the domain of the northern spotted owl. Because little of this low-elevation forest was included in the wilderness, it is here that you find the most blatant examples of corporate resource extraction policies. The cut-and-run attitude that once prevailed has been greatly ameliorated by the tree farm, but a farm is not a wilderness and a clear-cut makes a lousy place to hike (though, oddly enough, cross-country skiers find clear-cuts to offer excellent opportunities for tele-marking).

Higher up the western slopes of the Cascades, between 2,000 and 4,000 feet, Douglas fir and western hemlock give way to Pacific silver fir and mountain hemlock. At elevations where winters are long and cold, Alaska cedars and subalpine firs grow smaller and more slowly than the trees of lower elevations. Pockets of meadows are interspersed among these trees. It is at these elevations, between 4,000 and 6,000 feet, that hikers find their wilderness nirvana of wildflowers and mountain vistas. Marmots and pikas are the most often spotted animals of these heights, though mountain goats also feed amid the exposed rocks and meadows.

Above 6,000 feet, only the hardiest of plants survive. Few trees can live at this elevation in these mountains. Winter snows are often more than 30 feet deep and linger well into the middle of summer, often keeping passes and higher trails closed until late July or August. However, the distinctive Lyall's and alpine larches do manage to survive. Unlike the vast majority of conifers, these trees turn a bright golden yellow in the autumn and drop their needles. Glacier lilies, columbines, and lupines fill the meadows at these elevations.

The eastern slopes of these mountains receive far less precipitation than do the western slopes, and consequently different species of trees dominate the forests. The single most pronounced characteristic of these east-side forests is that they are more open and less dense. In the lower east-side elevations, farthest from the Cascade Crest, the distinctively cinnamon-barked ponderosa pine dominates the forest. Higher up on the eastern slopes grow a much greater variety of conifers than on the western slopes. Elk and mule deer are frequently spotted in the drier, more open east-side forests.

Ringing the Alpine Lakes Wilderness are several towns that have both cultural and recreational importance. On the west side of Snoqualmie Pass, **North Bend** may induce a feeling of déjà vu in first-time visitors. Used in the filming of the once-popular TV series *Twin Peaks,* this town, and nearby natural attractions Mount Si and Snoqualmie Falls, were once as familiar to television viewers as Beverly Hills or Manhattan. Over on the east side of the pass, the town of **Roslyn** achieved the same sort of notoriety when it served for years as the set of the *Northern Exposure* TV series. Roslyn started out as a coal-mining town and still wears a rugged look.

Serving as the eastern gateway to Stevens Pass is the town of **Leavenworth,** a bizarre Bavarian theme town that seems to have been transported in its entirety from the Alps. What with cuckoo-clock shops, bratwurst restaurants, and a nutcracker museum, the town is a blatant tourist contrivance. Yet Leavenworth is redeemed by the fact that it is surrounded by alpine scenery that lends the Bavarian theme credence. Mountain slopes rise steeply all around the town, and in its center, the tumbling waters of the Wenatchee River and Icicle Creek come together. As the site of the ranger station for this district of the Wenatchee National Forest, Leavenworth is also of great importance

to backpackers heading into the Alpine Lakes Wilderness, which lies just south of town. Leavenworth marks the eastern edge of the wilderness. On the town's eastern outskirts, apple orchards cover the floor of the Wenatchee Valley, and hanging from these trees are the millions of red delicious apples that are shipped to the supermarkets of America.

Covering an area roughly 30 by 45 miles, the central Washington Cascades east of Seattle are compact enough to be driven around in a single day and close enough to the city to be accessible after work on a weekday. Yet the Alpine Lakes Wilderness is large enough that it takes nearly a week to walk the segment of the Pacific Crest Trail that passes through this wonderland of alpine meadows, glacier-carved granite, and sparkling lakes. If ever there were a wildland to make life in the city bearable, this is it.

Parks & Other Hot Spots

Alpine Lakes Wilderness

North of Snoqualmie Pass, south of Stevens Pass, and south of Leavenworth. Tel. 206/888-1421 (North Bend Ranger Station), 509/674-4411 (Cle Elum Ranger Station), 509/782-1413 (Leavenworth Ranger Station). Hiking, backpacking, fishing.

Lying within an hour's drive of Seattle, the Alpine Lakes Wilderness is one of the most visited wildernesses in the country. One trip into this rugged landscape of glacier-carved granite dotted with 800 crystal-clear lakes is enough to explain why this wilderness is being loved to death. So great are the numbers of people willing and able to hike here that many areas now require advance-reservation permits not only for overnight visits but for day hikes as well. Summer weekends may not get as crowded as the streets of downtown Seattle, but you certainly will have a hard time finding any solitude. However, those hardy souls willing to hike beyond the realm of day hikers and overnight backpackers can still hope to find a little bit of heaven amid the alpine lakes.

Henry M. Jackson Wilderness

North of Stevens Pass, northwest of Little Wenatchee Rd. Tel. 509/763-3103 or 509/664-2704 (Lake Wenatchee Ranger Station), or 360/677-2414 (Skykomish Ranger Station). Hiking, backpacking, fishing.

Encompassing the high country directly north of Stevens Pass and in the Monte Cristo Peaks region, this wilderness adjoins the much larger Glacier Peak Wilderness. The Pacific Crest Trail enters this wilderness just north of Stevens Pass and heads north toward Glacier Peak. There is also access to the west side of the wilderness from the Monte Cristo Road, which is closed to most motor vehicles but is open to mountain bikes. This makes combination mountain-biking and hiking trips into the wilderness an interesting alternative here. On the east side of the wilderness, there is access off FS 6500, the Little Wenatchee Road.

Lake Wenatchee State Park

East of Stevens Pass 3 miles off U.S. 2 on Wash. 207. Tel. 509/763-3101. Camping, hiking, fishing, canoeing, boardsailing, swimming, cross-country skiing, snowshoeing.

This park at the south end of Lake Wenatchee is a year-round recreational destination. In summer the sandy beach, good canoeing, and proximity to hiking and mountain-biking trails make the park very popular. In winter there are many miles of groomed cross-country ski trails within the park. The park also flanks the Wenatchee River as it flows out of the lake. Up the lake can be seen the mountains of the Alpine Lakes Wilderness.

The U.S. 2 Corridor ◆ What to Do & Where to Do It

BIRD WATCHING

Along **Icicle Creek,** just outside Leavenworth, you may spot bald and golden eagles, osprey, great blue herons, and, during the summer, nesting waterfowl,

including harlequin ducks. Just a few miles north of Wenatchee, off U.S. 97 Alt., is the **Swakane Wildlife Area** on the north side of Swakane Creek. In this canyon, look for golden eagles, valley quail, blue grouse, and several species of woodpeckers, among other birds.

BOARDSAILING

Lake Wenatchee, with its reliable afternoon winds in the summer, is the region's best windsurfing spot. Launch sites include the beach at Lake Wenatchee State Park and the Glacier View Campground up the south shore of the lake. This lake is popular with waterskiers, so be prepared for noise and wakes.

CROSS-COUNTRY SKIING

Leavenworth is the center of cross-country skiing for the U.S. 2 corridor. Here you'll find several systems of groomed trails, one of which starts on the edge of downtown Leavenworth. If you're looking for a different sort of cross-country skiing experience, consider a stay at one of the cabins at **Scottish Lakes Back Country Ski Trails.** Located at 5,000 feet in the Chiwaukum Mountains south of Lake Wenatchee, these cabins are 8 miles from the nearest paved road. Access is provided by snowcat or snowmobile. In the vicinity of the cabins, there are 15 miles of marked ski trails and lots of wide-open slopes for telemark skiing. The cabins are operated by **High Country Adventures,** P.O. Box 2023, Snohomish, WA 98291-2023 (tel. 800/909-9916 in western Washington, or 206/844-2000). Rates start at around $75 per person for one night or $100 per person for two nights.

Ski rentals are available at the Stevens Pass Nordic Center and in Leavenworth at **Gustav's X-C Ski Rental Shop,** 617 U.S. 2 (tel. 509/548-4509), **Leavenworth Outfitters Outdoor Store,** 21312 Hwy. 207 (tel. 509/763-3733), and **Leavenworth Ski & Sports,** U.S. 2 next to the Icicle Inn (tel. 509/548-7864), which also offers ski lessons.

GROOMED TRAILS

Stevens Pass Nordic Center

30 kilometers. Easy–most difficult. 760-foot elevation gain. Access: 5 miles east of Stevens Pass. Tel. 360/973-2441. Hours: Fri–Sun and holidays 9am–4pm. Trail fee: $7.50. Map: Trail maps available.

Located just east of Stevens Pass Ski Area, this trail system has trails groomed both for traditional track skiing and skate skiing. The trails lead up the Mill Creek Valley, which, unfortunately, is also used by a high-tension power line. When skiers aren't in the woods, they are in view of these crackling power lines, which detract immensely from visual appeal. Although there are fun stretches of trail here, the system has one major flaw—it's all uphill from the start. It's not that it's a steep climb, it's just that you don't get any fun downhills to keep you interested. Once you do reach the top end of the trail system, it's all downhill. At least there are plenty of curves to keep things interesting. This system is basically geared toward advanced skiers, who get the best views and greatest variety of terrain. There is only one trail here for beginning skiers—a road that runs straight up the valley. Novices will have much more fun skiing the groomed trails in Leavenworth or at Lake Wenatchee State Park.

Lake Wenatchee State Park

35-kilometer trail system. Easy–most difficult. Up to 400-foot elevation gain. Access: 22 miles north of Leavenworth. Take U.S. 2 to Wash. 207. Map: Trailhead maps.

Lake Wenatchee State Park's ski trails are divided into two systems, one on each side of the Wenatchee River. The south trail system is the more extensive and leads through the park forests, along the shore of the lake, and onto the open flats of the Kahler Glen Golf Course. There are good views from both the Lakeshore Trail and the Kahler Creek Loop around the golf course. There are also good views of the Wenatchee River from both north and south trail systems. The Kahler Creek

Loop also connects to the 15-kilometer Nason Ridge Trail, which climbs 1,400 feet to a viewpoint of the lake. This trail is recommended only for advanced skiers. When skiing the north area's outer loop, ski in a clockwise direction to avoid a steep descent at the west end of the trail.

Leavenworth Winter Sports Club Trails

30 kilometers total in three trail systems. Easy–most difficult. Up to 200-foot elevation gain. Access: Icicle Rd. at golf course and at fish hatchery, also at Leavenworth Ski Hill north of town (follow signs from U.S. 2). Tel. 509/548-5115. Hours: Daily 9am–5pm. Trail fee: $6–$7. Map: Trailhead maps.

The Leavenworth Winter Sports Club maintains three systems of ski trails in the Leavenworth area. The most easily accessible of these systems are the 15 kilometers of trails that begin along the river at the end of Ninth Street in downtown Leavenworth. These trails, which are suited to everyone from beginners to advanced skiers, cover rolling terrain in a park and golf course. By starting a tour of these trails at the far end (where there is a parking lot at the golf course off Icicle Road), you can ski back to town, have a snack or espresso, and then ski back to your car.

Farther out Icicle Road, there is another system of trails adjacent to the Leavenworth fish hatchery. The terrain here is flat and the trails are packed into a compact area, which makes this a good spot for beginners. The trails meander along the banks of the Icicle River and a canal. For more challenging ski trails, head out to Leavenworth Ski Hill on the north side of town. These latter trails, totaling 5 kilometers and including 2 kilometers of lighted trails, are designed for intermediate and advanced skiers and offer some good views. All trails are groomed for both traditional and skate skiing.

UNGROOMED TRAILS

Chiwawa Road Sno-Park

13 miles of trails. Easy and most difficult. Up to 600-foot elevation gain. Access: 22 miles north

of Leavenworth. Take U.S. 2 to Wash. 207, and after crossing the Wenatchee River, take the right fork onto Chiwawa Loop Rd. Map: Lake Wenatchee Ranger District Cross-Country Ski Guide.

At this sno-park just east of Lake Wenatchee State Park's north area, there are three loop trails. Two are rated "Easy" and one is rated "Most Difficult." The most entertaining of these trails (and my favorite area trail) is the See 'n' Ski Trail, which parallels the Wenatchee River for much of its 5-mile length. This trail rolls up and down through the forest along the river and then loops back through the forest farther from the river bank. Occasionally this trail is even groomed. The second "Easy" trail, Squirrel Run Trail, is much less interesting. The third trail, which begins off the Squirrel Run, is for experienced skiers only and should not be attempted when conditions are icy. The trail climbs 600 feet in 2 miles to reach a ridge top with excellent views of the surrounding mountains and the Plain Valley.

Heather Ridge

4 miles of trails. Most difficult. 1,200-foot elevation gain. Access: On U.S. 2, 49 miles east of Monroe at Stevens Pass. Map: Green Trails Stevens Pass.

Also known as Skyline Ridge and located across U.S. 2 from Stevens Pass Ski Area, this ridge is a favorite with telemark skiers. Moderate south-facing slopes dotted with trees create ideal glade skiing conditions that keep tele-skiers coming back again and again. On clear days the views are stunning, but if it hasn't snowed in a while, the snow conditions won't be very good. In fresh snow, climbing skins are a necessity. The route up the ridge begins behind the ski area buildings on the north side of the highway. Follow snow-covered roads leading north (uphill), until the last road disappears. From this point continue climbing up to Skyline Lake, the favored spot for beginning the descent. Keep in mind that the east slopes here are more avalanche prone than those to the west.

DOWNHILL SKIING & SNOWBOARDING

Stevens Pass

On U.S. 2, 49 miles east of Monroe at Stevens Pass. Tel. 206/634-1645 in Seattle, or 206/353-4400 in Everett (snow report, tel. 206/634-0200 in Seattle, or 509/663-7711 in Wenatchee). 36 trails; 11 lifts; 1,800 vertical feet. Lift hours: Daily 9am–10pm. Adult lift tickets (9am–10pm): $34 weekends and holidays, $18 Mon, $23 Wed–Fri.

Stevens is probably the most popular ski area for Puget Sound skiers and snowboarders, and the major reason for this is snow, snow, and more snow! While it's true Stevens doesn't get the big dumps that Mount Baker gets, it's a whole lot closer to Seattle. Many are the weekends that Stevens gets 6 inches of fresh snow while Crystal, Snoqualmie, and White Pass get rain. There is plenty of vertical here and terrain to suit any person's level of expertise, with the exception of beginning skiers. If you're planning to teach a friend to ski or ride, don't come here. The Daisy chair runs are too flat, and Brooks is too steep for a novice.

Experienced skiers will find the runs off the Double Diamond and 7th Heaven chairs to be, well, heavenly. If you feel like getting off the beaten paths, work your way over to Big Chief Bowl or Tye Bowl. There are also endless acres of diamond skiing on the "back side," which can be accessed from either the Tye-Mill or Double Diamond chairs. You can usually ski the back side all day and still find caches of untracked powder late in the afternoon. Just keep in mind that lift service back here usually stops at 3:30.

Intermediate skiers and snowboarders will find an endless series of excellent trails accessed by all the lower lifts. You never get bored here, which is another reason the resort is so popular with locals. You want bumps? Try Chief. You want to fly? Try the jump park under Brooks. You want speed? Try the Upper Housewives run off the Hogsback chair.

It's worth noting that if you like night skiing, don't go anywhere else in

Washington. They keep this place lit up like they're expecting the mother ship. All of the lower lifts, including the Skyline Express chair (the only night skiing high-speed quad in the state), are open for night skiing, which costs only $12 Sunday through Thursday.

Leavenworth Ski Hill

On the north side of Leavenworth; follow the signs from U.S. 2. Tel. 509/548-6975. 2 trails; 2 rope tows; 400 vertical feet. Adult lift tickets: $7.

What is a Bavarian village without a ski hill? Leavenworth, Washington State's pseudo-Bavarian town, wouldn't know since it has its own family ski area, albeit a small one. With Stevens Pass only 36 miles away, it's hard to imagine why anyone would bother with this tiny slope, but low prices and convenience make Leavenworth Ski Hill popular with both families and beginning downhillers. If you're in town and just want a few quick runs without any hassle, give it a try. It's worth coming up here just to see the old, abandoned ski jump.

Mission Ridge Ski Area

12 miles southwest of Wenatchee. Tel. 509/663-7631 (800/374-1693 for snow report). 35 trails; 4 lifts, 2 rope tows; 2,200 vertical feet. Lift hours: Daily 9am–4pm (late Dec–late Feb, Thurs–Sat 4–9pm). Adult lift tickets: $30 weekends and holidays, $20 Mon–Fri.

Mission Ridge is the easternmost of Washington's major Cascade ski areas and consequently claims the most sunny days and best powder snow in the Cascades. This alone should have you scheduling at least one trip out here each year. Since you can use Leavenworth as a base and ski here one day and at Stevens Pass the second day, Mission Ridge is a great weekend destination if you live on the west side of the mountains. However, with only four lifts, it can't handle a lot of traffic.

If you're looking for new runs and generally better conditions than on the west side, Mission Ridge is definitely worth checking out. Intermediate skiers will find an abundance of interesting runs here. My favorite is the Bomber Bowl, which is named for a bomber that crashed here in 1944. This run skirts the base of the Bomber Cliffs and offers excellent bowl skiing off its upper slopes. Advanced skiers also have plenty of chutes, the Outback, and Windy Ridge to keep them screaming. Snowboarders have their own park with a half pipe at the top of Lift 1. With only two green runs, though, this isn't the place for beginners. Child care is available and a free bus operates from Wenatchee.

FISHING

The **Skykomish River,** on the west side of Stevens Pass, is one of Washington's best winter steelheading rivers with the season running from December to April. The river also holds sea-run cutthroats and summer steelhead. Along the 25 miles of this river between Index and its confluence with the Snoqualmie, there is lots of access off of U.S. 2, which parallels the river. The stretch from Gold Bar down is good drift-boat water, and it is along this stretch that most anglers are to be found. Above Sunset Falls, the **South Fork Skykomish** has excellent fishing for stocked rainbow trout during the summer. With U.S. 2 running alongside the river here, there is plenty of access. The **Foss River** and the high-altitude lakes it drains also offer some fairly productive fishing. It is a long, steep hike up to most of the lakes.

If you're out for salmon, you can still fish the **Skykomish** for coho (silvers), but you currently have to release any Chinooks or pinks you catch. Over on the east side, **Icicle Creek,** just outside Leavenworth, has a short summer salmon season for fish headed upstream to the Leavenworth Fish Hatchery.

Fly anglers will find plenty of good waters along U.S. 2. The **Foss River,** which feeds into the South Fork Skykomish River, is fairly good, and you can try your hand along the **South Fork** itself. Outside Leavenworth, there is good fly-fishing on the **Wenatchee River,** and between the Icicle Bridge in Leavenworth and Lake Wenatchee, this river is open to artificial lures and flies only. **Chiwaukum Creek,** which feeds into the Wenatchee about midway through this section of river, is subject to the same regulations and is a good trout-fishing stream with good access. **Icicle Creek** also provides good fly-fishing waters. However, the favorite fly-fishing stream in the area is probably the **Little Wenatchee River,** which flows into Lake Wenatchee. This river has good access, has lots of campgrounds along its length, and offers particularly good fly-fishing from August through the end of the season.

If you want to take a fly-fishing class while you're in the area, contact **English Flyfishing School of Leavenworth** (tel. 509/548-5218 or 509/763-3429), which teaches its classes on the Wenatchee River and Icicle Creek. A one-hour class is $30.

Lake Wenatchee, at 5 miles in length, is the biggest lake in the area and holds kokanee, as well as Dolly Varden and rainbows. To fish for kokanee, you'll need a boat. Nearby **Fish Lake** holds both trout and bass. South of Leavenworth, several of the lakes in the Alpine Lakes Wilderness have been stocked and provide good fishing action. **Colchuck Lake,** though accessed via a steep hike, is a good possibility, but for a real surprise, try **Eightmile Lake,** where you might hook into a Mackinaw. Cutthroats and rainbows are, however, more common.

HIKING & BACKPACKING

South of U.S. 2 lies the Alpine Lakes Wilderness, which is the most heavily visited wilderness in the state. So popular is the **Enchantment Lakes** area of this wilderness that overnight hiking permits for the area are limited between June 15 and October 15 and are issued by advance reservation. Popular destinations included in the Enchantment Permit Area include all of the Enchantment Lakes, Snow Lakes, Nada Lake, Colchuck Lake, Stuart Lake, Eightmile Lake, and Caroline Lake. Telephone reservations are taken by **Reservations Northwest** (tel. 800/735-2900) beginning on May 1. A fee of $7 per reservation is charged. Reservations are taken until seven days before the planned start of a trip; you must set your itinerary at the time you make your reservation, and groups are limited to eight people.

To acquire a permit, you're going to have to really work hard. Start calling months in advance of your planned visit, keeping in mind that weekends in July and August are, of course, the most sought-after times to hike here. If you can get through on the phone (one person I met on the trail tried for three months), and you can get a reservation, you will be mailed your permit and can head straight for the trailhead on the day your trip is to begin. One secret worth knowing is that if you make your reservation for the Enchantments, it also permits you to stay at Snow Lakes, but if you make a reservation for Snow Lakes, you cannot stay at the Enchantments. If you cancel your trip, please let the ranger station know so they can put your sites back in the reservation pool.

If you don't get a reservation by phone, you can put your name in the **day-of-departure lottery** that is held daily at exactly 7:45am at the Leavenworth Ranger Station. The first five people chosen from the hat get permits for that day, though no parties will be split up. So, if four people have already been chosen and your party of six gets chosen next, you all get to go. Your best bet for getting in on this day-of-departure lottery is to come sometime in September or early October. Other areas within the wilderness have trailhead self-issue permits for both day hikers and overnighters.

Foss Lakes

15 miles round-trip to Angeline Lake. Strenuous. 3,150-foot elevation gain. Access: From U.S. 2 in Skykomish, drive 1.8 miles east, turn south on FS 68 (the road starts out paved but turns to gravel), continue 4.8 miles, turn left on FS 6835, and continue 1.8 miles to the trailhead. Map: USGS Big Snow Mountain; Green Trails Skykomish (175) and Stevens Pass (176).

If this hike had a snow-covered peak in the distance and a few clear-cuts in the foreground, it would be the quintessential Northwest hike. There are cascading waterfalls, some very tall, all along the trail, and the sound of falling water always fills the forest. Huge old-growth trees, some 10 to 12 feet in diameter, flank the trail.

One is so large I thought it was a rock out-crop the first time I passed it. There are nurse logs, banana slugs, great huckleberry fields, and 10 lakes, each with its own char-acter. When I hiked the trail one drizzly autumn afternoon, I counted 16 species of fungi, 8 species of ferns, and 8 varieties of moss. Now if all that doesn't add up to a Northwest hike, I don't know what does.

The trail shows signs of damage from the February 1996 floods. It starts out as a cobbled dry streambed and soon crosses Foss Creek on logs. The first lake reached by the trail is Trout Lake, formed when a landslide blocked the West Fork Foss River. The rising waters killed the trees on the banks of the creek and these skel-etal trees still rise from the water. The landslide also formed a nice swimming hole if you don't mind cold water. From Trout Lake it is a steep climb, crossing talus fields with slippery, jagged footing, up to a trail junction. The right fork leads to Malachite Lake, a very clear cirque lake that is a bit quieter than the other lakes because it is off the main trail. The left fork leads to Copper Lake, a large lake the color of verdigris. This lake is ringed by rocky crags on one side, while on the other, the trail passes through dense for-est on its way up to Little Heart Lake. This latter lake is smaller than Copper Lake and isn't as pretty, but it does have good campsites.

Beyond Little Heart Lake, the trail climbs 500 feet to crest a ridge with a good view of the lakes and then drops down to Big Heart Lake. As you have probably already guessed, this last ridge weeds out a lot of hikers who decide Little Heart Lake is far enough. So, if you're looking for solitude, try looking at Big Heart Lake or beyond. The maintained trail comes to an end at the outlet of Angeline, but that doesn't mean you have to stop hiking here. After setting up a base camp on one of the lakes, you can strike out for Chetwoot Lake, which has the most dis-tinct trail, or Otter Lake, Azurite Lake, or Delta Lake.

Because these lakes are well stocked with fish, this trail sees a lot of use by an-glers. An ominous sign at the trailhead warns hikers that camera surveillance is used here to reduce car break-ins.

A trailhead host is also sometimes in resi-dence here to further dissuade thieves.

Merritt Lake and Nason Ridge

7.4 miles round-trip to Merritt Lake; 12.4 miles round-trip to Alpine Lookout. Strenuous. 2,000-foot elevation gain to Merritt Lake; 3,250 feet to Alpine Lookout. Access: Drive 14.5 miles east of Stevens Pass on U.S. 2, turn left onto FS 657, and continue 1.5 miles to the end of the road. Map: USGS Mount Howard; Green Trails Wenatchee Lake.

It's a steady climb up to Merritt Lake on the south flank of Nason Ridge, but the views, the subalpine scenery, and the lake's setting make it all worthwhile. Rock and forest are constant companions both on the switchbacking trail up from U.S. 2 and at Merritt Lake itself. Openings as you climb provide ever-widening views down the Nason Creek Valley, through which runs the highway. Be forewarned, how-ever, that bugs can be bad at the lake. Try coming in late summer or early fall to avoid them. If, after reaching Merritt Lake, you still have lots of energy and feel like an-other 5 miles of hiking, strike out for the Alpine Lookout atop Nason Ridge. As you climb the 2.5 miles to this ridgetop lookout, the views just get better and better; at the lookout you'll have unob-structed views south to the Stuart Range and north across Lake Wenatchee to Dirtyface Mountain. However, what makes this lookout particularly interesting are the mountain goats that are often seen in the area, usually in early morning or late afternoon. Your best bet for spotting goats would be to pitch camp at Merritt Lake and hurry up here just after dawn, or lin-ger until it's almost too late to get back to the lake before dark.

Enchantment Lakes

23 miles round-trip. Strenuous. 5,900-foot el-evation gain. Access: From Leavenworth, drive south on Icicle Rd. (on the west side of town) for 4 miles to the large trailhead parking lot. Map: USGS Mount Stuart and Liberty; Green Trails Enchantments (209S).

Only *You* Can Prevent Forest Fires!

The slightly threatening image of Smokey the Bear, that icon of the wilderness aesthetic, probably haunts the memories of every American who has ever built a fire in the woods. For nearly half a century his visage has gazed out at campers from roadside signs throughout the forests of the west. And now we find that Smokey lacked scientific basis for his pronouncements of gloom and doom concerning forest fires. The myth of Smokey is slowly but surely being debunked. Fires are good for the forests of the west. At least they would be if forest fires hadn't been suppressed for the past century.

In a land where lightning is a frequent occurrence and summers are hot and dry, fire is as natural and necessary as winter's snows. The eastern slopes of the Cascades are just such an area. Examination of ponderosa pines from east-side forests has shown that prior to the advent of fire suppression practices, fires swept through these forests approximately every 10 years. The plant community here is uniquely adapted to this fire cycle. The cones of lodgepole pines are sealed by resins that are melted by low-intensity fires, freeing seeds to fall to the ground and germinate. Ponderosa pines have thick, fire-resistant bark. Grasses resprout from their roots, and some native willows send up shoots that grow more than 1 inch per week immediately following a fire. However, for nearly 100 years forest fires have not been allowed to burn naturally. Had they been allowed to do so, the forests we see on the east side of Stevens and Snoqualmie passes would be very different places.

"We came to a glorious forest of lofty pines . . . perfectly open and unencumbered with brush wood, so that traveling was excellent," wrote Lt. Edward Beale in 1858 when he passed through the forests of the Cascades' eastern slopes. Photos taken in these forests in the late 19th century show a very different forest than what we see today. Huge, widely spaced ponderosa pines grew above a forest floor of grasses. Today, many east-side forests are overgrown with young, unhealthy trees. These trees are susceptible to attacks by insects and many forests have been ravaged by pine beetles and spruce budworms. These forests now are filled with dead and dying trees, fuel for future fires.

In the summer of 1994, forest fires swept through the mountains around Leavenworth, burning right down to the edge of town and destroying several homes along Icicle Road. The fires were initially seen as a devastating event, but now, with the knowledge of the importance of fire to the area's ecosystem, the fires are being seen as a chance to return these forests to a natural cycle in which fire plays a vital role.

Just don't take this as license to ignore what Smokey the Bear has taught us over the years. These forests are adapted to *natural* fires, not man-made ones (although there are plenty of habitats in the West that once existed only because of regular burning by Native Americans). As you head up the trail to the Enchantments, contemplate the future of the fire-scarred landscape above Icicle Creek. One day a very different forest will grow here, and perhaps it will be a little bit closer to what nature intended for these mountains.

If there is a single most popular backpacking trip in the state of Washington, this is surely it, and consequently, this is one of the few places in the Northwest where it is necessary to make a reservation for a backcountry campsite. Don't come up here expecting solitude. No matter, though; this is the grandest landscape in the Northwest, unduplicated until you reach California's Trinity Alps or the

Yosemite high country. The scenery is so breathtaking that it is impossible to complain about other hardy hikers enjoying the setting as well. And *hardy* is the key word—once you're done fighting the red tape of the permit process, it'll be time to take on the unforgiving trails and the elements.

The Enchantments, a string of rock-rimmed lakes high on the north slopes of the rugged Stuart Range, more than live up to their name. Throughout the basin that holds these lakes, water cascades over glacier-scarred rocks, and stunted trees struggle to survive in the harsh climate. Meadows fill the spaces between exposed granite outcroppings. Rising above the lakes are unbelievably jagged peaks including The Temple, Little Annapurna, and the pyramidal Prusik Peak. All around you shimmering granite thrusts skyward. Divided into the Upper and Lower Enchantments, these lakes show signs of very recent glaciation. In fact, the upper lakes, some of which are never completely free of ice, were hidden beneath a glacier within the past century. The Enchantments beg to be explored at a leisurely pace. Trails lead around lakes and off into hidden corners of the basin. Everywhere you turn a new vista unfolds.

Although the first 7 miles of trail (which unfortunately now lead through several miles of hillsides blackened by fire) provide a good tread and an easy, switchbacking route; from Snow Lakes to the Enchantments the route you'll follow really stretches the definition of "trail." This stretch climbs straight up the mountain, sometimes requiring hand-over-hand scrambling on smooth rock.

The weather here is highly capricious; snow can fall any month of the year, and the wind blows almost constantly. With few protected campsites, reconcile yourself to a night of bad weather should you be caught up here when the weather changes. Camping down at Snow Lakes and day hiking up to the Enchantments is an option that avoids both bad weather and a steep climb with a heavy pack. And if all the hardships described here make this sound like a miserable place, it isn't. Despite all, a trip to the Enchantments is well worth the effort.

Upper Icicle Creek Area/Lake Mary

16 miles round-trip. Strenuous. 3,300-foot elevation gain to Lake Mary; 3,900 feet to Mary Pass. Access: From Leavenworth, drive the Icicle Rd. 20 miles to its end. Map: USGS Chiwaukum Mountains; Green Trails Chiwaukum Mountains (177).

So you're despondent because you didn't get a permit for the Enchantments. Buck up, matey; in fact, head up this trail and you'll get over it in a hurry. Maybe this area isn't quite as beautiful as the Enchantments, but it's pretty close. In some ways, it is an even better hike. For instance, instead of hiking straight uphill from the trailhead, you start this hike with a leisurely stroll for 2 miles up Icicle Creek to the Frosty Creek Trail. Only on this latter trail do you begin to climb. In the next 5.5 miles, you climb 2,800 feet, passing a trail to Lake Margaret, to reach Frosty Pass. It is here that the forests end and alpine meadows take over. It is these meadows, and the wandering they inspire, that make this hike so enjoyable. At Frosty Pass, the trail forks. Take the right fork and follow the ridgeline until you come to a short trail down to Lake Mary, where there are numerous good campsites.

Using Lake Mary as a base, there are excellent day hikes to be done among these high-rolling grasslands. A hike 0.75 miles up to Mary Pass provides the greatest variety of options. You can choose between a way trail that leads to within about 500 feet of the summit of Snowgrass Mountain (climbing equipment is needed above this point) or you can hike down Upper Florence Lake. You could also continue on to Ladies Pass and then down to Lake Flora. Alternatively, you could hike back to Frosty Pass and then descend north 1 mile and then climb 1.5 miles east to Grace Lake.

If you can arrange a car shuttle (or don't mind 3 miles of hiking on Icicle Road), you could also return to the road by way of Chatter Creek Trail, which will allow you some extra miles of wandering at elevation. This route takes you over Mary Pass and down to Upper Florence Lake, up to Ladies Pass and down past Lake Edna, then up once again on the flanks of

Cape Horn, down a bit, then up around Grindstone Mountain before beginning the steep descent along Chatter Creek. From Lake Mary it is about the same distance to either trailhead.

Lake Stuart/Colchuck Lake

9 miles round-trip to either lake (13 miles total for both lakes). Moderate–strenuous. 1,600-foot elevation gain to Lake Stuart; 2,100 feet to Colchuck Lake (2,500 feet total for hike to both lakes). Access: From Leavenworth, drive the Icicle Rd. 8.5 miles, turn left onto FS 7601, and continue 4 miles to the trailhead. Map: USGS Chiwaukum Mountains and Mount Stuart; Green Trails Enchantments (209S).

Another backup plan for when your Enchantment Lakes permit doesn't pan out is a hike up to Colchuck Lake. This lake lies across the challenging Asgaard Pass from the Enchantments and is just as pretty. Plus, it is close enough for a day hike, unlike the Enchantments. The drawback is that everyone else seems to know of the beauty and accessibility of Colchuck Lake, so expect crowds. Also, be prepared for a strenuous climb up to this mountain-encircled lake. Lake Stuart may not be as spectacularly scenic as Colchuck Lake, but it does have the rocky summit of glacier-draped Mount Stuart rising beyond its shores. This lake also benefits from a trail that climbs about 600 feet less, and that may see fewer hikers. Pick which of the two you feel up to, or visit them both. If you are considering the Asgaard Pass route into the Enchantments, be aware that it is a very difficult scramble over the rocks at the pass and many a hiker has suffered a twisted ankle or worse up there.

The trails to Lake Stuart and Colchuck Lake start at the same trailhead, but 2.5 miles up, the trail splits with the west fork leading to Stuart Lake and the east fork leading to Colchuck Lake. Either lake is an excellent destination for a day trip or overnight hike (limited overnight permits are available; reserve far in advance).

MOUNTAIN BIKING

Although there is some very good riding to be had in the Leavenworth area, it is primarily on logging roads and ORV trails. The roads are worthwhile mostly because they provide great views of the surrounding mountains and valleys. The ORV trails, designed for motorcycles, can be a blast, with lots of ups and downs, but are best ridden on weekdays when they aren't crowded with high-powered bikes.

If you'd like to do a guided ride down from Sugarloaf Lookout, the highest point on Entiat Ridge, which divides the Wenatchee Valley from the Entiat Valley, contact **Vertical Adventures** (tel. 509/548-9104 or 509/763-9014) at Coles Corner (the turnoff for Lake Wenatchee from U.S. 2). They'll drive you to the top of this ridge so you can have a totally downhill experience. Similar guided mountain-bike rides are also offered by **Leavenworth Outfitters Outdoor Center,** 21312 Hwy. 207 (tel. 800/347-7934 or 509/763-3733). Both of these shops also rent mountain bikes.

Leavenworth Ski Hill

3 miles of trails. Easy. 200-foot elevation gain. Access: North of downtown Leavenworth at Leavenworth Ski Hill (follow signs from U.S. 2). Map: Trailhead map.

Although there are only about 3 miles of trails here, they have a lot of ups and downs that make them a lot of fun. In the winter these are moderate and advanced cross-country ski trails. Once you have ridden all these trails in one direction, you can turn around and ride them in the reverse direction for a completely different experience.

Boundary Butte

13 miles. Strenuous. 1,500-foot elevation gain. Strenuous. Access: From downtown Leavenworth, drive U.S. 2 toward Wenatchee; after crossing the bridge on the edge of town, turn right onto E Leavenworth Rd., and then left onto Mountain Home Rd. Continue up this road until it turns to gravel and continue to a closed spur road on the right and park. Map: Leavenworth Ranger District Map.

This steep climb to the top of Boundary Butte offers the best views of Leavenworth and the Icicle Valley. From the summit of this butte, you'll also be able to see the Stuart Range and Icicle Ridge. Do some stretching at trailhead; there is no warming up on this ride—as soon as you're in the saddle you're pedaling uphill. Pass the Mountain Home Lodge, and continue climbing through ponderosa pine forest with views down into the valley. At 4.5 miles, reach a saddle with a four-way junction. Turn left onto FS 500 here to continue climbing another 2 miles to Boundary Butte. The last half-mile is the steepest and roughest of the entire ride. Once at the top, relax and take in the views before starting the fast, fun downhill ride. Coming down, you can take an alternate double-track route for part of the descent by turning right onto FS 555 about 1 mile below the summit. In another mile, take a dirt road to the right to continue downhill. This stretch of road has numerous large berms across it, so stay alert. When this road ends at FS 7300, take a right and continue back down to your car. Watch out for washboard on this road.

Wenatchee River Road

8.5 miles. Easy. 500-foot elevation gain. Access: Drive 11 miles north of Leavenworth on U.S. 2, cross the Wenatchee River, pass the Tumwater Campground, and watch for rough-dirt FS 7906 on the right in 0.6 miles. Pull off and park where you can. Map: Green Trails Leavenworth.

This dirt road heads north from U.S. 2 at the north end of Tumwater Canyon and follows the Wenatchee River from both high above and from down at water level. Because this is a road ride and there isn't a lot of elevation gain, it is a good choice for novice riders. Although the ride is through the forest on a gated road, there are a couple of houses back here, so you might encounter a car or a barking dog. From the gate the road climbs on a slope 400 feet above the river and provides good views before dropping quickly through the forest. Pass one house in the woods, and then come to a second in a large clearing. The road weaves past this second house and continues descending to reach the river at the 2-mile point. For the next 2.25 miles, the trail stays close to the river and there are lots of inviting places to stop. When

you reach the "No Trespassing" signs, it's time to turn around.

Chickamin Ridge

16.6 miles. Strenuous. 1,800-foot elevation gain. Access: From Lake Wenatchee State Park, off U.S. 2, cross the Wenatchee River and take the right fork onto Chiwawa Loop Rd. (FS 62). In 1.3 miles, turn left onto Chiwawa River Rd., drive 9.7 miles to FS 6210, turn right, and continue a half-mile to the Chikamin Creek trailhead. Map: Green Trails Plain.

Chikamin Ridge is motorcycle country, with trails built for speed and power. However, these same trails, when ridden in a downhill direction, can be a lot of fun for experienced mountain bikers (as long as you don't encounter too many motorcycles). To start this ride, head back out to FS 6210, turn right, and begin 7.4 miles of steady uphill climbing. On the way up this road, you'll pass a couple of other trails, including, at 3.25 miles, the Minnow Ridge Trail, which is part of the downhill route. After climbing 1,620 feet, reach the Chikamin Tie Trail and take a well-deserved rest (surely not your first on this climb). At this point, check your brakes, and then head downhill through a clearcut on a steep trail. Switchbacks tend to be paved with cement blocks to prevent erosion caused by spinning motorcycle tires. You'll need good control and balance on this trail; many places are deeply rutted. Catch your front tire in one of these ruts and it's endo time.

In 2.1 miles, come to a fork in the trail. Take the right fork and in another 0.1 miles reach the Minnow Ridge Trail (the left fork is the Chikamin Creek Trail, which traverses a steep hillside to return back to the trailhead in about the same distance). The Minnow Ridge Trail is a rollicking good roller coaster of a ride through dense forests on sometimes good firm trail, sometimes dusty, pummy trail, but it's all single-track. As you roll up and down this ridge, keep an eye out for the viewpoint over the surrounding valleys and mountains. At about the 15.5-mile point, the trail drops steeply off Minnow Ridge in a series of switchbacks, before making the final fast run back to the car. Just before you reach the trailhead, you'll merge with the Chikamin Creek Trail.

From this same parking area, you can also ride the Lower Chiwawa Trail (another motorcycle trail) down valley to Deep Creek Campground. To access this trail, head up the trail from the parking lot, cross the creek on a bridge, climb up above the creek, and turn right at the trail junction. From the campground, ride down FS 6101, turn right on FS 6100, and then turn right onto FS 62 to return to your car. This loop is about 20 miles long.

PACKSTOCK TRIPS

If you want to ride the high country on a multiday pack trip, or would simply rather have a horse carry your gear while you hike, contact **Icicle Outfitters & Guides,** P.O. Box 322, Leavenworth, WA 98826 (tel. 800/497-3912, 509/784-1145, or 509/763-3647), or **Eagle Creek Ranch,** P.O. Box 719, Leavenworth, WA 98826 (tel. 509/548-7798). Both of these outfitters offer a wide range of trips to remote areas within the Wenatchee National Forest. Expect to pay around $135 per person per day for a deluxe pack trip.

ROAD BIKING

White River and Little Wenatchee Roads Ride

26 miles. Moderate. 600-foot elevation gain. Access: From Lake Wenatchee State Park, off U.S. 2, drive 6 miles up Wash. 207, past the Lake Wenatchee Ranger Station to the Cougar Inn. Park here.

If you enjoy forest rides, you'll love this pedal through the forests along both the White and Little Wenatchee rivers up at the west end of Lake Wenatchee. From the Cougar Inn, continue in the same direction you were driving for 1 mile to a fork in the road. The right fork is White River Road (FS 6400) and the left fork is Little Wenatchee Road (FS 6500). Take the right fork and ride up this scenic, gently climbing road for 6 miles, sometimes with the river right beside the road, until the pavement runs out. If you are on a mountain bike, you can continue another

3 miles to White River Falls. Turn around for a fun coast back down the valley.

Back at the fork, take a right and head up the Little Wenatchee Road, which starts out by crossing a wide, flat plain created by the meandering White River. Rounding the foot of Wenatchee Ridge, the road then heads up the Little Wenatchee River valley. At times the road is completely shaded by the dense forests, but at other times there are views of the surrounding ridges and peaks. At 6 miles from the road fork, reach Little Wenatchee Falls, which is the turnaround for this ride and is a good place for a picnic. If you still have energy and are up to some more climbing, you can continue another 6 miles beyond here to the end of pavement and another 3 miles beyond that to the end of the road.

Leavenworth to Cashmere Orchard Ride

27 miles. Moderate. 600-foot elevation gain. Access: Start this ride at the Lions Club Park on U.S. 2 in the center of Leavenworth.

Downriver from Leavenworth, the Wenatchee Valley quickly becomes apple-orchard country. A ride through the back roads of the valley rolls through these orchards, with views of the high mountain ridges on either side of the valley. From downtown Leavenworth, ride toward Wenatchee, but before crossing the bridge on the edge of town, turn left onto Chumstick Road (Wash. 209). Within a half-mile, turn right onto North Road, a winding, hilly road that leads to the tiny orchard town of Peshastin in 4 miles. Ride through Peshastin to U.S. 2 and continue a short ways along the highway before turning left onto Saunders Road. This road loops around and then crosses U.S. 2 to become Deadman's Hill Road (yep, there is a hill here, but it won't kill you). This road winds along and eventually dead-ends at Pine Flats Road. Turn left. Follow this road to its end and turn right onto Stines Hill Road, which will take you into Cashmere, which, following in the footsteps of Leavenworth, tried to fashion itself after an "Early American" town (it didn't go over like Leavenworth). While in town, be sure to stop in at Aplets and Cotlets for some free samples of these unusual candies.

The return route begins by crossing the river from downtown Cashmere and heading up U.S. 2. This is the only relatively long stretch of highway riding on this entire route and lasts only about 2 miles, at which point you turn right onto North Dryden Road to wind your way through orchard country once again. At the end of this road, ride the highway again to cross the river and turn right onto Saunders Road. From here on out, you'll be backtracking. When Saunders Road loops back to the highway, turn right and soon right again onto North Road for the last 5 miles back to Leavenworth.

ROCK CLIMBING

Leavenworth is at the center of Washington's most popular sport-climbing area and offers lots of good climbing. Anyone serious about climbing in this area should buy a copy of local climber Viktor Kramar's *Leavenworth Rock* (Snow Creek Design, 1996). This book has detailed route descriptions for all the most popular climbs in the area. If you're more a mountaineer than a sport climber, pick up a copy of Fred Beckey's *Cascade Alpine Guide, Volume 1* (The Mountaineers, 1987), which has detailed descriptions of climbing routes for peaks and crags from here to the Columbia Gorge.

The most popular spot is **Peshastin Pinnacles State Park,** 2 miles west of Cashmere. This small park was created specifically as a climbing park in 1991 after the land, which had been privately owned and was closed to climbing due to liability concerns, was sold to the Trust for Public Land. This organization developed facilities at the base of the rocks and then sold the land to Washington State Parks and Recreation. The rocks here are 200-foot-high sandstone slabs and spires with many climbing routes in a wide range of difficulties.

The next most popular climb is probably **Snow Creek Wall,** which is a mile or so up the trail to the Enchantment Lakes. To reach the trailhead, drive 4 miles up Icicle Creek Road from the west side of Leavenworth. Another popular climb is up

Castle Rock, which is above U.S. 2 in Tumwater Canyon about 2 miles outside Leavenworth.

Over on the west side of Stevens Pass, there is good climbing at the **Index Town Walls** outside the town of Index, which is better known as the launch site for rafting and kayaking the infamous Skykomish River. Mountaineers and other climbers inclined toward big challenges can take on the fortress-like crag of Mount Index. Just north of Stevens Pass summit, **Ramone Rock** also attracts a good number of sport climbers.

If you want to take a rock climbing class while you're in the area, contact **Wave Trek** (tel. 800/543-7971 or 360/793-1705), which is just outside the town of Index.

SNOWSHOEING

Groomed trails for snowshoers? Sounds pretty strange, but that's exactly what you'll find at the Stevens Pass Nordic Center, where snowshoers are welcome to walk on the groomed skate-ski lane (but not in the tracks). For this, you'll have to pay the same $7.50 trail fee that skiers pay. The Nordic center is open Friday through Sunday and holidays from 9am to 4pm. Other days of the week, you can use the trails without paying a fee.

For less regimented snowshoeing, try wandering around at Lake Wenatchee State Park, where you can stay off the groomed ski trails and still find a lot of places to go. Best of all, there are good views along the lakeshore here.

Snowshoes can be rented from **Leavenworth Outfitters Outdoor Center,** 21312 Hwy. 207, Leavenworth (tel. 800/347-7934 or 509/763-3733), which also offers guided snowshoe hikes in the Lake Wenatchee area. The folks here can also point you in the direction of good snowshoeing.

SWIMMING & TUBING

The mountains of this region are filled with glaciers, so no matter where you go, you can expect the water to be cold. However, this doesn't stop people from going swimming. The beach at **Lake Wenatchee State Park** is a good spot for families, and it has a great view. Right in Leavenworth, people swim in **Icicle Creek,** despite the name and cool temperatures, and at Barn Beach and Blackbird Island, which are in the downtown riverfront park. For more natural swimming holes, head farther up Icicle Creek. On the **Wenatchee River,** there is a great swimming hole at Swiftwater Picnic Area in Tumwater Canyon, and other pull-offs within this steep-walled canyon also provide access to good swimming holes.

WALKS & NATURAL ROADSIDE ATTRACTIONS

Deception Falls

100 yards–0.5 miles. Easy. 50-foot elevation gain. Access: East of Skykomish 6 miles on U.S. 2.

There oughtta be a law against building freeways over waterfalls. These sublimely beautiful granite waterfalls would be a fine destination for a hike. Instead, however, they are less than 100 yards from a parking lot tucked under a highway bridge with trucks and cars roaring by overhead. Still, the falls' triple chutes are gorgeous, and if you look downstream and cover your ears, you'd never know you were under a highway. There is also a half-mile interpretive trail through some old growth. Signs in the parking lot explain the railroad history of the Stevens Pass area.

Old Pipeline Trail

3 miles round-trip. Easy. 100-foot elevation gain. Access: From Leavenworth, drive 1.7 miles west on U.S. 2 to a public fishing area.

This trail takes its name from the fact that it follows the route of a pipeline that once carried water to power an electrical turbine that powered trains through the long Cascade Tunnel. Today the pipeline is abandoned and the section across the Wenatchee River is now used as a bridge for this trail. After crossing the bridge to the other side of the river, the trail heads upstream, passing little sandy beaches and providing a new perspective on the walls of Tumwater Canyon, through which the trail passes. High on the rock walls on the highway side of the river, rock climbers can often be seen ascending Castle Rock. At 1.5 miles, reach a large pile of rocks that blocks the entrance to an old pipeline tunnel. This makes a good turnaround point for this hike.

WHITEWATER KAYAKING & CANOEING

On the Skykomish, **Wave Trek** (tel. 800/543-7971 or 360/793-1705) offers kayaking classes and gear rentals. In the Leavenworth area, you can rent canoes and sit-on-top kayaks from **Leavenworth Outfitters Outdoor Center,** 21312 Hwy. 207 (tel. 800/347-7934 or 509/763-3733).

CLASS I

The **Skykomish River,** which drains down the west side of the Cascades along U.S. 2, is, in its upper reaches, the state's premier kayaking river. However, way down in the flatlands, it still is a pretty river. If you're looking for an easy quick-water paddle, then the run from Sultan down to Monroe should keep you happy. All along this stretch of river, woods hug the riverbanks, and in summer, there are lots of gravel bars to stop on. This is a prime steelheading river, so remember to give anglers a wide berth. Put in at the small park at the confluence with the Sultan River on the west side of the town of Sultan. Take out at the Wash. 203 bridge on the south side of Monroe.

There isn't a lot of easy Class I water in the Leavenworth area, but there are at least a couple of places where novice paddlers and anyone else in search of leisurely moving water can head to. The run down the **White River** into the west end of Lake Wenatchee is a longtime favorite in the area. The scenery is fantastic, with constantly changing views as the river meanders back and forth across its floodplain. Put in up the White River Road where the river runs alongside the road, and take out on the north shore of the lake. To get here, take Wash. 207 off of U.S. 2 and continue on around the lake to its far end.

Down at the other end of the lake, where the **Wenatchee River** flows out of the lake, there is another good Class I stretch. Starting at Lake Wenatchee State Park, you can paddle 7 miles down the river to the town of Plain for a good half-day trip. Although there are vacation cabins along this stretch of river, it is still quite scenic, with lots of wildlife to be seen.

CLASS II

The **Skykomish River,** which is legendary among Washington paddlers, is more than just the Class III and IV water above and below the town of Index. If Class II Sky water is all you can handle, there's still a great run for you. Put in at Big Eddy, at the U.S. 2 bridge, 2 miles east of Gold Bar, and have a blast paddling the 9 miles down to the park at the west end of Sultan (at the confluence with the Sultan River). This run is mostly fast water with only three real rapids.

In the Leavenworth area, the 12-mile run down the **Wenatchee River** from the town of Plain to Tumwater Campground at the start of the almost unrunnable Tumwater Canyon is a fun and popular run. This run can be extended by starting up at Lake Wenatchee and doing the Class I run down to Plain. Just don't forget to take out at the U.S. 2 bridge over the river!

CLASS III

The **South Fork Skykomish River** is where aspiring Sky paddlers cut their teeth. The 9-mile stretch of river from the community of Skykomish down to Baring is filled with lots of Class II and III rapids that help paddlers develop their skills. One of the nicest aspects of this run is that it is possible year-round, a rarity in western Washington. However, the water is always cold, even on the hottest day of summer. Put in at the U.S. 2 bridge, 1 mile east of Skykomish, and take out 2 miles west of Baring at Barclay Creek. The Money Creek Campground makes a good alternative put-in or take-out about 4 miles into the run.

The **lower Wenatchee River,** from Leavenworth down to Monitor (18 miles), is one of the most popular stretches of river in the state. Run by numerous commercial rafting companies, these waters are crowded on weekends. The river here is big and pushy with lots of big rapids.

However, there are also long stretches of easy water in between the rapids, which gives you a chance to catch your breath and take in the views. About midway through the run there is a dam that must be portaged on the right side. Just above the town of Cashmere, you come to Granny's Rapid and the huge wave known as Suffocator. Be prepared. Unfortunately, the river is always in sight of the highway, so don't come here expecting a wilderness experience. This is a snowmelt run that is best done between April and early July.

CLASS IV & ABOVE

The 7-mile upper **Skykomish River** run, beginning at the community of Index, is the single most popular stretch of kayaking water in the state. Flowing beneath the ramparts of Mount Index and Mount Persis, this cold, green river tumbles through more than half a dozen major rapids on this fast and demanding run. The biggest and most infamous of all the rapids here is the Class IV+ Boulder Drop about 2 miles into the run. Depending on the flow, Boulder Drop is run differently through the section of lined-up boulders known as the Picket Fence. Ask a local, or better yet, don't paddle this run without someone who knows the river to guide you through the first time. Although this river is most popular during snowmelt season from April to July, it is also run during the middle of the rainy season (winter). As kayakers in wetsuits unload their gear, skiers headed to Stevens Pass shake their heads at the seeming insanity that would prompt anyone to get on an ice-cold river in the middle of winter. You gotta do what you gotta do. This run can be started either on the North Fork or South Fork of the Sky (as it's known). The north fork put-in is just across the bridge from the tiny community of Index and is the easier access point.

However, launching on the South Fork, at the foot of Sunset Falls, adds one more rapid to the run. To reach this latter put-in, turn right off of U.S. 2 just before crossing the South Fork bridge, which is only 0.3 miles west of the turnoff for Index. Drive down this dirt road a half-mile to a pull-off and hike down to the river. When the water level is up, the Sky pushes to solid Class IV+ water, and Boulder Drop becomes a terrifying Class V. Don't even think about it unless you're a seasoned expert paddler and have already run this river at lower levels.

Upstream from Index, there is more Class IV+ paddling on the **North Fork of the Sky.** The usual put-in is at or just above the bridge at Galena, which is 10 miles upriver from Index. About 1.5 miles above Galena is the Class VI Drumbeater Rapids. This is a 12-mile run down to Index.

If you're a kamikaze Class IV paddler searching for whitewater in the Leavenworth area, you've got a couple of impressive choices right outside town on **Icicle Creek.** The upper run starts at Big Slide Creek and ends 4 miles downstream at Bridge Creek Campground. This upper run has stupendous scenery if you can take time out from dodging boulders to even notice the views. The lower run starts at Snow Creek (trailhead for the Enchantment Lakes) and ends 2 miles downstream at the Leavenworth Fish Hatchery.

WHITEWATER RAFTING

The **Wenatchee River** is Washington's most popular commercially run river, and on summer weekends, these waters are littered with brightly colored rafts. What makes this river so popular are the many Class III rapids. Boulder Bend, Rock 'n' Roll, and Suffocator are just some of the named rapids that strike fear and longing in the hearts of novice rafters as they negotiate their way from Leavenworth to Cashmere. From April to July numerous commercial rafting companies run this river. Try one of the following companies: **All Rivers/Wenatchee Whitewater & Company** (tel. 800/743-5628 or 509/782-2254), **Alpine Adventures** (tel. 800/926-RAFT or 509/548-4159), **Cascade Adventures** (tel. 800/723-8386), **Leavenworth Outfitters Outdoor Center** (tel. 800/347-7934 or 509/763-3733), **Osprey Rafting Co.** (tel. 800/743-6269 or 509/548-6800), **River Recreation** (tel. 800/464-5899 or 206/831-1880), or **River Riders** (tel. 800/448-RAFT or 206/448-RAFT).

Although more popular with kayakers than rafters, the **Skykomish River** is a monster of a river on the rainy west side of the Cascades. With the Class V Boulder Drop rapid as the centerpiece of the run from Index to Gold Bar, this trip is meant for people who already have some rafting experience. This river is also run from April to July and sometimes in October and November when there has been heavy rain. Companies running the Skykomish include Cascade Adventures, River Recreation, and River Riders. See above for phone numbers.

WILDLIFE VIEWING

In the late summer and early autumn, **salmon** can often be seen in the Wenatchee River from the **Old Pipeline Trail** along the river in Tumwater Canyon west of Leavenworth. There is also a salmon-viewing area at **Rocky Reach Dam,** between Wenatchee and Chelan on the Columbia River. Stop by in the fall to see salmon.

The I-90 Corridor ◆ What to Do & Where to Do It

BIRD WATCHING

At **Gold Creek Pond,** off I-90 (exit 54) at the north end of Keechelus Lake, you can see a variety of waterfowl, including nesting Canada geese and wading birds. Red Mountain, west of Swauk Pass off U.S. 97, is one of the best raptor-watching locations in the state. Both bald and golden eagles, as well as Cooper's and sharp-shinned hawks, can be seen here. September and October are the best hawk-watching months. To reach Red Mountain, take FS 9738 west to FS 9702. From November to February, bald eagles can be spotted roosting in the Yakima Canyon south of Ellensburg on Wash. 821, and along the banks of Umtanum Creek, which flows into the Yakima Canyon from the west. Birders will find excellent riparian habitat that is home to several species of songbirds and woodpeckers, valley quail, and chukar partridges. Along the length of the Yakima River, watch for prairie falcon and other raptors.

CROSS-COUNTRY SKIING

GROOMED TRAILS

Ski Acres/Hyak Nordic Center

55 kilometers. Easy–most difficult. Up to 1,500-foot elevation gain. Access: Take exit 53 off I-90 and continue east. Hours: Mon and Thurs–Fri 9am–5pm, Wed 9am–10:30pm, Sat 8:30am–10:30pm, Sun 8:30am–5pm (holiday hours differ; call ahead). Trail fee: $8 upper trails, $6 lower trails. Map: Trail maps available at Nordic center.

A lot of people balk at the thought of paying money to use cross-country ski trails, but the trails of this commercial system are so well laid out, so varied, so extensive, and offer such stunning views that anyone would be foolish *not* to do some skiing here. The upper trails, which include the Mount Catherine loop trail, have it hands down over the lower trails. However, in order to ski these trails, you definitely need to be an intermediate-level skier. First of all, just to get to the trails, you have to ride a chairlift up the mountain. Once off the lift, you have to begin dealing with a variety of hills, both long and short, steep and gradual. And just remember that for each exhilarating downhill swoop, you'll have an equal uphill slog.

The grand tour here is the loop around Mount Catherine, which should be done counterclockwise to take full advantage of a perfectly sloped, intermediate-level descent that goes on for around 4 kilometers. Talk about a fun run! Skiing counterclockwise will also allow you to ascend (instead of descend) one of the steepest sections of trail in the system. Telemarkers have their own play area on the open slopes encircled by the Windy Acres Trail, and down along Ollalie Meadows, you'll find a cozy warming hut. From nearly anywhere on this system of trails, you'll have a view of some sort.

In addition to the big loop around the mountain, there are more than a dozen shorter loops to keep you entertained and to add mileage to your workout. When you're done for the day, you have two choices. You can ride down the ski lift, which usually has two downloading periods each day, or you can ski down on trails that are marked for Nordic skiers (although some of these trails are none too easy). Be prepared to deal with schussing skiers and kamikaze snowboarders.

The lower trails here are short and are preferred by students, families, and novice skiers. They also offer a couple of short black-diamond trails where intermediate skiers can gain a bit more confidence and improve their downhill skills. The lower trails also offer some of the only Nordic trails in the Northwest that are lighted for night skiing (unfortunately, they're all beginners' trails).

Lake Keechelus Sno-Park (Iron Horse State Park)

14 miles round-trip. Easy. 100-foot elevation gain. Access: Take exit 54 off I-90 and turn south. At the stop sign, go left and then turn right onto the Keechelus boat ramp road (signed). The sno-park is 1 mile down this road. Map: Green Trails Snoqualmie Pass.

This sno-park provides access to Iron Horse Trail along the shore of Lake Keechelus. This trail follows an abandoned railroad grade (which is where "Iron Horse" comes from) and serves as a great introduction to cross-country skiing. The trail is flat, wide, and well groomed (once you get beyond the footprints and post holes near the parking area), which makes it a great place to learn skiing basics and develop confidence. Unfortunately, the views of the lake are limited, but they are quite impressive. If you have two cars, you can arrange a 7-mile one-way ski from this sno-park to the Price Creek Eastbound Sno-Park, which is at a rest area on eastbound I-90.

To reach this sno-park, cross the dam at the east end of the lake and follow the marked ski trails. Although there is a trail that begins about halfway across the dam, the trail at the far end is easier for novice skiers. Also consider starting this route at Price Creek; this way, you'll ski uphill for the first half of your tour and downhill on the way back. Although the gradient is barely perceptible, everything helps when you're a novice. It is also possible to ski the Iron Horse Trail to the Crystal Springs Sno-Park. However, between the dam and Crystal Springs, the trail crosses two avalanche slopes, requiring skiers to detour down onto a busy snowmobile trail for a while.

Price Creek Eastbound

5 miles. Easy–more difficult. 100-foot elevation gain. Access: Take I-90 east from Snoqualmie Pass for 9 miles to the signed sno-park. Map: Green Trails Snoqualmie Pass.

This sno-park is a rest area during the summer months and lies at the eastern end of Lake Keechelus. From the sno-park, groomed trails lead both east and west and can be linked together to form a pleasant, easy 5-mile loop. I suggest starting a tour here by skiing west toward the lake. The trail drops down a bit through a deciduous forest before climbing to the dam that forms Lake Keechelus (at the trail fork, you can go either way). The trail then follows the top of the dam all the way to the other side of the lake, where it connects to the Iron Horse Trail. Turn left onto the skiers-only Iron Horse Trail (not to be confused with the snowmobile route to the immediate left). Follow this groomed trail for 1.5 miles before turning left onto a snowmobile route. This stretch of trail passes through an avalanche zone, and, if there has been a recent heavy snow or rainfall, you should descend from the Iron Horse Trail to the snowmobile route, which is outside the avalanche zone.

Pass through the Crystal Springs Sno-Park, cross the bridge over the Yakima River, and turn left into the Crystal Springs campground, where you'll pick up groomed trail again. In the campground, a couple of picnic tables in a rustic shelter beside the river are a great spot for lunch (if you ski this loop in reverse, you could have a picnic on the dam with a magnificent view of the lake and surrounding mountains). From the campground, it's about 1 mile back to the sno-park, the trail meandering through some big trees, along the river, and up and down a few gentle hills. This area gets my vote for the best

spot for beginning skiers. Unfortunately, there aren't a lot of parking spots here. If the sno-park is full, continue east to the Crystal Springs Sno-Park (a snowmobile area), from which you can access the loop described above.

If you want to ski a more difficult route, add another 5 miles to your tour, and don't mind sharing the trail with roaring snowmobiles, then, from the south end of the Lake Keechelus dam, continue straight ahead on FS 5483, which climbs steadily to gain more than 600 feet of elevation before reaching the left turn onto FS 5484, which leads up and over Dandy Pass before dropping back down to FS 54 and the Crystal Springs Sno-Park. From the pass, there is a great view of Mount Rainier to the south. If you are doing the loop clockwise, head up FS 54 from the Crystal Springs Sno-Park to FS 5484 and return on FS 5483 to the Lake Keechelus dam. Another alternative is to ski up the Iron Horse Trail to Lake Keechelus Sno-Park (see above for details).

Cabin Creek Sno-Park

12 kilometers. Easy–most difficult. 200-foot elevation gain. Access: Take exit 63 off I-90. Map: Green Trails Snoqualmie Pass.

A total of more than 12 kilometers of impeccably groomed trails maintained by the Trollhaugen Nordic Club make this a favorite of Seattle skinny skiers. The flat trails attract families and novice skiers, while the more challenging loop trails off the main road provide great workouts for anyone working on technique, stamina, or speed. These trails were laid out for racing, and skate skiing is the preferred technique here. The black-diamond trails are suitably challenging and lead to some of the best views on this system of trails. Lots of rolling hills provide plenty of short ups and downs that make this one of the best laid-out and most interesting ski-trail systems in the state. On days when there are races being held here, the trails are closed to the public. These trails also provide access to the Amabilis Mountain. To reach the trails from the parking area, walk across the bridge over the interstate.

UNGROOMED TRAILS

Gold Creek Sno-Park

2–7 miles round-trip. Easy–most difficult. 2,800-foot elevation gain. Access: Take exit 54 off I-90 at Snoqualmie Pass and drive to the north side of the interstate. Map: Green Trails Snoqualmie Pass.

As the closest sno-park to Seattle, Gold Creek is always jammed on weekends with both skiers and snowmobilers, and parking spaces fill up early. However, on a weekday, there may only be a couple of other cars here. There are three different tours starting here, including the maze of trails through the flats along the valley floor, the trail up to Kendall Knobs, and the route up Mount Margaret.

The easiest trails are those in the flats surrounding Gold Creek Pond, which though not groomed are quite easy and offer good views of the Gold Creek Valley, which is one of the few vistas in the area that is not marred by clear-cuts. However, the valley floor is now up for sale, and as vacation cabins are built, you can expect more and more NO TRESPASSING signs to go up.

For a more challenging tour with inspiring views, head up toward the Kendall Knobs on the road that heads due north from the west end of the sno-park. This road climbs steadily for more than 3 miles before offering skiers a choice of hills to ascend. The western hill is favored by telemark skiers, who are among the most avid users of this area. Dubbed Telemark Hill, this clear-cut slope, with its views across the valley to the downhill ski areas, is a telemark playground. For more staid skiing, head up to the east knob for excellent views of the surrounding mountains and valleys. Even if you don't make it all the way up here, you'll find great views of the Gold Creek Valley to the east and Guye Peak to the west at about the 2-mile mark where the trail makes a couple of big switchbacks. Before attempting this route, be sure you have plenty of confidence in your downhill skills, all of which will be challenged by the rutted, often icy trail, which on weekends is a veritable obstacle course of skiers.

Telemarkers who can put up with skiing more than 2 miles alongside the interstate accompanied by speeding snowmobiles may actually enjoy the Mount Margaret route. The trail climbs almost 3,000 feet in 4.5 miles to a point just shy of the summit of Mount Margaret. Needless to say, the views are superb, and the clear-cut slopes offer hours of telemarking fun. This route starts at the east end of the sno-park and follows the service road beside the interstate before starting its switchbacking climb to the summit of Mount Margaret.

Amabilis Mountain

8 miles round-trip. Most difficult. 2,000-foot elevation gain. Access: Take exit 63 off I-90. Map: Green Trails Snoqualmie Pass.

It's a long, hard climb to the top of this mountain 10 miles east of Snoqualmie Pass, but the views from the summit are stupendous. The trail, which makes a loop around the top of the mountain, follows logging roads for the most part, so the gradient isn't too steep. But still, I wouldn't want to come down off Amabilis when it's icy. Along the route up, you'll ski in and out of clear-cuts and the views just get better as you get higher. Near the summit, you finally start to get views of Mount Rainier. Start this tour on the groomed trails at the Cabin Creek North Sno-Park, following the right fork at the start of the ski trails. This fork climbs gradually to intersect the ungroomed Amabilis Mountain Road, which climbs to the right at a steeper gradient than that of the groomed trail.

About 2 miles after leaving the groomed trail, you'll reach a major switchback to the left. At this turn another road goes straight. This latter road is the return leg of the loop you will be skiing around the mountain's summit. Follow the switchback around to the left and stay on this main road all the way to the open ridge top of the mountain and then follow the ridgeline road to the south. There are superb views from here, with Kachess Lake spread out below and the mountains of the Alpine Lakes Wilderness to the north.

On a cloudy day, you may want to pick somewhere else to ski. Not only will you not get the views, but you can easily lose the road up here and get lost. Ski along the ridge for slightly more than 1 mile, and, at the south end of the clear-cut, turn to the right and follow the edge of the forest less than 0.25 miles to intersect another logging road. Go right on this road and follow it steeply downhill for about 1 mile to intersect your uphill tracks. Alternatively, you could turn around after skiing the ridgeline and return the way you came.

DOWNHILL SKIING & SNOWBOARDING

The Pass

Access: Exit 52 and exit 53 off I-90 east of Seattle. Tel. 206/236-1600. 65 trails; 23 chairs; 2,200 vertical feet. Hours: Alpental, Tues–Fri 9am–10:30pm, Sat 8:30am–10:30pm; Snoqualmie, Tues–Fri 9am–10:30pm, Sat 8:30am–10:30pm, Sun 8:30am–10:30pm; Ski Acres, Mon and Wed–Fri 9am–10:30pm, Sat 8:30am–10:30pm, Sun 8:30am–9pm; Hyak, Fri 5–10:30pm, Sat 8:30am–10:30pm, Sun 8:30am–6pm; longer hours during holidays. Adult lift tickets: Mon–Tues $14, Wed–Thurs $16, Fri $18, Sat–Sun $28.

Consisting of four different ski areas all merged together under a single management, this is the closest downhill skiing to Seattle. It is also one of the lowest-elevation ski areas in the state, and consequently gets off to a late start some years. Many skiers find these slopes rather tedious. There isn't a whole lot of variety in the terrain—it's either steep or flat—and the runs, especially those of the Snoqualmie ski area, have a monotony bordering on the absurd. Yet the lifts stay full on weekends with Seattleites who just can't seem to ignore the fact that it takes less than an hour to get up here. Why bother spending more time in the car just to get to better slopes?

If you're looking for challenging terrain, I suggest heading to the Alpental ski area. You can't see it from I-90 and somehow that just makes skiing here feel better. This area has lots of challenging steep runs and a more remote, alpine feel to its setting. Aspiring Warren Miller screen stars can head for the unmarked chutes of the Back Country. Snowboarders should head straight to Hyak, the most easterly of the ski areas at The Pass, or to the runs off the Silver Fir lift at the adjacent Ski Acres area. In these two areas, boarders will find a half pipe and plenty of great hits along the edges of runs that have been cut through the trees. The massive lighting system and proximity to Seattle make The Pass particularly popular for night skiing.

FISHING

Above Snoqualmie Falls, the **Snoqualmie River** supports both rainbow and cutthroat trout populations and is popular for fly-fishing. The **Cle Elum River,** both above and below Cle Elum Lake, is stocked with rainbows throughout the summer, but the crowds that flock to the many campgrounds in the area keep the pressure on this river. The **Yakima River,** between Ellensburg and Yakima, offers superb angling for wild trout up to 24 inches in both spring and fall. During the fall, the low water makes wading the preferred method of going after these fish. In spring, float fishing from a raft or boat is preferred. All wild trout must be released unharmed. This lake is a favorite of fly anglers.

The Snoqualmie Pass area's three large lakes—**Keechelus, Kachess,** and **Cle Elum**—are all popular kokanee lakes. Additionally, Cle Elum and Kachess have a few good-sized Mackinaw. All three lakes also have plenty of rainbows, cutthroats, and Dolly Vardens. Nearby Lake Easton, site of a state park, is popular for its stocked rainbows. Many of the lakes of the **Alpine Lakes Wilderness** are also stocked with trout.

HIKING & BACKPACKING

If you are looking for a long hike through this region, nothing can compete with the 67 miles of the **Pacific Crest Trail** between Snoqualmie Pass and Stevens Pass. Along this route, which includes a total of more than 10,000 feet of climbing, there are more than a dozen lakes, many of which are among the most beautiful in the aptly named Alpine Lakes Wilderness, through which the trail passes. To do this hike, you'll need to arrange to have someone pick you up at the far end or set up a car shuttle.

Mount Si

8 miles round-trip. Strenuous. 3,100-foot elevation gain. Access: From I-90, take the North Bend exit (exit 31), drive into town, turn right at the stoplight onto North Bend Way, continue through town, turn left onto Mount Si Rd., turn right after crossing the Snoqualmie, and continue 2.5 miles to the trailhead. Map: USGS Mount Si, Snoqualmie, North Bend, and Bandera; Green Trails Mount Si (174) and Bandera (206).

This is it! The single most popular hike in the state of Washington, and the second most popular summit hike. If you don't believe me, just join the line of hikers huffing and puffing their way to the top on a sunny Saturday in August and you'll know it's true. Why do they come? Is it the view from the top? Is it the ease of access from downtown Seattle? Is it the fact that anyone who has driven I-90 east of Seattle has had their attention pulled from the highway by this mountain rising straight up from the valley floor outside North Bend? Perhaps it's all of these. I think it's the fact that Mount Si slaps the viewer in the face and issues a challenge that simply cannot go unmet.

Mount Si, at 4,167 feet in elevation, hardly even deserves to be called a mountain in a state filled with lofty peaks, yet it is far more impressive in stature than the vast majority of peaks in the state. Mount Si rises without preliminary or foothill from the flat floor of the Snoqualmie Valley in much the way that Half Dome and El Capitan rise from the floor of the Yosemite Valley and, as in the Yosemite Valley, owes its cliffs to glaciers that once scoured out the Snoqualmie Valley. So, why not go climb a mountain. This trail just might turn you into a peak bagger.

From the trailhead, climb 1 mile to the first view. From here it is another 2 miles, past a mix of old-growth Douglas firs and snags left from past fires that have swept across this mountain. At the 3-mile point there are campsites for those who want to stay to see the lights of Seattle twinkling far below. The last 1 mile of trail switchbacks steeply up to the Haystack

Basin, which is below the summit crag known as The Haystack. This basin is the goal of most hikers, and from here the views are dizzying. Directly below lies North Bend, and in the distance can be seen Seattle, Puget Sound, and the Olympic Mountains.

Snow Lake/Gem Lake

8 miles round-trip to Snow Lake; 11 miles round-trip to Gem Lake. Moderate–strenuous. 1,300-foot elevation gain to Snow Lake; 1,700 feet to Gem Lake. Access: Take exit 52 off I-90 at Snoqualmie Pass and drive north of the interstate on Alpental Rd. to the ski area and trailhead parking. Map: USGS Snoqualmie Pass and Bandera, Green Trails Snoqualmie Pass (207).

This is the most popular hike in the Snoqualmie Pass area and for good reason. Snow Lake is absolutely beautiful! Imagine hiking steadily uphill through dense forest for 3.5 miles with little more than a couple of down-valley views to keep your appetite for scenery sated. Suddenly you crest a saddle and come face-to-face with a ridge top of granite rocks. Now this is getting interesting; then you realize that behind the rocks and 400 feet below you lies a stunning subalpine lake. The waters along the shore are a Caribbean turquoise hue, while out in the center of the lake, a midnight blue hints at the lake's depth. From this ridge, the trail drops down, crossing a talus slope, before reaching the lake. A side trail leads past the ruins of a cabin built in 1932 and down to several lake access points, while the main trail leads around the east side of the lake a half-mile to the outlet stream, which is crossed on a huge log.

If you're satisfied with your hike thus far, you can just lounge on the rocks by the lake and soak in the scenery. However, if you are up for more hiking, take the trail that leads uphill from the log, and in 1 mile of steady climbing through open forests alternating with pocket meadows and granite outcroppings, you'll come to Gem Lake, which though pretty, is but a diamond in the rough compared to Snow Lake. However, if you continue around Gem Lake on the trail above the east shore, and then climb up to a saddle above the lake (this trail leads to Wildcat Lakes, 2 miles distant), and then keep climbing just a little bit higher on a narrow trail, you'll come to one of the most spectacular campsites in this wilderness. This campsite is perched on a narrow ridge with views in two directions.

Needless to say, the crowds descend on beautiful Snow Lake (fewer reach Gem Lake) daily throughout the summer. Try an early morning or late afternoon hike to avoid the crowds, and please, stay on the trails and use designated campsites and day-use sites. This area has been pounded.

Denny Creek–Melakwa Lake Trail

9 miles round-trip. Strenuous. 2,300-foot elevation gain. Access: Take exit 47 off I-90, follow signs to Denny Creek Campground, drive 0.2 miles past the campground, turn left over a bridge, and continue 100 yds. on this dirt road to the trailhead. Map: USGS Snoqualmie Pass, Green Trails Snoqualmie Pass (207).

One look at the cars in the trailhead parking area for this hike may convince you to just keep driving east to less accessible trails, but keep in mind that most of the people who come in those cars never make it past Denny Creek Waterslide, a stretch of water-worn granite that is an extremely popular play area during the summer. Beyond the waterslide, the number of people on the trail becomes progressively fewer the higher you hike (switchbacks have a way of doing that). So maybe there will still be trailside traffic jams as far up as Keekwulee Falls, but these are often the alternate destination of those not interested in getting wet at the waterslide.

For those willing to tough out the switchbacks, the trail crosses open talus slopes as well as cooler forests before finally reaching Melakwa Lake, which lies at the foot of rugged Chair and Kaleetan peaks. Crystal-clear waters ringed by patches of subalpine forest and massive granite boulders are a cooling payoff for anyone who makes it up this far. After resting a while, you can hike most of the way around the lake and even scramble up to Melakwa Pass and look down into the valley of the South Fork Snoqualmie River. There are designated campsites both at

the point where the trail reaches the lake and across the lake in a patch of trees.

One rather disturbing aspect of this hike is that it starts out *in the middle of* I-90. The trail, though deep in the woods, is actually in the median strip of the interstate at a point where the uphill and downhill lanes are separated by more than a quarter-mile. The Denny Creek trail starts between the lanes and then passes under the interstate at a point where the cars are high overhead on an elevated roadway. Don't expect to hear the twittering of birds at this point.

Granite Mountain

8.6 miles round-trip. Strenuous. 3,800-foot elevation gain. Access: Take exit 47 off I-90, then, on the north side of the interstate, turn left and continue a half-mile to the trailhead. Map: USGS Snoqualmie Pass, Green Trails Snoqualmie Pass (207).

There are those who like to hike to lakes, and those who prefer the challenge of summiting a peak; if you're one of the latter, Granite Mountain is for you. Not nearly as crowded as Mount Si (though don't expect solitude on a summer weekend), Granite Mountain offers superb views over the Snoqualmie Pass area and beyond. The hike starts on the Pratt Lake Trail for 1 mile of climbing through the low-elevation forests just off I-90. When the Granite Mountain Trail branches off to the right, you have a half-mile breather of easy walking through the trees, but at the end of this section, the trail breaks out into an old burn where the views, and the switchbacks, begin. This south-facing slope heats up in the summer, so bring lots of water. One consolation is that, though you'll be sweating profusely, every time you stop to cool off, you'll have glorious views.

About midway up the mountain, the trail traverses east, across a shaded gully that is often snow-filled and prone to avalanches sometimes as late as June. Wait until July and you'll have safety and wildflowers (wait until September and have huckleberries). Above this traverse, there are more switchbacks, though the trail becomes less steep. At the top, you reach the lookout and views of Mount Rainier, Mount Baker, Glacier Peak, and the Stuart Range.

Spectacle Lake-Mineral Park

26 miles round-trip. Moderate–strenuous. 2,675-foot elevation gain. Access: Take Roslyn exit (exit 80) off I-90, drive north to the stop sign on Wash. 903, turn left, drive through Roslyn, continue 15 miles (passing Cle Elum Lake), turn left onto FS 46 (which crosses the Cle Elum River), continue 4.7 miles, turn right onto FS 4616 (signed for Cooper Lake), continue past the campground, turn left onto FS 4616113, and continue 1 mile to the trailhead. Map: USGS Snoqualmie Pass and Kachess Lake, Green Trails Kachess Lake (208).

And a spectacle this lake is indeed! As far as I'm concerned, there is no more beautiful spot on the south side of the Alpine Lakes Wilderness. Spectacle Lake, a convoluted collection of coves rimmed by granite and patches of subalpine evergreens, is surrounded on three sides by jagged peaks that give the lake basin a rugged and remote quality that is belied by the long, though not-too-difficult, trail in. From the trailhead at Cooper Lake, hike 5.5 miles to Pete Lake, which is as far as many hikers ever get in this area (which means this lake is crowded on weekends). From here it is another 3.75 miles to the side trail that leads very steeply for a half-mile up to Spectacle Lake (4,350 feet). Don't despair when you see the roots and rocks you have to scramble up to reach the lake; it's well worth the effort. Once you reach the lake, sit down and catch your breath; you'll likely be breathless both from the climb and from the beauty of your surroundings.

Granite bedrock, scraped into graceful curves by ancient glaciers, sweeps down into the clear lake waters in many places, and exploring the lake's shore is one of the biggest treats of this hike. High above tower the jagged peaks of the Three Queens to the south, Chikamin Ridge and Chikamin Peak to the west, and Lemah Mountain to the north.

As pretty as it is by the lakeshore, an even more spectacular view can be had 2 miles beyond Spectacle Lake at Spectacle

> "Climb the mountains and get their good tidings. Nature's peace will flow into you as sunshine flows into trees. The winds will blow their freshness into you, and storms their energy, while cares will drop off like autumn leaves."
>
> —John Muir

Point (5,475 feet), where the trail to Mineral Park crosses a saddle between the Three Queens and Chikamin Ridge. From this vantage point, you can see how amazingly convoluted Spectacle Lake really is and you have an even more dramatic view of the surrounding peaks. To reach Spectacle Point, follow the trail that heads south (and uphill) from the east end of the lake. Having made it this far, you owe it to yourself to wander the remaining 1.5 miles down into Mineral Creek Park where you can walk around Upper Park Lake, and, if it is late enough in the summer, pick huckleberries until you've had your fill. This hike can be done as an overnight, but really deserves two nights so that you can explore the various trails in the area.

Tuck Lake and Robin Lakes

14 miles round-trip. Strenuous. 2,900-foot elevation gain. Access: From I-90, take exit 80 toward Roslyn and follow signs for Salmon la Sac Campground, which is 16 miles from Roslyn. At Salmon la Sac, turn right onto gravel FS 4330, and continue 12.5 miles to the end of the road and the Hyas Lake/Deception Pass trailhead. Map: USGS Mount Daniel and The Cradle; Green Trails Stevens Pass (176).

Almost as beautiful as the fabled Enchantments, and almost as difficult to reach, the Robin Lakes are a good alternative for anyone who was unable to secure an Enchantments permit. This area offers the same landscape of glacier-polished granite, though on a smaller scale.

The trail starts out at a very gradual ascent along the valley floor. After 1.5 miles of hiking through dense forest, reach the shore of Hyas Lake with a view of Cathedral Rock across the water. The trail follows the shore of the lake for a mile, then begins to climb more steeply as it heads up toward Deception Pass. After about a half-mile of climbing, you'll come to a trail junction, with the trail to Tuck Lake and Robin Lakes heading off to the right. This trail seems deceptively mild mannered at first, but soon turns nasty as it tilts at a crazy angle to climb straight up the mountainside. At times you'll have to use your hands to pull yourself up over rocks and downed trees. Finally, at 6 miles from the trailhead, you break into the open high on the mountainside and are treated to a gorgeous view of Hyas Lake below and Cathedral Rock across the valley. However, the real treat lies to your back. Tucked into a bowl on the side of the mountain, with hardly 100 square feet of level ground in this crazily tilted landscape of rock and twisted trees, are the captivating waters of Tuck Lake (5,630 feet). At the point where the trail first reaches the lake, a small island lies just offshore. On the far side of the lake, steep rocky slopes rise high above the surface of the water. To the right, a jumble of rock outcroppings is mixed among the trees, and shelters a tiny tarn.

To continue up to the Robin Lakes, which are even more ruggedly beautiful, follow whatever trails you can that lead counterclockwise around the lake. After passing the tarn, head up the rocky ridge. If you find yourself descending or staying level for more than 20 feet or so, you're probably on the wrong trail. The trail (if you can call it that) up to Robin Lakes twists and turns to find the easiest route among the jumble of glacier-smoothed granite boulders, but eventually breaks out onto open slabs of rock surrounded by heather meadows. At this point just follow the cairns uphill to reach a shoulder 100 feet above Lower Robin Lake (6,160 feet). The trail then leads down to the lake and up the basin to Upper Robin Lake. Granite is everywhere with heather and stunted conifers clinging to whatever thin cups of soil they can find amid the rocks. The bare rock is perfect for wandering on and a whole weekend could be spent just

exploring this high basin. Two things to consider when planning to hike up here: Campsites are at a premium on weekends, and the weather can be bad.

HOT SPRINGS

Goldmeyer Hot Springs (tel. 206/789-5631), located on private land within the Mount Baker–Snoqualmie National Forest, are among the nicest little developed springs in the state. By developed, I mean there are cement pools and a small building here, but the springs are still remote and just a step above primitive. From the parking area on FS 5620, it is a short walk to the springs, which are reached by crossing the river on a footbridge. A fairly substantial fee is charged for the use of these springs, but the setting is quite idyllic. Because the springs are on the Middle Fork Trail along the Middle Fork Snoqualmie River, they make a great destination for a hike through the forests along the river. To reach the hot springs, take exit 34 off I-90, go north on Edgewick Road, and turn right onto Middle Fork Road (FS 56) at the yield sign. In 10 miles, turn right onto FS 5620 and continue another 9 miles to the hot springs parking area.

MOUNTAIN BIKING

So you finally put your old road bike out to pasture and bought a new fat-tire bike with 21 gears and all you've done since then is ride the paved Burke–Gilman Trail. It's time to get some gravel in those treads, so why not start with something easy. **Iron Horse State Park,** a linear park along the route of an abandoned railroad, is the perfect trail on which to get a feel for off-road biking. It's close to Seattle, it has a very gentle incline, and along the way, there are some nice views of Lake Keechelus and the peaks of the Snoqualmie Pass area. Best of all, you can, if you don't suffer from claustrophobia, pedal through the 2.5-mile-long Snoqualmie Tunnel, which goes under Snoqualmie Pass. At 113 miles, this trail is too long for most riders to do in a single trip, so break it up into a few sections. If you arrange a car shuttle, you can also do segments one way (preferably downhill) and save yourself the possible boredom of riding back on the same trail.

In addition to the rides listed below, the **Ski Acres Mountain Bike and Hiking Center** (tel. 206/434-7669, ext. 3372 or 206/236-1600) at Snoqualmie Pass provides 30 miles of trails accessed by the Silver Fir ski lift. These are the same trails that by winter serve as cross-country trails. Some are gravel roads and others are single-track. There is a lot of climbing to be done here, but a ride on the chairlift gets you over the worst of it. Lift rides are $8 if you have your own bike and $6.50 if you use one of the center's rental bikes ($15 per half day). The trails are open with the chairlift operating Friday through Sunday. Mountain-biking classes are also offered here.

If you'd like to have a guide lead you around this area and tell you a bit more than you would learn on your own, contact **Mountain Outfitters,** P.O. Box 1163, North Bend, WA 98045-1163 (tel. 206/409-0459), which leads rides on the Iron Horse Trail. This company also offers a shuttle service, so you can ride the Iron Horse one way without having to bring two cars yourself. Bike rentals are also available.

If you don't mind riding with motorcycles and ORVs and are looking for miles and miles of challenging riding, head for the **Taneum Creek/Manastash Ridge area** of the Wenatchee National Forest due south of Cle Elum. Here you'll find a maze of logging roads and ORV trails that will suggest loop rides of varying lengths. At the **Cle Elum Ranger Station,** 803 W Second St., Cle Elum (tel. 509/674-4411), you can pick up a copy of the *Kittitas County Off-Road Vehicle Recreation Guide,* a map of the area's trails and logging roads. Most rides in this area include between 1,000 and 1,500 feet of climbing. There are several campgrounds in the area, so you can spend a weekend exploring. Some of the more fun trails include Taneum Ridge, Taneum Creek, and Manastash Creek. To reach this area, take exit 93 off I-90 and follow signs for Taneum Creek.

Middle Fork Road and Trail

13 miles (or more). Moderate. 450-foot elevation gain. Access: Take exit 34 off I-90, follow Edgewick Rd. north, and at the yield sign, turn right onto Middle Fork Rd. (FS 56). Follow this road 10 miles and park in the Middle Fork trailhead before crossing the Taylor River. Map: USFS North Bend Ranger District.

The Middle Fork Snoqualmie River is paralleled by both a rough forest road and a rough trail. Together the two can be combined into one of the most fun mountain-bike rides in the region. From the trailhead parking lot, continue up FS 56 for a half-mile and turn right onto FS 5620. Ride this road for 6 miles, through ups and downs that are more fun than challenging, to the Dingford Creek Trail parking area. Turn right and ride down to the river and cross on a footbridge. On the far side of the bridge, turn right to head down the trail toward your car, or, if you've got lots of energy, turn left and head up the trail as far as you feel like riding (it's 6.8 miles to the end with about the same amount of elevation gain that it took to reach this trail junction), and then turn around for the downhill ride back to the car. The trail is a roller coaster of a ride winding through the forest, and is much more enjoyable than the rough road section of the ride. Much of the trail is actually on a long-abandoned old logging railroad bed, which means the gradient is quite easy.

Iron Horse Trail/West Side Segment

29 miles round-trip. Moderate. 1,300-foot elevation gain. Access: Take exit 38 off I-90, drive east on Homestead Valley Rd. almost to the point where it rejoins I-90, and turn right onto FS 9020. The parking lot is a short distance up this road. Map: USFS North Bend Ranger District.

The closest segment of the Iron Horse Trail to Seattle also happens to include the greatest elevation gain. From the trailhead it is a steady 11-mile climb up to the west entrance of the Snoqualmie Tunnel, which is open from May 1 to October 31. As you climb up to the tunnel, you will have nearly constant views of I-90 and the South Fork Snoqualmie Valley. This is a very different perspective than what most people are used to from I-90; here you are high above the valley floor. There are good views of the mountains on the north side of the valley.

At the tunnel entrance, turn on the bike headlight or headlamp flashlight that you of course remembered to bring with you, put on the sweater and rain gear that you also remembered, and prepare for the most bizarre mountain-bike riding in the country. For the next 2.5 miles you pedal through the dank recesses beneath Snoqualmie Pass. Water drips (and sometimes pours) from the ceiling. In the distance a tiny speck of light indicates the far end of the tunnel. It really isn't that bad after you get used to it. If it is summer, as you exit the far end of the tunnel you will be struck by the sudden blast of warm air on the outside. After removing your tunnel gear, continue down the trail less than 1 mile to the Keechelus Lake trailhead. Here you can head down to the lake for a picnic before turning around to head back through the tunnel and down the west slope. If you can arrange a car shuttle, start here and make the ride a downhill run from the far side of the tunnel.

Iron Horse Trail/Keechelus Lake Segment

22 miles. Easy. 100-foot elevation gain. Access: Take exit 62 off I-90, drive south past the Crystal Springs Campground, cross the Yakima River, and continue on this road until you cross the Iron Horse Trail. There is a gravel parking area on the left. Map: Green Trails Snoqualmie Pass.

As an alternative to all that uphill pedaling on the west side of the tunnel, you can start near Crystal Springs Sno-Park and ride up a more gradual section of the trail. This segment passes above the shore of Keechelus Lake for more than 5.5 miles. There are several places along this stretch of trail where you could scramble down to the lake if you were so inclined. From the trailhead, it is 8.5 miles to the west entrance to the Snoqualmie Tunnel. Switch on your light and put on your rain gear before heading into the dark, cold, and dripping tunnel. At the far end take a break and enjoy the views down the South Fork Snoqualmie Valley before heading back through the tunnel and to the trailhead.

Amabilis Mountain

10.5 miles. Strenuous. 2,100-foot elevation gain. Access: Take exit 63 off I-90 and turn right into the sno-park parking area. Map: Green Trails Snoqualmie Pass.

If you're looking for a ride on the Iron Horse Trail, with significantly more cardiovascular challenge than either of the two rides mentioned previously, then you may want to consider this grueling (though rewarding) challenge. Starting just off the interstate, this ride follows logging roads to the summit of Amabilis Mountain, where there are excellent views in all directions. From the parking area, cross the bridge over the freeway and continue straight on FS 4822. In about 0.25 miles, turn right onto FS 4822 and begin climbing through a combination of impressive old-growth forest and depressing clearcuts. Continue following FS 4822 through its many switchbacks, noting FS 118 at a wide switchback to the left about 2.5 miles from the start of FS 4822. This side road is your route back down from the top.

As you near the clear-cut summit of Amabilis Mountain, impressive views open up. To the south is Mount Rainier, to the west is Keechelus Lake, to the east is Kachess Lake, and to the north is jagged Chikamin Ridge in the Alpine Lakes Wilderness. Continue to the south along the ridge top until you reach the edge of the summit clear-cut, which is just past a tempting viewpoint on the left. At the edge of the clear-cut, watch for a double-track trail on the right, and follow this trail along the edge of the trees for 0.3 miles to intersect FS 118. Turn right on this rough road and ride downhill to return to FS 4822, which will take you back to the bottom.

PACKSTOCK TRIPS

If you're interested in exploring the mountains of this area from horseback, contact **Three Queens Outfitter/Guide Service,** 211 Seaton Rd., Cle Elum, WA 98922 (tel. 509/674-5647), or **High Country Outfitters,** 3020 Issaquah Pine Lake Rd., Suite 544, Issaquah, WA 98029 (tel. 888/235-0111 or 206/392-0111). Both outfitters offer a variety of trips from drop camps to deluxe guided outings. Expect to pay around $200 per person for an overnight trip.

ROAD BIKING

Because I-90 is the only road over Snoqualmie Pass, there isn't a lot of good road biking in this area. However, if you are looking to do a longer ride, combine the ride below with a tour of the Snoqualmie Valley below Snoqualmie Falls (see chapter 3 for details).

Snoqualmie Falls–Mount Si Loop

14 miles. Easy. 250-foot elevation gain. Access: Take exit 31 (North Bend) off I-5 and drive north to the Snoqualmie Valley Historical Museum and Information Center.

Before you start this ride, duck into the museum (if it's open) to learn a bit about the history of the area. Once your mind is filled with visions of long-gone hops farms, ride into town, passing Mar-T Cafe, which was made famous for its "damn good pies" on the *Twin Peaks* TV series. Keep those pies in mind at the end of the ride. Continue straight past the Mar-T and head out of town on Snoqualmie–North Bend Road. After crossing the river, angle right onto Boalch Road to avoid traffic as you pedal the 2.5 miles to Snoqualmie. This unusual little tourist town has an excursion train and is home to a huge collection of old railroad engines and rolling stock. After checking out the trains, head back the way you came and turn left on Meadowbrook Way to cross the Snoqualmie River.

Once across the bridge, turn left on Mill Pond Road and ride 1.5 miles on this riverside road to the junction with Wash. 202. Turn right onto the highway to reach the Snoqualmie Falls overlook. Feeling like a gourmet lunch? Try the Salish Lodge. Backtrack to Mill Pond Road but turn left onto 66th Street instead of right onto Mill Pond and start pedaling up the steepest hill of the ride. From 66th, turn right onto Tokul Road, continuing to climb. In less than 1.5 miles, turn right on 53rd Way, which becomes 369th Avenue. In under 1 mile, turn right on 60th Street. In 1.3 miles

turn left on Reinig Road to begin the most scenic stretch of the ride.

Reinig Road passes between two rows of 70-year-old sycamore trees that once lined the main street of the town of Snoqualmie Falls, which was washed away by a flood. Ahead you have a breathtaking view of the glacier-carved cliffs of Mount Si. At 428th Avenue, turn right and cross both the north and middle forks of the Snoqualmie River. Turn right onto 108th Street and then left onto Ballarat Avenue to reach North Bend Way, the town of North Bend's main street. Turn right and head for the Mar-T. After your pie, just head down North Bend Boulevard to return to your car.

ROCK CLIMBING

There are several areas along I-90 that offer good climbing and a wide variety of routes. **Little Si,** the diminutive peak adjacent to the ever-popular Mount Si, is a couple of miles up a hiking trail and offers climbing on good metamorphic rock known for its big rhino jug handholds. To reach Little Si, take exit 31 off I-90, turn left at the end of the ramp, go 0.75 miles to a stoplight, turn right onto North Bend Way, continue 1.25 miles, turn left on Mount Si Road, cross a bridge in a half-mile, and turn left into the trailhead parking lot.

Another favorite climbing spot in the area, known simply as **Exit 38,** is, you guessed it, at exit 38 off I-90. To reach these walls, take a right at the bottom of the ramp (if you're coming from the east) and go about a half-mile to a metal barrier on the right. Park here, and follow the trail for half a mile to the first wall, which has some good 5.6 to 5.11 climbs. After you've done these climbs, you can continue around the wall to the right to the top of the train trestle, where there are more climbs possible.

SEA KAYAKING & FLAT-WATER CANOEING

Cooper Lake, located 21 miles northwest of Roslyn (the town that doubled as Cicely, Alaska, on the TV show *Northern Exposure*), is one of the only lakes in the area that is both accessible and restricted to nonmotorized boats. For this reason, it has become a magnet for canoeists and sea kayakers. The lake's walk-in campground fills up early on weekends and almost every campsite has a boat or two beside its tents. What makes this lake so appealing other than its lack of motorboats are its clear waters, horsetail marshes, and forested shoreline. However, it is the view that makes Cooper Lake truly memorable. Lying just northwest of the lake are the crags of Chikamin Peak and Lemah Peak, which are within the Alpine Lakes Wilderness. At the far end of the river from the campground, the Cooper River can be explored upstream a little ways. However, don't even think about paddling down the Cooper River from here; not too far downstream, the river plunges over an unrunnable waterfall (below this waterfall, however, whitewater kayakers do challenge the whitewater). There are a few primitive campsites on the far side of the river if the walk-in campground is just too crowded for your tastes. This lake is a true gem!

To reach Cooper Lake, take exit 80 off I-90, drive through Roslyn, and continue 15 miles (passing Cle Elum Lake) to a left turn onto FS 46 (Cooper Lake Road). Continue on this road for 4.5 miles to a right turn down to Cooper Lake and the Owhi Campground, where there is easy access to the water.

Although far more popular with powerboats, the three large dammed lakes of the Snoqualmie Pass area—Keechelus Lake, Kachess Lake, and Cle Elum Lake—also see their share of paddlers. **Keechelus Lake** is the most easily accessible, with a boat ramp near the Hyak ski area at the north end of the lake. However, the presence of I-90 along the lake detracts considerably from its appeal. **Kachess Lake,** when full, is the nicest and has a large campground on its northwest shore. **Cle Elum Lake** is the most distant from Seattle, but also has campgrounds. However, anyone driving this far usually continues to Cooper Lake. **Lake Easton,** a small lake just south of Kachess Lake and adjacent to I-90, is perhaps more interesting than the larger lakes. Lake Easton State Park provides access to the lake. On the three larger lakes, afternoon winds are a problem. It's best to plan your paddling for the morning hours.

SNOWSHOEING

On winter weekends, the Forest Service leads easy and informative snowshoe nature walks at Snoqualmie Pass. The fee for these walks is $10, which includes snowshoe rentals. To find out when these walks are scheduled, stop in at the Snoqualmie Pass Visitor Information Center (tel. 206/434-6111). Any of the sno-parks in the area also offer access to good snowshoeing; just remember to stay out of groomed ski tracks. The Gold Creek Sno-Park, because of the variety of terrain available, is about the best place to access some easy snowshoeing.

SWIMMING & TUBING

On the Snoqualmie River above Snoqualmie Falls, there is a swimming hole at a bend in the river beside the **Reinig Sycamore Corridor.** To reach this spot, take Wash. 202 to the southern outskirts of Snoqualmie, turn north on Meadowbrook Way, cross the river, turn right on Mill Pond Road, then right again onto Reinig Road, and park in the pull-out on the right. A trail leads down to the water. Don't worry—you're still a long way from the falls at this point. Below the falls, there is a comparable swimming hole just above the **Plum's Landing** boat launch at the junction of Fish Hatchery Road and 372nd Avenue. Unfortunately, this is a Department of Game parking lot for which you'll need a parking permit. If you don't have a permit, park at the boat ramp and walk up Fish Hatchery Road.

The most popular summer swimming hole in this area is the **Denny Creek waterslide,** a natural, water-smooth slab of granite over which flow the cold waters of Denny Creek. The waterslide is 1 mile up the trail from the parking lot and is packed with screaming kids on summer days, when children by the busload are brought in to enjoy this blissful corner of the wilderness. If you can hit this place on an uncrowded weekday afternoon, it is nice for cooling off. However, if cars fill the parking area, you might want to skip it and head over the pass to **Lake Easton State Park,** where you'll find a beach with more room for the crowds.

Northwest of the town of Roslyn, there are several places where people cool off in the summer. The **Cle Elum River** above Cle Elum Lake is a favorite for tubing and casual rafting, while **Cle Elum Lake** itself also offers a much larger body of water for you to swim in if you can handle the cold water. Above Cle Elum Lake, the small **Cooper Lake,** on which no motorboats are allowed, is another good choice for a quick, chilly dip.

The most popular splashy playground in the area is the **Yakima River.** Where it flows through the Yakima River Gorge it is restricted to nonmotorized boats, which makes it popular with tubers, rafters, and canoeists. Raft rentals are available from **River Raft Rentals,** 9801 Hwy. 10, Ellensburg (tel. 509/964-2145).

WALKS & NATURAL ROADSIDE ATTRACTIONS

Snoqualmie Falls

1 mile round-trip. Easy. 300-foot elevation gain. Access: Take exit 27 and follow signs to the falls.

Oohing and aahing out-of-state relatives being chauffeured around the region by lucky residents are the mainstay of visitors to this impressive waterfall outside North Bend. But with a luxury resort hotel at the top of the falls, there are also those stressed-out executive types hanging around on the weekends. Whether or not you fit into either of these categories, you should be sure to stop and have a look, and if you were a fan of *Twin Peaks,* then it's déjà vu time.

Twin Falls State Park

3 miles round-trip. Easy. 500-foot elevation gain. Access: Take exit 34 off I-90, go south on Edgewick Rd., and in a half-mile, turn left onto SE 159th St. The trailhead is in 0.75 miles at the end of this road. Map: Trailhead map.

A 1.5-mile trail along the South Fork Snoqualmie River leads from the parking lot to this impressive pair of waterfalls. A footbridge crosses the river between the two falls, while a separate short trail leads to an observation deck below the lower falls. The trail continues past the falls for another 1 mile to connect with the John Wayne Trail in Iron Horse State Park.

Asahel Curtis Nature Trail

1.25-mile loop. Easy. 80-foot elevation gain. Access: Take exit 47 off I-90, turn right at the stop sign, turn left onto FS 55, and continue a half-mile to the trailhead parking lot. Map: Trailhead map.

This short interpretive trail leads through one of the last groves of old-growth Douglas fir trees in the Snoqualmie Valley. The trail makes a quick introduction to the Northwest's ancient forests. On the dark forest floor, orchids, ferns, mosses, and other wildflowers can be seen in the late spring. You might also see pileated woodpeckers or winter wrens, depending on the time of year.

WHITEWATER KAYAKING & CANOEING

CLASS I

On the west side of I-90, the **Snoqualmie River** provides some fun Class I paddling above the famous Snoqualmie Falls. This 4.25-mile stretch of river moves fairly quickly most of the time, and there are some gravel bars and sweepers to negotiate, which adds a bit of a challenge. The view of Mount Si from the put-in is superb. This run can be done any time of year. To reach the take-out, drive to Snoqualmie Falls outside Fall City. From the falls, drive south on Wash. 202, and just past Salish Lodge, turn left onto Mill Pond Road, which very soon is right beside the river. To reach the put-in, continue in the same direction on Mill Pond Road, and turn right on Reinig Road. When this road comes to an end at a T intersection, turn right, cross a bridge over the North Fork Snoqualmie River, and then, just before crossing the second bridge, turn left onto an abandoned road. Park your car and haul your boat 200 feet down a wide trail beside the bridge.

On the east side of Snoqualmie Pass, the **Yakima River** provides an entirely different sort of experience. This river flows through a deep basalt-walled canyon between Ellensburg and Yakima, and most of the land is public. Although Wash. 821 parallels the river the entire way, this 17-mile run has a wonderfully remote feel to it. The abundant sunshine in the summer gives it a classic western feel. The water moves swiftly through the Yakima River Canyon, but stays in the Class I to I+ range, perfect for novice paddlers and canoeists in search of a scenic and relaxing day's paddle. The take-out is at the Roza recreation site, 7 miles north of I-82 on Wash. 821. To reach the put-in, continue north on Wash. 821 for 17 miles to Ringer Road, where there is a boat launch. There are also many other boat launch sites along the river if you want a shorter run. Late spring and early summer are the best times to do this run.

CLASS II

The I-90 corridor is a beginning and intermediate kayakers' wonderland. Nowhere else in the state are there so many Class II stretches of river in such close proximity. Starting on the west side, the first, most convenient, and perhaps most popular run is the **Powerhouse Run on the Snoqualmie River** below Snoqualmie Falls. This run is only 1 mile long, but it's such a blast that paddlers just do it over and over throughout the day. Best of all, the flow is regulated, which means this run can be done any time of year. However, it is at its most popular in the late summer when just about every other river on the west side of the Cascades is too low. To reach the take-out at the Plum's Landing boat ramp on Fish Hatchery Road, take Wash. 202 out of Fall City heading toward Snoqualmie Falls. After 1 mile, turn right on Fish Hatchery Road and continue 1.5 miles to the boat ramp. To reach the put-in, continue upstream less than 1 mile on Fish Hatchery Road and park outside the powerhouse fence, which is at the base of a trail from the top of Snoqualmie Falls.

The Snoqualmie River has three forks—the North, Middle, and South—and of these, the South and Middle forks have good Class II runs. The most accessible is the **North Bend Middle Fork run.** This 4.5-mile run is pretty straightforward and offers novice paddlers a chance to work on their basic skills. The take-out is on Ballarat Road north of downtown North Bend off North Bend Way. The put-in is at the bridge on Tanner Road, which is off North Bend Way at the east end of North Bend. The **upper Middle Fork run** is the most scenic of the runs in the area and has the greatest sense of wilderness. This run covers about 7.5 miles of river. The put-in is 10 miles or so up the Middle Fork Road (FS 56) at the Taylor River, and the take-out is 5 miles out of North Bend at a concrete bridge. To reach Middle Fork Road, go north on 140th Street at the east end of North Bend. The **South Fork run** starts not far out of North Bend and covers less than 4 miles. This run offers lots of good play waves, boulder gardens, and eddy hopping. There is also a weir toward the end of the run that should be scouted. To reach the take-out, take exit 32 off I-90, go right on 436th Avenue, and continue about a half-mile. To reach the put-in, take I-90 east to exit 34, go south on Edgewick Road, turn left in a half-mile, and continue a half-mile to Twin Falls State Park.

On the east side of Snoqualmie Pass, there is good Class II paddling on the Cle Elum and Yakima rivers. Although the Yakima Canyon section of the **Yakima River** is by far the more popular run on this river, the 14-mile stretch from the Teanaway River to near the town of Thorp offers much more lively water with lots of fun Class II water. The dry east-side scenery is a welcome switch from the dark, forested runs of the west side. The take-out is on Wash. 10 about 4 miles west of the junction with U.S. 97 (west of Ellensburg) and above a diversion dam. The put-in is also on Wash. 10 and is less than a half-mile downstream from the mouth of the Teanaway River. This is a good late spring or early summer run.

For a fun weekend camping and kayaking trip, head over to Salmon la Sac Campground on the **Cle Elum River** northwest of Roslyn on Wash. 903. The 4-mile run from the campground down to Cle Elum Lake is a lot of fun and can be run several times in a day. Once you've mastered this run, you can move upstream to more difficult waters. There are two other campgrounds along the river downstream from Salmon la Sac and plenty of open camping as well.

CLASS III
Both the **North Fork Snoqualmie River** and **Middle Fork Snoqualmie River** have Class III runs, but both have problems. The run on the North Fork starts on private forest lands and is often inaccessible due to a locked gate. The Middle Fork run is more accessible, but has a monster Class IV rapid in the middle of the run and consequently is best run only by paddlers with Class IV experience (or who are ready to have their first). This latter run is downstream of the upper Middle Fork Class II run mentioned above.

CLASS IV & ABOVE
If you're looking for some challenging Class IV whitewater, the **Cle Elum River** upstream of Salmon la Sac Campground is your best bet on the east side of Snoqualmie Pass. The river is paralleled by FS 4330 for more than 8 miles, providing ample put-in and take-out opportunities. The biggest challenge on this run is Triple Falls, a trio of 6-foot-high waterfalls about 3 miles into the run. To reach Salmon la Sac, drive to Roslyn and continue on Wash. 903 to the campground. The rapids beside the campground are the site of an annual kayak slalom competition. If you're good enough to push the outer limits of runnability, there is also a 1.5-mile, Class V run on the nearby Cooper River. The put-in is below a 50-foot waterfall and the run is a nonstop adrenaline rush through a steep, rocky gorge.

WHITEWATER RAFTING

This area doesn't have any rivers that are run by commercial rafting companies. However, the **Yakima River Canyon** is a popular spot for a leisurely float on Class I waters. There are numerous river access points along Wash. 821, which parallels the river from just south of Ellensburg to just north of Yakima. The favorite float is

from the boat launch 5 miles south of Ellensburg down to the Roza Dam. Along this stretch of river, basalt cliff walls rise up from the water. If you're interested in rafting here, you can rent rafts from **Richies River Rentals** (tel. 509/453-2112).

WILDLIFE VIEWING

If you'd like to catch a glimpse of spawning **kokanee salmon,** which turn a bright red during the September-to-October spawning season, stop at **Gold Creek Pond** just off I-90 at the north end of Keechelus Lake. An interpretive trail and viewing areas have been built along the stream bank near the pond so that the fish can be easily observed.

In the **Yakima Canyon,** south of Ellensburg on Wash. 821, sharp-eyed visitors may be able to spot **California bighorn sheep** on Manastash Ridge, which forms the northern gateway to the canyon.

Campgrounds & Other Accommodations

CAMPING

A certain percentage of campsites at many National Forest Service campgrounds can be reserved at least five days in advance by calling the **National Forest Reservation Service** (tel. 800/280-CAMP). To make a reservation you'll need to know the name of the campground you want to stay at and the dates you plan to visit. The reservation fee is $7.50.

ALONG U.S. 2
There are only a few campgrounds along U.S. 2 on the west side of Stevens Pass. Any of these make good choices if you are here to do some kayaking on the Skykomish River. The first campground that you'll come to is at **Wallace Falls State Park** (6 campsites), north of Gold Bar. Farther east are **Money Creek** (21 campsites) and **Beckler River** (27 campsites), near the town of Skykomish. Up the North Fork of the Skykomish River is **Troublesome**

Creek (25 campsites), a campground particularly popular with whitewater kayakers.

The Lake Wenatchee area is one of the most popular summer camping destinations in the state and there are lots of choices in the area. If you want creature comforts (hot showers) stay at **Lake Wenatchee State Park** (197 campsites), which is at the south end of the lake. This campground has a sandy beach and a great view up the lake. Farther up the south shore of the lake, the Forest Service's **Glacier View Campground** (20 campsites) provides a similar lakeside atmosphere with walk-in campsites. Right outside the entrance to the state park, you'll find the **Nason Creek Campground** (68 campsites), which has some nice sites right on this large creek. Northwest of Lake Wenatchee, there are several campgrounds along both the White River and the Little Wenatchee River. These include **Napeequa** (5 campsites), **Grasshopper Meadows** (3 campsites), and **White River Falls** (5 campsites) on the White River, and **Soda Springs** (5 campsites), **Lake Creek** (8 campsites), **Little Wenatchee Ford** (3 campsites), and **Theseus Creek** (3 campsites) on the Little Wenatchee River. Any of these makes a good base for hikes in the Glacier Peak Wilderness, mountain biking in the Chikamin Ridge area, or paddling on the White River of Lake Wenatchee.

In the Leavenworth area, **Tumwater Campground** (80 campsites) is the biggest campground, and though it is right on the bank of the Wenatchee River, the proximity to U.S. 2 means it gets some traffic noise and is always full on weekends. Up Icicle Road on the west side of Leavenworth, there are six campgrounds. These include (in the order of their proximity to Leavenworth) **Eightmile** (25 campsites), **Bridge Creek** (6 campsites), **Johnny Creek** (16 campsites), **Ida Creek** (10 campsites), **Chatter Creek** (12 campsites), and **Rock Island** (22 campsites). Eightmile is the closest to the Enchantment Lakes trailhead if that is where you are heading. Chatter Creek is a good choice if you want to do day hikes into the Alpine Lakes Wilderness.

ALONG I-90

Along the I-90 corridor, there are only a couple of campground choices on the west side of Snoqualmie Pass. **Tinkham Campground** (47 campsites) at exit 42 off I-90 is the closest Forest Service campground to Seattle. It is set on the bank of the South Fork Snoqualmie River, but has only 5 campsites right on the river. Tinkham is quieter than nearby **Denny Creek Campground** (39 campsites), which is so close to the freeway that campers are lulled to sleep by the roaring of trucks. However, it is a nice forest campground with sites on the creek. Over Snoqualmie Pass there are a couple of campgrounds that are so close to the freeway that they should be considered only in emergencies. **Crystal Springs** (30 campsites) is definitely for emergencies only, and **Lake Easton State Park** (140 campsites) has more amenities, including a swimming beach, but noise is still a problem.

Kachess Campground (180 campsites), near the north end of Kachess Lake, is the biggest and most popular campground in the area. Powerboating and fishing are the most popular activities here, but there are also some nearby trailheads providing access to the Alpine Lakes Wilderness. The Cle Elum Lake area offers the I-90 corridor's greatest concentration of campgrounds. **Wish Poosh** (39 campsites) is set on a marshy area on the bank of the lake, while the **Cle Elum River Campground** (35 campsites) is right where the Cle Elum River flows into the lake. **Red Mountain** (9 campsites) is a little farther up the river. **Salmon La Sac** (112 campsites) is this area's biggest and busiest campground and is also on the bank of the Cle Elum River. These latter two campgrounds are particularly popular with whitewater kayakers. **Owhi Campground** (23 campsites), on Cooper Lake 4.7 miles up FS 46 from Salmon la Sac Road, is my favorite area campground. All the sites are walk-ins and are close to the shore of the lake. No motors are allowed on this lake, which makes this campground very popular with canoeists and sea kayakers. To reach the campgrounds in the Cle Elum Lake area, take the Roslyn exit (exit 80) off I-90, drive north to the stop sign, and turn left on Wash. 903.

INNS & LODGES

ALONG U.S. 2

Bush House Country Inn

300 Fifth St. (P.O. Box 359), Index, WA 98256. Tel. 800/428-BUSH or 360/793-2312. Fax 360/793-3673. 11 rms (all with shared baths). $59–$80 double. MC, V.

Purchased recently by a member of the famous Nordstrom department-store family, this historic lodge is a quiet and out-of-the-way spot for a weekend retreat. The lodge makes a good base if you are here to do some hiking, whitewater kayaking, downhill skiing, or rock climbing. Antique furniture reflects the inn's heritage, but the overabundance of stuffed animals doesn't quite seem the style of the folks who frequent this neck of the woods.

Run of the River Bed & Breakfast

9308 E Leavenworth Rd. (P.O. Box 285), Leavenworth, WA 98826. Tel. 800/288-6491 or 509/548-7171. 6 rms. $90–$140 double. AE, DISC, MC, V.

This log house on 2 acres outside of Leavenworth is one of the Northwest's most tranquil B&Bs. Set on the banks of the Icicle River, the view is as soul satisfying as they come. Step through the front door and you enter a house full of bare wood, hand-hewn log furniture, and exposed stones (both in the fireplaces and entry floor). Upstairs guest rooms have lofts that are great spaces for a bit of quiet reading, but for a moment of solitude, the log porch swings just can't be beat. Novice bird watchers will appreciate the binoculars in every room, and bicycling, hiking, and cross-country skiing maps are available.

ALONG I-90

Salish Lodge

37807 SE Fall City–Snoqualmie Rd. (P.O. Box 1109), Snoqualmie, WA 98065. Tel. 800/826-6124 or 206/888-2556. 91 rms, 4 suites. $165–$295 double; $500–$575 suite. AE, CB, DC, DISC, MC, V.

Set at the top of 270-foot Snoqualmie Falls and only 35 minutes east of Seattle on I-90, Salish Lodge is a popular weekend getaway spot for folks from Seattle. With its country lodge atmosphere, the Salish aims for casual comfort and hits the mark. Guest rooms are furnished with wicker and Shaker furnishings and have down comforters on the beds. With fireplaces and whirlpool baths in every room, this lodge is made for romantic weekend getaways, but does nicely as a base for hikes and bike rides in the area.

7

THE MOUNT RAINIER &
MOUNT ST. HELENS AREAS

MOUNT RAINIER NATIONAL PARK AND MOUNT ST. HELENS National Volcanic Monument are two of Washington State's biggest tourist attractions. On summer weekends busloads of tourists descend on these two mountains, camcorders whirring and cameras clicking. Stuck trying to find a parking space at Paradise on Mount Rainier or at Coldwater Ridge on Mount St. Helens, you can easily begin to wonder why you even bothered coming. Who wants to deal with parking problems and traffic jams in the mountains after dealing with commuter traffic all week? But beyond the designated viewpoints, beyond the last NO PARK-ING signs, beyond the visitor centers where people crowd around videos to "experience" the mountain outside, there lie two mountains that together sum up the past, the present, and the future of the Cascades. For anyone willing to expend a little energy to get away from the roadside crowds, these mountains have secrets to share—mountain goats and marmots, steaming waterfalls in fields of ash and ominous walls of ice deep in the rain forest, instant canyons and buried lakes, prostrate forests and thousand-year-old giants.

Despite what you might think, should you visit on a dreary October day, Mount Rainier was not named for its climatological proclivities. It was named in 1792 by Captain George Vancouver for Rear Admiral Peter Rainier, a man who never even laid eyes on this peak. Mount Rainier had for centuries been known as *Takhoma* or *Tahoma* by local Native American tribes. (Today that name is affixed not to this majestic peak but to a city roundly vilified for its industrial sprawl—Tacoma.) Although these early peoples feared the snowy heights of this mountain, on its flanks they hunted deer, elk, and mountain goats and gathered huckleberries. Today's Puget Sound residents see Mount Rainier as a symbol of the wild Northwest, a land that lies within easy reach. On sunny days when, as they say in Seattle, "The mountain is out," Mount Rainier is a constant reassurance of the beauty that lies beyond the sprawl of suburbia.

While most mountains of the West were seen only as obstacles by pioneers, 14,411-foot Mount Rainier so captivated early settlers in the Puget Sound area that as early as the 1850s, less than a decade after Seattle was founded, aspiring mountaineers were heading for its snow-clad slopes in hopes of conquering this majestic mountain. In 1857, an army lieutenant, August Valentine Kautz, made it to within 400 feet of the summit, and in 1870, General Hazard Stevens and Philemon Van Trump made the first recorded ascent of the mountain (trapped near the summit at dark, they survived the night huddled in ice caves formed by sulfurous steam vents that kept the air temperature near 170°F). In 1884, James and Martha Longmire opened the mountain's first hotel, the Mineral Springs Resort, at a spot that now bears their name. In 1899, Mount Rainier became the nation's fifth national park, and by 1916, the trail system now known as the Wonderland Trail was completed, forming a loop nearly 100 miles long around the mountain.

Because of its massive system of glaciers and unpredictable weather, Mount Rainier is an unforgiving peak. Many climbers have died on its slopes, yet each year more than 8,000 climbers set out for the summit of this dormant volcano. However, only about 4,500 ever reach the top of this peak. The rest are turned back by bad weather, altitude sickness, exhaustion, and hazardous glacier crossings. This is not a mountain to be treated lightly, and because of its reputation for difficulty, it often serves as a training ground for climbers planning expeditions to other famous peaks around the world.

Although Mount Rainier is a magnet for climbers, these adventurers make up only a tiny fraction of the 2 million visitors who come to the park each year. This mountain is really all about hiking through alpine meadows, and that is the main activity pursued by the vast majority of park visitors, most of whom visit during the short summer season that lasts only from July to September in the higher elevations.

According to local legend, Martha Longmire, who helped found the first hotel in the area, exclaimed, "It looks just like paradise," upon her first visit to the subalpine meadows that now bear that name. It is these meadows, now the site of the seasonal Paradise Lodge and the Henry M. Jackson Memorial Visitor Center, that are the most popular spot in the park. Wildflowers color the slopes here, and the vast bulk of the mountain rises so steeply overhead that it is necessary to strain one's neck to gaze up at the summit. On a sunny summer weekend, it is sometimes necessary to park more than a mile away from Paradise and walk up, on forest trails or along the road, to the meadows.

To understand how enamored of Mount Rainier were early Northwest residents, it is only necessary to look at the names that were affixed to the mountain's topography. Of course, there are many memorial names, including the Kautz and Van Trump glaciers. However, these are to be expected on a mountain that has been attracting climbers for more than a century. There are other names that truly reflect the beauty of this mountain: Paradise, Sunrise, Wonderland Trail, Reflection Lakes, Sunset Amphitheater, Fairy Falls, Sunbeam Creek, Mount Wow, Elysian Fields, Summerland, Grand Park. Seeing names such as these on a map, how can a hiker not long to explore this landscape? Do the Elysian Fields live up to their name? Is Paradise really a paradise? There's only one way to find out—by pulling on those hiking boots and hitting the trail.

While Mount Rainier clings to its legendary beauty, seeming never to age, nearby Mount St. Helens (8,366 feet) has become a freak of nature. People come to marvel at its ugliness, but once upon a time, Mount St. Helens was the queen of Cascade peaks, as beautiful, say oldtimers, as Japan's famous Fujiyama. But when, on May 18, 1980, this volcano blew its top, people turned their backs on the once-beautiful mountain. They went elsewhere to do their hiking, they found other lakes and rivers to fish, and they kicked their crampons into snowfields on other summits. Mount St. Helens became a mountain to be ogled from the safety of an overlook parking lot, but not something to be explored on foot. After being declared a national volcanic monument, these noninteractive visits were encouraged by the monument's management through the construction of roads and visitor centers, but few trails.

Slowly but surely this is changing. In the years since the 1980 eruption, new trails have been built. Climbing to the rim of the crater that now serves as the summit for Mount St. Helens has become a Northwest must for hikers. Trails through the blast zone now provide a backcountry glimpse into the awesome power of nature, while older trails through alpine flower gardens reveal the

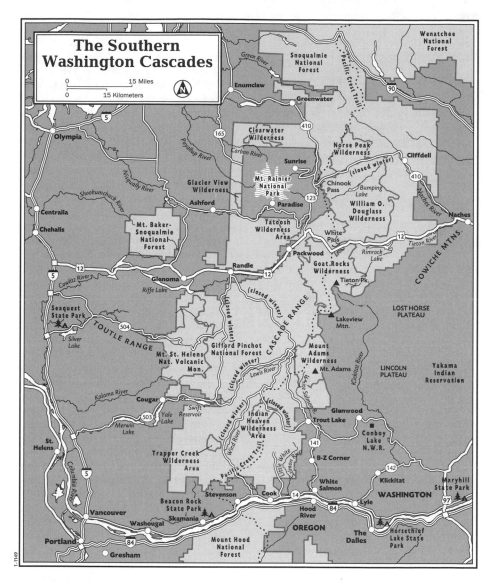

The Southern Washington Cascades

0   15 Miles
0   15 Kilometers

mountain's pre-eruption beauty. Beauty and the beast now coexist side by side on Mount St. Helens, with the north side showing the mountain's more violent character and the south side remaining relatively unchanged.

Surrounding the national park and the national monument are three different national forests—Mount Baker–Snoqualmie, Wenatchee, and Gifford Pinchot. Within these national forests are seven wilderness areas and thousands of miles of logging roads and trails. Although the wilderness areas do attract their share of hikers, it is primarily to Mount Rainier and Mount St. Helens that both day hikers and backpackers head for dramatic scenery. On the other

hand, it is outside the park and the monument that mountain bikers, anglers, skiers, and kayakers find places to play. Whatever your preferred sport or sports, you're likely to find plenty of opportunities for pursuit within this region of volcanic peaks.

The Lay of the Land

Mount Rainier and Mount St. Helens lie toward the southern end of the Washington Cascades. Here, the crags of the North Cascades are replaced by a volcanic landscape of rolling green hills punctuated by Rainier and St. Helens and, to the east,

> "Every one of these parks, great and small, is a garden filled knee-deep with fresh, lovely flowers of every hue, the most luxuriant and the most extravagantly beautiful of all the alpine gardens I have beheld."
>
> —John Muir, after a visit to Mount Rainier in 1888

two other volcanic landmarks—Mount Adams and the Goat Rocks—the latter but a remnant of an ancient volcano, and the former, a snowcone as impressive as Mount Rainier (see chapter 8 for details on Mount Adams, which is most readily accessible from its south side). Although Mount Rainier National Park and Mount St. Helens National Volcanic Monument comprise only a small area of this region, they are by far the most interesting landmarks and consequently dominate outdoor activities in the same way that they dominate the horizons.

With four separate entrances, 378-square-mile Mount Rainier National Park is served by four different state highways. **Wash. 410** leads to the northeast corner of the park before continuing eastward to Yakima along the bank of the Naches River. This highway provides access to Sunrise via the White River park entrance in the summer, but by winter is closed at the turnoff for the popular Crystal Mountain ski area. Although this is the most direct access to the national park from the Seattle area, it is not the most popular entrance. **Wash. 706,** which leads to the Nisqually park entrance, is the busiest route into the park. This is due to the fact that it provides the quickest access to the Paradise area, which is the most beautiful and popular road-accessible spot in the park. In the southeast corner of the park, **Wash. 123,** which leaves U.S. 12 northeast of Packwood, provides access to the Ohanapecosh Campground and the Stevens Canyon entrance to the park. This highway is closed in the winter. In the

northwest corner of the park, **Wash. 165** leads southwest from Wash. 410 to the Carbon River entrance and also provides access to Mowich Lake.

Likewise, there are several routes to Mount St. Helens National Volcanic Monument. The main tourist route is up **Wash. 504,** the Spirit Lake Highway, which leads past no less than five visitor centers, three of which are operated by the national monument. This highway leaves I-5 at Castle Rock and leads west into the heart of the blast zone on the north side of the mountain. **Wash. 503,** which leaves I-5 at Woodland, leads to the south side of the monument. This highway provides access to a variety of hiking trails in the summer, cross-country ski trails in winter, and the main climbing routes to the summit of the volcano. Connecting Wash. 503 on the south side of the park with U.S. 12 on the north side of the park are a network of forest service roads (**FS 90, FS 25,** and **FS 99**), which together provide access to some of the most spectacular regions of the park, including several trails that lead into the blast zone.

Running east to west between the park and the monument is **U.S. 12,** one of the few year-round highways through the Cascades. This highway not only provides easy access to both Mount Rainier and Mount St. Helens, but it also leads to the White Pass ski area and is paralleled by the Cowlitz River on the west side and by the Tieton River on the east side. Flanking this highway east of Mount Rainier are the William O. Douglas and Goat Rocks wildernesses.

Morton, Randle, and **Packwood,** three of the largest towns in the area, are found along this highway. Throughout this entire region, there are but a smattering of towns, most of which are timber-dependent mill towns. Different from so many other national parks around the country, no tourist blitzkriegs have sprung up to separate vacationers from their cash. **Ashford,** outside the Nisqually entrance at the southwest corner of Mount Rainier National Park, is the closest thing there is to a tourist town around here. A few motels, some cabins, and a couple of rustic restaurants are all you'll find. There's not a McDonald's in sight. This lack of tourist infrastructure stems from the fact that most people visit Mount Rainier (and Mount St. Helens as well) on a day trip from Seattle or Portland.

It is said that Mount Rainier makes its own weather, and more often than not, it isn't what people consider good weather. Because it rises more than 1 mile above the surrounding landscape, Mount Rainier interrupts the eastward flow of moisture-laden air that comes in off the Pacific Ocean. Forced upward into colder altitudes, this moist air dumps its load of water on the mountain. At lower elevations on the west side, this moisture falls as rain, which creates a rain forest in the Carbon River valley. However, at higher elevations, the mountain's precipitation is in the form of snow. On average, more than 620 inches of snow fall each winter on Mount Rainier, but in the winter of 1971–72, 1,122 inches (93.5 feet) of snow was recorded at Paradise, setting a world annual snowfall record.

Such massive amounts of snowfall are the reason that Mount Rainier is the single most glaciated mountain in the contiguous 48 states. So much snow falls each winter that it cannot all melt over the short months of summer. Each year the snow accumulates, eventually compressing into ice that adds to the mountain's glaciers. There are 26 named glaciers on Mount Rainier and another 50 unnamed ones. Among these are the largest (Emmons) and the lowest (Carbon) in the U.S. south of Alaska.

These glaciers in turn feed half a dozen rivers. The **Muddy Fork** of the **Cowlitz River** and the **White River** take their names from the color that glacial flour (silt) imparts to them. Fortunately, the **Carbon River** is not as black as its name implies. This river instead takes its name from the coal deposits found in the area. The **Nisqually,** the **Puyallup,** and the Cowlitz all retain names given to them centuries ago by the region's Native American tribes. All of these rivers eventually flow westward to the Puget Sound, with the exception of the Cowlitz, which flows into the Columbia River. The **Tieton**

and **Naches** rivers and their tributaries, all of which have their sources to the east of the national park, flow eastward, descending from lush mountain forests into the dry lands of the eastern slopes of the Cascades.

Even before it lost its topmost 1,300 feet, Mount St. Helens was not a tall mountain in comparison to its volcanic neighbors. At 9,677 feet tall, this mountain had only small glaciers on its slopes. However, elevation alone did not account for this lack of glaciation. Mount St. Helens was for the most part such a young volcano that its upper slopes had not even existed during the last ice age. Had this mountain's glaciers been larger, the mudflows that swept down the Toutle River might have been far more devastating than they were.

"It was a big brown cat with a long tail," she was explaining excitedly to her husband as I walked past. "It just walked off across that hillside." I was hiking the Skyline Trail above Paradise at the time, and I found it hard to believe that a cougar could have just walked in broad daylight across an area in which several hundred hikers were wandering. However, in a national park, where animals need not fear death from humans, you never know. Yes, cougars live within this park, as do black bears, but neither is seen very often. Much more commonly spotted large mammals are the park's deer, elk, and mountain goats. Deer, mostly black-tailed, are the most frequently spotted and can be seen along any of the park's roads and on trails from the lowland river valleys up to the subalpine meadow country. Elk, much larger and more majestic in stature, are less in evidence than the deer, but can sometimes be seen in the Sunrise area in the summer and throughout the eastern regions of the park during the autumn. Mountain goats, which are actually not goats but a long-haired relative of antelopes, keep to the rocky slopes of alpine and subalpine meadows during the summer.

Perhaps the most entertaining and enviable of the park's wild residents are its marmots. These largest members of the squirrel family spend their days nibbling wildflowers in subalpine meadows, and stretching out on rocks to bask in the sun. In meadows throughout the park, these bloated sybarites seem oblivious to human presence, contentedly grazing only steps away from hikers.

Marmots share these subalpine zones with pikas, tiny relatives of rabbits, that are more often heard than seen. Living among the jumbled rocks of talus slopes, pikas skitter about their rocky domains calling out warnings with a high-pitched beep that is surprisingly electronic in tone.

Even unexpected wildlife sometimes pops up to surprise visitors to Mount Rainier. While paddling our canoe around Mowich Lake once, my wife and I found ourselves being closely observed by a curious river otter. After losing interest in us, the otter ducked back under the surface of the lake, and we watched its torpedo-like body disappear into the dark depths.

Monkeyflowers, elephant's heads, parrot's beaks, bear grass—this grass menagerie represents just a small fraction of the variety of wildlowers to be found on the slopes of Mount Rainier. This mountain's subalpine meadows are among the most celebrated in the Northwest. Bold swaths of color sweep across these mountainsides each summer as the white of snow melts away to once again reveal the greenery that lies hidden most months of the year. Although not as colorfully named as the flowers mentioned above, lupines, asters, gentians, avalanche lilies, phlox, heather, and Indian paintbrush all add their own distinctive splashes of color to these slopes. About the only thing more impressive than the flowers on Mount Rainier is the array of photographic equipment lugged out onto trails for capturing the floral displays on film.

The meadows at Paradise are much wetter than those at Sunrise, which lies in a rain-shadow zone and consequently is relatively dry. In the northwest corner of the park, the Carbon River valley opens out toward the Pacific Ocean and channels moisture-laden air into its depths. As a result, this valley is a rain forest where tree limbs are draped with mosses and lichens, and Douglas firs and western red cedars grow to enormous proportions. However, it is in the southwest corner of the park,

in the Grove of the Patriarchs near the Stevens Canyon park entrance, that some of the oldest trees stand—Douglas firs more than 1,000 years old and western red cedars more than 25 feet in circumference.

Mount St. Helens lies only 50 miles southwest of Mount Rainier, across a vast expanse of clear-cuts that, so the story goes, President Carter mistook for the work of the volcano when he made a fly-over inspection of the region in the wake of the eruption. These forests are among those at the heart of the battle to preserve the last old-growth forests of the Northwest. Little of this land is protected in wilderness areas, and logging roads now lace a landscape once considered the most likely holdout of the elusive bigfoot.

The statistics surrounding the eruption of Mount St. Helens are mind-boggling. More than 540 million tons of ash spewed forth from St. Helens and eventually fell over 22,000 square miles of land. Ash was detected as far away as Denver, Colorado. Before the eruption, Mount St. Helens had remained draped in snow and glacial ice throughout the year, but when the eruption was over, 70% of this frozen water was gone, sent down the mountain's slopes as a slurry of earth and water traveling at up to 80 miles per hour.

This massive debris flow was caused in part by the massive landslide that triggered the eruption. The slide moved roughly two-thirds of a cubic mile of earth, much of which fell into Spirit Lake, causing a huge wave that splashed 800 feet up the opposite shore of the lake. When the earth had settled into place, Spirit Lake was as much as 250 feet higher than it once was, and former resorts were buried beneath this massive slide. A square mile of blast-killed trees now covers the surface of the lake.

The speed at which the landslide moved was dawdling compared to the 670 miles per hour at which the blast itself traveled. Equivalent in power to 21,000 nuclear bombs of the size that was dropped on Hiroshima, the blast leveled 150 square miles of forest. Millions of trees now lie like giant toothpicks bleaching in the sun where they fell. Their angle of repose points away from the blast's origin and serves as a blueprint of the blast's progress. In some places trees still stand, not knocked over by the blast but simply cooked in place by air at approximately 500° F. In other places, patches of forest actually survived the blast, protected by ridgelines that deflected the fury of the fiery winds.

One of the strangest phenomena surrounding the eruption of Mount St. Helens was the cone of silence around the volcano when it erupted. So violent and so sudden was the eruption that sound waves blasted upward and outward. For up to 60 miles around, the eruption occurred without a sound. However, 150 to 200 miles away a window-shaking boom was heard, and as far away as 690 miles, people could still hear the sound of the volcano's blast.

Since 1980, flora and fauna have slowly been recolonizing the ash-covered slopes of Mount St. Helens. Most majestic of the park's residents is the herd of elk that has taken up residence in the mudflat meadows in the valley of the North Fork Toutle River. In mountain streams, trout managed to survive the blast by swimming from one pool of cool water to the next, and Coldwater Lake, which didn't even exist before the eruption, soon had a population of cutthroat trout. Since then, this lake on the west side of the monument has also been stocked with rainbow trout.

While much of the devastated land was publicly owned, much was also privately owned timberland. Today public land and private land are flip sides of a grand experiment. On public land, nature has been allowed to do the regenerating, while on private lands, massive reforestation programs have been instituted. Millions of trees have been planted on the denuded mountainsides outside of what is now Mount St. Helens National Volcanic Monument. Today these mountain-sides are slowly trading the gray of volcanic ash for the green of growing trees.

The Cascades are not dead; they're just sleeping. This fact was driven home with cataclysmic finality when Mount St. Helens erupted on May 18, 1980. From past geologic records, it seems likely that Mount St. Helens will continue to be active, though on a smaller scale, for several more decades. But what of Mount Rainier—could it do the same? Of course not; it's a national park. Wrong! Snow and glaciers notwithstanding, Rainier has a heart of fire. Steam vents at the mountain's summit are evidence that, though this volcanic peak has been dormant for more than 150 years, it could erupt again at any time. However, scientists believe that Rainier's volcanic activity occurs in 3,000-year cycles, and luckily we have another 500 years to go before there's another big eruption. So, go ahead and plan that trip. Whether you visit Mount St. Helens or Mount Rainier, only the scenery will blow you away.

Parks & Other Hot Spots

Mount Rainier National Park

Four entrances: Nisqually (Wash. 706, southwest corner), Stevens Canyon (Wash. 123, southeast corner), White River (Wash. 410, northeast corner), Carbon River (Wash. 165, northwest corner). Tel. 360/569-2211. Admission: $10 per car per week. Camping, hiking, backpacking, mountain biking, fishing, bird watching, wildlife viewing, cross-country skiing, downhill skiing.

At 14,411 feet, Mount Rainier, the highest mountain in Washington, is a sort of combination totem and weather vane for the citizens of the south Puget Sound area. When "the mountain" is out, it is a signal to all outdoors enthusiasts to call in sick and head for the hills. Consequently, Mount Rainier National Park is a favorite playground. So much so, in fact, that on summer weekends it becomes a human zoo, with crowds, traffic jams, and parking lots to rival those of any shopping mall. However, along the park's hundreds of miles of trails, anyone with stamina and sturdy footgear can escape the crowds. During the winter months the park puts on a completely different face, and on weekday afternoons, the guttural croaking of ravens is often the only sound to break the silence at Paradise, the park's most popular driving destination.

The Nisqually entrance on Wash. 706, just east of Ashford, is the park's main entrance and is in the southwest corner. However, the northern entrance, on Wash. 410, provides easier access from the north, especially if your goal is the Sunrise area. In the northwest corner, there is an entrance along the Carbon River off Wash. 165. At the southeast corner, the Ohanapecosh entrance, off U.S. 12, provides access from Yakima. During the summer, it is also possible to enter the park from the east on Wash. 410, which also leads to Yakima by way of Chinook Pass. In winter, only the Nisqually entrance is open.

Longmire, just inside the Nisqually entrance, serves as a welcoming center for the park. Here you'll find a museum, visitor center, general store, hiker information and permitting center, post office, year-round lodge, and restaurant. Although it sounds as though this must be a small city, it is actually quite compact and rarely very crowded.

Climbing up from Longmire, the next stop is Paradise, the busiest spot in the park. Here you'll find the Henry M. Jackson Memorial Visitor Center, the park's main visitor center, which houses a snack bar and the only public showers in the park. Interesting exhibits make this stop worthwhile. Paradise is also the site of the seasonal (May to October) Paradise Inn, a historic mountain lodge (much the worse for wear) that houses a restaurant and a lounge. Rainier Mountaineering, which offers mountaineering classes and leads summit climbs, also has its facilities here at Paradise.

In the southeast corner of the park, just outside the Stevens Canyon park entrance, there is a campground and small visitor center at Ohanapecosh. North of here, there is another visitor center at Sunrise, and in the Sunrise Lodge, there is a snack bar/restaurant. Sunrise is the second most popular spot in the park after Paradise, and offers similar views and meadows.

There are five drive-in campgrounds within the park, though only one, the Sunshine Point Campground, stays open throughout the year. None of these campgrounds takes reservations. See "Campgrounds & Other Accommodations," below, for details.

Mount St. Helens National Volcanic Monument

Three main entrances: Wash. 504 (west side; access Coldwater Ridge and Johnston Ridge), Wash. 503 (south side; access Ape Cave and climbing route), FS 99 (east side; access Windy Ridge). Tel. 360/247-3900. Camping, hiking, mountain biking, spelunking, fishing, wildlife viewing, cross-country skiing, downhill skiing.

It may seem strange to choose a landscape devastated by a massive volcanic eruption for a pleasant day's outing, but, hey, you take your pleasures where you find 'em. Sure you might not want to do an overnight backpacking trip through the monument, but the ascent to the volcano's rim has become a classic Northwest outing whether in summer or in winter. The national monument also has numerous trails that make for excellent day hikes, and there are several short interpretive trails that are quite informative about both the eruption and the renewal of life within the areas devastated by the 1980 explosion. Not only are there hiking and cross-country ski trails here, but there are places to fish or paddle a canoe, and even a cave to explore. However, the vast majority of visitors just drive to one or more of the many visitor centers and viewpoints and call it a day. If, on the other hand, you're willing to pull on some hiking boots and hit the trail, you'll get a whole new perspective on what was once regarded as the most beautiful of the Cascade peaks.

Within or associated with the national monument there are three interpretive and information centers along the Spirit Lake Highway (Wash. 504). The first of these is the Mount St. Helens Visitor Center, 5 miles east of I-5. Although located a long way from the volcano, it serves as a good introduction to the monument and the volcano. The Coldwater Ridge Visitor Center is another 42 miles up the Spirit Lake Highway and has fascinating exhibits and an excellent view of the mountain. Currently, this is the busiest of the monument's visitor centers. However, in the summer of 1997, the Johnston Ridge Observatory is scheduled to open even farther up the Spirit Lake Highway and will provide the closest

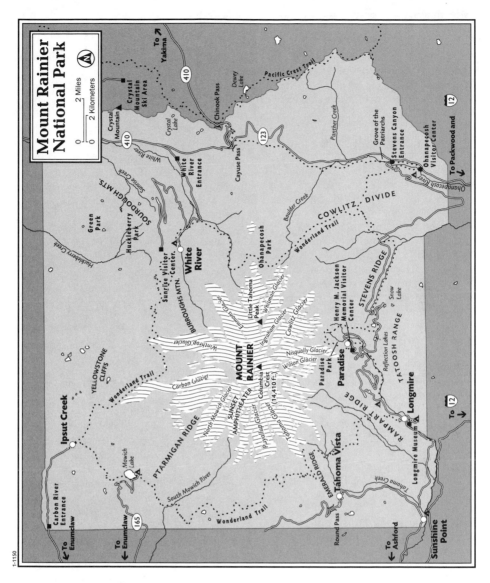

road-accessible view of the blown-out north side of the volcano. This should prove to be the most popular visitor center in the park.

On the east side of the monument, the drive up to Windy Ridge, for many years the closest road access to the crater, is not for the faint of heart. This narrow, winding road requires a driver's total attention, yet out the car window lies a scene of such devastation that it is nearly impossible to concentrate on the road. Despite the white-knuckle driving, this road is always busy with traffic because it leads to the best views in the monument. It also accesses several trails that lead through the blast zone. At **Windy Ridge Viewpoint,** a vast pumice plain stretches out, and 361 steps lead up to a breathtaking view of the crater and Spirit Lake.

The south side of Mount St. Helens was the least affected by the eruption. Today forests still stand on these slopes. At **Ape Cave,** an ancient lava tube can be explored (lanterns are available for rent). There are several good hiking trails on this side of the mountain, including the popular climbing route to the summit. Some of the trails here are also open to mountain bikes. The south side is also popular in winter with cross-country skiers and snowmobilers.

There are no campgrounds within the monument, but there are several nearby. Currently, there is no admission charge for the monument, but there is talk of instituting one.

Glacier View Wilderness

North of Wash. 706 (off FS 59) just east of the Nisqually entrance to Mount Rainier National Park. Tel. 360/497-1100. Hiking, fishing.

This small wilderness area is tacked onto the southwest corner of Mount Rainier National Park. Meadows and a couple of low peaks that provide unobstructed views of Mount Rainier's west face are the main goals of the short trails within this wilderness. However, more adventurous backpackers can use the trails as their route into the national park by way of Gobbler's Knob and Lake George. This side of the national park is the least visited and most remote, and therefore is the best area for solitude seekers.

Norse Peak Wilderness

North and east of Wash. 410 and accessed from Crystal Mountain Rd. and Wash. 410 east of Chinook Pass. Tel. 509/653-2205. Hiking, fishing, cross-country skiing.

Lying northeast of Mount Rainier National Park and Wash. 410, this wilderness overlooks the Crystal Mountain ski area. The dramatic cliffs and spires of Fife's Peak, visible from the Fife's Ridge Trail off Wash. 410 west of the Hell's Crossing Campground, are the most eye-catching focal point of this wilderness. Near Crystal Mountain, Norse Peak itself is a popular goal, with both hikers and cross-country skiers.

William O. Douglas Wilderness

South of Wash. 410 and north of U.S. 12; accessible from Chinook Pass, White Pass, and Bumping River Rd. Tel. 509/653-2205. Hiking, fishing.

Lying between Wash. 410 and U.S. 12 due east of Mount Rainier National Park, this large wilderness area preserves drier east-slope forests. Because this wilderness lacks much in the way of dramatic focal points, it is little visited. Consequently, it makes an excellent choice if your goal is solitude rather than dramatic scenery. There are several small lakes within the park, and Mount Aix and Goat Peak offer superb views of Mount Rainier.

Goat Rocks Wilderness

South of U.S. 12; accessible from forest roads southeast of Packwood, White Pass, and FS 1000 southwest of Rimrock Lake. Tel. 360/494-0600. Hiking, fishing.

Lying to the southeast of Mount Rainier National Park, this wilderness encompasses the craggy remains of an ancient volcano. The Goat Rocks are hung with small glaciers that perch above meadows and offer some excellent hiking amid alpine scenery that is far less crowded than similar landscapes within the national park. The Pacific Crest Trail meanders through some of the most beautiful and rugged portions of this wilderness.

Tatoosh Wilderness

North of U.S. 12 at Packwood; accessible off FS 5270 and FS 5290/5292. Tel. 360/494-0600. Hiking, fishing.

Lying just to the south of Mount Rainier National Park and contiguous with the park, this small wilderness area effectively expands the boundaries of the park. The heart of the wilderness is the Tatoosh Range, the rugged wall of mountains seen to the south from Paradise and the Reflection Lakes area. The Tatoosh Range is unique in this area in that it is composed of granite, unlike the rest of Mount Rainier. No trails lead into this wilderness from the national park.

Mount Adams Wilderness

Southeast of U.S. 12 at Randle; accessible from Wash. 131/Cispus Rd. (FS 23). Tel. 509/395-3400. Hiking, fishing.

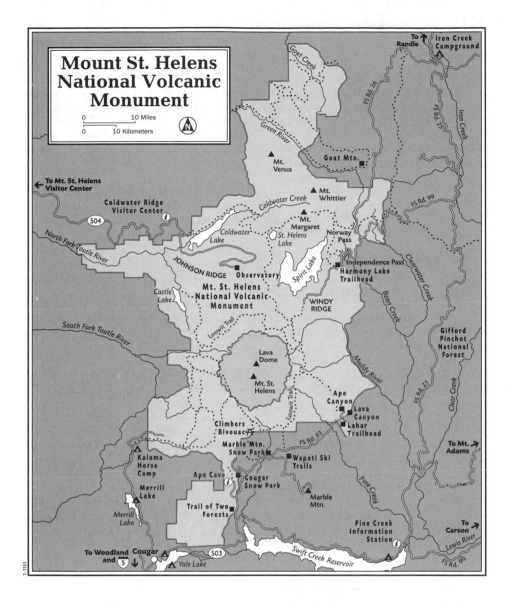

Mount St. Helens National Volcanic Monument

0   10 Miles
0   10 Kilometers

To ↑ Randle   Iron Creek Campground

Goat Creek

FS Rd. 26

FS Rd. 25

Iron Creek

Green River

Mt. Venus ▲

Goat Mtn. ▲

To Mt. St. Helens Visitor Center ←

Coldwater Creek

Mt. Whittier ▲

FS Rd. 99

Coldwater Ridge Visitor Center ⓘ

504

Mt. Margaret ▲

Coldwater Lake

St. Helens Lake

Norway Pass

North Fork Toutle River

JOHNSON RIDGE   Observatory ■

Spirit Lake

Independence Pass ■
Harmony Lake Trailhead

Clearwater Creek

Mt. St. Helens National Volcanic Monument

Castle Lake

WINDY RIDGE

Bean Creek

Gifford Pinchot National Forest

South Fork Toutle River

Loowit Trail

Lava Dome ▲

Muddy River

Clear Creek

Mt. St. Helens ▲

Loowit Trail

Ape Canyon ■

Lava Canyon ■
Lahar Trailhead ■

FS Rd. 25

Climbers Bivouac ▲⏚

Marble Mtn. Snow Park ■

Wapati Ski Trails ■

FS Rd. 83

To Mt. ↗ Adams

Kalama Horse Camp ▲

Ape Cave ⓘ

Cougar Snow Park ■

Marble Mtn. ▲

Pine Creek

Merrill Lake

Trail of Two Forests ■

Merrill Lake

To Woodland and 5 ↓   Cougar ▲

503

Yale Lake ▲

Swift Creek Reservoir

Pine Creek Information Station ⓘ

To ↗ Carson

Lewis River

FS Rd. 90

1-1151

Encompassing all of Mount Adams, this wilderness area is most easily accessible from the south, which is also the side from which most climbers make the ascent to the summit of Mount Adams. (See chapter 8 for information on the southern reaches of this wilderness.) There are, however, also trails leading into the wilderness from the north and west sides, and these trails are most easily accessed from Randle or Cougar. High subalpine meadows, a trail that goes almost all the way around the mountain, and fewer other hikers are what draw people to this wilderness.

Mount Rainier National Park & Surrounding Areas ◆ What to Do & Where to Do It

BIRD WATCHING

In **Mount Rainier National Park,** keep your eyes out for white-tailed ptarmigans around Paradise or Sunrise or anywhere near the tree line. Also look for calliope and rufous hummingbirds, which frequent wildflower meadows. Around Sunrise, you are also likely to spot mountain bluebirds.

East of Mount Rainier, off U.S. 12, you'll find good raptor viewing at Timberwolf Mountain (no wolves here anymore). Goshawks and golden eagles arc frequently spotted. Also to be seen here are a variety of songbirds and blue grouse. To reach **Timberwolf Mountain,** take U.S. 12 east from White Pass past Rimrock Lake, turn left onto FS 1500, and then left again onto FS 190.

CROSS-COUNTRY SKIING

GROOMED TRAILS

Mount Tahoma Trails Association Trail System

Easy–most difficult. Variable distance and elevation gain. Access: Drive to Ashford, just west of the Nisqually entrance to Mount Rainier National Park on Wash. 706, and follow signs to snoparks. Map: Mount Tahoma Trails Association map; Green Trails Mount Rainier West.

This system of trails west of Mount Rainier National Park is divided into three districts and includes almost 90 miles, of which about 20 miles are groomed on a regular basis. The system includes a wide variety of trails, from those that novices enjoy to difficult backcountry tours.

Novices should head to the 92 Road Sno-Park, which is the first sno-park in the system as you approach from the west. The sno-park is at 3,400 feet at the end of a 6.5-mile gravel road. From here, the groomed Champion Trail heads out through young tree farms atop a ridge with occasional impressive views. It is 3 miles and a 900-foot climb up to the Copper Creek Hut, which makes a great lunch spot. Along the way, you'll be treated to views of both Mount St. Helens and Mount Rainier. The Champion Trail can also be skied to Copper Hut from the east by parking at the 59 Road Sno-Park (8-mile round-trip ski, 1,000-foot elevation gain). This latter sno-park also provides access to many miles of intermediate-level ski trails to the north off Champion Trail.

Advanced skiers and telemarkers will want to explore the trails from the Road 1 Sno-Park, which is south of Ashford and

well signed on U.S. 12. The trails in this area involve lots of climbing (typically more than 2,000 feet) and provide access to lots of open slopes for tele-skiing. There are also two huts in the area—High Hut and Snowbowl Hut—that make good destinations and overnight accommodations (by reservation only).

For information, maps, or hut reservations, contact Mount Tahoma Trails Association, P.O. Box 206, Ashford, WA 98304 (tel. 360/569-2451), or stop by their headquarters in Ashford (usually open on winter weekends).

White Pass Nordic Trails

15 kilometers of trails. Easy–most difficult. 300-foot elevation gain. Access: At White Pass, 85 miles east of I-5 on U.S. 12. Trail fee: $8. Map: Trailhead maps.

Located across the highway from the slopes of the White Pass downhill area, this system of trails, groomed both for skate skiing and for traditional track skiing, are aimed primarily at novice and intermediate skiers. The trails meander through forests and across open slopes, providing plenty of ups and downs to keep things interesting. The main loop is around White Pass Lake, but other trails head off through the forest to the north and east of the lake. Advanced skiers will be disappointed with these trails since they offer only one short (0.7 kilometers) "Most Difficult" trail. However, for other skiers, these trails are a lot of fun.

UNGROOMED TRAILS

Reflection Lakes/Mazama Ridge

5.5–7 miles. Easy–most difficult. 800–1,500-foot elevation gain. Access: Mount Rainier National Park. Enter through the Nisqually gate on Wash. 707 east of Ashford and continue to the end of the plowed road at Ashford. Map: USGS Mount Rainier National Park; Green Trails Mount Rainier East.

On a clear day this popular route, which begins at Paradise at 5,400 feet in elevation, is one of the best half-day ski trips in the Northwest. First there is the superb

Outdoor Resources

RANGER STATIONS & INFORMATION CENTERS

Mount Rainier National Park, Tahoma Woods, Star Route, Ashford, WA 98304 (tel. 360/569-2211). Henry M. Jackson Memorial Visitor Center (tel. 360/569-2211, ext. 2328); Ohanapecosh Visitor Center (tel. 360/569-2211, ext. 2352); Sunrise Visitor Center (tel. 360/569-2211, ext. 2357); Hiker Information Line (tel. 360/569-2211, ext. 3317).

Mount St. Helens National Volcanic Monument, 42218 NE Yale Bridge Rd., Amboy, WA 98601 (tel. 360/750-3900 or 360/750-3903 for recorded information).

Visitor centers: Mount St. Helens NVM Visitor Center (tel. 360/274-2100 or 360/274-2103 for recorded information);

Mount St. Helens NVM Coldwater Ridge Visitor Center (tel. 360/274-2131 or 360/274-2103 for recorded information).

Mount Adams Ranger District, 2455 Hwy. 141, Trout Lake, WA 98650 (tel. 509/395-3400).

Naches Ranger District, 10061 U.S. 12, Naches, WA 98937 (tel. 509/653-2205).

Packwood Ranger District, 13068 U.S. 12, Packwood, WA 98361 (tel. 360/494-0600).

Randle Ranger District, 10024 U.S. 12 (P.O. Box 670), Randle, WA 98377 (tel. 360/497-1100).

White River Ranger District, 853/857 Roosevelt Ave. E, Enumclaw, WA 98022 (tel. 360/825-6585).

---

close-up view of Mount Rainier and the jagged peaks of the Tatoosh Range that hems in the southern skyline. Then there is a long, easy stretch of downhill road for warming up, followed by a more challenging climb on a narrow trail that leads up and over forested Mazama Ridge. Finally, open rolling meadows beside the frozen Reflection Lakes present a classic Nordic setting. Perhaps what's equally satisfying about this ski tour is the absence of the crowds and cars that haunt these regions during the summer months. Peace and quiet abound here when snow covers the landscape.

The route starts at the southeast corner of the Paradise parking lot and follows the Paradise Valley Road for a long curve around to the far side of the valley. At the head of the valley, after crossing the second bridge, you can leave the road and climb Mazama Ridge on an unmarked though popular route (Most Difficult route). Once you've topped the ridge, gradually descend following the length of it to reach the Reflection Lakes basin. This route requires navigation abilities and adds an extra 550 feet of climbing.

If you're not up for it, continue on the road until you see a sign marking the Mazama Ridge Bypass Trail, which climbs the ridge through the forest (More Difficult route). This trail bypasses the end of the ridge, which is prone to avalanches. However, if the threat of avalanches is low (check at the Jackson Visitor Center or Paradise Ranger Station), you can bypass this steep section of trail and continue around to the lakes on what becomes Stevens Canyon Road (Easy route). If you are able to take this route, you will get a great view of Narada Falls (an alternate starting point for this ski route). After exploring the open rolling meadows around the Reflection Lakes, you can ski farther on Stevens Canyon Road for a new perspective on the mountain or for a closer look at Lake Louise, which lies east of, and much lower than, the Reflection Lakes.

Upon returning to your car, consider taking the steep trail that leads up from near Narada Falls. This trail begins just after the bridge over the Paradise River on the road leading down to Narada Falls from Paradise Valley Road. Shortly before reaching Paradise, the trail crosses Barn Flats, a great place to just ski around in circles practicing your skills.

Two other unmarked trails start at Paradise, both leading uphill across open slopes. Both the Deadhorse Creek Trail (1.75 miles round-trip) and the Edith Creek Basin Trail (1.5 miles round-trip) will challenge your downhill abilities. The latter trail is subject to avalanches, so this route should be taken only when the avalanche danger is low.

Paradise Spring Skiing

3–9 miles round-trip. Most difficult. 1,000–4,500-foot elevation gain. Access: Drive to the Nisqually entrance of Mount Rainier National Park on Wash. 706 and continue to Paradise. Map: USGS Mount Rainier National Park; Green Trails Mount Rainier East.

Telemark skiers who just can't bear to put their skis away even after other people have brought out backpacks and swimming suits can take a drive up to Paradise and find, well, a telemarker's paradise. The slopes above Paradise Lodge usually stay covered with snow well into June, and one needs only ski uphill 1.5 miles to the Glacier Viewpoint to get in a fine 1,000 feet of vertical. If you crave a longer run or the snow level has risen above these slopes already (maybe its July and you still want to ski), continue uphill following the Skyline Trail and then the route toward Camp Muir, which is 4,500 feet above Paradise. Below this climbers' camp are permanent snowfields that offer ski mountaineers a chance to hone their skills.

Be aware of avalanche dangers and pay attention to the weather, which can turn bad very quickly at this elevation. If these high slopes get socked in, it can be very difficult and dangerous finding your way down. To the west of these slopes, the mountain drops off into the Nisqually Glacier. Stay clear!

Suntop Sno-Park

10 miles (Huckleberry Creek Rd.); 10 miles (to Sun Top Mountain). Easy (Huckleberry Creek Rd.); Most difficult (Sun Top Mountain). 700-foot elevation gain (Huckleberry Rd.); 2,200-foot elevation gain (Sun Top Mountain). Access: Drive east 24 miles from Enumclaw and turn right onto FS 73 (Huckleberry Creek Rd.). Map: Green Trails Greenwater.

There is a very disappointing lack of good, easily accessible cross-country skiing on the north side of Mount Rainier. This is the only sno-park that provides access to snowmobile-free trails, and as such is a magnet for the area's Nordic skiers. There are two routes here—one for novice skiers and one for advanced skiers. The novice route follows Huckleberry Creek on FS 73 (Huckleberry Creek Road) for almost 5 miles. About 0.75 miles before reaching the turnaround point (the bridge over the creek), there is an avalanche chute. You may want to turn around here unless you have some knowledge of avalanches and know that the danger is low.

The route up Sun Top Mountain is decidedly more challenging, primarily because of the amount of climbing to be done (and of course the control required for the downhill return as well). Views of Mount Rainier and the surrounding mountainous country are the reward for the energy expended in climbing this road route. The usual turnaround for this ski route is at the saddle below the southern slope of Sun Top. Above this point, steep, open slopes are highly prone to avalanches.

Crystal Mountain Backcountry

4–9 miles. Most difficult. 1,500–2,700-foot elevation gain. Access: Drive Wash. 410 southeast from Enumclaw and turn left onto Crystal Mountain Rd. at the gate on Wash. 410. Drive to the downhill ski area. Map: USGS Mount Rainier National Park; Green Trails Bumping Lake.

Crystal Mountain is one of the top ski areas in Washington, and although there are no marked cross-country ski trails here, backcountry skiers do find their way onto area slopes. And they have a blast! This is backcountry tele-skiing terrain, and before heading out, you should be aware of the current avalanche danger.

The easiest and most rewarding destination here is Silver Basin, to the southwest of Hen Skin Lake. This area can be reached by skiing up to the top of the Quicksilver run and then continuing on to the southwest. Once you reach the basin, open slopes await.

More adventurous skiers familiar with avalanche dangers can ski to Norse Peak northeast of the ski area by roughly following the Bullion Basin Trail from the top of the Gold Hills ski lift. Stay clear of the avalanche-prone slopes north of Bullion Creek and west of the ridge that runs north to Norse Peak. It is about 9 miles round-trip and a 2,700-foot climb to Norse Peak and its views. However, the real attraction of this route is the excellent open slopes that are perfect for telemarking.

DOWNHILL SKIING & SNOWBOARDING

White Pass

85 miles east of I-5 on U.S. 12. Tel. 509/453-8731 (509/672-3106 for snow report). 30 trails; 4 lifts (including 1 high-speed quad); 1,500 vertical feet. Lift hours: Daily 9am–4pm (night skiing on weekends from mid-Dec to early Mar and on holidays). Adult lift tickets: Mon–Fri $14–$19, Sat–Sun $30.

Though this ski area is fairly small, it keeps its customers happy by providing a high-speed detachable quad lift, snow that is generally a little bit lighter than at ski areas closer to Seattle, and, best of all, slopes that have been used by at least one Olympic skier as a training ground. The biggest drawback here is that almost all the trails lead back to the same two lifts, which causes a bottleneck at the base of the slopes. Cultivate patience. Novice skiers and snowboarders may appreciate that a lower slope lift pass is available for only $10. This pass will provide you with enough slope to help you work on your turns and get the feel of downhilling.

Crystal Mountain

39 miles east of Enumclaw on Hwy. 410. Tel. 360/663-2265 (206/634-3771 in Seattle for snow report, or 206/922-1832 in Tacoma). 55 trails; 10 lifts (including 1 high-speed quad); 3,100 vertical feet. Lift hours: Mon–Fri 9am–4:30pm, Sat–Sun and holidays 8:30am–4:30pm; night skiing Fri–Sun 4–10pm mid-Dec to late Mar. Adult lift tickets: $30 Sat–Sun and holidays, $25 Mon–Thurs, $28 Fri.

Crystal Mountain is a very deceptive mountain. From the main lodge, you don't get any idea of how extensive the runs here are. It is only once you get halfway up the mountain that you begin to grasp how much skiable terrain there is here. The mix of runs for different ability levels and varied terrain have made this the favorite ski area of Seattleites, even though it is the farthest of that city's nearby ski areas.

Though more advanced skiers wait for a good, heavy snowfall before heading up here to track some fresh snow, the ski area is well known for the superb job it does in grooming its runs. Well-groomed runs make this a great place for beginner and intermediate skiers to work on their technique. Intermediate skiers will find the greatest variety of runs off the Rainier Express high-speed quad. From here lots of steep runs drop down into the Snorting Elk Bowl, where many skiers spend the entire day. Diamond divers will want to get to the top of Silver Queen Mountain on the High Campbell lift. From the top of this crag, there are chutes galore, and if you traverse across Silver Ridge, you'll often find untracked snow even late in the day. Snowboards will find perfect terrain with lots of hits, even early in the year, on the Downhill, CMAC, and Queens runs off Rendezvous chair.

The children's day care is some of the best in the Northwest and accepts children ages six months and older. Other services and amenities that make this a very user-friendly ski area include parking lot shuttle buses, a family drop-off area right at the lodge, and several lodges and condominiums right at the base of the ski runs.

FISHING

One of the best things about fishing in Mount Rainier National Park is that no fishing license is required. The bad thing is that the fishing isn't very good.

The Pacific Crest Trail in Southern Washington

Although it briefly ducks across the boundary into Mount Rainier National Park, the Pacific Crest Trail through this region lies almost entirely outside the park. Within this region of the Cascades, the PCT passes through four wilderness areas—Norse Peak, William O. Douglas, Goat Rocks, and Mount Adams. North of Naches Pass, which lies at the north end of the Norse Peak Wilderness, the trail passes through some of the most heavily clear-cut forests in the state. Unless you are intent on bagging the entire trail, this stretch is worth missing.

The 23-mile stretch of the PCT between Naches Pass (accessible from FS 70 off Wash. 410 east of Greenwater) and Chinook Pass traverses the Norse Peak Wilderness. Along the route, the trail passes through many miles of subalpine meadows with the most attractive being those closest to Chinook Pass near Sourdough Gap. Several sheltered basins, filled with wildflowers and dotted with subalpine trees, make superb camping spots. Lake Basin is perhaps the most pleasant. Views of Mount Rainier, Mount Adams, and Mount St. Helens appear from the highest points along this stretch of trail. However, civilization intrudes on the trail in the form of views down onto ski lifts at Crystal Mountain ski area.

The 29.5-mile stretch of the PCT between Chinook Pass and White Pass traverses the William O. Douglas Wilderness. At the north end, near Chinook Pass, the trail briefly enters Mount Rainier National Park as it passes through beautiful subalpine meadows. The trail near the road here may be the most crowded piece of PCT in the state. However, after you pass Dewey Lake, the crowds thin out considerably. Toward the southern end of the wilderness, the trail passes by dozens of small lakes in a wide plateau dimpled by hundreds of small ponds. Although beautiful, this plateau is plagued by mosquitoes in early summer. South of here, as it approaches White Pass, the trail is very popular with horse riders.

The 30-mile stretch of the PCT through the Goat Rocks Wilderness between White Pass and Walupt Lake is one of the most dramatic sections in Washington. The trail follows the knife-edge, rocky ridges of the Goat Rocks Crest and climbs up to a high point of more than 7,000 feet, with outstanding views to both the east and west. This stretch of trail is very narrow, very exposed, and popular with horse riders. Be prepared for storms throughout the summer.

The 22.5-mile stretch of trail through the Mount Adams Wilderness passes through sublimely beautiful subalpine meadows on the flanks of Mount Adams, but unfortunately, the trail spends all but about 5 miles in forests without any views.

However, there are some fish out there, and you're welcome to try your hand at catching a few. Lots of people do. Just remember that only artificial lures and flies can be used within the park and some posted waters are closed to fishing.

For the most part, glacial silt keeps Mount Rainier's rivers too cloudy for fishing in the summer. The trout don't strike because they can't see anything. The **Ohanapecosh River** is one exception. This river in the southeast corner of the park flows clear throughout the summer and is designated fly-fishing only. Anglers are also encouraged to release the wild trout they catch. Most of the park's many lakes have one or another species of trout in them, but in most cases you're going to have to hike in to do your fishing. Some shorter hikes include **Sunrise Lake** below Sunrise Point, and **Louise, Bench,** and **Snow lakes** east of Paradise off the road to the Stevens Canyon park entrance.

Outside the park, the fishing is a bit better. South of the park, off U.S. 12, the **Cowlitz River** is planted with rainbow trout each summer. East of the park (and east of White Pass) off this same highway, the **North Fork Tieton River** is a favorite of fly anglers, who hook into cutthroats, rainbows, and Dolly Vardens. As of 1996, most of the South Fork Tieton River was closed to fishing. The main **Tieton River** is well planted with hatchery rainbows during the summer. Along the route of Wash. 410, the **Naches River, Little Naches River, American River,** and **Bumping River** all provide good trout-fishing waters, and fly-fishing is particularly popular. These rivers all have roads paralleling them, which means plenty of good access. The American and the Naches are regularly stocked with rainbow trout each summer.

Lake anglers will also find a few choices outside the park. South of Elbe off Wash. 7 (west of Ashford and the Nisqually park entrance), **Mineral Lake** is stocked with rainbow trout, but it's the 10-pound giants that really get people out on this lake. This lake also has German browns and cutthroats. Boats can be rented at Mineral Lake Resort (tel. 360/492-5367) right in the town of Mineral. The resort also has a bait and tackle shop. You'll need a boat to get around this fairly large lake. Nearby **Alder Lake,** a large reservoir, offers good late-winter and early-spring fishing of rainbows and kokanee. At White Pass on U.S. 12, **Leech Lake** holds some eastern brook trout and is restricted to fly-fishing only. No motors are allowed on this lake. East of the park there are also a couple of reservoirs that attract anglers with boats. **Rimrock Lake,** on U.S. 12, is a popular kokanee lake, with good fishing for these landlocked salmon throughout the summer and into the fall. **Bumping Lake** also has kokanee, though they don't get very big.

If you're fishing east of the national park, you can pick up fly-fishing supplies at the **Little Bug Shop,** 18421 Wash. 410, Naches (tel. 509/658-2319), which also offers fly-fishing classes and guided fishing trips.

HIKING & BACKPACKING

If you're looking for solitude on the trails, then you've come to the wrong place. The trails in Mount Rainier National Park, especially those with views and meadows,

stay packed throughout the summer. This crowding is exacerbated by the fact that there are only a few places where it is possible to drive to the high elevations where the meadows are to be found. On any trail leading out of Paradise or Sunrise, you're likely to see a lot of people, and for the first mile or so the smell of perfume is more common than the fragrance of wildflowers.

If you feel trapped by such hordes and want to escape from trails that feel like rush hour on the freeway (if you can read the label on these jeans, you're too close), you'll have to work a bit harder. Try entering the park through the **Carbon River entrance** in the northwest corner. In 1996 this road was closed to motor vehicles due to flood damage (which made it a great mountain-bike ride), but even when it is open, it is relatively quiet. **Mowich Lake,** which serves as the trailhead for the beautiful **Spray Park,** is an exception. Spray Park sees hundreds of hikers' feet on a sunny weekend. **Mystic Lake** and **Moraine Park** do not.

Other less-crowded trails to try include the **Shriner Peak Trail** between Cayuse Pass and the Stevens Canyon entrance and any trail off the **West Side Road,** a gravel road that is closed to motor vehicles but open to hikers and mountain bikers. By riding a bike up this road, you can reach trails that are rarely hiked anymore.

INSIDE MOUNT RAINIER NATIONAL PARK

Wonderland Trail

93 miles. Allow 10–14 days. Strenuous. 21,000-foot elevation gain. Access: This hike can be started from Longmire, Paradise, Sunrise, Mowich Lake, or Carbon River. Map: USGS Mount Rainier National Park; Green Trails Mount Rainier East, Mount Rainier West, and Greenwater.

Sure, hiking the Pacific Crest Trail is the ultimate hike, but few people have the time to do more than a few sections of that trail per summer. No, the ultimate Northwest hike has to be the Wonderland Trail circuit of Mount Rainier. This round-the-mountain trail takes in all the best Mount Rainier has to offer and can be done in a typical two-week vacation. This makes it very popular with young and old hikers alike, and I've met more than a few people on this trail who seemed to be on their only backpacking trip of the year. Overloaded and out of shape is not the way to start this circuit, so think long and hard before throwing in the camp-stove espresso maker and the portable trail shower. You'll feel those ounces before this hike is done.

Most people doing the entire trail cache food in one or two places along the way such as at Mowich Lake or Sunrise. Fuel can be cached only at Sunrise and can be purchased only at Longmire. Food caches must be in rodent-proof containers. For specific instructions on how to arrange a food cache, contact the park at 360/569-2211.

Backcountry camping within the national park is restricted to designated campsites and cross-country camping (at least 0.25 miles from the trail). Most hikers opt for the designated campsites, which tends to determine how far you must hike each day. If the campsite you want is full, you might have to hike much farther than you intended to reach the next one. Park rangers tend not to bring up the subject of cross-country camping and need to be prompted on where are likely places to get off the trail and pitch camp. Many areas are restricted, and in other areas, you can't find any flat ground that isn't near the trail. Be flexible. It is also advisable to start your hike midweek when it is more likely that you will be able to get the campsite you want. Longmire makes a good starting point because it is near the most convenient west-side entrance (Nisqually). Starting here also puts Sunrise and Mowich Lake at good points in the trip for food caches.

For information on hiking the Pacific Crest Trail through this region, see the sidebar on the subject.

space). Map: USGS Mount Rainier National Park; Green Trails Mount Rainier East.

This may be the most crowded trail in Mount Rainier National Park, but there's a reason for that—the views are awesome and the wildflowers are stupendous. Paradise has been one of the park's main destinations for nearly a century, and in that time, this area has been hammered. However, the wildflowers that have always been the big draw here continue to paint the hillsides in a rainbow of colors by late July. Through these swaths of living color runs a maze of trails, and the Skyline is the most popular.

From the upper parking lot near the Paradise Ranger Station, take the stone steps that lead up beside the rest rooms. This will put you on the start of the Skyline Trail, which for the first part is paved but climbs at a grueling angle. After leaving the pavement behind for gravel, the trail climbs by way of stairs for a ways, levels a bit near the Glacier Vista, and then switchbacks to climb steeply on a trail cut into the rock to 6,800-foot Panorama Point. From here you can see not only the Nisqually Glacier below and to the west, but also (on a clear day) mounts Adams, St. Helens, and Hood.

Although the Skyline Trail contours across the slope at this point, a steep snowfield usually keeps the trail closed and hikers must climb a bit higher to the High Skyline Trail, which loops around to rejoin the Skyline Trail on the far side of the snowfield. Below this junction, you can choose to shorten your hike by a mile by taking the Golden Gate Trail back to Paradise. Otherwise, stay on the Skyline Trail, past Sluiskin Falls, to loop through more beautiful meadows. At the point where the Golden Gate Trail rejoins the Skyline Trail, you pass Myrtle Falls, even more beautiful than Sluiskin Falls. The last bit of trail is once again paved.

Skyline Trail

5 miles. Moderate. 1,500-foot elevation gain. Access: Drive to the Nisqually entrance of Mount Rainier National Park on Wash. 706 and continue to Paradise (arrive early if you want a parking

Naches Peak Loop

5 miles. Easy. 750-foot elevation gain. Access: Drive Wash. 410 southeast from Enumclaw to Chinook Pass. Map: USFS Mount Rainier National Park; Green Trails Mount Rainier East.

There are very few places in the Northwest where you can drive to the timberline to start a hike. Mount Rainier has three such spots, which is partly why the national park is so popular. Chinook Pass sees far fewer visitors than do Paradise and Sunrise, the park's other two road-accessible timberline locations. So, if you want to hike beautiful wildflower meadows with fewer people (though still far more than anyone really wants to encounter), try this loop, which is in meadows for almost its entire distance around the steep-sided Naches Peak.

From the parking area just over Chinook Pass to the east, hike back toward the pass and cross the highway on a wooden bridge. You very quickly leave the roar of the highway behind, so don't despair. The trail circles around the east side of Naches Peak, crossing through meadows that usually harbor snowfields into late July. The trail passes a couple of small lakes before reaching an overlook with a view of the much larger Dewey Lake and the valley of the American River stretched out far below. As the trail curves around to the west, you pass a trail junction. Keep right to continue the loop, or, if you want some extra mileage, go left to descend to Dewey Lake. At about the point you reach the trail junction, an astounding view of Mount Rainier fills the horizon. This view becomes your constant as you descend slowly through beargrass meadows to cross Wash. 410 at the very popular Tipsoo Lake picnic area. Cross the highway and hike up the east side of the lake to continue back up to Chinook Pass and your car.

Summerland Trail

8.5 miles. Moderate. 1,500-foot elevation gain. Access: Take Wash. 410 southeast from Enumclaw for 38 miles, turn right at the White River entrance to Mount Rainier National Park, and continue 3 miles to a roadside parking lot at Fryingpan Creek. Map: USGS Mount Rainier National Park; Green Trails Mount Rainier East.

This trail is one of the most crowded in the park, as you will discover as soon as you try to find a parking space in the small trailhead parking area. However, if solitude is not your priority, you'll find that this trail is a cross section of all that Mount Rainier has to offer: old-growth forests, brushy avalanche slopes, wildflower-filled alpine meadows, in-your-face views of the mountain, and the high probability of seeing both elk and mountain goats.

For the first 3 miles, this trail keeps to the floor of the Fryingpan Creek valley. The route is through a quiet, dark forest and gains elevation at a very gradual pace. At 3 miles, however, the way breaks out of the forest into sunlight (well, sometimes) to climb across a brushy slope that is swept clean of trees by winter avalanches. After crossing Fryingpan Creek, the trail then begins the steep 1-mile climb to the subalpine meadows at Summerland. It is here, at 5,900 feet, that you come into the views. To the west, Mount Rainier and the massive Emmons Glacier loom, and to the southwest stands the bear rock buttress of Little Tahoma, below which is the Fryingpan Glacier, which feeds the creek up which you just hiked. To the north is Goat Island Mountain. Keep your eyes peeled for goats on the rocky slopes above, and if it is late enough in the season for the snow to be clear of Panhandle Gap, continue hiking up to that point, which is on the Wonderland Trail. You will leave the greenery behind at Summerland if you choose to climb up to Panhandle Gap, but you will stand a greater chance of spotting goats.

There is a campsite at Summerland, but it fills early on weekends (like on Thursday or Friday). Don't count on making this an overnighter, but you never know, you might get lucky. Your odds of seeing goats are definitely better early in the morning and late in the afternoon.

Sourdough Ridge/Burroughs Mountain Loop

7 miles round-trip. Moderate. 1,000-foot elevation gain. Access: Take Wash. 410 southeast from Enumclaw for 38 miles, turn right at the White River entrance to Mount Rainier National Park, and continue to the end of this road at Sunrise. Map: USGS Mount Rainier National Park.

After Paradise, Sunrise, a parkland of alpine rock gardens, meadows, and subalpine forest, is the most popular spot in Mount Rainier National Park, and just as at Paradise, there is a maze of trails here. This loop takes in all the best views, plenty of meadows, rocky slopes, and a couple of lakes. Before starting, check to see if the two snowfields on Burroughs Mountain have melted enough for this hike to be safe. The snowfields usually linger until late July.

From the northwest corner of the parking lot, head uphill across the meadows toward Sourdough Ridge. The plants that grow in alpine meadows are extremely fragile, and the meadows here are among the most heavily trampled in the park. Years of people wandering at will across the meadows have left large sections dead and have exposed the fragile soil to erosive forces. As you hike up to Sourdough Ridge, you can see some of the extensive restoration that is being done in an attempt to slow erosion and restore alpine plants in this area. Signs that tell people to stay on the trail are everywhere, but still people wander off the trails.

Once you reach the Sourdough Trail, turn left and climb steadily along the ridge with Mount Rainier in constant view. From a couple of points, you can gaze north into Huckleberry Park at the headwaters of Huckleberry Creek. On the horizon are the Stuart Range, Glacier Peak, and Mount Baker. Continue up the ridge, crossing a talus slope, to Frozen Lake, where icebergs can often be seen even late in the summer. Just above this lake there is a five-way trail junction. Take the lefthand uphill fork toward the two Burroughs peaks. First Burroughs is 1.25 miles up this trail and Second Burroughs is another half-mile beyond. From either mountain, and from along much of the trail for that matter, there are breathtaking views of Mount Rainier, Emmons Glacier, and Winthrop Glacier. After you've had your fill of the views, look for a trail leading down the other side of the mountain from First Burroughs. This trail drops down to Shadow Lake and the Sunrise walk-in campground. Find the Sunrise Rim Trail along the south side of the lake and follow this trail through forest and pocket meadows back to Sunrise.

Berkeley Park/Grand Park Trail

13 miles round-trip. Strenuous. 700-foot elevation gain in, 1,500 feet out. Access: Take Wash. 410 southeast from Enumclaw for 38 miles, turn right at the White River entrance to Mount Rainier National Park, and continue to the end of this road at Sunrise. Map: USGS Mount Rainier National Park; Green Trails Mount Rainier East.

If the crowds at Sunrise have you thinking maybe you should have stayed home where you could get some peace and quiet, then you need to head for Grand Park. With no designated campsites, this high, dry tableland meadow is open to cross-country camping, which means anyone up here is tucked at least 0.25 miles off the trail. Grand Park is, as its name implies, quite grand. It is a vast meadow from which a huge dome of stars can be seen on clear nights and a full moon is an invitation to stay up half the night. By day, Mount Rainier rises to the south. Come early in the summer when the park is still green, and bring plenty of water (there's none up here).

The trail to Grand Park is even more enjoyable than the parkland itself, but you'll encounter lots of other hikers along the way. You'll also encounter marmots nibbling wildflowers, and if you're lucky, as my wife was, you might see a bull elk materialize from out of the clouds. Start this hike by getting out of Sunrise almost any way you can. Your destination is Frozen Lake to the east of the parking lot. This small lake can be reached by hiking north from the parking lot to Sourdough Ridge and then east, or you can hike the old road toward Sunrise Campground and then climb a side trail up to the lake, or you can hike the Sunrise Rim Trail to Shadow Lake and then backtrack on the abandoned road to the side trail to the lake. The Sourdough Ridge Trail is the most scenic, the road is the easiest, and the Sunrise Rim Trail is the shadiest (yes it can be hot up here).

From 6,700-foot Frozen Lake, descend toward Berkeley Park, keeping right at the junction with the trail to Mystic Lake. As you descend into the greenery of Berkeley Park, you will be serenaded by Lodi Creek. At 4 miles from Sunrise, reach Berkeley Park camp in the trees. From here, it is another 2.5 miles, most of it uphill, to the plateau of Grand Park. Be sure to stock up on water as you cross the stream beyond Berkeley Camp. Once at Grand Park, head out across the meadows and find a nice grove of trees to tuck your camp into.

Moraine Park/Mystic Lake Trail

12 miles round-trip. Strenuous. 3,800-foot elevation gain. Access: Take Wash. 410 to Buckley, turn south on Wash. 165, and follow signs to the Carbon River entrance to Mount Rainier National Park. Map: USGS Mount Rainier National Park; Green Trails Mount Rainier West.

Beginning in the park's only rain forest, this trail ascends slowly for 3 miles along the banks of the Carbon River until reaching the snout of the Carbon Glacier. This is the lowest elevation glacier in the contiguous states and appears out of the dark forest as a noisy behemoth filling the narrow valley. Gushing out of the base of the glacier are the waters that form the Carbon River. Because of ice and rockfall off the glacier face, it is inadvisable to get too close.

At this point, the trail crosses a suspension bridge over the Carbon River and begins a grueling climb up to the meadows of Moraine Park. As you climb above the glacier, the trail is rocky and slippery, and at times cut into the rock face of the Northern Crags (my knees took a beating that lasted for months when I descended this stretch of trail in too much of a hurry). At Moraine Park, the way finally flattens out and then drops a bit to Mystic Lake and the designated campsites. Using a lake campsite as a base, you can explore high on Curtis Ridge, the glacier's lateral moraine, in the land of rock and ice and wind. If you crave rugged beauty and awesome sunrises, consider camping at one of the rock shelters that climbers have built atop Curtis Ridge over the years. These roofless shelters afford a bit of protection from the wind and offer views that make "totally awesome" sound like a major understatement.

OUTSIDE MOUNT RAINIER NATIONAL PARK

South Fork Tieton Headwaters

16 miles. Moderate. 1,500-foot elevation gain. Access: From U.S. 12 east of White Pass, turn south on FS 12 (Tieton Reservoir Rd.), drive 4.5 miles (passing the southeast corner of Rimrock Lake) to FS 1000, turn left, and continue 14 miles to a gate at Conrad Meadows. Map: USFS Goat Rocks Wilderness; Green Trails White Pass and Walupt Lake.

Source of the Cowlitz, Cispus, Klickitat, and Tieton rivers, the Goat Rocks are the craggy, glacier-clad remnants of an ancient volcano. Visible from Mount Adams and the southeastern slopes of Mount Rainier, these crags sit off by themselves, a tiny island high enough to shelter small glaciers on their steep slopes. Today this area is preserved as the Goat Rocks Wilderness. Several trails lead into the wilderness, including the Pacific Crest Trail, which passes along the dramatic Goat Rocks crest. However, the most interesting subalpine scenery and best off-trail exploring in the wilderness is up the South Fork Tieton Trail on the east side of the wilderness.

This trail starts amid a patchwork of private and public land in Conrad Meadows and parallels a logging road for the first 2 miles before beginning its climb onto the flanks of 8,201-foot Gilbert Peak, the highest point in the Goat Rocks Wilderness. About 4 miles into the hike, the trail divides at the start of a loop around the headwaters of the South Fork Tieton River. Go left to reach Surprise Lake, popular with horse packers, in about 1 mile, or go left and climb steeply to gain the wide-open spaces below the summit of Gilbert Peak. Here, the streams that feed the South Fork flow through flower-filled meadows surrounded by colorful rock outcroppings and dotted with stunted subalpine trees. About midway around the loop, a side trail branches off and meanders through meadows under Gilbert Peak's Meade and Conrad glaciers. Strike out through this high, isolated country, find the perfect campsite, and then begin exploring to your heart's content. When it comes time to return, continue around the loop, and once the loop is completed, backtrack 4 miles to the trailhead.

Adams Creek/Killen Creek Meadows

10 miles round-trip (basic trip). Moderate. 2,250-foot elevation gain. Access: From Randle on U.S. 12, drive south on Wash. 131, and in less than 2 miles, turn left onto FS 23. Follow this road (first paved, then gravel) for 32 miles, turn left onto FS 2329 at the sign for Tahklahk Lake Campground, and continue past the campground less than 2 miles to the Divide Camp trailhead. Map: USFS Mount Adams Wilderness; Green Trails Mount Adams West, Blue Lake.

What Bird Creek Meadows are to the southeast side of Mount Adams, Adams Creek and Killen Creek meadows are to the northwest side. This hike starts from just beyond Takhlahk Lake Campground, one of the most scenic campgrounds in the state, which makes this a good choice for a day hike or a backpacking trip. Start by hiking steadily up the Divide Camp Trail beside Adams Creek. The trail passes through forests and occasional clearings. About 2 miles up the trail, a side trail leads 0.25 miles to Divide Camp, which lies at the base of a lava flow beside the springs that are the source of the Lewis River. Continuing up the main trail, reach the Pacific Crest Trail in another 0.8 miles from the junction with the spur trail to the springs. At this point, you reach the meadow country, where views of Mount Adams and colorful displays of wildflowers are a constant distraction. Although you could strike out off trail from here to find a campsite, you might want to turn left on the PCT and continue 1.2 miles to the junction with the Killen Creek and High Camp trails. The latter trail goes right off the PCT and leads another 800 feet up the mountain in 1 mile. The views just get better as you climb, but you can expect to see quite a few hikers on this stretch of trail, which is also the approach route for the North Cleaver summit climb. Directly above lies the massive Adams Glacier. Again, head off the trail and find a campsite.

Alternatively, from the Divide Camp–PCT junction, you can contour southwest on the PCT through meadows and forests for 2 miles to the large Mutton Creek lava flow. The trail through this lava flow is almost a half-mile long. There are a couple of streams along the stretch of trail leading to the lava flow, so you could find someplace in this area to pitch camp.

If you have a few days for exploring, this area makes a superb base camp. From the PCT–High Camp trail junction, it is about 8 miles around the mountain to the tundra country of 7,770-foot Devil's Gardens. This barren, windswept slope is the highest point on the Highline/Round-the-Mountain Trail (which doesn't actually go all the way around the mountain). Along the way to this point, the trail passes below both Lava Glacier and Lyman Glacier and crosses the top of an immense lava flow.

Beyond Devil's Gardens, the trail enters the Yakama Indian Reservation and, in 2 miles or so, leads to the breathtakingly beautiful Avalanche Valley below the awe-inspiring wall of Roosevelt Cliff. However, you may have to get a permit to enter the reservation. Be sure to check first either at the Mount Adams Ranger District (tel. 509/395-3400) or the Yakama Indian Nation (tel. 509/865-5121).

HORSEBACK RIDING

Although there are no horse-rental stables within Mount Rainier National Park, in Elbe, on the road to the Nisqually park entrance, you can do some guided horseback riding at **EZ Time Outfitters,** 18703 SR 706 (tel. 360/569-2449), which is open throughout the year and offers rides of from one hour to several days. East of White Pass just a few miles, you'll find **Indian Creek Corral** (tel. 509/672-2400) near the shores of Rimrock Lake. Also, 19 miles east of Chinook Pass on Wash. 410, you'll find **Susee's Skyline Packers** (tel. 206/472-5558) on Bumping River Road. Expect to pay around $15 per hour at any of these stables.

MOUNTAIN BIKING

In addition to the trails listed here, both **Crystal Mountain** and **White Pass** ski areas have trails and dirt roads open to mountain bikers during the summer months. Crystal Mountain is by far the more popular of the two areas and is known for its grueling climbs and brake-burning downhills. Luckily you can avoid much of the climbing by riding the lifts up. The lifts generally run only on weekends, so come on a weekday only if you want a *real* workout.

Westside Road

18.4 miles round-trip. Moderate. 1,820-foot elevation gain. Access: Drive Wash. 706 to the Nisqually entrance of Mount Rainier National Park, continue 1 mile, turn left onto Westside Rd., and continue 3 miles to the gate and parking area (in winter and spring, this road is gated near the main road, which adds 6 miles to this ride). Map: USGS Mount Rainier National Park; Green Trails Mount Rainier West.

No trails within the national park are open to bicycles. However, the Westside Road, a gravel road that is closed to motor vehicles, is a pretty good substitute. This road used to provide access to campgrounds and picnic areas, but in 1967 a massive debris flow swept down Tahoma Creek from the Tahoma Glacier and washed out not only a good chunk of the road but a campground as well. Such debris flows (known as a *jokulhlaup*) carry a mix of ice, water, sediment, and rocks and move at speeds up to 20 miles per hour. Anything in their path they destroy, as can be seen near the start of this ride. Here the valley is a scene of devastation nearly as total as anything on Mount St. Helens. The valley for hundreds of yards across is littered with splintered and upended trees, some 3 feet in diameter. The only rough section of this whole ride is where the road crosses a creek in the zone of destruction. Otherwise the road is well graded and hard-packed. Most of the way is through forest, but there are a few viewpoints along the route. One of the best reasons to ride this road is the chance to get on some of the little-used west-side hiking trails (closed to bikes). Try strapping some hiking boots on your bike.

From the 2,880-foot trailhead, the road climbs steadily to Tahoma Vista at 2.1 miles. From here you can catch a glimpse of the mountain through the trees growing around an old picnic area. A trail leads

from here up Tahoma Creek to Indian Henry's Hunting Grounds. Continuing on, the road climbs another 480 feet in 1.6 miles to Round Pass, the site of a memorial for 32 U.S. Marines who died in a plane crash on South Tahoma Glacier on December 10, 1946. A trail from the pass leads to Lake George, where there are campsites. From the memorial, there is a good view of the mountain. From the pass, the road drops down 500 feet in 1.4 miles to the South Puyallup Trailhead, which leads up to the snout of Tahoma Glacier in about 2.5 miles. From here, the road begins climbing again. At 8 miles it crosses St. Andrews Creek, where a trail leads up to the pretty St. Andrews Park area. Beyond the creek, the road continues another 1.2 miles to 4,200-foot Klapatche Point, which is the turnaround point for the ride.

Bethel Ridge

8 miles. Easy. 500-foot elevation gain. Access: Take U.S. 12 east from White Pass for 18 miles, turn left on FS 1500 (Bethel Ridge Rd.), continue up this road 7 miles to FS 324, and park near this road junction. Map: USGS Tieton Basin; Green Trails Rimrock.

Sometimes all that's needed to make a perfect ride is a breathtaking view. This is just such a ride. Short and to the point is the best way to describe Bethel Ridge. You start out at 5,600 feet and pedal steadily uphill on a gravel road that crosses a rubble-strewn mountainside. As you climb, the views across the Tieton River valley grow ever more expansive and the mountain across which you are pedaling becomes ever more steep-sided, until finally you top out at a 6,150-foot-high plateau with 1,000 feet of sheer basalt cliffs dropping off not 20 feet away from the road, which at this point becomes a rocky, rutted 4 x 4 trail paralleling the edge of the cliffs. Stretching for more than 2 miles and curving around to the south, these cliffs are a sight rarely equaled in the Northwest. Way off to the south, you can see Mount Adams if it's a clear day. The 4-mile point makes a good turnaround. The views don't change much and the 4 x 4 trail begins to descend. However, if you're interested in a longer ride, you can continue many miles in this direction on dirt roads that lead into the Oak Creek Wildlife Area, which is known for its wintering elk herd.

Little Naches Valley Trails

Varies (most rides are under 20 miles). Strenuous. 800–2,400-foot elevation gain. Access: Drive Wash. 410 east from Chinook Pass 23 miles, turn left on FS 19 (Little Naches Rd.), and continue 2.5 to 2.75 miles to campgrounds. Map: USFS Naches Ranger District.

To the east of the national park, the Naches Ranger District of Wenatchee National Forest abounds in trails that are open to bicycles. Unfortunately most are also open to motorcycles. However, if you're willing to share the road, you'll find many miles of great riding out here. Connecting the trails are a maze of logging roads and 4 x 4 trails. The essentials for riding are a good map of the district and a list of trails (available from the ranger station). The Little Naches River corridor is particularly generous in its offerings of single-track. The Little Naches Valley Trail parallels the river and FS 19 heading upriver from Kaner Flat Campground. Almost opposite this campground is Crow Creek Campground, from which three excellent trails—West Quartz Creek, Fifes Ridge, and Sand Creek—all begin. Any of these trails can be ridden as a loop by combining it with logging roads. Fifes Ridge has the best views while Sand Creek is the most fun. This is the perfect spot for a multiday mountain-bike camping trip.

Skookum Flats/White River Trails Loop

11 miles. Strenuous. 800-foot elevation gain. Access: Take Wash. 410 east from Enumclaw, pass through Greenwater, and continue 11 miles to a right turn onto FS 7160 (Buck Creek Rd.). Map: USGS Sun Top; Green Trails Greenwater.

Located just outside the northern boundary of the national park, this loop parallels both the White River and Wash. 410, sticking close to the valley floor the entire way. However, though this ride does not climb any mountains, it is plenty challenging. In fact, it is extremely technical (one of the

most technical rides around) and is absurdly so when wet weather makes the trail's many roots and rocks seem Teflon coated. Check your dental insurance and wear a new helmet. Pick a dry day in late summer if you want to do any rock hopping or stump jumping. The early section of the ride passes through beautiful and dark old-growth forest and stays close to the river much of the time. Other than the technical thrill of it all, these are the only scenic rewards of this trail.

From the Buck Creek Road parking area, cross the White River and turn right on Skookum Flats Trail (No. 1194). Keep to the right at the first couple of trail junctions, but after crossing Buck Creek, keep left as you pass a trail that leads down to a suspension bridge over the White River. In another 4 miles, turn right onto gravel FS 73, cross the river, and turn right onto the Dalles River Trail (No. 1204A), which leads to the Dalles Campground. Pedal through the campground to Wash. 410 and cross the highway onto FS 7150, which curves to the right to parallel Wash. 410. In just over 1 mile, you are forced down onto the busy highway (which luckily has wide shoulders), but your stay on pavement is brief. In 0.4 miles, watch for a trail on the left and climb steeply from the highway to pick up the White River Trail (No. 1199). Follow this trail upvalley, through many twists and turns, past the Camp Shepard Boy Scout Camp, to a signed junction just before the 11-mile mark. Turn right here to drop down to Wash. 410, turn left on the highway, and continue less than 0.25 miles to your car.

Evans Creek Trails

Varies up to 20 or 30 miles. Moderate–strenuous. Up to 1,500-foot elevation gain. Access: From Buckley on Wash. 410, drive south on Wash. 165 following signs toward Mowich Lake. Watch for the Evans Creek Trails sign and turn left onto FS 7920 to reach the parking area. Map: Maps of these trails are available from the White River Ranger Station in Enumclaw (tel. 360/825-6585).

Located off the road that leads to Mowich Lake in the northwest corner of the national park, these ORV trails are just outside the park on national forest land. The network of trails is designed for, and most popular with, motorcyclists, but if you enjoy challenging riding, you'll likely enjoy this area. If you can, come on a weekday to avoid the motorcycle crowds (the walk-in campground at Mowich Lake makes a good base). Although this is clear-cut country, there are enough views of the mountain that it is easy to forget how butchered the foreground is. Once here and armed with a map, head out on whatever looks like a good route. There is such a maze of trails and logging roads here that it is easy to get lost, but the area isn't really all that big. Even if you are lost, it won't take too long to get unlost.

MOUNTAINEERING

Each year more than 8,000 people set out to climb to the 14,411-foot summit of Mount Rainier. That only slightly more than half make it to the top is a testament to how difficult a climb this is. Although the ascent does not require rock-climbing skills, the glacier crossings require basic mountaineering knowledge, and the 9,000-foot climb from Paradise is physically demanding. Also, the elevation often causes altitude sickness. This is not a mountain to be attempted by the unprepared or the untrained. Over the years, dozens of people have died attempting to reach the summit. Because of the many difficulties presented by summit ascents of Mount Rainier, this mountain often serves as a training ground for expeditions headed to peaks all over the world.

The easiest and most popular route starts at Paradise at 5,450 feet and climbs to the stone climbers' shelter at 10,000-foot Camp Muir. From here, climbers, roped together for safety, set out in the middle of the night to reach Columbia Crest, the mountain's highest point. From the summit on a clear day, seemingly all of Washington and much of Oregon stretches out below.

The best way for most people to climb Mount Rainier is with **Rainier Mountaineering, Inc.,** 535 Dock St., Suite 209, Tacoma, WA 98402 (tel. 206/627-6242; fax 206/627-1280) in winter, or Paradise, WA

98398 (tel. 360/569-2227) in summer, which offers a variety of mountaineering classes as well as guided summit climbs. A one-day basic climbing class combined with the two-day summit climb costs a little more than $400.

PACKSTOCK TRIPS

If you'd like to do a hike with a llama, contact the **Llama Tree Ranch** (tel. 206/491-LAMA), which offers "llunch with a llama," a 4- to 5-hour hike in Gifford Pinchot National Forest just outside the national park, for $35. Longer trips are also available.

SEA KAYAKING & FLAT-WATER CANOEING

Located in the northwest corner of the national park, **Mowich Lake** is a pristine little lake with a peekaboo view of the mountain from its west side. The water is incredibly clear and it's fun to paddle around gazing down into the deep at the many large logs and boulders lying on the bottom. Early morning and late afternoon are particularly good times for a paddle. In the morning you might catch sight of an otter as my wife and I did. The curious animal checked us out for almost a minute before diving into deep water in search of the lake's crayfish, no doubt. In the evening, deer often feed in the small meadows along the shores of the lake. A walk-in campground beside the lake makes this a particularly great spot for a weekend camping and paddling trip. Yes, there are even a few fish in the lake if you want to try your luck.

SNOWSHOEING

If you've never tried snowshoeing and want to, visit Mount Rainier National Park on a winter weekend or holiday when free ranger-led snowshoe walks lasting about 90 minutes are offered. If after getting a taste for snowshoeing you want to do more, you can rent snowshoes by the day in Longmire at the gift shop beside the National Park Inn.

One of the better snowshoeing routes in the national park is the marked route from the Paradise parking lot behind the Jackson Information Center to the Nisqually Glacier overlook. This **Nisqually Vista Trail** is only 1.25 miles long and twists and turns as it meanders up and down hills. At the turnaround, you're treated to a great view of the glacier and the rest of the mountain.

Lower down on the mountain, at Longmire, snowshoers can make a 4.6-mile loop up **Rampart Ridge.** This steep trail requires some route finding and the snow level is not always reliable, but if conditions are right, it makes for an enjoyable and rigorous hike. Another good snowshoeing trail in this same area is the trail to **Carter Falls,** which starts above Longmire just before the Cougar Rock campground. This 2.2-mile round-trip trail follows a section of the Wonderland Trail, which goes all the way around the mountain. It's all uphill to Carter Falls.

SPELUNKING

Although there aren't any big caves to explore in these parts, there are a couple of small ones that you can duck your head into. **Layser Cave Archeological Interpretive Area** is only 32 feet deep, but is historically significant because as long ago as 6,000 years it was used by Native Americans, who sheltered here to skin deer and elk they had killed in a nearby box canyon. The trail is only 0.25 miles from the parking area and has interpretive signs explaining its prehistoric use. To reach the cave, drive south from Randle on Wash. 131, turn left on Cispus Road (FS 23), and 7 miles from Randle turn left on FS 083, and continue 1.5 miles to the trailhead.

The area's other cave, **Boulder Cave,** is actually a 400-foot-long natural tunnel formed as Devil's Creek has slowly eroded the basalt walls of a gorge just off the Naches River. This cave is up a 0.75-mile trail from the road, and there are several smaller caves in the area. To find the caves, drive 26 miles east of Chinook Pass on Wash. 410 and watch for the "Boulder Cave National Recreation Trail" sign between mileposts 95 and 96.

SWIMMING & TUBING

On a hot summer day, hiking in Mount Rainier Park leads one to dreaming of a cool dip. If this happens to you, forget about dangling your toes in glacial runoff and head west from the Nisqually park entrance to the town of Elbe and drive south 3.75 miles on Wash. 7. Turn left at the sign for Mineral Lake and in 1.5 miles you will come to **Mineral Lake** and the quaint little long-ago resort community of the same name. From the road on the west side of the lake there is an excellent view of the mountain, and though the swimming area is little more than a gravel beach beside a boat ramp, the waters are clear and fairly warm by Northwest standards. Enjoy.

For information on swimming beaches at **Mayfield Lake,** see the "Swimming & Tubing" section, under "The Mount St. Helen's Area—What to Do & Where to Do It," below.

WALKS & NATURAL ROADSIDE ATTRACTIONS

In addition to the walks listed below, there are a few roadside attractions within the national park that should not be missed. **Reflection Lakes,** south of Paradise on the road to the Stevens Canyon park entrance, are a favorite of photographers. As their name implies, these small lakes are natural reflecting pools that perfectly frame the mountain. Be here at sunrise for the best shot. **Tipsoo Lake,** at Chinook Pass on the east side of the park, is a tiny alpine lake surrounded by meadows. Naches Peak rises directly above the lake, and Mount Rainier looms in the distance. A trail circles the lake and there is a picnic area.

Pinnacle Saddle

3 miles. Moderate. 1,150-foot elevation gain. Access: Take Stevens Canyon Rd. 1.5 miles east from the Longmire–Paradise Rd. and park at Reflection Lakes. The trail starts on the south side of the road. Map: USFS Mount Rainier National Park; Green Trails Mount Rainier East.

Every time I go to Paradise, I find myself marveling at the rugged Tatoosh Range to the south as much as I gaze up at Mount Rainier to the north. If this small but rugged mountain range south of the mountain has also captured your attention, you'll be pleased to know that there are a couple of short trails that lead up amid these crags. This trail, which is a bit strenuous and hazardous to be considered a casual walk, is nonetheless a quick trail excursion for anyone short on time. The goal of the trail is the 6,000-foot saddle below Pinnacle Peak. From the saddle, there is an outstanding head-on view of Mount Rainier to the north (no need to strain your neck here as you do at Paradise). To the south rise Mount Adams and the Goat Rocks. The trail up to the saddle crosses steep snowfields that usually linger late into the summer. A misstep on any of these snowfields can have serious consequences. This trail sees a lot of hikers for the simple reason that it starts at the popular Reflection Lakes pull-off.

Snow Lake

2.5 miles round-trip. Easy. 350-foot elevation gain in, 300 feet out. Access: Drive 1.2 miles east of Reflection Lakes on Stevens Canyon Rd. (the road from Paradise to the Stevens Canyon entrance of the national park). The trail starts on the south side of the road. Map: USFS Mount Rainier National Park; Green Trails Mount Rainier East.

Smaller crowds than at Paradise or Sunrise, two little lakes, and fine subalpine scenery beneath the jagged peaks of the Tatoosh Range make this the best short hike in the park. Slightly shorter and with significantly less climbing than the trail to Snow Lake, this trail climbs through subalpine meadows past patches of snow that usually linger through the summer. After passing through a silver forest of trees killed by a fire almost a century ago, the trail reaches Bench Lake, which sits on a wide, flat bench. Climb a little more to reach Snow Lake, where there are two campsites (reservations required). Above this cirque lake rise steep walls that are capped by the pinnacle of Unicorn Peak, from which flows Unicorn Creek, the source of Snow Lake. Truly this is a landscape that would please a unicorn.

Grove of the Patriarchs

2 miles. Easy. 50-foot elevation gain. Access: From the Stevens Canyon entrance to the national park, drive west 0.25 miles to the trailhead. The trail is on the north side of the road. Map: USFS Mount Rainier National Park; Green Trails Mount Rainier East.

Located on a small island in the middle of the Ohanapecosh River, the Grove of the Patriarchs is a stand of ancient trees, including a pair of Douglas firs more than 1,000 years old. Giant Western red cedars also can be seen in this shady grove. The crystal-clear waters of the Ohanapecosh are almost reason enough to hike this trail, and if the water weren't so cold, it would be impossible to keep people from turning this into the park's favorite swimming hole.

Carbon River Rain Forest Trail

0.3 miles. Easy. No elevation gain. Access: Take Wash. 165 south from Wash. 410. Map: Not necessary.

Rain forests seldom occur this far inland, but because the Carbon River valley opens to the west, straight into the mouth of storms off the Pacific, it receives the highest rainfall of any area in Mount Rainier National Park and is the site of the park's only rain forest. This short trail is best appreciated on a gloomy, overcast day when a true feel for life in a rain forest can be experienced. Be sure to bring rain gear.

Nisqually Vista

1.2 miles round-trip. Easy. 200-foot elevation gain. Map: USGS Mount Rainier National Park; Green Trails Mount Rainier East.

Mount Rainier is the most glaciated peak in the contiguous 48 states, and if you're short on time but still want a close-up view of one of the mountain's many glaciers, this is your best bet. The trail, which starts behind the Henry M. Jackson Memorial Visitor Center at Paradise, involves far less climbing than most Paradise trails, and leads to an overlook of the ice fall at the snout of Nisqually Glacier. From the glacier far below, the noise of falling slabs of ice can often be heard.

WHITEWATER KAYAKING & CANOEING

Of all the rivers in the Mount Rainier area, the **Tieton River,** east of White Pass and paralleled by U.S. 12, is probably the most well known among paddlers. This river is unusual in that its season is three or four weeks in September when the waters of Rimrock Lake are drawn down by the Rimrock Dam. When this happens, the Tieton turns into a nonstop joyride. Because Washington's Cascades offer very little else in the way of runnable rivers at this time of year, the Tieton turns into an absolute zoo. Rafting companies bring customers by the busload, and seemingly everybody in the state who owns a paddle shows up here at least one of the weekends the river is on. Kayakers are a minority, but if you don't mind dodging rafts as you paddle, this is still a fun run with hardly an eddy to take a breather in. The river divides nicely into a Class II run and a Class III run. It is the upper Class III run that is so popular with commercial rafting companies.

The **Naches River,** east of Chinook and Cayuse passes on Wash. 410, is another of this area's rivers that presents a wide array of options to paddlers. From Sawmill Flats Campground down to the mouth of the Tieton River there are 26 miles of Class II and Class III waters. To this add the lower 5 miles of the American River, which flows into the Naches at Sawmill Flats. Do the math and you'll find that this is a perfect destination for a long weekend of paddling.

The **Cispus River,** south of Randle off U.S. 12, is another of the area's rivers that has lots of different runs of different levels. Between the FS 28 (Cispus Road) bridge and the confluence with the Cowlitz there are 16 miles of Class II and III waters. Above this bridge the river roars through rapids running up through Class V into the realm of death-wish falls.

With the exception of the Tieton River, all the east-side rivers listed here should be run in snowmelt season (early summer), which is really the only time these rivers have enough water in them for good paddling.

CLASS II

On the **Cispus River,** there is a popular Class II run (with one Class III rapid close to the end) that starts at the FS 28 (Cispus Road) bridge and ends at the Iron Creek Campground. To reach the take-out, take Wash. 131 (Woods Creek Road) south out of Randle and continue on FS 25. After crossing the river, turn left into the campground. To reach the put-in, continue east from the campground on FS 76 to FS 28 (Cispus Road), turn left, and continue to the bridge.

The Mount Rainier area's most enjoyable Class II run is the 9-mile stretch of the **Cowlitz River** from La Wis Wis Campground down to the Skate Creek Road bridge in Packwood. This run is big on scenery, with views of Mount Rainier from the lower stretches. Along the way there are lots of fun rapids as you float through impressive old-growth forests. Be aware, however, that this water is icy cold snowmelt. Dress appropriately. Late spring to mid-summer is the season for this river.

The **Tieton River's** Class II run begins at Windy Point Campground and continues 8.5 miles down to the confluence with the Naches River. The action is nearly continuous and the gradient is still close to 50 feet per mile. This stretch of the river is prone to logjams, so ask around before throwing your boat in the water and taking off. Because of the fast, constant flow of this river, there is rarely time or space to exit should you need to. Also, remember to take out before you hit the Naches River, which has a nasty weir across it just downstream from the Tieton confluence.

The **Naches River,** between Sawmill Flat Campground and Cottonwood Campground, is a fun and scenic 7-mile run. With basalt cliffs rising overhead and ponderosa pines lining the river, this is a classic eastside run. Both campgrounds are on Wash. 410 east of Cayuse and Chinook passes.

CLASS III

On the **Cispus River** upstream from its confluence with the Cowlitz just above

Riffe is a 7.5-mile Class III run. This run starts at Iron Creek Campground and continues down to a take-out on the right just after entering the Cowlitz River. At high water, the Cispus-Cowlitz confluence can be very tricky. This stretch of the Cispus has lots of boulders and a few ledge drops as well. To reach the take-out, take Savio Road off U.S. 12, 2 miles west of Randle; turn left on Kiona Road and right on Falls Road to reach a boat ramp on the Cowlitz River. To reach the put-in, drive back to Randle, head south on Wash. 131 (Woods Creek Road), continue on FS 25 to the bridge, and turn left to the Iron Creek Campground.

The upper stretch of the **Tieton River,** from below the dam to Windy Point Campground, is a 15-mile rush with a gradient of 52 feet per mile. This ain't no pool-drop river either, so don't expect to take a breath after you get your boat wet. The action is nonstop, steep, and narrow. With so many rafts grabbing all the fun waves, you'll need to do a lot of backpaddling and ferrying to catch the fun stuff free of wave-stealing rubber. If you can steal a glance around as you roar down this river, you'll be awed by the basalt cliffs that rim this valley. About halfway through this run there is a river-wide weir that must be portaged on river left. Keep an eye out for that horizon line.

The **Naches River** below Cottonwood Campground has several Class III stretches of water. For a short, fun run, put in at Cottonwood and take out 5 miles downstream at the Nile Road bridge just off Wash. 410. For a longer run, you can continue all the way to the mouth of the Tieton River, but before the Tieton there is a dam to portage, and after the Tieton mouth there's an even more dangerous dam. It's about 19 miles from Cottonwood Campground down to the mouth of the Tieton.

CLASS IV

The **Cispus River** between the FS 23 and FS 28 bridges, the **Little Naches River** above the Little Naches Campground, and the **American River** below Hell's Crossing Campground provide expert paddlers with some Class IV rapids in this region.

WHITEWATER RAFTING

The **Tieton River,** which flows out of Rimrock Lake (a dammed reservoir) on the east side of White Pass, is one of the Northwest's most unusual rafting rivers. The rafting season on this river lasts only about three weeks and is created by the annual September drawdown of water from the reservoir. When the gates are opened and water pours out of the lake into the river, a dozen or so rafting companies are there with clients ready to ride the river's constant Class III waters. The trip is steep, fast, and unrelenting, with no time to drift lazily along as on so many other raft trips. The river flows through a dry, east-side canyon where basalt cliffs and brown grasses set the tone.

Companies offering trips on the Tieton include the following: **All Rivers Adventures** (tel. 800/74-FLOAT or 509/782-2254), **Alpine Adventures** (tel. 800/926-RAFT or 509/548-4159), **Osprey Rafting Co.** (tel. 800/743-6269 or 509/548-6800), **River Recreation Inc.** (tel. 800/464-5899 or 206/339-9133), and **River Riders** (tel. 800/448-RAFT or 206/448-RAFT).

WILDLIFE VIEWING

Hunting is prohibited within Mount Rainier National Park, and consequently **deer, elk,** and **mountain goats** within the park have lost their fear of humans. Anyone hiking the park's trails in the summer can expect to encounter some of these large mammals. Deer are the most commonly spotted, although it is the park's mountain goats that seem to command the greatest interest. Look for goats on **Goat Island Mountain,** across the White River valley from Sunrise (use binoculars), on the **Summerland Trail** (see "Hiking & Backpacking" above), on **Mount Fremont** (5.5 mile round-trip hike from Sunrise), and at **Skyscraper Pass** (7-mile round-trip hike from Sunrise). You can also look for mountain goats outside the park near the summit of **Timberwolf Mountain** (no wolves here anymore), which is north of Rimrock Lake on U.S. 12. To reach Timberwolf Mountain, take FS 1500 north from just past Hause Creek Campground and then turn on FS 190.

However, among the most commonly spotted animals in the park are **marmots,** which resemble beavers but live in alpine meadows. These shaggy squirrel relatives are often seen lying on rocks and soaking up the warmth of the sun. They often allow people to approach quite close, but when alarmed, will let loose with an ear-piercing whistle.

The **Oak Creek Wildlife Area,** 18 miles northwest of Yakima on U.S. 12 near the junction with Wash. 410, is a winter feeding area for **Rocky Mountain elk,** which are supplied with supplemental hay to maintain the health of the herd. Nearby, on the **Old Naches Road** that parallels U.S. 12 beginning at the U.S. 12–Wash. 410 junction, **California bighorn sheep** may also be spotted during the winter months at another feeding station.

Just off U.S. 12, east of White Pass, you can see spawning kokanee salmon, a landlocked variety of sockeye salmon, in the vicinity of Rimrock Lake. Good viewing spots include the section of the **North Fork Tieton River** between Rimrock and Clear Lakes, the upper end of **Clear Lake,** and **Indian Creek,** which flows into Rimrock Lake near its west end.

The Mount St. Helens Area ◆ What to Do & Where to Do It

BOARDSAILING

Riffe Lake, a large reservoir on the Cowlitz River north of Mount St. Helens, is the premier boardsailing lake in this region. Thermal winds blow across the lake almost every afternoon in the summer, and at the east end of the lake, there is a designated sailboard launching area at **Glenoma County Park.** This park is about 38 miles east of I-5 on U.S. 12. Watch for the sailboard sign on the highway (and bring mosquito repellent; the bugs are horrible around here).

CROSS-COUNTRY SKIING

Cougar Sno-Park

Up to 15 miles round-trip. Easy–most difficult. Up to 1,300-foot elevation gain. Access: Take exit 21 (Woodland) off I-5, drive 35 miles east on Wash. 503, passing through the town of Cougar, and turn left onto FS 83 (signed Ape Cave). Continue another 3 miles to the sno-park. Map: Green Trails Mount St. Helens NW.

The fairly new system of marked ski trails at the Cougar Sno-Park offers an alternative to the trails at Marble Mountain. Together the two sno-parks provide great variety. The trails at this sno-park, a system of loops and a long-distance trail that leads all the way to Kalama Horse Camp, have lots of good views. Although there is plenty of elevation gain, it is fairly gradual for the most part. These trails stay close to FS 81, which is a popular snowmobile route, and the road is a fast alternative return route for these trails. Goat Marsh, which is at the end of a half-mile spur trail from near the junction of FS 81 and FS 8123, makes a good destination for a long ski. If you ski the trails up and return on the road, this route is about 14 miles. The springs of the Kalama River, at the base of a lava flow, make a good destination for a 10-mile ski. Because this sno-park is at only 2,200 feet, snow is not reliable. Call the Mount St. Helens National Volcanic Monument (tel. 360/247-3900) and check the snow level before heading up here.

Marble Mountain Sno-Park/Wapiti and Sasquatch Ski Trails

Up to 15 miles round-trip. Easy–most difficult. 100–750-foot elevation gain. Access: Take exit 21 (Woodland) off I-5, drive 35 miles east on Wash. 503, passing through the town of Cougar, and turn left onto FS 83 (signed Ape Cave). Continue another 6 miles, passing the Ape Cave turnoff, to the end of the road. Map: Green Trails Mount St. Helens NW; trailhead maps.

This is the biggest and most popular sno-park on Mount St. Helens and is used by both skiers and snowmobilers, so expect a lot of racket around the parking lot. However, because there are several systems of skier-only trails, you can quickly escape the noise. The easiest trails are the Wapiti Loops, which are just east of the sno-park. These trails pass through gently rolling forested terrain before reaching the open spaces of Wapiti Meadow. They are a good choice for beginners or for a warm-up.

The Sasquatch Loops northeast of the sno-park are longer and more challenging trails that require quite a bit of climbing, which means that you get much better views as well. These trails start about 1.8 miles from the sno-park and can be accessed either by following the Pine Marten Trail or the FS 83 snowmobile route. One of the most popular routes (and my personal favorite) is the challenging loop up to June Lake and back down the Swift Creek Trail. The Pika Trail provides a traverse between June Lake and the Swift Creek Trail. This route begins 1 mile east of the sno-park off either the Pine Marten Trail or FS 83 and ascends steeply and steadily with frequent good views of Mount St. Helens looming above.

June Lake, though little more than a pond, is tucked under forested cliffs down which cascades a waterfall. The lake's opposite shore is a snow-covered lava flow. After making the traverse on the Pika Trail, it is possible to continue another 2.2 miles upslope to the start of the climbing route. Beyond this point, you have to have a permit. From here, it is a long, though only moderately difficult, ski to the sno-park. Climbing skins are a good idea.

Mount St. Helens' Summit

10 miles round-trip. Most difficult. 5,700-foot elevation gain from Marble Mountain Sno-Park; 4,500 feet from Climbers' Bivouac. Access: Take exit 21 (Woodland) off I-5, drive 35 miles east on Wash. 503, passing through the town of Cougar, and turn left onto FS 83 (signed Ape Cave). Continue another 6 miles, passing the Ape Cave turnoff, to the Marble Mountain Sno-Park at the end of the road. Map: Green Trails Mount St. Helens NW.

For backcountry skiers, this is one of the classic trips of the Northwest. It is a long, uphill trudge and climbing skins are a necessity, but the payoffs are the vast, untracked slopes that are a tele-skier's dream come true. Before making this ascent, you should be familiar with travel through avalanche country and have good winter climbing technique. Be especially careful on the crater rim, where corniches sometimes extend 100 feet over the edge! Although the view from up top is grand, for most skiers, it is the return descent that is the real goal of this trip. It is possible to make the summit in a day, but many skiers choose to make an overnight trip. June Lake makes a good campsite, especially if you are getting a late start. Late spring is the best time to make this climb, and by early summer you can start from the Climbers' Bivouac and cut off 1,200 feet of climbing. To make the summit climb, you'll need a permit, which can be picked up at Jack's Restaurant in Yale, 23 miles east of I-5 on Wash. 503.

The route is very straightforward. Head uphill from the Marble Mountain Sno-Park on Swift Creek Trail to the top of Monitor Ridge and then on to the summit. Be prepared. This is a grueling climb.

Lahar Trail

12 miles. Moderate. 400-foot elevation gain. Access: Take exit 21 (Woodland) off I-5, drive 35 miles east on Wash. 503, passing through the town of Cougar, and turn left onto FS 83 (signed Ape Cave). Continue another 6 miles, passing the Ape Cave turnoff, to the Marble Mountain Sno-Park at the end of the road. Map: USFS Mount St. Helens National Volcanic Monument; Green Trails Mount St. Helens NW.

I don't like noise, and I most emphatically don't like noise in the wilderness. Consequently, throughout this book I have recommended mostly cross-country ski trails on which a skier does not have to contend with snowmobiles. However, sometimes a route is just too good to leave out, even if it means dealing with whining snowmobiles. This is such a trail.

What makes this trail so worthwhile is the landscape and view at the end of it. The vast lahar (flow of mud and ash) that swept down the southeast flank of St. Helens is, by winter, a vast plain of snow. Though far from untracked (remember the snowmobiles), it is a fascinating field upon which to wander. Looming over you at all times is the wall of white marking the slope of the volcano.

FISHING

From superb steelheading on the Kalama River to tiger muskies in Mayfield Lake, this region has a wide variety of fishing options. If you have a boat, the many reservoirs in the area are favorites, especially if you like quantity.

Both the **Kalama River** and the **Cowlitz River** provide excellent summer steelheading, though all wild steelhead must be released. These rivers are popular with drift-boat anglers, though there are also plenty of places to fish from shore. The section of the Kalama River from Summers Creek upstream to the 6420 Road is fly-fishing only betwen June 1 and March 31. The Kalama also has cutthroat trout, which start biting around August when they return from saltwater. However, the Cowlitz may be a bit better for cutthroat, and is a good fly-fishing stream. Try woolly buggers early or late in the day. Again, all wild fish must be released. These two rivers also get runs of spring Chinook, but it is the summer steelhead that are the real draw.

The **Lewis River** below Merwin Dam is good for both winter and summer steelheading due to the many hatchery fish that are stocked. This lower section of the river also sees some sea-run cutthroat as well as salmon. The lowest section is even open for fishing year-round (check the regs.). In the upper stretches of the river, the Lewis River Power Canal often is very productive. Above Eagle Cliff Bridge at the east end of Swift Reservoir, it's all catch-and-release on artificial lures and flies only. Above Merwin Dam, in **Merwin Reservoir,** small rainbows and kokanees are the main catch, with cutthroats and Dolly Vardens out there too. **Yale Reservoir,** upstream of Merwin Reservoir, holds the same species of fish, but they tend to get a bit bigger here. In either lake, the best fishing isn't until the water warms up in late summer. Still farther upstream, **Swift Reservoir** offers the same sort of fishing as at the other two reservoirs. A boat is a necessity to fish any of these lakes with some degree of success.

Coldwater Lake, formed when the entire north slope of Mount St. Helens slid into the valley of the North Fork Toutle River and spilled 1,500 feet up a ridge and over into the valley of Coldwater Creek, has been stocked with rainbow trout that have now grown to good size. There are only three shoreline spots where you can fish, so it's a good idea to bring a boat or a float. Just remember that only electric motors are allowed on this lake. Fly-fishing can be very productive, with woolly buggers working well. Currently the limit is one 16-inch or larger trout per day, and only artificial flies and hooks are allowed.

On the south side of the mountain and outside the monument border, **Merrill Lake** provides a similar fishing experience to that of Coldwater Lake. Merrill is a fly-fishing-only lake, with float tubes being the favored fishing method.

A very different sort of lake fishery exists on **Mayfield Lake,** a large reservoir on the Cowlitz River. This lake has been stocked with tiger muskelunge (muskies), which are known as powerful fighters. This is one of the few lakes in the Northwest with tiger muskies, and the lake's record as of summer 1996 was 46.5 inches and 28.2 pounds. For bait, tackle, and advice on fishing this lake, stop in at Fish Country Sports Shop (tel. 360/985-2090) on U.S. 12, 12 miles east of I-5.

Shallow, weedy, warm **Silver Lake** attracts yet another breed of angler. This is a warm-water fishery, with largemouth bass, crappie, and perch. There are, however, also some trout. Weed-eating grass carp were recently introduced here to try to control the rampant growth of aquatic plants that have nearly completely clogged this lake.

HIKING & BACKPACKING

Hiking on Mount St. Helens is unlike hiking anywhere else in the Northwest. The most interesting trails lead through the blast zone, the slowly regenerating wasteland on the north side of the mountain. Within this area there are no trees and consequently no shade. Wear sunscreen and carry lots of water. The wind here tends to kick up a lot of dust, so sunglasses and a bandanna for covering the nose and mouth can be useful. If you plan on doing a long hike through the blast zone, wear good, sturdy boots.

In addition to the trails listed here, there is a round-the-mountain trail on Mount St. Helens as there is on most Cascade volcanic peaks. It is known as the **Loowit Trail** and was named for the Indian maiden who, in an ancient legend, was turned into the beautiful peak that once stood here. The Loowit Trail is 27 miles long, but can be accessed only by other trails, so if you want to hike all the way around, you'll have to add another 5 miles or so just to reach it. Few people make this hike in one trip because water is scarce and the whole north side of the mountain is a restricted area where camping is prohibited. Several of the trails listed below utilize portions of the Loowit Trail.

Summit Hike

9.5 miles round-trip. Strenuous. 4,500-foot elevation gain. Access: From the town of Cougar on Wash. 503, drive 7 miles east to FS 83, turn left and continue 3 miles to FS 8100, turn left and continue 1.75 miles to FS 830, turn right and continue 2.75 miles to the climbers' bivouac. Map: USFS Mount St. Helens National Monument; Green Trails Mount St. Helens NW.

Mount St. Helens was once the most beautiful of all the Cascades volcanoes and was a popular climb. Today, though the mountain is 1,300 feet lower than it once was and lacks that perfect profile, it is still a very popular climb. If done after the snow melts off in late summer, this is not a technical climb, just a long, dusty slog. The chance to hike to the rim of this famous volcano is, however, an adventure that should not be passed up.

Although there are two routes to the crater rim of Mount St. Helens, the route up Monitor Ridge is the easier. This trail

starts out with 2 miles of hiking through forest before reaching a junction with the Loowit Trail. This marks the start of the hard part—the Monitor Ridge lava flow. For the next 1.8 miles, the trail scrambles upward over jagged lava before reaching the ash slopes below the rim. From the top of the lava flow, it is another 0.8 miles and 1,000 feet of struggling through this unstable footing, often with the winds whipping up clouds of gritty pumice. Goggles or sunglasses with side shields are a good idea, as is some sort of scarf or bandanna to cover your face. Once at the rim, you can gaze down into the crater at the lava dome that formed after the eruption. To the north, all is a wasteland. Naked, fire-seared rock drops away below your feet, and in the distance, log-clogged Spirit Lake appears, a pale ghost of its former self. All around rise other volcanoes—Mount Rainier, Mount Adams, Mount Hood—quiet for now. But for how long?

A permit is required to climb Mount St. Helens, and from May 15 to October 31, reservations are accepted and a quota is instituted (summer weekends book up months in advance). As of 1996, 60 permits per day were issued by reservation and another 40 unreserved permits were available each day at Jack's Restaurant and Store, 5 miles west of Cougar on Wash. 503. From November 1 to May 14, self-issue permits are available at this same store, which also doubles as the climber's register, where all climbers must sign in and out. However, as of late 1996, there was talk of changing the permit program, so be sure to call the Mount St. Helens National Volcanic Monument (tel. 360/247-3900) before making plans.

Sheep Canyon Loop

7 miles. Moderate–strenuous. 1,900-foot elevation gain. Access: From I-5 at Woodland, drive 30 miles east on Wash. 503 almost to the town of Cougar and turn left onto FS 8100 (signed Merrill Lake). In about 11 miles this road turns to gravel and then becomes FS 8123; continue another 7 miles from this point to the trailhead. Map: USFS Mount St. Helens National Volcanic Monument; Green Trails Mount St. Helens NW.

Located on the southwest side of the volcano off the main tourist routes, this trail is less popular than others listed here. Consequently, you'll see far fewer hikers. This hike includes a good mix of the old St. Helens and the new St. Helens—green trees and silver snags, rainbow-hued meadows and gray ash.

The trail starts out in forest, ascending beside Sheep Canyon, which was scoured by mudflows when the volcano erupted. Today this canyon is a scar amid the forests on the volcano's flank. In a half-mile, pass a bridge over Sheep Canyon. This will be your return trail. Continue climbing through old-growth noble fir forest to reach the Loowit Trail at 2 miles from the trailhead. Turn left here, cross the head of Sheep Canyon, and continue climbing just a bit more to reach the high point of this hike at 4,700 feet. Drop down from this point through more than a mile of meadowlands, ablaze with wildflowers in July. At the far end of these meadows, you enter the south edge of the blast zone. Here, trees were not blown over, but instead were killed where they stood by the intense heat of the eruption.

Shortly after reaching this dead zone, the trail climbs to the top of a ridge for a view of the heart of the blast zone. To the north lies the new; to the south lies the old. Imagine all the miles of meadows and forests that once stretched onward from this point. All gone in an instant. Drop down though this ghostly forest to a junction with the Toutle Trail at about 2.75 miles from the Loowit–Sheep Canyon Trail junction. At the Toutle Trail junction, you reach the rim of the South Fork Toutle River canyon. This canyon was laid waste by a huge mudflow that formed when glaciers above melted suddenly. If you want to walk amid the destruction, turn right and drop down to the river; otherwise, turn left to complete this loop hike. In 1.5 miles, which includes 600 feet of climbing, you will reach the bridge over Sheep Canyon. Although impressive, the destruction below the bridge is paltry compared to that of the Toutle River and the blast zone. Turn right on Sheep Canyon Trail to return to the car.

Lava Canyon Trail

3.3 miles. Moderate. 1,000-foot elevation gain. Access: Take exit 21 (Woodland) off I-5, drive 35 miles east on Wash. 503, passing through the town of Cougar, and turn left onto FS 83 (signed Ape Cave). Continue another 11 miles, passing the Ape Cave turnoff, to the end of the road. Map: USFS Mount St. Helens National Volcanic Monument; Green Trails Mount St. Helens.

The history of Lava Canyon is as fascinating as any on this mountain, and knowing this canyon's past should be enough to make anyone want to have a look. Prior to the eruption, there was no Lava Canyon. There was an unremarkable, forested valley. However, when surveyors returned to the area after things had calmed down, they discovered that a mudflow had scoured this valley down to a 3,500-year-old basalt lava flow that had been buried for centuries. The Muddy River had carved its way down through different layers of both smooth and columnar basalt, which lay on top of each other in striking contrast. Follow the layers and you'll see how they flowed down this canyon. Today the Muddy River once again plunges down the spectacular gorge it carved so long ago. And now a trail almost as dramatic as the canyon follows the flow of the river down to a huge freestanding plug of basalt known as "The Ship."

I don't have a fear of heights, but this trail made me nervous. In fact, it made me more nervous than any trails I've ever hiked on my many treks in Nepal. However, the trail did not induce the same feelings of uneasiness in my wife. The first 0.75 miles of the trail is an easy stroll, guaranteed *not* to induce vertigo. However, once you cross the bouncy suspension bridge and head downstream on the section of trail marked "Most Difficult," you'll see what made me nervous. The trail becomes very narrow, cut into steep cliffs, with the muddy gray waters thundering below. Then there are the metal ladders— one to get you down to the base of "The Ship" and one to get you up to the top of this monolith. The floods of February 1996 did considerable damage to the ladders, which had not been repaired by the late summer of that year. From the top of "The Ship," you have an excellent view of the many waterfalls that cascade down through this canyon. From "The Ship," head back the way you came. Even if you have no tendencies toward acrophobia, I don't recommend this trail when it is wet or icy!

Loowit Falls/Plains of Abraham Loop

9 miles round-trip. Moderate. 800-foot elevation gain. Access: From U.S. 12 in Randle, drive 20 miles south on FS 25, turn right onto FS 99, and continue 17 miles to Windy Ridge. Map: USFS Mount St. Helens National Volcanic Monument; Green Trails Mount St. Helens NW.

If you want to gaze into the mouth of the mountain, this is the trail. Starting from Windy Ridge, the trail leads 4.5 miles to 200-foot-tall Loowit Falls, which cascades down from the crater. In a region of abundant waterfalls, this would hardly be remarkable, but this waterfall is 100°F. Before you hot-springs junkies start stripping down, be aware of the warnings about harmful bacteria in these waters. Also, anyone hiking this trail should know that this is a restricted area and off-trail hiking is prohibited (fines start at $100).

This hike starts out with 2 miles of hiking up a gated gravel road that is designated as the Truman Trail, named for Harry Truman, the old man of the mountain who refused to leave his Spirit Lake resort. Harry, and his resort, were buried under 200 feet of rubble when the mountain blew. Before the end of this road/trail, you'll see on your left the Abraham Trail, which leads to the desert-like Plains of Abraham, 2 miles distant. With the steep slope of the mountain rising above it, the plains are a dramatic sight well worth the 4-mile round-trip detour. At the end of the gravel road, take the trail to the left (Windy Trail) to continue on toward Loowit Falls. If you want outstanding views of the lava dome within the crater and don't mind adding 4 miles to your hike, keep to the right on the Truman Trail for another 2 miles to the views and then return. Windy Trail climbs steadily across a barren, windswept pumice plain with views of Spirit Lake below. After about 4.25 miles, the 0.25-mile spur trail to Loowit Falls heads off to the left. After marveling at these steaming hot falls, head back the way you came.

Norway Pass and Mount Margaret Trail

5 miles round-trip to Norway Pass; 11 miles round-trip to Mount Margaret. Moderate–strenuous. 900-foot elevation gain to Norway Pass; 2,300 feet to Mount Margaret. Access: From U.S. 12 in Randle, drive 20 miles south on FS 25, turn right onto FS 99 and continue 9 miles to FS 26, turn right and continue 1 mile to the Norway Pass Trailhead. Map: USFS Mount St. Helens National Volcanic Monument; Green Trails Spirit Lake.

The view from Norway Pass, with Spirit Lake at your feet and the gaping maw of the blown-out north side of Mount St. Helens staring you in the face, is among the most breathtaking in the monument. Trees cover the surface of the lake, and steam rises from the lava dome that has grown within the confines of the volcano's crater. For an even more impressive view, and a longer hike, you can continue on from Norway Pass to 5,858-foot Mount Margaret, another 2.5 miles beyond the pass. From the summit of this low peak, you not only have the view of Spirit Lake and the crater of St. Helens, but also mounts Rainier, Adams, and Hood. Save this hike for a clear day. Return the way you came. It is also possible to hike 3.5 miles southward to Independence Pass from Norway Pass if you have arranged a car or bicycle shuttle back to the Norway Pass Trailhead.

MOUNTAIN BIKING

If you'd like to have a guide lead you through a maze of logging roads in the middle of the blast zone and see Mount St. Helens the way few people do, contact **Volcano View Mountain Bike Tours,** P.O. Box 539, Castle Rock, WA 98611-0539 (tel. 360/274-4341). Trips offered by this husband-and-wife company are aimed at beginning and intermediate riders, with their most popular ride being almost all downhill. Bike tours, which last about 8 hours from pickup to drop-off, are van supported and cost $50 per person.

If you are so inclined you could explore these same logging roads on your own. Just head up the gravel roads off Spirit Lake Highway near the Coldwater Lake Visitor Center. Although riding here involves more than 1,000 feet of climbing, the views are stupendous.

Lewis River Trail

22 miles round-trip. Moderate–strenuous. 800-foot elevation gain. Access: From I-5, take exit 21 (Woodland) and drive east on Wash. 503 for 46 miles, turn right onto FS 90 and continue 15 miles to the Lewis River Campground. Map: USGS Spencer Butte; Green Trails Lone Butte.

This ride enjoys a near-legendary status among mountain bikers from both Washington and Oregon. The excellent, hard-packed trail parallels the wild Lewis River and is a roller-coaster ride that will keep you grinning from start to finish. Aside from the roaring river to keep you company, there are humongous old-growth trees, and in winter you might come across the river's resident elk herd. Ride the trail down and the FS 90 back up to your car (or bring two cars and leave one at the bridge on FS 9039 about 5.5 miles after turning onto FS 90).

Unfortunately, both the trail and the road to it were severely damaged by the February 1996 floods. By the end of summer 1996, neither the trail nor the road had been repaired, and though an alternate, though circuitous, drive over remote logging roads could get you to the trail, you still couldn't ride more than about 7 miles once you got there, and even this was interrupted by mud slides that had to be negotiated. Hopefully both trail and road will be repaired by the time you read this, but call the Randle Ranger Station (tel. 360/497-1100) first to be sure.

Marble Mountain

13.5 miles round-trip. Moderate. 1,500-foot elevation gain. Access: Take exit 21 (Woodland)

off I-5, drive 35 miles east on Wash. 503, passing through the town of Cougar, and turn left onto FS 83 (signed Ape Cave). Continue another 7 miles to the June Lake Trailhead. Map: USFS Mount St. Helens National Volcanic Monument.

If the Ape Canyon Trail is just too rigorous a workout for you, consider this option. This out-and-back ride on gravel logging roads climbs to the top of Marble Mountain for a view as good as any you'll find on this south side of St. Helens. From the 4,128-foot summit of this little peak, you can see all of Mount St. Helens's nearby volcanic relatives (Rainier, Adams, and Hood). Start this ride by heading back down paved FS 83 to the Marble Mountain Sno-Park. Opposite the sno-park, turn left onto FS 8312 and ride this road to the top of Marble Mountain. On the high-speed cruise back down, slow down to enjoy the view of St. Helens if you can.

Ape Canyon Trail

12 miles round-trip. Strenuous. 1,300-foot elevation gain. Access: Take exit 21 (Woodland) off I-5, drive 35 miles east on Wash. 503, passing through the town of Cougar, and turn left onto FS 83 (signed Ape Cave). Continue another 11 miles, passing the Ape Cave turnoff, to the end of the road. Map: USFS Mount St. Helens National Volcanic Monument.

If you don't mind aching muscles and being soaked with sweat for the chance to pedal through an otherworldly landscape of ash and pumice dumped by the 1980 eruption of Mount St. Helens, then you will not want to pass up an opportunity to ride this trail. Why the monument even allows bikes on the trail is a mystery to me, but as long as they do, it will remain one of the most fascinating rides in the world.

Although this trail leads to the Plains of Abraham, it is more like riding to the gates of hell. After slogging up a grueling single-track climb that will make your thighs and lungs scream for mercy, you pass out of the lush old-growth forest through which you have been pedaling and into fields of ash and pumice. Ever pedaled through sand? This is just as bad.

All around you is devastation, a wasteland. After sucking down a bottle or two of water, the grin breaks over your face. There is no other ride like it in the universe. After pedaling the ash for a while, you start dreaming about that downhill cruise. Just remember that I want to come back here, and if you run over a hiker, this trail will most certainly be closed to bikes. Control your speed and stay alert.

ROAD BIKING

Spirit Lake Highway

12–40 miles round-trip. Strenuous. 900-foot elevation gain from Elk Rock; 3,100 feet from Hoffstadt Bluffs. Access: From exit 49 on I-5, drive east 27 miles on Wash. 504 to the Hoffstadt Bluffs Visitor Center.

Thighs of iron? Think there's nothing more fun than a grueling hill climb? In training for the Tour de France? If this is you, then you won't want to miss the opportunity to do this ride. It's a long, grueling climb up the Spirit Lake Highway to the Coldwater Ridge Visitors Center, but if your legs are up to it, the rewards are worth the effort. So, don't let your spirits flag. First, there is the head-on view of the blown-out north side of Mount St. Helens; then there is the return trip, which is almost entirely downhill from Elk Rock to Hoffstadt Bluffs, and perhaps most important, there are no parking problems at Coldwater Ridge. Though this road sees a lot of traffic, it is new, has wide shoulders, and is closed to commercial traffic, so there are no trucks to blow you off the road. You can start riding at a number of points. From Hoffstadt Bluffs Visitor Center, it's a 40-mile round trip. From the Forest Learning Center, it's a 28-mile round trip. From Elk Rock Viewpoint, it's a 12-mile round trip.

From Hoffstadt Bluffs, the road climbs and climbs and climbs for 14 miles to reach Elk Rock Viewpoint, the highpoint of the ride. At this point you get your first view of the blast zone, and off in the distance Mount Adams can be seen. From here the road drops 700 feet and then regains 200

feet to reach the Coldwater Ridge Visitor Center.

Blast Zone Loop

38 miles. Strenuous. 3,000-foot elevation gain. Access: From U.S. 12 in Randle, drive 10 miles south on FS 25 to the Iron Creek Picnic Area.

If you haven't had enough punishment yet, try this second Mount St. Helens ride, which has just as much climbing as the road up to Coldwater Ridge. Passing through the heart of the blast zone on the east side of Mount St. Helens, this ride is one of the most spectacular in the Northwest. It is a very different trip from the Spirit Lake Highway. This road is narrow and winding, and much of the route is in the wastelands devastated by the 1980 eruption. From the Iron Creek Picnic Area, ride back north on FS 25 to the FS 26 junction and turn left. Here begins the long, slow climb up through the blast zone. As you climb, the views of millions of blown-down trees become more and more astonishing and the gash in the north side of the mountain becomes ever more ominous.

At 14 miles you reach Ryan Lake, where there is an interpretive center. Drop 200 feet (smiling all the way) and then continue climbing past the Norway Pass Trailhead (where you could go for a hike if you need some time out of the saddle). There is also drinking water here. About 1 mile past this trailhead, after another brief downhill, reach the FS 99 junction at Meta Lake. Here you can join the crowds ogling the miner's car that was thrown through the air by the force of the eruption, or hike the 0.25-mile trail to Meta Lake. This is your only other source of water on this route.

If you're a cycling masochist, you can continue another 8 miles and 1,200 feet up to Windy Ridge at 4,170 feet. Sane people should instead turn left here onto FS 99 and continue climbing 2.5 miles to Bear Meadow, at 4,120 feet. This is the high point of the ride. From here, the 17 miles back to the start (turn left when you reach FS 25) are almost all downhill. Enjoy!

SEA KAYAKING & FLAT-WATER CANOEING

Although Spirit Lake was once the center of summertime boating on Mount St. Helens, today the only place to put a boat in the water is at **Coldwater Lake,** which didn't even exist before the eruption. Located at the foot of Coldwater Ridge near the end of the Spirit Lake Highway (Wash. 504), this lake was formed when the north slope of Mount St. Helens collapsed. The massive landslide spilled into the North Fork Toutle River valley, up and over a 1,500-foot ridge, and into the valley of Coldwater Creek. The debris blocked the canyon and the flow of the creek, and slowly the 5-mile-long Coldwater Lake was formed.

Today this lake has a paved road right to its shore, is stocked with trout, and is a great place to do a little paddling amid the devastated landscape. A paddle through this lake is unlike any other canoe or sea kayak experience you'll ever have. Though the lake's shore sees throngs of casual strollers (down from the visitor center on the hill above the lake), it is still a fascinating place to get the paddles wet. To reach the lake, drive Wash. 504 to the Coldwater Ridge Visitor Center and follow signs to the boat ramp. No motors are allowed on the lake, which keeps it nice and quiet.

SNOWSHOEING

Although climbing Mount St. Helens is far more popular in the summer months than it is when snow blankets the mountain's slopes, there are still quite a few hardy souls who venture up this quiescent volcano in winter. Skiing is a far more popular way to make the **summit climb** here (see "Cross-Country Skiing," above), but you can also do it with snowshoes if you are in good shape. Just remember to pick up your climbing permit at Jack's Restaurant in Yale, 23 miles east of I-5 on Wash. 503. Another good snowshoeing route is the loop up **June Lake Trail** and down the **Swift Creek Trail.** This route covers less than 5 miles but has plenty of great views. Should you follow it, try to stay out of the ski tracks as much as

possible so as not to make descents more treacherous for skiers. The starting point for either of these hikes is the **Marble Mountain Sno-Park,** where you should also be able to pick up a simple map of area ski trails.

SPELUNKING

Lava tubes form when a lava flow cools around its outer edges and eventually forms an arching roof over still-flowing lava. The lava, now insulated from outside air, can continue flowing through this tunnel. When an eruption stops, the hot lava can flow out of the tube and form a tunnel. Often portions of roof will collapse over the years and tunnels will be divided into caves. Such tunnels are common throughout volcanic areas of the Cascades. However, none are as long as **Ape Cave** on the south side of Mount St. Helens.

Ape Cave, the longest continuous lava tube in the continental United States, was discovered in 1946. The cave was named by a local Boy Scout troop that called themselves the Mount St. Helens Apes. The scout troop in turn had taken its name from an incident in the 1920s in which an apelike creature was seen on the mountain (later admitted to have been a hoax). Still, it is fun to imagine this cave as the former home of bigfoot.

However, there is nothing to fear from the big hairy beasts of Northwest legend, and armed with a powerful flashlight or lantern, you can see for yourself that there are no apes in this cave. The cave is divided into two sections, both of which are accessed from a stairway entrance near the Ape's Headquarters cabin off FS 83 north of Cougar. The 0.75-mile-long lower section, which has a high ceiling and sandy floor, is the easier to explore. This is a dead-end cave, so after exploring to its end, you'll have to return the way you came. The 1.5-mile-long upper cave has an exit at the far end and an above-ground trail to return you to your car. This section of the cave is much more difficult to explore. You'll have to do some scrambling over piles of rock. At the Ape's Headquarters cabin, you can visit the information center, where you can learn about lava tubes and rent a lantern for $4.

SWIMMING & TUBING

At Mayfield Lake, on U.S. 12 between I-5 and Morton, there are a couple of good swimming beaches. **Mayfield Lake County Park,** on the south side of the lake and right off the highway, is the more convenient of these beaches. On the north side of the lake, there is **Ike Kinswa State Park.** Both of these parks have wide lawns for spreading blankets on, and both stay busy mostly with local families throughout the summer.

WALKS & NATURAL ROADSIDE ATTRACTIONS

In addition to the trails listed below, the 2.5-mile **Woods Creek Watchable Wildlife Trail,** mentioned below under "Wildlife Viewing," makes a good, easy walk through a variety of habitats, including and old-growth forest.

Quartz Creek Big Trees Trail

0.5 miles. Easy. No elevation gain. Access: From Randle, on U.S. 12, drive south 9 miles on FS 25, turn right onto FS 26, continue 8 miles south, and turn right on FS 2608. Map: USFS Mount St. Helens National Volcanic Monument.

After seeing the devastated forests of the monument, you may be in need of a little reassurance that vertical forests really do still exist. This is the place to find that reassurance. The big trees along this trail really do live up to their name, with some reaching 10 feet in diameter. These Douglas firs are as much as 750 years old. Most amazing is that only a mile away, there are nothing but skeletons of trees that once were as majestic as these.

Harmony Trail

2 miles round-trip. Moderate. 600-foot elevation gain. Access: From the junction of FS 26 and FS 99 south of Randle, drive 3.5 miles west to the Harmony Viewpoint. Map: USFS Mount St. Helens National Volcanic Monument; Green Trails Spirit Lake.

This is the only trail that leads down to Spirit Lake, once the jewel of Mount St. Helens and the site of a very popular mountain resort. Today all is a wasteland. Even the lake can hardly be considered the same lake. Today the lakeshore lies 200 feet higher than it did before the eruption. From the shoreline, there is a view up the lake to the lava dome inside the crater.

WHITEWATER KAYAKING & CANOEING

Maybe it comes from living so close to a mountain with such a violent temper, but the rivers surrounding Mount St. Helens seem to have developed an attitude. They're steep and powerful, boulder-clogged and jammed with ledge drops. Only the best of paddlers should even think of bringing a boat on a vacation in this neck of the woods. If, however, you have honed your skills on gnarly Class IV waters and find that only such waters can keep you interested in paddling, then you'll find area rivers entertaining (to say the least).

CLASS I

This region has very little in the way of Class I waters, but if that's your speed, try the **Lower Cowlitz River.** This shallow, clear-flowing river maintains a good clip even in its lower stretches where it passes through wide-open farmland. Mount St. Helens and Mount Rainier show themselves in the distance, and there are islands for picnic stops. This is a favorite steelheading river and drift boats usually far outnumber canoes. From the Cowlitz Trout Hatchery northeast of Toledo on Spencer Road down to the I-5 bridge is a 14-mile run that can easily be done in half a day. To reach the take-out, take exit 56 off I-5, drive north on South Jackson Highway 2 miles, and turn left on Mandy Road to reach the boat ramp almost directly underneath the I-5 bridge. To reach the put-in, continue north on South Jackson Highway, turn left on Wash. 505, drive through Toledo and turn right on North Jackson Highway, and then right again after about a mile. An almost immediate left onto Spencer will take you to the fish hatchery, where you'll find a boat ramp down a gravel road. This is a great summer run.

CLASS II

Above the Cowlitz Trout Hatchery on the **Lower Cowlitz River** there is also an easy Class II run. This 8-mile run begins further up Spencer Road near the Cowlitz Salmon Hatchery. This is a lively stretch of water, though it has only a single Class II rapid. Another easy Class I–II run in this area is the **lower Kalama River.** The last 10 miles of this river before it empties into the Columbia River are fast and shallow. There are a couple of easy Class II rapids near the start of the run and then things quiet down. The take-out is a fishing access west of I-5 on Kalama River Road (exit 32). To reach the roadside put-in, drive 6 miles east of I-5 on Kalama River Road. Both of these are fun summer runs.

CLASS III

Most people never think to experience Mount St. Helens from the water, but it was in the river valleys that the volcano had some of its most far-reaching effects. The Toutle River is still choked with ash as it carves its way down through the thick layer of debris that was sent downstream by the eruption. Class III paddlers can get a look at this lunar riverscaping as they paddle through ash-colored water between ash-colored banks on the **South Fork Toutle River,** which flows into the main Toutle River a couple of miles east of Silver Lake. Put in at the end of the road at Harrington Place. Pick your own take-out.

If you like beautiful scenery and good whitewater, the **North Fork Lewis River** is for you. Although the run down the last 6 miles of the river before it flows into Swift Creek Reservoir isn't very long, it has lots of Class II and III rapids. It also provides some unexpected scenery in the form of two waterfalls, one of which flows through two natural arches before cascading into the Lewis. Along the way there are also views of Mount St. Helens to the north. The take-out for this run is the Eagle Cliffs Bridge at the east end of the reservoir. To reach the put-in, cross the bridge and follow FS 90 less than 6 miles to Rush Creek, turn left after crossing the creek and continue 1 mile down to a river access.

CLASS IV & ABOVE

How many Class IV runs can you have in one small area? Quite a few actually. The **East Fork Lewis River** and the **North Fork Lewis River** are well separated but both have Class IV runs. On the East Fork, this water is above Sunset Falls off County Road 12/FS 42 east of Moulton Falls. On the North Fork, the upper Lewis River run begins below the Lewis River Falls at a bridge over the river. The take-out is above Curly Creek Falls at Rush Creek. This run is accessed from FS 90 east of Cougar and Swift Creek Reservoir (this road was closed throughout 1996 because of flood damage).

The **Kalama River,** which flows down from the southwest flank of St. Helens, also offers nearly 25 miles of runnable water that is mostly Class III but with occasional Class IV rapids thrown in to keep paddlers below the expert level at bay. The uppermost put-in for running this river is northwest of Merrill Lake and below Kalama Falls. Take-outs are located at regular intervals along Kalama River Road, which parallels the river from I-5 eastward.

If you've ever thought it would be interesting to paddle a river on the moon, you can get the earth-bound visual equivalent by launching into the ash-filled waters of the **Toutle River.** This is the river that took almost the full brunt of St. Helens's eruption and today is still something of a wasteland. The river carves its way through a thick blanket of debris deposited when the eruption sent the entire north side of the mountain flooding down this valley. The **Green River,** a tributary of the Toutle that enters east of 19 Mile Camp, was spared the mudflows that inundated the Toutle and is a river of normal Cascade character. Fast and relentless, this river rarely gives paddlers time to think, and because road access is poor, once you're on, you're on for the whole run (about 12 miles).

WILDLIFE VIEWING

At the **Forest Learning Center** at milepost 33.5 on the Spirit Lake Highway (Wash. 504), you can gaze down into the Toutle

River valley where a large herd of **elk** can usually be seen grazing or resting in the meadows on the valley floor. You'll need binoculars to get a good look at the herd. At the **Woods Creek Watchable Wildlife Trail** on FS 25 south of Randle, you can often see **beaver** keeping busy on their ponds. This 2.5-mile trail is opposite the Woods Creek Information Center.

Campgrounds & Other Accommodations

CAMPING

A certain percentage of campsites at many National Forest Service campgrounds can be reserved at least five days in advance by calling the **National Forest Reservation Service** (tel. 800/280-CAMP). To make a reservation you'll need to know the name of the campground you want to stay at and the dates you plan to visit. The reservation fee is $7.50.

IN & NEAR MOUNT RAINIER NATIONAL PARK

There are five main campgrounds within Mount Rainier National Park, all of which are available on a first-come, first-served basis and stay full on summer weekends. Arrive early. The fees range from $6 to $10 per campsite per night. No electrical or water hookups are available. Only the Sunshine Point Campground stays open all year. The rest are open only from late spring through late fall.

The **Ohanapecosh Campground** (205 campsites), located in the southeast corner of the park, is the largest but is a long ways from the alpine meadows that are what most visitors want to see. The closest campground to Paradise is **Cougar Rock** (200 campsites), where you should try to get a site at the far end of the C, D, or E loop where you'll be camped under huge old-growth trees. The **White River Campground** (117 campsites) is close to Sunrise, which is one of the most spectacular spots in the park (this is my favorite of the park's drive-in campgrounds). The **Sunshine Point**

Campground (18 campsites), near the Nisqually (southwest) entrance to the park, is small but is the only park campground that is open year-round. Up in the northwest corner of the park, there is **Ipsut Creek Campground** (29 campsites), which in 1996 was accessible only by foot due to flood damage on the Carbon River Road that leads to the campground.

In addition to drive-in campgrounds and the many backcountry camps, there are two walk-in campgrounds that often have spaces available even on weekends. **Mowich Lake Campground** (10 campsites, seasonal) is in the northwest corner of the park not far from Ipsut Creek Campground, and the sites are only 100 yards from the parking lot. If you're prepared for a longer walk in, consider the **Sunrise Campground** (8 campsites, seasonal), which is between 1 and 1.5 miles from the Sunrise parking area depending on which route you take to the campground. This is probably the least used campground in the park and puts you in the middle of a maze of fabulous hiking trails. The drawback is hordes of day hikers traipsing through all day long.

When the park campgrounds are full, try **La Wis Wis** (100 campsites, seasonal), a national forest campground on U.S. 12 and the Cowlitz River near the Ohanapecosh entrance. Old-growth trees and the riverside setting make this a pleasant place. There are also numerous unremarkable National Forest Service campgrounds along U.S. 12 east of White Pass and along Wash. 410 east of the park. These latter campgrounds are going to offer your best chances of finding a campsite on a Friday or Saturday night in summer. The campgrounds along Wash. 410 tend to be less crowded since they are harder to reach and are not near any fishing lakes.

IN & NEAR MOUNT ST. HELENS NATIONAL VOLCANIC MONUMENT

West of the monument, **Sequest State Park** (92 campsites, 16 with full hookups; year-round), set amid impressive old-growth trees on Wash. 504 about 5 miles off I-5, is the closest public campground to

Coldwater Ridge. This campground is set on Silver Lake (good fishing) and is also the site of the Mount St. Helens Visitor Center, which makes this an excellent base camp. For reservations, call Reservations Northwest (tel. 800/452-5687).

Mount St. Helens Adventure Tours, 980 Schaffran Rd. (P.O. Box 625), Castle Rock, WA 98611 (tel. 360/274-6542; fax 360/274-8437), offers a couple of unusual camping experiences in the area west of the monument. Eco Park at Mount St. Helens, at milepost 25 on the Spirit Lake Highway (Wash. 504), has 10 tent and 10 RV sites, but it also rents yurts, wood-floored tents, and basic cabins with rates starting at $35. The yurts, tents, and cabins make year-round visits possible and are basically a step up from camping in your own tent but not as luxurious as a motel. Unique in the area, the yurts are comfortable and fun. Also operated by this company is a tent-and-breakfast tour that includes a night in a large, wood-floored tent, plus dinner and breakfast for $75 per person.

South of the monument, there are a couple of conveniently located campgrounds on Yale Lake—**Cougar** (45 campsites, seasonal) and **Beaver Bay** (63 campsites, seasonal)—and another near the east end of **Swift Reservoir** (93 campsites, seasonal). These campgrounds are more popular with anglers than with visitors to the monument. For more solitude and quiet, try the little **Merrill Lake Campground** (11 campsites, year-round), which is operated by the Washington Department of Natural Resources. This is a good choice for exploring the monument, as well as flat-water canoeing, fly-fishing, and mountain biking. Although a bit out of the way for exploring the monument, the **Lower Falls Campground** (43 campsites, seasonal) on the Lewis River is a beautiful spot set beside the waterfalls for which it is named. This campground is popular with mountain bikers out here to ride the Lewis River Trail.

East of the monument, **Iron Creek Campground** (98 campsites, seasonal), a Forest Service campground, is the closest to Windy Ridge and is the area's most popular campground with people exploring

the monument. This campground is set amid old-growth trees on the bank of the Cispus River.

INNS & LODGES

IN & NEAR MOUNT RAINIER NATIONAL PARK

Paradise Inn

P.O. Box 108, Ashford, WA 98304. Tel. 360/569-2275. 126 rms (95 with bath), 2 suites. $65 double with shared bath; $92–$118 double with bath; $124 suite. AE, CB, DC, DISC, MC, V. Closed early Oct to mid-May.

Built in 1917 high on the flanks of Mount Rainier in an area aptly known as Paradise, this rustic lodge offers breathtaking views of the mountain and nearby Nisqually Glacier. Cedar-shake siding, huge exposed beams, cathedral ceilings, and a gigantic stone fireplace all add up to a quintessential mountain retreat. A warm and cozy atmosphere prevails. Guest rooms vary in size and amenities, so be sure to specify which type you'd like. Miles of trails and meadows spread out from the lodge, making this the perfect spot for some relatively easy alpine exploring.

National Park Inn

P.O. Box 108, Ashford, WA 98304. Tel. 360/569-2275. 25 rms (18 with private bath). $61 double without bath, $84–$113 double with bath. AE, CB, DC, DISC, MC, V.

Located in Longmire in the southwest corner of the park, this rustic lodge was opened in 1920 and fully renovated in 1990. With only 25 rooms and open all year, the National Park Inn makes a great little getaway or base for exploring the mountain. The inn's front veranda has a view of Mount Rainier, and inside there's a guest lounge with a river-rock fireplace that's perfect for winter-night relaxing. Guest rooms vary in size, but come with rustic furniture, new carpeting, and coffeemakers. In the winter, this lodge is popular with cross-country skiers. Cross-country ski rentals are adjacent.

Alta Crystal Resort

68317 S.R. 410 E, Greenwater, WA 98022. Tel. 360/663-2500. 25 rms. $85–$165 single to quad. AE, MC, V.

Though this condominium resort is most popular in winter when skiers flock to Crystal Mountain's slopes, there is also plenty to do in summer. Accommodations are in one-bedroom and loft chalets. The former sleep up to four people and the latter have bed space for up to eight people. No matter what size condo you choose, you'll find a full kitchen and fireplace. This is the closest lodging to the northeast park entrance and the Sunrise area. An outdoor pool and nearby hiking trails provide summer activities.

Hotel Packwood

102 Main St. (P.O. Box 130), Packwood, WA 98361. Tel. 360/494-5431. 9 rms (2 with bath). $25–$30 double with shared bath, $38 double with private bath. No credit cards.

Two stories tall with a wraparound porch and weathered siding, this renovated 1912 hotel looks like a classic mountain lodge even though it is right in the middle of this small town. The tiny rooms are for those who aren't finicky. Packwood is about 10 miles from the southeast entrance to the park.

NEAR MOUNT ST. HELENS NATIONAL VOLCANIC MONUMENT

Blue Heron Inn Bed & Breakfast

2846 Spirit Lake Hwy., Castle Rock, WA 98611. Tel. 360/274-9595. 6 rms. $95–$125 double. MC, V.

Set on 5 acres of land beside Silver Lake, this inn has an excellent view of Mount St. Helens. Lots of decks provide plenty of places for relaxing and soaking up the view, and during cooler weather, you can sit by the fire in the parlor. This inn is by far the best bet for accommodations in the area and is adjacent to the Mount St. Helens Visitor Center.

8

THE COLUMBIA GORGE, MOUNT HOOD & MOUNT ADAMS

SEATTLEITES MAY CLAIM THAT THEIR BACKYARD MOUNTAIN IS *THE mountain*, but Portlanders have their own major peak in their backyard and one in the neighbors' yard, as well, plus an impressive gorge separating the two. Mount Hood, roughly 60 miles east of Portland, and Mount Adams, north across the Columbia River in Washington, loom up as natural gateposts flanking the deep, wide gash of the Columbia Gorge. Together this trio of natural attractions provides Portlanders (and numerous visitors) with enough outdoor options to keep them busy year-round: From waterfall walks in the gorge to summit climbs on both Hood and Adams, from downhill skiing at five ski areas to summer snowboarding on glacier-clad mountain slopes, from single-track trail riding to Class IV paddling, this area offers an amazing variety of outdoor activities no matter what the season.

It is in the summer that this area really reaches the zenith of its outdoor-sports potential—and popularity, though you might think otherwise when stuck in an après-ski traffic jam after a day at one of Mount Hood's ski areas. A friend once told me about two guys she met on a plane flying into Portland. Their minds were reeling at the prospect of their impending multisport vacation. It was July and their plans included early skiing on Mount Hood's Palmer Glacier, mountain biking on miles of single-track, afternoon boardsailing in the gorge, whitewater kayaking on the White Salmon River, and a quick climb to the top of 12,276-foot Mount Adams. Maybe they'd throw in some paragliding or road biking or flyfishing, just for good measure. But you get the picture—come summer the gorge area offers up all four seasons of the outdoors on a platter. Best of all, using the town of Hood River as a base of operations, all this great stuff is within an hour's drive.

The Columbia Gorge lies less than 20 miles east of downtown Portland, though in the past few years suburban sprawl has pushed the edges of the metropolitan region right to the mouth of the gorge. Luckily, the gorge has been somewhat protected since 1986 under the federal designation of Columbia Gorge National Scenic Area, though not without controversy (see the sidebar). Development has been limited within this stunningly beautiful landscape of basalt cliffs, ribbon-like waterfalls, and lush fir forests. The millions of motorists who pass through the gorge each year are treated to scenic vistas that, on foggy days, come close to duplicating those Chinese scroll paintings of vertical mountains dotted with twisted pine trees. I enjoy the gorge through my windshield as much as the next driver, but there's a whole lot more to the Columbia Gorge than you could ever hope to notice as you speed through at 65 miles per hour.

Boardsailors the world over know this already. The gorge, specifically right around the town of Hood River, has become the center of the universe for boardsailors who just can't get enough air. As the only low-elevation break in the Cascade Range, the Columbia Gorge acts as a massive wind funnel. When the dry high-desert lands east of the Cascades warm up in the summer, cooler air off the Pacific gets sucked up the river. Conversely, in winter, when the eastern desert is much colder than the maritime region west of the Cascades, cold winds blast out of the east, often bringing extreme conditions. High winds and long, wide stretches of water produce perfect conditions for high-speed, big-air sailing. With the summer winds rushing upriver against the current, wind-generated waves often reach 6 feet. Combine these watery ramps with winds over 30 knots and what you get is a playground on which world-class boarders perform awesome aerial acrobatics. Rest assured that mere mortals can sail here too. Conditions aren't always so extreme. It's even possible to learn the very basics of sailing on the gorge, in protected waters and wind shadows, that is.

There are, however, days when the wind just doesn't blow. When boardsailors here are becalmed, though, they don't sit around in pubs despondently quaffing pints of Full Sail Ale. No, they drop their kayak in some nearby whitewater, or hop on their mountain bikes and head for the hills. In winter, when checking the wind direction can mean checking to see which way the icicles are pointing, everyone heads up to the ski slopes on Mount Hood. And in July, dedicated telemarkers even ski off the summit of Mount Adams for up to 7,000 vertical feet of untracked snow. Consequently, in the past few years, Hood River has been attracting mountain-biking and snowboarding pilgrims along with all the boardheads.

Flanking the gorge to the north and south at roughly equal distances from the river are Mount Adams and Mount Hood. Of these two snow- and glacier-clad volcanic peaks, Mount Hood is the more accessible and developed. Mount Adams, which lies partially in the Yakama Indian Reservation, has no paved roads leading to it, no ski areas, no lodges, and consequently is a much less visited mountain.

The Lay of the Land

For the sake of this book, I have defined the gorge much as the federal government did in defining the boundaries of the Columbia Gorge National Scenic Area—from the Sandy River in the west to the Deschutes River in the east. I've also included Mount Hood, which, as far as Hood River residents are concerned, is but an extension of the gorge. Finally, the southern slopes and foothills of Mount Adams are covered here, because this area is most commonly accessed from White Salmon and Carson, both of which are in the Columbia Gorge.

The Columbia River is an old river—so old that it predates the Cascade Range, through which it slices. As the mountains, including 11,235-foot Mount Hood and 12,276-foot Mount Adams, arose (often in violent volcanic upheavals), the river continued to cut downward toward the ocean. Consequently, this is the only sea-level route through the Cascades. However, it has not been mountain building and volcanic upheavals that have shaped today's gorge so much as it has been floodwaters during the ice age.

The 4,000-foot-high basalt walls of the Columbia Gorge, today laced with waterfalls, once sloped gently down to the waters of the Columbia River. However, about 12,000 years ago floodwaters of inconceivable proportions swept down the Columbia River. These waters were released from huge lakes that developed repeatedly behind glacier-formed ice dams far to the northeast in present-day Montana. Floodwaters washed across central Washington, scouring everything in their path and leaving behind such natural phenomena as huge dry waterfalls and river channels left high and dry with no river nearby (Grand Coulee). When the floods reached the Cascade Range, they were forced into the relatively narrow valley of the Columbia River. Sometimes reaching heights of 1,000 feet and moving with tremendous speed, these floodwaters scoured out solid basalt mountains, leaving the gorge as we see it today—a huge U-shaped valley. Just as in the Sierra Nevada's Yosemite Valley, where glaciers carved away the sides of granite mountains, leaving streams to flow over vertical precipices, so too were the streams that once flowed into the Columbia left to cascade off high cliffs. Today, the Columbia Gorge has the highest concentration of waterfalls in the United States.

The gorge, because of its unique geography and topography, is a meeting point between two very distinct climatic zones. To the east lies the high desert; to the west lie lush green slopes that are watered throughout the year by rain clouds sweeping in off the Pacific. Consequently the gorge has developed a unique botanical mix and is well known for its spring wildflower displays. There are 15 wildflower species that are endemic to the gorge (found nowhere else). Many of these are to be found on steep basalt walls that are kept constantly moist by mists from waterfalls. The narrow cleft of the Oneonta Gorge is the best place to see such natural hanging gardens. Other good wildflower displays can be found on Dog Mountain in Washington, where meadows are filled with brilliant yellow balsamroot in May, and at Rowena Dells, where a high plateau is carpeted with wildflowers between March and May.

Because there is little flat land within the gorge, few towns of any size ever developed within its confines. At its western end, on the outskirts of Portland, there is **Troutdale,** which was once mostly a place to pick up fishing gear, but is now better known for a malignancy that seems to be afflicting many scenic areas across the nation—the factory-outlet mall. Just about the last thing you see before driving into the gorge today is this bastion of crass commercialism. Midway through the gorge stands the **Bonneville Dam,** which marks the end of the Lower Columbia and is located just beyond the end of the tidewater. Above the dam is the community of **Cascade Locks,** which today is best known as the point from which summer paddle-wheeler trips depart. Also here is the **Bridge of the Gods,** the only bridge across the river between Portland and Hood River. This bridge takes its name from a Native American legend of a stone bridge that once crossed the river at this spot. In fact, geologists believe that a natural bridge, caused by a massive landslide, did at one time exist here. The landslide, which took place about 1,000 years ago, blocked the river and created the Cascades for which Cascade Locks was named.

Almost directly across from Cascade Locks, on the Washington side of the river, is the town of **Stevenson,** site of the very informative **Columbia Gorge Interpretive Center** (tel. 509/427-8211) and the luxurious **Skamania Lodge** golf and conference resort (see "Inns & Lodges," later in this chapter). Continuing east on this side of the river brings you past some of the most legendary boardsailing spots in the gorge. Just past the bridge to Hood River lie the twin towns of **Bingen** and **White Salmon**—the former a gritty mill town, the latter a theme-town wannabe that once adopted a Bavarian theme in its business district but was never able to parlay gingerbread into tourist dollars.

The town that has dominated tourism in the gorge is **Hood River,** directly across the river in Oregon. Here, old Victorian homes have been renovated by boardheads looking to live in one of the world's perfect sailing spots. Board and sail shops line the streets of Hood River, as do espresso places and microbreweries. During the summer months it's as much a "scene" as any ski resort in winter. If you don't sail, you'll feel decidedly left out here.

Anchoring the eastern end of the gorge, on the Oregon side, is **The Dalles.** This is pilgrim country, a town built on helping pioneers get down the river; to this day, though it has some good sailing spots and a few board shops, it still seems to be all business, with a cloud-piercing church steeple as the city's most prominent architectural landmark.

Transportation and logging were long the mainstays of the gorge economy. Towns such as Hood River, Bingen, White Salmon, and Stevenson, all set at the foot of the gorge's cliffs, bluffs, and mountains, developed around lumber mills. However, in the wake of overcutting, mill automation, log exports to Japan, and designation of spotted owl habitat, these towns have

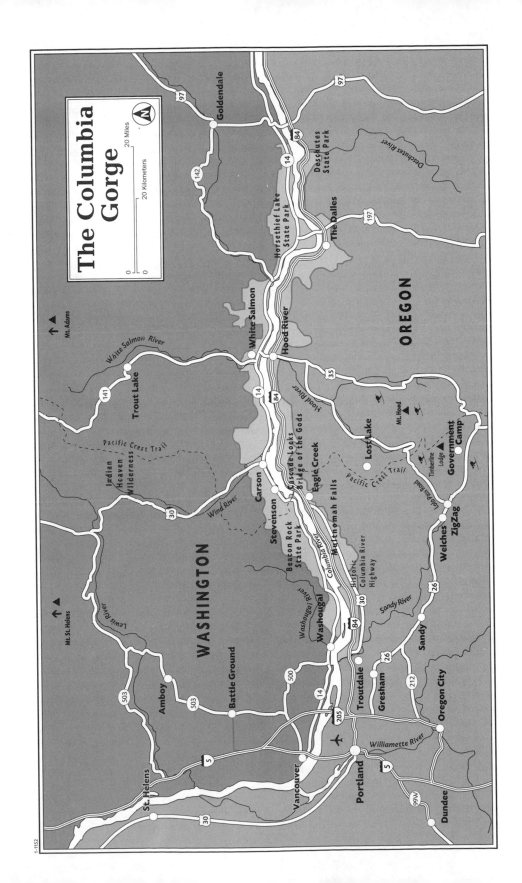

The Columbia Gorge

20 Miles

20 Kilometers

WASHINGTON

OREGON

Mt. St. Helens

Mt. Adams

Mt. Hood

St. Helens

Amboy

Battle Ground

Vancouver

Portland

Dundee

Oregon City

Gresham

Sandy

Troutdale

Welches

ZigZag

Government Camp

Sandy River

Williamette River

Lewis River

Washougal

Washougal River

Carson

Stevenson

Trout Lake

White Salmon River

Indian Heaven Wilderness

Pacific Crest Trail

Wind River

Beacon Rock State Park

Cascade Locks

Bridge of the Gods

Eagle Creek

Multnomah Falls

Columbia River

Historic Columbia River Highway

Hood River

Lost Lake

Timberline Lodge

Pacific Crest Trail

Lolo Pass Road

White Salmon

Hood River

Horsethief Lake State Park

The Dalles

Goldendale

Deschutes River

Deschutes State Park

5

30

503

503

500

205

99W

212

26

26

84

14

14

30

30

141

142

97

97

35

197

1-1152

watched their once-thriving mill economies dwindle. Today it's boardsailing and scenic vistas that the gorge's economy hinges on, and together these two are beginning to spread the name of the Columbia Gorge beyond the boundaries of the Pacific Northwest.

Parks & Other Hot Spots

Rooster Rock State Park

25 miles east of Portland, off I-84. Picnic areas, beach, boat ramp. Swimming, boardsailing, sea kayaking, fishing.

One of the largest and most popular recreation spots in the gorge, this state park has acres of green lawns, tall trees, long beaches (including one that is clothing optional), a boat launch popular with anglers, and of course its namesake rock, which is a basalt tower that rises above the trees along I-84. Boardsailing is popular here, and if you happen to have a sea kayak, this is one of the best places in the gorge to do a bit of paddling. Be forewarned, however, that on weekends crowds fill up the huge parking lot in a hurry. Weekdays, on the other hand, are much less crowded. Traffic noise from the interstate can be annoying.

Multnomah Falls

31 miles east of Portland, off I-84. Tel. 503/695-2372. Viewpoint, interpretive center, restaurant. Hiking.

At 620 feet high, this waterfall is the fourth highest in the United States and even has its own exit off I-84. The falls are by far the most visited spot in the gorge, and at their base you'll find a restaurant, snack bar, souvenir shop, and interpretive center. The falls themselves are divided into upper and lower falls, with an old pedestrian bridge over the creek between the two levels. Seen from below, this bridge seems to almost float in the middle of the falls. This is big-time photo-op terrain. Few of the visitors to the falls ever make it past the bridge, but a paved trail leads all the way to the top, and unpaved trails

lead onward from there. A reminder of the fact that the Columbia Gorge is still eroding took place in 1995 when a piece of rock the size of a school bus broke loose from the cliffs alongside Multnomah Falls and came crashing down into the pool at the waterfall's base. Luckily, no one was killed.

Eagle Creek Recreation Area

41 miles east of Portland, off I-84. Picnic area, camping, hiking, swimming, mountain biking.

Since the opening of the Historic Columbia River Highway back in 1915, Eagle Creek has been one of the gorge's most popular destinations. This isn't surprising when you see this small gorge-within-a-gorge. The clear waters of Eagle Creek, the precarious trail blasted into steep basalt cliffs, and a couple of waterfalls naturally designed for cooling off on a hot summer day are the payoff for putting up with the crowds here. The picnic area is extremely popular on summer weekends and a campground and fish hatchery further add to the overall appeal. To escape the crowds you need only be willing to hike beyond High Bridge on the Eagle Creek Trail.

Beacon Rock State Park

35 miles east of Vancouver, Wash. (or 7 miles west of Bridge of the Gods), off Wash. 14. Picnic area, camping, hiking, rock climbing, bird watching, fishing, sea kayaking.

If not for the farsightedness of an early recreationist, Beacon Rock would now be rubble at the mouth of the Columbia River. Despite the fact that this massive 848-foot-tall block of rock is the second largest freestanding monolith in the world (only the Rock of Gibraltar is larger), there were those people earlier in this century who thought this would be a great source of rock for jetties to protect the mouth of the Columbia. Henry Biddle thought differently and in 1915 he bought the rock and spent the next three years building a trail to the top. Today that precarious trail of steel girders and stairs remains, and the hike to the top of the rock is a highlight of any trip to the gorge. Beacon Rock offers

Outdoor Resources

RANGER STATIONS & OTHER SOURCES OF INFORMATION

**Columbia River Gorge
National Scenic Area**
USDA Forest Service
902 Wasco Ave., Suite 200
Hood River, OR 97031
Tel. 541/386-2333

Hood River Ranger District
6780 Hwy. 35 S
Mount Hood–Parkdale, OR 97041
Tel. 541/352-6002

Skamania Lodge
Forest Service Information Center
Stevenson, WA 98648
Tel. 509/427-2528

Wind River Ranger District
1262 Hemlock Rd.
Carson, WA 98610
Tel. 509/427-3200

Mount Adams Ranger District
2455 Hwy. 141
Trout Lake, WA 98650
Tel. 509/395-2501

Zigzag Ranger District
70220 E Hwy. 26
Zigzag, OR 97049
Tel. 503/622-3191

Mount Hood Information Center
65000 E Hwy 26
Welches, OR 97067
Tel. 503/622-7674 or
   503/622-3360

Barlow Ranger District
780 Court St.
Dufur, OR 97021
Tel. 541/467-2291

Ripple Brook Ranger District
61431 E Hwy. 224
Estacada, OR 97023
Tel. 503/630-4256

Estacada Ranger District
595 NW Industrial Way
Estacada, OR 97023
Tel. 503/630-6861

EQUIPMENT SHOPS

Cascade Outdoor Center
311 Oak St., Hood River
Tel. 541/387-3527

---

the most challenging rock climbing in the gorge, and at the foot of the rock is a side channel of the Columbia that is great for sea kayaking.

Horsethief Lake State Park

8.5 miles northeast of The Dalles. Take U.S. 197 north and then Wash. 14 east. Tel. 509/767-1159. Petroglyph tours, camping, canoeing, fishing, swimming, rock climbing.

Though many people know this park as a boating, swimming, and fishing spot, to me it is most importantly the home of **Tsagaglalal,** an ancient Native American petroglyph also known as "She Who Watches." This wide-eyed, square-mouthed face is unforgettable and has become the preeminent symbol of Native American history in this region (sort of the Kokopelli of the Northwest). You'll see likenesses of Tsagaglalal on jewelry and other gifts and souvenirs for sale in the gorge and throughout the Northwest. In addition to this petroglyph, there are hundreds of others scrawled on the rocks that litter the hillside within this park. Tours to visit the park's famous petroglyphs are offered April through October on Friday and Saturday mornings at 10am by reservation only.

Mount Adams Wilderness

45 miles north of Hood River Bridge. Take Wash. 141 north to Trout Lake and then head north on FS 17 (the right fork at the gas station) for 2 miles and take a left onto FS 80 (signed South Climb). Tel. 509/395-2501. Hiking, mountaineering, cross-country skiing.

Though located in Washington, Mount Adams is difficult to reach from that state's population centers; Portland residents, who have an easier time getting to the mountain, simply tend to overlook it. Mount Adams is, consequently, a great place to get away from the crowds that jam the trails on Mount Rainier and Mount Hood. It is also the easiest to climb of the major Cascade Range peaks in Washington and Oregon. The buff of bod consider this peak little more than a day's stroll, but mere mortals tend to look on it as a very strenuous day's hike. If you're not into peak bagging, do as the day hikers do and come for the Monet-like displays of wildflowers that cover the slopes and meadows in July and August. Bird Creek Meadows (see the "Hiking & Backpacking" section under "The Gorge's Washington Side," below) is the best known of these wildflower areas. Winter snows that linger well into the summer attract backcountry skiers and occasional snowboarders.

Indian Heaven Wilderness

From Wash. 14 in Carson, drive 6 miles north on Wind River Rd., then turn right onto FS 65. Continue north for roughly 20 miles to trailheads. Also accessible by driving west from Trout Lake on Wash. 141 to FS 24 to Cultus Lake Campground. Tel. 509/395-2501 or 509/427-5645. Hiking, fishing.

Located southeast of Mount Adams, this wilderness area encompasses a lake-studded plateau that, while not high, has an abundance of scenery. All trails into the wilderness lead uphill through generally uninteresting forest, but once you reach the plateau, the landscape opens up into glades, meadows, and lakes. In late summer and early fall, the huckleberry bushes that blanket the region are covered with succulent berries that make this the best time of year to hike here. The wilderness's name is a reference to the fact that for centuries this has been an important berry-gathering ground for the region's Native Americans, who still have exclusive rights to pick berries in certain areas.

Mount Hood Wilderness

Access from Timberline Lodge off U.S. 26 at Government Camp, Cloud Cap and Mount Hood Meadows ski area off Ore. 35, and Lolo Pass Rd. off U.S. 26 at Zigzag. Tel. 503/622-3191 or 503/666-0701. Hiking, mountaineering, fishing, cross-country skiing.

This wilderness area takes in the summit and much of Mount Hood's lower slopes. It is here that you will find the mountain's most beautiful meadows (aside from Mount Hood Meadows, which are the site of a ski area). The wilderness is most easily accessed from ever-popular Timberline Lodge, and consequently, this is where you'll find the greatest crowds on the trails. In addition to this 47,100-acre wilderness, there are two smaller and less-visited wilderness areas on Mount Hood. These are the **Salmon–Huckleberry Wilderness** south of Zigzag and the **Badger Creek Wilderness** east of Ore. 35. A sno-park permit is necessary to park at Timberline Lodge from November 15 to April 15 unless you are a hotel guest.

Columbia Wilderness

Accessible from trails along I-84 between Bonneville Dam and Starvation Creek State Wayside and from Wahtum Lake off FS 13 west of Dee, which is southwest of Hood River. Tel. 503/622-7674. Hiking, fishing.

The Columbia Wilderness lies to the south of the Columbia Gorge toward its eastern end. This low-elevation wilderness is characterized by dense forests and deep creek drainages. The Eagle Creek Trail is the most popular access into the wilderness. On the southeast side of the wilderness, Wahtum, Rainy, and North lakes attract anglers. Because of its low elevation, this place is only lightly visited.

Bull of the Woods Wilderness

50 miles south of Estacada. Take Ore. 224 south for 26 miles, then continue on FS 46 to FS 63 to FS 6340 to FS 6341. Tel. 503/630-6861. Hiking, fishing.

Located southeast of Estacada at the headwaters of the Collawash River (a tributary of the Clackamas River), this wilderness lies mostly within the Mount Hood National Forest but also in Willamette National Forest. The wilderness is at a relatively low elevation in mountains that predate the main Cascade Range and is characterized by dense forests of Douglas firs and other conifers. Most visitors come for the fishing in the area's many small lakes, though the hike to the top of 5,523-foot Bull of the Woods Mountain attracts a nonangling crowd. In spring and fall when high-elevation trails are closed by snow, this is a good place to escape the city and the crowds. The hike to Pansy Lake is the most popular in this wilderness.

The Gorge's Oregon Side ◆ What to Do & Where to Do It

BOARDSAILING

First and foremost, the gorge today is about boardsailing. Though there are a few places where beginners can give it a try, the gorge is primarily for the experienced sailor. Not only are there gale-force winds and a powerful current, but there are also all those other boardheads to contend with. Oh yeah, and then there are the barges— big barges, barges that wouldn't slow down for you even if they could. On a day when the winds are nukin' (as they like to say in Hood River), boardsailing here is akin to sailing in a hurricane through the Strait of Hormuz.

For any and all board needs, Hood River is the place to head. Here you'll find dozens of board shops, sail and boom makers, masseuses to knead your aching muscles, brew pubs, and pizza places— basically everything you could ask for. The following shops can help outfit you for sailing the Gorge: **Big Winds,** 505 Cascade St. (tel. 541/386-6086); **The Gorge House,** 13 Oak St. (tel. 541/386-1699); **Windwing Hood River,** 315 Oak St. (tel. 541/386-3861); or **Hood River Windsurfing,** 101 Oak St. (tel. 541/386-5787). Or, for a real deal, check out **2nd Wind Sports,** 210 Oak St. (tel. 541/386-4464), which sells both new and used sailboards and other sports equipment.

If it's lessons you need, there are plenty of places in Hood River willing to get you started or help you fine-tune your high-wind skills. Try the **Rhonda Smith Windsurfing Center,** Port Marina Park (tel. 541/386-WIND); **Sail World Hood River,** 112 Oak St. (tel. 541/386-9400); or **Hood River Windsurfing,** 101 Oak St. (tel. 541/386-5787).

For more information on sailing the gorge, you might want to contact the **Columbia Gorge Windsurfing Association,** P.O. Box 182, Hood River, OR 97031 (tel. 541/386-9225), or the **United States Windsurfing Association,** 202 Oak St., Suite 200, Hood River, OR 97031 (tel. 541/386-8708).

Most gorge windsurfing sites charge a $2 to $3 access fee.

Rooster Rock State Park

Take exit 25 off I-84. Recommended sail size: 3.5–4.5, occasionally as small as 2.5.

This is the closest boarding spot to Portland, and unlike other spots in the gorge, it gets east winds only. Consequently, it is popular in spring and fall when "nuclear" east winds blow down off the high desert. You won't find the standing waves that are so common farther east (so no airtime), but consistent 30-knot winds keep the speed freaks happy.

The Hook

In Hood River. Take exit 63 off I-84, then head north to a left onto Riverside Dr., right on N Eighth St., and left on Portway Ave. Recommended sail size: 4.5–5.0.

This is perhaps the best spot in the gorge for beginners and offers a nice quiet bay where you can practice the basics: uphauling, tacking, jibbing, and water starts. There are three launch sites, each of which will send you into different conditions. The east launch sends you into the bay, while the west site is perfect for practicing water starts (west winds will blow you back to the beach). The north launch provides immediate access to the swells and high winds of the main channel, where west winds often kick up 3- to 4-foot swells.

Hood River Sailpark

In Hood River. Take exit 64 off I-84, then north almost to the bridge and left on W Marina Rd. to Hood River Marina. Recommended sail size: 5.0–6.0.

This used to be *the* place to go boarding and was where lessons were given by Hood River windsurfing schools. Today many other spots have become more popular, but this place still offers plenty of conveniences.

Event Site

In Hood River. Take exit 63 off I-84, then head north on N Second St. Recommended sail size: 4.5–5.5.

These days this is just about the most popular of Hood River's launch sites, and it's packed on summer weekends when the winds are blowing. The winds here are typically lighter than over at the Hatchery across the river. This is a popular slalom spot and attracts quite a few intermediate sailors.

Rowena

Take exit 76 off I-84, then head north to Mayer State Park. Recommended sail size: 3.5–5.0.

If you aren't yet ready to take on the swells at the Hatchery or Doug's Beach, you might want to spend some time at this ever-more-popular spot. Rowena gets good west winds but doesn't build the swell of other sites, which makes this a good slalom spot. Lots of grass for rigging. Be aware of submerged rocks downriver along the shore.

Dalles Riverfront Park

Take exit 85 off I-84, then head north and follow signs. Recommended sail size: 5.0–6.0.

If you've never sailed the gorge, this is just about the best place to get started. The winds are usually light and luckily tend to blow you back to shore instead of out into the channel. A little pond within the park is meant to be used for practicing water starts. More advanced sailors will often find conditions good for slalom and speed sailing. There's plenty of grass for rigging and a sandy beach for launching.

FISHING

Whether you're after hefty salmon, massive sturgeon, wily steelhead, smallmouth bass, or perhaps rainbow trout, there are plenty of places to get your line wet up and down the length of the Columbia Gorge. The **Sandy River,** at the west end of the gorge, is one of the top 10 steelhead rivers in Oregon. And the many streams that come pouring down off the cliffs in the gorge support populations of rainbow and cutthroat trout. At the far east end of the gorge, the **Deschutes River** is legendary among fly-fishers for its native redside rainbow trout. The peak season for rainbows runs from May to October. Up and down the gorge, summer steelhead run primarily from August to October, with winter steelheading peaking between January and March.

Though for many people a big salmon is the prize catch of the Columbia, there are those dedicated anglers who go after the true giants of this river—the sturgeons. These ancient fish grow to massive proportions and hide out in deep holes in the middle of the river. If you haven't got a boat to head out to these holes, you can still fish for sturgeon from the riverbanks near the Bonneville Dam.

If fly-fishing is your passion, you'll want to stop in at the **Gorge Fly Shop,** 416 Oak St., Hood River (tel. 541/386-6977), for flies, gear, and advice. This shop also offers a guide service. A half day runs $85 and a full day $150. Alternatively, if landing big fish is what turns you on, you could hire a guide to take you where the fish are sure to be biting. Try **Mike's Guide Service,** P.O. Box 387, Cascade Locks, OR 97014 (tel. 541/374-2228), which is run by Mike Claggett. A half day runs $60 and a full day $110 to $125.

HIKING & BACKPACKING

Wahkeena Falls to Multnomah Falls

5.6 miles. Moderate. 1,500-foot elevation gain. Access: Take exit 28 off I-84 and drive east on the Historic Columbia River Hwy. for 2.5 miles to Wahkeena Falls. Map: Geo-Graphics Trails of the Columbia Gorge.

Multnomah Falls, with its own pull-off from I-84, is the busiest spot in the gorge. It doesn't lose anything being viewed from a vantage among the stiff-necked masses at the base of the falls, but my favorite way to visit Multnomah makes it the destination of a hike that starts at Wahkeena Falls. This trail climbs steeply from the base of Wahkeena Falls and continues up Wahkeena Creek (passing Fairy Falls). In 1.6 miles, you'll pass the junction for Angel's Rest, but continue to the left and eastward, climbing up to the trail's high point of 1,600 feet. This area was partially burned during a 1991 fire that closed the Perdition Trail, which ran parallel to, but lower than, this trail. That trail remains closed to this day.

You'll reach the Larch Mountain Trail (it's 5 miles up to the top of Larch Mountain, which has great views) 1.2 miles beyond the Angel's Rest junction. Take a left and head downhill toward Multnomah Falls; another mile's walk will lead you past several smaller waterfalls before reaching the Multnomah Falls overlook. Far below, you'll see the hordes gathered at the bottom of the falls and on the bridge that is less than halfway up from the base. From here on out you'll be dealing with the crowds. It's 1.4 miles on a paved trail from here down to the base of the falls.

At the base you'll appreciate that, at 620 feet high, these are the fourth-highest falls in the U.S. From the Multnomah Falls base you can walk back to Wahkeena Falls and your car along the historic highway (less than 1 mile). Otherwise, you can hike back up to the top of the falls and return the way you came.

Oneonta Gorge/Horsetail Falls/Triple Falls Loop

4.5 miles. Moderate. 550-foot elevation gain. Access: Take exit 35 off I-84 and drive west 1.5 miles to Horsetail Falls. Map: Geo-Graphics Trails of the Columbia Gorge.

Four waterfalls are the main attraction of this hike, and parts of the trail parallel the amazing little Oneonta Gorge (staying high above the stream on trail cut into the cliff face). However, the best part of a hike here is the chance to do a bit of Utah-style canyoneering before or after hiking the trail. From the parking area, you can walk directly up the narrow slot of the Oneonta Gorge. There is no trail down in these narrow recesses of the gorge; you'll be walking through the water. Be sure to bring sandals or shoes that can get wet. Most of the way, the gorge is no more than 20 feet wide, and hanging from its moist and shady walls are several species of plants that are endemic to the Columbia Gorge.

If it's too cold for stream walking or you just aren't in the mood to get your feet wet, you can still have a fun time exploring the waterfalls along this trail. From the Horsetail Falls parking area, head up the trail less than 0.25 miles to Ponytail Falls where the trail passes behind the falls. Continuing onward, you'll come to a clifftop overlook in about 0.5 miles and then after another 0.5 miles you'll reach the metal footbridge over Oneonta Creek and the 60-foot Oneonta Falls. Shortly beyond the bridge, turn left at a trail junction and head toward Larch Mountain. In about 1 mile, you'll come to Triple Falls, so named for the three distinct streams that form the falls. Backtrack on this trail, and when you reach the junction leading to Oneonta Falls, continue straight to the historic highway in a little less than a mile from the junction. From here it is necessary to hike 0.5 miles along the highway to return to the Horsetail Falls parking area.

Angel's Rest

3 miles round-trip. Moderate. 1,460-foot elevation gain. Access: Take I-84 to exit 28 (Bridal

The Columbia Gorge National Scenic Area

Created on November 17, 1986 by none other than President Ronald Reagan, the Columbia Gorge National Scenic Area was the first area in the nation to receive such a designation. What exactly is a national scenic area? That was what everyone living in the gorge wanted to know at the time it was being created, and visitors still ask the question as they explore this spectacularly beautiful area.

Basically, the objective in designating 285,000 acres of the gorge as a national scenic area was to preserve its look. Since the land within the gorge is a patchwork of private and public land, there was the potential for private land to be developed in ways that would not be compatible with the gorge's importance as a major natural attraction. Needless to say, the gorge experience just wouldn't be the same if every acre of forest was clear-cut, if factories lined I-84, and if tract housing sprawled eastward from Portland. If the measure were to be proposed today, landowners in the gorge would be screaming that the government was infringing on their property rights—and in fact that is more or less what they claimed a decade ago.

As it happens, fears over government "land grabbing" haven't been realized, but then again neither has the gorge been as protected as proponents of the national scenic area had envisioned. Although the Columbia River Gorge Commission oversees land-use practices within the gorge, the commission's jurisdiction does not extend to the 13 designated urban areas that are found within the gorge. These include Hood River, Stevenson, White Salmon, Lyle, Bingen, and other smaller communities, all of which can approve developments that would not be acceptable outside their designated urban areas. With these urban areas covering substantial acreages within the gorge, and with the recent growth throughout the gorge, urban sprawl on a small scale is beginning to show itself. The bluffs outside White Salmon are now lined with expensive homes—exactly what the national scenic area designation was supposed to guard against.

With the rising cost of lumber, trees within the gorge have become increasingly valuable. Pressures have grown to clear-cut within the gorge, and on private land that's just what has been happening. Though you aren't likely to see the effects of this logging as you drive through the gorge on I-84 or Wash. 14, a hike to the top of Dog Mountain or any of the other mountains on the Washington side of the gorge will provide a different perspective.

However, despite the inadequacies of the national scenic area designation, it is clear that the Columbia Gorge is more protected than it would be otherwise. Sure, most of the gorge's hiking trails were already protected on federal and state lands, and sure, many of the views would still be the same because they are already protected in wilderness areas.

But if the gorge were completely unprotected against rampant development, there would be an incessant gnawing away at its private lands, the integrity of the gorge would be compromised, and a visit to this unique feature of the western landscape would be far from the natural experience that it is today.

Veil) and continue east a hundred yards or so to the junction with the old Historic Columbia River Hwy. Park in the dirt lot at the junction. The trail begins across the old highway. Map: Geo-Graphics Trails of the Columbia Gorge.

It may be a hell of a walk up to this rock outcropping high above the Columbia River, but once you've reached the top, you're just a little bit closer to heaven. Angel's Rest, a basalt outcropping on a bare windswept ridge, offers splendid views west down the gorge as far as Portland. Because of the angle of this rocky ridge, it tends to deflect the gorge's famous winds, which rage through notches in the rocks and have over the centuries sculpted both the trees and the rocks. The top of the ridge is, however, wide and flat, and you needn't worry too much about being blown over the cliffs. Masochists may want to head for Devil's Rest, which is not too far away as the crow flies but is another 4.5 miles on trails 415 and 420.

Eagle Creek

4.2–12 miles round-trip. Moderate–strenuous. 400-foot elevation gain to Punchbowl Falls; 1,200 feet to Tunnel Falls. Access: Exit 41 off I-84. Map: Geo-Graphics Trails of the Columbia Gorge.

What with the families and scout troops and couples strolling along, the walk up the Eagle Creek Trail is hardly a wilderness experience, and though it's easier to find a parking space in downtown Portland than here on a sunny summer Sunday, Eagle Creek remains the quintessential gorge hike. Eagle Creek, a gorge within *the gorge,* slices down through steep basalt walls into which have been hacked a 6-foot-wide rough pathway that is certainly not for the acrophobic. At times a heavy chain anchored to the rock wall provides a handhold for the faint of heart and unsure of foot. However, if you don't suffer from fear of heights, you can't help but ooh and ahh over the views of the creek far below and the lush forested mountainside on the opposite side of this gorge. After about a mile, the trail enters the forest and remains there for the rest of the route.

During the summer months, it's a good idea to get an early start both to get a parking space and to avoid the hot afternoon sun that bakes the black basalt walls along the trail.

The goal for most hikers on this trail is Punchbowl Falls, though before you ever reach the spur trail to these falls, you'll pass a short side trail that leads to an overlook onto Metlako Falls. The deep green pool at the base of Punchbowl Falls is a favorite cooling-off spot and is the destination of most people hiking this trail. If this hasn't been enough of a hike for you, you can continue to High Bridge (a 6.6-mile round-trip) or Tunnel Falls

(a 12-mile round-trip). The former is a footbridge across a narrow gorge, while at the latter, the trail passes through a tunnel behind the falls. If your goal is to lose the crowds, you'll likely do so beyond High Bridge.

Rowena Dell/Tom McCall Preserve

2.2–5.6 miles. Easy–moderate. 250–1,250-foot elevation gain. Access: Take exit 69 (Mosier) off I-84 and drive 6.5 miles east on the Historic Columbia River Hwy. to the Rowena Crest Viewpoint. Map: At trailhead.

Site of the 230-acre Tom McCall Nature Preserve, this is one of the best places in the Columbia Gorge to see spring wildflowers. Because of its unique character, the area was purchased by the Nature Conservancy, and on spring weekends the Conservancy offers guided hikes and has volunteers answering questions about the unusual plants to be found here.

Consisting of rolling meadows high above the Columbia River, Rowena Dell has superb views from just about anywhere. The trails wander through the meadows, past small ponds, and out to viewpoints. There are two main trails here. The easier leads 1.1 miles gradually downhill past small ponds to a dizzying viewpoint overlooking the river. The more difficult trail leads 1.7 miles (and 1,000 feet in elevation) up to Tom McCall Point.

HORSEBACK RIDING

The Columbia Gorge isn't really cowboy country, but if you want to saddle up a palomino (or bay or roan or Appaloosa), **Shadow Mountain Ranch** (tel. 541/374-8592), west of Hood River in Wyeth (take exit 51 off I-84), will take you on the trail. A one-hour ride costs $20 and a two-hour ride costs $35. South of Hood River, you can ride at **Fir Mountain Ranch,** 4051 Fir Mountain Rd. (tel. 541/354-2753), which charges similar rates.

MOUNTAIN BIKING

In the past few years Hood River has become one of the nation's mountain-biking meccas. This has come about not just because there are dozens of miles of great single-track and forest roads nearby, but because—and this might be the biggest contributing factor to the sport's growing popularity here—the wind doesn't always blow in Hood River. When the winds aren't blowing, boardheads need some other sport to occupy their time, and mountain biking has become the second-string sport of choice (though whitewater kayaking is pretty popular too). Only a couple of rides are listed here; the best rides, those that make this a national fat-tire destination, are far enough out of town that I have stuck them in the Mount Hood section later in this chapter.

If you don't have a bike and want to rent one or just need directions or a part for your bike, stop by **Discover Bicycles,** 1020 Wasco St. (tel. 541/386-4820) or **Mountain View Cycles,** 411 Oak St. (tel. 541/386-2453) in Hood River, or **Life Cycles,** 418 E Second St. (tel. 541/296-9588) in The Dalles. If you want a guide to show you the best trails, contact **Gorge Mountain Velo** (tel. 541/337-2222, ext. 275), which does guided trips in the area.

Gorge Trail

4–20 miles round trip. Easy–moderate. 750-foot elevation gain. Access: Take exit 41 (Eagle Creek) and park near the main rest rooms. The trailhead begins up the paved road to the left. Map: Geo-Graphics Trails of the Columbia Gorge.

Currently there are only a couple of sections of this low-elevation trail open to mountain bikers. However, because these sections are short, they make good introductions to single-track riding for beginners. The 2-mile trail from Eagle Creek to Cascade Locks, which in its middle section is actually on an abandoned part of the old Columbia River Highway, has a little bit of everything you can expect on a good mountain-bike trail—roots, rocks, some wet spots, a few switchbacks, some steep pitches, a few views, and some smooth hardpack for easy cruising. Try this trail first before committing yourself to more serious single-track riding. A longer section of the trail heads west from Eagle Creek and continues to Dodson, about

8 miles away. If you're full of energy, you can add a hike up Eagle Creek and a dip in the cold waters after your ride.

Post Canyon Road

6–8 miles. Moderate–difficult. 700-foot elevation gain. Access: From downtown Hood River, go 1.9 miles west on Oak St. and turn left on Country Club Rd. Continue 1.5 miles and turn right onto Post Canyon Rd.

Located just west of downtown Hood River, Post Canyon is far more than just a road; it's a mountain-biker's playground with many miles of gravel roads and trails. This is Hood River's backyard bike zone, where local cyclists head for a quick after-work ride. The network of gravel and dirt roads and single-track trails lends itself to rides of varying lengths. A moderately difficult favorite is the Seven Streams Loop, which includes—you guessed it— seven stream crossings, and which can be connected to the more challenging Upper Post Canyon Loop.

Start this ride by heading up Post Canyon Road from the beginning of gravel for 1.3 miles to a dirt trail on the left. Follow this trail uphill for 0.8 miles and turn left to reach a gravel road in another 0.2 miles. Turn right here and continue another 0.2 miles to a right onto another 0.4 miles of trail. From the end of this section, it's a right onto a gravel road for another 0.2 miles, and then downhill for 0.2 miles on a dirt road. At this point, you can turn right and head downhill on good single-track to return to the starting point, or turn left on a gravel road for 0.6 miles to a right turn onto another gravel road. From this junction, it's 0.2 miles, across a clear-cut with views of both Mount Hood and Mount Adams, to a right turn onto almost 1 mile more of single-track riding. From the end of this stretch of trail, turn left onto a dirt road for 0.3 miles and then turn left again onto 1.4 miles of single-track that will take you all the way back to Post Canyon Road (you rode some of this trail coming in), where you turn right to reach your starting point. I know all this sounds complicated, but the other choice is to simply get yourself good and lost and then meander the best you can back downhill to Hood

River. If you're lucky, you won't end up on top of Mount Defiance.

ROAD BIKING

Hood River-Parkdale Loop

35 miles. Strenuous. 1,500-foot elevation gain. Access: Take exit 64 off I-84 and follow signs to Ore. 35. Park your car across from the China Gorge Restaurant, which is just across a bridge from downtown Hood River.

This ride makes for a good workout, since it's virtually all uphill from Hood River to Parkdale. Luckily, the climb is gradual, if a bit long. The route passes through the famous Hood River apple orchards, which makes spring (blossom time) and fall (harvest season) the best times to do the ride. Start by heading south (uphill) on Ore. 35, which sees a lot of fast traffic but has a wide shoulder, making it a good cycling road. Between here and the community of Mount Hood (13 miles up the road), you have frequent views of its namesake mountain. If you don't mind a bit of extra climbing, you can take an alternate, less traveled route up the east side of the valley. Watch for Eastside Road and the sign to Panorama Point (well worth a stop), and just follow this road up to Fir Mountain Road, where a right turn will return you to Ore. 35. This is actually a more scenic route. In the community of Mount Hood there is the Mount Hood General Store, which is everything a good general store should be plus a bit more. This is a great place to rest on the front porch and have a snack.

At the general store, turn west off of Ore. 35, cross a bridge over the East Fork of the Hood River, and continue toward the community of Parkdale, which is 2 miles up the road in the heart of apple-orchard country. This picturesque old farm community reminds me of a little New England village (though my wife, who is from the Northeast, disagrees). Parkdale is also the end of the line for the Mount Hood Scenic Railroad. Here you'll find old wooden commercial buildings that have been restored and converted into shops,

eating spots, and a museum. This is the turnaround point, and from here it is almost all downhill.

Follow signs for the community of Dee (basically just a lumber mill), which is 5.4 miles north of Parkdale on the Middle Fork of the Hood River. From the lumber mill continue north, paralleling the Hood River, into the town of Hood River. In 6.5 miles watch for the River Bend Country Store, which is known for its pies and huckleberry shakes. From here, cross Hood River and in 0.8 miles turn left onto Portland Road. Pedal 2.1 miles west and turn right onto Country Club Road, which after 3.4 miles and several jogs crosses Post Canyon Road. Turn right here and in 0.3 miles you will pass Flerchinger Vineyards. With the ride almost over, why not try sampling some wine? From the vineyard, it's 0.4 miles to Frankton Road. Turn left here, go 0.2 miles, and then turn right onto May Street. In 1.5 miles reach 13th Street, make a left, go 0.3 miles, and then turn right onto State Street, which in 0.6 miles will take you past the edge of downtown Hood River. From here it's another half-mile down State Street and across the bridge over the Hood River to where your car is parked.

Historic Columbia River Highway (Hood River to the Dalles)

20–40 miles round-trip. Moderate. 650-foot elevation gain. Access: Take exit 69 (Mosier) off I-84 and find a place to park in town. Alternatively, if the tunnel on the old highway has been reopened, take exit 63 (Hood River) off I-84 and drive south on Ore. 35 to the parking lot across from the China Grove Restaurant.

A clear day in spring is the perfect time to do this ride, which can be started in either Hood River or Mosier. The route climbs up from river level to the Rowena Dell bluffs where you'll be pedaling through meadows carpeted with wildflowers. Spectacular views along the Rowena Dell section take in both the gorge and Mount Adams.

By the time you read this, it should be possible to bicycle from Hood River all the way to The Dalles on the Historic Columbia River Highway. One stretch, from

Hood River to Mosier, may even be closed to cars most of the time. This stretch of road, which passes through the Mosier Tunnel, was closed after the construction of I-84, when rubble was used to fill in the tunnel. In 1995 and 1996 work was being done to clear the Mosier Tunnel and once again open this section of road. Between Hood River and Mosier, the road passes through dense forest with, unfortunately, the roar of the interstate drifting up from below. There are only a few peekaboo views of the river and the far side of the gorge. If the tunnel has not been reopened, you can start this ride in Mosier. If the tunnel has opened, the ideal ride might be Hood River to Rowena Dell and back.

After passing through Mosier, the road climbs onto the exposed, windswept bluff known as Rowena Dell. This section of the route provides outstanding views, though at the cost of several steep climbs. Along the way, you can stop and take a walk around the Nature Conservancy's Governor Tom McCall Preserve, which is best visited in the spring when the wildflowers are in bloom. From this point, it's mostly downhill to The Dalles. The last few miles are past strip malls and industrial areas, so if you haven't arranged a car shuttle in The Dalles, you might want to turn around at Mayer State Park, which is just downhill from Rowena Dell. For some it'll be worth continuing another 4 miles to Crates Point, where in the past there have been living-history programs.

SEA KAYAKING & FLAT-WATER CANOEING

Because of the combination of winds (which can go from nonexistent to gale force in a matter of hours), currents, tides, and barge traffic, sea kayaking is not as popular on the Columbia River as it might at first seem it should be. However, that's not to say that there aren't places to dig in a paddle. **Rooster Rock State Park,** with its sloughs and craggy scenery, is a good spot for an easy paddle (if the winds are calm), and if you're confident in your paddling skills, you can head across the river from here to the **Cape Horn** area on the Washington shore. Strangely eroded cliffs

rise straight out of the water and provide some interesting exploration.

SWIMMING

Rooster Rock State Park has one of the most popular swimming beaches on the Columbia. It's long and sandy and gets crowded enough on summer weekends to be a real beach scene miles from the nearest ocean. If you're into skinny dipping, you'll even find your own stretch of clothing-optional beach here at the north end of the park and down a long trail through willow flats that are often knee-deep in water. Some sort of water sock or sandal is a good idea for getting out to this section of beach.

More protected waters can be found at **Benson State Park,** where there is a small beach on a lake just across I-84 from the Columbia. To reach the park, take exit 30 off I-84. More adventurous types can cool off in the waters below **Punchbowl Falls** on Eagle Creek. These impressive falls are encircled by basalt cliffs that form a dark little gorge. Foolhardy types often jump from the cliff at the top of the falls. It's a 2-mile hike up the Eagle Creek Trail to reach the falls, but this spot is still very crowded on weekends. To reach Eagle Creek, take exit 41 off I-84.

WALKS & NATURAL ROADSIDE ATTRACTIONS

In addition to the following, some of the areas previously mentioned under hiking also lend themselves to short walks. If you don't have the time to hike the **Oneonta Trail,** it is still fun to get your feet wet on a summer day by hiking up the creek that flows through the moss-draped walls of this narrow little gorge east of Multnomah Falls on the Historic Columbia River Gorge. There is also no need to walk very far to enjoy the wildflowers of Rowena Plateau at the Nature Conservancy's **Tom McCall Nature Preserve** east of Hood River on the historic highway.

Portland Women's Forum State Park

Access: From I-5, take exit 17 and drive 9 miles along Ore. 30 (Historic Columbia River Highway).

This little park is nothing more than an overlook at the western end of the Gorge, but the perspective it provides is as good as any you'll get with so little effort. To the east, rank upon rank of the Gorge's basalt walls can be seen marching down to the waters of the Columbia. By stopping at this park, you can avoid the crowds at the Vista House, the cliff-top building you can see in the near distance. This is also often a good place to experience the famous Gorge winds. I once watched a small plane trying to fly up the Gorge against gale-force head-winds. It seemed to be advancing at a walker's pace. When it finally gave up and turned around, it disappeared within seconds.

Multnomah Falls

0.5 mile to bridge. Easy. 200-foot elevation gain. Access: Take exit 31 off I-84, or take exit 17 and follow the Historic Columbia River Highway.

At 620 feet high, Multnomah Falls is the fourth highest waterfall in the United States and the tallest in Oregon. Falling in two cascades (542 feet and 78 feet), it is a narrow plume of water that is among the busiest tourist attractions in the state. A paved trail—short but steep—leads from the base of the falls, where there is an informational exhibit, and a restaurant and gift shop. Most people make the footbridge in front of the falls their destination. This bridge overlooks the pool at the base of the upper cascade. Not even frigid winter weather can keep the crowds away from this waterfall. When temperatures drop below freezing, people come to see the columns of ice created by the falls. If you take the Historic Columbia Gorge Highway to get here, you will pass by many other smaller waterfalls as well.

WHITEWATER KAYAKING & CANOEING

With three good paddling rivers in the immediate vicinity, the Hood River area is becoming popular with paddlers (as well as boardsailors). However, only one of the area's whitewater rivers is on the Oregon side; see "The Gorge's Washington Side & Mount Adams—What to Do & Where to Do It," below, for information on the White Salmon and Klickitat rivers. If you need paddling gear or want to rent a boat or schedule some instruction, check in at **Cascade Outdoor Center,** 311 Oak St., Hood River (tel. 541/387-3527), or **Hood River Outfitters,** 1020 Wasco St., Hood River (tel. 541/386-6202).

Hood River

5–19 miles. Flow: 700–800 cfs. Class III–V. Put-ins/take-outs: In Hood River at the Hood River Marina; south of Hood River near Odell on Tucker Rd.; and on the Odell–Lost Lake Rd.

This river drops steeply down from the east side of Mount Hood and offers challenging paddling for much of its length. In fact, the river keeps up a good, fast flow right into the Columbia River. For a solid Class III paddle of about 5 miles, put in at Tucker Bridge on the back road from Hood River to Dee and Parkdale. If you want more challenging water, continue upriver to either Dee or White Bridge Park on the West Fork Hood River. At higher flows, these upper sections are Class IV and V.

The Gorge's Washington Side & Mount Adams ◆ What to Do & Where to Do It

BIRD WATCHING

The Columbia Gorge isn't especially well known for its birding, but there are a few places here on the Washington side where you can break out your binoculars and your bird book and give them both a bit of use. East of Washougal, near milepost 31 on Wash. 14, you'll come to **Franz Lake National Wildlife Refuge** (tel. 509/427-5208). Migratory birds and swans are the big draw here. At **Beacon Rock State Park,** there is a nesting pair of peregrine falcons. If you're lucky, you might spot them from either the trail that climbs to the top of the rock or from the boat ramp below and to the west of the rock. Continuing east, you can pull off just before Stevenson and scan **Hegewald Pond** for waterfowl. Perhaps better than all of these small viewing areas are the waters and marshes of **Conboy Lake National Wildlife Refuge** (tel. 509/364-3410), which is located outside the small community of Glenwood. During the spring and fall migrations, this refuge is filled with swans, ducks, geese, and sandhill cranes.

BOARDSAILING

Although many of the best sailing spots in the gorge are here on the Washington side, most of the shops offering sales and rentals of gear are across the river in Hood River. (See the boardsailing section, above, in "The Gorge's Oregon Side—What to Do & Where to Do It" for more information.) However, in Stevenson you'll find **Waterwalker,** 371 SW Hwy. 14 (tel. 509/427-2727), which rents boards and offers classes.

Bob's Beach

In downtown Stevenson, just off Wash. 14. Recommended sail size: 4.5–5.5 (west wind); 3.0–4.5 (east wind).

Bob's Beach is one of the few spots in the gorge that gets both east and west winds, so no matter what the conditions, you'll probably be able to do some sailing here. Swells regularly reach 3 feet on either wind. With a lawn stretching down to a narrow launch area, this is not a big place, and parking is limited. Arrive early.

Home Valley

16 miles west of the Hood River Bridge at Home Valley Park. Recommended sail size: 4.5–6.0.

With its family-oriented park, sand beach, and flat water, this is a popular spot with beginning and intermediate sailors, and is a good place to initiate yourself into the gorge sailing scene. Whether the winds are out of the east or west, this spot is sailable, but westerly winds offer slightly better conditions. The launch site is on a small, wind-protected cove, and the barge lane

is on the far side of the river—two plusses for beginners. There's also a campground here.

Swell City

4 miles west of the Hood River Bridge. Recommended sail size: 4.0–4.5.

As the name implies, this spot is legendary for its swell, which can reach 6 to 8 feet on a strong west wind. When there are conditions like these, the most skilled sailors vie both for the limited parking spaces and for the superb port and starboard ramps that are perfect for catching serious air. This may be the closest the gorge comes to having the locals-only sort of attitude associated with California waves. If you don't know the rules for riding this sort of swell, it's best to stay on shore. The best swell is at "In-Betweens," an area halfway between here and The Hatchery. Stay out of the wind shadow east of Ruthton Point, which is directly across the river.

The Hatchery

3.5 miles west of the Hood River Bridge. Recommended sail size: 3.5–4.5.

If you've seen jaw-dropping photos of unbelievable aerial maneuvers taken in the gorge, chances are they were taken here at The Hatch. A favorite spot both with expert sailors and those who just want to watch (or take pictures), The Hatchery is a real scene on days when the wind is raging out of the west and kicking up 6- to 8-foot swells. Under these conditions, the experts who sail here spend almost as much time in the air as they do on the water. Stay away from the Oregon shore, where you'll run into dead air and submerged pilings.

Bingen Sailpark

1.5 miles east of the Hood River Bridge at the Bingen Marina. Recommended sail size: 4.5–5.5.

Uncrowded and well set up for sailing, this is a good intermediate spot and is on during a west wind. The swell rarely goes above 1 to 2 feet, so you can just let it rip and work on your speed and slalom technique or do a little bump and jump.

Doug's Beach

13 miles east of the Hood River Bridge on Wash. 14. Recommended sail size: 3.5–4.5.

This is another of the gorge's top spots for big swells, with those 6- to 8-foot waves running before the west winds. Expect crowds and aggressive sailing and don't even think about launching here if you aren't confident in your ability to handle extreme conditions. The starboard ramps produce some of the most consistently superior airtime in the gorge.

Avery

8.5 miles east of The Dalles Bridge. Recommended sail size: 3.5–4.5.

With consistent 2- to 4-foot swells, Avery is a great bump-and-jump spot, and a good place for intermediate sailors to work their way up toward the really big swell. Occasionally the swell here will go up to 6 feet, and when it does, there are some good starboard ramps.

CROSS-COUNTRY SKIING

There isn't any reliable cross-country skiing in the gorge itself, but north of the gorge up the Wind River and White Salmon River valleys there are a few sno-parks.

Upper Wind River Sno-Parks

1–12 miles. Easy–most difficult. 200–550-foot elevation gain. Access: 25 miles north of Carson off Wash. 14. Map: Ski trails map available at Wind River Ranger Station, Carson (tel. 509/427-3200).

Located off the beaten track but close to Portland, the ski trails of the Upper Wind River are a great alternative to overcrowded trails on Mount Hood. The trails, which follow both unplowed roads and designated ski trails, pass through forests and clear-cuts that provide occasional views of Mount Adams, Mount Rainier,

and Mount St. Helens. There are seven sno-parks in the area, so you'll have plenty of options if you decide to come back several times or do more than one route in a day. Among the most popular trails are those starting at Old Man Pass, which is the site of the first sno-park in the area that is not shared with snowmobilers.

If you're looking for less-crowded conditions, you can continue onward to some of the more distant sno-parks, but you'll have to share several of these with the snowmobiles. At Old Man Pass you'll find more than a dozen miles of groomed trails (no skate-skiing lane, though) plus several more miles of ungroomed trails. The standard route here is to follow the long-but-easy 11-mile Hard Time Loop, which contains gentle ups and downs and has a few distant views from clear-cuts it passes through. An alternative is to do the 5.2-mile Scenic Loop. However, only part of this loop is groomed, so you may only want to try it either after someone else has broken trail or when there is just a light covering of fresh snow on top of hardpack. Add a 3- to 4-mile round trip to McClellan Meadows, and you'll have a good day's ski. The ski trails of the Upper Wind River Recreation Area are at a fairly low elevation (between 3,000 and 4,000 feet), and consequently, snow cover is unpredictable. Before heading up this way, be sure to call the Wind River Ranger Station for trail and road conditions.

Atkisson Sno-Park, Trout Lake

7–11 miles. Easy–more difficult. 300–1,100-foot elevation gain. Access: 6 miles west of Trout Lake on Wash. 141. Map: Ski trails map available at Mount Adams Ranger Station, Trout Lake (tel. 509/395-2501).

Of the four sno-parks in the Trout Lake area, the Atkisson Sno-Park offers the most interesting options for both short and long ski tours. This sno-park is used by both skiers and snowmobilers, so be prepared for a lot of noise in the parking area. However, there are many miles of skier-only trails in the area, so you won't have to worry about getting run over while out on the trail. One of my favorite trails here is a

7-mile loop that leads past the Ice Cave and the Natural Bridges, both of which were formed by lava tubes. The cave can be difficult to get into during the winter because of ice on the steps leading into it. The well-marked ski route heads northwest from the sno-park, and you have the option of skiing on either the north or south side of FS 24. Whichever side you choose, you can make a loop by skiing the other side on your return route. The cave entrance is about 0.75 miles from the sno-park on the southern trail. Either trail will lead you to FS 041 in about 1.5 miles. From here ski south to FS 050 and turn right and follow signs for the Natural Bridges Loop. The bridges are sections of a lava tube that is now mostly collapsed. Don't get too close to the edge or you may find yourself at the bottom of this deep trench.

For a ski tour with views, take the Peterson Ridge Trail, which follows the ski trail north of FS 24 as far as FS 2420 before turning right and heading north. The trail passes Lost Meadow before finally reaching the top of the ridge at about 5 miles from the sno-park. To return, ski back the way you came.

There are many more miles of ski trails in this area that are worth exploring, and one of the best ways is by staying at the U.S. Forest Service's ranger cabin. The cabin houses up to four people and costs $35 per night for two people and $45 per night for four people. Reservations are taken beginning October 1, and weekends are usually filled by the end of the day. It's much easier to get a weekday reservation. The cabin is less than 3 miles from the sno-park.

Mount Adams Summit

12–24 miles. Most difficult. 6,000-foot elevation gain. Access: From Trout Lake, head north on FS 17 (the right fork at the gas station) for 2 miles and take a left onto FS 80 (signed "South Climb"). Drive this road as far as it is clear of snow, or if late in the summer, to the Cold Springs Campground, 15 miles from Trout Lake. Map: USFS Mount Adams Wilderness.

For experienced backcountry skiers, the ascent (and, more importantly, the descent) of Mount Adams is a Northwest classic rivaled only by the run down sister peak Mount St. Helens. This is primarily a late spring or early summer ski trip, but can be done into late summer if the snowpack is heavy.

The route up follows the South Climb Trail from Cold Springs Campground. Once beyond Morrison Creek, follow the cairns up to a wide, flat shelf known as the Lunch Counter. Above the Lunch Counter, there's a very steep 2,500-foot climb to the false summit, beyond which is a fabulous wide bowl. Above the bowl is another steep section that leads up to the true summit. When coming down, keep to the west so as not to ski off the edge of Suksdorff Ridge. It's a long way down to the Mazama Glacier. Oh, and another thing—when you're on the summit, keep away from the east side, where Klickitat Glacier drops off with disconcerting precipitousness.

If you're heading up for an overnight and have a lot of friends coming with you, you can have your gear hauled up as far as Morrison Campground by Phil Zoller, who operates a snowcat service for skiers and snowshoers. You can't ride in his snowcat, but you can skijore (i.e., be pulled on a rope) behind it. The snowcat can carry gear for eight to nine people. Phil charges $500 for the service, so you'll definitely want to split the cost with some friends. Even if you don't make the summit, the snowcat does a good job of grooming trail for you and at the very least you'll get an 8- to 9-mile downhill run. For more information, contact **Phil's White Water Adventures** (tel. 800/366-2004 or 509/ 493-2641).

FISHING

Due to fish hatcheries, several of the rivers feeding into the Columbia on the Washington side of the gorge have good salmon runs. The **Wind River** has a good spring Chinook run (just don't fish too close to the hatchery). At the mouth of the **Little White Salmon River,** anglers gather on **Drano Lake** for much of the year to fish for coho and both spring and fall Chinook. The wide, flat water at the mouth of the **White Salmon** is another very popular and productive fishing area if you have a small boat.

Just across the Bridge of the Gods, in **Icehouse and Little Ash lakes,** you'll find good fishing for stocked rainbow trout early in the season starting in late April. **Tunnel Lake,** just east of Drano Lake, is another gorge lake that is stocked with rainbows for the opening of trout season. For productive lake fishing throughout most of the summer, head to **Horsethief Lake** at the east end of the gorge. Here you'll find not only rainbows but largemouth and smallmouth bass as well as other warm-water fish.

Up near **Trout Lake** and Mount Adams, you'll find good fishing in many of the lakes in the **Indian Heaven Wilderness,** as well as in the **Forlorn Lakes** and **Goose Lake,** which are just outside the wilderness area on the southeast side. Up in the **Yakama Indian Reservation, Bird and Bench lakes** are both stocked with large and small rainbows. You'll need a reservation fishing permit, but these are inexpensive and available at the lakes.

Miller's Sports, 290 E Jewett St., White Salmon (tel. 509/493-2233), is a good source of fishing gear and advice on fishing local waters. If you want to go out with a guide, contact **Northwest Guide Service,** 202 Woodard Creek Rd., Skamania, WA 98648 (tel. 509/427-4625), which is operated by Mike McGillivary. Rates for salmon, steelhead, or sturgeon trips are $55 per person for a half day and $100 for a full day.

HIKING & BACKPACKING

IN THE GORGE

Silver Star Mountain

6.6 miles round-trip. Moderate–strenuous. 2,015-foot elevation gain. Access: From Portland, take I-5 north to exit 1A (eastbound Wash. 14) and drive 16 miles to the Washougal exit (15th St.). Turn left and drive north on what becomes 17th St. and then Washougal River Rd. In 7 miles turn left at a small Bear Prairie sign and head steeply uphill. In 3.2 miles turn left onto Skamania Mines Rd., which after about 3 miles crosses a bridge and becomes a gravel road.

You'll pass a major gravel road coming in from the right and then, in 0.2 miles, you'll come to a fork with a wooden sign that reads PICNIC AREA 6 MILES, ROAD 1200, YACOLT 22 MILES. Take the left fork at this sign and continue for almost 6 miles to a pass with parking for several cars. Map: USGS Larch Mountain.

Though only 4,390 feet tall, Silver Star Mountain has the feel of a peak many times higher and is a totally unexpected bit of alpine scenery far removed from the more obvious alpine destinations in this area. This high-altitude atmosphere stems from the fact that the Yacolt Burn of 1902 completely denuded the upper slopes of the mountain, which has yet to reforest. Consequently, Silver Star Mountain's upper slopes are meadows of wildflowers that put on a beautiful show in June and July each year. On a clear day, the view from the summit takes in Mount St. Helens, Mount Rainier, the Goat Rocks, Mount Adams, Mount Hood, Mount Jefferson, and the Three Sisters. From here you also get an unusual view of the Columbia Gorge all the way east to Dog Mountain and can see all the way west to Saddle Mountain on the Oregon coast. An additional attraction of this trail is the chance to visit an area of Native American pits that were dug into a scree slope centuries ago. It is believed that the pits were used for vision quests, and when you see the location, high on a rocky ridge with snow-capped mountains all around, you'll understand why. This ridgetop aerie lends itself to contemplation and meditation.

The trail up Silver Star Mountain is actually a steep and rocky abandoned road that once provided access to a fire lookout that was destroyed long ago. From the parking area, take the trail (actually an old abandoned road) that heads steeply uphill through forest to the north of the road (don't take either of the two trails on the south side of the road). A hundred yards up the trail, take the right fork at a sign for the Tarbell Trail. The first mile of trail is through shady forest, which makes the steep grade a little easier to take. The remainder of the trail is almost all in meadows with views to the west that give no hint of the views to be had from the summit. All through these meadows are impressive rock outcroppings that invite a bit of scrambling. Even more tempting is the columnar basalt plug of Sturgeon Rock, which lies just west of the summit of Silver Star Mountain. Though you can make it to the peak and back in a leisurely 5 hours, if you have more time to spend, there is plenty of interesting exploring to be done on meadow-covered slopes adjacent to Silver Star Mountain.

Dog Mountain

6 miles round-trip. Strenuous. 2,850-foot elevation gain. Access: 12 miles east of the Bridge of the Gods on Wash. 14. Map: Geo-Graphics Trails of the Columbia Gorge.

Though it is a long—and often very steep—hike to the top, Dog Mountain is one of the most rewarding hikes in the gorge. The views along the trail, stretching far down the gorge and across to Mount Hood, are superb. In late spring and early summer, the wildflower displays on Dog Mountain's meadows are beautiful with balsamroot, penstemons, paintbrush, and phlox coloring the slopes. Today there are two routes to the top of this 2,948-foot mountain. The old route is by far the steeper, but it offers the best views. The new route, which climbs more gradually across the mountain's western slope, stays in forest with only occasional glimpses downriver. The preferred route seems to be to hike up the new trail and down the old trail, though this might actually be harder on your knees than the reverse routing. The best time to go is on a sunny day in spring, but expect crowds on weekends. Bring plenty of water and raingear just in case: Because Dog Mountain sits smack in the middle of the gorge's wind tunnel, it is a blustery place and tends to snag every rain cloud passing by.

Catherine Creek

2–6 miles. Easy. 300-foot elevation gain. Access: Take Hwy. 14 east from Bingen for 5 miles and turn onto C. R. 1230 at Rowland Lake and drive 2 miles. Map: USGS Lyle.

Known for its impressive displays of wildflowers in early spring, Catherine Creek flows through a small canyon with lava terraces and a natural basalt arch. There are also views of Mount Hood and Mount Adams, as well as the Columbia Gorge. The Forest Service is currently working on creating an established network of trails in the area, but even in the absence of these trails, the area can just be wandered, following existing trails and old gravel roads.

ON MOUNT ADAMS'S SOUTH SIDE & IN THE INDIAN HEAVEN WILDERNESS

Bird Creek Meadows

6.5 miles. Moderate. 900-foot elevation gain. Access: From the gas station in Trout Lake, head north on FS 17 (the right fork), which, in 2 miles becomes FS 82. This will become FS 8290 and enter the Yakama Indian Reservation, where it becomes Road 285. At Mirror Lake, turn left to go to Bird Lake or stay straight for the Bird Creek Meadows picnic area and trailhead. There is a $5 day-use fee for visiting the reservation. Map: USFS Mount Adams Wilderness.

If there are more beautiful spots in the Northwest, they are few and far between. Set on the southeastern flanks of Mount Adams on the Yakama Indian Reservation, Bird Creek Meadows are laced with meandering streams, framed by waterfalls and deep canyons, and ablaze with wildflowers in July and early August. Though it is possible to make this a day trip from Portland, it is more enjoyable to camp out at one of the campgrounds here on the reservation. You'll find the most convenient campsites on Bird and Mirror lakes, although the former should be the campground of choice because of its closer proximity to the meadows.

My favorite loop hike here starts at Bird Lake at the southwest corner of the lake. Along the way there are waterfalls, streams, views both east and south, and of course, meadows and wildflowers everywhere. From Bird Lake, hike 1.5 miles to the Round the Mountain Trail. For a glimpse of a beautiful creek, turn left on this trail and hike west for a half-mile or so to Crooked Creek, a picturesque little stream that meanders through a flat meadow and more than lives up to its name. From here, backtrack and continue east to the Flower Trail. Head uphill on this trail and watch for a trail to the left in about a half-mile. Take this trail uphill and in another half-mile you will reach the Hellroaring Meadows viewpoint. This is a great spot for lunch and has a dizzying view down into Hellroaring Meadows, 1,200 feet below.

From here, backtrack to the Flower Trail and turn left to continue around this loop trail. In about a half-mile, reach the Round the Mountain Trail again and turn right. In another 100 yards or so, turn left onto the Bluff Lake Trail, which descends to Bluff Lake in about 0.75 miles. This lake makes a great place for a refreshing swim. Be sure to hike out past the south end of the lake for a blufftop view. From this lake, it is another half-mile back downhill to Bird Lake.

Mount Adams Summit

12 miles. Strenuous. 6,676-foot elevation gain. Access: From Trout Lake, head north on FS 17 (the right fork at the gas station) for 2 miles and take a left onto FS 80 (signed South Climb). Follow signs for the South Climb Trailhead at Cold Springs Campground, which is 15 miles from Trout Lake. Map: USFS Mount Adams Wilderness.

If you've ever dreamed of being a mountaineer, this is the mountain on which to make your dreams come true. With a minimum of equipment and training, it's possible to bag this peak in a single long day, though it is much easier as an overnight trip. There are no crevasses to cross, so all you really need is crampons and an ice ax and a knowledge of how to glissade down snowfields. The summit trail starts at Cold Springs Campground at the end of a very bad road that is just barely passable to regular passenger cars. From here it is a steady 2-mile climb up to Morrison Creek on a wide trail that was once a road used by sulfur prospectors early in this century. At Morrison Creek you'll find good campsites and the last reliable flowing water (from here on up, you'll have to melt snow). This makes a good base camp, though it makes for a long walk to the summit (you'll need to start out around 3am if you want to reach the summit before the snow gets too mushy).

Beyond Morrison Creek, you'll likely be walking on snow much of the time, even in late summer. There are several campsites along this stretch of the route, and the farther up you get, the less you will have to climb the next morning (which means you can sleep later). It's a steady slog up the snow here to a flat bench known as the Lunch Counter at 9,300 feet. Rising above this point is the false summit at the top of a very steep 2,300-foot snowfield. This is the real make-or-break point of the climb. If you aren't totally disheartened by the sight of this slope, and can make it to the top, you should have no trouble making it to the true summit. From this false summit, the trail levels for roughly a half-mile as it contours around a huge bowl with the summit rising above. The final 600-foot climb to the top is on a slope marginally less steep than the one above the Lunch Counter, but because it isn't nearly as long and because the end of the climb is in sight, it feels much less daunting.

From the summit—a football-field-size expanse of snow with an old sulfur miners' shack in the southwest corner—the views are (as you would expect) quite astounding. To the north you can see Mount Rainier, Mount Baker, and Glacier Peak and to the south Mount Hood, Mount Jefferson, and the Three Sisters. Just to the west is Mount St. Helens, and way off in the Coast Range, you can see Saddle Mountain (a popular Coast Range hike). To the east lie the vast, dry expanses of the Columbia Plateau of eastern Washington.

Round the Mountain Trail-PCT-Highline Trail

27 miles. Strenuous. 4,300-foot elevation gain. Access: See "Bird Creek Meadows" above for access information. Map: USFS Mount Adams Wilderness.

For those who are goal oriented and loop obsessed, the name "Round the Mountain Trail" seems like an invitation to a superb hike around Mount Adams. Unfortunately, the name is a misnomer. This trail does not go around the mountain, and consequently, it is very difficult to make a circumambulation of Mount Adams. The trail extends from Bird Creek Meadows in the south to Devil's Gardens in the north. However, because the east side of the mountain is within the Yakama Indian Reservation and includes two deep gorges that are very difficult to hike through, there is a large gap that prevents hikers from completing a circle around the mountain. Also, because the roads from the south side to the north side are so long, rough, and circuitous, this trail does not lend itself readily to a car shuttle (you'll spend almost two days just driving the shuttles). If you're determined to do this trail, consider doing it in sections as out-and-back trips, or spend a week on a single out-and-back hike.

Indian Heaven Wilderness

10–18 miles. Moderate–strenuous. 750–1,550-foot elevation gain. Access: From Wash. 14 in Carson, drive 6 miles north on Wind River Rd., turn right onto FS 65, and continue another 20 miles north to the Thomas Lake Trailhead. Map: USFS Indian Heaven Wilderness.

Late summer or early fall is the time to hike this lake-filled wilderness area. It is then that the huckleberries are ripe and the leaves of these low-growing berry bushes have turned the forest floor a bright flame red. You also won't have to deal with mosquitoes this late in the year. Although the trail in from Cultus Creek Campground on the north side of the wilderness is probably the most popular route into Indian Heaven, I prefer hiking in from the west. This route hits you with four lakes in the first mile (Dee, Heather, Thomas, and Eunice) and keeps on providing distracting bodies of water at regular intervals of less than a mile.

Blue Lake, about 3 miles from the trailhead, is particularly attractive. From the east end of Blue Lake, head north on the PCT, passing Lake Sahalee Tyee and skirting the base of conical East Crater before arriving at Junction Lake in another

2 miles from Blue Lake. This makes a good turnaround point for a day hike. If you plan on overnighting, continue north on the PCT another 1.5 miles to Deer Lake and leave the PCT on a trail heading east. In 1 mile come to Cultus Lake and watch for a trail junction on the south side of the lake. Turn right here and hike 2 more miles to Wapiki Lake, which is surrounded by steep slopes and has several good campsites. On your return route, you can scramble up Lemei Rock, west of Lake Wapiki, for an overview of the wilderness, and then, once you have hiked back to Cultus Lake, take the Lemei Lake Trail 1.9 miles to Junction Lake. From here, return the way you came.

Racetrack Trail

5 miles. Moderate. 800-foot elevation gain. Access: From Wash. 14 in Carson, drive 6 miles north on Wind River Rd., turn right onto FS 65, and continue another 16 miles north to the Racetrack Trailhead. Map: USFS Indian Heaven Wilderness.

As the name Indian Heaven implies, this area was once a popular gathering ground for the area's Native American tribes. They came in the late summer and early fall (as so should you) to gather huckleberries and socialize. Gambling was always a popular pastime, as was horse racing after area tribes acquired steeds sometime in the 18th century. One spot in particular, a wide, flat meadow, was for a century or more the site of annual races, and so many hooves raced across this meadow that a trench was worn into it along the route of the 2,000-foot-long racetrack. Today this Indian racetrack is still visible and makes a fascinating destination for a moderate hike. Though the racetrack itself is not overly impressive, the history of the area makes this an interesting hike.

From the trailhead, hike through forest, crossing Falls Creek at 0.25 miles, to Racetrack Meadow at 2.5 miles. In early summer there is a shallow pond at the edge of the meadow, but by huckleberry season, the pond usually dries up. For an overview of the racetrack, continue another mile up the Red Mountain Trail to a knoll below the lookout.

HORSEBACK RIDING

North Western Lake Riding Stables (tel. 509/493-4965), off Wash. 141 north of White Salmon, is another option in the area. They charge $18 for 1 hour and $34 for 2 hours. A much better deal is offered by **White Eagle Vision Expeditions,** 401 Ekone Ranch Rd., Goldendale, WA 98620 (tel. 509/773-4536), which offers half-day rides for $35 and full-day rides for $75. These folks also offer overnight and multiday trips.

HOT SPRINGS

After a hard day of raging on the nuclear gorge winds or pedal pumping down rocky single-track trails, if your muscles need a good soak in some hot mineral springs, you've got a couple of choices. Located just north of the town of Carson, **Carson Hot Springs** (tel. 509/427-8292) offers sex-segregated soaking pools that are offered in conjunction with a postsoak wrap in warm blankets. Add a massage on top of this and you'll be more than ready to do it all over again the next day. A soak costs $8 and a one-hour massage is $32.

If, on the other hand, you prefer soaking al fresco and au naturelle, you'll want to opt instead for the **Wind River Hot Springs** (also known as St. Martin Hot Springs). These springs are accessed by way of private property, the owner of which has given up on trying to keep trespassers out. The solution has been an honor-system pay box with a fee being charged both for parking and for each person using the springs. These springs, of which there are two, are set on the rocky east bank of the Wind River and are a hike up a trail (through poison oak), and then a scramble over rocks along the edge of the river. The first spring is the coolest and can be submerged under river water during the spring snowmelt season. The farther pool is higher up above the river and is both more reliably accessible (though harder to find) and warmer. It's also cleaner than the first spring. Because the owners

of this property do not condone or welcome public use of these springs, please show the utmost respect for them.

MOUNTAIN BIKING

Hospital Hill

7 miles. Strenuous. 1,300-foot elevation gain. Access: From Wash. 14 in Bingen, head uphill toward White Salmon and turn right at the sign for the hospital. Just before the hospital, watch for the trail to the left of a power substation. Map: None available.

When I suggested to my wife that we ride the Hospital Hill trail, she was convinced that it took its name from where you would end up after a ride here. On the contrary, this lung-busting ride takes its name from the location of the trailhead beside the Skyline Hospital. There is, however, one hazard on this trail that could easily make you pay a visit to its namesake—poison oak. The nasty plants are everywhere, almost unavoidable at times, so try to wear long sleeves and long pants and be sure to wash yourself and your clothes as soon after finishing the ride as possible.

This is a dry-side ride and starts out in oak grasslands that are gloriously golden (and hellishly hot) in high summer. Those same open slopes that provide awesome views of the gorge also allow the sun to bake you as you struggle upward in granny gear. To get on the right track, go through the gate and take the right fork, an old gravel road. From here on out, just keep to the main road and keep climbing at all trail junctions. Eventually, after 3.5 miles, you top out in high pastures interspersed with patches of forest. Just before reaching the top, you get a view of Mount Hood, and at the top itself, Mount Adams is visible. Continue on the main track to a second gate, go through the gate, and watch for a trail on the left after about 20 feet. So begins the hardpacked single-track payoff for the grunt of a ride up to the top of this hill. From here on down, it's smooth riding, mostly through blessedly cool forest, often with bermed curves that let you cruise without cramping your fingers. After you pass through a rocky, open stretch of trail, be sure to catch the continuation of the fun, which dives off to the left. Eventually you'll come out in downtown White Salmon and have to continue downhill to the turnoff for the hospital. Take lots of water!

Nestor Peak/Buck Creek Trail System

11 miles. Strenuous. 2,500-foot elevation gain. Access: Take Wash. 141 north from White Salmon and turn left at the sign for Northwestern Lake. Cross the bridge and continue straight to the Buck Creek Trail System signboard. Map: Available at trailhead.

Dubbed Nestor the Molester by local riders, the loop up to Nestor Peak and back is a favorite of serious riders looking for a real workout. The loop starts with an endurance-testing 6-mile granny-gear climb on gravel roads N-1000 and N-1600 (a right fork at about 5 miles). Top out just below the summit, where there is a fire lookout. Take a well-deserved rest and soak in the views of the gorge and Mount Hood (and work on your finger exercises while you relax). From here it is 5 miles of almost continuous downhill single-track that will have your fingers cramping up after only the first mile, but the superb condition of this mostly forest trail will have you grinning from ear to ear if you're a fan of screaming downhill trail rides. In the middle section there is a bit of flat double-track that leads to a downhill section of road N-1000.

Avoid the section of trail that leads uphill from the double-track; it only loops back around to the main trail after some steep uphill trail (you had enough uphill riding on the road to the top of Nestor Peak). After picking up the trail again, you'll face an incredibly steep downhill section (that is currently being bypassed) before bottoming out at the Buck Creek Loop. If you want to add some more single-track to your ride, you can do this loop, which passes Buck Creek Falls; otherwise, watch for a short connector trail that leads down to a gravel road. Turn right on this road and coast down to the starting point signboard. Carry lots of water and energy food.

ROAD BIKING

BZ Corners-Glenwood Loop-Trout Lake Loop

46 miles. Strenuous (because of distance and initial climb). 1,800-foot elevation gain. Access: From White Salmon, drive 9 miles north on Wash. 141 to BZ Corners.

Although this is a long ride with quite a bit of climbing early in the route, the views are stupendous. I would be hard-pressed to come up with a more beautiful ride anywhere in the state (no offense to the San Juan Islands). Park your car in the crossroads community of BZ Corners and head up the BZ Corners–Glenwood Road. This is a steady 2.5-mile climb, but then the road levels out for a couple miles as it passes through the pastures of Gilmer. From here the road climbs again for 1.5 miles to another pasture area. In less than 9 miles you get your first glimpse of Mount Adams, and then in another 2 miles you begin passing the vast prairie-like marshlands of Conboy Lake National Wildlife Refuge. Mount Adams serves as the too-stunning-to-believe backdrop to this bucolic scene.

At 19.5 miles into the ride, you reach the community of Glenwood, where there are old homes and churches as well as a deli. Turn left in Glenwood on the Trout Lake–Glenwood Road and in 5 miles you'll pass the entrance to the wildlife refuge. The headquarters are 1 mile down a gravel road. Beyond here the road becomes rolling, and in another 5 miles, you begin the 1.75-mile steep descent into the town of Trout Lake. Where the road bottoms out, there are lush green pastures and a great view of Mount Hood. In another mile, Mount Adams suddenly appears, closer than ever, around a bend in the road. At just over 35 miles from your starting point, roll into Trout Lake, where you can rest and carb load at Bonnie's Place Cafe or drop by the general store. From here it is 11.5 miles back to BZ Corners on Wash. 141, which sees a lot of fast traffic but has a good shoulder. At BZ Corners, you can replenish yourself at the Logs Restaurant.

ROCK CLIMBING

Although the gorge doesn't offer much in the way of rock climbing, despite the preponderance of rock, there are a couple of good spots here on the Washington side of the river. **Beacon Rock,** located 35 miles east of Portland in Beacon Rock State Park (7 miles west of the Bridge of the Gods), is an 850-foot-tall andesite monolith looming over the Columbia River. For hikers, a fascinating network of metal stairs and catwalks leads to the top of the rock on the west side. However, climbers will want to head to the east side and around to the south where more than 60 climbing routes await. This is not a place for inexperienced climbers. Most of the routes range from 5.6 to 5.11A.

Two major drawbacks of climbing here are falling rocks (wear a hard hat) and poison oak (wear long sleeves, cover your legs, and wash yourself and your clothes as soon after finishing your climb as possible). Also, be aware that Beacon Rock is closed to climbing between March and June or July due to the presence of a peregrine falcon nest in the middle of the climbing area. If it's early summer and you've decided to climb here, call first to make sure the closure has been lifted.

Way out at the east end of the gorge, you'll find **Horsethief Butte,** a good bouldering and top-roping area. The rocks that provide the climbing here have attracted people for thousands of years and are covered with petroglyphs. Consequently, climbers are requested not to chalk their holds, which in the long run might obscure some petroglyphs. Nearby Horsethief Lake State Park has the most famous petroglyph in the gorge. It is known as Tsagaglalal (She Who Watches), and looks much like the face of a bear. It can be visited only on ranger-guided walks. To reach Horsethief Butte, drive 3 miles east of The Dalles Bridge to Wash. 14, turn right, and continue another 3 miles to a small bridge. The butte is on the south side of the highway.

SEA KAYAKING & FLAT-WATER CANOEING

Because of the high winds, sea kayaking in the gorge is often an iffy proposition.

However, when the winds are calm, there are some good places to paddle. One of the most beautiful stretches of river lies just east of the town of Stevenson. Here cliffs rise straight up from the water and are topped with dense forests. Tiny coves and islands offer places to explore. You can start a paddle to this area either at the east end of Stevenson or from the west end of town on sheltered **Rock Creek Lake.** This latter spot is a good place to paddle around if the winds on the river are too strong. There are islands in the lake and lots of birdlife. If you head out of this lake and paddle downriver, you can also gain access to **Ash Lake,** another small lake worth a bit of exploring.

West of Stevenson (and west of the Bridge of the Gods), there is more good paddling at the foot of **Beacon Rock.** A boat ramp within the riverside section of Beacon Rock State Park provides access to a slough directly beneath the towering monolith. For a short but interesting paddle around **Pierce Island,** which is directly across the slough from Beacon Rock, head up the slough and then out into the main river. Turn downriver to reach the downstream end of the slough and access back to the boat ramp. There are actually three islands in the area, and you can paddle around all three if you want to lengthen your paddle. Plenty of beaches provide lunch spots.

If you want to rent a sit-on-top kayak or go on a guided tour in a standard sea kayak, contact **Waterwalker,** 371 SW Hwy. 14 (P.O. Box 102), Stevenson, WA 98648 (tel. 509/427-2727). Sit-on-tops rent for $16 a half day, and 3-hour guided sea kayak tours are $50. This shop also rents mountain bikes and sailboards and offers sailboard lessons.

If you're a canoeist searching for a quiet mountain lake, try **Goose Lake** or the nearby **Forlorn Lakes,** all of which are located off FS 60 west of Trout Lake. These lakes offer good canoeing in a remote forest setting. Goose Lake lies at the north end of Big Lava Bed in Gifford Pinchot National Forest. The ancient lava flow forms the south end of the lake, and ghostly tree skeletons rise up from the lake's waters. There is a campground and a boat ramp here. Two miles north lie the much smaller Forlorn Lakes, which are popular with campers. You can paddle around the different lakes and spend a pleasant few days up in this area.

SPELUNKING

Bring plenty of warm, waterproof clothes if you want to do any spelunking in this area. The only cave of note is the **Ice Cave,** west of Trout Lake in Gifford Pinchot National Forest, which certainly lives up to its name. Cold air trapped in the cave during the winter combines with groundwater seepage to form the sort of cave formations you would expect to find in limestone caverns; only here the stalactites and stalagmites are all made of ice. Back in the old days, this cave used to provide ice for the towns of Hood River and The Dalles.

The Ice Cave is actually a lava tube formed when molten lava crusted over but continued to flow below the surface. When the hot lava drained from the tube it had formed, it left a cave (lava tube). This particular cave is blocked off at its lower end, and consequently, cold air collects in the cave. In spelunking parlance, the main section of the cave is referred to as a *glaciere* (a cave that traps cold air and forms ice). Over the years the land has collapsed in several places and divided the cave into four sections, which together add up to a total of about 650 feet of cave. If you want to explore past the main section, you'll need, in addition to warm clothing, hiking boots, head protection, and a dependable source of light (plus a back-up light).

The Ice Cave is 5 miles west of Trout Lake on Wash. 141 (which becomes FS 24). If you continue a little bit farther west on FS 24, you'll come to several natural bridges that were formed when a lava tube collapsed.

SWIMMING

On a hot summer day, it's hard not to think about going for a swim when the waters of the Columbia River are stretched out in front of you. Finding an appropriate place to do your swimming, however, is a bit more difficult. In the town of **Stevenson,** there is a public beach on the river right downtown. Six miles east of Stevenson, you'll find a protected swimming beach at **Home Valley Park.** This is also a popular boardsailing spot. North of Trout Lake, Wash. 141 becomes FS 24 and leads to **Goose Lake,** which is on FS 60. This forest lake is at the north end of an ancient lava flow, and though the waters are chilly, it's an interesting spot (sun-bleached skeletons of trees rise up from the waters of the lake). Other possible places to cool off in the Mount Adams area include **Bird, Bench, and Bluff lakes,** all of which are on the Yaka-ma Indian Reservation. Bird Lake and Bench Lake both have campgrounds and are accessible by a very bad dirt road (four-wheel-drive is recommended if you're heading to Bench Lake). Bluff Lake is about 0.75 miles from Bird Lake by trail.

About midway between Bingen and Lyle, you'll find **Rowland Lake,** through the middle of which passes Wash. 14 on a narrow causeway. This lake is popular with anglers and has a boat ramp, but it's also possible to do a bit of swimming. East of The Dalles, you can cool off at **Horsethief Lake State Park,** where lake waters adjacent to the river provide a calm place to swim.

WALKS & NATURAL ROADSIDE ATTRACTIONS

Beacon Rock

1.8 miles round-trip. Easy. 600-foot elevation gain. Access: From I-84 take exit 44, cross the Bridge of the Gods, and drive 7 miles west on Wash. 14. Map: Green Trails Bridal Veil.

Beacon Rock is the second largest monolith in the world and the trail to the top is not for acrophobics. Built between 1915 and 1918 by Henry Biddle, this trail consists primarily of wood and steel walkways and stairs that have been bolted into the sheer cliff walls. The climb is, of course, steep, but at least it's short. Parking is to the east of the rock and the trail begins on the east side, passing through several hundred yards of forest before breaking clear on a rock-strewn scree slope. From here things get steep. A gate at this point enforces the rule closing the rock after dark. As you climb, the trail twists and turns around the west and south face of the rock with ever-more impressive views at each landing or switchback. Directly below lies a shallow slough with a small marina and boat ramp, while stretching off to the east is a lush, green pasture.

WHITEWATER KAYAKING

A designated National Scenic River, the **White Salmon** is a narrow spring-fed river draining north from the slopes of Mount Adams. This is by far the area's most popular kayaking river both because of its year-round flow and because of its proximity to Hood River. The most popular run is the 5-mile section from BZ Corners to Husum. This run has lots of Class III+ rapids and two Class IV drops—BZ Rapids at the start and Husum Falls at the end. This latter is a 15-foot waterfall that can be run on the right (or portaged on the right well above the falls). Below these falls there are another 3 miles of Class II water perfect for novice paddlers. Above BZ Corners are 10 miles of Class IV and V rapids to challenge expert paddlers. These upper runs are primarily snowmelt runs.

Trout Lake Creek, which feeds into the White Salmon at the town of Trout Lake, is one other popular run in this area. At only 2.8 miles, it's over pretty quick, but in that short distance it manages to slip in a lot of Class II and even one Class III and one Class IV drop. The put-in is on Guler Road and the take-out is at River Road Bridge (on Little Mountain Road).

In the winter, the area's top paddlers head for the **Wind River,** which offers 11 miles of almost continuous Class IV and V waters (plus unrunnable Shepherds Falls) from fall through early summer. It's definitely a good idea to make your first run on this river with someone who knows it well. Stabler is the upper put-in; High Bridge is the lower put-in/take-out. The lower take-out is on the Columbia River.

Equally challenging and also recommended only for expert paddlers are the runs on the **Washougal River,** just east of Vancouver. With several 15-foot ledge drops and a couple of mandatory portages, you have to stay alert to make it down this river without going for a swim. The river's two forks are runnable throughout the rainy season and attract a few kamikaze paddlers. The easiest run, which consists of Class III and IV water, starts at 10-Mile Bridge and ends 2.5 miles outside of Washougal at a boat ramp.

Popular both with commercial rafting companies and kayakers, the **Klickitat River,** at the east end of the gorge, winds its way through a dry east-side landscape. Sometimes ponderosa pines line the banks, and sometimes sheer cliffs of columnar basalt rise hundreds of feet up from the water. The runnable sections of this river begin just outside the Yakama Indian Reservation and extend to 5 miles before the Columbia River, with the season starting around Memorial Day and running into July (snowmelt season). In the last few miles before reaching the Columbia, the river passes through a narrow gorge filled with Class VI water. Avoid it! Along its length this river has runs for just about everyone. The 16-mile run from Leidl Campground to Klickitat Springs is a Class II run with the best scenery on the river. Above Leidl Campground, the river offers pretty continuous Class III and the occasional Class IV sections. The 12 miles below Klickitat Springs is Class II+ to Class III, a happy median between the two upper runs. Just don't miss your take-out at the fishing access area 4 miles outside of Lyle or you'll end up in the Class VI gorge.

WHITEWATER RAFTING

Of course there's no rafting within the Columbia Gorge itself (the winds would just blow you around at their whim). The gorge's rafting takes place on four of the rivers flowing into the gorge on the Washington side. The spring-fed **White Salmon River,** though narrow and fairly shallow by late summer, offers the longest rafting season (March through October). The **Klickitat River** surges with glacial meltwater and rages during the spring and early summer. The season on this latter river stretches from April through June. The **Washougal River,** at the east end of the gorge, sees much less commercial raft traffic than these other two rivers but is run by at least one company during the spring. The **Wind River** is small, steep, and exciting, with a short spring snowmelt season. Companies offering trips on these rivers include **AAA Rafting,** P.O. Box 203, Husum, WA 98623 (tel. 800/866-RAFT or 509/493-2511); **Phil's White Water Adventure,** 38 Northwestern Lake, off Hwy. 141 (tel. 800/366-2004 or 509/493-3121); and **Renegade River Rafters,** P.O. Box 263, Stevenson, WA 98648 (tel. 509/427-RAFT). Half-day trips on the White Salmon cost around $45, and full-day trips on the Klickitat cost around $70.

If you want to do a bit of leisurely do-it-yourself rafting or tubing, the **Washougal River** is perfect. The water is warm (as Northwest rivers go) and the road that parallels the river makes it easy to walk back to your car after floating down the rocky river for a mile or two. If you have two cars, you can do a shuttle and make it a longer trip. To reach the Washougal River, take the Washougal exit off Wash. 14 and drive straight north on 15th Avenue (which becomes 17th Avenue and then Washougal River Road). A park 3.3 miles up the river from Wash. 14 makes a good starting point for a float.

The Mount Hood Area ◆ What to Do & Where to Do It

CROSS-COUNTRY SKIING

With several groomed trail systems and numerous sno-parks providing access to marked but ungroomed ski trails, Mount Hood is a very popular weekend destination in the winter. If you don't have your own skis, you can rent them at both Portland area **REI** stores, 1798 Jantzen Beach Center (tel. 503/283-1300), and 7410 SW Bridgeport Rd., Tigard (tel. 503/624-8600); **Oregon Mountain Community,** 60 NW Davis St., Portland (tel. 503/227-1038); **Otto's Cross Country Ski Shop,**

38716 Pioneer Blvd., Sandy (tel. 503/668-5947); and at many other ski shops around Portland, in Sandy, and at Government Camp. Ski rentals and lessons are also available at the **Mount Hood Meadows Nordic Center** (tel. 503/337-2222, ext. 262). Guided one-day and overnight backcountry ski trips are offered by **Adventure Out,** P.O. Box 1408, Hood River, OR 97031 (tel. 541/387-4626).

GROOMED TRAILS

Trillium Lake Basin

3–12 miles. Easy–more difficult. 230-foot elevation gain. Access: 57 miles east of Portland in Government Camp. The Mazama Sno-Park is opposite the Timberline Rd., and the Trillium Lake Sno-Park is opposite the Snow Bunny winter play area. Map: Geo-Graphics Mount Hood Wilderness Map.

This system of trails is among the most scenic and popular on Mount Hood, and because of the easy terrain, it's popular with novice skiers. The only problem is that all routes into the lakes basin are steep, narrow descents that are often hardpacked and icy. If you can't negotiate the initial downhill, just take off your skis and hike down, being sure to keep to the edge of the trail so as not to further add to the difficulties of this trail for other skiers. Of the two sno-parks providing access to this area, Trillium Lake offers the easier descent.

What attracts skiers to this area are the flat meadows and expansive views, especially those to be had from Summit Meadows and from the south end of Trillium Lake. To reach the former area, ski down the Snow Bunny Hill from the Trillium Lake Sno-Park for a half-mile until you reach the Airstrip Junction and then turn right to reach the meadows in less than 0.25 miles. You can easily spend a lot of time just playing in this beautiful meadow with Mount Hood looming in the distance. To reach the equally scenic shore of Trillium Lake, continue almost to the north end of the meadow and watch for a trail leading west and then south. This is the Trillium Lake Loop Trail and will take you to the dam at the south end of the lake in

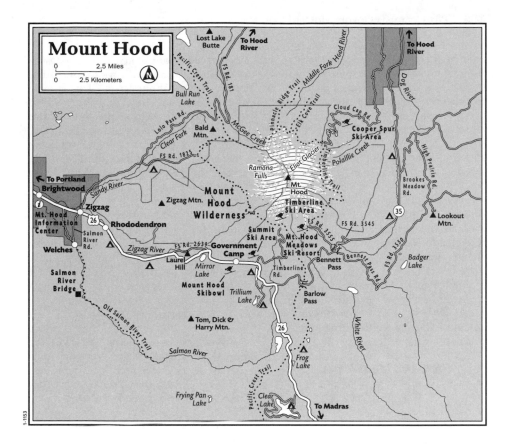

less than 2 miles. From here, ski north 1.5 miles to the airstrip junction to return to the sno-park for a total distance of 4.7 miles.

If you would like to add more miles, consider the Mud Creek Ridge Trail, which heads southeast from the Trillium Lake Loop Trail about halfway up the eastside of the lake. This trail climbs gradually for 1.8 miles to the Jefferson Viewpoint, from which you can see Mount Jefferson far to the south. From here you can head back the way you came, or if you are out for distance and have the endurance, there are many more miles of trails looping through the area of clear-cuts to the south of here. Be sure to carry a good map.

Teacup Lake

Varies up to 18 kilometers. Easy–most difficult. 75-foot elevation gain. Access: 11.1 miles east of Government Camp on Ore. 35. Fee: $3 donation. Map: Available at trailhead.

These 18 kilometers of groomed ski trails are maintained by the Oregon Nordic Club with track for both diagonal and skate skiers. The many kilometers of trails here have something for skiers of all abilities and pass through both shady forests and open clear-cuts and meadows. These latter have a superb view of Mount Hood. A favorite easy route heads up Teacup Road, turns right on Lakeside, then right again on Stump Street, which connects with Hood River Road. Larch Lane, a right off this road, will connect you to Meadow Trail, which returns to the trailhead (and warming hut).

This loop covers just under 7 kilometers, but you can add more distance by following any of the many other trails (both intermediate and advanced) that branch off from this route. For practicing your snowplow technique, nothing beats the Screamer Hill Trail. If views are your goal, head for the Mountain View Loop Trail.

Mount Hood Meadows Nordic Center

Up to 15 kilometers. Easy–most difficult. 100-foot elevation gain. Access: 12 miles northeast of Government Camp on Ore. 35. Fee: $9. Map: Available at Nordic center.

Although the nine loop trails here are immaculately groomed, they, and the entire Nordic center, seem to be just an afterthought at this downhill area. The steep price of trail passes and limited length of the trails makes this center far less popular than nearby Teacup Lake. The trails here spend a lot of time wandering around the outskirts of the parking lot before setting off into the trees. However, you will eventually end up in the beautiful Hood River Meadows, and one trail leads to picturesque Sahalie Falls. It's worth skiing here once, just to see what the trails are like.

UNGROOMED TRAILS

White River Sno-Park

Up to 12 miles or more. Easy–most difficult. 100–1,000-foot elevation gain. Access: 7 miles east of Government Camp on Ore. 35. Map: Geo-Graphics Mount Hood Wilderness Map.

For some inexplicable reason I keep being drawn back to this overcrowded and oft-abused sno-park (there are actually two sno-parks—White River East and White River West—of which White River West is the more popular). Heavy usage by families out for some fun and frolicking leave the snow a horrendous mess of footprints, dog tracks, snow angels, and sled runs, but what a view! It's worth the crowds and crummy snow just to be able to take in the view. Needless to say, save this one for a clear day.

White River is a wide, flat valley that beckons skiers immediately upvalley with the awesome view. However, the down-valley view, though lacking the bulk of Mount Hood for a centerpiece, is equally beautiful. The goal of most skiers is the steep slope of a gravel pit less than half a mile upvalley from the parking area. This slope is a perfect place to practice your telemark technique. If you want to get some distance between you and the

crowds, continue up the river valley as far as you can, which will bring you to the moraines of the White River Glacier. If you prefer skiing a narrow trail through the trees, follow the sign at the west end of the sno-park for the Yellowjacket Trail. However, for the least crowded trails, either park at the White River East sno-park, or cross the highway from the White River West parking lot and head down the valley. When you feel you've had enough, turn around and head back up the valley with Mount Hood filling your field of view. From this side of the highway, it is also possible to follow trails south to connect with Barlow Pass trails or north to connect with Bennett Pass trails.

Bennett Pass Sno-Park

4.8 miles round-trip to Gunsight Notch; 8.6 miles round-trip to Bonney Junction. Moderate. 350–700-foot elevation gain. Access: 9.7 miles east of Government Camp on Ore. 35. Map: Geo-Graphics Mount Hood Wilderness Map.

As the highest pass on Mount Hood, Bennett Pass has some of the most reliable snow on the mountain. So, if it is early in the season and you just can't wait another week, or if it has been a lousy snow year, this is the place to head when you want to strap on your skis. From the parking area, which is almost directly across the street from the entrance to Mount Hood Meadows Ski Resort, the trail, an unplowed forest road, leads gradually uphill through dense forest. Along the way, there are a few outstanding views down into the valley of the East Fork Hood River. The only thing marring these views are the many clearcuts, visible as patches of white surrounded by dark forests.

Keeping to the left at forks (except one left fork that leads immediately uphill at a steeper gradient) will lead to Gunsight Notch, which is at the end of a stretch of trail known as the Terrible Traverse. Early in the year, or when the snow isn't too deep, there is nothing too terrible about this traverse. However, when the snow gets deep, what was a fairly level road cut across a cliff becomes little more than a wide shelf on a very steep slope.

This area is prone to avalanches and should not be crossed for a while after a heavy snowfall. If there has been heavy snow, your best bet is to check with a ranger before planning to ski beyond this point. Otherwise, at a little over 2 miles from the trailhead, there is a good turn-around point. If you haven't had enough skiing yet, you can explore some of those right forks you passed by on the way up here.

If the Terrible Traverse is passable, you can continue through the natural rock gates of Gunsight Pass (great views here) to Bonney Junction and from there up the Gunsight Ridge Trail. It is also possible to put together a few different loops that drop down to the East Fork Hood River Trail and return to the sno-park by way of the Pocket Creek Tie Trail.

DOWNHILL SKIING & SNOWBOARDING

There are five ski areas on Mount Hood. These range in size from the tiny, family-oriented Summit and Cooper Spur areas to the world-class Mount Hood Meadows complex. Both Timberline and Mount Hood Meadows now offer summer skiing high on the ice fields of Mount Hood's upper slopes. To park at any Mount Hood ski area between November 15 and April 15, you'll need to have a sno-park permit ($10 seasonal, $3 daily). However, Washington, Idaho, and California sno-park permits are valid.

Mount Hood SkiBowl

In Government Camp, 55 miles east of Portland on U.S. 26. Tel. 503/272-3206 (503/222-2695 for snow report). 65 trails; 4 chairs, 5 surface tows; 1,500-foot vertical drop. Lift hours: Mon–Tues 1–10pm (9am–10pm on holidays), Wed–Thurs 9am–10pm, Fri 9am–11pm, Sat 8:30am–11pm, Sun 8:30am–10pm. Adult lift tickets: Daily (9am–closing) $29, night skiing $13 (4:30pm–closing); snowboard park $10–$15.

As the closest ski area to Portland and the largest lighted night-skiing area in the country, SkiBowl is great for after-work skiing (lift tickets are only $13 for night skiing). However, its low elevation usually

makes it the last of Mount Hood's ski areas to open each season. Lift tickets here are more reasonable than those at Mount Hood Meadows, but the ski area is not as well maintained, and lifts show their age. However, with more expert runs than any other ski area on the mountain, SkiBowl draws a lot of experienced skiers, especially for the steep runs off the Upper Bowl Chair directly above the west lodge. Snowboarders will want to head directly to the Multorpor area (east lodge) where they'll find a snowboard park off the Cascade Chair. Beginners will find good, wide runs off of the Lower Bowl Chair.

There is no day care here. A shuttle runs between the ski area's east and west sections.

Summit Ski Area

In Government Camp, 54 miles east of Portland. Tel. 503/272-0256. 5 trails; 1 chair, 1 rope tow; 500-foot vertical drop. Lift hours: Sat–Sun and holidays 9am–4pm. Adult lift tickets: $12 full day, $10 half day (begins at 1pm).

Skiers have been schussing down the little hill at this tiny ski area since 1927, which makes this a historic ski area if nothing else. These days, what with all the competition from the mountain's bigger ski areas, Summit attracts primarily families with small children who want to do a bit of tubing or sledding. However, easy runs and low ticket prices make this a good place for your first forays into the world of downhill skiing or snowboarding. The day lodge rents skis and snowboards and lessons are offered.

Timberline Ski Area

Just past Government Camp, 60 miles east of Portland off U.S. 26. Tel. 503/231-7979 in Portland, 503/272-3311 outside Portland (503/222-2211 for snow report). 31 trails; 5 lifts (including 1 express quad); 3,500-foot vertical drop in winter, 2,500-foot vertical drop in summer. Call for lift hours. Adult lift tickets: $29 Sat–Sun and holidays, $23 Mon–Fri.

This is the highest ski area on Mount Hood, and though its trails are considered a bit monotonous by many area skiers, the presence of the historic Timberline Lodge lends this ski area a unique atmosphere that is not duplicated anywhere in the Northwest. The most popular winter runs are those off the Miracle Mile lift, which rises above treeline to 7,000 feet. However, this is always the last lift to open due to the high winds that keep sweeping the upper slopes clean of snow during the early weeks of the ski season. For the full Timberline experience, make sure that Miracle Mile will be running before buying your lift ticket. Snowboarders have a couple of designated snowboard parks, including the Bone Zone, which is just east of the top of the Blossom lift. Runs at Timberline tend to be poorly marked, so be sure to get a map and familiarize yourself with the mountain before heading out on the slopes. A Betsy chair provides beginning skiers a place to practice for only $14 a day.

Timberline is also one of the only ski areas in the country that offers skiing throughout the summer. Runs, which are for advanced skiers only, are on the Palmer snowfield high above Timberline Lodge. The top of this lift is at 8,500 feet. Summer ski schools and training camps for Olympic teams are popular here.

There is no day care available. Raz Transportation (tel. 503/231-7979) operates a ski bus from three Portland locations.

Mount Hood Meadows

35 miles south of Hood River on Ore. 35. Tel. 503/337-2222 (503/227-7669 for snow report). 82 trails; 9 chairs (including 3 high-speed detachable quads); 2,777-foot vertical drop. Lift hours: Mon–Tues 9am–4pm, Wed–Sun 9am–10pm. Adult lift tickets: $35 day (9am–4pm, 11am–7pm, 1–10pm); $28 half day (noon–4pm); $15 night skiing.

This is the largest ski resort on Mount Hood, with more than 2,000 skiable acres, 2,777 vertical feet, and a wide variety of terrain. With three detachable high-speed quad lifts, it also moves a lot of skiers up the mountain. For those who need even more extreme skiing conditions than the lifts can provide, there are snowcats that

can take you another 1,000 feet higher up Mount Hood's slopes for a total run of 4,000 vertical feet, which is one of the longest continuous runs in the country. The Cascade Express is the chair of choice for nearly everyone who comes here. This chair takes you to the top of the ski area and accesses both the wide-open (and corniched) intermediate slopes of Texas, Boulevard, and Catacombs and the steeper bowls of Heather Canyon where the black-diamond crowd hangs. Wedged in between these two sides of the ski area are enough runs through the trees to get lost for days.

The diverse array of runs here (emphasis on cruisers) and the three high-speed quads make this the most popular ski area on the mountain. However, high prices and a lack of a snowboard park send many thrifty chute divers and shredheads to SkiBowl instead. Mount Hood Meadows now has a summer ski season that lasts until early July.

Cooper Spur

27 miles south of Hood River off Ore. 35. Tel. 503/230-2084 in Portland, 503/352-7803 on the mountain. 10 trails; 1 T-bar, 1 rope tow; 500-foot vertical drop. Lift hours: Thurs–Fri 4:30–10pm, Sat 9am–10pm, Sun 9am–4:30pm. Adult lift tickets: $10 day (9am–4:30pm); $5 night skiing (4:30–10pm).

This family ski hill offers the closest downhill skiing to Hood River, and though the area is small, the hill is steep enough to get in a few intermediate runs and even a couple of advanced runs. This is a good place to get in some practice if you aren't sure you want to spend the big bucks at one of the major ski areas.

FISHING

The trout season on Mount Hood's rivers and streams runs from the fourth Saturday in May through October 31, while steelhead can be fished through December 31 (only barbless hooks November 1 through December 31). Keep in mind that only fin-clipped hatchery steelhead can be kept (subject to catch limits). However, if you're lake fishing, you can fish all year. In many of the mountain's waters, rainbow trout are stocked throughout the summer.

Lost Lake, on the north side of Mount Hood, is as good a place as any to try your luck. Even if the fish aren't biting, you still get a drop-dead view of Mount Hood to keep you interested in staying out just a little bit longer. Rainbow, brook, and German brown trout as well as kokanee salmon are the quarry here (rainbows are stocked). The best fishing is early in the summer before the lake gets fished out. The best results are to be had from rowboats drifting in the shallows. Light spinning tackle and a small flatfish or spruce fly should get some fish interested.

The **Salmon, Sandy, and Zigzag rivers,** which all flow westward off of Mount Hood, provide good rainbow and steelhead fishing (some say the Sandy is the best year-round steelhead river in the state), and in the Salmon, there are also cutthroat trout. Although these three rivers also have runs of coho and spring Chinook salmon, fishing for these is prohibited. If fly-fishing is your passion, you'll want to head out of Rhododendron on the Salmon River Road. Upriver from the Salmon River Road bridge as far as Final Falls, the river is fly-fishing only.

For tips, gear, or to arrange a guided fly-fishing trip, contact the **Fly Fishing Shop** (tel. 503/622-4607) in Welches (on the road to Government Camp).

For information on fishing the **Clackamas and Molalla rivers,** see chapter 9.

FLAT-WATER CANOEING

Several lakes on the flanks of Mount Hood provide pleasant settings for a bit of flat-water paddling. **Lost Lake,** on the north side of Mount Hood off FS 13 southwest of the community of Dee, is by far the most popular and scenic; on a clear, wind-free morning the reflection of Mount Hood in this lake's waters is sublime. If you're looking for someplace to do a lot of exploring and even a bit of portaging, head south of Mount Hood to the **Ollalie Scenic Area,** where there are more than 30 lakes crammed together in an area of dry, east-side forests. This is about as close as

you'll come in the Northwest to a big north-woods experience and is a great place to practice for that Boundary Waters trip you've been planning. Guided one-day and overnight backcountry ski trips are offered by Adventure Out, P.O. Box 1408, Hood River, OR 97031 (tel. 541/387–4626).

Unfortunately, only six of the area lakes are accessible by road. Try a paddle around **Ollalie Lake** and a portage over to **Monon Lake** for a satisfying canoe experience. The best way to reach Ollalie Lake is to take FS 42 south from U.S 26 east of Blue Box Pass and follow the signs, or take FS 46 southeast from Ore. 224 east of Estacada. Either way you'll spend a lot of time on bad gravel roads. Closer to Government Camp, you'll find plenty of shoreline to explore on **Timothy and Clear lakes.** Timothy Lake is just off U.S. 26 east of Blue Box Pass, and Clear Lake is a bit farther off U.S. 26 (south on FS 42 and then west on FS 57).

HIKING & BACKPACKING

Ramona Falls

6.9 miles round-trip. Moderate. 1,000-foot elevation gain. Access: Take E Lolo Pass Rd. north from U.S. 26 at Zigzag, and in 5 miles turn right onto FS 1825. From this point, follow the signs for less than 3 miles to the Ramona Falls trailhead. Map: Geo-Graphics Mount Hood Wilderness Map.

This low-elevation hike is popular year-round and leads through dense forests along the Sandy River on the southwest side of Mount Hood. The destination of the hike is the fan-shaped Ramona Falls, which cascades 120 feet down a wall of columnar basalt. From the trailhead, hike up the Sandy River for 1.2 miles to the old trailhead (if you have a mountain bike, you can ride the old road to this upper trailhead) and cross the river on a footbridge. After crossing the river, you will come to a junction. Both trails lead to the falls, forming a loop trail. I prefer to hike counterclockwise on this loop, taking a right and hiking through dry, open forest with occasional views of Mount Hood. From the trail junction, it is 2.1 miles to the falls. After lingering (and perhaps lunching or even camping) by the falls, continue on around the loop, which now passes through denser, darker forest at the foot of impressive basalt cliffs. On this side of the loop, it is 2.4 miles back to the trail junction. If you're up for a longer hike, head up the Pacific Crest Trail 0.6 miles from the falls to a junction with the Yocum Ridge Trail. This little, uncrowded trail leads 4.7 miles up to alpine meadows with superb views of the Cascades.

Mirror Lake Trail

4 miles round-trip to Mirror Lake; 6.4 miles round-trip to Tom, Dick, and Harry Mountain. Easy–moderate. 700-foot elevation gain to Mirror Lake; 1,500 feet to Tom, Dick, and Harry Mountain. Access: The trailhead is off U.S. 26, 2 miles west of Government Camp. Map: Geo-Graphics Mount Hood Wilderness Map.

This is the single most popular hiking trail on Mount Hood, so don't come expecting to leave humanity behind. On summer weekends the parking area stays full all day, and crowds gather on the trampled shore of the lake to ooh and ahh at the sight of Mount Hood reflected in the waters of aptly named Mirror Lake. This trail is especially popular with families that have small children. The trail is just long enough to wear the kids out without being so long that they shift into whine mode.

If you're looking to escape the crowds (or at least part of them), continue from the south side of the lake up the trail that leads to the top of rocky Tom, Dick, and Harry Mountain, the ridge that you see directly to the south of the lake. Though the trail itself isn't too interesting, once you reach the top, you can gaze down at the people crowding the lakeshore or up at the bulk of Mount Hood, seemingly at arm's length. The winds often whip across this mountaintop, but there are a few shelters that have been excavated from among the jumble of rocks on the summit. In winter this mountain provides some of the slopes for the Mount Hood SkiBowl ski area. In late August, this trail has some of the best

huckleberry picking on the mountain (bring containers).

Cairn Basin/McNeil Point

9.5 miles round-trip. Moderate. 2,100-foot elevation gain to McNeil Point. Access: Take E Lolo Pass Rd. north from U.S. 26 in Zigzag, and in 4.2 miles turn right onto FS 1825. After 0.7 miles, continue straight ahead, following FS 1828 and signs for the Top Spur Trail. It is another 7.1 miles to the trailhead. Map: Geo-Graphics Mount Hood Wilderness Map.

I probably shouldn't say this, but this is the best overnight backpacking destination on Mount Hood. Meadows, views, streams, and high-elevation exploring make this a great place to spend a night or two. Unfortunately, a lot of people share my opinion and the area gets crowded on weekends. Try to visit on a weekday. After a half-mile of climbing through dense forest, the Top Spur Trail joins the PCT at a poorly marked four-way junction. Take the PCT (the middle trail), which soon crosses the steep, meadowed, southern slopes of Bald Mountain. (Can you guess how this mountain got its name?) Shortly after crossing the meadows and re-entering the forest, watch for an indistinct and unmarked trail to the left (it's at a wide, flat spot in the trail and leads steeply up an embankment). Take this trail less than 0.1 miles to the Timberline Trail and take a right.

This trail climbs steadily along a ridge, reaching small meadows with good views in about 1 mile and finally arriving at the meadows below McNeil Point in less than 2 miles. From here a vast expanse of meadows extends upslope and invites careful exploring (follow the existing paths and try to stay off the fragile meadows). The trail then alternates between forest and meadow and passes two picturesque ponds as it continues another 1.5 miles to Cairn Basin, where there is an old stone shelter. Just beyond the ponds, at a stream crossing, an unmarked trail leads uphill to McNeil Point. Below Cairn Basin is the beautiful Eden Park, which can be visited on a 2.9-mile loop out of the basin. Be sure to camp on bare ground among the trees and not on the meadows.

Cooper Spur

7.2 miles round-trip. Moderate–difficult. 2,800-foot elevation gain. Access: Drive 24 miles south of Hood River (or 16.6 miles north from the U.S. 26 junction) on Ore. 35 and turn onto Cooper Spur Rd. In 2.4 miles, turn left onto FS 3512, following the sign for the Cooper Spur Ski Area. From the ski area, continue 10 miles, mostly on rough gravel road, to the trailhead at Cloud Cap Campground. Map: Geo-Graphics Mount Hood Wilderness Map.

If you're a fan of windswept and treeless alpine scenery, then you'll love the high-altitude hiking on Cooper Spur. This was once one of the most popular areas on Mount Hood, as evinced by the Cloud Cap Inn, which was built in 1889. This hike, which follows the highest hiking trail on the mountain, offers far-reaching views that include Mount Adams and eastern Oregon. This hike starts by heading south out of Cloud Cap Campground on the Timberline Trail. The trail starts in the forest but rapidly climbs out of the trees into a landscape of rocks and diminutive, ground-hugging wildflowers.

From 1 mile up the trail at the Cooper Spur shelter (6,650 feet), you can continue climbing for another 2.5 miles to 8,515 feet, where a rock commemorates a 1910 Japanese climbing party. Along the way, you'll have a stupendous view of the north side of Mount Hood, as well as Eliott Glacier, which is the second largest glacier in Oregon. Above this point, the trail is used only by climbers and crosses dangerous snowfields.

Another option, if you don't feel like doing so much climbing, is to just continue on the Timberline Trail after reaching the Cooper Spur shelter. Cairns mark this trail as it traverses snowfields and rocky slopes high on Mount Hood's eastern flanks. Once up at elevation, you can just follow the trail (which sometimes isn't that easy to follow as it crosses snowfields), or wander around soaking up the high-altitude vistas. An alternate trail leads back to the trailhead from the Cooper Spur shelter by way of the Tilly Jane Campground and adds an extra 0.6 miles over the backtrack route. Though this isn't exactly an undiscovered corner of the mountain, it is far less crowded than greener areas and is way less crowded than the trails around Timberline (which as far as I'm concerned are some of the least interesting on the mountain).

Timberline Trail

40.7 miles. Strenuous. 9,000-foot total elevation gain. Access: There are several trailheads for accessing this trail. The easiest and most popular is at Timberline Lodge (off U.S. 26 at Government). Next most popular is probably Cloud Cap Campground (see "Cooper Spur" hike above for access information). Map: Geo-Graphics Mount Hood Wilderness Map.

Built primarily by the Civilian Conservation Corps (CCC) during the 1930s, the Timberline Trail (#600) encircles Mount Hood and is this mountain's quintessential hike. Although the trail stays primarily at or around timberline, over its length it loses and gains around 9,000 feet, with a low point of 3,200 feet and a high point of 7,320 feet. Because Mount Hood creates its own climate, hikers on this trail will pass through a wide range of life zones ranging from dry pumice slopes to lush forests of Douglas fir to rocky alpine scree slopes. Along the way there are numerous meadows, waterfalls, stream crossings (most unbridged), and even the historic Timberline Lodge, where, if you're so inclined, you can stop for a beer or a gourmet meal or even a night in a comfortable bed!

Most people take four or five days to do this hike. A fairly comfortable pace that has you stopping at good campsites would start at Cloud Cap Saddle Campground on the northwest side of the mountain and hiking in a clockwise direction. From this starting point, you'll hike up above timberline for 3 miles (often crossing snowfields even in late summer), pass through the Mount Hood Meadows ski area (site of glorious meadows that are among the most beautiful on the mountain), and reach good campsites near the Umbrella Falls Trail junction in 9.5 miles. It's then 3.7 miles farther to Timberline Lodge and another 5.2 miles to the campsites at Paradise Park. From here it's a long 15.7 miles to the beautiful meadows of the Cairn Basin/McNeil Point area (you could split this section into two days and stop at

Ramona Falls or at the Muddy Fork of the Sandy River). Another 8.1 miles through the enchanting meadows of Eden Park and Elk Cove will bring you to your starting point at Cloud Cap Saddle.

HORSEBACK RIDING

During the summer, guided horseback rides are offered at **Mount Hood Ski Bowl** (tel. 503/272-3206 or 503/222-2695) in Government Camp.

HOT SPRINGS

Bagby Hot Springs, at the end of a 1.5-mile trail through old-growth forest, is one of the most developed of Oregon's "natural" hot springs. It is also one of the most popular hike-in hot springs in the state. Consequently, weekends see big crowds, lines for the tubs, and occasionally unruly behavior. Though I like the dugout canoe-style soaking tubs and the overall rusticity of the soaking rooms here, it's all too much of a scene, and besides, who wants to breathe second-hand cigarette smoke and listen to half a dozen different conversations while soaking in a hot tub? For a more relaxing experience, come early on a weekend in the spring or fall. To reach the Bagby Hot Springs trailhead, drive Ore. 224 south from Portland through Estacada and, 0.5 miles past the Ripplebrook Ranger Station, turn right onto FS 46. In 3.5 miles, turn right on FS 63, and in another 3.5 miles turn right onto FS 70 and continue for 6 miles to the trailhead.

MOUNTAIN BIKING

Mountain biking is rapidly advancing in popularity in this area, and though these mountains are laced with logging roads, they are not the preferred routes of mountain bikers. Because the national forests of this region are so heavily logged outside wilderness areas, hikers tend to stick to the more pristine wildernesses. This leaves trails outside wildernesses to the mountain bikers (and, unfortunately, to ORVs). Because it is a little bit less straight up and straight down, the east side of Mount Hood is more popular with mountain bikers.

In addition to the trail rides listed below, you can also do some downhill riding at **Mount Hood SkiBowl,** which during the summer runs its lifts for mountain bikers and people using the alpine slide (a sort of summertime luge run). They charge $8 for you to haul your bike to the top of the mountain or $15 for an unlimited all-day pass.

Surveyor's Ridge

10–37 miles. Moderate–strenuous. 2,700-foot elevation gain. Access: From Hood River, drive north on Ore. 35 for 26.5 miles to FS 44 and turn left; from Government Camp, drive U.S. 26 to Ore. 35 and continue 14 miles north to FS 44. Continue for 3.6 miles to the signed Surveyor's Ridge Trailhead. Map: USFS Mount Hood Ranger District Map.

This trail is about the single most popular mountain-biking route on Mount Hood, but even so, there are still so few riders out here that you can hardly call it a crowded trail. The 17 miles of ridge-hugging trail (mostly single-track) and great views of Mount Hood, Mount Adams, Mount Rainier, Mount St. Helens, and the acres of orchards in the upper Hood River Valley are the main reasons for this trail's popularity. As an added bonus, there are plenty of wildflowers in June and July. Because several gravel roads cross the trail at different points, it is possible to bail out early and head back to your car whenever you get tired. If you opt to do this, just follow FS 17 and/or FS 44 back to your starting point.

If you arrange a car shuttle you can make this a very easy downhill coast. Drop one car at the Hood River Ranger Station or on FS 17 at the northern trailhead. If you don't opt to do a car shuttle, you'll be pedaling back uphill on paved and gravel roads at the end of your ride. Though this return route is on good roads, it is a long and tedious ride.

The preferred way to do this ride is to start at the southern trailhead and ride north (downhill) on mostly single-track trail. From the trailhead, pedal east for 1.5 miles to the small Cooks Meadow. Shortly after starting out, watch for a view of Mount Adams and Mount Rainier. Past

Cooks Meadow, you'll ride a short stretch of gravel road before picking up single-track again (just follow the signs for Trail 688). From here on out it is smooth riding as far as the power lines at around 13 miles. If you want to continue on the trail from here, you'll have to push your bike up a steep hill under the power lines, but you'll then be rewarded with a quick ride to Bald Butte, with its great views. The power lines also make a good turnaround point if you plan to head back to your car; this option makes for a 20-mile loop.

If you are continuing down to a second car at the northern trailhead or ranger station, you can also turn right at the power lines and head downhill on a gravel road that soon connects to mostly paved FS 17. Turn left on FS 17 and begin a smooth 6-mile descent to Ore. 35 (4 miles to the northern trailhead). From Ore. 35, it is 4 miles back up to the ranger station.

If done uphill, this trail can also be combined with the Dog River Trail (see below) and a return on Ore. 35 for a strenuous but very rewarding loop of around 37 miles.

Dog River Trail

6.5 miles one-way. Strenuous if going uphill, moderate if doing it downhill only. 2,000-foot elevation gain or loss (if you do the trail from the bottom). Access: From Hood River, drive north on Ore. 35 for 26.5 miles to FS 44 and turn left; from Government Camp, drive U.S. 26 to Ore. 35 and continue 14 miles north to FS 44. Continue for 3.6 miles to signed Surveyor's Ridge Trailhead. The lower trailhead is just before the bridge over the Hood River (19 miles south of the town of Hood River). Map: USFS Mount Hood Ranger District Map.

If you're a masochist, start this trail at the bottom, load up with about a gallon of water, and spend half a day pedaling up 2,000 steep feet of narrow single-track. If you like to have fun, arrange a car shuttle and start at the top for a freewheelin' race to the bottom. Got any doubts about how I like to do this trail? For the most part, this is a trail for the hard-core mountain biker, but it also has several rock outcroppings worth stopping at, and the numerous ridge-side views across the Dog

River and Hood River valleys to Mount Hood make this a very pleasant ride for the casual cyclist. Just make sure your brakes are in good order.

The unmarked trail starts directly opposite the Surveyor's Ridge Trailhead on an old dirt road that leads gradually downhill through dense forest for a ways before becoming steeper. About 0.75 miles down the trail, the main Dog River Trail branches to the right (an alternative, the Zig Zag Trail, goes left) and becomes less steep. For the next few miles the trail contours along the mountainside with easy ups and downs that make for an absolute joyride. When you come to a gravel logging road, just keep going downhill until the road dead-ends; the trail continues from the end of the road and immediately drops down a set of killer switchbacks before becoming a more gradual descent again. At the bottom, the trail empties onto a dirt road. Continue downhill and you will soon come to Ore. 35.

Knebal Springs-Bottle Prairie Loop

10 miles. Moderate. 2,400-foot elevation gain. Access: From Hood River, drive north on Ore. 35 for 26.5 miles to FS 44 and turn left; from Government Camp, drive U.S. 26 to Ore. 35 and continue 14 miles north to FS 44. Continue for 7.3 miles to the Knebal Springs/Bottle Prairie Trailhead (do not follow signs for Knebal Springs Campground). Map: USFS Mount Hood Ranger District Map.

Far less demanding than some of the other single-track rides in this area, this loop does still have a few steep pitches where you may have to walk your bike. However, the grades are mostly fairly gentle and much of the trail is smooth and fast. From the Knebal Springs Trail parking area off FS 44, head east on a dirt road for less than 0.5 miles and watch for the signed Bottle Prairie Trail to the left. This trail leads uphill through open forests (stay left at the fork) and meadows past the Perry Point viewpoint trail (worth a detour). Continue on this trail through a long descent that ends with a steep drop to a stream and then an equally steep climb up to near the Knebal Springs Campground. From the campground, head uphill on paved FS

1720 for 2 miles to the Knebal Springs Trail (this is a long, slow climb). The trail then gets very steep and sometimes very soft and dusty, but if you persevere, you'll be treated to a nice view of mounts Hood and Adams at the top and almost 2 more miles of smooth fast riding through forests and clear-cuts (the last stretch is a quick drop back to the parking area).

Gunsight Trail

20 miles. Moderate. 2,500-foot elevation gain. Access: The trailhead is on Ore. 35 at Bennett Pass, which is 6.6 miles from the U.S. 26 junction. Map: USFS Mount Hood Ranger District Map.

This ride is a combination of good dirt road, very rocky road, and excellent single-track. The view from Gunsight Butte near the turnaround point is one of the high points of the ride and provides the best view. From the Bennett Pass Sno-Park parking area, head east on FS 3550. This road is a steady (and sometimes steep) uphill climb to Gunsight Notch, a rock through which the road has been blasted and crosses a cliff just before the notch. From here the trail drops a little and then continues climbing until, at 4.4 miles, you reach a road junction and the start of the Gunsight Ridge Trail.

Here you have a choice—you can turn left and ride the road to Gunsight Butte or Gumjuac Saddle and return to this point on the trail, or you can head left up the trail (which parallels the road) and return on the road (or go both ways on the trail). If you've got plenty of time, I recommend riding the trail both ways (the road from here to Gumjuac Saddle is a real bone shaker). The only benefit of riding the road is that you get good views into the Badger Creek Wilderness. If you opt to ride up the road, keep left at the fork by Windy Camp and head toward High Prairie. Whatever you choose to do, you'll have fun on the mostly smooth trail as it follows the ridgeline through forests, pocket meadows, and across the shoulder of rocky Gunsight Butte. There are great views of Mount Hood from the butte and a couple of other spots along the trail.

MOUNTAINEERING

Mount Hood is one of the most frequently climbed glaciated mountains in the country, and though the climb to the summit isn't exactly a Sunday stroll, neither is it a grueling expedition. The climb can be done in a day from Timberline Lodge if you are already familiar with the requirements of climbing and crossing snowfields and glaciers. If you aren't yet in possession of these skills, you can learn the necessary techniques and make your first ascent with **Timberline Mountain Guides,** P.O. Box 340, Government Camp, OR 97028 (tel. 800/464-7704; fax 503/272-3677), which charges $245 per person for a two-day course that includes a Basic Snow Course and an ascent of Mount Hood. Timberline Mountain Guides also offers several other courses and leads climbs on other Cascade peaks.

ROAD BIKING

If you've got thighs of steel (or are working on it), the pedal up to **Timberline Lodge** from either **Gresham** or **Hood River** makes for a killer century ride. However, if you're only up to a lesser challenge, just start from someplace closer to the mountain (Sandy or Zigzag on U.S. 26 or Parkdale or Cooper Spur on Ore. 35). If you do the full century, you'll climb 5,000 feet or more, but keep in mind that you then get to scream back down much of that elevation gain. Though both of these roads see a lot of traffic (Ore. 35 is a bit less traveled), both have wide shoulders most of the way.

ROCK/ICE CLIMBING

During the summer months, when the lowlands are baking, the glaciers on Mount Hood offer experienced climbers a chance to do a bit of refreshingly cool ice climbing in glacier crevasses. For information, consult **Timberline Mountain Guides** (tel. 503/636-7704), which offers a couple of different ice-climbing courses.

WHITEWATER KAYAKING & CANOEING

For information on paddling the **Sandy, Clackamas, and Molalla rivers,** see chapter 9. See "The Gorge's Oregon Side" section above for info on paddling the **Hood River.**

Skilled paddlers familiar with the hazards of remote rivers, Class IV rapids, and avoiding logjams may want to check out the **White River** on the south side of Mount Hood. The best runs on this river are the two runs, totaling 23 miles, between Keeps Mill and Tygh Valley. This is beautifully remote canyon country on the dry east side of the mountain. The upper run (12 miles) is almost nonstop Class III to III+ water with one Class IV rapid, while the lower run (11 miles) is mostly Class II+ with a Class IV rapid at the end.

Making this river even more challenging are the many logjams that pile up every year. Stay alert! It's probably a good idea to run this river with someone who's made the runs before; it's a long way to help if you have a problem. Snowmelt season is the time to run the White River. To reach the Keeps Mill put-in, take U.S. 26 east from Government Camp to Ore. 216 east (toward Maupin). In about 3 miles, turn north (left) on Keeps Mill Road for 0.75 miles. To reach the first take-out, continue east on Ore. 216 past Pine Grove to Victor Road. Turn right here and drive 2.4 miles (through three 90° curves) to a left turn onto White River Crossing Road and continue another 1.8 miles to the river. To reach the second take-out, continue north from the first take-out to the town of Wamic and then drive east to Tygh Valley and turn south on Tygh Valley Road to reach a bridge over the White River.

SWIMMING & TUBING

For a brief month or so in late summer, several of the lakes on the flanks of Mount Hood warm up enough to actually be swimmable. **Lost Lake** is my personal favorite simply for its fabulous view of Mount Hood. Nearby, yet much smaller and less crowded, is **Wahtum Lake.** Other swimmable lakes in the Mount Hood vicinity include **Trillium Lake,** just east of Government Camp; **Clear Lake,** farther east on U.S. 26; and **Timothy Lake,** which is also off U.S. 26 a bit farther east than Clear Lake and a bit farther off the highway. Also near Timothy Lake is the tiny **Buck Lake,** which is as picturesque a swimming lake as you're likely to find in these parts. To reach Buck Lake, head west from Timothy Lake on FS 5810 for about 5 miles to the signed Buck Lake turnoff. It's a short hike to the lake.

Campgrounds & Other Accommodations

CAMPING

A certain percentage of campsites at many National Forest Service campgrounds can be reserved at least five days in advance by calling the **National Forest Reservation Service** (tel. 800/280-CAMP). To make a reservation you'll need to know the name of the campground you want to stay at and the dates you plan to visit. The reservation fee is $7.50.

THE OREGON SIDE

Campgrounds on the Oregon side of the Columbia Gorge all suffer from the same drawback—traffic noise. Not only is there the roar of trucks on the interstate, but a very busy railroad also runs alongside the freeway. If you're a light sleeper, or simply didn't plan a camping trip so you could feel like you were stuck between the Indy 500 and freight yards, I suggest camping somewhere other than in the gorge. If you absolutely must stay here, below are some choices.

Ainsworth State Park (45 campsites with full hookups; seasonal), 3.5 miles east of Multnomah Falls, is most recommendable for the fact that it has showers. Farther east, at exit 41 off I-84, there is **Eagle Creek Campground** (18 campsites; seasonal), which is the oldest campground in the National Forest system and is popular for its access to the Eagle Creek Trail.

There is also access to a short mountain-bike trail. At exit 51 off of I-84, there is **Wyeth Campground** (14 campsites; seasonal), a U.S. Forest Service campground on the bank of Gordon Creek. **Memaloose State Park** (110 campsites, 43 with full hookups; seasonal; reservations tel. 800/542-5687), which is accessible only from the westbound lanes of I-84, is located right on I-84, 11 miles west of The Dalles, and is named for the nearby island where local Native American tribes once buried their dead. Kayakers planning to paddle the Hood River should check out **Tucker County Park** (34 campsites; seasonal; reservations tel. 541/386-4477), which is set on the bank of the Hood River south of the town of Hood River.

THE WASHINGTON SIDE MOUNT ADAMS AREA

The Washington side of the Columbia Gorge is a little bit quieter than the Oregon side. There's no freeway, but there are busy railroad tracks. If you're here in the gorge to do some boardsailing, or just to see the gorge, you've got several choices. **Beacon Rock State Park** (35 campsites, including 2 primitive sites; year-round), which is 6 miles west of the Bridge of the Gods on Wash. 14, is about the quietest setting in the area and has access to hiking trails, rock climbing, and sea kayaking. **Home Valley Park** (23 campsites), which is 9 miles east of Cascade Locks in the trees right on the Columbia, is a favorite of boardsailors due to its good beach. **Horsethief Lake State Park** (14 campsites, including 2 primitive sites), which is 2 miles east of the junction of U.S. 197 and Wash. 14 (east of The Dalles), is set amid the grass-and-basalt landscape of the far eastern gorge. Nearby **Maryhill State Park** (50 campsites with full hookups, 3 primitive sites), which is just across the Sam Hill Bridge from Biggs, Oregon, on Wash. 14, is popular with the RV and fishing crowds. Because it's on the Columbia, this campground is also popular with boardsailors.

If you're heading up to the summit of Mount Adams, you'll want to camp at the **Cold Springs** (open camping, no designated sites) or **Morrison Creek** (12 campsites) campgrounds. The former is the better choice if you are planning on bagging the peak. To reach these two campgrounds, take FS 17 north out of Trout Lake (right fork at the gas station if you are coming north on Wash. 141 from White Salmon) and watch for a left fork onto FS 80. This will become 8040 (and then FS 500 if you are going to Cold Springs). No drinking water is provided at either of these campgrounds.

If you're up this way to take in the wildflowers at Bird Creek Meadows, you'll find campgrounds at **Bird Lake** (20 campsites; seasonal), **Bench Lake** (34 campsites; seasonal), and **Mirror Lake** (10 campsites; seasonal). To reach these campgrounds, head north out of Trout Lake on FS 17 and continue up FS 82, which becomes FS 8290 and then FS 285. Be forewarned, however, that the roads up here are best suited to four-wheel-drive vehicles, but Mirror Lake and Bird Lake can usually be reached in a regular passenger car. Because of snow, these campgrounds are usually not accessible until sometime in July.

If your intention is to explore the Indian Heaven Wilderness on day hikes or do some mountain biking in the area near Trout Lake, then the campgrounds at **Goose Lake** (20 campsites; seasonal) and **Forlorn Lakes** (8 campsites; seasonal) west of Trout Lake off Wash. 141/FS 24 are going to be your most scenic choices. However, these are also very popular campgrounds and fill up early. No drinking water is available.

ON MOUNT HOOD

If you're heading up this way to do some mountain biking, the **Sherwood** (14 campsites; seasonal) and **Robinhood** (24 campsites; seasonal) campgrounds, both on Ore. 35 south of Hood River, make excellent base camps. More remote campgrounds popular with mountain bikers include **Knebal Springs** (16 campsites; seasonal), **Pebble Ford** (4 campsites; seasonal), **Eightmile Crossing** (24 campsites; seasonal), **Lower Crossing** (3 campsites; seasonal), and **Fifteenmile** (6 campsites; seasonal), all of which are on or off of FS 44, which happens to cut through the heart of mountain-bike trail country. If you're out to do some high-altitude hiking, the **Alpine Campground** (16 campsites; seasonal) above Government Camp near Timberline Lodge, and the **Cloud Cap Saddle** (3 campsites; seasonal) and **Tilly Jane** (14 campsites; seasonal) campgrounds off Ore. 35 at the end of Cooper Spur Road/FS 3512, are good bets. The latter two are more remote and consequently easier to get a site at, but keep in mind that no drinking water is available at Tilly Jane.

Though **Lost Lake Campground** (91 campsites), on the north side of Mount Hood up Lost Lake Road from the town of Dee (southwest of Hood River), is a busy place, the setting on the lake is spectacular, and if you've got a canoe, all the better. Canoeists and anglers headed for the Ollalie Lakes area (south of Mount Hood off U.S. 26 by way of FS 42 and FS 4220) should try at the **Peninsula Campground** (35 campsites) first; it's got the best overall location. There are, however, five other lakeside campgrounds in the Ollalie Lakes Basin.

Paddlers may also want to check out the five campgrounds on **Timothy Lake** and see which strikes their fancy. These campgrounds include **Pine Point** (20 campsites; seasonal), **Gone Creek** (50 campsites; seasonal), **Hoodview** (43 campsites; seasonal), and **Oak Fork** (47 campsites; seasonal). For more seclusion than the above campgrounds can provide, try the walk-in or paddle-in **Meditation Point Campground** (4 campsites; seasonal).

INNS & LODGES

THE OREGON SIDE

Inn at the Gorge

1113 Eugene St., Hood River, OR 97031. Tel. 541/386-4429. 1 rm (without bath), 3 suites (all with bath). $62 single; $78 double. MC, V (add 5% surcharge).

Though this bed-and-breakfast is housed in a 1908 Victorian home, it is still a casual sort of place catering primarily to boardsailing enthusiasts (board-heads, to those in the know). Each of the three suites here has a kitchenette, so you can save money on your meals while you're in town. There's a storage area for boardsailing and skiing gear, and mountain bikes are available for guests. The innkeepers are avid board-sailors themselves and can steer you to the best spots for your skill level.

THE WASHINGTON SIDE

Skamania Lodge

P.O. Box 189, Stevenson, WA 98648. Tel. 800/221-7117 or 509/427-7700. 195 rms, 6 suites (all with air-conditioning, TV, and telephone). $95–$160 double; $185–$585 suites (lower rates in winter). AE, CB, DC, DISC, MC, V. Free parking.

Skamania Lodge has the most spectacular vistas of any hotel in the gorge. Although golf seems to be the preferred sport around here, the hotel is well situated for whether you brought your sailboard, hiking boots, or mountain bike. The interior decor is classically rustic with lots of rock and natural wood. To reach the hotel, take I-84 to Cascade Locks, cross the Bridge of the Gods, and continue east to Steven-son on Wash. 14.

Bingen School Inn

Humboldt and Cedar sts., Bingen, WA 98605 (just east of the turnoff for White Salmon). Tel. 800/827-4331 or 509/493-3363. $11 per bed in dorms; $29 double, $39 June 1–mid-Sept. MC, V.

Bingen is a lumber mill town just across the river from Hood River, and the Bingen School Inn, as its name implies, is an old school that has been turned into a hostel. The folks who stay here come from all over the world but share a love of the outdoors. Boardsailing is the main topic of conversation around the hostel, but when there aren't any winds, guests usually head off on their mountain bikes, catch a raft trip, hike, or practice their rock-climbing skills on the hostel's indoor climbing wall.

Accommodations, in old school rooms, are very basic (beds are banged together from two-by-six lumber). Mountain bikes and sailboards can both be rented at the hostel.

ON MOUNT HOOD

Timberline Lodge

Timberline, OR 97028. Tel. 800/547-1406 or 503/231-7979. Fax 503/272-3710. 60 rms (50 with bath). $62 double without bath, $92–$162 double with bath. AE, DISC, MC, V. Sno-park permit required to park in winter.

Constructed during the Great Depression as a Works Progress Administration (WPA) project, this classic mountain lodge overflows with craftsmanship. The grand stone fireplace, huge exposed beams, and wide plank floors of the lobby impress every first-time visitor. Rooms vary in size considerably, with the smallest rooms lacking private bathrooms. However, no matter which room you stay in, you'll be surrounded by the same rustic furnishings. Of more importance to most visitors are the ski lifts right outside the front door, the summer skiing, and hiking trails that pass right by the lodge. A pool, sauna, hot tub, excellent restaurant, and two lounges complete the picture here. Basically, this is the best place to stay on Mount Hood no matter what time of year.

The Inn at Cooper Spur

10755 Cooper Spur Rd., Mount Hood, OR 97041. Tel. 541/352-6692 or 541/352-6037. 6 rms, 5 cabins, 3 suites (all with TV and telephone). $78 double; $139 cabin double or quad; $10 for each additional person. AE, MC, V.

If you are looking to get away from it all, try an off-season stay at this surprisingly remote lodge. During ski season, though, you might find it difficult to get a reservation. The inn consists of a main building and a handful of modern log cabins that are certainly the more enjoyable rooms. These cabins have two bedrooms and a loft area reached by a spiral staircase. There are full kitchens for those wishing to do their own cooking. Facilities include whirlpools, tennis court, croquet, basketball, and cross-country ski rentals.

Lost Lake Resort & Campground

P.O. Box 90, Hood River, OR 97031. Tel. 503/386-6366. 7 cabins, 1 apartment. $40–$95 cabin; $95 apartment. No credit cards.

Rustic is the watchword here, where cabins don't have their own plumbing. However, token-operated showers are available in communal facilities. The lake offers scenic canoeing with a view of Mount Hood, good fishing, chilly swimming, and hiking trails. This has long been a popular family vacation spot, and the lake gets very crowded on weekends.

9

THE WILLAMETTE VALLEY:
Portland To Eugene

THE WILLAMETTE VALLEY IS OREGON'S AGRICULTURAL HEARTLAND, its industrial center, and is home turf for an awful lot of people—more than 70% of the state's population lives within 20 miles of the Willamette River. With nearly two million people residing in the valley, you might think the region would be of little interest to the outdoors oriented. However, for all those people crammed into its cities and towns, the Willamette Valley's outdoor offerings are among the most important in the state. It is these stress-relieving quick getaways that make life in the cities bearable. When there isn't the time to head all the way into the mountains or over to the coast, there are always places within 30 minutes or an hour that will provide a quick commune with nature, a workout, or simply a chance to breathe in some fresh air.

Today there are more than 150 public parks, boat launches, and parcels of undeveloped public land along the Willamette River. These public lands make the river an extremely popular recreational area with anglers, powerboaters and water skiers, kayakers and canoeists. Along the banks are also many miles of bike paths and bird-watching areas. This robust recreational scene would be a shock to someone who knew the Willamette 50 years ago: By the early part of this century it had become so polluted by industrial effluents and urban sewage that the river was effectively dead. However, after World War II, the slow process of cleaning up the river began, and by the early 1970s, the cleanup of the Willamette had become a national success story. About this same time, the Willamette River Greenway Program was established. This program was aimed at preserving the river's cultural, historical, natural, and recreational character. To this end, state and local governments began establishing a system of riverside parks up and down the length of the river.

Strict land-use regulations formulated in the 1970s and targeted at preserving prime farmland in the valley have limited suburban sprawl; as a result, even residents of inner-city Portland are usually no more than a 30-minute drive from the country. Though more than a century of farming and urban growth have left very little wild land in the Willamette Valley, patches of forest have been preserved in various places. Among these are Forest Park in Portland, Skinner Butte and Mount Pisgah Arboretum outside Eugene, and the Dunn and McDonald forests outside Corvallis. Several lowland areas have also been preserved as national wildlife refuges, including Sauvie Island refuge northwest of Portland, Ankeny and Baskett Slough refuges outside Salem, and William L. Finley refuge south of Corvallis. The bucolic farmland of the Willamette Valley is particularly popular with bicyclists who take to the quiet back roads of the valley on tours that travel through historic towns, past covered bridges, and through fertile farmland.

Although the Willamette River is a fairly tame river as it flows through the valley, there are numerous smaller and more lively rivers feeding into it. These rivers for the most part are not among the most celebrated rivers in the state, but they do provide the region's paddlers and anglers with a good variety of recreational opportunities. Ranging from the quiet waters of Sauvie Island's Gilbert River to the challenging whitewater of upper Clackamas, there are places for paddlers of all skill levels to get a paddle wet. Likewise, anglers, whether after salmon, steelhead, sturgeon, trout, catfish, or bass, will find fishing holes where they can try their luck.

The Lay of the Land

The **Willamette River** stretches for roughly 150 miles, from south of Eugene, where it originates in two separate forks, to northwest of Portland, where it flows into the Columbia, winding past **Sauvie Island,** the largest freshwater island in the U.S., in its last sluggish miles. Along its length, it is flanked by the Coast Range on the west and the Cascade Range on the east. This positioning between two mountain ranges helps provide the valley with its mild winter climate and its hot summer weather. The Coast Range traps much of the moisture coming off the Pacific and leaves the Willamette Valley with an average of around 45 inches of rain per year. This rain falls mostly between October and June, leaving summers sunny enough for the valley's residents to dry out and get in enough outdoor recreation to see them through the long, dreary months of the rainy season.

Over countless millennia, the Willamette River has meandered back and forth across its valley, creating the wide, relatively flat plain. Adding topographical relief and visual interest to the wide floodplains are the occasional hills and small mountain ranges, including the **Tualatin Mountains** west of Portland, the **Chehalem Mountains** north of Newberg and McMinnville, the **Eola Hills** west of Salem, and the **Coburg Hills** east of Eugene. Also dotting the valley are numerous ancient volcanoes, among which are several within the Portland city limits. These include **Mount Tabor, Powell Butte,** and **Rocky Butte,** all of which are city parks.

Rising from two forks—the **Coast Fork** and the **Middle Fork**—in two different mountain ranges and flowing 300 miles from its sources to the Columbia, the Willamette is also fed by dozens of smaller rivers and streams. Together these waterways drain 12,000 square miles of land. Though it is temporarily tamed by numerous dams in its upper reaches, the Willamette is a wild, tumbling mountain stream as it flows down from its mountain sources. Surprisingly, the river maintains this character right through downtown Eugene and on northward as far as Corvallis. North of Corvallis, however, the river deepens and widens, taking on a more controlled appearance—with the exception of dramatic **Willamette Falls** in Oregon City, that is.

This controlled appearance, however, can still be deceiving, as valley residents learned during the floods of February 1996. The worst floods in decades turned vast areas of the valley into lakes, flooded thousands of homes and businesses, and came within inches of spilling over into the streets of downtown Portland. The damage caused by these floods was compounded by the amount of urban and suburban development that has taken place in recent years close to the river. The prestigious Portland suburb of Lake Oswego, which skirts a man-made lake just off the Willamette, was among the town's most heavily damaged by the floods. At one point floodwaters were actually flowing against the normal current up into the lake.

Floodwaters once kept much of the Willamette Valley wet for a large portion of the year, but today dikes, levees, and drainage ditches have reduced the valley's wetlands to a fraction of their historic area. The region's wildlife refuges are now helping to preserve habitat for such wild residents of the region as dusky Canada geese, bald eagles, Roosevelt elk, sandhill cranes, great blue herons, and numerous species

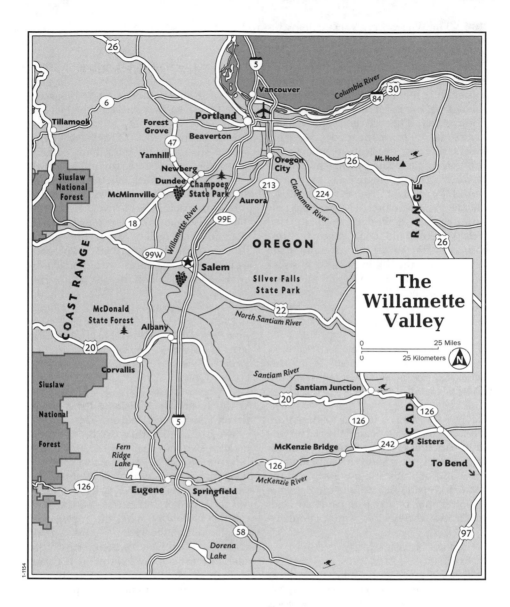

The Willamette Valley

0   25 Miles
0   25 Kilometers

of ducks. With the exception of the Sauvie Island Wildlife Management Area (home to a small population of bald eagles), the greatest concentration of wildlife refuges is in the central valley near Salem and Corvallis. These areas attract birders throughout the year, but especially during the winter when overwintering waterfowl crowd the refuges.

Parks & Other Hot Spots

Listed from north to south, these landmarks will help you orient yourself to this region.

Forest Park

In Portland; numerous entrances throughout the West Hills, including the upper end of NW Thurman Street, NW Saltzman Rd. (off U.S. 30), and NW Germantown Rd. (between NW Skyline Blvd. and U.S. 30). Walking, mountain biking, horseback riding.

Covering 4,800 acres and stretching for 8 miles from northwest Portland, this park is exactly what its name implies—a forested park. Through the forest wind dozens of miles of trails popular with walkers, picnickers, mountain bikers, joggers, and equestrians. Though there aren't many viewpoints within the park, and what views there are take in primarily the industrial wastelands of northwest and north Portland, the park is extremely popular simply because it provides a chance to hike in forested mountains only minutes from downtown Portland. Leif Erickson Road and the fire lanes that cross it are the domain of the city's mountain bikers, while the Wildwood Trail provides hikers with an escape from the two-wheeled demons.

Tryon Creek State Park

In Portland; from I-5, take the Terwilliger Blvd. exit and drive 2.2 miles south to the park entrance. Picnic areas, nature center, walking, hiking, road biking.

For people living on the south side of Portland, Tryon Creek State Park serves the same function as Forest Park. Deep woods tracked by banana slugs and carpeted with ferns and delicate trillium flowers are the draw. This park is also the starting point of a combination of bike paths and bike lanes that lead all the way to downtown Portland.

Sauvie Island

Take U.S. 30 for 10 miles northwest from downtown Portland to the Sauvie Island bridge. Walking, road biking, sea kayaking, fishing, swimming, bird watching, boardsailing.

Miles of sandy beaches on the Columbia River, hiking trails through wetlands full of waterfowl and bald eagles, and flat bicycling through idyllic farmland make this island (which some say is the largest freshwater island in the country) a popular destination on summer weekends. Adding to the appeal are all the fruit stands and pick-your-own farms that make a summer outing here a real treat. The island also provides a couple of flat-water canoeing or sea kayaking opportunities, as well as some spots that are popular with boardsailors.

Lewis and Clark State Park

Take exit 18 off I-84. Rock climbing, hiking, swimming, fishing, kayaking, tubing.

Located at the mouth of the Sandy River on the east side, this park lures anglers, swimmers, picnickers, tubers, and rock climbers. Anglers make up the majority of visitors much of the year, with steelhead and salmon being the elusive piscine prey. This is also one of the few rock-climbing sites in the Portland area. The park's Broughton Bluff, though dirty and plagued by poison oak, is popular with sport climbers who need a quick fix.

Oxbow County Park

From Portland, take I-84 east to exit 16A, drive south to Division St., and turn left. Follow signs to park. Camping, hiking, rafting, kayaking, fishing.

With old-growth forests and the Sandy River, a designated Wild and Scenic River, flowing through it, this park is the closest park to Portland that has a truly rugged Northwest feel to it. Sure the park has manicured lawns, group picnic areas, and a campground that stays packed throughout the summer, but rafters and kayakers run the whitewater here, and anglers pull steelhead from the water. The hiking trails serve as an excellent introduction to the ancient forests of the Northwest; the park is also the best place on the Sandy River to watch the annual Chinook salmon run (see "Wildlife Viewing," below, in "Portland to Salem—What to Do & Where to Do It").

Champoeg State Park

South of Newberg; from Newberg, take Ore. 219 south 4 miles and follow signs; from I-5, take exit 278 and drive 5 miles west. Historical museum, picnic areas, camping, hiking, road biking, fishing, canoeing.

With more than 3 miles of paved bike paths, an equal number of hiking trails, river access, and a campground, this historical park preserves a small piece of rural Willamette Valley for urban refugees

Outdoor Resources

CLASSES & OUTINGS

In the Portland area, **Portland Community College** (tel. 503/977-4933) offers classes in rock climbing, whitewater kayaking, and sea kayaking. **Portland Parks & Recreation** (tel. 503/823-5132) also offers a wide variety of seasonal outdoor sports classes and trips. Guided hikes, canoe trips, and bird-watching excursions are offered throughout the year by **Metro Regional Parks and Greenspaces** (tel. 503/797-1850). The **Tualatin Hills Parks & Recreation District** (tel. 503/644-3855) also offers similar outings, as well as canoe classes and guided rafting trips.

In the Eugene area, **Lane Community College** (tel. 541/726-2252) offers a wide variety of outdoor skills classes and tours throughout the year and throughout the region. Everything from sea kayaking to rock climbing to canoeing to cross-country skiing is covered by these trips. Call for a current listing of classes. The **City of Eugene Library, Recreation, and Cultural Services** (tel. 541/687-5333) offers a similar variety of classes and trips.

EQUIPMENT SHOPS

The Mountain Shop
628 NE Broadway, Portland
Tel. 503/628 288-6768

Oregon Mountain Community
60 NW Davis St., Portland
Tel. 503/227-1038

REI
1798 Jantzen Beach Center, Portland
Tel. 503/283-1300 or 360/693-0209

REI
7410 SW Bridgeport Rd., Tigard
Tel. 503/624-8600

REI
Third Avenue and Washington Street, Eugene.
Tel. 541/465-1800

Santiam Outfitters/Independence Mountaineering
237 NE High St., Salem.
Tel. 503/585-2628.

---

to have a look at on days off. The park also serves as the start of one of my favorite bike routes.

Willamette Mission State Park

North of Salem; from I-5, take exit 263 and drive 1.8 miles west on Brooklake Rd., turn right on Wheatland Rd., and continue 2.5 miles north to the park. Picnic areas, hiking, road biking, canoeing, fishing, bird watching.

Created to preserve the site of the first mission in Oregon (one of the first settlements of any kind in this region), this state park also has a few miles of hiking trails and is the site of the largest cottonwood tree in the country. There is also good bird watching and river access for canoes and sea kayaks.

Silver Falls State Park

East of Salem; from Portland, take the Woodburn exit off I-5 and follow Ore. 214 southeast for 30 miles to the park; from Salem, head east from I-5 on Ore. 22 for 10 miles, take the Ore. 214 exit (signed Silver Falls State Park), and continue 16 miles to the park. Nature center, picnic areas, camping, hiking, road biking, horseback riding, fishing, canoeing.

With its numerous waterfalls and miles of forest trails, this park is a popular weekend destination throughout the year. Come in the spring, and you'll likely encounter newts crossing the trails. Any time of year adults and children are fascinated by the many waterfalls, some of which it is possible to walk behind. Short and long hiking loops can be found here.

SOUTHERN WILLAMETTE VALLEY: CORVALLIS TO EUGENE

McDonald and Paul M. Dunn State Forests

North of Corvallis; from Corvallis, take Ore. 99W north for 4–6 miles. Hiking, mountain biking, horseback riding.

These two research forests, both affiliated with Oregon State University, are known in the Corvallis area primarily for their many miles of great mountain-biking roads and trails. However, the trails in the McDonald Forest are also popular with hikers and equestrians. The few hilltop viewpoints are the most popular destinations.

Alton Baker Park and Skinner Butte Park

Downtown Eugene; Alton Baker is off Centennial Blvd. and Skinner Butte Park is at the north end of High St. Picnic areas, road biking, canoeing, whitewater paddling, fishing, rock climbing.

These two parks, lying on either side of the Willamette River in downtown Eugene, are this city's outdoor playground for grown-ups and children alike. With more than a dozen miles of paved jogging, walking, and bicycling paths, the parks stay busy year-round. Other attractions include flat-water canoeing on the Alton Baker Canoe Path, whitewater paddling on the Willamette, and rock climbing at the Skinner Butte Columns.

Elijah Bristow State Park

Southeast of Eugene; from I-5, drive 8.5 miles east on Ore. 58. Picnic areas, hiking, mountain biking, horseback riding, canoeing and kayaking, fishing.

Several miles of trails open to hikers, mountain bikers, and horseback riders are the sole appeal of this park along the south bank of the Willamette River. The terrain is flat and for the most part the park is a weekend picnic area. However, the section of hiking trail along the river is

pleasant enough and the mountain biking is perfect for beginners.

Portland to Salem ◆ What to Do & Where to Do It

BIRD WATCHING

Set at the confluence of two rivers, the Portland metro area is laced with waterways and wetlands that attract a wide variety of waterfowl, as well as eagles that feed on ducks and their kin. The city's mascot is the great blue heron, and indeed these gangly, squawking birds are a common sight throughout the area. Out at Smith and Bybee lakes at **Heron Lakes Golf Course,** there is a heron rookery that is one of the best places in the area to spot great blue herons. Another heron rookery can be found in **Molalla River State Park** just north of Canby. The best all-around bird-watching sites include **Sauvie Island,** much of which is set aside as a wildlife refuge. The best viewing time is during the winter months when you can see Canada geese, swans, and numerous species of ducks. All these waterfowl attract a fair number of bald eagles, which feed on dead and dying ducks. Other good birding spots include **Oak Island, Beggars Tick, Oaks Bottom, Jackson Bottom,** and **Forest Park.**

For more information on birding in the area, stop by or call the **Portland Audubon Society,** 5151 NW Cornell Rd. (tel. 503/292-WILD). See also the "Outdoor Resources" sidebar, above.

BOARDSAILING

Though the area's serious boardheads all head up the Columbia Gorge to Hood River and its legendary raging winds, beginners head to **Vancouver Lake Park** just across the Columbia River in Vancouver, Washington. To reach the lake from Portland, go north on I-5 to Vancouver, take the Fourth Plain exit, and drive west 9 miles to the park.

One of the best beginner windsurfing spots in Portland is **Willamette Park** on the

Willamette River south of downtown. The park entrance is at the corner of Macadam Boulevard and Nebraska Street. Nearby is **Gorge Performance Windsurfing,** 7400 SW Macadam Blvd. (tel. 503/246-6646), which rents sailboards for $35 a day.

Another good spot, though with a considerable current that may dissuade novices, is **Sauvie Island,** where miles of beaches bounded by shallow waters provide ample opportunities to practice uphauling. The winds here are rarely, if ever, as strong as in the gorge. Just remember to stay out of the way of the freighters. To reach Sauvie Island's bea-ches, take U.S. 30 west from Portland toward Scappoose and turn right over a bridge onto the island and continue straight ahead for 1.8 miles to a right turn onto Reeder Road. Follow this road for 20 miles until you reach the beach parking areas.

FISHING

There aren't too many cities where you can catch a 25-pound salmon within the city limits, but—since the cleanup of the Willamette River in the 1960s and 1970s—you can number Portland among them. Or at least it would be if the salmon population wasn't on a such a spiral toward extinction. Today most salmon anglers head out in boats with fish finders and the salmon hardly stand a chance. However, there is still some bank fishing to be done on the Willamette from the **seawall in downtown Oregon City.** The area below Willamette Falls in Oregon City is one of the busiest fishing holes in the Portland vicinity. Migrating spring Chinook, summer and winter steelhead, and sturgeon are all taken in these waters with regularity. If you're going to be bank fishing from this high wall, just be sure you've got a strong rod and line.

If you're interested in pulling in some big catfish, head for **Multnomah Channel,** which runs up the west side of Sauvie Island. There are several access points and boat ramps on either side of the channel. You can also fish this channel for sturgeon, spring Chinook, largemouth bass, and panfish.

The **Clackamas River,** though it still supports reduced steelhead and salmon runs, is a surprisingly poor fishing river. Speculation is that upstream logging leaves so much silt on the bottom of the river that the trout population is severely reduced. Whatever the reason, you'll likely do better fishing another river. The **Molalla** is a good choice in the same area. There is a wild winter steelhead run (December through April) and a hatchery summer steelhead run (May through July). Upstream of the town of Liberal, in the wild section of the river, rainbows are stocked. This section of the river also has lots of bank access as it passes through BLM land.

On the east side of the city, the **Sandy River** provides some of the best steelheading in the state with both summer and winter runs. There are also three salmon runs on this river—spring Chinook (April through June), fall Chinook (August through October), and coho (September through October). **Lewis & Clark State Park, Oxbow Park,** and **Dodge Park** all provide good public access.

Salmon and sturgeon are the primary goals of anglers on the **Columbia River,** and if you want to fish this river, you just about have to have a boat. The only productive salmon fishing from shore takes place along the beaches of **Sauvie Island** during the spring Chinook run in March. If you do have a boat, there is often good fishing for coho and fall Chinook at the **mouths of the Sandy, Cowlitz, Kalama, and Lewis rivers** in August and September. During the summer months, these same river mouths are popular with steelheaders.

HIKING

The northern Willamette Valley has hundreds of small parks, but it is to the region's largest parks that people head when they want a quick escape from city life. Such places as Forest Park, Oxbow Park, and Powell Butte Park (all in the Portland metro area) offer hiking in forests that could easily be national forests rather than urban enclaves of nature.

Council Crest

3.8 miles. Moderate. 700-foot elevation gain. Access: From Terwilliger Blvd. (an extension of SW Sixth Ave.) just south of downtown Portland, turn right onto Sam Jackson Dr. and watch for the Marquam Nature Center parking area on the right. Map: None available.

Surrounded by affluent residential neighborhoods in the West Hills less than a mile from downtown Portland, this trail is another of the city's pocket wild areas. The trail up to Council Crest climbs steadily through a dark forest dominated by Douglas firs and western red cedars. Though you can see houses on the edge of the ravine that this trail follows, there is still a feeling of having escaped the city. From the top of Council Crest, there are expansive views. This trail is a good west-side option if you have already hiked the trails in Forest Park.

Powell Butte

1.2–9 miles. Easy–moderate. 300-foot elevation gain. Access: Take SE Powell Blvd. east from I-205 and turn right into the park at SE 162nd Ave. Map: On board at park trailheads.

If you happen to be on the east side of Portland and need a quick hiking fix, this park is your best bet. Once a dairy farm, Powell Butte is topped by rolling pastures that are now crisscrossed by hiking trails. From these open fields, on a clear day, you'll get one of the best views in Portland, with Mount Hood, Mount St. Helens, and Mount Adams all visible on the horizons. Dense forests cover the steep lower slopes of the butte, and by combining a trail to the bottom with some hiking up in the meadows, you can get a good workout and feel as if you've been off in the deep woods for a while.

If you want views, take the Mountain View Trail to the summit and then loop around the top of the hill on the Orchard Loop Trail. To add some forest walking, take the Wild Hawthorne and Mount Hood trails. You can add more meadows by looping back to the parking area on the Meadowland Trail. Keep eyes and ears alert for mountain bikers. Parking is near the top of the butte.

Wildwood Trail, Southern Section

7 miles. Moderate. 800-foot elevation gain. Access: From U.S. 26, take the zoo exit. Maps: Trailhead maps or Portland Parks and Recreation's Forest Park map.

Stretching for 27 miles from Washington Park to NW Germantown Road, the Wildwood Trail is an urban anomaly. How many other cities can claim a hiking trail of such a length within the city limits? Along its length, it passes through the wilderness of Forest Park and the tree collection of the Hoyt Arboretum and passes by historic Pittock Mansion, the Japanese Garden, and the Washington Park Zoo. My favorite section starts at the southern end of the trail, just beyond the zoo. Though this section of the trail has the most urban feel, it also offers the best views, a great variety of terrain, and the options to visit some of Portland's top attractions. The trail starts from the parking lot below the Vietnam Veterans Memorial and is well signed for its entire length. A spur trail drops down to the Japanese Garden, which is well worth a visit. From here, you pass through the Hoyt Arboretum with its groves of stately redwoods and ponderosa pines. Beyond here, the trail spends a mile in native forest before reaching the historic Pittock Mansion, which was built between 1909 and 1914. On a sunny afternoon, the neatly manicured lawns around the mansion just beg weary hikers to lay down for a rest, but it's hard to close your eyes when the best view in Portland stretches out beneath you. The mansion is open for tours. From here, head back the way you came to the Hoyt Arboretum and turn right onto the Creek Trail. Follow this to a left onto the Hemlock Trail to return to your car.

Warrior Rock, Sauvie Island

7 miles round-trip. Easy. No elevation gain. Access: From Portland, take U.S. 30 for 10 miles northwest to the Sauvie Island bridge, cross the bridge, and continue 1.8 miles to a right on

Reeder Rd. (after stopping at the market to get a parking permit). Follow Reeder Rd. to its end in 12.6 miles (it becomes gravel for the last 2.2 miles). Map: USGS St. Helens.

This flat trail is a good choice for late summer (when the blackberries are ripe) and through the autumn (when the leaves are off the trees and you get more glimpses of the river through the trees). The trail starts out across cow pastures before diving into the forest, where it remains for the next 3.0 miles. Alternatively, you can hike for a mile along the beach before it becomes too narrow. Though this area looks unpopulated today, before the arrival of whites in the Northwest, it supported several Native American villages, including one by Warrior Rock (hence the name). The turnaround point is the end of the island, where there is a lighthouse and a view of the town of St. Helens. If it's a hot day, don't miss the opportunity to go for a swim whenever the urge strikes. You don't even need to bring a bathing suit. This is a clothing-optional stretch of beach, and you can expect to see several nude bathers. Alternatively, you can preserve your modesty by sticking to the trail.

Silver Falls State Park

7.2 miles. Moderate. 600-foot elevation gain. Access: From Portland, take the Woodburn exit off I-5 and follow Ore. 214 southeast for 30 miles to the park. From Salem, head east from I-5 on Ore. 22 for 10 miles, take the Ore. 214 exit (signed Silver Falls State Park), and continue 16 miles to the park. Map: Trailhead maps or USGS Drake Crossing.

This state park east of Salem is one of the most popular inland parks in the state, and because of its low elevations, it makes a good hiking spot during those months of the year when snow keeps hikers out of the mountains. Miles of trails here meander through mossy, old-growth forests, but it is the falls for which the park is named that are the main attraction. Several of these waterfalls have trails that actually go behind the cascading water and through caves that have been carved out by Silver Creek. This loop hike, which starts at the

South Falls parking area, takes in 10 waterfalls, the highest of which is 177 feet tall. From the parking lot, follow signs to South Falls, which you can walk behind. From these falls, head north to Lower South Falls, which also have a trail behind the water. Beyond these falls, you can cut your hike and head back to the car or continue past Lower North, Drake, Double, and Middle North falls. Beyond this latter waterfall, a short-cut trail leads back to the parking area. If you're up for the full hike, take the left fork and continue past Twin Falls to hike behind North Falls where a spur trail leads to Upper North Falls. From this point on, the trail parallels the road for 2.5 miles but does pass by Winter Falls. Needless to say, kids love hiking behind the waterfalls here.

Opal Creek

10 miles round-trip. Easy–moderate. 200-foot elevation gain. Access: From Salem, drive 22 miles east on Ore. 22 to Mehama and turn left onto Little North Santiam Rd. Continue straight on this road for 15 miles to the end of pavement and then continue another 1.3 miles on gravel to a fork in the road. Take the left fork, FS 2209, for another 4 miles to a locked gate and large parking area. Map: Trailhead maps; USGS Elkhorn and Battle Ax.

When I first moved to Oregon in 1990, I very soon learned about the battle to save the Opal Creek watershed from the loggers' chain saws. As one of the largest intact old-growth watersheds in the state, it was coveted by logging companies. The long fight to save this beautiful area was finally won (at least somewhat) late in 1996 when the Opal Creek Wilderness was created. Although many environmentalists feel that not enough land and not enough protection have been extended to the Opal Creek watershed, at least it is now somewhat preserved. Don't come to Opal Creek looking to be awestruck by giant trees. The hike, though pleasant enough, is more about what you can't see than what you can see. Sure, the creek is beautiful, sometimes aquamarine, sometimes opalescent as it tumbles over eroded bedrock. And sure, the 3- to 6-foot-diameter tree trunks rising skyward are majestic—with the grand patriarchs, the trio of 1,000-year-old red cedars at the end of the trail, especially so. But far more impressive is the unseen forest beyond, where nature goes about its business unseen and unmolested by people.

The hike starts out with 2.5 miles on the dirt road that leads to Jawbone Flats, which was once a mining town but now is an environmental education center operated by the Friends of Opal Creek organization that fought so hard to preserve it. The actual Opal Creek Trail begins a half-mile before Jawbone Flats and follows the Little North Santiam for its first mile. The trees at the beginning of the trail are among the most impressive of the hike—an extensive forest of tall, thick trunks rising limbless and straight. At the 1-mile point, the trail passes the picturesque Opal Pool and heads up Opal Creek. At 2.5 miles from the start of the trail (5 miles from the parking area), you reach a grove of three western red cedars that are roughly 1,000 years old. These trees make a good turnaround point. All along the trail there are good campsites beside both the river and the creek, and if it's a hot day, there are several good swimming holes (the best is below Sawmill Falls just downstream from the start of the trail).

HORSEBACK RIDING

If you want to get back in the saddle, you can rent horses at **Beaverton Hill Top Riding Stables,** 20490 SW Farmington Rd., Beaverton (tel. 503/649-5497), which charges $20 per hour, or at **Lakeside Horse Rentals** on 162nd Avenue off Foster Road (tel. 503/761-1753), which charges $13 per hour.

MOUNTAIN BIKING

Leif Erickson Road

12 miles one-way. Easy–moderate. 350-foot elevation gain. Access: The eastern access is at the top of NW Thurman St. at a locked gate. The western access is on NW Germantown Rd. downhill to the north from NW Skyline Rd. (this parking area is highly prone to car cloutings). Map: Portland Parks Department Map or trailhead maps.

Running the length of Forest Park, Leif Erickson Road offers Portland mountain bikers a dozen miles of easy dirt road on which to keep in shape. The old road, built in 1915 as part of a plan to develop these hillsides, contours through the park winding in and out of ravines, with countless easy ascents and descents that give you a chance to catch your breath before the next climb. Adding excitement and challenge to this easy, popular, and often crowded road are several fire trails that run up and down slope from Leif Erickson Road. These trails are what lure serious riders into this urban forest. The steeply pitched fire trails offer breath-stealing, granny-gear climbs and screaming, kamikaze downhills. All in all it's a great place to prepare for the next race or just go for a leisurely ride through the woods. On weekends, especially in summer, the road sees a lot of use from strolling families and joggers. Stay alert, especially for small children, who tend to be unpredictable and unaware.

Powell Butte Nature Park

5 miles. Moderate–difficult. 300-foot elevation gain. Access: Take SE Powell Blvd. 3.5 miles east from I-205 to SE 162nd Ave. and the park entrance. Map: Trailhead map.

What Leif Erickson Road and the Forest Park fire lanes are to Portland's west side, Powell Butte is to its east side. Though at 570 acres considerably smaller than Forest Park, Powell Butte offers more varied terrain, and among Portland's hard-core mountain bikers is *the* place to ride. The butte was once a dairy farm and its summit is still a rolling pasture with superb views of Cascade peaks. Set out across these meadows and then dive into the forest on the Mount Hood Trail, which leads 300 feet down to the base of the butte. Now comes the workout. From here, you have to climb back up to the meadows on steep trails that stay muddy and slippery for at least half the year. Good luck, and I hope you brought a change of clothes. If a loop around the butte has left you grinning from ear to ear, why not do it all over again in reverse? It's a totally different trail!

Banks/Vernonia State Park

20 miles one-way. Easy–moderate. 700-foot elevation gain. Access: There are six trailheads. The Banks trailhead is northwest of Banks on Ore. 47. The Vernonia trailhead is on the south side of town in Anderson Park. Map: Trailhead maps.

Once a railroad right of way, this rails-to-trails park stretches between the logging community of Vernonia and the farm town of Banks. However, the best sections of the trail are the upper stretches closest to Vernonia, and these happen to be paved. So, if you want to do a pleasant 14-mile ride on your road bike, head up to Vernonia. Because this was once a railroad track, the incline is almost imperceptibly gradual, which makes for easy riding (bring the family). Currently, there are 7 miles of paved pathway, and another 5 miles were scheduled for paving in 1997. This still leaves 8 miles of gravel through the middle section of the trail. Unfortunately, the floods of 1996 caused a massive washout about midway through this gravel section of trail. As of late 1996, this washout had still not been repaired. Two of the most interesting sections of trail are bypasses around old railroad trestles that loom high above the present trail.

Hagg Lake

11 miles round-trip. Easy–moderate. 50-foot elevation gain. Access: Drive south for 3.5 miles from Forest Grove on Ore. 47 and turn right onto Scoggins Valley Rd. Map: Not necessary.

The trail around Hagg Lake was closed to bicycles for five years before being reopened in 1996, and is now once again one of the more fun mountain-bike rides in the Portland area. The trail circles the lake (actually a reservoir), with lots of short steep climbs and descents along the way. The views are great and the trail passes through forest and meadows. If you should

tire of the trail, there are lots of places where you can ride up to the excellent paved road that circles the lake (a favorite of road bikers). Once on the road, just take the shortest route back to your starting point. The main drawbacks of this trail are numerous hikers on summer weekends and muddy conditions in the winter.

ROAD BIKING

Sauvie Island

24.2 miles. Easy. No elevation gain. Access: From Portland, take U.S. 30 for 10 miles northwest to the Sauvie Island Bridge and park in the parking area on the far side of the bridge.

Sauvie Island, a long, flat island at the confluence of the Willamette and Columbia rivers, is Portland's fruit bowl, a vast expanse of truck farms providing the city with fresh fruits and vegetables throughout the summer. The rural flavor offers a quick escape from Portland's urban crowding, and consequently, the island's flat roads are a favorite of area cyclists, especially on summer weekends when fruit stands and pick-your-own farms are open. Add to this the chance to cool off at a river beach and you've got the perfect summer ride. Start this ride just over the bridge onto the island, where there is a large gravel parking lot (the only public parking area on the island for which you do not need a parking permit). From the parking area, go right on Gillihan Road. In 6.1 miles, you'll come to the intersection with Reeder Road. Turn right and continue 5.9 miles up this road. If you happen to be on a mountain bike, you can continue all the way to the end of this road, which is gravel for the last 2.2 miles. Beginning just before the end of the pavement, there are miles of sandy beaches (some of which, farther along, are clothing-optional). This is the turnaround point for the ride and is a great place for a swim on a hot day.

Returning back to the junction with Gillihan Road, turn right to continue around the island. After 4.4 miles, reach a T-intersection with Sauvie Island Road and turn left. If you want to add some more miles to your ride, turn right on Sauvie

Island Road, which parallels Multnomah Channel for 6.5 miles.

Skyline Boulevard

21 miles. Moderate. 600-foot elevation gain. Access: From downtown Portland, take W. Burnside Rd. uphill and turn right on NW Skyline Blvd. to a parking area on the left at Willamette Stone State Park.

This is the quintessential Portland-area bike ride, and on a summer weekend, there will be a steady stream of cyclists heading out and back on this scenic ridgetop road. Although in recent years Skyline Boulevard has become lined with "McMansions," there are still places where you can gaze down on the Tualatin Valley far below. This is an out-and-back ride (unless you want to create a loop that loses and then regains several hundred feet of elevation), so you can turn around wherever you want. A good place to start this ride is just west of the intersection of Skyline and Burnside/Barnes Road. Here you'll find several parking spaces at the side of the road. Cornelius Pass Road, where there is a small store, makes a good turnaround point and snack stop.

Hagg Lake

11.6 miles. Moderate. 750-foot elevation gain. Access: From Forest Grove, take Ore. 47 south 4.5 miles and turn right onto Scoggins Valley Rd.

With its wide shoulders, easy grades, and scenic views of Hagg Lake (actually a reservoir), this ride is another Portland area favorite. Because the road is used almost exclusively by park traffic, it is in excellent shape. Just remember that the park sees a lot of traffic on summer weekends. For quiet riding, come in the off-season or on a weekday. There are several picnic areas that can turn a ride around the lake into a fun outing. Several alternative starting points can add mileage and additional rural scenery to a ride in this area. You could start your ride at the junction of Ore. 47 and Scoggins Valley Road and add 8 miles to the ride. Alternatively, you could add 14 miles to your ride if you start in Forest Grove, head south on Ore. 47 to

Dilley, meander through this tiny rural community, then continue south on Patton Valley Road, which parallels Ore. 47. From Patton Valley Road, ride west on Scoggins Valley Road to the lake. For still more length, you can continue south and then west on Patton Valley Road to the quaint village of Cherry Grove for an additional 24 miles or so.

French Prairie Loop

23 miles. Moderate. 200-foot elevation gain. Access: From Newberg, take Ore. 219 south 4 miles and follow signs; from I-5, take exit 278 and drive 5 miles west.

Starting in Champoeg State Park, this ride includes 4.6 miles of bike path through the park, a quiet stretch of road along the Willamette River (now lined with the homes of the wealthy), and a visit to the historic town of Aurora, which is now filled with antique stores.

From the Riverside day-use area parking lot, follow the paved bike path eastward. The trail crosses pastures and oak groves before entering the thick forest along the bank of the Willamette. There are occasional glimpses of the river through the trees, but mostly this is just a quiet forest pedal. After 4.6 miles, the trail comes to an end and becomes Schuller Road. At the end of this road, turn left onto Butteville Road and then left again onto Butte Street at the bottom of the hill. Passing through the tiny community of Butteville, this road parallels the Willamette, passing many large new homes and older vacation cabins along the way, for 4.5 miles. After 2 miles, watch for a turnoff into a small park that is part of the Willamette River Greenway, the ambitious plan to preserve as much of the river as possible in a natural state. At the end of this road, turn left and cross over I-5. On the far side of the interstate, turn right onto Airport Road and continue 3.5 miles down this road, passing a large golf course and going straight at a stop sign, until the road comes to an end at a T-intersection. Take a left here, cross the Mill Creek bridge, and enter the historic community of Aurora in 0.2 miles.

This town was founded in 1855 as an experiment in Christian communal living and lasted barely 20 years. Today, Aurora is one of the Northwest's premier antique-shopping towns and dozens of its old restored buildings now house antique stores and malls. There are also several places around town to eat or get a snack and an espresso. You may want to stop at the local museum. After having a look around, head back out of town the way you came in (Ehlen Road). After the stoplight at Wilsonville–Hubbard Highway in 1.0 mile, take an immediate left onto Donald Road and continue for 4 miles (crossing back over I-5) to the farm community of Donald. Continue straight through this town, and in just under a mile, go straight onto Yergen Road. After another mile, turn right on Case Road and head north back toward Champoeg State Park. At the end of this road, turn left onto Champoeg Road, and in less than 1 mile you will be back at your car. If it is a summer weekend, you might want to detour 1 mile west from the intersection of Case Road and Champoeg Road to Champoeg Cellars and sample a few of their wines. Then again, you might want to save this detour until after you're back in your car.

ROCK CLIMBING

Although the rock climbing around Portland isn't the greatest, at least there are some easily accessible rock walls. The most popular of the area climbing spots is the **Madrone Wall** (Carver Cliffs), which is located 2 miles east of the crossroads community of Carver on Ore. 224 (take Ore. 224/212 east from I-205). The trail is behind a locked gate on the north side of the highway, and there is lots of roadside parking on the south side of the highway. This long basalt wall is a short hike in from the road and offers enough climbing routes over a large enough area that it doesn't get too crowded. Big red-barked madrone trees provide shade that makes climbing here fun even in the heat of summer. Lots of variety and plenty of bolted routes.

Broughton Bluff is the next-best climbing spot in the metro area. These basalt crags are convenient to Portland and could be classified as part of the Columbia Gorge if you wanted to claim to have climbed in the gorge. You'll find Broughton Bluff in

Lewis and Clark State Park just east of Troutdale off I-84 (exit 18). The bluffs, which include 13 major walls, the highest of which is about 150 feet, are visible from the interstate and look down on the Sandy River. To reach the rocks from the parking lot of the state park, walk upriver along the road and watch for a trail on your left that climbs through the forest.

Dirty and noisy (I-205 is right at your back), **Rocky Butte,** an abandoned rock quarry, is the least favored of Portland's climbing crags, but is still fairly popular due to its proximity to Portland and ease of access. This is a great spot for traverse practice and top roping (the access is from the top of the quarry), and has more than 100 climbs. To reach Rocky Butte, take the 82nd Avenue exit off I-84 and follow 82nd Avenue north for 1 mile to NE Fremont Street. Follow this street (it will become NE 91st Avenue) almost to the tennis courts and park in one of the small turnouts.

Portland Rock Climbs, A Climber's Guide to Northwest Oregon (Tim Olson, 1993), has an excellent section on Columbia Gorge ice-climbing.

In addition to the climbing spots listed above, you'll find a couple of good rock gyms around the Portland area. These include **Portland Rock Gym,** 2034 SE Sixth St. (tel. 503/232-8310), and **Stoneworks Inc. Climbing Gym,** 6775 SW 111th Ave., Beaverton (tel. 503/644-3517). Both of these gyms offer classes. The two Portland area **REIs** (1798 Jantzen Beach Center, tel. 503/283-1300 or 360/693-0209; and 7410 SW Bridgeport Rd., tel. 503/624-8600) also have climbing walls, but these are used only for climbing classes. All the above also offer climbing classes. If you'd like to do your learning outside, contact **AdventureSmith Guides** (tel. 503/293-6727). **Portland Community College** (tel. 503/977-4933) also offers rock-climbing classes.

SEA KAYAKING & FLAT-WATER CANOEING

Both canoes and sea kayaks can be rented at **Ebb & Flow Paddlesports,** 0604 SW Nebraska St. (tel. 503/245-1756), which is only a couple of blocks from the Willamette River. Double sea kayaks rent for $26 for a weekday half day and $39 for a weekend full day. **Sportcraft Marina,** 1701 Clackamette Dr., Oregon City (tel. 503/656-6484), also rents canoes and sea kayaks. Rates are $21 for a half day and $30 for a full day. The **Portland REI,** 1798 Jantzen Beach Center (tel. 503/283-1300 or 360/693-0209), also rents both canoes and sea kayaks for between $28 and $40 a day, while the **Tigard REI,** 7410 SW Bridgeport Rd. (tel. 503/624-8600), rents only canoes ($28 to $35 a day).

For more information on paddling in this area, contact the **Lower Columbia Canoe Club,** 7905 SW Canyon Lane, Portland, OR 97225 (Internet address: http://www.teleport.com/nonprofit/LCCC), or the **Willamette Kayak & Canoe Club,** P.O. Box 1062, Corvallis, OR 97339. See also the "Outdoor Resources" sidebar, above.

Vancouver Lake

1–2 hours. Easy. Access: From Portland, take I-5 north across the Columbia River to Vancouver, take the Fourth Plain exit, and go west to Lower River Rd.

Located on the outskirts of Vancouver, Washington, across the Columbia River from Portland, shallow Vancouver Lake is a popular spot with beginning paddlers. The scenery isn't too impressive (suburban homes line the east shore), though if you head to either the north or south end of the lake, you'll find marshy areas to explore. During the winter, you're likely to see quite a few waterfowl on the lake, and great blue herons are common throughout the year. During the summer, sea kayak rentals and lessons are sometimes available here.

Ross Island

3–4 hours. Moderate. Access: From downtown Portland, take SW Macadam Blvd. south to SW Nebraska St. and turn left into Willamette Park.

The most popular Portland paddle is around the Willamette River's Ross Island and on down the river to downtown Portland. This easy paddle is popular because it provides a bit of the city and a bit of the country. Starting from the boat landing at Willamette Park (at the corner of SW Macadam Blvd. and SW Nebraska St.), paddle across to the south end of Ross Island; depending on the wind conditions you may want to paddle down one side of the island or the other. However, the east side has a narrow channel and sees less powerboat activity. Along this stretch you'll pass steep forested banks both on the island and on the riverbank. A shallow slough makes an interesting place to explore and you might scare some resting fish in the mudflats. Continuing north around the island, you'll pass beaches that make good picnic spots. Toward the north end, you'll pass the entrance to a huge gravel pit that has removed a sizable chunk from the middle of this island. Barges loaded with gravel shuttle back and forth across the narrow channel to a pier on the east bank of the river. Stay clear of this area and any barges.

From the north end of the island, the look of the river changes rapidly as you enter downtown Portland. On the east are the noisy elevated roadways of I-5, above you the soaring Marquam Bridge. You'll pass by the Oregon Museum of Science and Industry, and though you may be tempted to tie up to their submarine, heed the signs! From here, cross to the far side of the river to the shores of Tom McCall Waterfront Park, which is the site of numerous summer festivals. The southern section of the park has a rocky beach where you can put ashore, but otherwise a high wall separates the park from the river. This is a good point at which to turn around. If you're hungry, you can tie up at the floating Newport Bay Restaurant and get a bite to eat. One of the reasons this paddle is so popular is that the put-in point is less than two blocks from the above-mentioned Ebb & Flow Paddlesports.

Multnomah Channel

2–4 hours. Easy–moderate. Access: Boat ramps are located at Brown's Landing off U.S. 30 just south of Scappoose and at the northern end of Reeder Rd. on Sauvie Island.

This waterway between Sauvie Island and the mainland is one of the Willamette River's connections to the Columbia River. It's nearly as wide as the Willamette, and along its length there are houseboat moorings, pastures, old log booms, and access to the Gilbert River, which flows out of Sturgeon Lake on Sauvie Island. If you just paddle the channel itself, you won't be having a wilderness experience but rather a glimpse into the variety of development along this stretch of water. The many houseboats are what capture most people's fancy. As you fantasize about this seemingly idyllic lifestyle, stop to think about the anxieties these people went through during the 1996 flooding. Friends of mine who live on a houseboat here nearly had their entire mooring break free, and their neighbors were without natural gas for months.

Sauvie Island's Lakes

2–4 hours. Easy–moderate. Access: Take U.S. 30 for 10 miles northwest from Portland, turn onto Sauvie Island, continue straight for 1.8 miles (after getting a parking permit at the market just over the bridge), turn right on Reeder Rd., and continue 12 miles to a boat ramp at the mouth of the Gilbert River.

For a more wildlife-oriented paddle than the one on Multnomah Channel, try the shallow lakes on Sauvie Island. There are more than 12,000 acres of lakes at the north end of this large island, and together these waters provide some of the best waterfowl habitat in the state. Consequently, this area offers the best bird watching in the Portland area, so be sure to bring your binoculars. You're likely to see several species of ducks as well as great blue herons, bald eagles, and maybe even sandhill cranes if you come in the spring or fall. From the boat ramp, you can paddle 3 miles up the muddy Gilbert River (the mouth is just to the south) to huge Sturgeon Lake, but keep in mind that this is a tidal river and you'll need to time your trip to the tides. Alternatively, you can paddle past the mouth of the Gilbert and up another channel to Crane Lake. One other alternative is to put in at Little McNary Lake, which you pass just before reaching the boat ramp. This is probably the most appealing of the three areas. However, whichever area you choose to explore, you'll certainly see plenty of birdlife.

Blue Lake, in northeast Portland between the airport and Troutdale, is the Portland area's favorite swimming hole and stays packed throughout the summer with families spending the day at the lake. To reach Blue Lake, take exit 17 off I-84 and drive north on Marine Drive. Equally popular but with a different crowd are the beaches along the north end of Reeder Road on **Sauvie Island,** which is north of Portland off U.S. 30. Here you'll find miles of sandy beaches (some of which are clothing optional). To reach these beaches, drive onto Sauvie Island, continue straight ahead for 1.8 miles, and then turn right onto Reeder Road. The beaches begin about 20 miles north and become less crowded the farther you go. Arrive early on a sunny weekend if you want a parking space and be sure to purchase your parking permit at the convenience store just over the bridge onto the island.

Less urban and more idyllic settings can be found on several of the area's smaller rivers. **Lewis & Clark State Park** and **Oxbow County Park** on the **Sandy River** east of Portland are both popular, though the water in this river stays fairly cold throughout the summer and the fast current can be treacherous. Good swimming spots on the **Clackamas River** can be found at **Barton Park,** 10.5 miles east of I-205 on Ore. 224, where kids can play in a quiet pond or strong swimmers can hop into the river above the boat ramp or do a bit of tubing. Farther up the Clackamas River, **Milo McIver State Park** has swimming, though it is in a fairly strong current. Keep in mind, however, that the Clackamas River is nearly legendary for its cold waters and has taken the lives of hundreds of people over the years.

The **Molalla River** offers slightly better swimming holes than the Clackamas. At the mouth of the river about 2.5 miles north of Canby, there is **Molalla River Park,** which has a sandy beach. Heading upstream, you'll find a fun little spot at the **Molalla River bridge** between Mulino and Liberal on Ore. 213. This swimming hole has a little waterfall and a pretty little pool. **Feyrer Park,** just east of the town of Molalla on Feyrer Park Road, is the most popular spot on the river. The park is quiet and shady and there are some rapids just upstream. Upstream from Feyrer Park, there are numerous river access points along **Dickey Prairie Road,** which parallels the river south of Feyrer Park. These sections are particularly good for tubing.

Down in the Salem area, the beach at **Willamette Mission State Park** (on the Willamette River) is an ever-popular swimming spot for families. This park is adjacent to the Wheatland Ferry, which is one of only three remaining car ferries on the Willamette River. To reach the park, take exit 263 off of I-5 and drive west on Brooklake Road. Turn right on Wheatland Road and continue north to signs for the park. For a more idyllic experience, head west of Salem to **Mill Creek,** where there are several swimming holes in and near **Mill Creek County Park.** Mill Creek is a narrow, rocky stream. To reach Mill Creek, take Ore. 22 west from Salem and watch for Mill Creek Road on the left between mileposts 4 and 5. Turn left here and watch for the first swimming hole in about 2 miles.

If you're heading to the coast on Ore. 18 on a hot summer day and you just can't wait to cool off, you can stop at **Blackwell Park** on **Willamina Creek.** Here you'll find a small beach, rapids, and even a rope swing. This park is 4.5 miles north of Willamina off Willamina Creek Road, which itself is on a business loop off Ore. 18.

The various forks of the Santiam River offer some of the best swimming holes in all of Oregon, but by far the greatest concentration of beautiful swimming holes is to be found on the **Little North Fork Santiam River.** To reach the Little North Fork, drive 22 miles east from Salem on Ore. 22 to Mehama and turn left on Little North Fork Road. All along this river there are numerous parks, campgrounds, and river access points. Try **North Fork Park, Bear Creek Park,** or **Salmon Falls Park.** Of all the swimming areas on this small, clear river, none can beat **Three Falls,** which is about 18 miles from Ore. 22. Take Little North Fork Road to FS 2207 (the last 2.5 miles are on gravel; follow the signs).

Chutes, pools, and a gravel beach surround a freestanding basalt wall and a natural stone pillar.

WALKS & NATURAL ROADSIDE ATTRACTIONS

If you're looking for a quick walk in the woods, the many miles of trails within Portland's **Forest Park** offer plenty of options. There are also some less obvious choices around the northern half of the Willamette Valley. See also the "Outdoor Resources" sidebar earlier in this chapter.

Camassia Preserve

1.5 miles. Easy. 100-foot elevation gain. Access: From Portland, take Macadam Blvd. south through Lake Oswego to West Linn, turn right on Willamette Falls Dr., follow this road for 0.3 miles, veer right onto Sunset Ave., and then turn right onto Walnut St. Map: Trailhead map.

Owned by the Nature Conservancy, this nature preserve has been set aside to protect a rocky hillside on which grows a rare patch of camas flowers that bloom in April and May. Once found extensively throughout the Northwest, camas plants provided, in their fleshy bulb, a staple food for the region's Native Americans. However, of the two species of camas growing in this region, only one, the purple-flowered camas, is edible. Often growing in the same place are white-flowered camas, which are highly poisonous (my advice is not to try eating any camas bulbs). Camas plants grow only in shallow wet soils, often on top of rock outcroppings, as is the case here. The fascinating landscape of this preserve consists of rocky outcroppings, benches, and cliffs surrounded by a mixed forest of deciduous and coniferous trees. Also common here is the nonnative Scotch broom plant, which has naturalized up and down the West Coast and displaces native plants wherever it takes hold. The Nature Conservancy has regular scotch-broom eradication outings here, in attempts to save this small patch of camas flowers. If you'd like to help pull scotch broom, contact the Nature Conservancy (tel. 503/230-1221).

Tryon Creek State Park

2–3 miles. Easy. 200-foot elevation gain. Access: From downtown Portland, take I-5 south to the Terwilliger Blvd. exit and drive 2.2 miles south to the park entrance. Map: Trailhead maps.

This little pocket of wilderness is a quick escape for residents of southwest Portland, and though the park is much smaller than Forest Park, it has the same sort of deep, dark forests. Plus, you can do your hiking on paved paths if you like. The trails here are particularly popular with families introducing their youngsters to hiking. There's a nature center too.

Champoeg State Park

2.1–4.4 miles. Easy. No elevation gain. Access: From Newberg, take Ore. 219 south 4 miles and follow signs; from I-5, take exit 278 amd drive 5 miles west. Map: Trailhead maps or Oregon State Parks' Champoeg Park Map.

It was here, on the banks of the Willamette River, that the Oregon country's first government was created (partly to create and fund a wolf bounty!). Today this park preserves rolling pastures, riverside forests, and stands of oak and cottonwoods that look much as they might have 150 years ago when this area was at the heart of Oregon's promised land. Paved and unpaved trails wind through this park. For a pleasant walk past numerous historic sites, start at the west end at the pavilion and head west to view some huge old cottonwood trees. After returning to the pavilion, head east along the river, and in about 1 mile cross Champoeg Creek on a road bridge and turn left to a nature trail that leads to the mouth of the creek. From here, you can return the way you came, make a loop with the bike path, or head up to the visitor center before returning to your car.

Willamette Mission State Park

2.5–4 miles. Easy. No elevation gain. Access: From I-5 north of Salem, take exit 263 and drive 1.8 miles west on Brooklake Rd., turn right on Wheatland Rd., and continue 2.5 miles north to the park. Map: Trailhead maps.

This park on the banks of the Willamette River was created to preserve a piece of early Oregon history. It was here that Methodist missionary Jason Lee established his first Willamette Valley mission in 1834. Frequent floods soon sent him south to found Salem, which became the first settlement in the Willamette Valley. However, history aside, the park offers a pleasant walk through forests and farmland and provides viewing decks overlooking fields and wetlands frequented by waterfowl during the winter months. One of the biggest attractions of this park is a giant cottonwood tree that is more than 26 feet in circumference and is said to be the largest in the world. Also, just outside the park is one of the last remaining car ferries on the Willamette River.

WHITEWATER KAYAKING & CANOEING

They don't call the mountains to the east of the Willamette Valley the Cascades for nothing. The many rivers and creeks flowing down into the Willamette from the east provide valley residents with many, many miles of excellent whitewater paddling. Whether you're looking for some easy Class I canoe paddling or some death-defying Class V drops, this area has lots to offer. Best of all, you never have to drive too far to find just the kind of water you're looking for.

Up at the north end of the valley just east of Portland lies the **Sandy River,** a designated National Wild & Scenic River, and one of the most accessible and popular paddling rivers in the state. The various runs provide something for paddlers of all skill levels. The rainy season and snowmelt season are the best times to run the Sandy, but the lower stretches of the river are very popular during the summer. The **Clackamas River** is as popular as the Sandy and offers the same sort of variety. It is here that the famous Bob's Hole Rodeo used to be held. Though the river gets low in the summer, it can usually be run throughout the warmer months. The waters of the Clackamas are infamously frigid.

The **Molalla River** is the Portland area's other popular paddling river, though it sees much less traffic than the Sandy or the Clackamas. Because the flow in the Molalla River falls dramatically in the summer, making the river virtually unrunnable, the Molalla is best run in the winter and spring, which means both the air and water will be cold. A wetsuit is a must if you're kayaking, and if you're doing one of the easier sections in an open canoe (say in late spring), be prepared to get wet and dress accordingly. In the Salem area, the **Little North Santiam** and **North Santiam rivers** offer year-round paddling on waters ranging from Class I to Class IV.

Whitewater Warehouse, 625 NW Starker Ave., Corvallis (tel. 800/214-0579 or 541/758-3150) offers rafting trips (Santiam, McKenzie, Rogue) and kayaking classes and also sells equipment. For more information on paddling in this area, contact the **Lower Columbia Canoe Club,** 7905 SW Canyon Lane, Portland, OR 97225 (Internet Web page: http://www.teleport.com/nonprofit/LCCC) or the **Willamette Kayak & Canoe Club,** P.O. Box 1062, Corvallis, OR 97339. Also see the "Outdoor Resources" sidebar earlier in this chapter.

CLASS I

On the **Sandy River,** the 4.5-mile run from Oxbow Park to Dabney State Park on Class I+ waters is the perfect beginner's run and is extremely popular in the summer. This run can also be extended another 3 miles to Lewis and Clark State Park on Class I waters. This lower section can be a pleasant paddle, but steer clear of fishing lines.

On the **Molalla River,** the 6-mile run from Feyrer County Park to the Ore. 213 bridge provides plenty of Class I+ water for beginning kayakers and canoers. You'll find Feyrer Park due east of the town of Molalla.

On the **North Santiam River** down in the Salem area, canoeists will enjoy the 19-mile Class I+ run from Stayton to Jefferson (put-in: south of Stayton on Stayton–Scio Road; take-out: just below bridge in Jefferson).

CLASS II

On the **Sandy River,** two Class II+ runs above Oxbow County Park (starting at either Revenue Bridge or Dodge Park) are favorites of intermediate kayakers. From Revenue Bridge to Dodge Park is 5 miles and from Dodge Park to Oxbow is 8 miles.

On the **Clackamas River,** the 5.5-mile stretch from Barton Park to Carver (Class II+) is one of the most popular stretches of river in the Portland area with canoeists. Several Class I and a couple of Class II rapids provide the sort of challenge that a beginning paddler won't find too daunting. There are a few houses along the banks here, but for the most part, the forests flank the river. In a couple of places, the river flows past eroded bluffs. The February 1996 flooding left several houses perched precariously close to the lips of these bluffs. The floods also scoured out the bottom of the river right down to sandstone bedrock and rearranged the channel. The 8-mile run from Milo McIver State Park down to Barton Park is another popular Class II+ run. From Carver down to Clackamette Park (Class II), at the confluence with the Willamette River, the Clackamas passes through suburbs that make this 8-mile run a much less appealing section of the river. There are also some bridge pilings in the river that require good boat-handling skills. To reach these sections of river, take Ore. 212/224 east from I-205 in Clackamas.

On the **Molalla River,** the 6-mile run from Glen Avon Bridge to Feyrer Park is a good introductory Class II run for novice paddlers. The biggest rapids are all in the first half of this run. To reach the put-in, cross the river at Feyrer Park and turn right on Dickie Prairie Road.

CLASS III & ABOVE

On the **Sandy,** the most popular run with intermediate and advanced kayakers is the 6.5-mile Sandy Gorge run from Marmot Dam to Revenue Bridge. This run has a lot of very challenging rapids, including the Rasp Rock, Drain Hole, and Revenue Bridge rapids. Be sure to scout when in doubt. Above Marmot Dam, the Sandy River has a lot of Class IV water and can be very technical in places.

The **Clackamas's** most famous waters are just above the North Fork Reservoir (take Ore. 224 southeast from Estacada). It is here that the famous Bob's Hole, site of the annual Bob's Hole Rodeo, once challenged experienced paddlers. However, the floods of February 1996 rearranged the river so much that Bob's Hole completely disappeared! This doesn't mean, however, that it isn't still the most popular and challenging run in the Portland area. From the put-in at Three Lynx Power Station, it is a 13-mile run on Class III and IV water to the reservoir. Many people have lost their lives on this stretch of river, so don't even think about trying it unless you are confident of your skills.

On the **Molalla River,** head upstream from Glen Avon Bridge to find several runs with Class III and IV water. The most famous run on this river is the Three Bears Run through rapids named, you guessed it, Papa Bear, Mama Bear, and Baby Bear. Oh yeah, and Goldilocks, too (by some wicked twist of paddler's humor the hardest of them). This run also goes through a beautiful narrow gorge below the Mama Bear Rapids. There are a couple more runs above the Three Bears, but these are not as popular. To reach this upper section, cross the river at Feyrer Park and turn right on Dickie Prairie Road. The uppermost put-in is at Copper Creek Bridge. Other put-ins/take-outs are at Turner Bridge and Table Rock Fork.

In the Salem area, the **North Santiam** and **Little North Santiam** rivers both offer lots of challenging Class III and IV waters. The drawbacks of some of these runs are mandatory portages. The most popular kayak run is from Packsaddle County Park to Mill City on the North Santiam (put-in: 3 miles east of Gates; take-out: Mill City bridge). This 6.5-mile run ranges from Class II+ to Class IV depending on the season and finishes with Mill City Falls, which you can opt out of after scouting it from the bridge that leads into Mill City. The run from Mill City down to Mehama is also popular with kayakers and offers plenty of Class II water in summer and Class III in the rainy/snowmelt season (put-in: Mill City bridge; take-out: Mehama bridge on Ore. 226). Experienced paddlers may also want to try the Class III and IV whitewater on the crystal-clear **Little North Santiam.** The 10-mile run from Elkhorn Valley Recreation Site to the Ore. 226 bridge in Mehama is the best on

this river, but does include the Class IV Troll's Teeth boulder garden (scout and portage if you're not up to it).

WILDLIFE VIEWING

Every year in mid- to late October, fall **Chinook salmon** head up the **Sandy River** to spawn. Spawning beds are up and down the river, but the best place to see these fish is at Oxbow Park. This park is the site of an annual salmon festival. For directions to the best viewing areas, ask at the front gate or head up to the far end of the park near the boat ramp and walk the bank of the river. Because much of the bank is raised above the river, you'll have a good viewing angle. This is about the only place you can count on seeing spawning salmon in the Portland area.

Corvallis to Eugene ♦ What to Do & Where to Do It

BIRD WATCHING

The **William L. Finley National Wildlife Refuge** (tel. 541/757-7236), 12 miles south of Corvallis off Ore. 99W, is perhaps the best bird-watching spot in the region, with wintering dusky Canada geese, ducks, and swans being the main attraction. This refuge has the largest remaining tract of Willamette Valley wet prairie and is managed primarily for dusky Canada geese, and is best visited between January and early March. By March the geese begin their northward migration to their summer nesting grounds on Alaska's Copper River Delta. In addition to Canada geese, you may also see a variety of migrating raptors in the autumn, rough-legged hawks in October, and bald eagles and peregrine falcons during the winter. Migrating songbirds pass through the refuge during the spring (May is the best month) and fall (August is best), and shorebirds stop here in April. Mallards, mergansers, and wood ducks are the primary summer inhabitants. Within the refuge, there are several short hiking trails through a variety of habitats.

Two other wildlife refuges in the area provide opportunities for similar birding experiences. The **Ankeny NWR** (tel. 541/ 757-7236) is 12 miles south of Salem off I-5 at the Ankeny Hill exit (exit 243). From the exit, go west 0.25 miles, turn right on Ankeny Hill Road, and proceed 1.5 miles north. **Baskett Slough NWR** (tel. 541/ 757-7236) is 11 miles west of Salem off Ore. 22.

BOARDSAILING

As elsewhere in the region, the winds in the Columbia Gorge keep local board-sailors happy even though it is a long drive away. Hey, when it's nukin', no drive is too long! However, for an easy sail or as a place to learn the sport, **Fern Ridge Reservoir,** 15 miles west of downtown Eugene, is a good quick fix. This huge lake is big enough that winds are fairly reliable and constant, which makes the lake popular with the local "yachting" crowd. There's a beach off Ore. 126 at **Perkins Peninsula Park** at the south end of the lake, but **Richardson and Orchard Point parks,** at the north end of the lake, are more popular launch spots (deeper water and no marshes).

Dorena Lake, southeast of Cottage Grove on Row River Road, is another fairly popular place to sail. This reservoir is quite a bit smaller than Fern Ridge and is located in the Cascade foothills. The beach at Baker Bay Park, on the south side of the reservoir, is the best sailboard launch area. To reach this park, turn south on Government Road about a half-mile before reaching the reservoir.

FISHING

How many townsfolk around the country can break out their fly-fishing gear right in the center of town? **Eugene** residents can—with plenty of bank access and several gravel bars and rapids right downtown, Eugene provides some good fishing for rainbow and cutthroat. Below Eugene, the water warms up and bass and panfish can be caught.

The **McKenzie River** drift boat is a mainstay of the Northwest fishing scene, so it is no surprise that the river that gave these boats their name is one of the best trout streams in Oregon. Ore. 126

parallels the river for much of its length and provides plenty of access points. Redside rainbow trout, brook trout, summer steelhead, and spring Chinook can all be caught in these waters, but be sure you know the current angling regulations before dropping a hook in the McKenzie's waters. One good spot is the first riffle below Armitage Park just outside Springfield. Each year in March, there is excellent fly-fishing here for winter steelhead.

Fall Creek, east of Eugene off Ore. 58 (turn north at Lowell and east at Unity), is well stocked with rainbow trout and also has a few native cutthroat. The best fishing is upstream from the Fall Creek Reservoir on national forest land. Here, you'll find a good hiking trail paralleling the creek and lots of deep pools. The **Row River,** southeast of Cottage Grove, is another good trout stream. For big trout try just below the Dorena Dam, and for the river's best trout fishing, head to the mouth of the river where it enters the Coast Fork of the Willamette River. The upper stretches of the **Long Tom River** (above Fern Ridge Reservoir) are also good trout fishing waters.

If you're interested in warm-water fishing, try **Dorena Lake** or **Cottage Grove Lake.** Dorena Lake is said to be one of the best catfishing lakes in western Oregon, and Cottage Grove Lake is well known for its trophy largemouth bass.

The Caddis Fly Angling Shop, 168 W Sixth St., Eugene (tel. 541/342-7005) has a fly-fishing hotline (tel. 541/485-2000, ext. 3906) and offers classes.

HIKING

Spencers Butte

1.5 miles round-trip. Moderate. 800-foot elevation gain. Access: Take Willamette St. south from downtown Eugene for 5 miles to a signed trailhead on the left. Map: Trailhead maps.

This is Eugene's backyard hike, the equivalent to the Wildwood Trail in Portland's Forest Park, and is part of the more extensive Ridgeline Trail system. If you do this loop trail counterclockwise, you'll start out with a fairly gradual incline through open fir forest, but the trail then gets steep—and even steeper as it leaves the shade of the forest for the dusty scramble to the top of this craggy butte. A clockwise hike starts you out steep and keeps you heading steadily and steeply uphill (sometimes on stairs). A jumble of rocks surrounded by meadows comprises the summit of Spencers Butte and makes for a perfect picnic spot. From here there's an excellent view of Eugene, the southern Willamette Valley, the Coast Range, and the Cascades, including Mount Jefferson and the Three Sisters. This lookout point gives a superb overview of the region's topography, making this hike a nice primer for any new resident of the area or anyone planning a move to Eugene. A sign at the base of the butte warns of three area hazards: rattlesnakes, dead trees, and poison oak. It is the latter that in my opinion is the most real hazard. There is poison oak almost everywhere the sun shines, so wear long pants and long sleeves and stay aware of the trailside vegetation. The densest stands are at the summit.

Mount Pisgah, Buford Park

3 miles round-trip. Moderate. 1,000-foot elevation gain. Access: Take the Ore. 58 (Oakridge) exit off I-5 and turn left onto Seavey Loop Rd. at the Mount Pisgah Arboretum sign in less than 0.25 miles. Follow this road for about 1.5 miles to the arboretum entrance. Map: Trailhead map.

Let's say you happen to be a recent California transplant and you miss those oak-studded golden hills that ring the Bay area. Don't let the long, wet winters make you miserable; indulge in a quick bit of nostalgia on the grassy slopes of Mount Pisgah. You could just about call this mountain the northernmost extension of California. In summer the hillsides are baked to a toasty golden color that's made all the more appealing by the dark clumps of oak trees. Yes, and there's even poison oak everywhere for that genuine California experience. It's a steady climb to the top, but the mountainside is beautiful and unlike any other Willamette Valley hike. Then there are the views, which take in farmland, mountains, and valley towns. Even if you've never lived in California,

you'll appreciate the beauty and convenience of this easy mountain hike.

Fall Creek (Dolly Varden to Bedrock)

10 miles round-trip. Moderate. 350-foot elevation gain. Access: From I-5, drive 14 miles east on Ore. 58 to Lowell and turn left. Drive north through Lowell to Unity and turn right. Follow North Shore Rd. around Fall Creek Reservoir to the Dolly Varden Campground 11 miles from Unity. Map: USGS Saddleblanket Mountain.

This low-elevation trail is open most of the year, which makes it a good choice for a rainy-season day hike. In the summer, when the pull is to the higher elevations, this trail still has the allure of numerous swimming holes that make even the hottest day of the year a good day to do this hike. The lower trailhead is across a bridge from the Dolly Varden Campground. From here, the trail heads upstream through dense forest with Fall Creek on your left. After 3.5 miles the trail crosses the road and then a bridge over Fall Creek to continue on the opposite bank. From here it is another 1.5 miles to Bedrock Campground and the best swimming hole on the creek. Pick a hot, sunny day so you can enjoy the cold water. You might also want to bring a fishing rod and do a bit of trout fishing along the way. From Bedrock Campground, hike back the way you came. This is a good hike for kids if you don't hike the full 10 miles.

Bohemia Mountain/Brice Creek

1.6 miles round-trip. Easy–moderate. 700-foot elevation gain. Access: Take the Cottage Grove exit of I-5 and head east toward Dorena Reservoir. Continue past the reservoir for 15 miles on Row River Rd. (which becomes FS 22). Follow signs for Bohemia Saddle and turn right onto FS 2212. From here it is 10 miles on mostly good gravel road to the trailhead. At road junctions, follow signs for Champion Saddle, Bohemia Saddle, and Fairview Peak (keep left at an unmarked fork 3.9 miles after turning onto gravel). Map: USGS Fairview Peak.

The trailhead for this craggy peak east of Cottage Grove may be difficult to reach, but the payoff is well worth the trouble.

Bohemia Mountain is one of the few places in western Oregon where gold was ever found and for a while boasted quite a little boomtown. Today, there are still a few active gold-mining claims in the area, and down below the peak there are old mining shacks that lend an air of ghost-town mystery to the hike. Though short, the trail is a steep climb to the rocky ramparts of the peak's summit. Here at the crest you'll find an abundance of wildflowers, including succulent-leaved sedums tucked into pockets in the rocks. An expansive view takes in the adjacent lookout-topped summit of Fairview Peak, lots of landscape-marring clear-cuts, and off to the northeast the Three Sisters and Mount Bachelor, and to the southeast Diamond Peak and Mount Thielsen.

This hike is short, so you might also want to hike down to the the the remains of Bohemia City (two buildings), which can be reached by heading downhill from the parking area at Bohemia Saddle. You can explore the meadows on the slopes of Fairview Peak and go say howdy to the firespotters in the lookout atop this latter peak. For a full day's outing, you can add a forest hike on the 5.5-mile-long Brice Creek Trail (you passed the trailheads on the way up FR 22) and maybe cool off in one of the beautiful swimming holes. The best spots are upstream from Cedar Creek Campground. Brice Creek is one of the most beautiful streams in western Oregon.

HORSEBACK RIDING

If you feel like doing a little horseback riding in the Eugene area, try **C Bow Arrow Ranch,** 33435 Van Duyn Rd. (tel. 541/345-5643), which is located 5 miles north of Beltine at exit 199 off I-5. Other choices in the region include **Cherry Creek Stables,** 25330 Cherry Creek Rd., Monroe (tel. 541/847-5785), and **Pruitt Equestrian Centre,** 81413 Clause Rd., Lowell (tel. 541/937-3265).

MOUNTAIN BIKING

Bike shops in Corvallis sell a mountain-bike map of McDonald and Paul M. Dunn forests. Be sure to pick up one of these before heading out to the popular biking areas. Otherwise, you're likely to get thoroughly lost on the maze of gravel roads through these two forests.

Bikes can be rented at **Pedal Power Bicycles,** 535 High St. (tel. 541/687-1775), Eugene.

McDonald Forest

5.6–16 miles. Moderate–difficult. 1,300–2,700-foot elevation gain. Access: Near Corvallis. McCulloch Peak trailhead is north of Corvallis on Sulphur Springs Rd., which is 1 mile west of Ore. 99W off Lewisburg Ave. The Baker Creek trailhead is 4 miles north of Corvallis at the gate on Oak Creek Dr., which is reached by driving west out of Corvallis on Harrison Blvd. Map: McDonald/Dunn Forests Multiple-Use Road and Trail Map (available at area bike shops).

This is the favorite riding spot of Corvallis mountain bikers, and though it does offer plenty of single-track riding, keep in mind that most trails are closed to bikes during the winter months. If you're looking for a challenging ride with a visual payoff, ride the 5.6-mile McCulloch Peak Loop, which follows the 700 road south from Sulphur Springs Road. To return to the trailhead, continue on the 700 road and take the 760 road fork. For some single-track riding, take the 8.3-mile Baker Creek Loop. The bike route heads north up the 600 road, then forks left onto the 620 road at the end of which the Alpha Trail connects to the 810 road. Follow this to a left turn onto the 800 road and another left onto the 870 road, which becomes the Alien Trail. This trail becomes the 682 road, which merges with the 680 road, which then feeds into the 600 road heading back toward the trailhead gate.

An alternative from the end of the Alien Trail/682 road is to turn right on the 680 road and then take a quick left onto the Extendo Trail. This trail ends at the 6020 road (turn left), which continues south to join with the 600 road (turn right) back to the gate. If you pick up the map listed above, many other routes should suggest themselves to you. If you're looking for a longer ride, you can connect these two loops by following the 680 road, which runs between the 700 road and the 600 road.

Most of the single-track trails here are closed during the winter due to muddy conditions. Please respect these closures, which are meant to preserve the quality of the trails for the dry season. Also be aware that the Alien Trail passes through Starker Forests company property; to ride it you'll need to get a use permit at their office: 7240 SW Philomath Blvd., Corvallis (tel. 541/929-2477).

Paul M. Dunn Forest

5.7–9.6 miles. Easy–difficult. 600–1,400-foot elevation gain. Access: The Berry Creek trailhead is at the 100 road gate on Tampico Rd. 4 miles northwest of Adair Village. The Forest Peak Loop trailhead is at the 300 road gate off Tampico Rd. Map: McDonald/Dunn Forests Multiple-Use Road and Trail Map (available at area bike shops).

Just a little bit farther north than the McDonald Forest, this is another state-owned research forest that opens its gravel roads to cyclists. These roads climb in and out of so many stream valleys that you'll swear you're on a roller coaster—just mind those fist-size paving stones! What you won't find here, however, are any single-track trails.

For an easy ride, try the 5.7-mile Berry Creek Loop. From the 100 road gate, follow the 100 road to the 190 road, which loops back to the 100 road (turn right). Then turn left on the 160 road and right on the 140 road, which leads into the 100 road (turn left) heading back to the gate. For a good view, take a short detour onto the 146 road.

For a more difficult route, there is the Forest Peak Loop. From the 300 road gate, follow the 300 road to its end, at which point it becomes the 290 road. Turn left onto the 200 road and then right onto the 130 road. A right onto the 131 road will bring you back to the 200 road (turn right). Then take a left onto the 250 road and another left onto the 300 road heading back toward the gate. Large paving stones along this route mean you'll have to concentrate on the road ahead, but there are some good views into the Soap Creek Valley.

Ridgeline Trail, Eugene

5 miles round-trip. Easy. 400-foot elevation gain. Access: From downtown Eugene, head south to 18th Ave. and turn left. At West Amazon Parkway, turn right and continue south on Hilyard St. to Fox Hollow Rd. Map: Trailhead maps.

This is Eugene's in-town mountain-bike riding area, and though the Ridgeline Trail isn't very long, it offers a lot of variety and some great views. There are currently two sections of the trail that are open to mountain bikes, and the best thing to do is ride the trail as an out-and-back ride rather than riding a loop, which would end up spending far too much time on residential streets. The trail passes through forests and open grassy slopes with good views. The most difficult sections are the rocky climb up from Dillard Road on the second leg of the trail and then the drop down to Spring Boulevard at the end of the trail. Watch out for poison oak.

Elijah Bristow State Park

Up to 10 miles. Easy. 50-foot elevation gain. Access: 8.5 miles east of I-5 off Ore. 58. Map: Trailhead maps.

If you're looking for a good place to give single-track trail riding a first try, this is your best bet in the area. With more than 10 miles of trails accessible to bikes and virtually no elevation gain, this park on the bank of the Willamette River offers easy riding. The only difficulties here are the occasional rocky sections of trail and the park's popularity with horseback riders. Be especially cautious around horses (it's often best to stop and dismount when being passed or passing horses). Otherwise, trails pass through meadows and forests and along the bank of the river. On a hot summer day you might even want to take a quick dip in the river. Bring some food; there are lots of great places to picnic.

Goodman Creek, South Willamette, and Eagles Rest Trails

8.5–16 miles. Moderate–difficult. 300–2,100-foot elevation gain. Access: The trailhead is a wide gravel parking area near milepost 21 on Ore. 58 southeast of Eugene. Map: USGS Mount June.

These trails on the south side of Dexter Reservoir just east of Lowell are among the most popular mountain-bike trails in the Eugene area, and for good reason. Miles of forest single-track offering grueling climbs, fast descents, creek crossings, technical sections, and even occasional views combine to make these trails ideal for a quick after-work ride or a whole day of punishing your thighs, lungs, and fingers. The most popular is the Goodman Creek Trail (8.5 miles round-trip), which, however, has seen so much abuse over the years that it should be ridden only at the very end of the summer when it has had a chance to dry out. This trail climbs about 650 feet, and you'll get the best charge out of it as an out-and-back ride, though a loop is possible using area logging roads. Slightly easier is the South Willamette Trail (9 miles round-trip), which climbs only 300 feet. Again out-and-back is best on this trail, because otherwise you have to ride busy Ore. 58 back to the trailhead. The toughest trail here is the Eagles Rest Trail (16 miles round-trip), which climbs 2,100 feet up to a viewpoint. The ride down is the real payoff.

Brice Creek Trail

11 miles. Moderate. 380-foot elevation gain. Access: From I-5, take the Cottage Grove exit and drive southeast on Row River Rd., passing Dorena Reservoir and continuing up the Row River. The road will eventually become FS 22. The lower trailhead is 1 mile past the Umpqua National Forest sign. Map: USGS Rose Hill.

This is by far the most beautiful ride anywhere in the area and offers not only superb views of Brice Creek and all its glorious swimming holes and waterfalls, but also includes quite a bit of fairly technical riding. However, the gradient is quite moderate, which makes this a fairly easy ride, especially if you are riding the trail downstream. Start this ride by heading uphill from the Brice Creek bridge for 5.5 miles on paved FS 22. When you reach the next bridge over the creek you'll see

the upper trailhead just across the bridge on the left. From here it's an easy roll down to the Lund Park Campground. Beyond here, the trail becomes slightly more difficult. Watch out for poison oak in any sunny stretches, especially at the lower end of the trail. An alternative is to ride the trail in both directions. Also in this same area is the much more demanding 12-mile Crawfish Trail ride, which starts across FS 22 from Cedar Creek Campground by climbing 3,450 feet up Adams Mountain Road to the summit of Adams Mountain. From here it is a steep 5-mile single-track run back down to FS 22, 1 mile east of Cedar Creek Campground.

ROAD BIKING

Because so many University of Oregon students in Eugene and Oregon State University students in Corvallis get around on bicycles, both of these cities are very bicycle-friendly. Eugene, in fact, is almost heaven as far as road biking is concerned. Not only are there the bike paths along the river, but within a short distance of the city are many excellent routes through relatively flat countryside. I'm a sucker for covered bridges, and so I've recommended the south Willamette Valley's three covered-bridge bike rides here. Even if the bridges draw no more than a shrug from you, you'll find the countryside different on each ride.

Bikes can be rented at **Pedal Power Bicycles,** 535 High St. (tel. 541/687-1775), Eugene.

Albany Covered Bridge Route

35.8 miles. Moderate. 450-foot elevation gain. Access: From I-5, take exit 242 or 244 and drive 8 miles east to Scio.

Beginning in the small town of Scio, this route visits three of the five covered bridges in the vicinity. Head east out of Scio on Ore. 226 for 2.3 miles and turn left on Richardson Gap Road. In 0.7 miles you'll come to the Shimanek Bridge (built 1966) over Thomas Creek. Cross the bridge, turn right, and ride 2.1 miles to Ore. 226 (a busy high-speed road with wide lanes but no shoulders), turn left, and continue 2.2 miles eastward to Camp Morrison Drive. Just off Ore. 226 on this road, you'll find the Hannah Bridge (built 1936) over Thomas Creek. From here you can either return the way you came or take Ore. 226 all the way to Richardson Gap Road. On this latter routing, it is 4.6 miles to Richardson Gap Road. From here, head south on Richardson Gap Road for 2.8 miles and turn left on Larwood Drive. In 4.7 miles, you'll come to the Larwood Bridge (built 1939) over Crabtree Creek. A shady park here is a great spot for a picnic lunch. The park also has rest rooms.

Continue through the bridge and, in 0.4 miles, turn right on Fish Hatchery Road. In 6.4 miles, this road merges with Ore. 226, which at this point has shoulders wide enough to be called extra lanes. In 1.8 miles, turn into the community of Crabtree on Cold Springs Road, go 0.4 miles to a stop sign, and turn right onto Crabtree Drive. Take an immediate left onto Hungry Hill Road and proceed 1.6 miles to the Hoffmann Bridge (built 1936) over Crabtree Creek. As you approach this bridge, notice how it both frames the forested hillside behind it and is also framed itself by the forest. Continue on Hungry Hill Drive for 2.6 miles to Ore. 226 and turn left. Ahead of you is the steepest and longest climb of this route (only 1.1 miles), but once you reach the top, it is a relaxing 2.0-mile coast downhill to Scio and your starting point.

Corvallis–Philomath Bike Path

11.4 miles round-trip. Easy. 400-foot elevation gain. Access: The bike path starts at the foot of Tyler Ave., just north of the Ore. 34 bridge.

If you're looking for a short, easy ride, this bike path is a good choice. Particularly popular with families on the weekends, the path starts in downtown Corvallis, passes through parks along the bank of the Willamette River, continues into the countryside, and comes to an end on the outskirts of Philomath.

Willamette River Greenway, Eugene

18 miles. Easy. No elevation gain. Access: Alton Baker Park off Centennial Blvd. (north side of Willamette) or Skinner Butte Park off High St. (south side of Willamette). Map: Trailhead maps.

Along the north side of downtown Eugene, lining both sides of the Willamette River, are two parks—Alton Baker and Skinner Butte—that together comprise the city's most popular recreation area. Running through these two parks (and extending east to Island Park in Springfield and west many miles along the Willamette) are nearly 20 miles of paved pathways that provide cyclists with superb riding through green lawns, past woodlots, across the Willamette on pedestrian bridges, and past a rose garden. Though you will have to watch out for pedestrians, in-line skaters, dogs, children, and other cyclists, you won't have to worry about cars (except on a few short sections that are on residential streets). Along the route, you can stop to go for a swim, do some fly-fishing, sunbathe, throw a Frisbee, rent a canoe, or turn off into downtown and get a latté or something to eat. Sounds perfect to me.

Eugene Area Covered Bridges

24.7 miles. Moderate. 600-foot elevation gain. Access: From I-5, head southeast of Eugene on Ore. 58 for 8 miles, turn left onto Wheeler Rd., and drive to Elijah Bristow State Park.

Southeast of Eugene, there are more covered bridges that readily lend themselves to a scenic bike ride. From any of the parking areas within the state park, head back the way you came a half-mile to Ore. 58 and continue east for 0.1 miles to a right fork onto Dexter Road. In another 2.1 miles turn right onto Lost Creek Road; continue south 0.6 miles to a right run onto Parvin Road and down a steep hill. In another 0.6 miles, turn right on Rattlesnake Road, go 0.1 miles, and turn left onto Lost Valley Lane. In 0.2 miles, turn left through the Parvin Bridge, which was built in 1921. From here, head north on Parvin Road, continuing straight on the road you came in on to return to Dexter.

In Dexter, turn right onto Ore. 58 and pedal 1.7 miles east to the turnoff for Lowell. You'll be riding along the south shore of Dexter Reservoir. When you turn off Ore. 58, you'll cross a new bridge adjacent to the old Lowell Bridge, a covered bridge built in 1945 but now closed to traffic. This is a popular fishing spot. Continue north across the causeway and through Lowell, following the road as it first jogs left and then right. As you pedal north out of Lowell, you will climb one of the only hills on this route, but it's fairly short. Coast down the other side to the crossroads of Unity (there's a general store here) at 2.8 miles from the Lowell Bridge. Directly in front of you, you'll see the Unity Bridge, which was built in 1936. You can ride through this bridge, but if you do, turn around and head west on Place Road. In 3.6 miles, take a right turn just before a stop sign to stay on Place Road. This will bring you to the Pengra Bridge in 0.8 miles.

From here, turn left onto Jasper–Lowell Road for 0.2 miles and then turn right on Pengra Road. This is one of the busiest sections on the ride. In about 2.5 miles you'll see ahead of you a large outcropping of rock rising high above the road. In 1.1 miles, reach Jasper and turn left to cross a bridge over the Middle Fork Willamette River. After crossing the bridge, take an immediate left onto Jasper Park Road. Follow this quiet road 1.5 miles through a residential neighborhood to Wheeler Road and turn left. Follow Wheeler Road for 4.8 miles, through several 90° turns to your starting point. If it's hot out, you may want to head down to the river on one of the park's trails, many of which are open to mountain bikes.

Cottage Grove Covered Bridge Loop

19 miles. Moderate. 500-foot elevation gain. Access: From I-5, take the Cottage Grove exit and drive 3 miles east on Row River Rd. to the signed Currin Bridge.

Okay, so I've got a thing for covered bridges. Even if for some reason you despise these river-spanning relics of slower times, you'll likely find it hard to argue with a bike trail and a swimming hole that help make this one of the best rides in the region. Start at the Currin Bridge, which was built in 1925 and is now closed to traffic. There is a small parking pullout adjacent to the bridge. From here, you have

two options: If the Row River Trail, a former railroad right-of-way, has been paved, head east on this. If it hasn't been paved, and you have a mountain bike, you'll definitely want to take this trail. Otherwise, head east on Row River Road for 1.2 miles and turn left at a fork to stay on this road.

Just past the fork, you will climb a hill and get your first glimpse of Dorena Reservoir. From the fork, it is 7.4 miles around the north side of the reservoir to Dorena Bridge, which was built in 1949 and was undergoing renovation in 1996. From here, head back along the south shore of the lake on Shore View Drive for 5.4 miles and turn left onto Garoutte Road. You'll immediately climb a steep hill, but on the other side, in 2.4 miles from the turnoff, you'll come to the Stewart Bridge, which was built in 1930 and is no longer open to traffic. Beneath this bridge is a popular little swimming hole. If it's summer, this is a great place to cool off after the hardest part of the ride. From here, turn right on Mosby Creek Road and pedal 1.1 miles to a right turn onto Layng Road. In 0.3 miles, you'll pedal through the Mosby Creek Bridge, which was built in 1920 and is the oldest covered bridge in the county. From here it is 1.1 miles north to your starting point at the Currin Bridge.

ROCK CLIMBING

Few cities in the country can boast great rock climbing right in the middle of the city, and few parks departments are so enlightened that they allow climbing on city rock. Eugene is very fortunate in this respect. At **The Columns in Skinner Butte Park,** rock climbers have access to a wall of basalt dihedrals that is the most conveniently located climbing spot in the state. This is a great place to practice top roping, and the dihedrals provide plenty of opportunities for finger crack climbing. Just remember that a local unwritten rule prohibits using bolts in this highly visible rock.

Rock-climbing classes are available in Eugene through **Lane Community College** (tel. 541/726-2252) and **City of Eugene Library, Recreation, and Cultural Services** (tel. 541/687-5333).

SEA KAYAKING & FLAT-WATER CANOEING

If you're looking for quiet water on which to do a little paddling, there's no better place in this area than the **Alton Baker Canoe Path.** This is actually two canals that were once a mill race, and you can easily portage between the two canals. You can even rent canoes, kayaks, rafts, and pedal boats on the canoe path at **River Runner Supply,** 2222 Centennial Blvd. (tel. 800/223-4326 or 541/343-6883), which is in Alton Baker Park. Rates range from $4 to $6 per hour. The convenient location and the presence of the canoe and kayak rental shop adjacent to the canals make this a popular spot to just play around on the water for a few hours. You can try different types of boats and see what kind you prefer. See also the "Outdoor Resources" sidebar earlier in this chapter.

SWIMMING & TUBING

The **Calapooia River** has very different characters depending on which side of I-5 you happen to be on. On the west side, it is a sluggish stream passing through farmland, but east of I-5 it becomes a lively little river with clear water, rocky banks, and some nice little waterfalls. The river's most convenient swimming hole is at **Pioneer Park** right in downtown Brownsville, 4 miles east of I-5 off Main Street. You'll find the best swimming hole behind some earthen mounds to the west of the baseball field. If you prefer waterfalls and boulders off which to leap, head east on Ore. 228 another 5.6 miles from Main Street to a pullout just before the entrance to **McKercher Park.** The water here tumbles over bedrock and breaks up into several chutes before flowing past some big boulders. There's even a tiny beach.

Up the **McKenzie River** from Springfield, you can cool off and go for a quick dip at the **Hendricks Bridge State Wayside,** where there is a small beach. The water here is quite shallow until you get over to the far side near the *Architectural Digest*–style home atop the rocks on the far bank. You'll find this wayside 12 miles east of I-5 on Ore. 126.

Fall Creek is one of the best swimming streams in the state. Between Dolly Varden Campground and Puma Campground there are numerous excellent swimming holes, each with its own unique character. To reach Fall Creek, take exit 188A off I-5 and drive 13 miles east on Ore. 58. Turn left on Jasper–Lowell Road and drive 3 miles north to Unity and turn right on Big Fall Creek Road. The first swimming hole, a small pool beside a bridge, is at **Dolly Varden Campground,** 10 miles east of Unity. If you want a larger pool, head up to **Big Pool,** which is 1 mile farther east. However, my personal favorite, Fall Creek swimming hole, is at **Bedrock Campground** another 3.5 miles up the road. Here the creek flows clear and cold past huge boulders and high cliffs that form a narrow gorge.

East of Cottage Grove, you'll find several great swimming holes on **Brice Creek.** Though **Wildwood Falls** at LaSells Stewart Park is one of the most spectacular, it is also rather littered and gets very busy and noisy on weekends. I prefer the beautiful holes upstream from **Cedar Creek Campground.** These are accessible from a trail that parallels the creek on the opposite bank from the campground. One of these holes is shaped like a swimming pool and another lies at the base of a picturesque waterfall. To reach Brice Creek, take exit 174 (Cottage Grove) off I-5 and drive 23 miles east on Row River Road (follow signs to Dorena Lake and continue east past the lake).

Slide Rock on **Lake Creek** is just about the most popular swimming hole anywhere near Eugene, and during the summer the crowds pack this place on weekends. However, over the years this swimming hole, with its slippery rocks for sliding down, has seen more than its share of mishaps, including broken bones and drownings. A waterfall, three deep pools, and a 100-foot-long natural waterslide make this as fun a summer play spot as you'll likely find anywhere. To reach Slide Rock, take Ore. 99 north from Eugene for 18 miles (almost to Junction City), turn left on Ore. 36, and drive 26 miles west to the parking area.

WALKS & NATURAL ROADSIDE ATTRACTIONS

Of course, the most popular places in the area for short walks and leisurely strolls are the paved pathways of **Alton Baker and Skinner Butte parks** in Eugene and **Riverfront Park** in Corvallis. However, there are also a few places around for less urban and more natural experiences.

Mary's Peak

2.2 miles. Easy. 500-foot elevation gain. Access: From Philomath, 6 miles west of Corvallis on U.S. 20, take Ore. 34 south toward Alsea for 10 miles and turn right onto the signed Mary's Peak Rd. From here it is less than 9 miles to the trailhead adjacent to the campground. Map: Trailhead maps.

The Coast Range, watered by almost constant year-round rains, supports some of the densest forests in the Northwest. Consequently, mountaintops in this range seldom offer much in the way of views. However, there are a couple of exceptions to this rule. The summit of Mary's Peak, the highest mountain in the Coast Range, is not forested but instead is capped by lush, gently sloping meadows. In July, these meadows are awash in color as tiger lilies, lupines, penstemons, paintbrush, and other wildflowers burst into bloom. Though you can hike up from the midway elevation of the peak, the trails that wind around at and just below the summit offer greater variety and less sweat. A combination of the Meadow Edge Trail and the old Summit Trail makes an easy and beautiful hike. This trail starts out in a dense stand of old-growth noble firs, a rarity in these mountains. The forest is so shady that no shrubs grow beneath the trees. Instead the ground is covered in summer by a lush green blanket of giant wood sorrel, bleeding hearts, and other shade-loving ground covers.

Unfortunately, though Mary's Peak is covered with gorgeous meadows, at the very summit is an ugly jumble of trailers and other equipment that comprise a weather observatory. Keep it to your back and the view is still breathtaking. The best time to do this hike is late in the afternoon

in July. When my wife and I hiked these trails, a buttery golden light was filtering through the blue-tinged branches of the noble firs as we spooked a black-tailed deer. On a clear day, this hike also affords a spectacular view of the Willamette Valley to the east and the Coast Range to the west, north, and south. The straight lines of valley farms are a striking contrast to the rolling ridge-lines and dark green forests of the Coast Range. It's even possible to see the ocean, as well as Mount Rainier.

William L. Finley National Wildlife Refuge Trails

1.2, 2.9, and 3 miles. Easy. 0–100-foot elevation gain. Access: 12 miles south of Corvallis off Ore. 99W. Map: Trailhead maps.

Although this wildlife refuge is most popular with bird watchers, you'll still enjoy the rural tranquility of the three loop trails here even if you don't know a bufflehead from a goldeneye. If you live in one of the Willamette Valley's burgeoning cities, it may break your heart to discover that this is what the entire valley once looked like, and not too many years ago either: rolling pastures, oak woodlands, marshes, and distant views of Cascade Peaks.

From the middle of this refuge, the views are expansive, with not a building in sight except for the historic farm buildings that still stand within the refuge. The first time I came here I was astounded by the refuge's remote feel. I had no idea anything like this still existed in the Willamette Valley. Of the three loop trails here—Woodpecker (1.2 miles), Mill Hill (2.9 miles), and Beaver Pond (3 miles)— the Woodpecker Loop, which passes through an oak woodland frequented by five species of woodpeckers, is my favorite. This trail ends at a viewpoint that takes in both Mount Jefferson and the Three Sisters. Unfortunately, the Mill Hill trail only circles this hill (no view), and the Beaver Pond is no longer frequented by any beavers. To learn more about birding within the refuge, see "Bird Watching," above.

Mount Pisgah Arboretum

1–3 miles. Easy. 100-foot elevation gain. Access: Take the Ore. 58 (Oakridge) exit off I-5 and turn left onto Seavey Loop Rd. at the Mount Pisgah Arboretum sign in less than 0.25 miles. Follow this road for about 1.5 miles to the arboretum entrance. Map: Trailhead maps.

In addition to the mountain-climbing Mount Pisgah Trail listed above under "Hiking," this arboretum has a network of easy trails along and close to the bank of the Coast Fork of the Willamette River. These trails pass through a number of different habitats, and along the way there are signs identifying the plants. Because the trails are through shady, cool forest, they make a better choice than the summit trail on a hot summer day. Better still, there are a couple of swimming holes along the bank of the river. Bring your bathing suit.

WHITEWATER KAYAKING & CANOEING

The south Willamette Valley offers some of the best and most convenient whitewater paddling in the state. The most popular runs are on the **Willamette** and the **McKenzie rivers,** both of which begin to develop the character of mountain rivers around Eugene. In addition to the runs listed below, there are many more small rivers and creeks in the region that provide more thrilling and technical runs. Among these are the **Calapooia River** east of Brownsville (20 miles of Class II and III water above McKercher Park), **Fall Creek** (Class II and III below Fall Creek Dam and Class III and IV between Bedrock Campground and Fall Creek Reservoir), and **Mary's River** west of Corvallis (19 miles of Class I and II water between Blodgett and Philomath).

You can rent canoes, kayaks, rafts, and pedal boats at **River Runner Supply,** 2222 Centennial Blvd. (tel. 800/223-4326 or 541/343-6883), which is in Alton Baker Park. Rates range from $4 to $6 per hour. The folks who run this tiny shop can also give you plenty of advice on running area rivers.

CLASS I

The 19-mile run from Armitage Park, on the **McKenzie River** just outside Springfield, down to Harrisburg (on the **Willamette River**), is one of the most enjoyable Class I stretches of river anywhere in the Willamette Valley (put-in: Armitage Park at Coburg Road bridge just south of Coburg; take-out: downtown Harrisburg boat ramp). The run actually starts out on the clear waters of the McKenzie River for about 4 miles before merging with the greener waters of the Willamette. Even in late summer, this is a big, pushy river, and though there are nothing but Class I riffles, the strong current, braided channels, and many sweepers and strainers require paddlers to stay alert for the entire length of the run. It takes about four hours to make the run, which makes it perfect for an afternoon paddle.

To lengthen this run, you can put in at Hayden Bridge, 8 miles upriver from Armitage Park. This section of river passes through the picturesque Coburg Hills. Paddling from Hayden Bridge to Harrisburg makes an ideal day-long paddle. To reach Hayden Bridge, take I-105 east from I-5 to Mohawk Road and go north a half-mile. From Harrisburg to Corvallis, an 8-hour, 29-mile run, is similar to the run from Armitage Park down, though the current slows a bit and there are fewer riffles or braided channels. There are, however, lots of strainers and sweepers as you approach Corvallis.

CLASS II

Paddlers in the Eugene area are privileged to have two superb Class II rivers in their backyard. East of Springfield, the **McKenzie River** offers 30 miles of runs that can be paddled year-round. Passing through farmland for most of its length, this section of the McKenzie offers novice paddlers a chance to do a bit of practicing and to get a feel for Class II rapids. With plenty of calm water between rapids, these sections are leisurely enough for paddlers to take their minds off the current from time to time. Because there are several parks and boat ramps along the river, you can do as much or as little of the river as you want. Popular runs include the stretches from Leaburg Dam to Hendricks Bridge Wayside (15 miles) and Hendricks Bridge Wayside to Hayden Bridge (15 miles). The river passes numerous islands along these sections, and for the most part, these can be paddled on either side. The biggest rapids are a half-mile above Hendricks Bridge Wayside and just above Hayden Bridge.

Even more convenient than the McKenzie is the **Willamette River** as it flows in from the east and passes through downtown Eugene. It's possible to play the several rapids that are bordered by Alton Baker Park and then paddle back upstream on the Alton Baker Canoe Path. An afternoon can easily be whiled away playing on the river in this manner. However, keep in mind that if you want to play the river in this fashion, you'll have to run the dangerous Class III "I-5 Rapids," which are formed by an old weir. The only safe way through this weir is the slot on the far right side, and at high water, even this can be chancy.

If you can handle the I-5 Rapids, a quick 7-mile run through the city can be started at Springfield's Island Park (just north of Ore. 126 on the east side of the Willamette), passing several fun rapids bordered by parks and greenways, and finished at the Beltline Bridge boat ramp. A longer run (13 miles) starts at Jasper County Park (off Ore. 222 just outside Jasper on the south side of the river) and ends up at Alton Baker Park (if you want to try the I-5 Rapids) or, alternatively, at Island Park in Springfield or the boat ramp on river right just before the I-5 rapids. This latter take-out allows you to portage to the Alton Baker Canoe Path, a 2-mile-long flat-water canal that bypasses the I-5 Rapids and leads to Alton Baker Park. Alton Baker Park and the boat ramp above the I-5 Rapids are both accessed from Centennial Boulevard.

CLASS III & ABOVE

It is the upper sections of the **McKenzie River,** above Leaburg Dam, that are the most famous and most popular stretches of the river. This is the water that commercial rafting companies run and that experienced kayakers play in. Although much of the water on the 40 miles of river between Ollalie Campground and Leaburg Dam is Class II or II+, there are numerous Class III rapids. Among the most famous are Fishladder (5 miles above Paradise Campground), the boulder

garden in the town of McKenzie Bridge, and Browns' Hole and Marten Rapids (above and below Ben and Kay Doris State Park respectively). Perhaps the most popular run on this section of the river is the 14-mile run from Finn Rock to Leaburg Dam. The 16-mile run from Paradise Campground to Finn Rock is the next most difficult section. Due to the continuous nature of the rapids, the run from Ollalie Campground to Paradise Campground is the most challenging section of the river. Numerous campgrounds and lodges along this stretch of the river cater to paddlers. All put-ins and take-outs are along Ore. 126 east of Springfield.

WHITEWATER RAFTING

Of Eugene's two whitewater rivers, the **McKenzie** gets the nod as the better river to raft and is among the most popular rafting rivers in the state. Both day trips and overnight runs can be done on this river. If opting for a multiday trip, you can even choose to stay in lodges rather than campgrounds. **Oregon Whitewater Adventures** (tel. 800/820-RAFT or 541/746-5422), **McKenzie River Rafting Company** (tel. 541/726-6078), and **Wilderness River Outfitters** (tel. 541/726-9471) all offer whitewater rafting trips starting around $45 per person. A slightly tamer whitewater experience can be had on the pontoon platform boats of **McKenzie Pontoon Trips** (tel. 541/741-1905).

Campgrounds & Other Accommodations

CAMPING

Because most land in the Willamette Valley is either urban or farmland, there are very few campgrounds in this region. In fact, the only major campground actually in the valley is at **Champoeg State Park** (48 campsites with full hookups). This campground is about midway between Portland and Salem and makes a good choice if you are planning some bicycle touring of the Yamhill Valley wine country. It is most popular with RVers and is set amid oak forests and manicured lawns. **Willamette City Park** (15 campsites), 1 mile south of Corvallis off Ore. 99W on SE Goodnight Street, is another option for camping on the river. If you happen to be paddling or powerboating down the Willamette, you'll have much better luck finding a place to camp. Along the length of the river are numerous primitive boat-in campgrounds. To find out where these campsites are located, get a copy of the **Willamette River Recreation Guide** from the Oregon State Marine Board (tel. 503/378-8587) or the Oregon Parks and Recreation Department (tel. 800/452-5687).

Your camping choices increase considerably as you head to either side of the valley and into the foothills of the Cascades or Coast Range. East of Portland, **Oxbow Park** (45 campsites; seasonal), on the Sandy River, offers campsites in a dark forest setting. This is a great choice for paddlers and anglers. To reach Oxbow Park, take exit 16a off I-84, drive south toward Gresham, and then follow signs to the park. East of Salem, **Silver Falls State Park** (104 sites, 53 with full hookups; seasonal), set amid the foothill forests, is a regional favorite. The hiking trails here wind past numerous waterfalls. To reach Silver Falls, take exit 253 off I-5 in Salem, drive east on Ore. 22, and then follow signs. In the coast range, **Mary's Peak Campground** (12 campsites; seasonal) is far removed from the mainstream of the valley and is actually atop the highest peak in the Coast Range. I include it here rather than in the Oregon coast chapter because of its relative proximity to Corvallis and the central valley. To reach Mary's Peak, take U.S. 20 west from Corvallis, go south on Ore. 34 at Philomath, and continue to the signed Mary's Peak Roade region along Fall Creek east of Eugene and Brice Creek east of Cottage Grove.

Along Fall Creek, you'll find several pleasant national forest campgrounds with great swimming holes and good fishing. These include (from west to east) **Dolly Varden** (5 campsites; seasonal), **Big Pool** (5 campsites; seasonal), **Bedrock** (18 campsites; seasonal), and **Puma** (11 campsites; seasonal). Bedrock gets my vote for best campground in the area because of its awesome swimming hole and distance from the road. To reach these campgrounds, drive east from Eugene on Ore. 58, turn north in Lowell, east at Unity, and then continue east past Fall Creek Reservoir.

Brice Creek is as beautiful as Fall Creek, and along its length are three small national forest campgrounds. **Cedar Creek** (8 campsites; seasonal) is the first and the largest and has campsites right on the creek. Smaller and less crowded are **Lund Park** (3 campsites; seasonal) and **Hobo Camp** (2 campsites; seasonal). To reach these campgrounds, drive east from Cottage Grove past Dorena Reservoir, turn left in Culp Creek, and continue past Disston.

INNS & LODGES

Campbell House

252 Pearl St., Eugene, OR 97401. Tel. 800/264-2519 or 541/343-1119. Fax 541/343-2258. 13 rms (12 with private bath), all with TV and telephone. $70–$225 double. All rates include full breakfast. AE, MC, V.

Located only two blocks from the Willamette and set on Skinner Butte overlooking the city, this large Victorian home was built in 1892 and now offers convenience and comfort. Guest rooms here vary considerably in size and price.

Springbrook Hazelnut Farm

30295 N Hwy. 99W, Newberg, OR 97132. Tel. 800/793-8528 or 503/538-4606. 5 rms (3 with private bath). $90–$125 double. All rates include full breakfast. No credit cards.

At only 20 miles from Portland, Springbrook Hazelnut Farm, a working farm, is a convenient rural getaway for anyone who craves a slower, old-fashioned pace. The four craftsman-style buildings are all listed on the National Register of Historic Places; this is a great base for bicycle explorations of the area.

Flying M Ranch

23029 NW Flying M Rd., Yamhill, OR 97148. Tel. 503/662-3222. Fax 503/662-3202.

28 rms, 7 cabins. Rooms $55–$75 double; cabins $80–$160 for one to six people. Campsites $11 per night. AE, DC, DISC, MC, V.

If you feel like mixing a bit of wine-country touring with the Wild West, the Flying M Ranch is the place for you. Located 4 miles down a gravel road at the foot of the Coast Range, this ranch on the North Yamhill River caters to folks who want to do a bit of horseback riding and play at being cowboys. The center of ranch activity is the big log lodge where every inch of wall space seems to display hunting trophies from musk-ox and buffalo heads to bearskins and even a stuffed cougar.

10

THE WEST-CENTRAL OREGON CASCADES

STRETCHING FROM MOUNT JEFFERSON IN THE NORTH TO DIAMOND Peak in the south, the central Oregon Cascades are a region of surprising diversity. Within the region are thousands of acres of black-rock lava flows seemingly as fresh as any in Hawaii; the largest glacier in the state; lakes that are among the purest in the world; groves of ancient Douglas firs; western red cedars and ponderosa pines; and six of the most ruggedly beautiful peaks in the state. If this all sounds like it ought to attract a lot of outdoors enthusiasts, you're absolutely right. Don't come up this way expecting solitude. This region is within easy weekend striking distance of Portland, Salem, Corvallis, Eugene, and Bend and sees heavy use by the state's weekend warriors. This isn't to imply, however, that you can't get away from it all and lose yourself among the region's rugged beauty—you can. You just have to do a bit of planning.

Almost all of the land encompassed by this chapter lies within the Willamette National Forest, which stretches for 110 miles from north to south and covers 1,675,407 acres. This is the most "productive" national forest in the country when it comes to cutting trees and producing lumber, which means that you can expect to see a lot of clear-cuts and logging trucks while you're up this way. For more than a quarter of a century, old growth trees within this national forest have been the focus of heated battles between logging interests and environmentalists determined to save the last remaining big trees in western Oregon. The battles started in the 1960s with French Pete Creek, which was eventually brought within the boundaries of the Three Sisters Wilderness. The most recent victory in the fight to save the region's old-growth forests came with the elevation to wilderness status of the Opal Creek drainage (see the northern Willamette Valley's hiking section in chapter 9). However, victories have been far fewer than defeats, and today there are few places in this region where you can see 1,000-year-old red cedars or Douglas firs 6 feet in diameter. But these places do still exist, and in this chapter, you can find out where.

Because this region extends from lush low-elevation valleys on the wet west side up over the High Cascade peaks and down into the eastern foothills, it offers year-round recreational opportunities. Above the big trees—the Douglas firs and western red cedars of the west side and the ponderosa pines of the east side—lie subalpine pumice plains and lava fields. These areas are the destination of skiers in winter and hikers in summer, and in their different guises through the seasons they remain exquisitely beautiful. Santiam Pass and Willamette Pass are the centers of winter activity in this region, with each pass claiming a downhill area and miles of cross-country trails. Stretching the entire length of this region is the Pacific Crest National Scenic Trail, which here passes through its most scenic Oregon miles. The highlight of the PCT in Oregon is the stretch through the Three Sisters Wilderness.

Mountain bikers will find in this region one of Oregon's best single-track destinations. The Oakridge area, on the southwest side of the region, has the most extensive network of single-track in the state. These rides range from flat novice rides to grueling hill climbs to technically demanding descents.

Anglers find a wealth of fishing streams and lakes. From fighting wild steelhead and redside rainbow trout in the McKenzie to 30-pound Mackinaw trout in Odell Lake, there is enough variety to keep most any angler content. Fly anglers will find challenging waters on the McKenzie and the North Fork of the Middle Fork of the Willamette. Several lakes in these mountains are even large enough and windy enough to be good windsurfing waters.

Because most of this land is within the Willamette National Forest, there are few lodges or hotels in this region. However, there are dozens of small national forest campgrounds, and many of these are relatively easy to get a site at even on summer weekends. Just remember that summer comes late in the High Cascades, with snowdrifts sometimes obscuring hiking trails well into July, and by late October the snow begins to accumulate once again. So the summer hiking season here is short, and shortened even more by the mosquitoes that make July a miserable month for hiking. The voracious bloodsuckers are so persistent and so dense that no amount of DEET can turn a July hike here into a pleasant experience. Wait until August, or be prepared to donate blood.

The Lay of the Land

For the purpose of this book, I am defining the central Cascades as those mountains flanking the **Santiam, McKenzie,** and **Willamette passes.** These passes are crossed by U.S. 20, Ore. 242, and Ore. 58, respectively. Of these three highways, only U.S. 20 and Ore. 58 stay open during the winter months. The narrow winding route over McKenzie Pass's famous lava beds is, unfortunately for novice cross-country skiers, closed during the winter months. If this highway were open during the snow season, it would undoubtedly be among the most popular cross-country skiing areas in the country.

On the west side of the Cascades, this chapter covers the areas east of Detroit Lake on Ore. 22, east of Cascadia on U.S. 20, east of Vida on Ore. 126, and east of Lookout Point Reservoir on Ore. 58. The eastern limits of this chapter lie just over the Santiam and McKenzie passes (Ore. 22/U.S. 20 and Ore. 126/242) in the north, while Crescent Lake and U.S. 97 mark the eastern limit of the Willamette Pass (Ore. 58) route.

Within this area there is an amazing diversity, from the dense, lush west-side forests that receive upward of 100 inches of rain each year to the dry ponderosa pine forests that begin just east of (and sometimes even west of) the Cascade crest. With the exception of Mount St. Helens in Washington, this stretch of the Cascades displays the most recent volcanic activity in the Northwest, with some major lava flows only a few thousand years old. However, the region also displays the effects of ice-age glaciers on its volcanic peaks. It is this combination of the effects of fire and ice that give the central Cascade peaks their distinctively rugged profiles. From north to south the major peaks of this region are Mount Jefferson, Three Fingered Jack, Mount Washington, North, Middle, and South Sister, Broken Top, and Diamond Peak.

Draining the slopes are three major rivers, each of which has multiple forks. From north to south these are the **Santiam River** (**North, Middle,** and **South** forks), the **McKenzie River** (**main stem** and **South Fork**), and the **Willamette** (**Middle Fork** and **North Fork of the Middle Fork**). Of these three rivers, the McKenzie is the most famous, both for its fishing and for its whitewater rafting.

Though most people traveling through the central Oregon Cascades see a single mountain range, there are actually two distinctive ranges lying side by side here. The peaks most people think of as the Cascades are the glacier-clad volcanic peaks that rise above the green, forested foothills. However, those very foothills are actually the remnants of a much older range of Cascade mountains, appropriately known as the **Old Cascades.** These mountains are not marked on any maps as a separate range, but geologically speaking, they are indeed very different mountains. The Old Cascades lie to the west of today's High Cascade peaks, and had their origins 15 to 30 million years ago. These mountains, too, were formed by volcanic activity, but later, the volcanic activity shifted eastward and these volcanic peaks were left to the forces of erosion. Today, these mountains have been weathered to low, rolling hills interspersed with craggy peaks such as **Rooster Rock** and **Iron Mountain.**

The area's more familiar Cascade peaks, including **Mount Jefferson, Three Fingered Jack, Mount Washington,** and the **Three Sisters,** are much more recent in origin. These peaks developed during the Pleistocene period between 1 million and 10,000 years ago. In fact, volcanic activity in this region continues to this day, though not on the grand scale of Mount St. Helens's recent eruption. Only 3,000 years ago, lava flowed out of vents on the flanks of Mount Washington and covered 75 square miles of the surrounding landscape. Today, these lava fields remain ragged and black, with only a few very hardy plants having yet taken hold. These lava flows often blocked rivers and streams, which has created many unusual features within this region. Waterfalls cascade over cliffs only to disappear into the ground. Rivers spring from nowhere or, as in the case of the McKenzie, disappear underground, leaving a dry waterfall. Lakes lack outlets, draining instead—with wild fluctuations—through porous lava rock. On the bottom of spring-fed **Clear Lake,** there is even a ghost forest of trees that were killed 3,000 years ago when lava blocked the McKenzie River near its source and formed this crystalline lake. Numerous hot springs also hint at the fires that still burn beneath the surface of these mountains.

Lava flows and glaciers have also given the region many of its lakes, and though Crater Lake, in southern Oregon, is the state's most awe-inspiring body of water, several lakes in this region come close. **Waldo Lake** rivals Crater Lake and Siberia's Lake Baikal in purity and clarity. Clear Lake is just what its name implies—a lake of astounding clarity. What the name doesn't say is that it is also an incredibly cold lake, fed by a 38° F spring.

The rugged glacier-clad summits of Mount Jefferson, Mount Washington, and the Three Sisters dominate the skyline at the north end of this region and are a constant pull on the eyes. For the best view, head up to McKenzie Pass on a clear summer day, and you'll be able to see Mount Washington and the Three Sisters rising above the pass's black lava fields. The Willamette Pass, on the other hand, lacks the sort of dramatic peaks that dominate the Santiam Pass/McKenzie Pass area. Only Diamond Peak rises above the hills and lesser peaks here.

Within this region there are few towns. A handful of small communities cater to vacationers and recreation visitors, but other than that, **Oakridge,** on Ore. 58, is the only real town in the region offering much in the way of conveniences. Oakridge is still a timber town, though barely hanging on to this meager economic base. In October 1996, it was further devastated when the Oakridge Ranger Station burned to the ground.

What all this means for outdoor-sports enthusiasts is lots to do throughout the year. Within this region are eight wilderness areas that together provide some of the best hiking in the state. Trout and salmon fishing attract anglers to the region's lakes, streams, and rivers. In the Oakridge area, mountain bikers have a network of trails unmatched anywhere in the Northwest. One of the state's finest road-bike rides also winds through these mountains. Wild rivers challenge paddlers while quiet lakes provide some of Oregon's only opportunities for canoe camping. Two ski areas and many miles of cross-country ski trails, both groomed and ungroomed, keep these mountains busy throughout the winter as well.

Outdoor Resources

Willamette National Forest
Supervisor's Office
211 E Seventh Ave.
(P.O. Box 10607)
Eugene, OR 97440
Tel. 541/687-6521

Sweet Home Ranger Station
3225 Hwy. 20
Sweet Home, OR 97386
Tel. 541/367-5168

McKenzie Ranger Station
McKenzie Bridge, OR 97413
Tel. 541/822-3381

Oakridge Ranger Station
46375 Hwy. 58
Westfir, OR 97492
Tel. 541/782-2291

Detroit Ranger Station
HC60, Box 320
Mill City, OR 97360
Tel. 541/854-3366

Blue River Ranger Station
Blue River, OR 97413
Tel. 541/822-3317

Lowell Ranger Station
Lowell, OR 97452
Tel. 541/937-2129

Rigdon Ranger Station
49098 Salmon Creek Rd.
Oakridge, OR 97463
Tel. 541/782-2283

Parks & Other Hot Spots

Because most of this region is within the Willamette and Deschutes national forests, there are few state parks. The main focuses of the region's outdoor activities are the national forest wilderness areas and the region's lakes and rivers.

Mount Jefferson Wilderness

North of Santiam Pass off Ore. 22 and U.S. 20. Tel. 541/854-3366 or 541/549-2111. Hiking, fishing.

Located north of Ore. 22 and U.S. 20, this wilderness is one of the most heavily used in the state. At its heart is 10,497-foot Mount Jefferson, the second-highest peak in Oregon and, according to many mountaineers, the most difficult climbing peak in the state. At the foot of this peak lies Jefferson Park, one of the most beautiful meadows in the Northwest. Also within this wilderness are the jagged pinnacles of 7,841-foot Three Fingered Jack and numerous good fishing lakes.

Three Sisters Wilderness

South of McKenzie Pass off Ore. 242 and east of FS 19 (Aufderheide National Scenic Byway). Tel. 541/822-3381 or 541/549-2111. Hiking, fishing.

Encompassing the Three Sisters (North, Middle, and South) as well as Broken Top, this is one of the most popular wilderness areas in Oregon. The area's jagged, glacier-clad peaks are popular with mountaineers, and its lakes are among the prettiest in the state. Pumice fields dotted with hardy, ground-hugging plants are an unusual and fragile feature of this wilderness. In the northwest part, lava flows create an eerie landscape. Trailheads are found along the south side of the McKenzie Pass Highway, south of the town of Sisters, and west of Bend. As far as I'm concerned, this wilderness *is* the central Oregon Cascades.

Menagerie Wilderness

Located 20 miles east of Sweet Home off U.S. 20. Tel. 541/367-5168. Hiking, fishing.

With names like Rooster Rock, Rabbit Ears, and Moose Mountain, it's easy to see how this wilderness area came by its name. Located north of U.S. 20 roughly 20 miles east of Sweet Home, the Menagerie Wilderness is relatively small and lies to the west of the more popular Three Sisters Wilderness. The mountains of this wilderness are part of the Old Cascades, the mountain range that formed some 25 million years ago. These mountains have weathered away to low rolling hills and are easily mistaken for the foothills of the much younger volcanic peaks of the current Cascade crest. There are a few short trails within this wilderness that are done primarily as day hikes.

Mount Washington Wilderness

Between Santiam Pass (Ore. 22/U.S. 20) and McKenzie Pass (Ore. 242). Tel. 541/549-2111. Hiking, fishing.

Easily accessible but little visited, the 52,516-acre Mount Washington Wilderness is a tortured landscape of jet-black lava fields spilling down from Belknap Crater. Rising above these lava fields is 7,794-foot Mount Washington. Most people approach this wilderness on short hikes from the McKenzie Pass area, where several short trails lead across the lava fields. Not surprisingly, overnight camping is unpopular amid the jumble of razor-sharp rocks in the lava fields. However, the Pacific Crest Trail does pass through this wilderness, and PCT hikers will find this stretch of trail particularly interesting, even if they are not enticed to linger.

McKenzie Pass

On Ore. 242 between McKenzie Bridge and Sisters. Camping, hiking, road biking, canoeing, fishing.

Though Ore. 242 over McKenzie Pass is closed during the winter months, during the months that it is open, it is the most scenic pass in Oregon. Consequently, it is a popular route with summer vacationers. The reason for the pass's popularity is the immense lava field through which the narrow, winding highway passes. Pullouts and a lava-rock observation building at the pass stay crowded throughout the summer and fall as people stop to marvel at the blackness all around. This road is very popular with bicyclists, who always spend a good deal of time at the pass recuperating from the long uphill pedal it took to reach this point. There are a couple of short trails here, and the Pacific Crest Trail also crosses the highway.

Waldo Lake and Waldo Lake Wilderness

North of Ore. 58 on FS 5897. Tel. 541/782-2291. Hiking, mountain biking, canoeing, fishing.

Waldo Lake, at 5,414 feet in elevation, covers 10 square miles and is 420 feet deep at its deepest. This is one of the purest lakes in the world—visibility in the lake's water reaches 125 feet, and, due in part to a lack of plants in the lake, the water purity rivals that of Crater Lake and Lake Baikal in Siberia. Encompassing the lands north and west of the lake is the Waldo Lake Wilderness. This wilderness area consists primarily of low, rolling hills dotted with small lakes. For this reason it is particularly popular with anglers. During the summer of 1996, a forest fire burned throughout the northern end of the wilderness for several weeks, burning right down to the lake's north shore. Be sure to find out about trail and forest conditions before planning a hike.

Diamond Peak Wilderness

South of Ore. 58 on FS 21 or FS 23. Tel. 541/782-2283. Hiking, fishing.

Though it is one of the highest peaks in the southern part of the Oregon Cascades, Diamond Peak just doesn't command much attention. Its low, humpbacked stature makes one wonder how it ever got such a superlative name. The wilderness surrounds the mountain and is bounded by Odell and Crescent lakes on the east. To the south of the wilderness is the Oregon Cascades Recreation Area, which is similar to a wilderness area but does not prohibit bicycles, motorcycles, or snowmobiles.

The Santiam & McKenzie Pass Routes ◆ What to Do & Where to Do It

CROSS-COUNTRY SKIING

An abundance of trails, a dozen sno-parks, and good views make the Santiam Pass area one of the best cross-country skiing spots in the state.

GROOMED TRAILS

Hoodoo Nordic Center

16.3 kilometers. Easy–most difficult. 600-foot elevation gain. Access: At Santiam Pass on U.S. 20, 82 miles east of Salem, Albany, or Eugene. Trail fee: $5 or $8 with rope-tow pass. Map: Trail maps available at Nordic center.

This Nordic center offers some of the most challenging groomed trails in the state on its Skyline Trail System, which is halfway up Hoodoo Butte. These trails loop around the south side of the butte for superb views of the Three Sisters and begin above the Manzanita Chair (ski up the downhill slopes). Although it is possible to ski all the way around the butte, it isn't easy and should be tried only in clear weather. The lower trail system is much less challenging, though it does have a 2.5-kilometer advanced loop. What this Nordic center lacks is much in the way of intermediate trails (a total of only 1.5 kilometers). Unless you're a novice or expert, try Mount Bachelor instead.

UNGROOMED TRAILS

Maxwell and Big Springs Sno-Parks

24 miles total. Easy–most difficult. 650-foot elevation gain. Access: 9 miles west of Santiam Pass on Ore. 22. Map: Imus Geographics Santiam Pass Recreation Area.

There are very few places in the Northwest where you can ski through old-growth forest. For that reason alone the trails at this sno-park should not be missed. There

is something ultimately magical about skiing through the quiet beneath massive Douglas firs that reach more than 100 feet skyward. The black trunks of the trees stand out in bold contrast to the snow. Despite the enchanting qualities of the forests here, these trails pass through disturbing amounts of clear-cut hillside—clear-cuts that until very recently were forests as awe-inspiring as those still standing in the vicinity. If you have not yet grasped the importance of halting the clear-cutting of the Northwest's ancient forests, a short ski here will certainly make a convert of you. To ski the old growth, head west from the parking area on the Mountain View Trail West. Once through the old growth, you can continue on the difficult Mountain View Loop or ski the easy middle loops. Directly across the highway from this sno-park is the Big Springs Sno-Park, which offers another 9 miles of easy ski trails. The Big Springs Loop offers the best views.

Lava Lake Trails

5.5 miles. Easy–more difficult. 600-foot elevation gain. Access: On U.S. 20, 3.8 miles west of the Ore. 22/U.S. 20 junction. Map: Imus Geographics Santiam Pass Recreation Area.

Of all the many sno-park trail systems in the Santiam Pass area, these trails offer the best views (from clear-cuts) as well as more awe-inspiring old-growth forest. The best route here connects the Pumice Loop with the Lava Loop for a 3.7-mile trail from which you'll get a view that takes in the Three Sisters, Mount Jefferson, Three Fingered Jack, and Mount Washington. Another good route heads 1.1 miles up the east leg of the Lava Flats Loop to Lava Lake, from which there are more views. Be forewarned, however, that parts of this trail are quite steep. From here it is possible to ski a half-mile to the Lava Lake East Access Trail, which connects to the trails at the Big Springs Sno-Park.

Roy Benson Sno-Park

18.3 miles total. Easy–more difficult. 300-foot elevation gain. Access: At Santiam Pass on U.S. 20, turn south at the Hoodoo Ski Area sign and

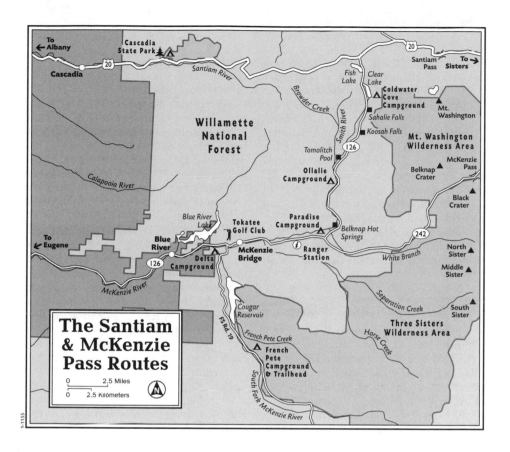

The Santiam
& McKenzie
Pass Routes

0   2.5 Miles
0   2.5 Kilometers

then left into the sno-park. Map: Imus Geographics Santiam Pass Recreation Area.

This large sno-park adjacent to the Hoodoo Ski Area is shared by both cross-country skiers and snowmobilers, but there are plenty of trails here that are closed to the noisemakers. These trails lead through a wide rolling plateau area with lots of open vistas. Some of these open areas are meadows and some are lakes, but for the most part, trails here pass through the area of Airstrip Burn, a forest fire that raged through this region in 1967. By far the most scenic route is the South Loop, which can be as short as 7.2 miles or as long as 10 miles depending on which trails you choose to ski. With the exception of the trail up Brandenburg Butte, this is an easy trail. Just be sure that at some point you ski south from the sno-park under the cliffs of Hayrick Butte. It is one of the most dramatic stretches of trail in the state. If you make this section the start of your trail, continue south to the shelter on Brandenburg Butte and then loop back to

the sno-park either on the Pacific Crest Trail, the Two Buttes Cutoff Trail, or the Circle Lake Trail. The 3.8-mile North Loop, which leads to the Blowout Shelter, is a good novice loop.

DOWNHILL SKIING & SNOWBOARDING

Hoodoo Ski Area

82 miles east of Salem on Ore. 22; 82 miles east of Albany on U.S. 20; 83 miles east of Eugene on Ore. 126. Tel. 541/822-3799 (800/949-LIFT for snow report). 22 trails; 3 lifts; 1,035-foot vertical drop. Lift hours: Thurs–Sat 9am–10pm, Sun–Tues 9am–4pm (open some Wednesdays). Adult lift tickets $22.

With only three lifts and a limited number of runs, this small ski area at Santiam Pass on U.S. 20 attracts primarily skiers from the Salem and Corvallis areas. The main attractions here are not great runs but rather low lift prices and proximity (it's another 90 minutes to Mount Bachelor).

The base elevation of only 4,668 feet means that Hoodoo frequently opens late and doesn't always get the snow that higher ski areas in Oregon get, so always call first. Although there is a 30%/40%/30% mix of expert, intermediate, and beginner runs, they tend to lack variety within each level. However, the location on the slopes of steeply pitched Hoodoo Butte provides good views of the surrounding peaks and Hayrick Butte, an adjacent butte of equal size but very different character. Your best bet here, if the weather is cooperating, is to ride the Green Chair to the top of the mountain. From here there are runs for all abilities.

FISHING

The upper **North Santiam River,** above Detroit Lake, offers lots of good trout water. The stretch between Idanha and Marion Forks is stocked each summer, but there are also plenty of wild fish as well. The best fly-fishing is above Marion Forks. Below Detroit Lake and the Big Cliff Dam, there is good steelhead fishing throughout the year. There's also a good spring Chinook run. Rainbow and cutthroat can also be taken on this lower section of the river. Try the numerous state parks, bridges, and boat ramps for good bank fishing below the dam. Above Detroit Lake, there is plenty of river access right along Ore. 22.

The **McKenzie River** is one of the most famous fishing rivers in Oregon, and it was here that the ubiquitous McKenzie River drift boat was developed many decades ago. Forget about the waters from Clear Lake (the river's source) down to Belknap Hot Springs; these waters are frustrating to say the least. The best all-around waters are those between Blue River and Leaburg Lake. Throughout the season, rainbow trout are stocked as far upstream as Paradise Campground. However, the real prizes of this river are the native McKenzie redside rainbows. Your best chance of hooking one is going to be above Paradise Campground. The **McKenzie River South Fork,** which enters the main river between Blue River and McKenzie Bridge, is another good trout stream and

is stocked with rainbows throughout the season. Above the Cougar Reservoir, there's a lot of good fly-fishing water.

Numerous guides work the McKenzie River, floating the sections both above and below Leaburg Dam in those famous drift boats. Among the more reliable guide companies are **Dave Helfrich River Outfitter** (tel. 541/896-3786); **Wilderness River Outfitters** (tel. 541/726-9471); and **Jim's Oregon Whitewater** (tel. 800/254-JIMS or 541/822-6003).

Numerous lakes in the area also produce some good fishing results, though for most lakes you'll need some sort of boat or float. **Clear Lake,** the source of the McKenzie, has some good-size brook trout, as well as wild cutthroat and stocked rainbows. This lake's crystalline waters make a fishing trip here an adventure even if you never hook a single fish. In the Santiam Pass area, **Lost Lake,** which has no outlet (it drains into lava beds), is stocked with both rainbows and Atlantic salmon, which makes it a very popular lake. Just over the Santiam Pass, **Suttle Lake** is known for its kokanee. May and June are the best months for these land-locked salmon. There are also large brown trout in this lake.

If you'd like to do a bit of hiking along with your fishing, there are a couple of good choices north of Ore. 22 east of Detroit Lake in the Mount Jefferson Wilderness. **Marion Lake,** north of Marion Forks, is well known for its large brookies and rainbows. Even though it is a 2.5-mile hike to this lake, many anglers carry in floats of some sort to improve their chances of catching one of the lake's big fish. Nearby **Pamelia Lake,** a 2.2-mile hike-in, is even more popular than Marion Lake. In fact, it is one of the most popular backpacking spots in the state and requires a reservation for overnighting. Anglers here also bring in inflatables of numerous varieties. There is such an overpopulation of cutthroat in this lake that a special bag limit of 30 fish is in effect as an attempt to reduce the population and increase the size of the fish. Fish here average only 6 to 8 inches, but you can keep anything you catch. They bite on just about anything.

HIKING & BACKPACKING

Jefferson Park

12 miles round-trip. Moderate. 1,450-foot elevation gain in, 1,150 feet out. Access: The trailhead is at the south end of Breitenbush Lake. From Detroit, on Ore. 22, head north on FS 46 to a right turn onto FS 4220 (signed Breitenbush Lake). The last 6 miles or so of road is rough gravel marked as not suitable for low-clearance vehicles. Map: USFS Mount Jefferson Wilderness.

My mind's eye pictures Shangri-La looking something like Jefferson Park. There's a valley. It's full of little lakes surrounded by flower-filled meadows. Rising above the valley is a glacier-clad peak. And to get to the valley, you have to hike uphill through forests for many miles (after first driving an incredibly bad road). Unfortunately, Jefferson Park looks like Shangri-La to a lot of other Oregon hikers as well, especially on August weekends. Sure there are comparable parks—in fact, better parks—on Mount Rainier, but here in Oregon, this is *the* place.

Covering roughly 1.5 square miles, the park contains five lakes and several smaller ponds. Together the meadows and lakeshores here provide ample opportunities for exploration over the course of a couple of days. Though there are other routes into Jefferson Park, I like the hike up from Breitenbush Lake, even though the drive to this trailhead is best suited to four-wheel-drive vehicles or cars and trucks with high clearance. This route starts on the shores of the lake and then climbs slowly but steadily through open forest with frequent views. Before reaching the high point atop Park Ridge, you pass by several tarns (glacier-carved pools) that produce a good crop of mosquitoes early in the summer. Here at the ridge, after 4 miles of climbing, you finally get a look at why it is you are hiking this trail.

Spread out in its entirety 1,150 feet below you is Jefferson Park. This aerie makes a perfect lunch spot. Once reconciled to losing almost all the elevation you just gained, head down the short, steep

2-mile descent to the floor of the park and start looking for a place to pitch your tent. Don't even think about camping near the lakes, which have been absolutely hammered over the years. Many areas around the lakes are simply closed to camping, while other sites are closed for restoration. If you head into the trees on the outer periphery of the park, you can still get away from the crowds.

If your car precludes using this route, you can start from the end of FS 2243, the Whitewater Road, which heads north from Ore. 22, 10.3 miles east of Detroit.

Canyon Creek Meadows

6 miles. Moderate. 1,400-foot elevation gain. Access: From U.S. 20, 8 miles east of Santiam Pass, turn north onto FS 12 and drive 4 miles north to FS 1230, continuing another 0.6 miles on pavement. In another 0.9 miles take a left fork onto FS 1234 and continue 5 miles to the trailhead at Jack Lake. Map: USFS Mount Jefferson Wilderness.

Of the two main trails to Three Fingered Jack, this is my favorite. Not only is it an easy hike, but for a mile or so the trail leads straight at this craggy peak, so you can marvel constantly as you walk. The trail starts beside tiny Jack Lake and very soon comes to a fork. This trail gets heavy use, and to limit the number of people you see along the trail, the forest service requests that you hike the Canyon Creek loop clockwise. So, take the left fork and climb gradually through a forest of spindly subalpine conifers for 2 miles to the first of two large meadows. It is here that you get your first view of Three Fingered Jack. The trail then climbs through trees for a bit and enters a second meadow on a steep slope. You get a view of a ridge that rises up in front of Three Fingered Jack. Exposed on the cliff face of this ridge are numerous multicolored layers of rock.

From here the trail gets steep as it climbs to a viewpoint above the third meadow. This last meadow is in a bowl at the base of the mountain and is backed by a curving ridge of brick-red rocks and cinder that flanks Three Fingered Jack on its north side. You can continue up to a better view and a small cirque lake. The loop trail back passes meadows that were once beaver ponds. You can still see many trees that they girdled, sometimes 5 feet above the ground, which indicates that the beavers were active even when snow lay thick at this elevation. At a pair of 12-foot falls on Canyon Creek, the trail back turns right. If you'd like to visit Wasco Lake, cross the creek on a foot bridge between the falls and continue another 0.7 miles.

Cone Peak–Iron Mountain Trail

8 miles round-trip. Moderate. 1,800-foot elevation gain. Access: The trailhead is 45 miles east of Sweet Home (0.7 miles east of Tombstone Pass). Map: USGS Harter Mountain.

With 18 different plant communities, more than 300 species of flowering plants, and more species of trees (17) in one area than anywhere else in Oregon, the Iron Mountain area is a botanical wonderland. Do this hike during the July wildflower season to fully appreciate the amazing variety of flowering plants. Iron Mountain is also the site of a forest-service fire lookout that is staffed in the summer. Although there is a steep short trail that climbs straight up Iron Mountain from U.S. 20, it is much more enjoyable to take the roundabout route up Cone Peak, across a saddle, and then up to Iron Mountain's summit. This route will take you through meadows on the slopes of Cone Peak as well as the meadows on Iron Mountain.

Rooster Rock

6.4 miles round-trip. Moderate–difficult. 2,300-foot elevation gain. Access: The trailhead (marked Trout Creek Trail) is 21 miles east of Sweet Home on U.S. 20. Map: USFS Menagerie Wilderness.

Located in the Menagerie Wilderness, Rooster Rock is just one of many rock outcroppings and spires in this section of the Old Cascades, which were formed 25 million years ago. High Cascades peaks such as Mount Hood, Mount Jefferson, and the Three Sisters are of much more recent age, geologically speaking. Keeping Rooster Rock company in

the Menagerie Wilderness are such named rock formations as Rabbit Ears, Turkey Monster, Chicken Rock, Cockatoo Tower, and Beetle Dome. These rocks are favorites of climbers, but also make this a popular hike for people who just like interesting panoramas.

There are actually two trails to the top of Rooster Rock—the steep trail and the steeper trail. I prefer the steep trail; it may be longer but it's easier—well, sort of. The best time to do this hike is in the late spring when the rhododendrons bloom. From the top of Rooster Rock, you can survey the surrounding menagerie of rocks, as well as a view down to the Willamette Valley. If you'd rather hike the steeper trail, continue 2.5 miles past the Trout Creek trailhead to the Rooster Rock trailhead.

McKenzie River Trail/Tamolitch Falls

4.2 miles round-trip. Easy. 200-foot elevation gain. Access: From McKenzie Bridge, drive Ore. 126 northeast for 14 miles and turn left at the Trail Bridge Reservoir/EWEB Powerhouse sign. After crossing the bridge, turn right onto a gravel road and drive 0.4 miles to the trailhead. Map: USGS Tamolitch Falls.

This magical mystery hike leads to one of the most astounding sights in the Northwest—the blue hole, at the base of dry Tamolitch Falls. If you've ever been to one of those miniature golf courses where they have a pond filled with water that's been dyed a bizarrely unnatural color of blue, then you know what to expect of this natural pool. I'll be a stinker and demystify the apparition: The pool is formed by the re-emergence of the McKenzie River after flowing underground for 3 miles through a porous lava bed. I think you'll agree that knowing where this water comes from doesn't alter its astounding beauty.

The 2.1-mile trail follows along the west bank of the McKenzie, sometimes at water level and sometimes high above, but always in earshot of this noisy, tumbling river. The trail begins in a dark forest of huge old-growth trees. These eventually give way to smaller trees as the trail passes through a lava field. Here the trail meanders through miniature canyons lined with jagged lava. In many places the rocks' ragged edges are considerably softened by the thick blanket of mosses, lichens, and sedums that have taken hold over the centuries since the lava ran red hot through this valley. The view of the blue hole 100 feet below you comes without warning at the crest of a short rise. Wide, deep, and the most amazing shade of turquoise, the pool is hauntingly silent compared to the roaring river only feet away at the pool's outflow. If you want to lengthen your hike, you can continue up the McKenzie River Trail from here for another 3 miles to see where the river disappears in a marshy area above a lava field.

Obsidian Trail

12 miles round-trip. Moderate–difficult. 1,800-foot elevation gain. Access: The trailhead is on Ore. 242 between mileposts 70 and 71 (6.2 miles west of McKenzie Pass). Map: USFS Three Sisters Wilderness.

This trail, leading to an area known as Sunshine, shares the dubious distinction, along with Pamelia Lake in the Mount Jefferson Wilderness, of being the most popular backpacking spot in the state. Consequently, as at Pamelia Lake, a Limited Entry Permit, available only in advance through the McKenzie Ranger Station (see the "Outdoor Resources" sidebar earlier in this chapter), is required for entry, whether you are here for the day or for an overnight visit. That said, what makes this area so popular? Well, there are the meadows and the lava flows; then again, there's the close-up view of Middle Sister and the trail up this peak (technical only at the very summit). Oh, wait a minute, I forgot to mention the area's obsidian flows, and the way the Obsidian Cliffs sparkle in the sun. . . .

You get the picture—this is a great place to spend a few nights camping and exploring. From the trailhead, take an immediate right-hand fork marked "White Branch Creek." The first 3.4 miles of trail are quite uneventful and pass through dense and often dusty forest. However, you eventually reach a wall of lava rock and climb up this wall onto the top of a lava flow with views of surrounding peaks. This half-mile-wide jumble of jagged rocks is

the wall protecting this little corner of paradise. On the far side of the lava flow, the meadows begin, and if you come in July, you will be greeted by a profusion of colorful wildflowers. Take the trail to the right and climb gradually to a plateau atop the Obsidian Cliffs. You will be surrounded by the sparkle of obsidian.

At the junction with the PCT, turn left and pass Obsidian Falls. The trail then climbs to another plateau and passes the Arrowhead Lakes and a view of North Sister before descending to the meadows known as Sunshine. At the four-way junction here, turn left to head back to your car. Continuing straight will take you to Collier Cone and the trail to Scott Lake (an alternative route back to the car that adds 3 miles to the hike), and turning right will put you on the climbers' trail up Middle Sister. Should you choose to camp here, observe all campsite-restoration closures and try to be inconspicuous—this is a place where carefully respecting the Nothing But Footprints maxim would really do a world of good.

HOT SPRINGS

Cougar Hot Springs, also known as Terwilliger Hot Springs, is my favorite in western Oregon. A lot of other people share my sentiments, and on a summer weekend day, there will be dozens of people here. Though the springs consist of several pools terraced down a gully, you will likely have to wait a bit for a space in one of the pools. Clear, hot water, old-growth trees, and a short hike are the factors that contribute to this springs' popularity. Over the years, volunteers have made many improvements to this "natural" hot spring, and today there is a pit toilet, a wooden structure where you can hang your clothes, and tree rounds paving the ground around the spring to reduce the amount of mud. No camping is allowed near the springs, and from dusk to dawn, no parking is allowed on the road near the trailhead. If you want to avoid the crowds, come on a weekday at dawn in the off-season. To reach the springs, turn south off of Ore. 126 onto FS 19 (the Aufderheide National Scenic Byway) between Blue River and McKenzie Bridge and continue

7.5 miles south to a parking area on the south side of the cove. The trail to the hot springs is across the causeway on the north side of the cove.

If you'd prefer a bit of solitude, try nearby **Bigelow Hot Springs,** which consist of a small, murky pool set beneath an overhanging rock beside the McKenzie River. Though the pool is within sight of a bridge, it remains fairly lightly used, in part because it is so inferior to Terwilliger Hot Springs. One plus here is that you can hop into the river and cool off for the ultimate invigorating experience. To reach these springs, drive 4 miles north of Belknap Hot Springs on Ore. 126 and turn left onto FS 2654 (Deer Creek Road). Park on the far side of the bridge and hike 100 feet downstream.

For those who prefer a more developed hot-springs experience, **Belknap Hot Springs,** east of McKenzie Bridge on Ore. 126, provides a small hot swimming pool beside the river. There are also cabins for rent here. A small fee is charged to soak in the pool. You'll find this hot-spring establishment about 5 miles east of McKenzie Bridge.

For a more zenlike experience, you'll have to pay. **Breitenbush Hot Springs,** located on the grounds of a New Age retreat center, is comprised of three natural hot springs set on the edge of a meadow. Two of these are pretty tepid and shallow, but the third is perfect. That's why it's the most popular. If you just want to soak in natural hot mineral waters, there is also a developed area where the tubs are different temperatures and include a cold tub. There's also a steam room here and meals are available in the dining hall. Keep in mind, however, that this place is popular and is not geared toward day-trippers. To use the tubs, you'll need to make a reservation by calling Breitenbush Community (tel. 503/854-3314).

MOUNTAIN BIKING

McKenzie River Trail

26 miles one way. Strenuous. 1,100-foot elevation gain north to south; 2,000 feet south to north. Access: The lower trailhead is on Ore. 126

at the McKenzie Bridge Ranger Station, 1.5 miles east of McKenzie Bridge. The upper trailhead is 2 miles south of the Ore. 126/U.S. 20 junction. Map: USFS McKenzie River Trail.

This long trail along the banks of the McKenzie River offers loads of variety, so no matter what your level of ability, you should be able to find a section that appeals to you. The uppermost section, from Clear Lake down to Trail Bridge Campground (12.5 miles), is the most scenic section of the trail, but it is also the most difficult, and is frequently used by hikers. This section passes along the shores of Clear Lake, through lava beds, and then drops precipitously down past Sahalie and Koosah falls. Below the Carmen Reservoir, the trail passes a marsh where the McKenzie simply disappears in most unriverly fashion. Three miles downstream, at the unnaturally blue pool at the base of Tamolitch Dry Falls, the river suddenly reappears. The trail then passes through a tire-shredding segment of highly technical trail that wanders through an ancient lava field.

The 13-mile lower section of the trail between the McKenzie Ranger Station and Trail Bridge Campground is a much easier stretch. The gradient is easy, there's no lava, and though you will have to deal with the odd root or rock, for the most part, you can just enjoy the forest scenery along the bank of the river.

Either section is best done with a car shuttle to avoid riding on busy Ore. 126. If you haven't got two cars, you can return to your starting point on the highway, or ride back on the trail. Also, you may want to know that there are 11 access points along the length of the trail, so should you want to bail out, you've got lots of options. Because of potential user conflicts, it's best to ride this trail uphill.

Cache Mountain Trail

17 miles. Moderate. 1,500-foot elevation gain. Access: Corbett Sno-Park, 17 miles west of Sisters on U.S. 20. Map: Mount Washington Wilderness.

Some people just feel a deep-down need to earn their fun. For them, fast, single-track descents just aren't as grati-fying if their thighs didn't burn, their hearts didn't pound, and their sweat didn't pour. If you're just such a mountain-bike masochist, then the Cache Mountain ride is for you. This ride starts with 9 miles of climbing on red-cinder forest roads. It's slow and it's steady, but in the first couple of miles as you pedal up FS 2076, you'll pass several small lakes that add a bit of interest to this stretch of the ride. Turning off onto FS 800, you begin the climb up the east side of Cache Mountain. Once you finally reach the top, you can sit down and catch your breath as you drink in the view of Mount Washington and its surround-ings. When you are sufficiently rested, check your brakes, and prepare to fly. It's 8 miles, all downhill, from here back to Corbett Sno-Park and your starting point.

ROCK CLIMBING

The many crags and pinnacles of the Menagerie Wilderness offer the best climbing in the region. Here you can climb such rocks as **Rabbit Ears** (260-foot twin spires), **Rooster Rock, Turkey Monster,** and **Cockatoo Tower.** Two trails lead into this wilderness from below Rooster Rock. The trailheads are 21 and 23.5 miles east of Sweet Home on U.S. 20.

SEA KAYAKING & FLAT-WATER CANOEING

If there is a lake anywhere in Oregon to convince you that you need a canoe or sea kayak, **Clear Lake** is it. More than living up to its name, this lake is the source of the McKenzie River and is formed by a spring on the northeast shore of the lake. The waters are so clear that it is easy to while away an entire afternoon just leisurely gazing down at the topography of the lake's bottom. Formed by a lava flow that blocked the McKenzie River 3,000 years ago, the lake still holds beneath its cold waters ghostly skeletons of perfectly preserved trees from the days when the lava flows filled this valley.

The key word here is *cold*. The waters that flow from the Great Spring, the source of the lake, maintain a constant year-round temperature of around 38°F.

Consequently, the lake stays cold through-out the year. Forget about doing any swim-ming here unless you've got a wetsuit. If your boat has a shallow enough draft, you should be able to paddle up a little riffle that forms between the main lake and the 100-foot-long creek that flows from the Great Spring. If you can make it up to the spring, you'll be drifting atop waters of a most amazing shade of blue. If you can't get your boat up the stream, you can walk here on a trail that comes close to shore just north of the spring. On the shores of the lake are both a campground and a rus-tic cabin resort.

Reservoirs generally don't make the best canoeing waters, but **Trail Bridge Reservoir** south of Clear Lake on Ore. 126 is an exception. The lake's waters are a fascinating blue-green color, and the long northern arm of the lake is fun to explore. This reservoir is unusual in that it is filled by a huge, long tunnel from nearby Smith Reservoir. The only drawback for canoe-ists is the traffic noise. Put in at the signed Trail Bridge Campground boat ramp off Ore. 126.

Scott Lake on the McKenzie Pass Highway offers the best views of any of the good canoeing lakes in this region. The lake—actually three lakes strung together by shallow channels—is perfect for explor-ing in a canoe or sea kayak, and the campground on the lakeshore makes this a good base for investigating the unusual volcanic features of this area. The view of South and Middle Sister from the lake is one of the most famous and photographed mountain vistas in the state.

Although located close to the highway, **Lost Lake,** just west of Santiam Pass, has enough ins and outs to its shoreline to make it fairly interesting to explore. This lake is stocked with Atlantic salmon, which makes it very popular with anglers. How-ever, trolling is prohibited with a motor running, so the lake stays pretty quiet. As with some other lakes in this region, Lost Lake has no outlet. The water simply seeps down through the porous volcanic soil beneath the lake. On the east side of the Santiam Pass, you'll find several more small lakes worth dipping a paddle into south of the Corbett Sno-Park. **Link Lake, Island Lake,** and **Meadow Lake,** all off

FS 2076, together make for a good day's worth of exploring.

As long as you stay out of the ski tracks, you'll be welcome on any of the ungroomed cross-country ski trails at Santiam Pass (see above under "Cross Country Skiing"). **Maxwell Sno-Park** is my favorite trail system in this area because of its old-growth trees. However, if you want breathtaking views, try snowshoeing between **Hayrick and Hoodoo buttes** from the parking lot of the Hoodoo Ski Area (just be sure to stay off the groomed trail). From here and the surrounding area there are views of Mount Washington, the Sisters, and Big Lake. From the pass between the buttes, you can continue around Hayrick Butte for a 4-mile walk or do an out-and-back around the south side of Hoodoo Butte. This route is unmarked, but because it follows a road, you aren't likely to get lost unless the weather turns bad. Pick a clear day for this one. Down at **Willamette Pass** there are several trail shelters that lend themselves well to overnight trips. See the "Cross-Country Skiing" section above for details. In this area, the 5-mile round-trip route to Gold Lake and the Marilyn Lakes is particularly rewarding.

The little-visited **Sawyer Ice Cave,** just off Ore. 126 south of the junction with U.S. 20, is a lava tube several hundred feet long. The cave traps cold air during the winter and, consequently, has ice in it for much of the year. The first section of the cave is close to the parking area. About 0.25 miles farther from the parking lot, there are two more sections of the lava tube.

Cascadia State Park, 14 miles east of Sweet Home on U.S. 20, sits on the banks of the South Santiam River and is home to one of the most spectacular swimming holes in the entire state. Known as **High Rocks,** this 300-foot-long gorge is a river lover's playground. You'll find trails down to the

gorge at turnoffs near Wolf Creek. Roughly a mile downstream from this point is another good swimming area where wide, flat rocks provide lots of sunbathing areas, and some small rapids provide tubing opportunities.

The reservoirs of Oregon are generally not among the finest of swimming holes in the state. However, one reservoir swimming area worth mentioning is the **Rider Creek Arm of Cougar Reservoir** south of McKenzie Bridge. This emerald-green cove lies along the trail to the popular Cougar Hot Springs, and before or after soaking in the hot pools, it's nice to do a bit of swimming in these cool waters.

At Santiam Pass, there are several lakes that are good for swimming. **Suttle Lake** is the largest of these, and though it has a designated swimming beach on its south shore, it is noisy with the roar of ski boats. For quiet waters, head over to **Scout Lake,** which is just south of Suttle Lake on FS 2066 and allows no motorboats at all. Also in this area is **Round Lake,** on the north side of U.S. 20 between Santiam Pass and Sisters. To reach Round Lake, take FS 12 north to the *second* left onto FS 1210 and drive this road 5.6 miles to the lake. There is a good view of Three Fingered Jack from the lake.

If you are driving the McKenzie Pass Highway (Ore. 242) during the summer, don't miss an opportunity to go for a swim in **Scott Lake,** one of the most picturesque lakes in Oregon. North and Middle Sister are perfectly framed by the waters of the lake, making this scene one of the most photographed panoramas in the state.

For information on swimming holes on the **Little North Santiam River,** see chapter 9.

Clear Lake

2.4 miles round-trip. Easy. 50-foot elevation gain. Access: From U.S. 20, drive 5 miles south on Ore. 126 and turn left at the Coldwater Cove Campground sign. Map: USGS Clear Lake or trailhead map.

Clear Lake, which is the source of the McKenzie River, is among the clearest (and coldest) lakes in Oregon. It's fed by a large spring that maintains a constant year-round temperature of only 38°F. This spring, on the northeast side of the lake, makes a good destination for a short hike. Starting at the boat ramp parking lot in the Coldwater Cove Campground, hike north, crossing two lava flows before reaching the Great Spring. The spring is set in a bowl surrounded by old-growth Douglas firs and is a most amazing shade of blue (a miniature version of the blue pool at the base of Tamolitch Dry Falls). Connecting the spring to the lake is a stream about 100 feet long. If you've decided you're up for a longer walk, you can hike all the way around the lake for a total of 5 miles of easy hiking.

Koosah and Sahalie Falls

2.2 miles. Easy. 200-foot elevation gain. Access: Across Ore. 126 from the turnoff to Clear Lake. Map: USGS Clear Lake.

Two waterfalls, 100-foot-high Sahalie Falls and 70-foot-high Koosah Falls, lie a few hundred feet off Ore. 126 just south of Clear Lake. The former has a well-marked and popular overlook parking area right on the highway, while the latter is accessed from Ice Cap Campground. However, a better way to see both of these falls, if you have an hour to spare, is on a 2.2-mile hike down the McKenzie River Trail from where it crosses Ore. 126 at the turnoff for Clear Lake. By visiting these impressive falls this way, you'll avoid the crowds, get in a bit of exercise, and see a bit more of this picturesque section of the McKenzie River. The trail follows the east bank of the river for a short distance and then crosses to the west bank.

Delta Old-Growth Grove

0.5 miles. Easy. No elevation gain. Access: At Delta Campground just south of Ore. 126 between the towns of Blue River and McKenzie Bridge. Map: Trailhead maps.

This short interpretive nature trail provides an informative introduction to the old-growth forest. Along the route, there are trees more than 650 years old and over 200 feet tall. The braided streams of Delta Creek, which flows into the McKenzie River at this point, are ideal habitat for young salmon and trout. This trail is a must if you are passing this way.

Proxy Falls and Linnton Lake

Proxy Falls 1.5-mile loop; Linnton Lake 2.8 miles round-trip. Easy. 200-foot elevation gain to Proxy Falls; 300 feet to Linnton Lake. Access: The Proxy Falls trailhead is 9 miles east of Ore. 126 on Ore. 242. The Linnton Lake trailhead is another 1.5 miles farther east. Map: USFS Three Sisters Wilderness.

Two 100-foot waterfalls are hardly worth mentioning in the Cascades, where falls are around every turn. However, there is something very different about one of the two falls. The trail to the falls traverses ancient lava beds that are now covered with moss and lichens. Vine maples, bright red in fall, grow among the jumble of rocks, and wherever there is enough soil, fir trees—some quite large and old—have grown. But what of the strange falls? The first you come to on this loop trail are straightforward enough—tall, mossy, shimmering white—but the second falls, now these are special. You see, lava does strange things, and here is one of the strangest. The trail leads to the foot of the noisy falls where there's a small pool, maybe 30 feet across, surrounded by rock walls. What's missing? The rest of the stream, of course. The pool has no surface outlet (at least not in the summer); the waterfall pours its water straight into a porous lava never to be seen again!

Linnton Lake is the site of another lava-lands phenomenon. This lake was created thousands of years ago when a lava flow blocked the creek here. Today the lava dam holds back the waters of Linnton Lake, which miraculously never overflows its banks. Instead, the waters seep down through the lava rock and likely resurface somewhere else as a spring. This trail passes through old-growth forest before reaching the lake and a view of Linnton Falls. There is a beach about halfway around the lake at the end of the trail.

Lava River Trail, McKenzie Pass

0.5 miles. Easy. 100-foot elevation gain. Access: On Ore. 242 at McKenzie Pass, 15 miles east of Sisters. Map: Not necessary.

For a quick spin through the lava fields at McKenzie Pass, try this easy paved trail that begins at the base of the Dee Wright Observatory, the lava-rock lookout building at the pass. This trail serves as an excellent introduction to the unusual geology of the region. Along the way there are great views of surrounding peaks. Sighting markers at the Dee Wright Observatory will help you identify all these peaks.

WHITEWATER KAYAKING & CANOEING

With more than 40 miles of fun Class II and III waters above Leaburg Dam, the McKenzie River is one of the most popular paddling rivers in Oregon. Although not as popular, the upper stretches of the North Santiam also offer challenging waters. For information on paddling the lower sections of the McKenzie and North Santiam rivers, see chapter 9.

CLASS III & ABOVE

The upper sections of the **McKenzie River,** above Leaburg Dam, are the most famous and most popular stretches of this river. This is the water that commercial rafting companies run, and that experienced kayakers play in. Although much of the water on the 40 miles of river between Ollalie Campground and Leaburg Dam is Class II or II+, there are numerous Class III rapids. Among the most famous are Fishladder (5 miles above Paradise Campground), the boulder garden in the town of McKenzie Bridge, and Browns' Hole and Marten Rapids (above and below Ben and Kay Doris State Park, respectively). Perhaps the most popular run on this section of the river is the 14 miles from Finn Rock to Leaburg Dam. The 16-mile run from Paradise Campground to Finn Rock is the next most difficult section. Due to the continuous nature of the rapids, the run from Ollalie Campground to Paradise Campground is the most challenging section. Numerous campgrounds and lodges along this stretch cater to paddlers. All put-ins and take-outs are along Ore. 126 east of Springfield.

The **Middle Santiam River,** east of Sweet Home, has a couple of Class IV runs, one of which is above the Green Peter Lake and Dam and the other of which is below the dam. The upper run (7 miles) starts at the fourth bridge over the river above the lake (7 miles from the lake). The lower run is short (only 2 miles), but because it is below the Green Peter Dam in dam-controlled waters, it can be run throughout the summer. Otherwise runs on this river are rainy season and snowmelt runs.

The **North Santiam River,** above Detroit Lake, offers another good snowmelt run. Starting at Bruno Mountain Road and ending at Detroit Lake, these 7 miles offer almost nonstop excitement and lots of fun play spots. If you want to avoid the Class IV Ricochet Rapid, put in at Whispering Falls Campground. Also be aware that if the lake level is low, there is a Class V drop right before reaching the lake and below the suggested take-out, which is down a dirt road beside a log-scaling station east of the town of Detroit.

WILDLIFE VIEWING

Twenty miles east of Sweet Home on U.S. 20, you can often see **Roosevelt elk** during the winter from a viewing platform on the Walton Ranch Interpretive Trail. The elk congregate in pastures along the banks of the South Santiam River.

The Willamette Pass Route ◆ What to Do & Where to Do It

BIRD WATCHING

The **Buckhead Wildlife Area,** just outside the town of Westfir, is a good place to do a little birding during the summer months. Located on the banks of the Willamette River and Buckhead Creek, the area's willow thickets attract several species of warblers. Also fairly common here are dark-eyed juncos, winter wrens, and sapsuckers. To reach this viewing area, turn off Ore. 58 just before Oakridge and follow signs toward Westfir. After crossing the first bridge, watch for a second bridge on the left in 1 mile. Take this bridge onto FS 5821 and continue 2 miles to the parking area.

Davis Lake, formed when lava flows blocked Odell Creek, fluctuates greatly in size over the course of the year. The marshes surrounding the lake attract a wide variety of birdlife including ospreys and bald eagles. This is also a nesting area for sandhill cranes. Many species of ducks can also be sighted here. The lake can be reached from Odell Lake over rough forest service roads that head north from the east end of Odell Lake. Alternatively, you can drive east on Ore. 58 to the Crescent Cutoff Road and take this road east to FS 46, which leads 8 miles north to the lake. The campgrounds at the south end of the lake provide the best access for bird watching.

BOARDSAILING

Strong, reliable winds blow through the Willamette Pass during the summer months, making **Odell Lake** a popular windsurfing spot. At Sunset Cove, on the north side of the lake, there is a sailboard launch area. However, this is also a boat ramp used by the anglers heading out to troll for Mackinaw trout. Stay alert. Winds tend to be best in the middle of the afternoon and die down around sunset, so don't get caught far offshore late in the afternoon.

Waldo Lake, 7 miles north of Willamette Pass on FS 5897, is the area's other good windsurfing lake. This large, deep lake is so big that winds coming over the Cascades can pick up speed and keep on track for a good, long reach. Windsurfers can do the same. The lake is also popular with sailboats, some as large as 26 feet or more. The Islet Campground is the most popular launch area. Winds here usually pick up around 10 or 11am.

CROSS-COUNTRY SKIING

Before doing any skiing in the Willamette Pass area, be sure to pick up a copy of Imus Geographics "Willamette Pass Oregon XC Ski Trails," a topographic map with easy-to-read routes and detailed descriptions of all area trails. These maps are available at Odell Lake Lodge, at the Willamette Backcountry Ski Patrol building at Gold Lake Sno-Park (open weekends only), and at ski shops in Eugene.

GROOMED TRAILS

Willamette Pass Nordic Center

20 kilometers. Easy–most difficult. 800-foot elevation gain. At Willamette Pass, 69 miles southeast of Eugene on Ore. 58. Tel. 541/484-5030, ext. 350, for information. Trail fee: $6. Map: A trail map is available at the Nordic center; Imus Geographics Willamette Pass Oregon XC Ski Trails.

This system of ski trails is groomed both for traditional and skate skiing and winds through the forests on the northwest side of the Willamette Pass ski area. Nordic trails even connect to the top of one of the downhill area's lifts, so Nordic skiers who don't want to bother trudging uphill can ride a lift up and then ski down onto the trail system. This Nordic system is generally open only on weekends.

Odell Lake Lodge

5 miles. Allow 1 1/2–2 1/2 hours. Easy–moderate. 100-foot elevation gain. 8 miles southeast of Willamette Pass; 77 miles southeast of Eugene on Ore. 58. Tel. 541/433-2540 for information. Trail fee: $4. Map: Trail map available at lodge.

Situated at the southern end of Odell Lake, these trails are maintained by Odell Lake Lodge, and though they are not groomed for skate skiing, they are better maintained than ungroomed trails in the area. This system of interconnected trails passes through young second-growth forest and through two small meadows. The terrain is gently rolling, which makes this a good spot for novice skiers. The groomed trails connect to ungroomed trails that lead farther afield to Fawn Lake, Crescent Lake, and the Maklak Loops. The greatest appeal of these trails is that they lead right to the front doors of the lodge's cabins. Such convenience is a rarity in the Northwest.

UNGROOMED TRAILS

Salt Creek Falls Sno-Park

3–8 miles. Easy–moderate. 100–1,500-foot elevation gain. Access: 20 miles southeast of Oakridge on Ore. 58. Map: Imus Geographics Willamette Pass Oregon XC Ski Trails.

These are the closest ski trails to Eugene, but because of the low elevation, snow is unreliable. If, however, the snow level is low enough, you might find fewer crowds here than up at the Gold Lake Sno-Park. Novice skiers will want to stick to the Salt Creek Road Trail, which ascends gradually almost to Gold Lake Sno-Park. This ascent means that you'll be skiing downhill all the way back to the car. Skiers looking for a more challenging ski tour will want to ski the Fuji Mountain Road Trail, which begins across the highway from the turnoff into the Salt Creek Falls Sno-Park. This is a demanding trail that gains 1,500 feet in 4 miles as it climbs to the Fuji Shelter, which is located at 5,600 feet. Along the way, there are several views south to Diamond Peak, which is also visible from the shelter. This shelter has a wood stove and a sleeping loft and is an excellent spot for an overnight trip. You can also get here from Gold Lake Sno-Park, though this latter route is more difficult than the trail from Salt Creek Falls. If you can arrange a car shuttle, you can make this a one-way trip.

Gold Lake Sno-Park

Distance varies. Easy–most difficult. 500-foot elevation gain. Access: At Willamette Pass, 69 miles southeast of Eugene on Ore. 58. Map: Imus Geographics Willamette Pass Oregon XC Ski Trails.

This is the largest sno-park in the area devoted exclusively to cross-country

skiers. From here trails lead south through the Westview Loops, which are at the north end of Odell Lake, though the lake itself is rarely visible. These loop trails offer a lot of variety and keep all levels of skiers happily striding and gliding. Just east of the Westview Loops is a section of the PCT from which there is a good view of Odell Lake. The Westview Shelter, atop a butte with a bit of a view (there's a better view from higher up on the butte), and the Bechtel Shelter (on the Bechtel Creek Trail southwest of the Westview Loops), are the two most popular skier destinations on this side of the sno-park. These shelters are available on a first-come first-served basis for overnight trips and are almost always full on weekends. Weekdays, however, the shelters see very little overnight use.

One of the more popular routes here is the Shelter Cove Trail, which leads down to the shore of Odell Lake at Trapper Creek Campground. This trail descends from the PCT at Pengra Pass to the east end of an active railroad tunnel that goes under the pass. Cautiously cross the tracks at this point to reach the West Odell Lake Road. Continue southeast to the campground, where there is an easy loop on flat terrain. The view down the lake is beautiful!

On the opposite side of Ore. 58 from the sno-park is the start of the Gold Lake Road, which leads in 2.2 miles to scenic Gold Lake, with connecting trails that lead to the two Marilyn Lakes. This is the most popular ski trail at Willamette Pass, especially with novice skiers. The trail is easy, with gradual ascents and descents, and the destination is both beautiful and has a shelter. However, along the way, there are no views and the heavy use often leaves this trail in poor condition, especially if the surface is the least bit icy. For a view of Diamond Peak, ski to the north end of Gold Lake on the Gold Lake Trail, which starts beyond the shelter at the end of the road. More skilled skiers will want to return via Marilyn Lakes Loop, a narrow trail that winds through the forest to two small lakes.

The trails to Gold Lake and Marilyn Lakes are the best in the area and offer some excellent scenery. From this sno-park, you can also ski to Waldo Lake.

Willamette Pass Sno-Park

6–9.5 miles. Moderate–difficult. 600–1,060-foot elevation gain. Access: At Willamette Pass, 69 miles southeast of Eugene. Map: Imus Geographics Willamette Pass Oregon XC Ski Trails.

The parking area for the Willamette Pass ski area also provides access to miles of cross-country ski trails, including the groomed trails of the Willamette Pass Nordic Center. If you aren't interested in paying to ski on groomed trails, park at the opposite end from the Nordic center. From here, the Pacific Crest Trail leads eastward to the Rosary Lakes area (6-mile round-trip). This route is a long, steady ascent that gains 600 feet before reaching Lower Rosary Lake. Returning back to the car makes this out-and-back 6-mile trip. From here, more experienced skiers can continue onward to Maiden Peak Saddle (from which there is a great view to the south of Odell Lake and Diamond Peak) and then continue north on either the Pacific Crest Trail or Skyline Trail to the Maiden Peak Trail. Take this latter trail west to Gold Lake and follow the Gold Lake Trail back toward Ore. 58. Shortly before reaching the highway, turn left onto the Willamette Pass Tie-In. This route forms a 9.5-mile loop that is quite challenging. Also keep in mind that any time conditions are icy, these trails become very difficult due to the elevation changes.

DOWNHILL SKIING & SNOWBOARDING

Willamette Pass

69 miles southeast of Eugene on Ore. 58. Tel. 800/444-5030 or 541/484-5030 (503/345-SNOW for snow report). 30 trails; 4 triples, 1 double; 1,563-foot vertical drop. Lift hours: Daily 9am–4pm (night skiing Fri–Sat until 9pm). Adult lift tickets $25 all day or $5 per hour (2-hour minimum).

A lack of variety in the terrain has always been the main failing of this ski area. Although the view from the lodge,

looking straight up at the Summit Lift toward the top of Eagle Peak, is enough to get any skier's blood pumping, the reality is a bit of a letdown. Sure, there are a couple of steep runs off the top, including the moguls on Success (directly below the Summit Lift), but all the runs descend at roughly the same slope with nothing unexpected along the way. However, if you're looking for steeper and deeper, this area isn't a complete wash. On the back side, hidden from view and accessed from Peak 2, are more than a half-dozen runs that offer much more challenging terrain than the runs on the south side of Eagle Peak. You'll find tight tree skiing, some rocky dropoffs for heart-stopping airtime, and more moguls than your knees will ever want to encounter. This side of the mountain also has one of the best views in the whole state. To the north can be seen Mount Bachelor, Mount Jefferson, Mount Washington, the Three Sisters, and even the tip of Mount Hood. Awesome!

Families will really appreciate the free day care, which is available by reservation and with a paid adult lift ticket.

FISHING

Odell Lake, deep, cold, and clear, is known for kokanee and Mackinaw that reach upward of 30 pounds. But to catch one of these behemoths, you'll likely need a boat. These fish stay deep and are most often caught by trolling between 50 and 120 feet down. Nearby **Crescent Lake** boasts similar catches, though not as often. On Crescent Lake, try fishing from shore in the early spring when the fish are hungry after a winter under the ice. Otherwise bring a boat and find out where the fish are biting before heading out. If you want to hire a guide to take you out on Odell Lake, contact the **Odell Lake Lodge** (tel. 541/433-2540).

Waldo Lake, even colder and deeper (420 feet) than Odell Lake and one of the purest lakes on earth, has a reputation as a tough place to catch fish, but if you're persistent, you might eventually land one of the lake's rainbows, brookies, or kokanees. June and October are the best months to fish this lake, but be forewarned that June is mosquito season.

Also in this area is **Gold Lake,** which is just west of Willamette Pass and 2 miles north on FS 500. This half-mile-long lake is fly-fishing only and has a good population of wild rainbows and brookies. These fish can get pretty big, but to catch them, you're going to need to get out on the lake. Just remember that no motors are allowed here.

If fly-fishing is your passion, head for the **North Fork of the Middle Fork of the Willamette River** north of Oakridge and Westfir. This is one of the finest fly-fishing streams in the state, and since it is not stocked, it holds only wild rainbows, cutthroats, and, in the uppermost 10 miles, brookies. Just be sure to keep an eye out for poison oak when tramping the banks here. This river is fly-fishing only from Westfir upstream, and the best time to fish is during the warmest months of summer and into the fall.

East of Oakridge, **Salmon Creek** provides good fishing for wild cutthroat and rainbows as well as stocked rainbows. Nearby **Salt Creek,** which parallels Ore. 58 all the way to Willamette Pass, is a notoriously poor trout stream. A habitat-enhancement program has been attempting to improve the fish habitat on this creek. Rainbows are, however, stocked between mileposts 38 and 48 on Ore. 58.

HIKING & BACKPACKING

French Pete Creek Trail

9.4 miles one-way. Moderate. 2,400-foot elevation gain. Access: The lower trailhead is 10.5 miles south of Ore. 126 on FS 19 (between Blue River and McKenzie Bridge and signed for Cougar Reservoir). The upper trailhead is reached by turning left off of FS 19 and crossing Cougar Dam. From here, drive FS 1993 for 15 miles east to Pat Saddle trailhead. Map: USFS Three Sisters Wilderness.

The battle to save the last big trees in the Northwest has been going on for more than two decades now and this is where it all started. When, in the 1960s, Congress failed to include any lowland old-growth forests in the newly designated Three

Sisters Wilderness, a cry went up for the inclusion of the French Pete Creek drainage. After years of protests by environmentalists, the area was finally added to the wilderness in 1978. The trail follows French Creek through its U-shaped valley, passing numerous groves of ancient Douglas firs and western red cedars.

This trail can be done as a one-way hike if you arrange a car shuttle. Start at the upper trailhead and it's all downhill. If you're looking for an easy hike, start at the lower trailhead and continue as far as you have time and energy to hike. However, if you're interested in seeing some of the oldest and largest trees, and don't mind doing more climbing as you return to your car, start at the upper trailhead and hike down Pat Creek. Roughly 2 miles of hiking will bring you to one of the oldest groves of trees along this trail.

Maiden Peak

11.6 miles round-trip. Difficult. 2,900-foot elevation gain. Access: From the Oakridge Ranger Station, drive 29 miles east on Ore. 58 and turn north on signed Gold Lake Rd. (FS 500). The trailhead is 1.5 miles up this gravel road near the Gold Lake Campground. Map: USGS The Twins and Waldo Lake.

The trail up this perfectly symmetrical cinder cone starts out climbing through dry, open forest with a few views, levels off to a steady climb, switches to a steep climb, and then makes a final steep scramble to the summit of Maiden Peak, the highest point in the region. You'd think that the distance and amount of climbing would keep the crowds away from this one, but that's just not the case. Because the treeless summit of Maiden Peak provides an astounding 360° panorama that takes in every Cascade Peak from Mount Hood to Mount Thielsen and all the large lakes in this region, this is the most popular hike in the area. Although the trail passes a few meadows and snowmelt ponds, most of the route is in forest. Just before reaching the summit, the trees become stunted and windblown, an indication that you don't want to do this hike if the weather is bad. Also near the summit is a small crater. Skyline Creek, passed at 2 miles into the hike, is the only reliable source of water, so carry plenty. Just beyond this creek, cross the PCT and continue another 3.6 miles to the summit.

Twin Peaks

6.6 miles. Moderate. 1,600-foot elevation gain. Access: From Ore. 58 west of Willamette Pass, drive north on FS 5897 (Waldo Lake Rd.) for 6 miles to the marked trailhead. Map: USFS Waldo Lake Wilderness.

So, maybe you aren't up for an 11.6-mile hike that climbs 2,900 feet, but you still want the payoff—a good view. No problem. Try this one. The trail climbs to the summit of a 7,360-foot volcanic peak that actually has two summits (hence the name). This hike starts at the north end of Waldo Lake, so it involves a bit more driving, but about half as much hiking and half as much climbing for a view that is quite a bit more than half as good as the view from Maiden Peak. The trail starts just before the turnoff for Shadow Bay and climbs gradually to cross the PCT in about 2 miles. From here the climb gets a bit steeper, and at the 3-mile point, after passing some small ponds, you reach red cinders and pumice and loop around the crater rim to the north twin. From the summit, you can see the Three Sisters, Mount Bachelor, Broken Top, and all of Waldo Lake. The saddle between the two twins is fun to explore, and if you cross to the south twin, you'll get a completely different view. Retrace your steps to return to the trailhead.

Waldo Lake Trail/South End

3.5–6.5 miles. Easy. 100-foot elevation gain. Access: From Ore. 58 west of Willamette Pass, drive north on FS 5897 (Waldo Lake Rd.) for 6.8 miles, turn left at the Shadow Bay Campground sign, and continue 2 miles to the boat ramp. Map: USFS Waldo Lake Wilderness.

Even though circumnavigating this lake on foot is hardly a wilderness experience (all those motorboats, sailboats, and boardsailors are hard to ignore), sections

of this trail at the north and south end have always been popular day hikes. The full circuit is an overnight trip for most people and along the west shore there are numerous pleasant campsites. Unfortunately, a forest fire in 1996 burned right down to the lakeshore at the north end of the lake, and this section of trail is no longer as pretty or as popular as it once was. So, I suggest doing a day hike at the south end of the lake.

From Shadow Bay boat ramp, follow the bay first east and then south before curving around to head west along the lake's south shore. It's a very easy 3.5-mile round-trip hike to the South Waldo Shelter, which is surrounded by meadows. Shortly before reaching the shelter, the trail reaches a sandy beach with an island just offshore. The water between the island and the beach is a beautiful Caribbean blue. If it's a warm day, it's impossible not to go for a quick dip here. If you're looking for a longer hike, Klovdahl Bay, another 1.5 miles up the trail along the west shore of the lake, makes an interesting destination. Here you'll see the concrete headgates of the diversion tunnel built between 1909 and 1914 by Simon Klovdahl. Had this tunnel been completed, it would have dropped the level of the lake by 25 feet. Luckily for us today, Klovdahl's crew mutinied before the tunnel could be finished. From here, hike back the way you came.

Indigo Lake–Sawtooth Mountain Loop

10.5 miles. Difficult. 2,000-foot elevation gain. Access: From Oakridge, drive 1.3 miles east on Ore. 58, turn south toward Hills Creek Reservoir, and before reaching the reservoir, turn right on FS 21 and continue 32 miles to a left turn onto FS 2154. Continue 9.3 miles (mostly on gravel) to Timpanogas Lake. Map: USGS Cowhorn Mountain.

This loop trail around Sawtooth Mountain is a very rewarding hike. It starts out at popular Timpanogas Lake, climbs easily to the shores of aptly named Indigo Lake, where there is a 1-mile loop trail around the lake, and then makes a rigorous climb up to the summit of Sawtooth Mountain.

Rising 1,400 feet above Indigo Lake, Sawtooth Mountain is a dramatic and rocky backdrop. Until a few years ago, if you wanted to climb to the summit of Sawtooth Mountain, you had to hike back downhill from Indigo Lake almost to the trailhead and then take the Sawtooth Mountain Trail back up. Now, however, it is possible to hike directly up from Indigo Lake by way of the Indigo Extension Trail, which leads 1.5 miles east to Windy Pass. From here, hike south to the shoulder of Sawtooth Mountain and then make your way to the summit for the view down to the lake. Back on the main Sawtooth Mountain Trail, continue for 3.5 miles to regain the trail up from Timpanogas Lake.

HOT SPRINGS

There are two natural hot springs in the Willamette Pass area. **McCredie Hot Springs,** located right on Ore. 58 on the banks of Salt Creek, is by far the more popular and is, in fact, the busiest and most accessible hot spring in the state. Unless you get here very early in the morning on a weekday, don't expect to have any of the many pools to yourself. Personally, I find these springs highly overrated. The traffic noise from trucks roaring by only a few feet away is the worst of it, but the water isn't all that hot either. You'll find the springs down a short path from a huge gravel pull-out 10 miles east of Oakridge.

For peace and tranquility, you'll do better to seek out **Wall Creek Hot Springs.** This small spring is at the end of a quarter-mile trail through mossy old-growth trees. The pool itself is a wide spot in the path beside the small creek that the trail follows from the parking area. The water is clear, though not much warmer than that at McCredie. However, the setting, beneath the big trees, is idyllic. Once again, the earlier you get here, the more likely you are to have it to yourself. To reach the springs, drive 2 miles east of Oakridge, then turn left onto Fish Hatchery Road. Drive 1 mile north to the stop sign at Salmon Creek Road and turn right. In 9 miles turn left onto FS 1934 (signed to Blair Lake) and continue 0.4 miles up

this gravel road to a pull-out on the left with lots of big fir trees.

MOUNTAIN BIKING

The forests around the town of Oakridge are rapidly developing a reputation as one of the premier mountain-biking areas in the Northwest. Many people speculate that this area has the potential to become another Moab. I'm not so sure about that, but I do know that the single-track riding around here is both abundant and superb. Listed below are just some of the best trails. Pick up the mountain-biking trail maps from both the Oakridge Ranger Station and the Rigdon Ranger Station for listings of many other good trails. The former ranger station is on Ore. 58 west of Oakridge, while the latter is on Salmon Creek Road east of Oakridge.

Larison Rock Trail

11.6 miles. Strenuous. 2,400-foot elevation gain. Access: From Oakridge, drive 1.3 miles east on Ore. 58, turn south toward Hills Creek Reservoir, and before reaching the reservoir, turn right on FS 21. After crossing the bridge over the Middle Fork of the Willamette River, turn right and park at the start of a gravel road. Map: USGS Oakridge.

Sometimes nothing will do but a long, hard climb and a freewheeling single-track descent—and that's exactly what this ride delivers. The ascent in this case is now on a superbly paved and little-used forest road that climbs more than 2,000 feet in 5 miles. Start out on FS 21 and in a half-mile turn right onto FS 2102. Sure it's not too exciting slogging away in granny gear, but just when you've had enough of this boredom, the trailhead appears. From here it's a half-mile to the top of Larison Rock, which peaks out above the surrounding forest and provides a view down on Oakridge and the surrounding valleys and peaks. Now comes the fun part. Scamper down off the rocks, saddle up, check your brakes, and let it rip. From here to the bottom of the trail, it's 3.5 miles of steady downhill. At the bottom, turn right onto FS 5852, which in 1.8 miles of almost flat riding will return you to your car.

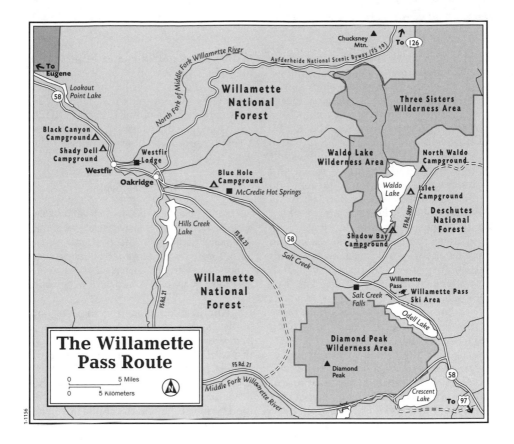

The Willamette
Pass Route

0   5 Miles
0   5 Kilometers

1-1156

Larison Creek Trail

21 miles. Strenuous. 1,200-foot elevation gain.
Access: From Oakridge, drive 1.3 miles east on
Ore. 58, turn south toward Hills Creek Reser-
voir, and before reaching the reservoir, turn right
on FS 21 and drive 3.5 miles to the trailhead.
Map: USGS Oakridge.

For a longer and more scenic ride in the
Oakridge area, try this loop that starts out
on paved forest roads but ends with a
6.5-mile single-track descent. Part of
this ride is on FS 2102, which is utilized
on the Larison Rock ride. Starting from
the trailhead on Larison Cove, an arm of
Hills Creek Reservoir, ride 3 miles back
down FS 21 and turn left onto FS 2102.
Ride up this steep, paved road for 1.5
miles and turn left onto gravel FS 101.
Ride this road through many easy ups and
downs for 9 miles and watch for the
Larison Creek Trail on your left. The
trailhead is in a fairly recent clear-cut, but
don't worry. This devastation will be left
behind as you descend to the old-growth

forests on the valley floor and near the
banks of Larison Cove.

Some of the descent is on fast, smooth
trail while other sections are quite
technical due to the numbers of tree
roots crossing the trail. The best part of
the entire ride is the last 1.8 miles along
the cove, which is dedicated to canoes
and is blissfully quiet. There are even
picnic areas, docks, and campsites here,
all for canoeists. When I rode this trail,
I kept spooking a bald eagle that also
seemed to appreciate the lack of ski
boats on this section of the reservoir. May
you be so lucky. The trail is also quite
popular with hikers, so watch your speed
on corners.

Youngs Rock—Moon Point Loop

18 miles. Strenuous. 3,150-foot elevation gain.
Access: From Oakridge, drive 1.3 miles east on
Ore. 58, turn south toward Hills Creek Reser-
voir, and before reaching the reservoir, turn right
on FS 21 and continue 19 miles to FS 2129.
Map: USGS Warner Mountain.

This loop is my all-around favorite ride in the Oakridge area. It's got everything—a long, slow climb to a viewpoint followed by an equally long but fast descent, meadows full of wildflowers, rocky cliffs, and dense old-growth forest. Start the ride by climbing for 9 miles on FS 2129 to the Youngs Rock/Moon Point trailhead. If you want to add another 4 miles and another viewpoint to your ride, continue climbing on the road for 2 miles to the Warner Mountain lookout. After soaking in the awesome panorama here, ride back down the road to the trailhead. From here on out, it's 6 miles of almost continuous high-speed single-track as you drop every one of those 3,150 feet you just climbed.

As you scream down this trail, don't forget to ride the quarter-mile out to Moon Point for the view of the region (it's less than a mile from the start of the single-track). At about 2.3 miles down the trail, you'll pass the shale-covered slopes of Youngs Rock. Scramble up to the top for a view that includes Diamond Peak, Dome Rock, and Sawtooth Mountain. On the way down you'll pass numerous little meadows, any one of which makes a great lunch spot. Make the ride in July and you'll be rolling through a Monet painting. When the trail bottoms out on FS 21 across from Campers Flat Campground, hang a right and ride back down FS 21 for 2.5 miles to your car.

Rigdon Fitness Trail

4.5 miles. Easy. No elevation gain. Access: 35 miles east of Eugene. Drive 2 miles east of Oakridge on Ore. 58, turn left onto Fish Hatchery Rd., continue 1 mile north, and park on the far side of the Salmon Creek bridge. Map: Not necessary.

If you've never had your bike off the pavement, or if you're simply looking for an easy trail or a place to warm up before a more strenuous ride, try this trail near the Rigdon Ranger Station. Set up as a parcourse fitness trail but evidently not often used for that purpose, the trail has a nice wood-chip surface for much of its length. The trail consists of several loops, all within earshot of Salmon Creek.

With occasional dips and humps and lots of curves, the trail can be fast and fun if you're so inclined, or it can be a leisurely pedal for the whole family. Unfortunately, the floods of 1996 washed out a section that ran alongside Salmon Creek. User detours have been cut around the washout.

Waldo Lake Loop

22 miles. Moderate. 200-foot elevation gain. Access: From Ore. 58 just west of Willamette Pass, drive north on FS 5897 (Waldo Lake Trail) for 6.8 miles to the Shadow Bay Campground turnoff, turn left, and continue 2 miles to the boat ramp. Map: USFS Waldo Lake Wilderness.

Imagine pedaling along the shore of one of the purest lakes in the world. The deep blue waters are studded with sailboats, and in the distance are the forest-blanketed conical peaks of ancient volcanoes. Near shore the water takes on a positively Caribbean hue. At lunch you stop not just for food but for a swim in the chilly-but-bearable waters. Along the route, marshes, islands, tiny coves, and forests remind you what a jewel this lake really is. Not a dream, a reality—the Waldo Lake Trail.

Of all the trails in this region, the Waldo Lake Trail is by far the most scenic, and though it never gains much elevation, it is a moderately difficult ride simply because of its length. Also keep in mind that on the west side of the lake, the trail runs between the lake and a wilderness area (closed to bikes, of course), and it's a long way to help. Be prepared and bring plenty of water and food. If you want, you can even turn the circuit around the lake into an overnight ride. Along the west shore, there are lots of primitive campsites.

There is only one fly in the ointment here—mosquitoes. Throughout the early summer months, mosquitoes plague the lake. Wait until late August or September to do this ride.

Windy Lakes

11.4 miles. Moderate. 650-foot elevation gain. Access: From the Crescent Lake junction on Ore. 58, turn right on FS 60 and follow signs for Crescent Lake campgrounds, keeping to the west side of the lake. Between Tandy Bay and Spring campgrounds, watch on the right for the steep, gated Summit Lake Rd. (FS 6010), a rough dirt road that leads 5 miles to Summit Lake and the trailhead. Map: USFS Diamond Peak Wilderness.

A string of at least 10 remote lakes, each seemingly a different shade of blue and separated by open forests and tiny meadows, make this one of the most idyllic rides in the state. Bring a bathing suit, pick your favorite lake on the outbound leg, and stop to swim on your way back. Lots of short ups and downs and an easy overall gradient make this an incredibly fun ride. Though you can turn it into a loop ride by dropping down to Crescent Lake on the Windy Creek Trail and then climbing back up to your car on Summit Lake Road (FS 6010), I much prefer riding back the way I came.

The trail starts on the shore of Summit Lake, by far the largest lake on this plateau west of Crescent Lake, and ambles along through scrubby forests and patchy meadows, crossing a wooden bridge over a creek before leaving this lake for the many smaller pools down the trail. With lots of ups and downs and more than enough roots and water bars to keep you paying attention to the trail, this is technically a moderately difficult trail. An alternative routing is to start on the Meek Lake Trail, which has its trailhead 1 mile before the trailhead at Summit Lake.

As at Waldo Lake, the mosquitoes in this area are positively terrifying during the early summer. Stay away!

ROAD BIKING

Aufderheide National Scenic Byway (FS 19)

58 miles. Strenuous. 3,000-foot elevation gain. Access: Start this ride at the north end at the Delta Old-Growth Grove.

In a state with an abundance of fabulous road-biking routes, this stands out as one of the very finest. The Aufderheide National Scenic Byway, one of the first in the nation, winds through the forests of the western foothills of the Cascades. Along its meandering route, it passes Cougar Reservoir and Terwilliger Hot Springs, trails through old-growth forests, and runs alongside the swimming hole–filled waters of the North Fork of the Middle Fork of the Willamette River. What this road does not pass is any towns, though it does pass numerous campgrounds.

Don't be deterred by the mileage listed above, which is the total length of the road from McKenzie Bridge to Oakridge. If you aren't up to such a distance, just pick a section that you can handle, or come for a weekend and do a couple of sections. No matter what section you ride, you'll have numerous distractions to get you off your bike. The hot spring is at the north end just off Cougar Reservoir, and the swimming holes are at the south end just a few miles north of Westfir.

SEA KAYAKING & FLAT-WATER CANOEING

Waldo Lake, one of the purest lakes in the world due to its lack of any permanent aboveground water input, is one of the best places in Oregon for a canoe-camping trip. Around the lake are numerous excellent campsites that allow canoeists to spend a day or a weekend exploring the crystal-clear waters. The most popular campsites are the two on Rhododendron Island just off the west shore of the lake. My favorite area for exploring is down at the south end. Put in at the boat ramp at Shadow Bay if you want to explore the little bays and islands down here. Wherever you put in, just be sure you get up early and do your paddling before the winds pick up at 10 or 11am, which they do with astounding regularity.

Though not as remote as Waldo Lake and much more popular with fishermen in motorboats, **Odell Lake** is another popular canoeing lake here in the Central Cascades. Each year in late July, the Odell Lake Canoe Race sends competitors paddling from one end of the lake to the other. The clear waters and a couple of campgrounds along the shore contribute greatly to the appeal.

Gold Lake, just west of Willamette Pass, is another excellent paddling lake in this area. Much smaller than Waldo or Odell, it is a restricted lake, which means no motorboats roaring around. The view from the north end takes in Diamond Peak, and also at this end are the marshes of the Gold Lake Bog Research Natural Area. This is a fly-fishing-only lake.

If you've got an inflatable and a foot pump, consider hiking in a half-mile to 40-acre **Betty Lake,** which is off the road leading to Waldo Lake.

Reservoirs generally aren't the best places to canoe or sea kayak. They tend to attract the waterskiing crowd, and who wants to deal with all that noise? However, **Hills Creek Reservoir** is one exception. Here you'll find the Larison Cove Canoe Area on a long, narrow cove that is closed to boats with motors. Along the 1.5-mile cove, there are several picnic areas, complete with docks and outhouses. At the far end of the cove there are even a couple of campsites. When I was here, I kept spooking a bald eagle that seemed to enjoy the quiet of the cove as much as I did. Larison Creek Trail heads upstream along the creek that feeds this cove and makes a great add-on to a bit of paddling on the cove. You'll find Larison Cove south of Oakridge on FS 21.

SNOWSHOEING

The sno-parks at Willamette Pass provide ample opportunities for exploring on snowshoes. Some of the better hikes are the **Gold Lake** and **Marilyn Lakes** trails, the trails **south of the Gold Lake Sno-Park,** and the trail to **Diamond Falls.** The numerous shelters in this area make this the perfect spot to try a bit of overnight snowshoeing. The **Westview and Bechtel shelters** south of the Gold Lake Sno-Park make good destinations, as does the Gold Lake Shelter.

SWIMMING & TUBING

If you love swimming holes on rivers, then you need to take a drive up the Aufderheide National Scenic Byway. This road parallels the **North Fork of the Middle Fork of the Willamette River.** Along the way there are numerous excellent swimming holes. In fact, once you get north of Westfir, virtually every pull-off along the highway is above a swimming hole. My favorite, however, is about 3.5 miles

north of the Westfir Covered Bridge. One warning—watch out for poison oak at any swimming hole along this river. In some places it's impossible to even get to the river without crashing through the noxious plants.

It may be hard to believe, but several of the lakes in this area actually get warm enough in the summer to offer relatively pleasant swimming. **Waldo Lake,** with its designated swimming areas and miles of shoreline, is the obvious choice here, and the beach at Islet Campground is about the most popular swimming area on the lake. For more secluded swimming, try **Bobby Lake,** which is only 1.5 miles by mostly flat trail from the Waldo Lake Road (the trailhead is 5.5 miles north of Ore. 58). Along the west shore of this lake is a large rock outcropping that angles down into a sandy bottom. This is an ideal place to swim and sunbathe.

On the opposite side of Waldo Lake Road from the Bobby Lake trailhead is the start of the Betty Lake Trail. It's only a half mile to **Betty Lake,** which is almost as nice a place for a swim as Bobby Lake. On the east side of Willamette Pass, **Crescent Lake's Simax Beach** enjoys near-legendary status with my wife, who spent a blissful afternoon here once playing in waters the color of the Caribbean. When the winds blow, you can almost body surf the waves that crash on this beach.

WALKS & NATURAL ROADSIDE ATTRACTIONS

Big Swamp Grove Trail (Middle Fork Trail)

4 miles. Easy. 100-foot elevation gain. Access: From Oakridge, drive 1.3 miles east on Ore. 58, turn south toward Hills Creek Reservoir, and before reaching the reservoir, turn right on FS 21 and continue 32 miles to FS 2153. Follow this gravel road another 3.5 miles to the trailhead. Map: Not necessary.

Located not far from Timpanogas Lake, this trail is long enough to be considered a hike, but the terrain is flat and it's easy enough that kids won't complain too much. The trail loop skirts the edge of Big Swamp, a marshy meadow. The trees along the edges of the swamp—Douglas fir, Engleman spruce, western red cedar, and western hemlock—are up to 350 years old and some reach 6 feet in diameter.

Salt Creek Falls

3.4 miles. Easy. 400-foot elevation gain. Access: 20 miles east of Oakridge on Ore. 58. Map: USFS Diamond Peak Wilderness.

Sure Salt Creek Falls is the second-highest waterfall in Oregon, but that alone is not what makes it worth a stop. Much more than just the height, the moss-draped basalt cliffs and drifting clouds of spray make this 286-foot waterfall one of the most picturesque in the state. The falls are just off the highway and can be seen as you drive eastward toward Willamette Pass. A short paved trail leads down to the falls overlook. From here the 3.4-mile loop trail to secluded, 100-foot-high Diamond Creek Falls begins. This easy trail passes the strangely named Too Much Bear Lake and provides dizzying views into Salt Creek Canyon.

WHITEWATER KAYAKING & CANOEING

This region doesn't have a lot of runnable water; the better stretches tend to be farther west and closer to Eugene. However, there are a couple of noteworthy runs in this area. One is simply fun and can be run by skilled canoeists, while the other stretch is a technical nightmare that only the most skilled Oregon paddlers ever try.

CLASS II TO III

The 10-mile stretch of the **Middle Fork of the Willamette River** from Oakridge down to Lookout Point Reservoir is a superbly fun Class II+ run. The rapids are frequent and long, so don't expect to spend much time just enjoying the scenery. This is a good run for novices to try after they have built up a few skills and some confidence. The only big drawback is the proximity of Ore. 58, from which the roar of trucks can be heard throughout the run. The put-in is at Greenwaters Park on the east side of Oakridge and the take-out is at Black

Canyon Campground on Lookout Point Reservoir. This trip can be done throughout the year and is great in late summer and early fall. In snowmelt season and after heavy rains, Hell's Gate Rapids, always the most challenging rapid on this run, bumps up to a Class III.

CLASS IV & ABOVE

If you're searching for the truly challenging rather than just the highly demanding, then you'll want to check out the unforgiving waters of the **North Fork of the Middle Fork of the Willamette River.** These waters, north of Westfir, are solid Class IV paddling with several Class V rapids thrown in as well. Does a gradient of 250 fpm give you some idea of what we're talking here? Don't even think about it unless you've run waters of this caliber before. What makes this run so tempting is its easy access. You can scout many of the rapids from the road as you drive north from Westfir on FS 19. One of the toughest rapids on this run is The Gorge, which is just below the second bridge north of Westfir. You can avoid this Class IV–V section by putting in at the first bridge above Westfir. The take-out is about a half-mile upstream from Westfir. The uppermost put-in is 4 miles above the second bridge. The total length of these runs is 13.5 miles. This is a rainy-season run.

Campgrounds & Other Accommodations

CAMPING

A certain percentage of campsites at many National Forest Service campgrounds can be reserved at least five days in advance by calling the **National Forest Reservation Service** (tel. 800/280-CAMP). State park campground reservations for both Oregon and Washington can be made by calling **Reservations Northwest** (tel. 800/452-5687). To make a reservation you'll need to know the name of the campground you want to stay at and the dates you plan to visit. The reservation fee for NFS campgrounds is $7.50, and for state parks it's $6.

THE SANTIAM & MCKENZIE PASS ROUTES

If you are heading up Ore. 22 toward Santiam Pass, I would stay away from campgrounds on Detroit Lake, which tend to be noisy with the water-ski and party crowd. Try **Whispering Falls** (16 sites) or **Riverside** (37 sites), which, however, both close down at the end of the summer but are quieter than lake campgrounds during the warm months. Even quieter campgrounds can be found north of Detroit near Breitenbush Hot Springs. These include **Humbug** (22 sites), **Cleator Bend** (9 sites), and **Breitenbush** (30 sites). Hiking and trout fishing are the main attractions of this area. If you can get a reservation to soak in the hot springs at Breitenbush Community, that's reason enough to camp here.

Heading east from Sweet Home, **Cascadia State Park** (26 sites) provides an ideal summertime campsite if you like to swim and splash in rivers. Farther east, **Trout Creek** (20 sites), **Yukwah** (20 sites), and **Fernview** (9 sites) campgrounds provide easy access to the interesting Rooster Rock Trail in the Menagerie Wilderness and the nearby Cone Peak/Iron Mountain Trail.

There are several campgrounds along the McKenzie River on Ore. 126. Of these, the **Delta Campground** (39 sites), set under huge old-growth trees between Blue River and McKenzie Bridge, is one of the finest. Rafters and kayakers tend to gravitate to **Ollalie Campground** (17 sites) and **Paradise Campground** (64 sites), which have the uppermost boat ramps on the river and are east of McKenzie Bridge. Between Paradise and Delta, you'll find **McKenzie Bridge Campground** (20 sites), another good choice in this area.

If you are up this way to hike, mountain bike, or do some flat-water canoeing, there is no better choice than Clear Lake's **Coldwater Cove Campground** (35 sites) on Ore. 126 just south of Santiam Pass junction. Clear Lake is one of the most beautiful lakes in the state. South of here on Ore. 126, the **Trail Bridge Campground** (28 sites) makes a good alternative to Coldwater Cove. It's on a reservoir, but motors are restricted and many of the campsites are walk-in tent sites.

Along the popular McKenzie Pass Highway (Ore. 242), there are only a few campground choices. **Scott Lake Campground** (20 sites), with its picture-perfect view of Middle and South Sister, is by far the best choice if you are tent camping. **Alder Springs Campground** (7 sites), west of Scott Lake, and **Lava Lake Campground** (9 sites), just east of McKenzie Pass on the edge of a lava field, are both good alternatives in this area, especially if you will be hiking into the Three Sisters Wilderness or bicycling over McKenzie Pass.

WILLAMETTE PASS ROUTE

If you are out here to do some mountain biking, there are several campgrounds worth trying along FS 21 (south of Oakridge) and its extensions. These include **Camper's Flat** (5 sites), **Secret Campground** (6 sites), **Sacandaga** (16 sites), and **Indigo Springs** (3 sites). All of these campgrounds provide easy access to the Middle Fork Trail and the Young's Rock–Moon Point Trail. Farther south, there is the **Timpanogas Lake Campground** (11 sites), which is the trailhead for the Indigo Lake/Sawtooth Mountain trail. There is also a hike-in campground just a short distance off the road at **Opal Lake** (1 site), which is near Timpanogas Lake. Just a few miles northeast of here is the **Summit Lake Campground** on a large lake that is also the trailhead for the Windy Lakes mountain-bike trail.

Northeast of Oakridge, there are a couple of more good choices reached by following Salmon Creek Road (FS 24). **Salmon Creek Falls Campground** (14 sites), 5 miles from Oakridge, is in a lush old-growth forest. The campground takes its name from two waterfalls on the creek. Farther east, **Blair Lake Campground** (8 sites) is a tranquil spot that does not allow motorboats. There is a mountain-biking trail here and fairly good fishing for stocked trout. All but one of the sites are walk-in sites.

On Waldo Lake, the **Islet Campground** (55 sites), with its sandy beach, should be your first choice. Since the forest fires in the summer of 1996, the **North Waldo Campground** is no longer a good choice here, so second choice should be **Shadow**

Bay Campground (92 sites) at the south end of the lake. If you have a boat, you can camp on **Rhododendron Island** (3 sites), where there are two designated campsites. There are also many paddle-up campsites on the west shore of the lake.

Gold Lake Campground (20 sites), just west of Willamette Pass on FS 500,is a quiet spot on a pretty lake that doesn't allow motorboats and is fly-fishing only. This is one of my favorite spots in the area. Both mountain-biking and hiking trails start here. Just over Willamette Pass, there are several campgrounds on Odell Lake. The **Sunset Cove Campground** (26 sites) is your best choice if you are here to windsurf. Otherwise, I would opt for the quieter **Odell Creek Campground** (22 sites) at the east end of the lake.

If you are driving the Aufderheide National Scenic Byway (FS 19), **Kiahanie Campground,** 18 miles northeast of Westfir, is a good choice, especially if you are trout fishing. Good choices farther north on this road include **Frissell Crossing** (12 sites), **Twin Springs** (5 sites, no water), **Homestead** (7 sites, no water), and **French Pete** (17 sites), all of which are on the banks of the South Fork of the McKenzie River. French Pete Campground lies at the mouth at French Pete Creek, which was the focus of one of the first battles to save the ancient forests of the Northwest. A hiking trail runs almost the entire length of this creek.

INNS & LODGES

SANTIAM & MCKENZIE PASS ROUTES

Eagle Rock Lodge

49198 McKenzie Hwy., Vida, OR 97488. Tel. 541/822-3962. 6 rms, 2 cottages. $90–$125 double (breakfast included). AE, CB, DC, MC, V.

Located 35 miles east of Eugene, this luxurious lodge is right on the McKenzie River and, consequently, caters primarily to rafters and anglers. However, this is not your average rustic fishing lodge. Rooms are furnished with antiques and original art, and romantic getaways seem almost as popular as active vacations with guests here. Decks and fireplaces and river views all add up to a very memorable setting. Guides and trips can be arranged and river-oriented packages are available.

Log Cabin Inn

56483 McKenzie Hwy., McKenzie Bridge, OR 97413. Tel. 541/822-3432. 8 cabins. $65–$75 double. DISC, MC, V.

Situated on 6½ acres in the community of McKenzie Bridge, this log lodge was built in 1906 after the original lodge, which had been erected in 1886, burned to the ground. In the lodge's heyday, its guests included President Herbert Hoover, Clark Gable, and the Duke of Windsor. Today you can stay in rustic log cabins, all but one of which have their own fireplaces. The one cabin without a fireplace does, however, have a kitchen, which the others do not have.

Belknap Lodge & Hot Springs

North Belknap Springs Rd., Belknap Springs, OR 97413. Tel. 541/822-3512. 10 rms, 4 cabins. $60–$90 room, $35–$60 cabin. MC, V.

At the end of a long day of hiking or mountain biking, a soak in the hot mineral pool here is guaranteed to soothe sore muscles. Set on the bank of the McKenzie, this lodge is an excellent choice if you play hard. The rooms in the main lodge are modern and feature a modern "country" decor. Some have antiques and some have good views of the river. If you're looking for a more rustic (read: very basic) accommodation, try a cabin (you provide the linens). More basic? Try the shelter, pitch a tent, or park an RV. Any way you look at it, the two hot pools are the main attraction.

WILLAMETTE PASS ROUTE

Odell Lake Lodge

P.O. Box 72, Crescent Lake, OR 97425. Tel. 541/433-2540. 12 cabins, 7 rms. $55–$200 cabin, $36–$45 room. MC, V.

Located at the east end of Odell Lake at the lake's outlet stream, this rustic cabin resort makes a good base of operations any time of year. There's a wide range of sizes in the cabins, the largest of which can accommodate 16 people. I like these much better than the rooms, which are quite small and directly upstairs from the dining room. During the summer this is a fishing lodge, and during the winter there are groomed cross-country ski trails. The lake and surroundings also offer good windsurfing, hiking, and mountain biking.

11

CENTRAL OREGON

ENTRAL OREGON, THE NARROW CORRIDOR JUST EAST OF THE Cascades that follows the Deschutes River along its south-to-north drainage from the Diamond Peak area, is essential to the sanity of many wet-side residents. It is to this sunny east-side recreational area that wet-siders flee when the relentless rains become so depressing that not even double lattés can raise their spirits. From the first lowland wildflower hikes of early spring to the last spring-skiing runs down the slopes of Mount Bachelor, this is a four-season destination. Through the summer, hikers and mountain bikers pick their way along trails that lead through forests and meadows to summit vistas and quiet mountain lakes. Rafters and kayakers challenge the rapids of the Deschutes River, the busiest recreational river in the state. In the fall, anglers stalk the Deschutes River's wily steelheads, while around Sisters, aspen groves paint the high country with splashes of gold. At the heart of this region is the community of Bend, the Northwest's only four-season resort community and home to half a dozen golf resorts and the best ski area in the Northwest.

I once asked a friend where she thought central Oregon started. "Over the Santiam Pass," she said. "Yes, but how far over the pass," I insisted. She hesitated, pondering for a moment. "Somewhere west of Sisters, you know, where it starts to smell different."

That's as a good a way as any to describe central Oregon. It just smells different. That smell is, of course, a direct result of what Willamette Valley residents see as central Oregon's most important defining feature—sunshine. Central Oregon lies in the rain shadow of the Cascades, and receives significantly more sunshine per year than the wet west side of the Cascades. An abundance of sunshine means a lack of rain and that is what is responsible for giving central Oregon its distinctive fragrance. Ponderosa pines, junipers, bitterbrush, and manzanita infuse the air with a decidedly different fragrance than do the Douglas firs, western red cedars, vine maples, and rhododendrons of the west side.

Receiving less than half the rainfall of the Willamette Valley, central Oregon marks the beginning of the high desert. Within barely a handful of miles after cresting a Cascade pass, the climatic change begins to make itself evident. Douglas firs immediately give way to lodgepole pines and then the stately cinnamon-barked ponderosa pines. Within a few more miles, the pines disappear and are replaced with junipers that can just barely qualify as trees. Another few miles and there is not even enough rainfall to support these shrublike trees. Bitterbrush, a fragrant sagelike shrub, and grasses become the dominant plants. This is the rain-shadow effect created by the Cascade peaks' snagging of most of the precipitation that drifts in off the Pacific Ocean.

Central Oregon is a land of year-round recreational superlatives. It has the best skiing (both downhill and cross-country, at Mount Bachelor Ski Area), the best rafting (on the Deschutes River), the best fly fishing (again, on the Deschutes River), the best mountain biking (outside Bend), the best rock climbing (at Smith Rock State Park), and, of course, the best weather. Add to this the biggest and best resorts in the state, and dozens of remote campgrounds, and you have a region tailor-made for outdoors enthusiasts of all types from backcountry backpackers to the ski-slope and hot-tub crowd.

The Lay of the Land

Encompassing the eastern slope of the Cascades, central Oregon is a narrow band of land between the lush west-side forests of the Cascade Range and the dry high desert of eastern Oregon. The region's northern boundary is the Columbia River, and for the purposes of this book, I am defining its southern boundary as the junction of U.S. 97 and Ore. 58. Although everyone has a different idea of where central Oregon ends and eastern Oregon begins, I have chosen to define the region's eastern boundary as that land lying along the corridor of the Deschutes River. However, I have also included Smith Rock State Park and Newberry National Volcanic Monument, both of which lie a bit east of the Deschutes River. In general, this definition encompasses those lands that western Oregonians see as their weekend sunshine getaway region. The **Deschutes National Forest** covers much of this land, though much also falls within the **Confederated Tribes of the Warm Springs Reservation.** In the north, private lands flank the narrow corridor of public land on either bank of the Deschutes River, and between Redmond and La Pine, much of the land is also private. It is within this latter area, a triangle of land that includes Sisters as its third corner, that most of the region's resorts are to be found.

Central Oregon could also be described as the lands of the **Deschutes River.** This north-flowing river, together with the **Little Deschutes River,** parallels the Cascade Range for nearly 200 miles, draining all the eastern slopes of the Cascades from Diamond Peak northward. Along its length, the Deschutes takes on many different characters. In its lower stretch, the river carves its way through the thick layers of basalt that covered much of eastern Oregon 13 million years ago. Today these brown canyon walls rise above slopes covered with gray-green bitterbrush that scents the air with a fragrance similar to that of sagebrush. This northern region of central Oregon is less visited than the lands farther to the south, due in large part to the fact that outside of the narrow band of land along either bank of the river, most of the land here is privately owned ranchland.

Roughly 100 miles south of its mouth, the Deschutes is joined by the region's two other important rivers, the Metolius and the Crooked. Today, at the point where these three rivers come together, lies **Lake Billy Chinook,** a large three-armed reservoir formed by the Round Butte Dam. The reservoir flooded these three rivers' deep canyons, creating a water wonderland similar to the desert reservoirs along the Colorado River in Arizona. Here, brown cliffs rise 400 feet straight from the water.

Flowing crystal-clear from huge springs at the base of Black Butte near the town of Sisters, the **Metolius River,** a designated National Wild and Scenic River, is one of the purest and coldest rivers in the state. Though short, at only 30 miles from its source to Lake Billy Chinook, it generates a lot of interest among both anglers and paddlers. Flowing through parklike groves of old ponderosa pines and eventually forming the southern boundary of the Warm Springs Reservation, this river is a remote jewel of a waterway. The **Crooked River,** which forms the third arm of Lake Billy Chinook after flowing across much of eastern Oregon, is another of the region's prime trout streams. However, this river is best known as the river beside which rises **Smith Rock,** one of the country's foremost rock-climbing spots. Preserved as a state park, Smith Rock is a jumble of orange rock rising 400 feet above the Crooked River, which here more than lives up to its name as it meanders back and forth around the cliffs. These rocks, comprised of rhyolite lava and welded tuff (volcanic ash), are all that remain of a larger volcanic peak that once bordered the river.

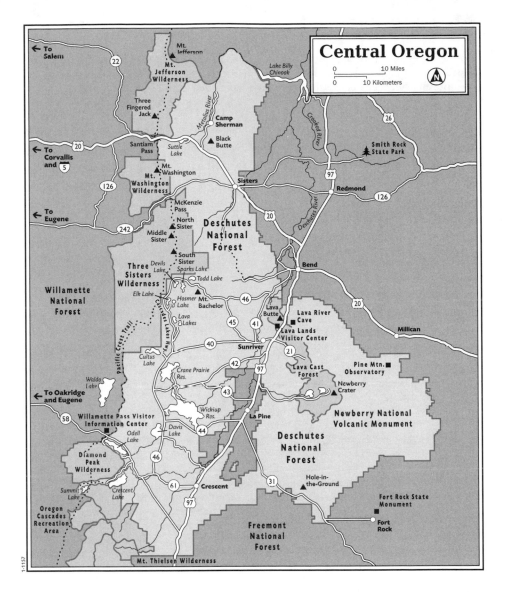

1-1157

Black Butte on the west and Smith Rock on the east mark the effective northern limits of central Oregon's lava lands. To the south of these two landmarks lies a volcanic landscape unequaled in the U.S. outside of Hawaii. Not only are the high Cascade peaks that dominate the western horizon of volcanic origin, but so too are the region's hundreds of buttes—cinder cones that stretch from Black Butte north of Sisters to Newberry Crater east of La Pine. The oldest of these cinder cones date back some 12,000 years, while the youngest are roughly 7,000 years old. Counted among the latter is **Lava Butte,** which rises 500 feet above the surrounding landscape south of Bend. As one of the youngest cinder cones in the region, Lava Butte still flaunts its volcanic heritage in its bare red and black cinder slopes. The variation in color from black to red was caused by the oxidation of minerals in cinders that repeatedly were hurled skyward and then fell back into the still-erupting crater of Lava Butte. However, the most famous of the region's hundreds of cinder cones is 9,065-foot **Bachelor Butte,** which rises 2,700 feet above the surrounding forests and is the site of the best skiing in the Northwest. This massive cone dates back 12,000 years and shows signs of ice-age glaciation on its slopes. Other noteworthy cinder cones in the region include **Pilot Butte,** a state park in Bend, and **Tumalo Mountain,** which lies across FS 46 from Bachelor Butte.

Although central Oregon as defined in this chapter is bordered by eight major Cascade peaks—Mount Hood, Mount Jefferson, Three Fingered Jack, Mount Washington, the Three Sisters, and Broken Top—that line up along its western horizon, four of these mountains (Hood, Jefferson, Three Fingered Jack, and Washington) are looked upon as mountains of the western Cascades. It is the latter four peaks that define central Oregon's high country. These mountains—10,094-foot **North Sister,** 10,053-foot **Middle Sister,** 10,358-foot **South Sister,** and 9,175-foot **Broken Top**—are visible from points throughout the region, but from nowhere is the view as dramatic as it is from U.S. 20 between Sisters and Bend. From this stretch of road the peaks rise in rugged, snow-clad grandeur above flat, brown rangeland. In truth, central Oregon has a quite valid claim to these peaks. Although they are accessible from the McKenzie Pass area in the west-central Cascades, the most common approach is from FS 46, which runs westward from the town of Bend. Although volcanic in origin, these four peaks are far more rugged and ragged than such obviously volcanic peaks as Mount Hood and Mount Jefferson. This different character is due in large part to the glaciation that has repeatedly scoured away at these peaks during various ice ages, and in the case of Broken Top, to a violent eruption that blew out much of this peak in the same way that Mount St. Helens erupted. Of these four peaks, which date back 2–2.5 million years, North Sister is the oldest and South Sister is the youngest. It is this latter peak that is the most likely of the region's volcanoes to one day awaken from its dormancy. For the time being, it is the easiest of the area's peaks to scale.

The land surrounding these peaks all falls within the Three Sisters Wilderness, an expansive wilderness area that is one of the most popular in the state. Within its boundaries are not only glaciated peaks but also hundreds of lakes. These lakes range from tiny high-altitude glacial tarns to much

larger lakes such as the immensely popular **Green Lakes.** The largest concentration of lakes lies to the southwest of South Sister amid forested rolling hills at around 5,000 feet in elevation. However, the region's most heavily visited lakes lies outside the wilderness boundary.

To the west of Bend, FS 46 and FS 42 together form an 80-mile loop road known as the **Cascade Lakes Highway.** As the name implies, this road connects a series of lakes lying just south and east of the Three Sisters Wilderness in the Deschutes National Forest. Ten lakes and two large reservoirs are the focal points of this highway and together provide the region with a wealth of summertime recreational activities. Although fishing is the most popular activity, canoeing, windsurfing, and swimming are also popular. All of these lakes in one way or another show signs of the region's volcanic activity. **Sparks Lake** has no outlet but instead drains through the porous volcanic soil beneath it. **Devils Lake,** lying at the foot of a massive wall of lava, is fed by springs that well up from beneath the lava field flanking the lake. The two **Twin Lakes,** which have neither surface inlets nor outlets, fill craters that were formed when lava exploded out of the ground.

South of Bend, the landscape takes on an otherworldly appearance as lava flows from volcanic eruptions 6,000–7,300 years ago blanket the land in shades of black and red. Stretching for 7 miles from Newberry Crater to Lava Butte lies a rift that spawned many of the region's cinder cones and poured forth the lava flows that are now protected within the **Newberry National Volcanic Monument.** One such lava flow, pouring out of Lava Butte, covered the land to the north and blocked the Deschutes River in several places. Over the centuries, the river has worn its way through these lava dams, leaving behind **Benham, Dillon, and Lava Island falls.** The most recent volcanic activity in the region took place 1,300 years ago, when lava poured out of Newberry Crater to form the **Big Obsidian Flow.** This astounding field of volcanic glass provided the region's Indian tribes with materials for tools and weapons, and was traded to other tribes throughout the Northwest.

Parks & Other Hot Spots

Cove Palisades State Park

5 miles west of U.S. 97 between Madras and Redmond. Hiking, boardsailing, fishing.

Set on the shore of Lake Billy Chinook (actually a reservoir), one of the most dramatic lakes in Oregon, this park is primarily used by anglers and water skiers who have come to fish and play beneath the high, brown cliffs that rim the lake. Located at the confluence of the Metolius, Deschutes, and Crooked rivers, Lake Billy Chinook consists of the three flooded arms of the aforementioned rivers. The park is one of the most popular in the state, due in large part to its location on the sunny east side of the Cascades within weekend-trip distance for Portlanders. The lake is best known for its kokanee fishing. There are a couple of short hiking trails here, plus the strange, untracked tableland atop a plateau called The Island.

Smith Rock State Park

3 miles east of Terrebonne off U.S. 97. Rock climbing, hiking, whitewater kayaking, fishing.

One of the nation's foremost rock-climbing meccas, Smith Rock rises from the scrublands of central Oregon like a huge orange-tinged castle. Its 400-foot crags rise up on the north side of the Crooked River, which snakes along in wide loops through the park. In the summer of 1996 a fire swept through the park, burning junipers and manzanitas that once gave the park's entrance area so much character. A little charred wood and ash has, however, had absolutely no effect on the numbers of climbers who flock to these walls from all over the world. For flatlanders, there are hiking trails, and kayakers sometimes paddle through here as they take on some of the nastiest water in the state, which lies just downstream from the park in the Crooked River Gorge. There is a "climber's bivouac" area, which is a nice way of saying, "If you ain't here to climb, don't even think about camping here."

Three Sisters Wilderness

South of McKenzie Pass off Ore. 242 and west of Bend off the Cascade Lakes Hwy. (FS 46). Tel. 541/549-2111. Hiking, fishing.

Encompassing the Three Sisters (North, Middle, and South) as well as Broken Top, this is one of the most popular wilderness areas in Oregon. The area's jagged, glacier-clad peaks are popular with mountaineers, and its lakes are among the prettiest in the state. Pumice fields dotted with hardy, ground-hugging plants are an unusual and fragile feature of this wilderness. In the northwest part of the wilderness, lava flows create an eerie landscape. Trailheads for this wilderness are found along the south side of the McKenzie Pass highway, south of the town of Sisters, and west of Bend. As far as I'm concerned, this wilderness *is* the central Oregon Cascades.

Newberry National Volcanic Monument

South of Bend between 4 and 22 miles along U.S. 97. Lava Lands Visitor Center, 58201 S Hwy. 97, 11 miles south of Bend. Tel. 541/593-2421. Hiking, mountain biking, canoeing, fishing, cross-country skiing.

Although Newberry Crater and its two lakes are not even remotely as visually breathtaking as Crater Lake, the two areas share much in common. First of all, neither is actually a crater. They are *calderas,* massive depressions formed when volcanoes emptied their entire contents and then collapsed. Here at Newberry Crater, there are two lakes—Paulina Lake and East Lake—instead of one, and motorboating is allowed. The forests surrounding these lakes are not the dense stands of ponderosas you find elsewhere in this region, and in fact are rather bleak and spindly at the east end of East Lake. However, to make up for this arboreal inadequacy, the monument abounds in lava flows, lava caves, and other volcanic features that together make a trip to Hawaii this winter altogether superfluous (well, maybe). The park's most fascinating feature, in my opinion, is the Big Obsidian Flow, which lies on the south side of the

Outdoor Resources

RANGER STATIONS

Bear Springs Ranger District
73558 Hwy. 216
Maupin, OR 97037
Tel. 541/328-6211

Bend/Fort Rock Ranger Station
1230 NE Third St., Suite A262
Bend, OR 97701
Tel. 541/388-5664

Sisters Ranger Station
P.O. Box 249
Sisters, OR 97759
Tel. 541/549-2111

EQUIPMENT SHOPS

Bend Mountain Supply of Oregon
2600 NE Division St., Bend
Tel. 541/388-0688

Sisters Mountain Supply of Oregon
148 Hood St., Sisters
Tel. 800/463-7590 or 541/549-3251

Eurosports
115 SW Hood St., Sisters
Tel. 541/549-2471

caldera between Paulina Lake and East Lake. A short trail leads up through this sparkling ridge of black volcanic glass. The park also has many miles of more strenuous hiking trails, two of which are also open to mountain bikes. One of these latter trails leads up to Paulina Lake along Paulina Creek, while the other is a trail along the entire rim of this vast caldera.

The Sisters Area, Smith Rock State Park & the Lower Deschutes River ◆ What to Do & Where to Do It

BIRD WATCHING

Within a few miles east of the crest of the Cascades, the landscape begins to grow drier, and barely 30 miles from the lush forests on Mount Hood, there is so little rainfall that only scrub junipers, bitterbrush, and other high-desert plants can grow. In this dry landscape, riparian areas are magnets for birdlife, and few places in the region exert a greater avian magnetic pull than the riparian zone around the **Oak Springs Fish Hatchery.** Here, springs drop from the canyon walls above the Deschutes River and support a dense greenway of white oaks, cottonwoods, and alders. Among these trees, you're likely to see Bullock's orioles, western tanagers, western kingbirds, screech owls, and many migratory songbirds, which pass through the area in May and June. To reach the fish hatchery, drive 6 miles north from Maupin on U.S. 197 and turn east at the sign. It is another 3 miles from the highway. One warning: The road into the fish hatchery is too steep for two-wheel-drive passenger cars during the wet winter months.

About 10 miles south of Madras on U.S. 26, the **Rimrock Springs Wildlife Area,** with its wetlands, riparian area, and drier uplands, attracts an amazing variety of birdlife including mountain bluebirds, Townsend's solitaires, yellow-headed blackbirds, ring-necked ducks, snipes, golden eagles, and great horned owls. Spring and fall are the best times to visit if you are looking to add some songbirds to your life list.

For good raptor watching, try **Smith Rock State Park,** where various trails can get you to bird's-eye elevations. Golden eagles, prairie falcons, and rough-legged and red-tailed hawks all frequent these cliffs, as do swallows, swifts, rock doves, and canyon wrens. The eagles and hawks nest here during the summer months, so keep scanning the cliff ledges and you might find a nest. In winter, bald eagles are sometimes spotted here. You'll find the park off U.S. 97, 3.3 miles east of Terrebonne.

The **Cold Springs Campground,** 4 miles west of Sisters on Ore. 242, is a good place to look for neotropicals that spend their summers here on the dry east side of the Cascades. The campground is in a stand of old-growth ponderosa pines interspersed with quaking aspens (these latter trees harbor the greater numbers of birds). Among the birds you might hope to see here are McGillivray's, yellow-rumped, and yellow warblers; black-backed, pileated, hairy, downy, and white-headed woodpeckers; and red-breasted and pygmy nuthatches.

CROSS-COUNTRY SKIING

In addition to the ski trails listed below, there are numerous sno-parks in the Santiam Pass area. See chapter 10 for details.

UNGROOMED TRAILS

Upper Three Creek Lake Sno-Park

2.6–12 miles. More difficult–most difficult. 1,500-foot elevation gain to Three Creek Lake. Access: From Sisters on U.S. 20, drive south on Elm St., which becomes FS 16. The sno-park is 11 miles from town. Map: USFS Three Sisters Wilderness Map.

Located south of Sisters, this sno-park provides access to the well-designed though not-very-scenic Warren's Loop and Nancy's Loop trails. They are intermediate-level trails and are each 2.6 miles long. Because they share a leg, they can be combined in a figure eight. For more challenging skiing and some truly outstanding views, continue south from these loops on the Snow Creek–Three Creek Loop Trail, which together add up to a 9-mile loop from the parking area. The Snow Creek Trail section of this loop leads through numerous meadows and open areas with views. If you can handle skiing 2 miles of trail each way with the snowmobiles, you'll reach the finest views in the area by skiing uphill to Three

Creek Lake and adjacent Three Creek Meadow. From here you can gaze up at the imposing cliffs of the Tam McArthur Rim, which rises 1,200 feet above the lake. The meadows and surrounding areas are perfect for a bit of off-trail exploring, but remember, it's 6 miles back to the car.

McKenzie Pass Lava Fields

12+ miles round-trip. Most difficult. 1,300-foot elevation gain. Access: From Sisters, drive west on Ore. 242 for 8.4 miles to a locked snow gate. Map: Geo-Graphics Three Sisters Wilderness.

If you've been over McKenzie Pass in the summer, you know what to expect—views, views, views. The big difference here between summer and winter is in color, or lack thereof. By summer the lava fields are jet black, but by winter, well, they're snow white. Though the ski up Ore. 242 is not that interesting (and is used by snowmobiles), the rarely-seen views awaiting you at McKenzie Pass more than make up for less-than-perfect skiing conditions. From the locked gate 8.4 miles west of Sisters, it is a 6-mile all-uphill ski to reach the lava fields, with only a single brief view at the midway point to keep your hopes up. However, once you're here, you aren't going to want to leave, so start early, bring lots of food and water, and plan to do some exploring. Head out across the bowls and slopes and have fun. The best time to do this ski is in the spring when the snow is good and firm. You also might be able to shorten your uphill ski a bit as well. If you head out this way in the middle of winter, pick a day that is absolutely clear with no chance of a change in the weather. This is no place to get lost. Also, a thin coating of new snow, say 2 to 4 inches on top of some hardpack, is just about perfect, and maybe someone else will have been good enough to have already broken trail for you. If you've got lots of stamina and are confident on skis, and the weather is good, don't pass up an opportunity to ski this route.

FISHING

Fishing in northern central Oregon means only one thing—**the lower Deschutes**

River. This stretch of river, from Pelton Dam to the Columbia River, is managed primarily for wild steelhead and the famed redside rainbow trout. Together these two types of fish provide fly anglers with nearly year-round action. This is a big, powerful river, with lots of rapids (which are popular with rafters). Because much of this section of the Deschutes is inaccessible except by boat, drift-boat fishing trips are very popular. Though fishing from boats or floats is prohibited, a boat can get you to some of the more remote holes.

From the mouth of the river upstream to several miles above Maupin, there are several good access points. From the mouth of the river at Deschutes River State Recreation Area (just off I-84 at exit 97), a trail leads up the east bank for 24 miles to Macks Canyon. Motor vehicles are prohibited on this trail, but mountain bikes are permitted and can negotiate all but the last few miles. Above Macks Canyon, a gravel road provides motor vehicle access from the south (off of Ore. 216 at Sherar's Bridge). More river access is possible above and below Maupin, where roads, some paved, some gravel, parallel the river.

The best steelhead fishing is from below Sherar's Falls to the mouth, though this does not mean that there aren't also plenty of steelhead above the falls. Summer steelhead are in the river from July through December, with the peak fishing season running September and October. Several very effective steelhead flies have been developed for the Deschutes, and you'd be well advised to have some on hand. These include the Deschutes Skunk, Deschutes Demon, and Macks Canyon.

The Deschutes' wild redside trout, a type of rainbow, are such fighters that friends of mine would rather drive three hours from Portland to fish the Deschutes than toss a fly in any nearer river. The best fishing for redsides is above Sherar's Falls, where current regulations restrict catches to two fish per day between 10 and 13 inches. This should give you an idea of how tightly managed the river is. You'll also catch the occasional brown or bull trout, but redsides are by far the most common.

The Deschutes has spring and fall salmon runs, but as elsewhere in the Columbia Basin, these runs have been severely reduced in recent years and fishing seasons have been closed at times. The 3-mile-long stretch of river below Sherar's Falls is the best salmon-fishing area and is the only section of the river that is open to bait fishing.

The region's other premier trout-fishing stream is the **Crooked River,** which flows into the Deschutes from the east at Lake Billy Chinook. The most productive and easily accessible stretch is just downstream from Bowman Dam, which forms Prineville Reservoir. Here the cold, clear lake water and a large insect population make for good fly-fishing. If you head out this way to fly-fish, be sure you come armed with a good supply of scuds (flies that imitate freshwater shrimp). If you ask any Crooked River angler what sort of fly to use here, you'll likely get a response something like, "Try a scud. If that doesn't work, try a scud. If that still doesn't work, try a scud." To reach this stretch of river, head east from Redmond to Prineville on Ore. 126 and then turn south on Ore. 27, which parallels the river for more than 20 miles. There are numerous campgrounds along this stretch of river.

Lake Billy Chinook, a reservoir at the confluence of the Metolius, Deschutes, and Crooked rivers, is remote and surrounded by high cliffs. The lake is well known as one of the better kokanee lakes in the state. In fact, there are so many kokanee in this lake that special catch limits are in effect; you can take up to 25 per day! The hope is that by allowing anglers to reduce the kokanee population, the remaining fish will grow larger. This is the only place in the state where bull trout can be kept (check regulations). Smallmouth bass fishing can also be productive here.

Boasting near legendary status, the spring-fed **Metolius River** is one of the hardest streams in Oregon to fish. Its cold, clear waters support populations of rainbow, bull, brown, and brook trout, and there is even a spawning run of kokanee that come up from Lake Billy Chinook, into which the river empties. The upper section of the river is fly-fishing only, and it is here that dedicated anglers try the hardest to match wits with the river's many wild trout. The crystal-clear water makes stealthy approaches imperative and a good reading on the current fly hatch is also a necessity. Cold, clear waters, abundant food, and fishing pressures over the years seem to have combined to make fish in the Metolius extremely wary of taking any artificial lures. You have to present the lure perfectly just to get a strike, but if you do get a bite and land a fish, it's likely to be larger than average. The Metolius is also known for its Dolly Varden trout, which are large and elusive. Try the shadows along deep banks and toss a big muddler minnow (a large, brown wet fly) at the bank. Also be aware that the left bank in the lower section of the river is on the Confederated Tribes of the Warm Springs Reservation and is closed to the public. Good luck.

For fly-fishing supplies and advice on fishing the Deschutes, stop by the **Deschutes Canyon Fly Shop,** 7 North Hwy. 197, Maupin (tel. 541/395-2565), or the **Gorge Fly Shop,** 416 Oak St., Hood River (tel. 541/386-6977). For fly-fishing supplies and advice on fishing the Metolius, check at **The Fly Fisher's Place,** 230 Main St., Sisters (tel. 541/549-3474), or the **Camp Sherman Store and Fly Shop** (tel. 541/595-6711) in Camp Sherman.

If you'd like a guide to take you out on the Deschutes, try **Travis Duddles** at the Gorge Fly Shop in Hood River (tel. 541/386-6977), **Glenn Summers** (tel. 541/296-5949), **Rick Wren's Fishing on the Fly** (tel. 800/952-0707 or 541/382-1264), or **Young's Fishing Service** (tel. 541/296-2544). **Somali Ranch,** P.O. Box 218, Tygh Valley, OR 97063 (tel. 503/483-2207), has 11 miles of private river access on White River for wild native Oregon redside trout.

HIKING & BACKPACKING

Lower Deschutes Trail

4.2 miles. Easy. 600-foot elevation gain. Access: Take exit 97 off I-84, 15 miles east of The Dalles. Map: USGS Wishram and Emerson.

Although the mouth of the Deschutes River, where it flows into the Columbia River, marks the eastern end of the Columbia Gorge National Scenic Area, this spot seems quite removed from the gorge.

Here you are solidly in the sagebrush country of central Oregon. The three hiking trails within this state recreation area provide a good overview of the Deschutes River Canyon. One trail leads along the riverbank past sumac thickets, meadows, and marshy areas. The other trail climbs up the side of the canyon and parallels the river at a high enough elevation that you gain a different perspective on the canyon and hike through dry sagebrush. The third trail climbs to Ferry Spring and the best views. All three trails can be linked together into an easy loop.

Start by hiking along the river on the Atiyeh River Trail for 1.4 miles to Moody Rapids (the last rapids on the river), then switchback up to the Upper River Loop Trail for 0.4 miles, where there is a good viewpoint beside the abandoned road that now serves as a mountain-bike trail. From here you can look upstream to Rattlesnake Rapids. If you had stayed on the river trail at Moody Rapids, you would have reached these rapids in 0.8 miles. From the Upper River Loop viewpoint, cross the dirt road and begin a 500-foot climb that leads to another, even better viewpoint. From here, the trail follows the rim of the canyon for a little ways, passing Ferry Spring, before dropping down to rejoin the Upper River Loop Trail. Turn right on this trail to return to the parking area. If you do this hike on a warm day, be sure to keep an eye out for rattlesnakes. Spring and fall are the best times; summers are just too hot for hiking amid all this rock.

Smith Rock State Park Trails

6.6 miles. Easy–moderate. 200–1,100-foot elevation gain. Access: From U.S. 97 in Terrebonne (6 miles north of Redmond), drive 3.3 miles east following signs to the park. Map: USGS Redmond.

Rising orange and jagged from the gray sagebrush lands of central Oregon, Smith Rock is impossible to ignore when driving north on U.S. 97 from Redmond and Bend. It catches the late afternoon light, and with some sort of magical magnetic pull, it captures the attention of drivers and forces them to turn their steering wheels at the small sign for Smith Rock State Park.

Although this park is most popular with rock climbers, there are also miles of hiking trails that follow the meandering Crooked River and climb up among the cliffs and crags for stupendous views. Though at first it seems you need to be carrying rock-climbing gear to gain entrance to this park, don't be put off by the hundreds of rock jocks who crowd here on weekends. You won't be able to escape them, but you can at least appreciate the rocks they climb as you keep your hiking boots firmly planted on terra firma.

There are two main hiking routes, both of which start 0.5 miles from the parking area on the far side of the footbridge over the Crooked River. The easier route goes left from the bridge and follows the bank of the river and eventually leads to a view of the park's most famous climbing rock— Monkey Face. This rock does indeed resemble a monkey's face when the light is just right. If you want to get a closer look at the cliffs that draw all these climbers, there are a couple of trails that lead up to the bases of some rock walls. Turn around north of Monkey Face at some balancing rocks. This route is a 6.6-mile out-and-back hike.

If you want a more adventurous hike, with 1,000 feet of climbing, go straight (instead of left) after crossing the bridge. This trail immediately begins climbing up a steep slope on a series of staircases. If it's summer, this is a miserably hot climb; be sure to bring water. When you finally reach the top, you'll find yourself atop a cliff-edged ridge. You can wander around marveling at the views and then head back for a hike of just over 2 miles or you can continue up the ridge and then angle around to the east. This trail eventually leaves the park and follows a dirt road south for a mile before picking up another park trail that starts near a canal. The trail leads steeply down to the river and returns you to the bridge. This loop covers a total of 5.3 miles.

Black Butte Trail

4 miles round-trip. Moderate. 1,650-foot elevation gain. Access: From U.S. 20, 6 miles west of Sisters, turn north on FS 11 and drive 4 miles to a signed left fork onto FS 1110. From here it is another 4 miles to the trailhead at the end of the road. Map: USGS Black Butte.

You just can't help but want to climb Black Butte. There it is, in your face every time you come around a bend driving between Santiam Pass and Sisters. A picture-perfect volcanic cone, Black Butte takes its name not from lava as do other cinder cones in the region, but from the dense forests of ponderosa pines that cover its flanks. The trail to the summit is one of the most popular in central Oregon, and rightfully so. The trail starts out on the west side of the butte and eventually circles around to the east side before reaching the summit. Along the way, openings in the trees keep offering different panoramas. Once you reach the barren summit, however, they all merge into one all-encompassing 360° view that seems to take in all of central Oregon as well as more Cascade peaks than I care to name. Do this hike in July and you'll be hiking through wildflowers for much of the route. At the top is a fire lookout that is staffed throughout the summer. Why not stop in and say hello?

Chambers Lakes

14.2 miles round-trip. Strenuous. 1,800-foot elevation gain. Access: From Sisters, drive west on Ore. 242 for 1.4 miles and turn left onto FS 15. Drive this gravel road for 15.2 miles to the Pole Creek trailhead. Map: Geo-Graphics Three Sisters Wilderness.

If the thought of the crowds at Green Lakes (see "Hiking & Backpacking" in "The Bend Area, Cascade Lakes Highway & Newberry National Volcanic Monument—What to Do & Where to Do It," below) has you thinking you might as well go to Seattle for the weekend, but you're dying to hike to some high-elevation lakes with knock-your-boot-socks-and-liners-off views, don't despair. You do have an option. The Chambers Lakes, a quartet of lakes in the saddle between Middle and South Sister, are surrounded by signs of recent glaciation and themselves are dyed amazing shades of blue by glacial flour.

I must admit, this landscape is not quite as benign as the soft pumice plain that surrounds Green Lakes, but it is certainly as dramatic, if not more so. The reason this hike isn't as popular as the hike to Green Lakes is that it is long and boring for much of the way. By late summer it is also hot and dusty, so bring lots of water, and drink it. After 5 miles of hiking through uninteresting forest (with the exception of a view of Middle Sister as you cross Squaw Creek), the trail finally climbs onto a sandy ridge, from which there are fabulous views. The 2-mile hike along this ridge to Camp Lake is a joy, at least when the wind isn't blowing, and tiny ground-hugging flowers color the gray ground. Because winds tend to funnel between South and Middle Sisters at this point, this area is almost always windy. However, there are somewhat sheltered campsites in the trees along the east shore of the lake. From Camp Lake, it is cross-country, up steep pumice slopes, to get views of the Chambers Lakes, which usually have chunks of ice floating on them even in late summer.

Tam McArthur Rim

5 miles round-trip. Moderate. 1,200-foot elevation gain. Access: From Sisters, drive south on Elm St., which becomes FS 16, for 15.7 miles. There is a parking area off the gravel road that leads to the Driftwood Campground. Map: Geo-Graphics Three Sisters Wilderness.

Named for Lewis "Tam" McArthur, who was secretary of the Oregon Geographic Names Board from 1916 to 1949, this 500-foot-high cliff serves as a dramatic backdrop for Three Creek Lake and Little Three Creek Lake. The hike to the top of the rim is not all that difficult, and hikers are rewarded with stunning views of the Three Sisters and Broken Top. In fact, you can see every major peak from Mount Adams southward to the Three Sisters.

The top of the rim is a fairly wide plateau that starts at about 7,100 feet. Consequently, only stunted trees can withstand the harsh winters of this rocky landscape. Once the trail reaches the rim, after a steep climb from the lake, it climbs much more gradually. An amazing viewpoint, a promontory surrounded on three sides by cliffs, makes an ideal turnaround point. However, if you have been bewitched by this flower-speckled high plateau, you can continue exploring to the west for more than 2 miles, which will bring you to an unusual butte named Broken Hand, from which it is just over 1,000 feet to the summit of Broken Top on a difficult climbers' trail (don't even think about it unless you know what you're doing and have climbing equipment). To get back, return the way you came.

HORSEBACK RIDING

Sisters fancies itself the wild West (in tasteful pastels), so if you get caught up in the spirit of things and just have to get back in the saddle, there are of course a couple of local stables to accommodate your need to play cowboy. **Black Butte Ranch Stables** (tel. 541/595-2061), located 7 miles west of Sisters off U.S. 20, offers rides through old-growth ponderosa to meadows with views of Mount Jefferson and the Three Sisters. A one-hour ride is $24. If you long to ride the purple sage (and green juniper) of the high desert, schedule a ride through **Eagle Crest Equestrian Center,** 1522 Cline Falls Rd., Redmond (tel. 541/923-2072), which offers one- and two-hour rides. Longer rides often head down into the Deschutes River canyon.

MOUNTAIN BIKING

With the exception of the Lower Deschutes River Trail, the mountain-bike rides in this section are all in the vicinity of the town of Sisters. This particular area is as much of a mountain-biking mecca as Bend, and trails tend to be well maintained and well marked. Mountain bikes can be rented in Sisters at **Sisters Mountain Supply of Oregon,** 148 Hood St. (tel. 800/463-7590 or 541/549-3251), and **Eurosports,** 115 SW Hood St. (tel. 541-549-2471).

Deschutes River Trail (Lower)

32 miles. Easy–moderate. 600-foot elevation gain. Access: Take exit 97 off I-84 east of The Dalles and follow signs 2 miles to the park. Map: USGS Wishram, Emerson.

Though this trail doesn't offer the sort of challenging climbs and steep descents that experienced mountain bikers crave, it does offer great central Oregon scenery, including rolling brown sagebrush hills, rugged basalt cliffs, and of course, the green waters of the Deschutes River. The trail starts in Deschutes River State Park and follows the east bank of the Deschutes River on what was once a railroad bed. The surface varies from packed dirt to jagged rocks, and, in the rainy months, includes a few shallow stream crossings. For much of the trail's length it remains high above the river, but there are spots where it dips down close enough that you can easily walk to the bank. Be alert for rattlesnakes.

About 2.5 miles from the start, you pass a section of trail where the railroad was cut into the basalt cliffs 40 to 50 feet high. At about 3.8 miles, you'll pass under 60–70-foot-high columnar basalt cliffs in which the basalt cooled in amazing flowing patterns that have cracked. Farther along you encounter more cliffs. Around 8 miles from the trailhead, watch for a large rapid in the river. This new rapid was formed in the summer of 1995 when a flash flood sent rocks crashing down from the hills on the opposite shore. Around 11 miles up the trail, you'll come to an abandoned and weather-beaten old Victorian farmhouse adjacent to some active corrals. At around 12 miles, the trail is surrounded by layered cliffs hundreds of feet high. Continuing another 4 miles will bring you to Macks Canyon, the current turnaround point of this trail. There is talk of bridging this gap with a trestle to accommodate hikers, mountain bikers, and horseback riders as well as to allow firefighters access to the area beyond Macks Canyon.

Green Ridge Trail

20 miles round-trip. Strenuous. 2,000-foot elevation gain. Access: From Sisters, drive 6 miles west on U.S. 20, turn right onto FS 11, and then left onto FS 1120. Continue 1 mile to the trailhead. Map: USFS Sisters Ranger District Map.

Sure, 2,000 feet is a bit of a climb, and granted, some of the trail is pretty steep, but once you make it to the top of Green Ridge, the terrain just rolls along with gentle ups and downs, which leaves you free to soak up the views. These encompass Mount Jefferson, Three Fingered Jack, and far out into the terra incognita of the Warm Springs Indian Reservation. This trail consists of good single- and double-track, and the ride back down from the ridgetop is the second highlight (after the views). The turnaround point is the fire lookout tower 10 miles from the trailhead. If there is anyone staffing the lookout when you show up, be sure to pay a visit. The view from here is the ultimate. To get back to your car, just head back the way you came. Sure, you could make a loop on logging roads, but none can compare with the trail.

Butte Loops Trail

11 and 13 miles. Moderate–strenuous. 500–1,300-foot elevation gain. Access: From Sisters, drive 6 miles west on U.S. 20 to the FS 11 and Indian Ford Campground. Alternatively, you can continue 3.5 miles on U.S. 20 to FS 2060 (George McCalister Rd.) and park on the south side of the highway. Map: USGS Black Butte or get mountain-bike map at Sisters Ranger Station.

Black Butte, the perfectly conical volcanic butte rising above the ponderosa forest due east of Three Fingered Jack and the main Cascades, dominates the entire Sisters region and is a magnet for hikers bound for the summit and its 360° panorama. Mountain bikers also head for Black Butte, but rather than heading to the summit, they circle the butte on old logging roads that have been closed to motorized vehicles and are now part of the roads-to-trails program that has made this area such a mecca for mountain bikers.

There are two Black Butte loops. The easier Lower Butte Loop, 11 miles long and climbing roughly 500 feet, loops back and forth along the south and west slopes of the butte. I prefer the more challenging and slightly longer Upper Butte Loop, which provides a few views, albeit not as grand as those from the summit, but views nonetheless, and passes through impressive stands of old-growth ponderosa pines. Bring plenty of water.

Sisters Mountain Bike Trail

16 miles. Easy. 200-foot elevation gain. Access: Start in downtown Sisters on U.S. 20. Map: A map detailing local mountain-bike trails is available at the Sisters Ranger Station.

This fairly easy trail starts about a quarter-mile south of Sisters on Elm Street (FS 16), but the ride is best started from downtown, where there is plenty of parking. Heading south on Elm, you'll see the trail on the left just after crossing over a small stream. This trail is fast and fun for the most part, with generally flat terrain and only a few rocky sections at the start of the trail. Luckily the trail is well marked as it crosses numerous jeep trails in the 5-mile section leading up to Peterson Ridge. The forest thoughout this section is mostly thinned, young pines. Not too picturesque, but this ride is mostly about the trail and not the scenery.

At 2.5 miles you cross a bridge of Squaw Creek Canal and then in another 2.5 miles begin climbing Peterson Ridge. From the top of the ridge, at a few rocky outcroppings that make perfect resting spots, there are great views of the Three Sisters, Mount Washington, Three Fingered Jack, and Black Butte. What you won't see from here is Sisters, which can be a bit disconcerting, since you really aren't that far from town. Nothing but forest seems to lie to the north. Continue on, following bike symbols and passing lava piles and more mountain views. After circling a particularly large pile of lava, the trail loops around and heads back to Sisters on the trail you rode out on.

PACKSTOCK TRIPS

Sisters is the llama capital of the Northwest, and ranches outside this western-theme town seem to have more llamas per square mile than Peru. Though these camel relatives are popular pack animals, there are surprisingly few llama-packing companies in this region. If you'd like to explore with a llama for company and to carry your gear, contact **Oregon Llamas** (tel. 541/595-2088).

ROAD BIKING

Sisters is the starting point for one of the finest bike rides in the Northwest. There are also some shorter rides possible in the area. Out near **Camp Sherman,** there are many miles of paved forest roads that see little traffic. A ride from Suttle Lake to Camp Sherman and on down the Metolius River as far as Lower Bridge Campground, where the pavement ends, makes a good day trip (32 miles). Alternatively, you could start in Camp Sherman and ride downriver, or start at the Head of the Metolius overlook. Most of this is fairly flat riding through open ponderosa pine forests.

McKenzie Pass (Sisters to McKenzie Bridge)

41 miles. Strenuous. 3,000-foot elevation gain. Access: This one-way route starts in Sisters at the junction of U.S. 20 and Ore. 242.

Though it's a grueling climb up to McKenzie Pass on Ore. 242, few over-the-mountains road-biking routes in the Cascades are as gratifying as this one. What makes this ride so memorable is the otherworldly landscape that is the payoff for pedaling all the way up to the pass. Here, a vast lava field stretches off in all directions. The jumbled black rocks create a landscape unlike any other in the state. The best way to do this ride is to start in Sisters and head west up to the pass. Although the lava fields are more striking when approached from the west, this involves more climbing and likely starting farther from the pass. If you have two cars, you can do a shuttle over the pass; if not, coast back down the way you came.

ROCK CLIMBING

Maybe the climbs aren't as long as those in the Yosemite Valley and maybe the rock isn't as clean as that Sierra granite, but neither of these factors has stopped **Smith Rock State Park** from becoming one of the world's top climbing areas. Walk the trails that lead to the park's hundreds of climbs and you'll hear quite a few languages other than English. Rising like a castle above the rolling high desert country just east of Terrebonne (yes, it is beautiful country), Smith Rock is much more than such a simple name implies. Comprised of volcanic tuff and rhyolite, it is a complex of pinnacles, columns, and massive walls covering 623 acres on a horseshoe bend in the aptly named Crooked River. As the single best climbing area in the Northwest, it attracts a lot of local climbers. Add to this the international crew, and, on a sunny spring weekend, you'll find hundreds of people heading up the rock.

Spring is the best season here. Summer can be scorchingly hot. In fact, during the summer of 1996 the park did indeed get scorched as a fire swept through it, burning the juniper, sage, and manzanita. Today, the once-beautiful high-desert landscape is nothing but ash, right up to the bases of the most popular climbing walls. However, it shouldn't take too many years for the area to green up again, and besides, when your nose is six inches from the rock, who cares what the land behind you looks like.

The obviously named and extremely photogenic **Monkey Face,** a massive 400-foot-tall column of rock rising above the river, is the quintessential Smith Rock climb. If you want to really challenge yourself, try the 5.13d route known as East Face of Monkey Face. Another climb here, known as Just Do It, ranks as a 5.14c and is one of the hardest climbs in the U.S. But don't worry—there are literally hundreds of easier climbs here.

Arrive early on weekends if you want to get a parking space. There is no official campground within the park, but there is a climbers' bivouac area that even has hot showers. No sleeping in cars is allowed. The daily park admission is $3 and the campsite fee is $4.

Before heading out here, you should pick up a copy of the *Climber's Guide to Smith Rock* (Chockstone Press, 1992) by Alan Watts. This is the Smith Rock bible and describes in detail the hundreds of routes among these rocks. You can pick up this book and other climbing supplies at **Redpoint Climbers' Supply,** 975 Smith Rock Way (tel. 800/923-6207 or 541/923-6207), at the corner of U.S. 97 in Terrebonne, and **Rockhard Climbing and Clothing Gear,** 9297 NE Crooked River Dr. (tel. 541/548-4786), right outside the park entrance. This latter shop is also famous for its huckleberry ice cream. If you've never done any climbing or want to improve your skills, both **First Ascent Climbing School & Guide Service** (tel. 541/548-5137) and **Vertical Ventures** (tel. 541/389-7937) offer classes here at Smith Rock.

SNOWSHOEING

For a longish, fairly strenuous walk, try climbing **Black Butte.** The Black Butte Trail proper is 2 miles long and climbs 1,600 feet. However, you won't likely be able to drive as far as the trailhead, so you'll need to add some mileage onto the 4-mile return trip on the trail. Try to pick a day when the snow level is fairly high, and you'll avoid a lot of trudging up the road.

SWIMMING & TUBING

Although it never gets very warm, **Three Creek Lake,** 16.3 miles south of Sisters on FS 16, is a picturesque lake set at the foot of dramatic Tam McArthur Rim. There are two campgrounds on the lake. In Sisters, FS 16 is Elm Street. Much warmer water can be found on a narrow stretch of the **Deschutes River near Cline Falls State Park.** This popular swimming hole is banked by bedrock that has been worn and smoothed by the action of the river over the centuries. The river carves a narrow stream through these rocks, and the current is so slow that it is possible to swim upstream. The main drawbacks here are noise from traffic on the bridge high overhead and the amount of litter. Otherwise, it is a very pleasant place to cool off. This swimming hole is below the Deschutes River bridge 4 miles west of Redmond on Ore. 126.

Farther north, you'll find beaches with designated swimming areas in **Cove Palisades State Park** on **Lake Billy Chinook.** Because this lake is popular with motorboats, it tends to be very noisy. To reach the park, follow signs from U.S. 97 about 8 miles south of Madras.

WALKS & NATURAL ROADSIDE ATTRACTIONS

Sherar's Falls

Access: From the town of Tygh Valley 7 miles north of Maupin on U.S. 197, drive 8 miles east on Ore. 216 to Sherar's Bridge.

Located at Sherar's Bridge, these impressive falls are the largest on the lower Deschutes River. The falls, which are visible from the road, are best visited during the middle of the day when the sun shines down into the narrow north–south canyon. For thousands of years Native Americans have fished for salmon at these falls. Today you can still see Indians fishing from seemingly flimsy wooden platforms built over the falls. Using dip nets, they catch salmon in much the same way they have since before recorded time.

White River Falls

0.6 miles. Easy. 200-foot elevation gain. Access: From the town of Tygh Valley 7 miles north of Maupin on U.S. 197, drive 4 miles east on Ore. 216 and turn into the Tygh Valley Wayside. Map: Not necessary.

Located on the White River 2 miles before this designated Wild and Scenic River flows into the Deschutes, these falls consist of three separate cascades in a narrow basalt gorge. The trail, which starts near the top of the 80-foot-high uppermost falls, leads down to the base of the lowest falls. It is possible to explore farther downstream, but poison oak is rampant through this canyon.

Crooked River Gorge

Access: Located 4 miles north of Terrebonne on U.S. 97.

The Crooked River, as it passes under U.S. 97 north of Redmond, carves a deep, narrow gorge that looks as though it could have been lifted straight out of the canyon country of southern Utah. There's a big rest area beside the gorge, with a paved path along the rim. Don't pass up an opportunity to gaze down into this almost-grand canyon.

Head of the Metolius

Access: West of Sisters on U.S. 20/Ore 22, turn north at the Camp Sherman sign and follows signs for the "Head of the Metolius."

The Metolius River, diminutive, pristine, and crystal-clear, is one of central Oregon's natural wonders. It wells up almost full-size from deep underground without so much as a trickle of introduction and races off downhill to its confluence with Lake Billy Chinook. The spot where the river emerges from its mysterious underground source is an often-visited short walk through an open forest of mature ponderosa pines near the community of Camp Sherman. These springs well up at the base of Black Butte on the butte's north side, and within a few yards the Metolius is a full-blown river. The springs are well marked and are just a short walk on a paved trail from the parking lot. Because it is a spring-fed river, the Metolius supports populations of several species of trout and is one of the state's most famous (and most difficult) trout streams.

WHITEWATER KAYAKING & CANOEING

Running the entire length of central Oregon from south to north is the Deschutes River, one of the busiest rivers in the Northwest. This river's character is very different in its upper and lower sections, but throughout its entire length it is a ruggedly beautiful stream. The lower 100 miles of river from U.S. 26 at Warm Springs are big and fairly wide with a strong current and numerous large Class III rapids. For this reason it is particularly popular with rafters. The river's popularity has brought restrictions in recent years in an attempt to control the watery traffic jams that occur on summer weekends. It is now necessary to get a Deschutes River Boater Pass before launching a boat on this stretch of river. Permits are available at sporting goods and rafting stores in Maupin and The Dalles. Two tributaries of the

Deschutes, the Metolius River and the Crooked River, are also runnable.

If you'd like to take a kayaking class in this region, contact **All Star Rafting & Kayaking** (tel. 800/909-7238, 503/235-3663, or 541/395-2201), which offers two-day beginner and intermediate classes throughout the summer.

CLASS III

The **Lower Deschutes River,** a designated National Scenic River, begins below Lake Billy Chinook at the U.S. 26 bridge just east of Warm Springs. From this put-in point, there are just under 100 miles of superb paddling, interrupted only once by the Class VI Sherar's Falls, 53 miles downriver from the U.S. 26 bridge. The Deschutes, from here to the mouth at the Columbia River, is the most popular stretch in the state, with numerous rafting companies running day trips on an 18-mile section on either side of the town of Maupin. In order to run either section of the Lower Deschutes in a single trip, you'll need raft support for a two- to three-day trip. However, it is also possible to bite off smaller sections of the river and do them as day trips. Of course, the most popular run would be the same stretch that the rafting companies do. This run starts just below Buckskin Mary Falls and includes such rapids as Boxcar, Wapinitia, Oak Springs, and the Elevators. For a shorter run with good road access, try putting in at Maupin and paddling down to the take-out above unrunnable Sherar's Falls.

Though small, the cold, clear **Metolius River** is one of the most fascinating rivers in the state. Fed by huge springs at the base of Black Butte, this river gushes from the ground fully grown and maintains its uniform size, temperature (around 43° F), and clarity all the way to the flat waters of dammed Lake Billy Chinook, only 30 river miles from the Metolius's source. Most boaters skip the uppermost 6 miles or so, both because of the lack of whitewater and because this section is heavily used by fly anglers, with whom boaters can come into conflict on this narrow stream. If you're looking for some fun Class III paddling, put in at Gorge Campground, 1 mile below which is the Gorge Rapid. Below here there are a couple of low bridges to be aware of, as well as other possible put-ins/take-outs. It is 7 miles from the Gorge Campground to the Lower Bridge Campground, and because a rough dirt road runs along the river for 8 miles below Lower Bridge Campground, it's possible to make a run of up to 15 miles without having to drive a long shuttle. Below Lower Bridge Campground, there is lots of Class II and III water. Just don't miss your take-out, because after the end of the dirt road, it's 9 miles down to Lake Billy Chinook with a car shuttle of around 40 miles. Oh yeah, and there's a Class IV rapid in the middle of it all.

CLASS IV & ABOVE

The **Crooked River** is the toughest river in this region—solidly Class III and IV for its 36 runnable miles, and at high water, the Class IV water bumps up to Class V. Running through the Crooked River Gorge, one of the ruggedest and most inaccessible canyons in the state, this river is not to be taken lightly. Only expert paddlers should even contemplate it and then only in the company of someone who knows the river. For a full description of this run, consult The Mountaineers *Soggy Sneakers, A Guide to Oregon Rivers,* which is written by members of the Willamette Kayak and Canoe Club.

WHITEWATER RAFTING

The **lower Deschutes River,** from the U.S. 26 bridge outside Warm Springs down to the Columbia River, is one of the most popular stretches of water in Oregon. Flowing through a dry sagebrush canyon lined with basalt cliffs, this section of the Deschutes provides lots of Class III rapids, and at almost 100 miles in length, multiday rafting trips are possible. So popular has this river become in recent years that weekends are bumper to bumper with rafts on the most popular stretches (on either side of Maupin).

Numerous rafting companies offer one-day trips on the Deschutes. These splash-and-giggle trips usually start at Harpham Flats just upstream from Maupin and end just above the impressive Sherar's Falls. Most companies also offer two- and three-day trips as well. Rafting companies operating on the lower Deschutes River include the following:

All Star Rafting (tel. 800/909-7238, 503/235-3663, or 541/395-2201), which also rents rafts and offers kayaking classes; **C&J Lodge** (tel. 800/395-3903 or 541/395-2404), which also operates a bed-and-breakfast inn for rafters in Maupin; **Deschutes River Adventures** (tel. 800/723-8464), which also rents rafts; **Deschutes Whitewater Services** (tel. 541/395-2232 or 541/395-2647), which also offers raft rentals and car shuttles; **Ewings' Whitewater** (tel. 800/538-RAFT), which also offers a combination rafting and mountain-biking trip; **Rapid River Rafters** (tel. 800/962-3327 or 541/382-1514); **Fantastic Adventures** (tel. 800/449-5640 or 541/389-5640); and **Cascade River Adventures** (tel. 541/593-3113 or 541/389-8370). Expect to pay around $65 for a one-day trip and up to around $390 for a three-day trip.

WILDLIFE VIEWING

If you're the kind of person who is thrilled simply to catch a glimpse of big trout and salmon, pay a visit to the Metolius River, where big rainbow trout can be seen beneath the Camp Sherman bridge on FS 1419. The Metolius also has a run of kokanee salmon that swim up from Lake Billy Chinook to spawn each year in September and October. You can tell these fish during spawning season by their distinctive red coloring.

The Bend Area, Cascade Lakes Highway & Newberry National Volcanic Monument ◆ What to Do & Where to Do It

BIRD WATCHING

The best bird-watching spot in the area is **Crane Prairie Reservoir,** where ospreys are so common that there is a designated osprey-viewing area on the west side. Here you are likely to see osprey nests and much osprey activity. Bald eagles, cormorants, spotted sandpipers, and terns can also be seen here. Ducks and geese are common. Expect to see wood ducks, scaups, goldeneyes, American wigeons, green-winged teals, and pintails. The reservoir is 54 miles southwest of Bend on the Cascade Lakes Highway (FS 46); the viewing area is a short walk from the parking lot. Another good Crane Prairie birding area is located at the Cow Meadow Campground at the north end of the reservoir.

BOARDSAILING

Though it can't compare with the windsurfing up in the Columbia Gorge, there is good sailing at Sunset View Beach on Elk Lake, which is 30 miles west of Bend on the Cascade Lakes Highway. The wide expanses of Wickiup Reservoir are also good for windsurfing, as are the deep waters of Paulina Lake in Newberry National Volcanic Monument. Board rentals and lessons are available from **Cascade Lakes Windsurfing** (tel. 541/389-8759).

CROSS-COUNTRY SKIING

Dry east-side snow, open forests, rolling terrain, and miles of trails combine to give the Bend area the best cross-country skiing in the state. Combine this with the occasional breathtaking view and the state's finest Nordic center, and you have a sure-fire combination for fun winter weekends. Cross-country skis can be rented at **Mount Bachelor Nordic Center** (tel. 541/382-2442) and a dozen or so other ski shops, most of which are along the roads leading from downtown Bend toward Mount Bachelor.

GROOMED TRAILS

Mount Bachelor Nordic Center

56 kilometers. Easy–most difficult. 100-foot elevation gain. Access: The Nordic center is located on the north side of Mount Bachelor's West Village parking lot, 22 miles west of Bend on the Cascade Lakes Hwy. (FS 46). Fee: $9.50. Map: Trail maps available.

This Nordic center at the base of Bachelor Butte offers 56 kilometers of groomed trails on a network of loop trails that provide an assortment of terrains and distances to please skiers of all levels. Groomed both for skate skiing and diagonal striding, this is the region's premier skate-skiing track and many races are held here throughout the winter. The wide trails provide ample space for passing and are so extensive that the crowds disappear among the numerous interconnected loops. A shelter near the far end of the intermediate trail system provides a place to warm up if you haven't already worked up a sweat. If you're an advanced skier, you can stride right onto Blue Jay's Way just outside the Nordic center for a challenging, if short, loop. Otherwise, you'll have to head to the far end of the intermediate trails to find some track to test your abilities. All in all, these trails are well worth the cost of the trail pass.

UNGROOMED TRAILS

Virginia Meissner Sno-Park

Up to 18 miles. Easy–more difficult. 350-foot elevation gain. Access: 13 miles west of Bend on the Cascade Lakes Hwy. (FS 46). Map: Bend Ranger District Winter Ski Trail Guide.

This is the closest sno-park to Bend and is ideal for novice skiers. With the exception of the Shooting Star Trail, which is rated "Most Difficult" in the downhill direction, all the trails are suitable to beginning skiers. Most of the trails are on forest roads, and though there are few views, the big cinnamon-barked ponderosa pines add a bit of visual interest. The Tangent Loop (5.9 miles) and the Wednesdays Trail (4.2 miles) have good basic loops that provide access to other trails if you want to add more miles. It is also possible to connect to the Swampy Lakes trails from here. This sno-park is named for Virginia Meissner, an avid local cross-country skier who taught classes and led Wednesday ski tours for many years. Meissner loved wildflowers, and that's where the names of the trails here come from.

Swampy Lakes Sno-Park

Up to 22 miles. Easy–most difficult. 180–900-foot elevation gain. Access: 16 miles west of Bend on the Cascade Lakes Hwy. (FS 46). Map: Bend Ranger District Winter Ski Trail Guide.

With four skier shelters scattered along more than 22 miles of loop trails, this is the most popular cross-country skiing area in the Bend area. As at other sno-parks, there are trails for all levels of ability and of varying lengths, so you can choose one to suit your skills. For a moderately easy 4-mile loop, the Swampy Lakes Loop is hard to beat. The trail passes through gently rolling forest of lodgepole pine with a few short, steep stretches that are difficult when the trail is icy and rutted. The destination is the wide expanse of shallow, marshy Swampy Lakes, across which this loop trail passes both at the north and south ends. The shelter is on the far side of the lake from the trailhead and a few hundred yards through the forest.

If it's a sunny day and views are what you're after, try the easy Nordeen Loop, an easy trail with great views! This loop trail covers 4.9 miles, and from the shelter at its far end, offers views across the dry plains of central Oregon and southeast to Newberry Crater. For a longer trail that will appeal to intermediate skiers, take the 4.6-mile Swede Ridge Loop, which leaves the Swampy Lakes Trail 1 mile from the sno-park. As the name implies, this trail climbs Swede Ridge, following gently graded roads to a shelter in a clear-cut with good views. The rest of the loop is on trails rather than roads and requires a bit more skill. The Swede Ridge Trail rejoins the Swampy Lakes Loop trail at the north end of Swampy Lakes.

If your downhill skills are good, and you're looking for a challenging trail that includes lots of climbing, consider the trail to the top of Vista Butte. This is a 7-mile round-trip route and involves 920 feet of climbing. However, the view from the top is well worth the effort.

Dutchman Flat Sno-Park/Mount Bachelor Parking Lot

Up to 15 miles. Easy–difficult. 350-foot elevation gain. Access: 22 miles west of Bend on the Cascade Lakes Hwy. (FS 46). Map: Bend Ranger District Winter Ski Trail Guide.

Dutchman Flat is the last sno-park before the Mount Bachelor Ski Area and provides access to the area's most varied and enjoyable marked ski trails. However, I prefer starting onto this area's trail not at the sno-park but at the Mount Bachelor Nordic Center, where you can ski a half-mile section of groomed ski track without having to pay a use fee. This brief taste of groomed trails may tempt you to forsake the backcountry on a day when the snow is fresh, deep, and untracked. There is a lot of variety in the terrain here. My favorite route in the area leads up to scenic Todd Lake on the Todd Lake Trail and then climbs the steep, forested mountain-side above the lake (on the Todd Ridge Trail) to Big Meadow, where there are acres and acres of flats to be skied. From here, the Big Meadow Trail leads downhill through Little Meadow to the Water Tower Trail and from there back to either the Nordic center or the sno-park.

Alternatively, it is possible to ski back on the 370 Road, which is, unfortunately, a designated snowmobile route. However, it is the fastest, most direct route back down. The road can be a real challenge, but can also be fast and fun if you are a strong intermediate skier. This entire route covers roughly 7 to 7.5 miles. For a shorter ski or to add some more miles, just link together some of the many interconnected trails north of Dutchman Flat. You can also ski from here eastward to Swampy Lakes on the Flagline Trail, which makes an interesting 8-mile route if you have a car shuttle.

Tumalo Valley Ski Trails

Up to 7.6 miles. Easy. 120-foot elevation gain. Access: 13 miles west of downtown Bend (take Galveston Ave. west and continue on Skyliners Rd.). Map: Bend Ranger District Winter Ski Trail Guide.

Starting at the site of the first ski hill in central Oregon, these trails don't always have enough snow to be skiable, but when they do, they offer a less crowded alternative to the sno-park trails on the roads to Mount Bachelor. There are only two short loop trails (1 and 2 miles), but it is an unmarked

road ski that is the main reason to venture out here. From the Skyliner Snow Play Area, it is 2.3 miles up FS 4603 to Tumalo Falls and the South Fork Shelter. Although the route passes through the still-regenerating area of the 1979 Bridge Creek Burn, the sight of the 85-foot-high waterfalls at the end of the trail is still a rewarding spectacle. From here ski back the way you came. It is also possible to ski from this area up to the Swede Ridge Shelter and connect to the Swampy Lakes trails.

DOWNHILL SKIING & SNOWBOARDING

Downhill skis and snowboards can be rented at Mount Bachelor and at a dozen or so ski shops between downtown Bend and the edge of town on the road leading to the ski area.

Mount Bachelor

22 miles west of Bend, on the Cascade Lakes Hwy. (FS 46). Tel. 800/829-2442 or 541/382-2442 (541/382-7888 for snow report). 54 trails; 10 chairs (including 6 high-speed detachable quads); 3,100-foot vertical drop. Lift hours: Mon–Fri 9am–4pm, Sat–Sun and holidays 8am–4pm. Adult lift tickets $35.

If you've ever seen a photo of Mount Bachelor (the mountain is officially called Bachelor Butte), you've known that one day you would, *you must,* take on these slopes. A cinder cone, 9,065-foot Bachelor Butte is perfectly conical and rises above treeline to create a vision of downhill perfection. Because Bachelor is on the east side of the Cascades, the snow is lighter than at most other Northwest ski areas and there is more sunshine. (Powder and sunshine? Sounds like the Rockies, doesn't it?) Consequently, this is about the only destination ski area in Washington or Oregon and has developed a national reputation. Though not yet as popular as Aspen or Sun Valley, Mount Bachelor has lured U.S. Ski, Cross-Country, and Snowboarding teams here to do their training.

With dozens of great runs and six high-speed quad chairs, you'll get plenty of runs in even on a crowded holiday weekend, and believe me, holiday weekends get crowded. If you're looking for some untracked powder, you're more likely to find it on the east side of the mountain, so head straight for the lifts that service the Sunrise Lodge. On days when the Summit Express lift isn't running, the Rainbow Chair will get you up above treeline to open slopes and untracked bowls. Unfortunately, this is not an express chair. When the Summit isn't open—which unfortunately is a rather frequent occurrence—advanced skiers head to the Outback area and up the small cinder cone to the west of the Red Chair. Skiers and boarders with suicidal tendencies will find the tree skiing here is as good as it gets. Snowboarders will find a snowboard park down the Chipper run off the Skyliner Express chair. In the winter of 1996–97, a new express quad chair opened up more steep runs on the northwest slope of the mountain.

Keep in mind that the ski season here usually lasts right up to the Fourth of July! Day care for children 6 weeks and older is available. The free Mount Bachelor Super Shuttle (tel. 541/382-2442) operates between Bend and the ski resort and leaves from the corner of Colorado Avenue and Simpson Street, where there is a large parking lot.

FISHING

Central Oregon offers some of the best fishing in the state, from deep-lake fishing for Mackinaw to fly-fishing on small creeks for little rainbows. The lakes along the Cascade Lakes Highway seem to lure the majority of anglers, but there is also good fishing along various stretches of the Deschutes River. However, this upper section of the Deschutes has nowhere near the reputation of its lower stretches. The many small hike-in lakes in the Three Sisters Wilderness also provide many good fishing opportunities.

Fly anglers in search of a good trout stream have several choices in the Bend area. First and foremost is, of course, the **Deschutes River.** Although not restricted to fly-fishing in the Bend vicinity, it is the preferred method, and the river lends itself well to this style of fishing. Upstream from Bend, the river changes character several times. The waters immediately up

from town are big and powerful and pass over several waterfalls. With numerous access points on both sides of the river and a trail that follows the west bank for nearly 9 miles from the Meadow Picnic Area to Benham Falls, this stretch is particularly popular with Bend residents.

Between Benham Falls and Wickiup Reservoir, there are 43 miles of river popular with drift boaters. However, keep in mind that this stretch is broken up into several specific sections by unrunnable waterfalls. Small rainbows make up the majority of the catch between Bend and Wickiup Reservoir, with some large browns pulled in occasionally. Although short (only 3 miles), the stretch of river between Wickiup and Crane Prairie reservoirs is a superb fly-fishing area flowing through meadows. The wild brook trout here can reach 5 pounds, and there are also some browns from Wickiup Reservoir. Upstream from Crane Prairie Reservoir to the river's source in Little Lava Lake, the Deschutes is little more than a creek, but the fly-fishing is still good for small rainbows and brook trout.

The **Fall River,** a short river that feeds into the Deschutes below Pringle Falls, is fly-fishing only and is one of the prettiest little streams in the region. FS 42, between Sunriver and Wickiup Reservoir, follows this river for much of its length, providing access. Rainbow, brook, and brown trout are all taken from this stream, with rainbows and browns being stocked.

The dozen lakes along the **Cascade Lakes Highway** (FS 46) are favorite fishing destinations in this region during the six or seven months that this road is clear of snow each year. The waters vary from small natural lakes to huge reservoirs. Consequently, there's a good variety of fishing opportunities available.

Sparks Lake, a large shallow lake formed when a lava flow blocked a creek, is one of the most picturesque lakes in the area, with Broken Top and Bachelor Butte visible from its waters. This is a fly-fishing-only lake, and though motors are allowed on the lake, they are prohibited while trolling. The lake's brook trout never get too big because the lake is only 10 feet deep at its deepest. Try the deepest waters during the late summer.

Of the many lakes on the Cascade Lakes Highway, none has a more far-reaching reputation than **Hosmer Lake.** This hidden jewel of a lake has been stocked with Atlantic salmon and also contains brookies and rainbows. To protect this unusual fishery, the lake is fly-fishing only and no motors are allowed. Atlantic salmon are catch-and-release, but other fish can be kept. Because the salmon, which can run 24 inches or more, tend to stay in deep water or at the mouth of the inlet stream at the north end of the lake, some sort of boat or float is a necessity here. Hosmer Lake is actually two lakes joined by a narrow channel. The upper lake is the shallower of the two sections. Surprisingly, this is where you'll find the salmon during the summer, when they are attracted to the cold waters near the mouth of Quinn Creek. In October, the fish move down to the deep water of the lower lake for the winter.

Of the two **Lava Lakes (Big and Little),** Big Lava is the more productive lake. Both lakes hold brook and rainbow trout. **Cultus Lake,** which is 200 feet deep, is primarily fished for its Mackinaw trout, which can reach 20 pounds. However, these big fish, which mostly keep to the deep water, are never easy to catch. Nearby **Little Cultus Lake** is good for browns and rainbows.

If you've got a boat and want to try for some big rainbows, head for **Crane Prairie Reservoir,** where these trout often reach 24 inches and 10 pounds. However, it is nearby **Wickiup Reservoir** that is the most productive and popular of the region's many lakes. Here, coho salmon and rainbow trout are stocked annually, and brown trout and kokanee populations sustain themselves. This reservoir is so large, with the best fishing in the submerged river channels out in mid-lake, that a boat is almost a necessity. Fluctuations in water level make fishing here a real challenge (the fish move around a lot). Easier fishing for stocked rainbows can be had within only a few hundred yards of Wickiup Reservoir's north shore at **North and South Twin lakes.**

For big deep-water fish, try **Paulina Lake** and **East Lake,** both of which are located in Newberry National Volcanic Monument, east of La Pine. In Paulina Lake, the brown trout and kokanee both grow to immense proportions. The state record for each has come out of this lake. East Lake, though it, too, produces trophy brown trout, is better known as a rainbow lake.

Fly-fishing supplies are available in Bend at **The Fly Box,** 1293 NE Third St. (tel. 541/388-3330), and **The Patient Angler Fly Shop,** 55 NW Wall St., Bldg. B (tel. 541/389-6208), and in Sunriver at **Sunriver Outfitters,** 56805 Ventura Lane, Sunriver Business Park (tel. 541/593-8814). These shops can also arrange guides and classes.

If you're not familiar with the local waters and decide you want to hire a guide to show you where to hook into a big one, try **John Garrison** (tel. 541/593-8394), **Deschutes River Outfitters** (tel. 541/388-8191), **High Cascade Descent Guide Service** (tel. 541/389-0562), **High Desert Drifters Service** (tel. 541/389-0607), or **Rick Wren** (tel. 800/952-0707 or 541/382-1264). Expect to pay between $125 and $175 for a day of fishing. Deschutes River Outfitters also operates a fly shop and offers rentals and instruction.

FLAT-WATER CANOEING

With its abundance of lakes, both large and small, the **Cascade Lakes Highway** west of Bend is an excellent destination for a weekend of flat-water paddling. My favorite lakes are Sparks and Hosmer.

How would you like to canoe a lava flow? No, you don't need an asbestos canoe. This lava flow has been cold for a few thousand years and now forms the southeast shore of 250-acre **Sparks Lake,** 24 miles west of Bend. Created thousands of years ago when a lava flow blocked a stream, this lake is only 8 feet deep at its deepest and has no outlet. The southeast shore, near the boat ramp, consists of blocky lava walls that look as though they might have been built by some lost relatives of the Incas. Several coves invite exploring, and tucked into the lava walls are little "water closets" (tiny coves surrounded by rock). One long cove leads to a fabulous campsite. Eagles, osprey, ducks, and deer can all be seen on or near the lake. The water level at this lake is extremely variable, depending in large part on snowmelt. By late summer there is often very little water left in the lake, which makes this a bad time to count on doing much canoeing here. Plan for the early summer months or early fall (after the first rains), and you should be fine. Also keep in mind that this lake is fly-fishing only. Motorboats are allowed, but they are limited to 10 miles per hour.

Just west of Sparks Lake lies **Devils Lake,** which, though hardly big enough to warrant unloading the boat for, is such an amazing color of turquoise that it is impossible to pass by. Almost equally interesting but with a completely different character, **Hosmer Lake** is most popular with fly-fishermen trying to catch the lake's famous Atlantic salmon (all catch-and-release). However, because Hosmer is actually two lakes connected by a narrow channel, and because the upper lake is surrounded by marshes, it is an excellent lake to explore in a canoe or sea kayak. Hosmer Lake is south of Sparks Lake along the Cascade Lakes Highway.

South of Hosmer at the north end of Wickiup Reservoir, the two **Twin Lakes** also provide some interesting canoeing. These lakes are almost identical in size and are both nearly circular due to their unusual origins. Both are *maars,* lakes formed when volcanic craters flooded, and neither has surface inlets or outlets. The spring-fed lakes are cold and clear and no motorboats are allowed. However, because South Twin Lake has a resort and campgrounds around its shores, it can still get crowded on summer weekends. For a quieter paddle, try North Twin Lake.

If you haven't got your own canoe, you can rent one during the summer months at **Elk Lake** (west of Hosmer Lake), **Cultus Lake** (south of Elk Lake), or **Paulina Lake** in Newberry National Volcanic Monument. However, these lakes are not as interesting to explore as Hosmer or Sparks.

HIKING & BACKPACKING

Deschutes River Trail

9.2 miles round-trip. Moderate. 300-foot elevation gain. Access: Drive the Cascades Lakes Hwy.

for 6 miles west from Bend, turn left at a sign for the Meadow Picnic Area, and continue 1.3 miles to the trailhead at the picnic area. Map: USGS Benham Falls.

This trail, shared by hikers and mountain bikers, parallels the Deschutes River west of Bend and offers great views of Lava Island Falls, Big Eddy Rapids, and Dillon Falls along its length. Because this is an out-and-back trail, you can vary the length of your hike to fit the time and energy you have to spend. For almost the entire length of this hike, you are close to the river. The trail passes through forests of tall ponderosa pines, and in its first mile skirts the edge of the lava flow that formed the Lava Island Falls. These first falls are an impressive sight as the Deschutes churns between rugged lava-rock banks. Above these falls, the river becomes much more placid, and the hike becomes a pleasant stroll through the forest.

Keep your eyes out for eagles, osprey, and other birdlife as you hike this 3.5-mile section to Dillon Falls. About midway through this stretch of trail, you'll pass Big Eddy Rapids. This is one of the most frequently run rapids on the Deschutes, and if it's a summer weekend, you'll certainly see rafts lined up to bounce through this churning whitewater. At Dillon Falls, the Deschutes pours over a 15-foot ledge and then roars through half a mile of boiling whitewater. Needless to say, the rafting companies put in below this unrunnable waterfall. Once again, this waterfall was created by lava flows that edged up against the river. From here, return the way you came.

Green Lakes

10 miles round-trip. Moderate. 1,200-foot elevation gain. Access: The Green Lakes trailhead is at the north end of Sparks Lake, 25 miles west of Bend on the Cascade Lakes Hwy. (FS 46). Map: Geo-Graphics Three Sisters Wilderness.

I'm probably not supposed to say this, but I would walk through miles of clear-cuts or tree farms or climb 3,000 feet on a bad trail to reach Green Lakes. Fortunately (or unfortunately, depending on your point of view), this isn't necessary. The trail to

Green Lakes is as rewarding as the destination. The trail follows Fall Creek all the way to the lakes, and what a beautiful, noisy creek it is, with numerous small waterfalls along its length. There are some small meadows 3 miles up the trail, and then in another half mile or so, you reach a long, level stretch of trail. Here meadows flank the meandering creek, and on the far side an obsidian flow forms a jagged, shimmering wall that obviously pushed the creek to its present location. Brown dippers (also known as water ouzels) frequently can be seen feeding along this stretch of creek. These birds, which look like large wrens, are distinctive for their habit of diving into rapids of mountain streams and for the way they comically bob up and down (the better to spot underwater insects) while standing on rocks in midstream. Above here you reach the wide basin that holds the aptly named Green Lakes. Flanking the basin on the west are South Sister and Broken Top, their red-cindered ramparts holding snow throughout the summer. Also to the west, an immense ghostly white lava flow forms a long wall of rock.

The Green Lakes area makes a good base for some exploration of this corner of the Three Sisters Wilderness, and days can be spent exploring from here. A couple of worthy destinations include the south side of Broken Top along the Crater Ditch Trail and the Park Meadows area. The trail to the latter is particularly rewarding. It climbs to a pass (from which much off-trail exploring can be done) before dropping through forest to the classically wild west meadow of Park Meadows, which has a view of Broken Top's north side. It's easy to imagine the ghosts of Jeremiah Johnson and Chief Joseph wandering this meadow. Because the Green Lakes area is so popular, camping is allowed only in designated campsites, and on summer weekends expect hundreds of people for company.

South Sister Climb

11 miles. Strenuous. 4,900-foot elevation gain. Access: The trailhead is at the Devil's Lake Campground, 27 miles west of Bend on the Cascade Lakes Hwy. Map: Geo-Graphics Three Sisters Wilderness.

Born of volcanoes and carved by glaciers, the Three Sisters are an extremely rugged trio of peaks. Most hikers who visit this area are content to simply gaze up at them from some Alpine meadow or lakeside resting spot. However, if you long to stand at the summit of one of these peaks, such a dream can be realized even if you've never roped up or don't know a carabiner from a crampon. The climb of 10,358-foot South Sister, though extremely strenuous, involves no technical climbing, just a lot of uphill slogging. To break up the monotony of climbing nearly 5,000 feet (in 5.5 miles), you can make a detour to Moraine Lake, which is set below a cliff on the flanks of the mountain and makes a good base for turning this hike into an overnight.

The trail starts out by crossing the highway and then climbs for 1.5 miles through dense forest. At a four-way junction with the trail that leads from Moraine Lake to Sisters Mirror Lake, you enter a sandy plateau area. Stay straight at this junction unless you plan to pitch camp at Moraine Lake. From the junction, it is an easy hike across the open plateau, which has views down to Moraine Lake and east to Broken Top. At 3 miles you pass a second trail that leads steeply down to Moraine Lake. This valley was carved by the Lewis Glacier, which also deposited the terminal moraine that lends its name to the lake.

Continuing steeply upward from this point, the views just get better and better as the landscape to the south opens up, exposing the many lakes of the Cascade Lakes Highway. In just over 1 mile, you come to a saddle where you can take a well-deserved rest and soak in the views. This saddle lies at the base of Lewis Glacier at the junction with the climber's trail from Green Lakes. Directly below to the south lies the Wickiup Plain and the adjacent lava field of Rock Mesa. To the east, Broken Top and Green Lakes are visible. From here on up to the summit, you'll be struggling against the unstable footing of pumice scree, which makes almost as miserable a hiking surface as loose sand. You may want to bring a hiking stick or ski pole to assist you with this last pitch. But it's only another 1.1 miles to the summit—persevere.

A little more than halfway up this last section, you'll reach the edge of South Sister's crater and get your first glimpse of the small pool of water that fills the crater. A little less than a half mile will bring you to the summit and the most awesome views in the state. Middle and North Sister are right there in your face, with glacial-blue Chambers Lakes dotting the saddle between here and Middle Sister. To the south, you can see Diamond Peak and Mount McLoughlin. To the west, the lush green forests of the western slopes of the Cascades roll off toward the Willamette Valley, while to the east, Bend and most of the high desert are visible. If you are headed back to Moraine Lake, be sure to take the upper trail. This is a much more scenic route.

Broken Top Trail

4.4–12 miles. Moderate. 400–1,100-foot elevation gain. Access: From Bend, drive 22 miles west on the Cascade Lakes Hwy. (FS 46) and turn north onto FS 370 (signed for Todd Lake). At the Todd Lake parking area, the gravel road turns to badly rutted dirt and begins climbing. In 3.5 miles turn left onto FS 380 and continue 1.3 miles to the trailhead. Map: Geo-Graphics Three Sisters Wilderness.

Although the Broken Top trailhead provides access to a trail to the popular Green Lakes area, this is a worthy destination in its own right. Twice I've come up here intending to hike to Green Lakes and got distracted by the high pumice plains and easy trails leading up the slopes of Broken Top. The hardest part of this trail is getting to the trailhead. FS 370 is an extremely rough road that is just barely passable to two-wheel-drive passenger cars. Although it is possible to start this hike from the FS 378 spur road off FS 370, this will deny you one of the most picturesque stretches of road in the state. Persevere and try to get your car all the way to the main trailhead, which is at 7,050 feet and is right at the Three Sisters Wilderness boundary.

From the trailhead, hike west on the wide path (once a continuation of the road). Before too long, this trail narrows down to a true footpath and begins dropping. Within less than a mile, you will reach sandy pumice fields that are dotted with ground-hugging wildflowers. At the second creek crossing, look to your right and you will see a faint trail leading up toward the summit of Broken Top. This trail climbs steadily for about 1 mile to reach the east side of Broken Top's serrated crater rim. As you hike up this trail, contemplate the massive eruption, similar to that of Mount St. Helens, that blew out this mountain's entire south face. Today, the layers of this stratovolcano are exposed to view in a fascinating progression of colors—red, black, and yellow. As you crest this shoulder of the mountain at 8,149 feet, you reach a glacier, at the foot of which lies a small lake with drifting icebergs.

If you prefer a hike with less climbing, stay on the main trail at the second creek crossing. The trail continues to drop and soon reaches a wide pumice plain and crosses a narrow canal. This is the Crater Ditch, an irrigation ditch fed by Crater Creek. From here, the trail traverses across the south slope of Broken Top and past Cayuse Crater as it winds its way to Green Lakes. It is around 5 miles from the trailhead to Green Lakes if you plan to make that your destination.

Tumalo Mountain

3.6 miles. Moderate. 1,200-foot elevation gain. Access: From Bend, drive 20 miles west on the Cascade Lakes Hwy. (FS 46) to the Tumalo Mountain trailhead on the right. Map: Geo-Graphics Three Sisters Wilderness.

If you're just looking for a short hike with good views, try this one. Tumalo Mountain is located directly across the Cascade Lakes Highway from the Mount Bachelor Ski Area, and though it is 1,300 feet shorter than Bachelor Butte, it provides an equally outstanding view of Broken Top and the South Sister. Best of all, you'll avoid the crowds and you won't have to hike beneath ski lifts. The first mile of this steep climb is through trees, but as you approach the summit, you break out into red-cinder fields. Both this mountain and Bachelor

Butte are large cinder cones that formed during this area's most recent period of major volcanic activity. From the summit, the nearly treeless 7,775-foot summit of Tumalo Mountain, Broken Top, and South Sister are right there in your face. Turn around 180° and you'll have an outstanding view of Bachelor Butte, on which you'll probably be able to pick out lots of people.

HORSEBACK RIDING

If you'd like to do a little horseback riding while you're in the area, contact **Saddleback Stables** (tel. 541/593-1221, ext. 4420) in Sunriver, where an hour's ride will cost $22.

MOUNTAIN BIKING

Hood River and Oakridge may have a lot of great mountain biking, but Bend has to be the best all-around mountain-biking region in the state. Where else can you ride the rim of a volcano that only 1,300 years ago was spewing out liquid obsidian? Where else can you ride right up to subalpine meadows with in-your-face views of Cascade peaks? Where else can you ride for miles through ancient lava flows linking pristine mountain lakes? Whether you're a total novice or a gonzo gearhead, there are trails here for you. Got a week and want to do some bike camping? The extensive network of trails and gravel roads in this area can link you north to Sisters and south to Waldo Lake for the most awesome trail trip imaginable. Happy trails, Dude!

In addition to the trails listed below, during the summer months, you can haul your bike to the top of Mount Bachelor on a ski lift for $9 and then ride down on 12 kilometers of marked mountain-bike trails. Bikes can be rented here as well. Bike rentals are also available at **Chrome Pony** (tel. 541/593-2728) in Sunriver next to Baja Norte.

Guided mountain-bike rides in Newberry National Volcanic Monument are offered by **High Cascade Descent Guide Service** (tel. 541/389-0562). Rates range from $37 to $50 depending on the length. An easy downhill ride includes stops at waterfalls and a natural waterslide. Guided rides are also offered by **Pacific Crest Mountain Bike Tours** (tel. 800/849-6589 or 541/593-5058) with rates ranging from $30 to $60.

Shevlin Park Loop

5.5 miles. Moderate. 100-foot elevation gain. Access: The park is 3 miles west of Bend on Newport Ave. Map: USGS Shevlin Park or Mount Bachelor Bike and Sport's Central Oregon Mountain Biking Trails Map (available at most area bike shops).

This park is a great place for riders of different levels. The trail up the west side of Tumalo Creek is flat, easy, and even, and passes through a little covered bridge. At the 2.8-mile point, however, the trail crosses the creek on a one-log bridge and turns nasty. Novice riders can stay on the west bank while more experienced riders can add the challenging east-bank trail to complete the loop. If you plan to ride the full loop (both banks), you should be aware that locals always ride this loop clockwise. From the parking lot, the trail leads down to Tumalo Creek and crosses the creek on a log bridge, which as of summer 1996 was broken and not likely to survive another winter.

Once on the far side of the creek, the trail climbs up from creekside meadows on a couple of tight, steep switchbacks. Once on the plateau above the creek, the trail gets much easier and follows a fast, flat dirt road for a ways before switching to rolling, narrow single-track. But after this easy stretch, the trail gets technical with lots of rocks, roots, and steep drop-offs. The last bit of east-bank trail is a steep, rocky descent that will have you carrying your bike and wishing you had on hiking boots.

At the bottom of this mountain-bike nightmare, the trail crosses the creek on a second log bridge. Those looking for more challenges can explore the trails that climb out of the stream valley on the west side. Locals often do several reps on the loop trail for a good workout. Cruisers can just go up and back on the west side for a leisurely 5.5-mile ride.

Deschutes River Trail

6 miles. Easy. 100-foot elevation gain. Access: Drive 7.5 miles west of Bend on the Cascade Lakes Hwy. (Ore. 46), turn left onto FS 41, and follow signs to Lava Island Falls. Map: Bend Ranger District Mountain Biking Route Guide or Mount Bachelor Bike and Sport's Central Oregon Mountain Biking Trails Map (available at most area bike shops).

This easy trail is one of the most scenic in the state and is a good one for novice mountain bikers who want to take a leisurely ride along the Deschutes River. The highlights of the ride are the views of Lava Island Falls, Big Eddy Rapids, and Dillon Falls. This is one of the most popular hiking trails in the Bend area, and consequently you need to be alert for hikers when riding. There are two ways you can ride this route. There is the narrow trail that parallels the river with views almost the entire way, and then there is the marked trail, which utilizes abandoned roads and a few short stretches right along the river. This latter route is the preferred route on weekends and anytime there seems to be a lot of hikers on the trail (cars without bike racks at the trailhead parking lot are a sure sign that this is the case).

This signed route utilizes gated FS 4120, which is now closed to motor vehicles. From the first gate at the Lava Island Falls south parking area, it is 0.75 miles to Big Eddy Rapids and a 0.75-mile stretch of single-track/double-track. The trail then returns to FS 4120 at another gate. Continue along this stretch of road, with a good view of the river, for 1 mile to a gate at the Dillon Falls parking area. From the falls overlook, a trail loops back downstream to rejoin FS 4120 for the ride back to the trailhead. If you want to ride the trail the whole way, pick a midweek day and do the ride before people get off work. It is also possible to continue all the way to Benham Falls for a 17-mile round-trip ride.

Swede Ridge Trail

9-mile loop. Easy–moderate. 450-foot elevation gain. Access: Drive 16 miles west of Bend on the Cascade Lakes Hwy. (FS 46) to the Swampy Lakes Sno-Park. Map: Bend Ranger District Mountain Biking Route Guide or Mount Bachelor Bike and Sport's Central Oregon Mountain Biking Trails Map (available at most area bike shops).

In the winter, the Swampy Lakes Sno-Park provides access to miles of cross-country ski trails, but by summer, these same trails make excellent mountain-bike trails. Novice mountain bikers will appreciate the easy gradients of the trails here, and the short distances and interconnected loops mean rides of varying lengths can be pieced together. One good ride in this area is out to the Swede Ridge Shelter. The route starts out by heading toward the appropriately named Swampy Lakes, on the far side of which there is a winter ski shelter. The trail passes the shelter and loops back across the marshes surrounding Swampy Lakes before reaching the spur trail that leads out Swede Ridge to the shelter. From the shelter, you can head back the way you came and finish the Swampy Lakes Trail loop for a ride on mostly single-track trails, or ride FS 110 to FS 4615 to FS 080 back to the Swampy Lakes Sno-Park. I recommend riding the trails; they're more fun.

370 Road Ride

12 miles each way. More difficult. 800-foot elevation gain. Access: Take the Cascade Lakes Hwy. (FS 46) 24 miles west of Bend, turn right onto FS 370, and drive to the Todd Lake parking lot. Map: USFS Three Sisters Wilderness.

If you like views and don't mind a bit of strenuous climbing to achieve them, then don't miss the 370 Road. This rough dirt track, popular with four-wheelers, remains barely passable to two-wheel-drive vehicles. However, outside of hunting season, the road just isn't that busy, which makes it an ideal mountain-bike road ride. The trail starts at Todd Lake and begins climbing almost immediately, sometimes steeply and sometimes gradually. As the road climbs it alternates between forest and large meadows that are among the prettiest in the region. If you want to see them when they're green and full of wildflowers, be sure to bring mosquito repellent. The views take in Broken Top, Bachelor Butte, Tumalo Mountain, and all the rolling forested lands to the south. Near the high point, a spur road leads to the boundary of the Three Sisters Wilderness and the Crater Ditch Trail to Green Lakes. Although the wilderness is closed to bicycles, a short hike makes a pleasant break from time in the saddle.

From here, you can continue northward on FS 370 all the way to Three Creek Lake. If you can arrange a car shuttle, you can make a one-way traverse from Todd Lake to Three Creek Lake or vice versa (you actually do less climbing if you start at Three Creek Lakes). You could also connect to the Metolius–Windigo Trail at Three Creek Lake and ride 18 miles of single-track down to Cold Springs Campground 4 miles west of Sisters on Ore. 242.

Sparks Lake–Lava Lake– Edison Butte Trail System

31-mile loop. Strenuous. 3,000-foot elevation gain. Access: Take the Cascade Lakes Hwy. (FS 46) 25 miles west of Bend to Sparks Lake, turn left, and then left again at the fork to the trailhead parking area on the immediate left. Map: Mount Bachelor Bike and Sport's Central Oregon Mountain Biking Trails Map (available at most area bike shops).

This trail is the essence of central Oregon mountain biking. The trail starts out by crossing lava beds for 3 miles on a trail that's a serpentine roller-coaster ride. However, sharp rocks, roots, and 8-inch-diameter water bars make it a bit of a technical challenge. At 2.5 miles, a 100-foot-long trail leads down to the south end of Sparks Lake (your only glimpse of the lake until the end of the ride). At 4.5 miles you'll pass through a forest with more dead trees laying on the ground than live ones standing up. At 5.25 miles you'll reach a junction, signed Lava Lake, to the left. If you continue straight ahead, you'll pass Hosmer Lake on a shorter, alternate loop ride. Take the left to Lava Lake instead and the trail continues descending through lodgepole pine forest and reaches Lava Lake in about 3.5 miles. From here, you

can bail out and ride 13.5 miles back to your car on pavement or take on the hardest section of this loop.

The trail from Lava Lake to Edison Butte and FS 45 climbs nearly 1,300 feet to a wide saddle between Bachelor Butte and Sheridan Mountain before descending almost all of that elevation you just gained. The last 2 miles of trail pass through more lava flows. At FS 45, turn left (north) and return on this paved road to the Cascade Lakes Highway (FS 46). Turn left, ride past Mount Bachelor Ski Area, and return to your car at Sparks Lake. This last section of the loop covers 10 miles of pavement and includes a 1,500-foot climb.

If you don't want to do the full loop, you have a couple of options. You can ride to Quinn Creek Horse Camp and return on the Cascade Lakes Highway for a 13.5-mile trip or you can ride to Lava Lakes and return on the highway for a 23.5-mile trip. The former route drops down past beautiful, pale-green Hosmer Lake and then parallels Quinn Creek before passing through a large meadow. The trail down to Quinn Creek is at points unrideable due to rocks, and there are several tight switchbacks. Persevere and at 6.5 miles you'll reach a bridge over the crystalline creek. Across the bridge, turn right and parallel this pretty creek for about a mile to reach Quinn Meadows. From the campground, follow the gravel access road to the highway. This is a very scenic route (though a bit difficult in places), but because it goes to a horse camp, it is best left for the fall, after the horse camp is closed for the season. Either of these loops includes only about 900 feet of climbing, and this is mostly on the paved return leg of the loop.

Peter Skene Ogden Trail

17.5 miles round-trip. Strenuous. 2,400-foot elevation gain. Access: Take U.S. 97 south from Bend for 22 miles, turn east on FS 21, and drive 2.8 miles to a left turn into the Ogden Group Camp. Map: USGS Paulina Peak and Finley Butte.

This trail, once one of the most popular downhill single-track rides in the region, is now closed to downhill mountain-bike travel. However, you can still ride it uphill, with a return on FS 500 to make a strenuous, though enjoyable, loop. The trail parallels Paulina Creek for its entire length, and along the way there are waterfalls and pools of refreshingly cool water. Because this trail includes a grueling, steep 6-mile climb, you are certain to work up a sweat long before you reach the top. Cool off in the creek, indulge in a bit of natural hydrotherapy, and you'll see why this has always been such a popular ride. When the climb is done, you can take a rest on the shore of Paulina Lake, and then feel free to fly down the dirt road (FS 500) that returns you to your starting point. There is something ultimately exhilarating about an 8-mile downhill coast on dirt.

Start this ride in the Ogden Group Camp and follow the marked trail uphill to Paulina Resort. At the resort, turn right on FS 21, cross the bridge over Paulina Creek, and turn right into the picnic area. FS 500 leads west and downhill from here, paralleling the creek and eventually leading you back to the group camp.

Newberry Crater Rim Trail

21 miles. Strenuous. 1,300-foot elevation gain. Access: Take U.S. 97 for 2 miles south from Bend, turn left onto FS 21, and continue 13 miles uphill to Paulina Lake and the Paulina Lake Lodge. Map: USGS Paulina Lake and East Lake.

Views, views, views! That's what this trail is all about. As its name implies, this trail circles the entire Newberry Crater (actually a caldera) and its two lakes—Paulina Lake and East Lake. This is another grueling ride, but the scenery should more than make up for the difficulty. You need to be in good shape to do this entire ride, but about halfway around, the trail crosses FS 21, which allows you a chance to bail out and save a few miles of riding. Start at the Paulina Lake Lodge and begin pedaling uphill on the Crater Rim Trail, which leads north from the lodge to the flanks of North Paulina Peak, climbing 1,100 feet in 4 miles. From here the trail winds its way—with ups and downs, of course—around the crater with frequent views. In the southeastern section, the trail crosses

FS 21, which leads steeply down to East Lake and back along the floor of the Crater to Paulina Lake. However, if you've still got the energy, the best is yet to come.

Between FS 21 and Paulina Peak, the trail passes above the Big Obsidian Lava Flow, the most impressive feature within Newberry Crater. When the trail reaches FS 500 on the south side of 7,985-foot Paulina Peak, you should ride to the top of the peak if you can summon up the energy. The view from the summit is superb and takes in four states. Riding back down to the trail, turn off the road, and begin a very steep and fast 2-mile descent to within a mile of Paulina Lake. The last stretch is on FS 500, the cinder road that goes to the top of Paulina Peak.

ROAD BIKING

Mount Bachelor Loop

64 miles. Strenuous. 2,600-foot elevation gain. Access: Start this ride just off U.S. 97 at the shopping plaza in Sunriver.

This is the area's classic ride and takes in all the best scenery as well as the best roads in the area. Although there is a significant amount of climbing, by riding the loop clockwise, you get to ride downhill on the steepest section of road. Starting in Sunriver, head west on Cottonwood Drive, which becomes Spring River Road and then Three Trappers Road (FS 40). This first section offers quiet riding through the forest with occasional views of the area's peaks.

After 21 miles, reach FS 46 and turn north to parallel the Deschutes River for a while. Pass Elk Lake at 33 miles, and reach the jewel-like Devil's Lake at the 37-mile point. You might as well take a breather here. Although you've been climbing steadily for the past 16 miles, just beyond here is where the real climb begins. From Devil's Lake, the road climbs past the ominous wall of a lava flow and then drops down to cross the meadows at the north end of Sparks Lake. Ahead you can see Bachelor Butte, over the flanks of which you must now climb. It's roughly 1,000 feet in elevation to the ski-area parking lot, where, if you're so inclined, you could ride the ski lift to the summit for the most stunning panorama of the whole ride, and if you happen to be riding a mountain bike, you could even ride down. From the ski area, it's all downhill, and a steep downhill at that (2,000 vertical feet in 15 miles). After 3 miles of downhill riding from the ski area, turn right on FS 45. From this turnoff, it is 12 miles down to FS 40 (Spring River Road) and another 4.5 miles back to Sunriver.

Crane Prairie Reservoir Loop

60 miles. Strenuous. 1,500-foot elevation gain. Access: Start this ride just off U.S. 97 at the shopping plaza in Sunriver.

If climbing 2,600 feet just doesn't appeal to you, no matter how spectacular the views, this ride offers a slightly less daunting climb and a whole lot more flat riding. Start the ride by heading south from Sunriver for 2 miles on Huntington Road, from which there are particularly sweeping mountain vistas. After turning west onto FS 40, you'll be heading toward the mountains and, for a while, paralleling the Fall River. Just north of Wickiup Reservoir, take the signed turnoff to the Twin Lakes. These lakes, which have neither inlets nor outlets, are examples of volcanic *maars* (craters) that have been filled by springs.

South Twin Lake is the prettier of the two and makes a great lunch stop. From here, continue west to the junction with FS 46 and turn north (right). Pedaling north, you'll have superb views of Broken Top, South Sister, Middle Sister, and Mount Bachelor. If you'd like to do a bit of osprey watching, look for signs to Crane Prairie Reservoir's osprey viewing area, which is a short hike from the parking lot. North of Crane Prairie Reservoir, turn east (right) at the FS 40 junction and head back toward Sunriver. This section of the loop includes the only long uphill section of the ride. Just keep telling yourself, "This hill will be over in 6 miles." Once over the top, it is a long descent back to Sunriver on a road that is sometimes quite rough.

Mount Bachelor to Lava Lake

20 miles. Easy. 1,900-foot elevation loss. Access: From Bend, drive 20 miles west on the Cascade Lakes Hwy. (FS 46) to Mount Bachelor Ski Area.

You want a route with no climbing, you say? No problem. If you can set up a car shuttle, you can enjoy my favorite section of the Cascade Lakes Highway, which begins at Mount Bachelor Ski Area, where you can park one car, and ends at Lava Lake, where you should park a second car. From Mount Bachelor, immediately begin a long, energizing descent from the pumice fields of Dutchman Flat to Lower Todd Meadow. After a short climb, you descend to the marshes at the north end of Sparks Lake, a lake that is slowly turning to meadow. Climb again before dropping past the unbelievably blue waters of Devils Lake, which is right beside the highway and makes a great place for a rest stop.

On the opposite (north) side of the highway, you'll find the Devil's Garden, where springs bubble up at the base of a ragged lava flow. Here the road curves around to the south and begins a long, straight section leading to Elk Lake, where you might want to go for a swim to cool off. You'll find a general store and diner where you can fuel up if you don't have a picnic lunch with you. From Elk Lake, continue south to Lava Lake and Little Lava Lake. The latter lake is spring-fed and the source of the Deschutes River. The only drawback of this particular ride is that you'll be pedaling away from the Three Sisters and will have to look back over your shoulder for the best views.

SNOWSHOEING

Marked cross-country ski trails offer the easiest snowshoeing routes, but remember to stay out of the ski tracks. Less than half a mile from the Mount Bachelor Nordic Center there are nearly 20 miles of marked cross-country ski trails. I recommend the hike up to **Todd Lake** and then around the lake as a good day's walk. If you have time and energy, consider climbing to the top of the ridge at the far end of Todd Lake. From here, you'll have a great view of the lake and the surrounding countryside. For some other suggestions, read the section on cross-country ski routes in the area.

If you'd rather strike out on a less traveled route, the 3.6-mile round-trip hike to the top of **Tumalo Mountain** (7,775 feet), though guaranteed to leave you with aching muscles, offers the best view this side of Mount Bachelor's summit. Tumalo Mountain is the conical peak just north of the Cascade Lakes Highway between the Vista Butte and Dutchman Flat sno-parks. The mountain can be climbed from either sno-park, though I prefer Vista Butte simply because it doesn't get the snowmobile traffic that Dutchman Flat sees. Although there is a marked hiking trail that starts about midway between the two sno-parks, you might have a hard time following the trail when the snow is deep. All you really have to do is head uphill, and, if you have the stamina, you'll reach the top. To get back down, just head downhill on the south side of the mountain and you'll eventually hit the highway.

There are guided, **ranger-led snowshoe walks** from Mount Bachelor's West Village on weekends at 9:30am and 1:30pm throughout the winter. These walks, which last about an hour, are free and snowshoes are provided, which makes this a great introduction to snowshoeing. If after going on one of these walks, you're interested in doing a longer outing, you can cross the parking lot to the Nordic center and rent a pair of snowshoes for $8 a day.

SPELUNKING

Central Oregon's volcanic legacy has left this region with numerous lava caves and lava tubes, several of which are fairly accessible. These caves formed when flowing basalt crusted over on the surface and acted as an insulator for still-flowing molten rock beneath the surface. When the eruption ended, lava flowed out of these underground channels, eventually emptying them and leaving long tubes through the solidified lava. In the thousands of years since these lava tubes were formed, many have collapsed either partially or totally. Before heading into any cave, be sure you have at least two reliable light sources such as a powerful flashlight and a propane lantern. Also be sure to dress warmly; most caves in the area maintain year-round temperatures just above 40° F.

The most visited of the region's caves is **Lava River Cave,** which, at 1 mile in length, is the longest lava tube in Oregon. This cave is located 1 mile south of the Lava Lands Visitor Center off U.S. 97 south of Bend. From May through October, a small admission fee is charged and propane lanterns can be rented. For a less crowded and more adventurous outing, try visiting the group of four easily accessible and well-marked caves off FS 18 southeast of Bend in the northern section of Newberry National Volcanic Monument. **Boyd Cave** is the first you'll come to and is 0.2 miles long. Hanging from the ceiling of this cave are lavacicles, similar to stalactites, but formed by dripping re-melted lava.

Skeleton Cave is the next along this route and can be explored for 0.6 miles. The third cave, **Wind Cave,** is the most challenging and rewarding to explore. Here you'll have to clamber over boulders, but you'll be rewarded with several high-ceilinged halls in the far reaches of this 0.5-mile–long cave. There is also a skylight in this cave. The fourth cave, **Arnold Ice Cave,** traps cold air during the winter, and water seeping into the cave freezes. Today the cave is completely blocked with ice. Because these and other caves in the area provide hibernation and nursery habitat for Townsend's big-eared bats, they now are subject to seasonal closures.

SWIMMING & TUBING

It gets hot around these parts in the summer, and what with all those lakes lying out there to the west and south of Bend, it's hard not to think about doing a bit of swimming. My all-around favorite place to swim in the area is **Todd Lake,** which lies just to the west of the Mount Bachleor Ski Area. Although the water here is a bit chilly, because the lake is a short walk from the parking lot, the crowds are small and there are no motorboats. More popular lakes along the Cascade Lakes Highway are those that have drive-in campgrounds and picnic areas, boat ramps, and plenty of room for motorboats. I tend to stay away from such lakes, but if you don't mind the conditions, try **Elk Lake,** which has several designated swimming areas. Perhaps the nicest is at the Beach Picnic Area on the south end of the lake. However, the Sunset View beach is also a popular place both with swimmers and boardsailors.

Farther south on the Cascade Lakes Highway, **Cultus Lake** has good swimming beaches and picnic areas. However, when my wife and I tried swimming here a couple of summers ago, we renamed this "Cold Us" Lake. Nearby **Little Cultus Lake** has a 10-mile-per-hour boating speed limit and consequently is a much quieter place to go for a dip. Continuing south, **North and South Twin lakes,** just north of Wickiup Reservoir, are interesting places to cool off. These lakes are maars (flooded craters) and have no surface inlets or outlets. Needless to say, the 60-foot-deep lakes are cold, but are also fairly quiet because motorboats are prohibited. North Twin is the quieter of the two lakes.

Closer to Bend, **Tumalo State Park** offers a chance to do a bit of swimming in a relatively slow section of the Deschutes River. You'll find this park 5 miles northwest of Bend off U.S. 20. If you feel like drifting down a lazy river in an inner tube, head south of Bend to the **Little Deschutes River.** In this same area, off U.S. 97, there are a few swimming options in Newberry National Volcanic Monument. **Paulina Creek,** which flows down from Paulina Lake, is paralleled for almost its entire length by the Peter Skene Ogden Trail. Along the creek's length, there are dozens of small waterfalls and several fairly large ones. Many of these falls have pools big enough for cooling off and even a bit of swimming. Try easily accessible McKay Falls just downstream from the McKay Crossing Campground. It's also possible to do a bit of swimming in both Paulina Lake and East Lake in the national monument. However, the waters of these lakes are quite chilly.

WALKS & NATURAL ROADSIDE ATTRACTIONS

Lava Lands Visitor Center and Trails

Access: 11 miles south of Bend on U.S. 97.

This visitor center (tel. 541/593-2421) serves as an introduction to the volcanic history and landscape of central Oregon and is built at the base of Lava Butte, a cinder cone that was formed 7,000 years ago. Outside the visitor center are two short interpretive trails through the surrounding lava flows. During the summer, a shuttle bus takes visitors to the top of Lava Butte, where there is another short trail (and great views of the region). This is the best place in the area to learn about central Oregon's unusual geology.

Lava Cast Forest

1 mile. Easy. 50-foot elevation gain. Access: From Bend, drive 14 miles south on U.S. 97, turn east onto FS 9720, and continue 9.5 miles on this gravel road. Map: Trailhead maps available.

Roughly 6,000 years ago, Newberry Volcano erupted and flooded the landscape to its north with lava. At the time, forests similar to today's forests were growing here, and as the lava flowed across the land, it flowed around trees and formed molds of their trunks. Lava Cast Forest is the greatest concentration of these lava molds (incorrectly known as lava casts) in the region. In some instances, the molds form holes in lava up to 15 feet deep. Along this well-marked trail, you can see these and many other signs of the area's volcanic heritage.

Big Obsidian Flow

0.7 miles. Easy. 250-foot elevation gain. Access: In Newberry National Volcanic Monument. From Bend, drive 22 miles south on U.S. 97, then 15 miles east on FS 21. Map: Trailhead map.

Throughout central Oregon, the evidence of past volcanic activity is everywhere. Lava flows blacken the landscape, cinder cones lift their conical slopes skyward, and lava tubes create caves beneath the forest. However, none of these attracts more curious visitors than the Big Obsidian Flow. Obsidian, the stuff of arrowheads, is a natural volcanic glass that forms when rhyolite lava seeps to the surface without ever encountering water. The smooth, glassy rock can be easily cracked, chipped, and flaked into razor-sharp edges, which made it the preferred material of ancient arrowhead makers. Here in Newberry National Volcanic Monument, one of the state's largest obsidian flows can be explored on this paved trail. Formed only 1,300 years ago, this obsidian flow is the newest lava flow in the state. Oh, and just in case you're wondering, if that same rhyolite lava were to encounter water, it would instantly vaporize the water, trapping thousands of tiny bubbles as it exploded and cooled, forming pumice.

Tumalo Falls

Access: 13 miles west of downtown Bend. Take Galveston Ave. to Skyliner Rd. and continue to the end (it is gravel for the last 2.5 miles).

These 85-foot falls are one of the Bend area's most popular natural attractions, and though there is a parking lot at the base of the falls, you can also hike several miles on easy trails that start at the falls picnic area.

WHITEWATER KAYAKING & CANOEING

The upper stretches of the Deschutes River have an entirely different character from the lower Deschutes. The most popular stretches of the upper river are Class I runs. However, separating these runs are Class IV, V, and VI waterfalls that offer hard-core whitewater paddlers some short but very challenging trips. Because the Deschutes River is dam controlled and fed by the Wickiup Reservoir, it has a fairly consistent level of water during the summer months and is perfect for paddling. During other months, the river's volume varies quite a bit depending on dam activities. For information and supplies, try

Bend Whitewater Supply, 413 NW Hill St., Bend (tel. 541/389-7191), which also offers kayaking classes.

CLASS I

The upper **Deschutes River** is an open-canoeists dream come true: miles of easy Class I waters, split up into distinct runs by several Class IV and V+ waterfalls. The uppermost run starts at Wickiup Reservoir and covers 9 miles in its run down to the Wyeth Campground, just above Class IV Pringle Falls. The forest setting and meandering nature of the river at this point make this the best of all the Class I runs outside Bend. To reach the take-out from U.S. 97, turn west onto Burgess Road (FS 43) about 4 miles north of La Pine (the turn is signed for Wickiup Reservoir). This road becomes Pringle Falls Loop. Just after crossing the Deschutes River above Pringle Falls, turn left into Wyeth Campground. To reach the put-in, continue west on FS 43 and turn left onto Wickiup Road, drive to the dam, turn left, and drive to the river at the far end of the dam.

The next run starts below Pringle Falls at Pringle Falls Campground and covers 16 miles before reaching Big River Campground. Although the paddling along this stretch of river is easy, you will have to make a 200-yard portage around the Tetherow Logjam 4 miles below the put-in. The upper section is through forest, while the lower, more meandering section is through grasslands with views of the mountains. The put-in is just downstream from Wyeth Campground (see above for directions). The take-out is on FS 42 (South Century Drive) at Big River Campground, which is reached from U.S. 97 by turning west onto Vandevert Road 4 miles south of Sunriver and then south onto South Century Drive (FS 42).

The next run covers the 18 miles between Big River Campground and Class V+ Benham Falls and is the least interesting of these three Class I runs. This run passes through residential areas and the Sunriver Resort, and the water gets crowded with resort guests in rental canoes, inner tubes, and the like. If you're looking for solitude, you might want to opt for one of the other runs. If you decide to

River Twister

Moving river waters are categorized on a scale of I to VI, with Class I waters being swift but lacking any real rapids and Class VI being those waterfalls that not even crazy people paid to advertise beer and other questionable sports products would attempt. So, how do you categorize a tornado? That's a question that Ed Wheeler, river guide for Cascade River Adventures, is probably still pondering.

On July 26, 1996, Wheeler was leading a boatload of six clients through the Deschutes River's popular Big Eddy run just upstream from Bend when a giant dust devil (or miniature tornado, depending on who you listen to) dropped onto the river. The twister sucked up water to a height of somewhere between 150 and 200 feet and barreled down the river straight for Wheeler's 1,000-pound raft. Everyone in the boat was more fascinated than fearful of this strange phenomenon, and no one thought to try to get out of its way. When the twister slammed into the raft, it lifted the boat 10 feet into the air, spun it around twice, and threw rafters and equipment into the river before depositing the raft back in the water, upside down. So powerful was the twister that it even sucked people's shoes right off their feet. Luckily no one was hurt, and everyone agreed it was the raft trip of a lifetime.

do this run, don't miss the take-out, which is at Benham Falls boat ramp, upstream from a footbridge and a logjam. To reach the take-out from U.S. 97, turn west onto FS 9702 just south of the Lava Lands Visitor Center and drive 5 miles to the Benham Falls Campground. To reach the put-in, drive back to U.S. 97 and follow the directions for the Pringle Falls–Big River Campground run above.

CLASS III

Between Dillon Falls and Lava Island Falls on the **Deschutes River,** there is a short (1.5-mile) run that is popular far beyond what its length would suggest. The reason for this popularity is the Class III Big Eddy Rapid in the middle of the run and the fact that local resorts and rafting companies send visitors by the hundreds down this stretch of water for a quick taste of whitewater. Big Eddy Rapid is sandwiched between Class II rapids, and together these waters provide enough play spots to make this a very entertaining run, plus it's very convenient to downtown Bend. Put in at Aspen Campground and take out on river left just upstream from Lava Island Falls, which are reached off Cascade Lakes Highway (FS 46) on FS 41.

CLASS IV & ABOVE

Between Lava Falls, just outside Bend, and Lake Billy Chinook on the **Deschutes River,** there are numerous, short Class IV runs, with a few Class V drops thrown in as well. All of these runs require expert paddling skills, not just because of the rapids but because paddlers must be on the constant alert for logs blocking the river. Don't set out on any run here without plenty of advice, an assessment of current conditions, and preferably, a local for a guide. Consult *Soggy Sneakers, A Guide to Oregon Rivers* for descriptions of individual runs.

WHITEWATER RAFTING

The **Deschutes River,** which passes through Bend, is the most popular river in Oregon for whitewater rafting. However, this river's most famous stretches of whitewater are nearly 100 miles north of Bend and are covered in "The Sisters Area, Smith Rock State Park & the Lower Deschutes River" section of this chapter. It is, however, possible to get a taste for whitewater rafting within 15 minutes of downtown Bend on the short-but-famous Big Eddy run. This stretch of water between Dillon Falls and Lava Island Falls covers only 3 miles, but in the middle of the run are the impressive Class III Big Eddy Rapids. There are also some Class II rapids for warm-up. Before you have enough time to catch your breath, it's all over, and you usually find yourself wondering why you didn't sign up for the all-day trip on the lower section of the Deschutes. Oh, well, there's always next time.

Companies doing the Big Eddy run include **Cascade River Adventures** (tel. 541/593-3113 or 541/389-8370), the **Inn of the Seventh Mountain** (tel. 541/382-8711, ext. 601), and **Sun Country Tours** (tel. 800/770-2161 or 541/382-6277). Expect to pay around $35 for this quick trip.

WILDLIFE VIEWING

At **Brown's Mountain Crossing** on the Deschutes River, you can see spawning kokanee salmon during September. There is a fish-viewing platform here. You'll find this viewing area on FS 42 (Cascade Lakes Highway/South Century Drive) between Wickiup Reservoir and Crane Prairie Reservoir.

Campgrounds & Other Accommodations

CAMPING

A certain percentage of campsites at many National Forest Service campgrounds can be reserved at least five days in advance by calling the **National Forest Reservation Service** (tel. 800/280-CAMP). State park campground reservations for both Oregon and Washington can be made by calling **Reservations Northwest** (tel. 800/452-5687). To make a reservation you'll need to know the name of the campground you want to stay at and the dates you plan to visit. The reservation fee for NFS campgrounds is $7.50, and for state parks it's $6.

THE SISTERS AREA, SMITH ROCK STATE PARK & LOWER DESCHUTES RIVER

Anglers and rafters have only a couple of developed campground choices along the lower Deschutes River. At the mouth, the **Deschutes River State Recreation Area** (30 campsites; open year-round) is convenient to I-84 and has good hiking and mountain-biking trail access. The other campground, **Beavertail** (21 campsites; open year-round) is 17 miles southeast of Maupin on the Deschutes River Road and is run by the Bureau of Land Management. Downriver from Sherar's Falls, there are also many undeveloped campsites along the river.

At Lake Billy Chinook, west of U.S. 97 between Madras and Redmond, there are several campgrounds. The most developed are the two at **The Cove Palisades State Park.** The Crooked River Camp (91 campsites; open year-round) is on the canyon rim while the Deschutes River Camp (181 campsites, 87 with full hookups; open year-round) is down below at the south end of the plateau known as The Island. Farther west, up the Metolius arm of the reservoir on FS 64, you'll find the forest service's more primitive **Perry South Campground** (63 campsites; seasonal). A little bit farther west is the **Monty Campground** (20 campsites; seasonal), which is the lowermost campground on the Metolius River's free-flowing waters (popular with anglers and kayakers).

Farther north on the Metolius River, there are eight forest service campgrounds strung along FS 14 north of Camp Sherman. All of these campgrounds are on the banks of the river and are most popular with anglers. From south to north these campgrounds are **Camp Sherman** (15 campsites; seasonal), **Allingham** (10 campsites; seasonal), **Smiling River** (37 campsites; seasonal), **Pine Rest** (8 campsites; seasonal), **Gorge** (18 campsites; seasonal), **Allen Springs** (17 campsites; seasonal), **Pioneer Ford** (18 campsites; seasonal), and **Lower Bridge** (12 campsites; seasonal). The first of these, the Camp Sherman Campground, is only 0.5 miles north of Camp Sherman, while the most remote, the Lower Bridge Campground, is 9 miles north (the last 0.5 miles of which is on a rough dirt road).

South of Sisters, at the end of FS 16, there are three campgrounds at or near Three Creek Lake. The first of these, **Three Creek Meadow Campground**

391 CAMPGROUNDS & OTHER ACCOMMODATIONS

(12 campsites; seasonal), is set on a large meadow, has a view of Tam McArthur Rim, and is adjacent to the hiking trail that leads to Park Meadows and on to Green Lakes. Of the two campgrounds on Three Creek Lake itself, I prefer **Driftwood Campground** (16 campsites; seasonal), which has a superb view of Tam McArthur Rim from its north-shore location and offers campsites that are a short walk from the road. **Three Creek Lake Campground** (10 campsites; seasonal) is at the south end of the lake and lacks views. All three of these campgrounds stay open in the fall.

Although signs as you enter **Smith Rock State Park** say that this is a day-use only park, there is actually a very popular campground, here known as a bivouac, used almost exclusively by rock climbers.

THE BEND AREA, THE CASCADE LAKES HIGHWAY & NEWBERRY NATIONAL VOLCANIC MONUMENT

The closest campground to Bend is **Tumalo State Park** (87 campsites, 22 with full hookups; seasonal), 5 miles northwest of Bend off U.S. 20. Nine of the campsites here (all in the A Loop) are on the bank of the Deschutes River. South of Bend, there are several more campgrounds along the banks of the Deschutes. **Dillon Falls Campground** (7 campsites; seasonal), off the Cascade Lakes Highway (FS 46) 6.5 miles west of Bend, is the closest of these and is set beside some of the most impressive falls on the river. The biggest campground in the area, and your best bet if you show up on a Saturday (or even late on a Friday night), is **La Pine State Park** (145 campsites, 95 with full hookups; year-round), which is accessible from U.S. 97 between Sunriver and La Pine. **Big River Campground** (5 campsites; seasonal), set on a meandering stretch of the river on FS 42 just west of Sunriver, is in an idyllic setting for a canoeing base camp. Farther up the river, **Pringle Falls Campground** (7 campsites; seasonal), off FS 43 northwest of La Pine, is another campground popular with canoeists.

Of the many campgrounds along the Cascade Lakes Highway (FS 46), **Todd Lake Campground** (7 walk-in campsites; seasonal), 25 miles west of Bend, is my favorite because it is enough of a walk from the parking lot to the campsites to discourage most car campers. Consequently, the lake stays fairly quiet. The view here is great, and there's good hiking, mountain biking, and flat-water canoeing nearby. **Devil's Lake Campground** (6 campsites; seasonal), also a walk-in campground, is another favorite of mine. The lake is an amazing color of turquoise and the campsites are well scattered.

Farther south, there are lots of campgrounds on the many lakes along this road. Some of my favorite campgrounds here include **Mallard Marsh Campground** (15 campsites; seasonal) and **South Campground** (23 campsites; seasonal), both of which are on beautiful Hosmer Lake, which is restricted to fly-fishing and on which no motors are allowed. On nearby Elk Lake, which is a good wind surfing spot, try **Point Campground** (9 campsites; seasonal). The campgrounds at **Lava Lake** (63 campsites; seasonal) and **Little Lava Lake** (14 campsites; seasonal) are also fairly quiet, and the view from Lava Lake is the finest at any campground on this stretch of road. Just north of Crane Prairie, there are nice campsites at **Cow Meadow Campground** (20 campsites; seasonal), which is on the bank of the Deschutes River, here barely more than a creek.

If you are headed to **Newberry Crater National Volcanic Monument** to do some fishing, hiking, or mountain biking, you've got lots of campground options. Most of the people who come to camp in the monument are here to fish. For these campers, **Paulina Lake Campground** (69 campsites; seasonal) and **Little Crater Campground** (50 campsites; seasonal) are the two Paulina Lake options. On East Lake, there are **Cinder Hill** (110 campsites; seasonal), **East Lake** (29 campsites; seasonal), and **Hot Springs** (42 campsites; seasonal). If you're looking for quiet and seclusion, try the two hike-in campgrounds on Paulina Lake. **North Cove** (6 campsites; seasonal) is 1.5 miles from the parking area and **Warm Springs** (5 campsites; seasonal) is 0.5 miles from the parking area (and near some elusive hot springs on the shore of the lake). Away from the lakes, there are two more campgrounds along Paulina Creek. **McKay Crossing** (10 campsites; seasonal) and **Prairie** (16 campsites; seasonal) both provide easy access to the Peter Skene Ogden Trail, which is popular with hikers and mountain bikers.

INNS & LODGES

THE SISTERS AREA, SMITH ROCK STATE PARK & THE LOWER DESCHUTES RIVER

Black Butte Ranch

P.O. Box 8000, Black Butte Ranch, OR 97759. Tel. 800/452-7455 or 541/595-6211. Fax 541/595-2077. 100 condos and homes. $80–$130 double; $160–$225 condos and houses. AE, DISC, MC, V.

This gated resort 8 miles west of Sisters is built on a former ranch and offers stunning views of the Cascade peaks across the meadows of a wide valley. The abundance of activities and recreational facilities is the main draw of this resort. Two 18-hole golf courses, an outdoor pool, tennis courts, recreation center, sports field, 16 miles of bike-and-jogging trails, canoe rentals, bicycle rentals, horseback riding, and whitewater rafting are all available to resort guests.

Kah-Nee-Ta Resort

P.O. Box K, Warm Springs, OR 97761. Tel. 800/554-4SUN or 541/553-1112. 139 rms, 4 suites, 25 cottages, 21 tepees. $115–$130 double; $185–$295 suite; $105–$200 cottage; $50 tepee. AE, CB, DC, DISC, MC, V.

This unusual resort 65 miles north of Bend is one of central Oregon's most popular sunny-side destinations. Operated by the Confederated Tribes of the Warm Springs Reservation on whose land the resort is built, Kah-Nee-Ta offers a wide range of accommodations from hotel rooms to cottages to R.V. sites to tepees. The Warm Springs Indians and the reservation both take their names from the hot springs that come welling out of the ground here. These springs feed a large outdoor pool,

as well as soaking tubs. Other facilities and activities include a fitness center, tennis courts, horseback riding, bicycle rentals, kayak rentals, and fishing-rod rentals.

Metolious River Resort

P.O. Box 1210, Camp Sherman, OR 97730. Tel. 800/81-TROUT or 541/595-6281. 11 cabins, 2 rms. $110–$130 double (lower rates in off-season). MC, V.

These shake-sided two-story cabins 14 miles west of Sisters offer modern amenities and styling with a bit of a rustic feel. Peeled log beds, wood paneling, riverstone fireplaces, and green roofs give the cabins a quintessential western appearance. Set on the banks of the spring-fed Metolius River not far from the river's source, the cabins are particularly popular with trout anglers.

THE BEND AREA, THE CASCADE LAKES HIGHWAY & NEWBERRY NATIONAL VOLCANIC MONUMENT

Inn of the Seventh Mountain

18575 SW Century Dr. (P.O. Box 1207), Bend, OR 97709. Tel. 800/452-6810 or 541/382-8711. 339 rms. $65–$109 double; $139–$285 condo. AE, CB, DC, DISC, MC, V.

This resort is the closest accommodation to Mount Bachelor and is especially popular with skiers in the winter. In the summer, an abundance of recreational activities turns the resort into a sort of summer camp for families. An 18-hole golf course, indoor and outdoor pools, whirlpools, indoor and outdoor tennis courts, an ice-skating rink, hiking/jogging trails, miniature golf course, playing fields, volleyball, basketball, massages, whitewater rafting, float trips, canoe trips, horseback riding, and mountain-bike rentals provide plenty of options for the active guest.

Mount Bachelor Village Resort

19717 Mount Bachelor Dr., Bend, OR 97702. Tel. 800/452-9846 or 541/389-5900. 80 rms.

$68–$105 double; $105–$285 1- to 3-bedroom (2-night minimum, discounts for 3 nights or longer). AE, MC, V.

Most of Bend's resorts cater to families in the summer months and consequently can be very noisy and crowded. If you'd rather be able to hear the wind in the trees, this condominium resort is the place to check out. Facilities include an outdoor pool, whirlpool, tennis courts, athletic club, and nature trail.

Sunriver Lodge & Resort

P.O. Box 3609, Sunriver, OR 97707. Tel. 800/ 547-3922 or 541/593-1221. Fax 541/ 593-5458. 299 rms, suites, and condos. $110–$129 double; $175–$195 suite; $184–$274 2- to 4-bedroom condos. Lower rates in off-season. AE, CB, DC, DISC, MC, V.

This sprawling resort has a wealth of activities and sports facilities available for active vacationers. Two golf courses, two pools, 28 tennis courts, indoor miniature golf, ice-skating rink, canoes, bicycles, horseback riding, fishing-gear rentals, massages, and whitewater rafting assure that most people staying here are, and stay, physically fit.

My favorite rooms are the loft suites, which have stone fireplaces, high ceilings, and rustic log furniture. Lots of pine trees shade the grounds, and there are 30 miles of paved bicycle paths connecting the resort's many buildings (two bicycles come with every room).

12

SOUTHERN OREGON

SOUTHERN OREGON IS AN ANOMALY. ASIDE FROM THE PEOPLE WHO live in the region, few Oregonians seem to be familiar with this jumbled landscape where three different mountain ranges come together. However, southern Oregon attracts people from all over the world. They come to gaze down on the sapphire jewel of Crater Lake (Oregon's only national park), to fly-fish for the legendary steelhead of the North Umpqua River, and to raft and fish the federally designated Wild and Scenic section of the Rogue River. With a climate and topography more akin to that of northern California, it hardly even seems appropriate to call this neck of the woods Oregon. Yet Oregon it is.

"It's the Climate" is the motto of the town of Grants Pass, and it's hard to dispute this claim. Southern Oregon is sunnier and warmer than the Willamette Valley to the north. However, when you consider that an average of 44 feet of snow falls on the rim of Crater Lake each winter—enough to keep the north rim of the lake closed each year until late July—you can't help wondering if this motto is just another example of the spin doctors at work. When winter's over, though, it really is the climate, and that is when this region truly shines. Even the fish are accommodating, with the best fishing on both the North Umpqua and the Rogue coming during the summer and fall months.

For the vast majority of people, Oregonians and out-of-staters alike, southern Oregon means one thing—Crater Lake. Even if this lake were not the deepest in the country, its astounding beauty would still be undeniable. It is as if the Grand Canyon has been filled with a starless night sky. Visitors to this national park have not even the slightest hint of the awesome grandeur that lies ahead as they approach the rim of Crater Lake, which makes the lake's sudden appearance 1,000 feet below all the more astounding. "I came, I saw, I left" might be the motto of most Crater Lake visitors, but if you're looking to interact with this awesome landscape, there are a few options, such as superb cross-country skiing and snowshoeing in winter, road biking around the Rim Road, and day hiking to the summits of several peaks, including that of 764-foot Wizard Island in the middle of the lake.

Crater Lake National Park is also the source of one of southern Oregon's other major recreational attractions. The Rogue River, which heads inside the boundaries of the park and carves its way through three mountain ranges—the Cascades, the Siskiyou Mountains, and the Coast Range—before emptying into the Pacific Ocean, first rose to national acclaim in the 1930s when Western author Zane Grey wrote of his life on the river in such books as *Adventures of Fishing, Tales of Freshwater Fishing,* and *Rogue River Feud.* This latter book focused on the battle between commercial and sport fishermen that arose early in this century when commercial fishermen intercepted the Rogue River's runs of salmon and steelhead at the mouth of the river and left sport fishermen with hardly a fish to strike at their flies. Today this river is managed for its famed sport fishing, but is also world renowned for its 35-mile-long Wild and Scenic stretch of Class III and IV whitewater. Along this stretch are several rustic lodges that make a three- or four-day float down the Rogue a luxury outing rather than a rugged adventure.

As famous as the Rogue River is, it is the North Umpqua that usually gets the nod as having not only the region's best fly-fishing, but of being the region's most beautiful river as well. Each time I visit the North Umpqua I am once again astounded by the blue-green waters. Crowded with rocks and lined with lush old-growth forests, this river has a pristine feel, despite the presence of Ore. 138 alongside the river for most of its length. In fact, though the traffic noises of this highway may intrude, the road provides excellent access for both anglers and paddlers. Approximately 31 miles have been federally designated as a Wild and Scenic River and these same miles are designated for fly-fishing only. Is it any wonder that fly anglers from around the country come here to fish?

As far back as the time when Zane Grey was fishing here, the importance of preserving the river's runs of salmon and steelhead had been recognized. In 1932, all fishing was banned on Steamboat and Canton creeks, two of the most important spawning grounds for the North Umpqua's fish runs. This far-sightedness is in large part responsible for this river continuing to have healthy fish runs. Although the North Umpqua could turn anyone into a fly angler, this beautiful river also offers aquatic options for the nonangler. Its whitewater is perfect for kayaking and rafting, and its swimming holes would make Huck Finn drool.

While Crater Lake pulls in view-seeking summer vacationers and the Rogue and North Umpqua attract dedicated anglers from around the country, this region's other outdoor activities and recreational areas remain largely overlooked by those who don't live here. If there is anywhere in the Oregon Cascades that is an undiscovered gem, it is the Ore. 140 corridor. Stretching from Medford to Klamath Falls, this road passes between two wilderness areas. Along the road's flanks are 9,495-foot Mount McLoughlin, the highest peak in southern Oregon and easily hiked in a day; 7,311-foot Brown Mountain, its slopes covered with boot-shredding lava flows and crossed by the Pacific Crest Trail; the massive Upper Klamath Lake, home to white pelicans, river otters, and the only marked canoe trails in the state; Great Meadow, site of some of the most splendid cross-country ski terrain in the state; and Lake of the Woods and Fish Lake, a pair of classic old Cascade summer-vacation lakes complete with rustic resorts and campgrounds.

This is, however, just one undiscovered corner of the region. Although remote, southern Oregon abounds in superlatives—the finest cross-country ski route in the state, the most interesting flat-water canoeing, the most challenging wilderness whitewater in the Northwest, the best bird watching in the state. Whether you're an Oregonian who has put off exploring this region or an out-of-state visitor drawn to the region to fish its famous rivers or to see Crater Lake, there is plenty to keep you busy should you wish to expand your adventure horizons.

The Lay of the Land

Southern Oregon has some of the most complex geography in the state. It is here that the Cascade Range, Coast Range, and Siskiyou Mountains all come together in a jumble of peaks and valleys. However, the lack of high peaks deceives many people into thinking this region is not as wild as more mountainous areas to the north and south, and it is partly this perception that has kept the region relatively undiscovered. With Mount Shasta, Mount Lassen, the Trinity Alps, and the Marble Mountains just south of the border in California, it is hard to get excited about the low peaks of southern Oregon.

While the high conical peaks of mounts Shasta and Lassen flaunt the volcanic heritage of the Cascade Range, here in southern Oregon signs of past volcanic activity are less vertical yet more dramatic. **Mount Mazama** once stood as tall as its neighbors

> **"The clearest way into the universe is through a forest wilderness." —John Muir**

to the south, but 7,700 years ago it erupted with almost unimaginable violence. When it had finished erupting, this volcano collapsed in on itself, forming a vast caldera 6 miles wide and 4,000 feet deep. Over the millennia, that caldera slowly filled with water to become today's **Crater Lake.**

Though Crater Lake is the most dramatic of southern Oregon's volcanic landmarks, many others exist. **Mount McLoughlin, Mount Bailey, Mount Thielsen,** and **Brown Mountain** are all volcanic peaks, and each in its own way shows a different face of volcanism. Although young by geological standards, 300,000-year-old Mount Thielsen has been around long enough to have suffered the ravages of ice-age glaciation. Where a conical peak once stood, there is now a needlelike crag, the hardened core of the volcano. Jutting skyward like an accusing finger, Mount Thielsen has come to be known as the "Lightning Rod of the Cascades," the rocks on its summit repeatedly melted by lightning.

In striking contrast, Mount Bailey, due west of Mount Thielsen on the far side of Diamond Lake, formed after the last ice age, and its rounded shape shows few signs of glaciation. It is this gentle slope that makes the peak such an ideal mountain to ski (snowcats carry skiers to the top of the slopes). At 9,495 feet tall, Mount Mc-Loughlin, at least when seen from the west, is a nearly perfect cone rising high above the surrounding landscape. Nearby Brown Mountain shows its volcanic heritage not only in its conical shape but in the mantle of lava it wears. Oddly enough this lava is far more black than brown when seen up close. Less readily recognizable as a volcanic feature is the caldera that comprises most of the Mountain Lakes Wilderness. Lying to the east of Lake of the Woods, this caldera was formed in much the same way that Crater Lake was formed. However, after the 12,000-foot

volcano that once stood here erupted, it left not a single deep lake, but rather several shallow ones. The volcanic Cascade Range is just one of the three mountain ranges in southern Oregon.

It is the **Siskiyou Mountains** that make this region so different from the rest of the state. These mountains are far older than either the Coast Range or Cascades and are composed primarily of a rock called serpentine. This glossy stone, which is often a bright green color, is high in heavy metals, which makes the soils of these mountains particularly poor (and which also led to a gold rush here in the 1850s and 1860s). Ridgelines throughout the Siskiyous support only rocky meadows and stunted pine trees. However, these plant communities are not the result of elevation but rather the poor quality of serpentine soils.

There are many plants that have adapted to these poor soils, and that has made the Siskiyou Mountains a region of botanical interest. With more than 1,000 plant species growing within these mountains, this is one of the most botanically diverse regions in North America. There are also more species of conifers here than anywhere else in the state. Among these are the Brewer spruce, which grows few other places. In 1946, 76,900 acres of the Siskiyous were set aside as the Kalmiopsis Wilderness to preserve the *Kalmiopsis leachiana* plant, a small shrub that resembles a dwarf rhododendron and grows almost exclusively in the Siskiyou Mountains. Because this plant has grown here since before the ice age, it is evident that these mountains were not scoured bare by glaciers as were so many other mountains in the Northwest.

Perhaps the most fascinating of the many unusual plants of the Siskiyou Mountains is the cobra lily *(Darlingtonia californica)*. Also known as pitcher plants, these insectivorous plants grow in boggy areas where the soils are so low in nutrients that the plants have adapted by extracting necessary nutrients from insects, which they digest with powerful enzymes inside their pitcher-shaped leaves. Cobra lilies can be seen at the Eight Dollar Mountain Botanical Area north of Cave Junction, while other rare and interesting

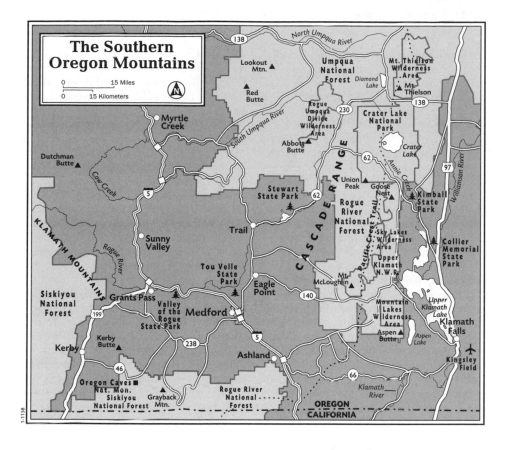

The Southern
Oregon Mountains

0   15 Miles
0   15 Kilometers

1-1158

plants can be seen at the Rough 'N' Ready Botanical Area south of Cave Junction.

The region's third mountain range, the **Coast Range,** is not as recognizable as a distinct range here in the south as it is further north along the coast. In its southernmost reaches it is intermingled with ridges of the Siskiyous.

Southern Oregon's two major rivers, the **North Umpqua** and the **Rogue,** are unique in that they are the only rivers in the state that head in the Cascade Range and empty into the Pacific Ocean. A third river, the **Klamath,** is even more impressive in that it heads on the east side of the Cascades and flows all the way through the Cascade Range. However, this river spends most of its length in California. The Klamath River flows out of **Upper Klamath Lake,** the largest lake in Oregon and an important resting stop on the Pacific Flyway used by migratory waterfowl.

Because this region is such a jumble of mountains and valleys, the highways that crisscross the area are meandering

roadways. Even **I-5,** the region's main transportation artery, wanders back and forth as it searches out the passes through this mountainous area. Heading east off of I-5 at Roseburg is **Ore. 138,** which follows the North Umpqua River for much of its length and leads to the north entrance of Crater Lake National Park. Heading northeast from Medford to the southern Crater Lake entrance is **Ore. 62,** which parallels the Rogue River for much of its length. Connecting Medford to Klamath Falls is **Ore. 140,** which passes Mount McLoughlin and the Lake of the Woods/Fish Lake recreational area. Still farther south, **Ore. 66** connects Ashland to Klamath Falls. Although there is a narrow, winding road from Grants Pass over the mountains to the coast at Gold Beach, the main route west from I-5 is **U.S. 199,** which heads southwest into the California redwood country.

Medford and **Roseburg** are the largest cities in southern Oregon, but these lumber-mill towns are overshadowed by

Ashland, home of the Oregon Shakespeare Festival and the region's cultural mecca, and **Grants Pass,** headquarters for Rogue River recreational activities. With its historic homes and restored gold-rush–era downtown, the town of **Jacksonville** just west of Medford corners the quaint market for this region. Each summer Jacksonville stages the Britt Festivals, a series of outdoor music and dance performances. The region's only other city is **Klamath Falls** on the dry east side of the Cascades. This town is surrounded by national wildlife refuges that attract an amazing variety and number of birds (and bird watchers).

Four different national forests— **Umpqua, Rogue River, Winema,** and **Siskiyou**—sprawl across the mountains of southern Oregon, and within these national forests are six wilderness areas. The Bureau of Land Management also has large land holdings here, including lands along the Rogue River's Wild and Scenic section. While the **Pacific Crest Trail** passes through here, it traverses some of its least interesting segments.

Parks & Other Hot Spots

North Umpqua River

Along Ore. 138 east of Roseburg. Tel. 541/496-3532. Camping, hiking, mountain biking, rafting, kayaking, fishing, wildlife viewing.

First made famous by Zane Grey, who came here to fish for steelhead, the North Umpqua has become legendary among anglers, and a long stretch of the river is open to fly-fishing only. The Steamboat Inn is the North Umpqua's premier fly-fishing lodge and is set on the bank of the river just downstream from Steamboat Creek, the main spawning stream for the North Umpqua's wild steelhead and salmon. Kayakers and rafters also find the blue-green waters of this river among the best in the state. For nearly 80 miles, from east of Idleyld Park to the Mount Thielsen Wilderness, the river is paralleled by the North Umpqua Trail. There are also numerous campgrounds, picnic spots, and boat launches along the stretch of the river that is federally designated as a National

Wild and Scenic River. Just north of the river between Steamboat and Toketee Reservoir is the small Boulder Creek Wilderness. Also along this river are several large rock formations that add grandeur to the river valley and attract a few rock climbers.

Crater Lake National Park

93 miles east of Roseburg on Ore. 138 (this entrance is closed in winter); 75 miles northeast of Medford on Ore. 62; 61 miles northwest of Klamath Falls on Ore. 62. Tel. 541/594-2211, ext. 402. Camping, hiking, road biking, fishing, cross-country skiing, snowshoeing.

Oregon's only national park preserves the deepest lake in the United States. Formed by the volcanic eruption of Mount Mazama 7,700 years ago, the sapphire-blue lake's surface is at the base of 1,000- to 2,000-foot-high cliffs that rise to an elevation of more than 8,000 feet. Rising up from the middle of the lake is 764-foot-high Wizard Island, which can be visited on informative boat tours that start from Cleetwood Cove on the lake's north shore. The high elevation of the crater rim and heavy winter snowfalls mean that the summer season here is short (and packed with people). Picnicking, walking and hiking, road biking around the Rim Drive, and cross-country skiing in winter are all popular park activities. The Pacific Crest Trail passes through the park, though at a distance from the lake's rim. There are even fish to be caught in the lake.

The lake was first discovered by whites when in 1853 prospectors searching for a lost gold mine stumbled upon the lake's rim. The Indian tribes of the region, which held the lake as sacred, had never mentioned its existence to the first explorers and settlers who arrived in this region. By 1886, soundings of the lake established its depth at 1,996 feet, making it the deepest lake in the United States. Sonar soundings later set the depth at 1,932 feet. In 1902, the lake was designated a national park.

The lake has no inlet or outlet streams and is instead fed solely by springs, snowmelt, and rainfall. Evaporation and ground seepage keep the lake at a nearly constant level. Because it is so deep, it rarely freezes

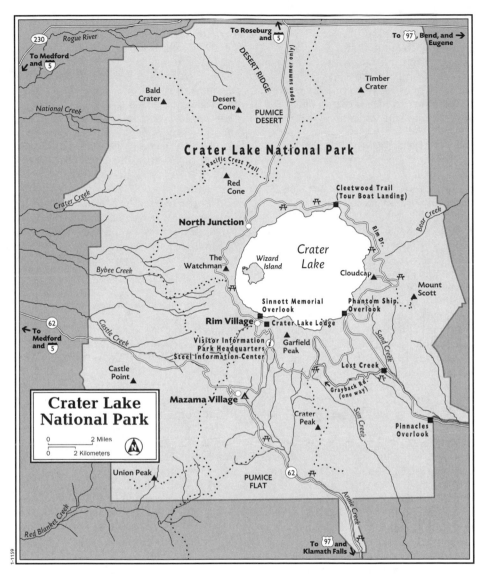

1-1159

over entirely, despite the long, cold winters at this elevation. The last time it froze completely was 1949.

The southern park entrance leads to the park's main tourist facilities. It is here that you'll find Mazama Village, which has a campground, motel, general store, and gas station; the Steel Information Center and park headquarters; and Rim Village, site of the Crater Lake Lodge, Rim Village Visitor Center, a gift shop, cafeteria, and, in winter, a cross-country ski and snowshoe rental shop.

Diamond Lake

76 miles east of Roseburg on Ore. 138; 4 miles north of Crater Lake National Park. Tel. 541/498-2531 or 541/793-3310. Camping, hiking, road biking, cross-country and downhill skiing, snowshoeing.

Though it can't hold a candle to nearby Crater Lake for beauty, this high Cascades lake still has a lot to offer. The lakeshore views of Mount Thielsen and Mount Bailey are reward enough for many of the folks who stay in the lake's many cabins and campsites. In summer, the lake is popular with families and good for canoeing and fishing. In winter, there are groomed cross-country ski trails, and snowcat trips for downhill skiers are offered to nearby Mount Bailey. The lake is also popular with snowmobilers.

Mount Thielsen Wilderness

East of Diamond Lake and Ore. 138 just north of Crater Lake National Park. Tel. 541/498-2531. Hiking, fishing, mountaineering.

Known as the "Lightning Rod of the Cascades," Mount Thielsen is a needlelike crag that rises to the east of Diamond Lake. This peak has been struck by lightning so often that its summit contains rocks that have actually been melted. Although the Pacific Crest Trail passes through this wilderness, there are few other trails. The ascent of Mount Thielsen, which is technical though fairly straightforward, is the main attraction. There are, however, a couple of small lakes as well.

Sky Lakes Wilderness

North of Ore. 140 and south of Ore. 62. Best accessed from Forest Service roads to the south and east. Tel. 541/885-3400. Hiking, fishing.

Dozens of lakes and ponds are scattered across the basin of this wilderness to the south of Crater Lake National Park. At more than 25 miles from north to south, the Sky Lakes Wilderness claims southern Oregon's longest wilderness stretch of the Pacific Crest Trail. Within this wilderness is 9,495-foot Mount McLoughlin, the highest peak in southern Oregon and a popular summit hike. This wilderness offers the best backpacking destinations in the southern Oregon Cascades.

Rogue River

The most famous stretch of the Rogue lies to the west of Grants Pass and is accessed from the Merlin–Galice Rd. (take exit 61 off I-5). Tel. 541/479-3735 or 541/770-2200. Camping, hiking, rafting, kayaking, fishing.

Perhaps the most famous river in Oregon, the Rogue is known for its superb steelhead and salmon fishing. While the Rogue stretches from Crater Lake National Park to the Pacific Ocean, the most interesting segment of the river is the federally designated National Wild and Scenic section that begins west of Grants Pass at the mouth of the Applegate River and extends all the way to Gold Beach. Within this stretch of river, the 35-mile portion between Grave Creek Bridge and Foster Bar is the most famous. This stretch is almost entirely inaccessible by road and in its lower reaches it passes through the Wild Rogue Wilderness. Although a hiking trail parallels this section, most people prefer to float the river in rafts, drift boats, and kayaks.

Kalmiopsis Wilderness

West of U.S. 199 and accessible from several roads in the Cave Junction area. Tel. 541/592-2166. Hiking, rafting, kayaking, fishing.

Encompassing the jumble of low mountains where the Siskiyous and the Coast Range come together, this 180,000-acre wilderness lies between U.S. 199 and the coast and is named for the kalmiopsis plant *(Kalmiopsis leachiana)*, which is endemic to these mountains and looks a bit like a dwarf rhododendron. The mountains here are characterized by serpentine, an often green, glossy rock. Flowing through this wilderness is a section of the Illinois River that is popular with rafters and kayakers. Even more challenging than the Rogue, the Illinois is not as well known outside the region.

Oregon Caves National Monument

50 miles southwest of Grants Pass off U.S. 199 at the end of Ore. 46. Tel. 541/592-2100. Spelunking, hiking, snowshoeing.

Although not especially large, Oregon Caves, which were discovered in 1874, are filled with fascinating formations created by the slow dripping of acidic water through the marble rock that forms this mountain. In 1909, the caverns and

Outdoor Resources

surrounding aboveground lands were designated a national monument to preserve what are some of the only true caverns in the state. Set high in the Siskiyou Mountains, the monument is surrounded by national forest.

Although there are no campgrounds within the national monument, there is a rustic lodge that was built in 1934. Campgrounds can be found in the national forest on the road that leads up to the caves. Hiking trails starting in the monument lead into the national forest and connect with trails that are open to mountain bikes.

What to Do & Where to Do It

BIRD WATCHING

For thousands of years birds have been gathering in the **Klamath Basin,** and as early as 1908, when President Teddy Roosevelt created the nation's first wildlife refuge, the importance of area wetlands was recognized. Although the lakes and marshes here at the base of the eastern slopes of the Cascades once covered more than 185,000 acres, today, due to the draining and conversion of these lands to agricultural uses, less than 25% of the wetlands remain. As an important stop on the Pacific Flyway, the Klamath Basin once saw more than 6 million waterfowl each spring and autumn. Today that number is down to just over 1 million birds, which represents approximately 80% of the waterfowl that use the Pacific Flyway.

Each season in this region presents different birding opportunities. Waterfowl numbers peak in March. Birds to look for include Ross's geese, ruddy ducks, northern pintails, northern shovelers, and cinnamon teals. In April and May songbirds and shorebirds proliferate. Look for American avocets and black-necked stilts. During summer, nesting waterfowl and marsh birds are abundant. Look for western and pied-billed grebes, American white pelicans (there are three breeding colonies in the Klamath Basin), white-faced ibises, sandhill cranes, great egrets, green-backed herons, double-crested cormorants, and various species of terns and gulls. Many of these species are most abundant in August and September. The autumn waterfowl migration begins in September when the first northern pintails and greater white-fronted geese arrive. By early November the number of waterfowl is back up around 1 million. Joining the earlier migrants are Canada, snow, and Ross's geese, as well as tundra swans, American wigeons, and green-winged teals. Winter is the time to observe the region's bald eagles. Also present at this time of year are golden eagles, northern harriers, rough-legged and red-tailed hawks.

However, as impressive as the region's waterfowl numbers are, the Klamath Basin is best known as the wintering grounds of the largest concentration of bald eagles in the contiguous United States. Between December and February, as many as 1,000 bald eagles gather here, with the greatest concentrations in California at Lower Klamath and at Tule Lake National Wildlife Refuges. However, up to 300 eagles roost each night in the ponderosa pines of the **Bear Valley National Wildlife Refuge** south of Klamath Falls off U.S. 97 near the town of Worden. Although access to this refuge is prohibited, it is possible to observe the morning mass fly-out from a side road west of U.S. 97 on the south side of Worden.

Right in the town of Klamath Falls, the **Link River Nature Trail** is a good place to look for waterfowl and songbirds, as well as white pelicans. However, it is a superb place to practice identifying swallows. Five species—tree, bank, northern rough-winged, cliff, and barn—are commonly sighted here. Also keep an eye out for black-crowned night herons. To find this trail, take the Oregon Avenue exit off U.S. 97 and go west to Moore Park.

North of Klamath Falls 50 miles (due east of Crater Lake) is the **Klamath Marsh National Wildlife Refuge,** which is a good place to see sandhill cranes, yellow rails, and shorebirds, as well as great gray owls, which live in the pine forests surrounding this large wetland. A 10-mile-long trail through the marshlands and forests is open for hiking, mountain biking, and skiing.

For more information on birding in this area, or to reserve one of the photo blinds at Lower Klamath or Tule Lake Refuge, contact the Refuge Manager, **Klamath Basin National Wildlife Refuges,** Route 1, Box 74, Tulelake, CA 96134 (tel. 916/667-2231). For further information, you can also contact the Klamath Basin Audubon Society, P.O. Box 354, Klamath Falls, OR 97601, which publishes the *Birder's Guide to the Klamath Basin.*

CROSS-COUNTRY SKIING

If you want to take some cross-country or telemark lessons or would like to do a guided day ski trip, contact **The Adventure Center,** 40 N Main St., Ashland, OR 97520 (tel. 800/444-2819 or 541/488-2819). Ski lessons are also available at **Diamond Lake Nordic Center** (tel. 800/733-7593). Diamond Lake Resort offers Crater Lake ski tours that include a snowcat ride to the north rim ski trail. Tours are $35 per person, but they operate only if there are at least 10 people going.

Cross-country skis can be rented at **Diamond Lake Resort** (tel. 800/733-7593), **Crater Lake's Rim Village ski shop** (tel. 541/594-2255), **Fish Lake Resort** (tel. 541/949-8500), and **Ashland Outdoor Store,** 37 Third St., Ashland (tel. 541/488-1202).

GROOMED TRAILS

Diamond Lake Nordic Center Trails

10.5 kilometers. Easy. 50 foot elevation gain. Access: 80 miles east of Roseburg on Ore. 138; 85 miles east of Medford on Ore. 62/Ore. 230. Tel. 800/733-7593. No trail fee. Map: Trailhead maps.

Though wide and well groomed, these are quite simply the most boring groomed cross-country trails I've ever been on. There's almost no topography and the monotonous appearance of the surrounding forests leaves little to distract you from your plodding. These trails make it painfully obvious that Diamond Lake Resort doesn't value cross-country skiers as much as it does snowmobilers, who get far more interesting trails to roar around on.

UNGROOMED TRAILS

Diamond Lake Trails

3–13 miles. Easy–most difficult. Up to 3,000-foot elevation gain. Access: Diamond Lake is 80 miles east of Roseburg on Ore. 138. Sno-parks can be found at both the north and south ends of the lake. Map: A rough map of ski trails is available from the Diamond Lake Resort Nordic Center.

On the North Shore, starting from the Diamond Lake Resort parking lot, is the Vista Trail, which heads west and climbs for 1.5 miles with good views of the lake along the way. Unfortunately, the snow cover is very unpredictable at this end of the lake and often there is not enough snow to ski this trail. From Diamond Lake Resort you can also ski the 11.5-mile Diamond Loop Trail that follows the route of the summer bike path that circles the lake.

On the east side of the lake, a challenging 13.5- to 14.5-mile loop is possible either from the Howlock Sno-Park (on the road to Diamond Lake Resort) or from the Thielsen Sno-Park on Ore. 138. This loop climbs more than 2,000 feet, much of it through scrubby forests with few views. The trail does, however, cross a couple of large meadows, the higher of which has a great view of Mount Thielsen. From the

Howlock Sno-Park, ski up the Howlock Mountain Trail for 3.4 miles, crossing Timothy Meadows, and go right on the Thielsen Creek Trail. In another 2.4 miles reach the meadow with the Mount Thielsen View. From here, turn right onto the Mount Thielsen Trail and continue climbing for another mile or so to the 7,300-foot high point of this loop. From here, ski down 3.2 miles, keeping right at the Pacific Crest Trail junction, to the Spruce Ridge Trail, which goes right and connects back up with the Howlock Mountain Trail in 2.5 miles. Go left to return to the sno-park.

Down at the south end of the lake are the South Diamond Sno-Park and the Three Lakes Sno-Park, both off Ore. 230. I prefer the latter sno-park, from which the Silent Creek Trail immediately leaves the snowmobile route and leads through scrubby forest to the bank of Silent Creek, a wide, shallow, spring-fed stream that lives up to its name. In about 2 miles, this trail crosses a road and a bridge over Silent Creek and continues to another bridge over the creek. Here, you can take a short trail to the right to visit tiny Teal Lake, which is usually covered with ice that is sometimes a beautiful shade of turquoise (not teal). Back on the main trail, cross the bridge and follow signs for the Diamond Lake Loop. This trail angles westward through the marsh at the south end of the lake before entering the forest again. A side trip across the marsh to the lakeshore is worthwhile and provides a good view of Mount Thielsen.

Back at the main trail, continue west until you cross a snowmobile road. Turn left onto this road and then take the next snowmobile route to the right. Within a half-mile another ski trail crosses this road. This is the ski trail to the summit of Mount Bailey. The full summit ascent is for experienced backcountry skiers, but the 750-foot climb to the Mount Thielsen viewpoint and Hemlock Butte shelter is a good intermediate route. For experienced skiers, the route onward from here to the summit, which is well above timberline, is the finest and most challenging in the area. Don't miss it. To return to the Three Lakes Sno-Park, turn left at the base of the Mount Bailey Trail to reach the Silent

Creek Trail and the route back to your car. This route, including the trip to the Hemlock Butte Shelter (but not the Mount Bailey summit climb), covers just over 10 miles.

Crater Lake Trails

2–33 miles. Easy–most difficult. 50–3,800-foot elevation gain. Access: 80 miles east of Medford at Rim Village in Crater Lake National Park. Map: Maps of the park's ski trails are available at the Steel Information Center at park headquarters.

Without a doubt, the rim of Crater Lake offers the best ski touring in the Northwest. In fact, it's some of the best in the country. Not only are there numerous views of sapphire-blue Crater Lake 1,000 feet below you, but the views to the west and the south take in Mount McLoughlin, Mount Shasta, and countless ridges and seemingly endless forest vistas as well.

The ultimate ski tour, of course, is the 30–33-mile circuit of the lake. Although this route has been done in a single day by racers, most skiers take three days and enjoy the views along the way. Because the weather is better and there's still plenty of snow, April and May are the most popular months to do this trip. The route is very straightforward, although you may have to do some route finding on the northeast side of the lake.

The West Rim Trail is the most popular day skiing area. The trail follows Rim Drive, which in summer is always clogged with cars circumnavigating the lake's rim. However, by winter the road is unplowed and snow cover turns it into a superb trail. Because the trail starts at 7,050 feet, this trail requires little climbing. However, if you want more exercise, just head down any of the open slopes that lead away from the lake. These slopes are perfect for practicing telemark turns. Views are to be had at the trailhead, in 1 mile at Discovery Point, in 2.8 miles on the south side of the Watchman, and in 3.8 miles at the Watchman/Wizard Island Overlook. Beyond this point there are many more viewpoints before reaching Cleetwood Cove trailhead at 10.4 miles from Rim Village. The West Rim Trail is best done in good weather and good snow conditions. The section of trail

around the Watchman, an 8,013-foot butte on the crater rim, crosses a known avalanche slope. The steepness of this slope also makes this a very difficult section of trail when the snow is icy or crusty. Consult with a ranger in the Steel Visitor Center at park headquarters for snow conditions before heading out. Because it is the most exposed, this trail also gets the worst winds.

Several other trails can be accessed from the West Rim Trail. These include the Dutton Creek Ski Route, which heads downhill from the West Rim trailhead to connect with the Pacific Crest Trail (PCT) in 2.4 miles and Ore. 62 in 4.5 miles. The PCT provides a less scenic alternative to the West Rim Trail. At 2.2 miles from the trailhead on the West Rim Trail, the Lightning Springs Trail heads downhill to the PCT, making possible a 13-mile loop that includes both the PCT and the West Rim Trail by way of the Dutton Creek and Lightning Springs trails.

For a warm-up, or to add a little more interesting terrain to your ski tour, try the Hemlock Trail, a 2-mile trail that starts on the east side of the Rim Village parking lot and meanders through forests and glades and up and down hills as it loops south of the Crater Lake Lodge. There are some good views to the south along this intermediate trail. Also behind the lodge is the Raven Trail, which leads steeply down to park headquarters and the East Rim Trail. This latter trail is for advanced skiers only.

The East Rim Trail is not nearly as popular as the West Rim Trail for the simple reason that it is between 4.25 and 5.4 miles to the first view of the lake (depending on where you start). This trail also has a lot more ups and downs. So, why would you want to do this section at all? To stay out of the wind, that's why. If after driving all the way here there's a gale-force wind blowing up the west slopes, you really don't have much choice.

The first section of the East Rim Trail is a steep, 600-foot descent to park headquarters. This 1-mile stretch of trail is popular with telemarkers, but can be avoided by novice and intermediate skiers by starting at headquarters. From headquarters it is a 2.3-mile ski to the junction with the Crater Peak Trail (if you've already seen the lake and are looking for a challenging trail, try this 5-mile round-trip route to the summit of 7,263-foot Crater Peak; this trail requires solid downhill skills), 3 miles to Vidae Falls, and 4.4 miles to Sun Notch, which is the first viewpoint onto the lake along this route. The next viewpoint onto the lake isn't until you reach Kerr Notch at 8.4 miles from the trailhead. This route passes two avalanche slopes, so be sure to check with a ranger to find out what the danger is. If it is high, there is an alternate route to avoid one of the avalanche slopes.

Fish Lake, Summit, and Great Meadow Sno-Parks

2–10 miles. Easy–more difficult. None–800-foot elevation gain. Access: 35–45 miles east of Medford or Ashland on Ore. 140. All three sno-parks are within 7 miles of each other between Fish Lake and the Ore. 140 junction with Dead Indian Memorial Hwy. Map: USFS Jackson–Klamath Winter Trails Map.

From the Fish Lake Sno-Park, intermediate skiers can head out a joint-use trail to the Lollipop Loops on the south side of the lake. These loops include almost 10 miles of marked trails.

Because it directly accesses an extensive network of marked ski trails, the Summit Sno-Park is a favorite of cross-country skiers. Intermediate and advanced skiers will want to do the 6.5-mile Lower Canal–McLoughlin Trail loop. This trail climbs about 800 feet on the Lower Canal Trail before looping back down to the sno-park. Along the route, there are great views of Mount McLoughlin and Brown Mountain. Some short, steep downhills are what warrant the difficulty rating. For a moderate 5-mile loop, ski up the Petunia Trail, go left on Big Mac, and return on Lower Canal. Open ridges along the Petunia Trail are great places to practice your downhill technique or telemark turns. For easy views of Mount McLoughlin, ski up Lower Canal Trail, go right on Pitt View (where you'll encounter the views), and then right again on McLoughlin and left on Petunia. This is a 4-mile loop.

With big, open meadows that become a vast expanse of crystalline white snow

in winter, the Great Meadow area truly lives up to its name. This is a great place to pretend you're in one of those classic Nordic skiing photographs: skiers kicking across a snowy plain with snow-coated pines in the background ... I'm sure you know what I'm talking about. This is a joint-use sno-park, so you'll find plenty of snowmobiles here as well. However, they have their own trails. Stick to the trails marked by blue diamonds and you shouldn't have to deal with the machines. These trails will take you along the edge of the meadow and then through the forest to trails along the shore of Lake of the Woods. Telemarkers will want to head south across the highway to the open slopes of Brown Mountain, which by summer are a vast expanse of lava.

Mount Ashland to Grouse Gap

6 miles round-trip. Easy–more difficult. 200-foot elevation gain. Access: From Ashland, take I-5 south to the Mount Ashland exit (exit 5) and drive 10 miles to Mount Ashland Ski Area. Map: USGS Mount Ashland.

This out-and-back ski route that follows an unplowed forest service road offers the second-best views of any ski trail in southern Oregon (Crater Lake has the best). The route follows the crest of the Siskiyou Mountains with views to the south of Mount Shasta, the Marble Mountains, and the Trinity Alps. At Grouse Gap, there is a ski shelter with a woodstove. This shelter makes a good turnaround point, but you can continue farther if you want. You'll find other cross-country ski areas back down the Mount Ashland Road. However, these don't offer the views of the crest route.

DOWNHILL SKIING & SNOWBOARDING

Mount Bailey Snowcat Skiing

Diamond Lake Resort, Diamond Lake, OR 97731. Tel. 800/733-7593 or 541/793-3333.

There isn't any heli-skiing in Oregon yet, but at Mount Bailey, adjacent to Diamond Lake, there is snowcat skiing that will get you into the untracked steep-and-deep stuff. Mount Bailey, the top of which is broad and treeless and lined with steep chutes, offers lots of runs of 3,000 vertical feet, and an average day here includes anywhere from 10,000 to 20,000 vertical feet of skiing. Only 12 people a day are taken out in the snowcat, which means plenty of untracked powder for everyone. The only drawback is that if you're a good skier, you'll find yourself doing a lot of waiting at the bottom for the less skilled skiers in the group. A day of skiing costs $160 ($120 before December 22 and after April 1), and multiday packages that include meals and lodging are available.

Mount Ashland Ski Area

15 miles south of Ashland (take exit 6 off I-5). Tel. 541/482-2897 (541/482-2754 for snow report). 23 trails; 4 lifts; 1,150 vertical feet. Lift hours: Sun–Wed 9am–4pm, Thurs–Sat 9am–10pm. Adult lift tickets $18 weekdays, $24 weekends.

It may be small, but Mount Ashland is a mogul-basher's heaven, and like the town of Ashland below, the ski area draws on the Bard of Avon for inspiration (all the runs and lifts have been given Shakespearean names). The Ariel lift accesses all the most heavily moguled runs, as well as the bowl skiing and chute diving off the Circe run. For long intermediate runs, drop off the Ariel chair onto Upper Dream and then take your choice of Caliban or Dream. This is definitely not a ski area for beginners, who will find only one short bunny slope and nothing to graduate to. Although there is night skiing here Thursday through Saturday, it is limited to the bunny slope and four intermediate runs.

Skis and snowboards can be rented at the ski area and in Ashland at **Ashland Mountain Supply,** 31 N Main St. (tel. 541/488-2749).

FISHING

If fishing is your passion, the steelhead and salmon of the Rogue and North Umpqua rivers probably already haunt your dreams. These two rivers attract anglers from all over the country with their promise of big fish. If you plan to fly-fish for steelhead on either of these rivers, you'll need an 8¹/₂- to 9¹/₂-foot 7- to 9-weight rod. Because both rivers are so heavily fished and have been for many years, fishing regulations are complex. Be very familiar with the regulations before you do any fishing.

The **North Umpqua** is the most renowned summer steelheading river in Oregon and was first made famous by Zane Grey. Today, 31 miles of the river from Deadline Falls to Soda Springs Dam is a federally designated Wild and Scenic River. This same 31 miles of river is also designated for fly-fishing only. Steamboat Creek, which flows into the river about midway through this 31-mile stretch, has been closed since 1932 to all fishing to preserve the spawning grounds of the North Umpqua's native summer steelhead. Consequently the waters just downstream from where this creek enters the North Umpqua are among the most famous in the Northwest. It is here that you'll find the Steamboat Inn, the foremost fly-fishing lodge in the Northwest. There are more than two dozen good steelhead holes in this area, which keeps it busy with anglers throughout the summer. However, there are also plenty of good holes farther downriver (try the big hole below Wright Creek Bridge). Good steelhead flies include Skunks, Green Butt Skunks, and leech patterns.

Fly-fishing supplies and equipment are available in Idleyld Park at **Blue Heron Fly Shop** (tel. 541/496-0448) just off Ore. 138, and in Steamboat at **Steamboat Inn** (tel. 541/498-2411). This latter shop is world famous and no fly angler should fish this river without first stopping in here for a few tips.

If you need a guide for the North Umpqua River, try **Larry Levine's River Wolf Guide Service** (tel. 541/496-0326), **North River Guide Service** (tel. 541/496-0309), **Jerry Q. Phelps** (tel. 541/672-8324), or **Summer Run Guide Service** (tel. 541/496-3037). Rates are generally between $100 and $200 per day.

Like the North Umpqua, the **Rogue River** is best known as a steelhead and salmon fishing river, with steelhead in parts of the river year-round and both spring and fall Chinook runs as well as a

How's the Fishin'?

One of the most frequently asked questions in southern Oregon is, "How's the fishing in Crater Lake?" The answer is, "Not too good." However, there are some rainbows and kokanee to be caught if you're willing to hike 700 feet down to Cleetwood Cove (and back up with your catch). No fishing license is necessary to fish the lake and there is no limit on how many fish you can take. In fact, the park service would be happy if more people fished this lake.

Until the end of the 19th century, there were no fish in Crater Lake, and it is perhaps partly for this reason that it is one of the purest lakes in the world. With no inlets or outlets, the lake was effectively cut off from any chance of naturally acquiring a fish population. However, in the late 19th century, the human hand intervened where nature feared to tread, and fish were introduced to the lake in hopes of attracting more visitors. Over the next 50 years

or so, rainbow, cutthroat, and brown trout, steelhead, and coho and kokanee salmon were stocked in the lake. However, only the rainbows and kokanee have survived since the discontinuation of this misguided program.

Other than the shores around Cleetwood Cove, the only other place to fish Crater Lake is from Wizard Island, where you may have good luck if you are stealthy enough and lucky enough. To fish from Wizard Island, take one of the early boat tours from Cleetwood Cove, get off on the island, and arrange to take one of the later boats back.

Two things to remember are that no live or organic bait is allowed in the lake, and cleaning fish in the lake is prohibited. In addition to lake fishing, Crater Lake National Park also offers stream fishing for several species of trout. However, for the most part, the park's streams are fairly inaccessible.

coho run. Of the steelhead, it is the summer-run "half-pounders" that are perhaps most famous. These small (under 2 pounds) fish are known for the fight they put up and show up in August and September. Much larger fish are around from May through July and September through November, at which time the winter steelheads begin showing up. Fishing the riffles in the Hellgate Canyon area is usually productive, though it is the lower Wild and Scenic section of the river that is most popular (and most remote, with no road access for 35 miles). This stretch is, for the most part, the realm of guided fishing trips. It is also here that some of the best salmon fishing is to be had. Although most salmon fishing takes place below Gold Rey Dam just east of Gold Hill, there is also good fishing for spring Chinook upriver from Shady Cove. While the Rogue River is best known for its steelhead and salmon fishing, the North, Middle, and South forks all hold trout, but it is the North Fork that offers the best fishing for both wild and hatchery trout.

If you're heading to the Rogue, fly-fishing supplies and equipment are available in Grants Pass at **McKenzie Outfitters,** 1470 NE 7th St. (tel. 541/474-0211), and in Merlin at **Silver Sedge Fly,** 325 Galice Rd. (tel. 541/476-2456). For general tackle, try **Skipper's Tackle,** 200 Galice Rd., Merlin (tel. 541/474-2838). If you want to do a guided fishing trip on the Rogue River, try **River Trips Unlimited** (tel. 541/779-3798), **Rogue Excursions Unlimited** (tel. 800/460-3865 or 541/826-6222), **Rogue River Raft Trips** (tel. 541/476-3825), or **Rogue Wilderness** (tel. 800/336-1647 or 541/479-9554). Other area guides include **Russ Nye** (tel. 541/474-7799) and **Geoff's Guide Service** (tel. 541/474-0602). Expect to pay between $85 and $130 for a day of fishing.

Aside from the steelhead and salmon fishing on the Rogue and North Umpqua, southern Oregon has lots of lakes that offer bass fishing. Some of these include **Lost Creek Reservoir** near Shady Cove on the Rogue River, **Galesville Reservoir** near Azalea north of Grants Pass, **Lake Selmac** west of Grants Pass, **Emigrant Lake** east of Ashland, and **Applegate Lake** southwest of Jacksonville. Up in the high country, there is good trout fishing at **Willow Lake, Fish Lake, Lake of the Woods,** and **Fourmile Lake** between Medford and Klamath Falls on Ore. 140, in **Upper Klamath Lake** (which produces lunker rainbows), and at **Diamond** and **Lemolo lakes** (good for brown trout) north of Crater Lake. At Diamond Lake, there is even charter fishing out of **Diamond Lake Resort** (tel. 800/733-7593). Most of these high-elevation lakes are stocked annually with brook trout. Lake of the Woods, Fourmile Lake, and Willow Lake also hold kokanee. For information on fishing in **Crater Lake,** see the accompanying sidebar.

One other southern Oregon river that warrants mention here is the **Williamson River,** which flows into the north end of Agency Lake, which in turn adjoins Upper Klamath Lake. This crystal-clear, spring-fed river is considered one of the premier trout streams in the West, and yet due to its remote location, it is little known outside the community of serious fly anglers. Collier State Park and the forest service's Williamson River Campground both provide access to this river. The trout here are trophy-size rainbows that come upriver from the lake to spawn.

HIKING & BACKPACKING

WITHIN CRATER LAKE NATIONAL PARK

Garfield Peak

3.4 miles round-trip. Moderate. 1,010-foot elevation gain. Access: Crater Lake National Park. Trailhead is at east end of Rim Village parking lot. Map: USGS Crater Lake West.

Sure the view from Rim Village borders on sublime, but the parking lot full of cars, families wandering along the rim trail, and general national park see-it-all-without-leaving-your-car atmosphere doesn't do this natural wonder justice. You'll leave most of the crowds behind, get in a good hike, and treat yourself to an even more breathtaking (literally, since the hike starts above 7,000 feet) view of the lake by hiking to the summit of 8,054-foot Garfield Peak, which lies just east of Rim Village. The route gains all its elevation in a short 1.5 miles of nearly constant switchbacks. From the summit, the entire lake is visible below, including the island called Phantom Ship, which is not visible from Rim Village. To the south, Mount Shasta can be seen.

Mount Scott Trail

5 miles round-trip. Strenuous. 1,480-foot elevation gain. Access: Crater Lake National Park. Trailhead is 14 miles east of park headquarters on East Rim Dr. and across the road from Cloudcap junction. Map: USGS Crater Lake East.

If the trail to Garfield Peak had a few too many other hikers on it for your tastes, try the trail to the top of 8,929-foot Mount Scott. This is the highest point within Crater Lake National Park, and the trail is longer and steeper and entails more elevation gain than the trail up Garfield Peak. These factors tend to weed out those folks who just aren't serious about their views. Needless to say, the views from the summit are the most far-reaching in the park, encompassing not only the entire lake but such surrounding peaks as Mount Thielsen, Mount Shasta, and Mount McLoughlin, as well as the vast expanse of Klamath Lake to the southeast. The views don't start until about a mile into this hike, so don't be discouraged. Carry plenty of water.

OUTSIDE THE NATIONAL PARK

Seven Lakes Basin and Devil's Peak

18 miles round-trip. Moderate. 1,700-foot elevation gain. Access: From Ore. 62 at Fort Klamath (south of Crater Lake National Park), go west on Nicholson Rd. for 4 miles, turn right onto FS 3334, and continue 6 miles to the end of the road and the Sevenmile Trailhead. Map: USGS Devil's Peak, USFS Sky Lakes Wilderness.

The Sky Lakes Wilderness, due south of Crater Lake National Park, more than lives up to its name. Within the wilderness, there are more than 50 named lakes and some 150 other ponds, and it is here, on a 7,300-foot saddle between Devil's Peak and Lee Peak, that the Pacific Crest Trail reaches its highest point in Oregon. As anywhere else, the lakes here are a magnet for hikers, and consequently, if you're looking for solitude, plan a weekday hike. The rocky landscape around Devil's Peak is as rugged as it gets in southern Oregon, while the lakes of Seven Lakes Basin, north of the peak, offer plenty of easy exploring and good swimming and fishing.

From the Sevenmile Trailhead, hike southeast, climbing gradually to meet the PCT in about 1.75 miles. Go left on the PCT and continue another 3 miles to the junction with the Seven Lakes Trail. Go right on this latter trail and wind your way past Grass, Middle, Cliff, and South lakes. Because Cliff Lake has the best view of Devil's Peak, it has always been the favored spot for campsites. For more solitude, try camping near one of the other lakes. After pitching camp, you can explore the other trails around the Seven Lakes Basin or head to the summit of Devil's Peak. To make the summit hike, continue south of South Lake on the Seven Lakes Trail and at the next junction go left. In another 0.25 miles, go left again on a trail that climbs almost to the summit of 7,431-foot Lucifer and a junction with the PCT. Go left here to continue to the summit of Devil's Peak (on a side trail off the PCT), from which you can see Mount Bailey and the Crater Lake Rim to the north, Klamath Lake to the southeast, and Mount Shasta to the south. From the summit, drop down to the east to pick up the PCT and go north. In about 2.5 miles, you'll come to a trail that leads back down into the Seven Lakes Basin.

Mount McLoughlin Trail

12 miles round-trip. Strenuous. 3,900-foot elevation gain. Access: From Ore. 140, turn north on FS 3661 (signed Fourmile Lake), go roughly 3 miles north, turn left on FS 3650, and continue 0.2 miles to the trailhead parking lot. Map: USGS Mount McLoughlin.

At 9,495 feet high, Mount McLoughlin is the highest peak in southern Oregon, and

dominates the skyline for miles around. Appearing perfectly conical from the west, this peak leaves no doubts about its volcanic origins. However, the view from the east, where this trail begins, is much more rugged, with steep cliffs gouged out of the higher slopes by long-gone glaciers. Although glacial ice is no longer carving away at this mountain, snow does usually linger near the summit throughout the summer. The trail starts in dense forest without views, but in 1.25 miles, there is a short side trail that leads to little Freye Lake, which does have a view of the mountain and is the best place to camp. From the Freye Lake junction, it's another 3 miles to timberline. Once you get up above timberline, you're walking on rock and shale on a ridge that drops off steeply on both sides. The view is enough to make you dizzy. From the summit, all of southern Oregon and much of northern California is spread out below you. To the east is the vast expanse of Klamath Lake. To the west you can see Medford, Mount Ashland, and the Siskiyou Mountains. To the south, in California, rises Mount Shasta. This hike can take all day, so bring plenty of water. Although not nearly as busy as the trails in Crater Lake National Park, this hike is popular.

Brown Mountain Trails

8–12 miles round-trip. Easy–moderate. 600–700-foot elevation gain. Access: On Ore. 140 east of Fish Lake, watch for the Pacific Crest Trail crossing. Map: USGS Brown Mountain.

While signs of past volcanic activity abound throughout the southern Oregon Cascades, it is only at Brown Mountain, between Fish Lake and Lake of the Woods, that you can hike across lava fields. Here, the Pacific Crest Trail crosses the western flank of the aptly named 7,311-foot Brown Mountain, and the High Lakes Trail and Fish Lake Trail traverse the lava fields on the mountain's northern slopes. For a good long exploration of the lava fields, start your hike where the PCT crosses Ore. 140. Heading south from the highway you are almost immediately into the otherworldly lava landscape. Within the first half mile, you begin to get a view up to the summit of Brown Mountain and north to Mount McLoughlin. There is also a brief glimpse of Fish Lake. However, on this unusual hike it is not the distant vistas but rather the foreground of gnarled lava boulders that is so captivating.

The 4-mile point, where the trail begins to descend toward Dead Indian Plateau, is a good place to turn around. To learn a bit about these lava fields, you might want to shorten your hike on the PCT and add some mileage on the High Lakes Trail, which winds its way east from the PCT to Lake of the Woods. Along this trail there are interpretive signs. If you are camped at Fish Lakes Campground, you can reach the PCT by hiking for 2 miles on the Fish Lake Trail. Both the Fish Lake and High Lakes trails intersect the PCT about 0.25 miles south of Ore. 140. Carry lots of water.

Rogue River Trail

41 miles one-way. Moderate–strenuous. 2,000-foot elevation gain. Access: At Grave Creek Bridge. Take exit 61 off of I-5 and drive 24 miles west on the Merlin–Galice Rd. Map: USGS Galice, Marial, and Agness.

This cliff-hanging trail must be the most fabulous low-elevation hike in the state. The valley of the Rogue is as awe-inspiring as the Columbia Gorge, but on a human scale. Along the river's banks great blue herons are a common sight. Once when my wife and I were hiking this trail, a heron erupted suddenly from the trees 10 feet in front of us with a primeval squawk that nearly scared us right over the edge of the cliff. River otters are also frequently seen from this trail. They fish for salmon and steelhead and eat them while lounging on riverside boulders. The deer that inhabit this valley have become very tame and frequently wander into camps. Black bears also occasionally visit camps, so be sure to hang your food at night.

Most people take four or five days to hike the trail, spending time leisurely exploring along the banks of the river, doing some fishing, and swimming in side creeks (Tate Creek, 33 miles down the trail, has a natural water slide 25 feet long). There are many good campsites and even several rustic lodges that are generally accessible only on foot or by boat. Should you want to hike unencumbered by a backpack, you could do a lodge-to-lodge hike on this trail.

Before starting down this trail, you may want to pick up *The Wild and Scenic Rogue River,* an informative map/brochure published by the Forest Service, and the BLM's *Rogue River Trail* booklet, a mile-by-mile description of the river. Both of these are available from the Rand Visitor Center, 14335 Galice Rd., Merlin, OR 97532 (tel. 541/479-3735), which is open daily between May 15 and October 15 each year.

Anyone who is allergic to poison oak may want to think twice about hiking here. This noxious plant lines the trail and at times grows as big as a tree, with branches arching over the trail! Ticks are also a problem.

Kalmiopsis Rim Trail to Eagle Mountain

5 miles round-trip. Easy–moderate. 900-foot elevation gain in; 500 feet out. Access: From U.S. 199 between Kerby and Selma, go west on Eight Dollar Rd., which becomes FS 4201. After crossing the bridge over the Illinois River, the road, now gravel, begins to climb and is sometimes very rough. Approximately 14 miles from U.S. 199, turn right on FS 142 and continue a half-mile past FS 141 (signed for Onion Camp). Map: USGS Pearsoll Peak and Josephine Mountain, USFS Kalmiopsis and Wild Rogue Wildernesses.

Superb vistas from a rocky serpentine ridge start within a few hundred yards of the trailhead on this ridgetop trail overlooking the Kalmiopsis Wilderness. The Kalmiopsis Rim Trail stretches for more than 40 miles along the east side of this wilderness, and though the section of trail between Onion Camp and Chetco Pass is outside the wilderness boundary, it is still one of the most scenic stretches. This out-and-back route spends most of its length in meadows and atop barren rock outcroppings and scree slopes. Tiny plants somehow manage to survive in this harsh environment, and contorted Jeffrey pines and mat-forming manzanita bushes dominate on this dry, windswept ridge. The trail climbs first toward 4,464-foot Whetstone

Butte, the summit of which can be reached by a bit of scrambling from the trail. From here, the trail drops down through the forest to a saddle below 4,399-foot Eagle Mountain. It is a steep climb on an open hillside to the wide, flat summit of Eagle Mountain. Far below to the east, you can glimpse the Illinois River, and to the west is the Chetco River. Beyond Eagle Mountain, the trail drops down to Chetco Pass and the views are less spectacular. There is no water along this ridge, which can get pretty hot in summer, so carry plenty.

HORSEBACK RIDING

Southern Oregon seems to have more opportunities for horseback riding than any other region of the state. Whether you want to ride the High Cascades around Diamond Lake or the oak savannahs around Ashland, there's a stable that can put you in the saddle. Rides generally start around $20 for one hour at any of these stables.

At the north end of Diamond Lake, which is just north of Crater Lake National Park's northern entrance, **Diamond Lake Horse Corrals** (tel. 541/793-3337) schedules rides between June and September. These trail rides wander through scrubby pine forests between Diamond Lake and Mount Thielsen. On the south side of the national park, horseback rides are offered by **Crazy Cayuse Ranch & Pack Station** (tel. 541/779-9121) at Union Creek Stables, which is located across from the Farewell Bend Campground just north of Union Creek Resort on Ore. 62.

At Lake Selmac, 23 miles south of Grants Pass on U.S. 199, **Lake Selmac Outfitters** (tel. 541/597-4989 or 541/597-4507) offers guided rides of varying lengths. Another option to the north of Grants Pass is Happy Trails (tel. 541/471-3733).

In the Ashland area, both **Circle C Stables,** 1275 Old Hwy. 99 (tel. 541/482-7463), and **Mountain Gate Stables,** 4399 Hwy. 66 (tel. 541/482-8873), take riders into the hills outside town for stupendous views of the valley. A little farther from town, there is **Green Springs Outback,** 11475 Hwy. 66 (tel. 541/488-5062), which leads rides through old-growth

forests and up to views of area lakes. In the winter, they offer horse-drawn sleigh rides.

HOT SPRINGS

Located not far from Toketee Lake off Ore. 138, **Umpqua Hot Springs** are perched on a hillside of travertine high above the North Umpqua River. The setting is unlike that of any other hot spring in the state, and the water is the hottest I've ever experienced in the Cascades. The natural travertine pool is covered by a well-made log lean-to, and a couple of small platforms look out over the river below. The springs are about 0.25 miles from the road across a footbridge and up a steep trail that can be very slippery and muddy in the rainy season. To reach the hot springs, follow signs to Toketee Lake from Ore. 138 about 20 miles west of Diamond Lake and continue past the lake. In 3 miles, turn right onto gravel FS 3401, and continue 2 miles to the hot springs trailhead on the left.

MOUNTAIN BIKING

North Umpqua Trail
(Tioga and Hot Springs Segments)

7–32 miles. Easy–strenuous. 300–1,500-foot elevation gain. Access: For the Tioga Segment, drive 6 miles east of Glide on Ore. 138 and follow signs to Swiftwater County Park; for the Hot Springs Segment, follow signs to Toketee Lake from Ore. 138 about 20 miles west of Diamond Lake. Map: USFS North Umpqua Trail Map; USGS Glide, Mace Mountain, and Old Fairview.

The North Umpqua Trail stretches for 79 miles from east of Glide to the Pacific Crest Trail in the Mount Thielsen Wilderness, and aside from the section of trail within the wilderness, this trail is open to mountain bikes. There are, however, segments of the trail that make for decidedly better riding. One good short section is the Hot Springs Segment, which goes east from Toketee Lake for 3.5 miles to cross FS 3401. This road can then be ridden back to the lake for a 7-mile loop ride. This is one of the only segments that can be ridden as a loop without venturing onto busy Ore. 138. This section starts out near the boat ramp and immediately crosses the river on a foot/bike bridge before heading upstream along the river. However, the best feature of this ride is its easy access to Umpqua Hot Springs, which are across a footbridge over the river and up a short, steep hiking trail.

The westernmost stretch of this trail, known as the Tioga Segment, is among the most popular sections. It is 16 miles long and includes both easy, rolling terrain and a steep climb up and around Bob Butte. Although you can loop back to the start on Ore. 138, traffic is much scarier than the worst section of trail. I prefer turning around and riding the trail back down. And no one says you have to ride the whole segment. Turn around when the trail ceases to be entertaining.

Diamond Lake Loop

21 miles round-trip. Moderate. 1,200-foot eleva-tion gain. Access: 76 miles east of Roseburg on Ore. 138, follow signs toward Diamond Lake Resort and park at the Howlock Mountain Trailhead beside the Diamond Lake Horse Cor-rals. Map: USGS Diamond Lake.

The Diamond Lake area just north of Cra-ter Lake National Park abounds in cross-country ski trails that when free of snow make excellent mountain-bike trails. Sev-eral of these trails combined with a few rough logging roads and a paved bike path can be strung together for a fun ride.

From the trailhead, ride south on the North Crater Trail, which parallels the east shore of Diamond Lake, though far enough away that you'd hardly know there was even a lake nearby. At about 4.5 miles, go right on a gravel road that will take you down to the lake, where you'll pick up the paved bike path almost directly across the paved lakeside road. Follow this bike path along the south shore of the lake around the Broken Arrow Campground. About 1 mile from the campground, watch for a trail on your left. Turn onto this trail and pedal past tiny Teal Lake. In 0.25 miles, go right on a paved road, and in another 0.25 miles, turn left onto Silent Creek Trail. This ex-quisite single-track parallels the beautiful

spring-fed Silent Creek. This 20-foot-wide stream is crystal clear, perfectly quiet, and bridged by numerous small logs that make the creek look like a ladder.

The trail parallels the creek for 1 mile, then curves into woods to meet the bot-tom end of Mount Bailey Trail, which you will soon be riding down. Take the rutted dirt 4 × 4 road to the left, not the trail, and start climbing steeply uphill. In the next 2.5 miles, you do just about all of the climbing on this ride. After this climb, the road drops down a steep, rocky stretch at the bottom of which you turn right onto another dirt road. In 0.75 miles you reach the end of your climbing as the road crosses the Mount Bailey Trail. Turn right and begin your freewheeling descent. In 0.5 miles, watch for a pile of rocks on the left. Scramble up to the top of these rocks, known as Hemlock Butte, for *the* view of this ride. Below is Diamond Lake and to the east rises Mount Thielsen. This is a great place for lunch!

From here, it's 1.5 miles to the bottom of the Mount Bailey Trail and the junction you rode through as you began your climb. Go left down the dirt road, and left again on the road that goes north along the lake's west shore. Watch for the bike path crossing and turn left onto the paved trail. Follow this path around the lake to Diamond Lake Resort and then ride out the resort's paved entrance road to the main road and turn left to return to the Howlock Mountain Trailhead.

High Lakes/Fish Lake Trail

25 miles round-trip. Easy–moderate. 700-foot elevation gain. Access: 1 mile west of Fish Lake and 1 mile south of Ore. 140 on Big Elk Rd. at North Fork Campground. Map: USGS Brown Mountain and Lake of the Woods South.

This is a very easy trail, too easy as far as some mountain bikers are concerned. However, it ranks high on the scenery scale, and there are few places in the coun-try where you can ride through lava flows as impressive as those through which this trail passes.

Starting at North Fork Campground, the trail follows the North Fork of Little Butte Creek for 0.5 miles. This is a picture-perfect trout stream flanked by meadows on both sides. Along the creek on the opposite shore can also be seen the first lava beds of this ride. Just before the Fish Lake Dam, the trail enters the woods, where it meanders for a half-mile before you get a view of the lake. Lots of rocks and roots along this stretch make it the most technical part of the ride. As the trail skirts the lake, there is a good view of Brown Mountain. From Fish Lake Campground, there are two choices: continue on the Fish Lake Trail or take the High Lakes Trail, which starts on the right just up the campground entrance road. Either way it is 2 miles of climbing to a junction with the Pacific Crest Trail (closed to bikes).

On the far side of the PCT begin 3 miles of riding through Brown Mountain's lava beds on an immaculate trail of crushed and packed cinders. Along the way there are interpretive signs explaining past volcanic activity in this area. The trail climbs another 200 to 300 feet. After leaving the lava, the trail is exceedingly flat for 2.5 miles as it skirts Lake of the Woods and then Great Meadows before ending at Ore. 140. Unless you have arranged a car shuttle, turn around and ride back the way you came.

A couple of other good mountain-biking trails in this area make it a great spot for a long weekend of riding. In addition to the High Lakes Trail, there are the Rye Spur Trail, which connects Ore. 140 with Fourmile Lake (ride a loop using FS 3661 as the uphill route), and the Brown Mountain Trail (which can be ridden as a 22-mile loop around Brown Mountain by utilizing the High Lakes Trail, Brown Mountain Trail, and several connecting forest service roads).

Lithia Loop

28 miles. Strenuous. 3,000-foot elevation gain. Access: Start this ride in Lithia Park in downtown Ashland. Map: USGS Ashland.

This gravel-road loop is the most popular mountain-bike ride in the Ashland area, and it is more of a training ride than anything else. The ride starts out with a grueling 7 miles of climbing before leveling off for 15 miles of rolling road through the hills high above Ashland. The last 6 miles are why anyone ever bothers—a straight shot of ear-to-ear-grinning, who-needs-breaks downhill screaming.

Start the ride by heading up Granite Road from the upper end of Lithia Park. This road becomes FS 2060 and climbs for 7 miles into the drainage of the Ashland Creek, which is the watershed for the city of Ashland. Once you finally top out (at 5,000 feet, by the way), this gravel road rolls up and down as it traverses the lower slopes of the Siskiyou Mountains. Finally you begin the payoff for all the grunt-work of getting up on these mountains—the 6-mile descent. But halfway down, watch for a trail sign on the right and hit the brakes. This is the White Rabbit Trail, a ridiculously fun 2.3-mile, 700-foot single-track descent to the suburbs of Ashland. This trail cruises through a bizarre forest of madrone trees, drops through tight switchbacks, spits you out onto bluffs with jaw-dropping views of the city far below, then shoves you through patches of poison oak that will have you regretting you ever took this route (wear long pants or tights and you'll save your skin). Finally, you wind up back on an incredibly steep paved road (Park Street) that is gated at the top of the hill. On the other side of the gate lie the suburbs. Drop down this road to a canal and hang a left onto the path beside the water. This path is a popular neighborhood dog-walking route, so you'll probably have to keep it slow. When the path narrows, bail out onto the roads again, drop down to Siskiyou Boulevard, and go left to get back to downtown Ashland and Lithia Park. Now that's a bike ride!

An alternative, if you can arrange a car shuttle, is to start at the top of Mount Ashland and ride 15 miles and 4,600 feet back down to town using the Bull Gap Trail to FS 2080 to FS 2060 to the White Rabbit Trail. Who says you have to pay to play?

Siskiyou Crest

30 miles round-trip. Moderate. 850-foot elevation gain. Access: From Ashland, take I-5 south to the Mount Ashland exit (exit 5) and drive

10 miles to Mount Ashland Ski Area. Map: USGS Mount Ashland and Siskiyou Peak.

While the Lithia Loop is a grueling climb that can be appreciated only by cyclists with thighs of steel, the Siskiyou Crest ride, which simply follows FS 20 from Mount Ashland Ski Area to Jackson Gap, is a scenic cruise suitable for novice riders. However, the views from this 6,600-foot subalpine ridge are so stupendous that no one should miss a chance to ride here. Visible to the south are Mount Shasta, the Marble Mountains, and the Trinity Alps.

Don't be discouraged by the distance, which is to Dutchman Peak. There is no need to ride all the way to enjoy the views. Turn around whenever you feel like it and you likely won't miss much other than the last steep 1.5-mile climb to the summit of Dutchman Peak. If you feel like climbing but don't want to do so many miles, ride the steep road to the summit of Mount Ashland. This road starts near the beginning of this ride.

Applegate Lake Loop/Payette Trail

18 miles round-trip. Moderate. 600-foot elevation gain. Access: From Ore. 238 in Ruch (west of Jacksonville), drive 14.5 miles south on Applegate River Rd., turn left onto FS 1075, cross the Applegate Dam, and continue less than 1.25 miles to the French Gulch Camp and Trailhead on the right. Map: USGS Carberry Creek and Squaw Lakes.

This is a great ride for novice mountain bikers (but only those who aren't highly allergic to poison oak). The fun, easy ride around emerald-green Applegate Lake includes 13 miles of single-track riding, most of which is nearly flat. The two trails that this route follows stay close to the lake most of the time and have good views of both the lake and the surrounding pine-forested mountains.

From the trailhead, head west on the Payette Trail along the French Arm of the lake and follow the convoluted shoreline for 9 miles to the Manzanita Trailhead on FS 1041. Follow this road as it parallels the lakeshore, and when you reach the paved Elliott Creek Road, turn right. In 1 mile turn right on Applegate River Road and then, in another 0.25 miles, turn into the shady Watkins Campground. The single-track begins again to the left as you enter the campground's parking lot. From here, it is just over 4 miles on the narrow single-track of the Da-ku-be-te-de Trail to Hart-tish Picnic Area, where there is a bit of paved trail before you have to rejoin Applegate River Road. Continue up this road and turn right over the dam to return to the French Gulch Trailhead.

Because the trail is often crowded by poison oak, long pants and long sleeves are a must. In fact, I'd recommend this primarily as a winter ride, when you're more likely to have your skin covered and there's less sap in the poison oak. This ride's other drawback is that the lake is rarely full of water and consequently often has a bathtub-ring appearance.

If you want a more challenging ride, try the Stein Butte Trail, which starts at the junction of Elliott Creek Road and FS 1041 and climbs more than 2,300 feet to Stein Butte. After 7.5 miles of single-track, you can loop back to the starting point on FS 1050 (which happens to be in California).

PACKSTOCK TRIPS

Crazy Cayuse Ranch and Pack Station (tel. 541/779-9121) at Union Creek Stables, which are located across from the Farewell Bend Campground just north of Union Creek Resort on Ore. 62, offers trips of varying lengths in the national forests surrounding Crater Lake National Park. **Greensprings Outback,** 11475 Hwy. 66, Ashland, OR 97520 (tel. 541/488-5062), which is located east of Ashland near Hyatt Lake, offers horse-packing trips ranging in length from three to ten days. **Lake Selmac Outfitters** (tel. 541/597-4989 or 541/597-4507), which has its stables west of Grants Pass, offers overnight rides into the Siskiyou Mountains. Expect to pay around $100 per night per person for pack trips.

ROAD BIKING

Diamond Lake Loop

10.5 miles round-trip. Easy. 100-foot elevation gain. Access: 76 miles east of Roseburg.

It isn't often that you find a paved bike path in the middle of the woods, which makes this ride something of an anomaly. The path circles Diamond Lake with views of Mount Bailey, Mount Thielsen, and the lake along the way. The path is easy, flat, and at least 6 feet wide. The most scenic part is the area west of Broken Arrow Campground (a good starting point) at the south end of the lake. Here, you'll ride through meadows and cross the whispering Silent Creek. The trail then heads up the west side of the lake through forests for quite a while, then crosses a road and begins to hug the shoreline, where you get your first views of the lake since leaving Broken Arrow. The east side of the lake, from Diamond Lake Resort at the north end to Broken Arrow Campground, is the most developed stretch of shoreline, and though there are good views of Mount Bailey, the paved roads, parking lots, and pizza parlor detract somewhat. Diamond Lake Campground sprawls through most of this area.

If you want to tack on some good road miles or feel like another nearby ride of roughly the same length, ride or drive 6 miles north on Ore. 138 to the Lemolo Lake road and continue another 3 miles to this attractive reservoir. A 12-mile-long road circles this blue-green lake. At the point where the road crosses the dam that impounds these waters, there are spectacular views—down into a gorge of the North Umpqua River and up to the pinnacle of Mount Thielsen.

Crater Lake Rim Road

33 miles. Moderate–strenuous. 3,800-foot elevation gain. Access: 80 miles east of Medford at Rim Village in Crater Lake National Park.

The 33-mile circuit of Crater Lake is one of the most popular road-bike trips in the state, despite the heavy car traffic with which riders must share the road. Although it would seem at first that this would be an easy trip, numerous ups and downs (especially on the east side of the lake) turn this into a very demanding ride. Also keep in mind that not only are there more hills on the east side, but there are also fewer views, which makes that side of the lake a bit tedious. A more view-packed alternative would be to do the 21-mile out-and-back ride from Rim Village to the Cleetwood Cove trailhead (and maybe add on a boat tour on the lake).

Ashland–Talent Loop

21 miles round-trip. Moderate. 500-foot elevation gain. Access: Start this ride at the Plaza in downtown Ashland.

From the Plaza, ride up Main Street and turn left on Oak Street, which leads downhill and out of town. In 1.3 miles, go straight on Eagle Mill Road, and in another 1.6 miles, take a right on Valley View Road—aptly named for its expansive views. In 0.7 miles, turn left onto West Valley View Road, where the big views of the hills continue. Although this road has no shoulders, it does not get much traffic. In 1.6 miles, turn left to stay on West Valley View. In another 0.9 miles, take a right on Talent Avenue, and in 0.4 miles, turn left onto Colver Road. In 1.5 miles, turn left on Adams Road, a gorgeous rolling route past farms, orchards, and pastures. Stay on Adams for 2.1 miles, and at Anderson Creek Road, go straight ahead on a great downhill stretch. In 0.9 miles, go left on Wagner Creek Road, and in another 0.9 miles, go straight onto Rapp Road at the stop sign. In 0.8 miles, turn left onto Talent Avenue, and in 0.6 miles, turn right onto Suncrest Road. In 0.5 miles, turn right onto the Bear Creek Greenway bike path, which follows the creek for 3.6 miles to Valley View Road. Turn left here and then right onto Eagle Mill Road to retrace your route back to Lithia Park. If you still have energy, finish your ride with a pedal to the top of the park and a coast back down.

To turn this ride into a half century, you could continue on back roads to the historic town of Jacksonville. This route adds roughly 24 miles and includes several steep hills. However, if you are up to it, it's a great ride. The route leaves the above ride from Colver Road just past the Adams Road turn. Turn left onto Pioneer Road and climb over a steep hill to Griffin Creek Road. Turn left and follow this road over another hill (the road becomes Poorman Creek Road). Turn right on Sterling Creek

Road and right again on Cady Road, which leads into Jacksonville. After exploring town, ride east on South Stage Road, turn right on Dark Hollow Road, and ride this road up another steep hill to return to Pioneer Road.

ROCK CLIMBING

The most popular climbing area in this region is located south of Ashland about 15 miles off Ore. 66 (turn right on Tyler Creek Road at milepost 15 and go 0.25 miles south). **Greensprings,** as this climbing area is known, consists of basalt columns, and though the wall isn't too big, it offers a lot of diversity. Because the wall faces south, it can get hot in summer, and is often warm enough for climbing in the middle of winter. Before heading out this way, you should pick up *A Climbers Guide to the Greensprings Climbing Area* by Mahlon Kerr-Valentic, which is available at Ashland outdoors stores. Oh, yeah—be sure to bring a helmet. There's a lot of loose rock here.

More remote and scenic climbing can be found north and west of Crater Lake at Mount Thielsen and Rabbit Ears. Along the North Umpqua River west of Toketee Lake there are numerous high rocks including Eagle Rock, Old Man Rock, Old Woman Rock, and several others, all of which are very close to the river and Ore. 138.

SEA KAYAKING & FLAT-WATER CANOEING

If you are in the Ashland area and would like to take a sea-kayaking class or go out on a guided sea-kayak trip, contact **Adventure Kayak Tours** (tel. 541/488-1914), which offers tours on Applegate Lake, the Upper Klamath National Wildlife Refuge, and the Lower Coquille River.

Toketee Lake

2 miles. Easy. Access: 21 miles west of Diamond Lake off Ore. 138.

This reservoir on the North Umpqua River is owned by Pacific Power and Light, and if you ignore the power lines overhead, a weird aqueduct dropping down a lakeside cliff, and all kinds of power-generation facilities, it's not a bad place to go for a paddle. The lake is a beautiful deep green color. Along some of its shores there are marshes to explore, while in other places basalt cliffs rise straight out of the lake. There is a boat ramp at the north end of the lake, but you can also put in at the adjacent campground for a short, swift ride a few hundred yards down the North Umpqua River into the lake. Toketee means "pretty" or "graceful" in the Chinook trading language once used by Northwest tribes, and that is an apt description of this lake (or would be if the Pacific Power and Light wasn't so much in evidence).

Lemolo Lake

2–10 miles. Easy. Access: 10 miles north of Diamond Lake off Ore. 138.

With its convoluted shoreline, Lemolo Lake, another North Umpqua reservoir, is a far more interesting place for a paddle than nearby Diamond Lake, and the winds here generally aren't as bad as on Diamond Lake. Even the view of Mount Thielsen seems to be a little bit better (although you're farther away here). The lake's waters are an amazing blue-green color. With two campgrounds right on the lake, and another one nearby on the bank of the North Umpqua, this lake is an ideal base for a multisport visit to the area—paddle here, mountain bike the North Umpqua Trail, fish the North Umpqua River.

Spring Creek

3 miles round-trip. Easy. Access: 6 miles north of Chiloquin at Collier State Park picnic area on the west side of U.S. 97 (go up the road past the logging exhibit).

Although short, this is one of the most astonishing stretches of flat-water canoeing in the Northwest. Spring Creek is an icy-cold, crystal-clear stream that gushes out of the ground in the middle of the forest and is 100 feet wide. In this first stretch, springs can be seen bubbling up through the sandy floor of the creek. The stream bottom is white sand in many places, and when the sun shines, the water takes on the turquoise hues usually associated with the Caribbean. From the picnic area, you can easily paddle upstream 1.5 miles to the headwaters, visit the springs, and then have a leisurely float back down. There are a few houses in the lower stretch, but above these, you'll be paddling through tranquil forests.

This creek is reminiscent of the spring-fed rivers of Florida, and it's easy to imagine manatees drifting lazily by. Actually, these waters hold so few nutrients that not much of anything grows in the creek other than the unusual plants known locally as mare's eggs. The leaves of these plants form water-filled spheres that look and feel like water balloons. You may also see ducks here, and the creek is planted with rainbow trout each fishing season.

Upper Klamath Canoe Trail

3.5–6 miles. Easy. Access: From Ore. 140, 7 miles east of Lake of the Woods, go north on West Side Rd. for 3 miles to Rocky Point Resort.

Well-signed canoe trails wander through marshlands here at the north end of Upper Klamath Lake. The bird watching, as elsewhere in this region, is excellent. Expect to see great blue herons, great egrets, American coots, double-crested cormorants, and numerous species of ducks and wading birds. If you're lucky, you might also spot some river otters as my wife and I once did while paddling around one evening at dusk. The four otters snorted and sniffed as they approached close enough to get a good look at us. Bald eagles are also frequently seen over these marshes.

There are two marked canoe trails here, one 3.5 miles long and the other 6 miles long. Start either loop by paddling north up Recreation Creek, with forest (and vacation cabins) on one bank and marshlands on the other. Eventually this creek narrows and meets Crystal Creek. Turn back south on this latter creek and, if you want to do the short loop, watch for the shortcut trail on your right after about 1 mile. To do the longer loop, continue south to the mouth of Crystal Creek, and go right to skirt the edge of the marsh back to Rocky Point. Be aware, however, that by late summer the water level here can be very low, and it may not be possible to paddle some of the trails.

Fish Lake

4–5 miles. Easy. Access: Ore. 140, west of Lake of the Woods.

Although motorboats are allowed on this 2-mile–long lake, there is a 10-mph speed limit, which keeps things quiet here, but what makes the lake an interesting place to paddle a canoe are the lava flows that form the south shore. Set out from the Fish Lake Campground on the north shore and paddle along the opposite shore, marveling at the jagged, 20,000-year-old lava. This is the most interesting and attractive of the area lakes. Two lakeside campgrounds and the rustic Fish Lake Resort (which rents canoes) provide options for those wanting to overnight here. The lake also holds some 6-pound rainbow and eastern brook trout, which should cause some paddlers to lengthen their floating time.

SNOWSHOEING

With its jewel of a lake for a centerpiece and views that extend all the way to Mount Shasta in California, **Crater Lake National Park** is a magnet for snowshoers. Though the **West Rim Trail** is the most popular spot to snowshoe (just as it is the most popular spot to cross-country ski), snowshoers have the advantage of being able to go where few skiers dare to go— up the slopes of **Garfield Peak.** This craggy summit rises 1,000 feet above Rim Village just east of Crater Lake Lodge. From its southern slopes there are views across the Klamath Basin. There are two possibilities for hiking up this peak. The shortest and most direct route begins at the east end of Rim Village near Crater Lake Lodge and heads up the southwestern slopes of the peak. These slopes are, however, somewhat avalanche prone and should be attempted only when the potential for avalanches is low (check at the Steel Information Center). The longer and safer route is to head up the East Rim Trail toward Sun Notch and then, from the highest point on this trail (less than 2 miles from the park headquarters), strike out across country ascending through forests and the exposed southern slopes of Garfield Peak.

If you've never snowshoed before, you can give it a try at **Rim Village** in Crater Lake National Park, where 1.5-hour guided snowshoe hikes are offered on winter weekends and holidays (November 25 to mid-April). Snowshoe rentals for these hikes are available at Rim Village for $4. The hikes start at 1pm.

The marked ski trail that heads along the **Siskiyou Crest** from Mount Ashland Ski Area and other cross-country ski trails in this area are also good places to snowshoe. In fact, **Mount Ashland Lodge** (tel. 541/482-8707), just a few miles downhill from the ski area, has snowshoes available to guests and has a fun annual snowshoe competition. Another good place to do some snowshoeing is in **Oregon Caves National Monument,** where summer's hiking trails make good snowshoeing routes.

SPELUNKING

Although you can't do any exploring on your own, the marble caverns of **Oregon Caves National Monument** (tel. 541/592-2100) can be visited on guided tours. These caves are located high in the Siskiyou Mountains, at the end of Ore. 46 from the town of Cave Junction. Discovered in 1874 by a hunter trying to save his dog from a bear, the caverns were designated a national monument in 1909 by President Howard Taft. The cave tours last a little more than an hour and cover about a half-mile of the caverns. These caverns are home to both Townsend's big-eared and Pallid bats. The caves are open for tours year-round and tickets are $6.

SWIMMING & TUBING

Southern Oregon abounds in great swimming holes. Whether you like leisurely long swims in lakes or quick dips in fast-flowing mountain streams, there are plenty of places around here to get wet.

Although **Crater Lake** is too deep to ever reach a truly comfortable temperature, plenty of people take the plunge each summer and do a few quick strokes to cool down after hiking the Cleetwood Cove Trail or after exploring Wizard Island. (If only they could move the lake to the *top* of Cleetwood Cove Trail!) Just north of Crater Lake, there are slightly warmer waters at **Diamond Lake,** where there are swimming areas at Diamond Lake Resort on the north end of the lake and at the South Shore Picnic Area. A few miles farther north, at Lemolo Lake, you'll find a swimming beach at **Poole Creek Campground.**

Although the **North Umpqua River** and its tributaries are best known for their fishing, these rivers and streams also have quite a few good swimming holes. The spots listed here are just a sampling. Do a little exploring on your own and you'll find lots of other good places to go for a dip. At the lower end of the river, the stretch between **Winchester** and **River Forks Park** (at the confluence with the South Umpqua) is a favorite tubing run. **Cable Crossing Park,** between mileposts 22 and 23, has a little of everything (if you're a strong swimmer)—rapids for tubing, a gravel-bar beach, and a long deep stretch for distance swimming—and is just about the best swimming hole on this river. It's at a broad and open spot, with deep-green water and big rocks to lie on. It's easy to miss this place; there's only one sign on the road. At the sign, turn down a steep section of pavement. Roughly a mile upstream, you'll find the **Hill Creek Wayside,** which is at a big deep spot in the river and has a tiny pocket beach. The pull-off is an angled spur as you're driving east. Between the **Susan Creek Picnic Area** and the **Susan Creek Campground** (between mileposts 28 and 29), there is a stretch of water that is good for tubing. A trail along the river connects the picnic area and the campground. Between mileposts 38 and 39, FS 38 goes north along Steamboat Creek and in 1.5 miles reaches the aptly named **Little Falls.** Here, beside the 10-foot-high falls that cascade over blocky basalt, there are big rocks from which to jump into a big pool. Natural stone steps lead down from the road.

The Rogue River, though better known for its raging whitewater and fighting steelhead, also has quite a few tame stretches that make good swimming holes. In the Grants Pass area, there are numerous riverside parks where you can do a little swimming. West of town, try **Schroeder Park** off U.S. 199 or **Whitehorse Park** off Lower River Road. East of town, you can swim at **Valley of the Rogue State Park** off I-5 and at **Savage Rapids Park** off Ore. 99. Farther east, there are a couple of good swimming holes in Gold Hill. The fast water below the **Gold Nugget Rapid** on the north side of Gold Hill is a fun place to do a little tubing (just stay out of the big Class IV rapids). For tamer water, head to **Gold Hill Beach Park** beside the bridge on the east side of town. Northwest of Grants Pass, try **Indian Mary Park** on Merlin–Galice Road west of Hellgate Canyon. Much farther upriver, north of the town of Shady Cove on Ore. 62, you'll find a nice swimming hole on Elk Creek at **Rogue Elk County Park.**

Ore. 140, between Medford and Klamath Falls, passes through some pretty forested lakes country. **Lake of the Woods** is the largest and busiest of these lakes and is popular with powerboats and water-skiers. Despite the noise and lakeside development, there are a couple of swimming areas that are good for families. West of here is the smaller **Fish Lake,** which has a 10-mph speed limit for boats and no designated swimming area. However, the trail along the north shore of the lake provides plenty of places to get down to the shore and get in the water. If you have your own boat, try heading to the lava flows on the south shore of the lake.

The **Applegate River,** west of Jacksonville, flows warm and gentle through a number of excellent swimming holes. **Applegate Wayside,** a private park across the street from the Applegate River Restaurant in the town of Applegate on Ore. 238, is in a narrow, rocky stretch of river and has long been a popular local swimming hole. If you're looking for more facilities and more legroom, continue west past Ruch and turn south on Hamilton Road to **Cantrall–Buckley Park,** a county park that charges a $3 day-use fee. A little bit south of this park on Applegate Road

(which goes south from Ruch), between mileposts 5 and 6, there is another small swimming hole with riffles above and pools below. The current makes this a good choice only for strong swimmers. Farther up Applegate Road is **Applegate Lake,** a dammed reservoir near the California line. At the Hart-tish Picnic Area on the lake's west shore, there is a large designated swimming beach backed by a beautiful big lawn. Nearby **Big Squaw Lake** has a more natural feeling and is surrounded by walk-in campsites. It is reached by taking FS 1075 for 8.2 miles from the Applegate Lake Dam.

The **Illinois River** (pronounced Ill-a-*noise* around these parts), which flows northwest from Cave Junction, has a reputation for being the wildest river in southern Oregon, but that doesn't mean there aren't a few quiet pools where you can go for a swim. In fact, this river has some of the prettiest little swimming holes in this corner of the state. Just west of Cave Junction on U.S. 199 is **Illinois River State Park,** which is a good family spot with a couple of beaches and a wide, calm spot where the water is fairly deep. There's also a nice picnic area here. Eight miles up Illinois River Road (FS 4103) from the blinking light on U.S. 199 in Selma, you'll come to the superb **Six Mile** swimming hole, which has a beach, bedrock, and boulders. There are views of mountains all around, rapids above and below the main beach, and lots of rocks for sunning or jumping off of. When I was here one September the water was refreshingly cool but still swimmable.

About 1.25 miles farther up this same road is **Store Gulch,** where there is a very large, deep swimming hole down a steep trail from the road. Unfortunately, there is lots of poison oak along the trail. The pull-off is on the left across from an abandoned building. There's a Store Gulch sign at a stream that runs by the old building. One last excellent swimming hole—**Illinois River Falls**—is located another 1.8 miles past Store Gulch and then a half-mile down a steep, rough road that is best attempted only in a four-wheel-drive vehicle. From the swinging bridge over the river, head upstream to the falls. Lots of rocks provide good sunning and jumping spots.

WALKS & NATURAL ROADSIDE ATTRACTIONS

IN CRATER LAKE NATIONAL PARK

Castle Crest Wildflower Garden

1 mile round-trip. Easy. 100-foot elevation gain. Access: Crater Lake National Park. Trailhead is at park headquarters. Map: Not necessary.

Summer is short on the rim of Crater Lake, so when the snow finally melts, wildflowers burst forth with nearly unrivaled abandon. This short trail meanders through one of the best displays of wildflowers in Crater Lake National Park. July and August are the best wildflower months.

The Watchman

1.4 miles. Moderate. 655-foot elevation gain. Access: Crater Lake National Park. Trailhead is 3.7 miles northwest of Rim Village on West Rim Dr. Map: Not necessary.

With a historic fire lookout perched on its summit, The Watchman is one of the high points on the crater rim. A short but steep trail leads to the top for an outstanding view of the lake with the conical Wizard Island rising from amid the deep blue of the foreground. This is the shortest climb you can do along the rim of the crater.

Cleetwood Cove Trail

2.2 miles round-trip. Moderate. 675-foot elevation gain. Access: Crater Lake National Park. The trailhead is on the north side of the lake, 4.5 miles east of the North Junction. Map: Not necessary.

This is the only trail to the shore of Crater Lake and stays busy with those who just want to get to the water and those who are headed to Cleetwood Cove to take a boat tour around the lake. Because the trail leads downhill, many visitors are lulled into thinking this is an easy trail. It's not! The climb back up from the water to the rim is strenuous and steep, though luckily it goes on for only a mile.

Wizard Island

2 miles round-trip. Easy. 765-foot elevation gain. Access: Crater Lake National Park. Take the Cleetwood Cove Trail (see above) and then a boat tour around the lake, disembarking on the island. Map: Not necessary.

Though it is small, Wizard Island is a great temptation to many Crater Lake visitors. The island, with its volcanic cone rising from the deep, is fun to explore for a few hours, and there is a trail to the island's summit. To spend some time here, take an early boat tour, get off on the island, and arrange to come back on a later boat. Because most of the hiking is on jagged lava rock, be sure to wear sturdy boots.

OUTSIDE THE NATIONAL PARK

Colliding Rivers

Access: On Ore. 138 beside the North Umpqua Ranger Station on the west side of Glide.

Here at the confluence of the North Umpqua and the Little River, these two rivers meet head-on in a churning stew of whitewater.

Toketee Falls

1 mile round-trip. Easy. 60-foot elevation gain. Access: Follow signs to Toketee Lake and then Toketee Falls Viewpoint from Ore. 138 about 20 miles west of Diamond Lake. Map: Not necessary.

Considered by many to be the most beautiful waterfalls in Oregon, Toketee Falls is a double cascade that drops a total of 120 feet. A viewing platform provides an excellent perspective on the falls. The trail meanders through shady forest along the bank of the North Umpqua. A huge, old wooden aqueduct runs along the access road to the trailhead.

Natural Bridge

Access: On a spur road from the Natural Bridge Campground at Union Creek, which is at the junction of Ore. 62 and Ore. 230 about 26 miles west of Crater Lake's Rim Village.

Although this bridge, little more than a lava flow that the river flows under instead of over, is not too impressive as natural bridges go, in a country where such geologic phenomena are scarce, it's noteworthy. If you feel like a hike, it is 3.5 miles from here to the Rogue River Gorge on the Rogue River Trail.

Rogue River Gorge

Access: At Union Creek, which is at the junction of Ore. 62 and Ore. 230 about 26 miles west of Crater Lake's Rim Village.

At 500 feet long, 25 feet wide, and 45 feet deep, the Rogue River Gorge could only be deemed petite by geologic standards, but what it lacks in size, it makes up in character. The gorge is a collapsed lava tube that was formed 1.25 million years ago when a lava flow filled the original valley of the Rogue, which now lies 650 feet below this current gorge.

Oux-Kanee Overlook

Access: From U.S. 97 about 3 miles north of Collier State Park, go west on FS 9732.

You would never think as you drive this stretch of highway that only a mile away is one of the most amazing sights in the Northwest. Oux-Kanee Overlook has a view of meandering Spring Creek, whose crystal-clear spring-fed waters are the color of the Caribbean when the sun shines. Surrounding the creek are pastures and pine forests and in the distance rise Mount Shasta and Mount McLoughlin. If you're anywhere in the area, don't miss this spot.

Hellgate Canyon

Access: From I-5, take exit 61 and drive 10 miles east on Merlin–Galice Rd.

Although nothing can take the place of looking *up* at the walls of Hellgate Canyon from water level, the view from the top of the 250-foot-high cliffs that form this narrow gorge on the Rogue River is still pretty impressive. Just don't come expecting to see some terrifically terrifying stretch of whitewater. The waters that flow through Hellgate Canyon are completely flat. I don't know how it got its name.

WHITEWATER KAYAKING & CANOEING

Southern Oregon is a paddler's heaven. It has the Northwest's most famous and most challenging long runs. However, it also has quite a few easier and shorter runs.

If the sight of the Rogue River has you wishing you were an experienced whitewater paddler, you're in luck—there are two kayaking schools in the area. **Sundance Expeditions** (tel. 541/479-8508) is one of the premier kayaking schools in the country. They offer a four-day instructional trip down the Wild and Scenic section of the Rogue River as well as a nine-day beginner's program that does a four-day trip down the river after five days of initial instruction. Sundance also does kayaking trips on the Illinois River. For a more low-key program, try **Siskiyou Kayak School** (tel. 800/571-3311 or 541/ 772-9743), a husband-and-wife operation run by Scott and Kelly Larson. They offer a variety of short classes, as well as a comprehensive five-day class that then heads down the Rogue River for four days.

Both **Sundance Expeditions** and **Siskiyou Kayak School** lead kayaking down the Rogue (Sundance also does the Illinois). **Siskiyou Adventures** (tel. 800/ 250-4602 or 541/488-1632) offers kayaking trips on the Rogue and Applegate rivers, and **Arrowhead River Adventures** (tel. 800/ 227-7741 or 541/830-3388) offers several different kayak trips on Class I and II waters of the middle Rogue River upstream from Gold Hill.

CLASS I

Cow Creek, which flows into the South Umpqua River north of Canyonville, is a pretty little stream, and its last 6 miles before it dumps into the South Umpqua make for an excellent Class I run. The only problem with this run is that the take-out is right at the Class II Lawson Bar, which you may find yourself accidentally running if your ferrying skills aren't too good. To reach the take-out, take exit 102 off I-5 and follow the road west to Lawson Bar. To reach the put-in, go back north on I-5 to exit 103 and go west 6.5 miles on Riddle Bypass Road to the Glenbrook Loop Bridge. If you don't mind running a couple of Class II rapids (or portaging them), you can continue down the **South Umpqua** another 9 miles to the town of Myrtle Creek. Together these two runs make a good day's outing. The Myrtle Creek take-out is beneath the bridge into town from I-5.

Although the **Rogue River** is better known for its more rambunctious stretches of water, it does have its tamer runs. One of the more enjoyable Class I runs is the 10-mile stretch from River's Edge Park just below Lost Creek Lake and the Cole Rivers Fish Hatchery (on Ore. 62) to Shady Cove County Park in the town of Shady Cove. Although this run is paralleled by the highway, the forested mountain scenery makes up for any traffic noises. This is the most challenging of the Class I Rogue River runs in the area, and some of the rapids verge on Class II. Below Shady Cove County Park, there is a 12-mile run to Tou Velle State Park. However, this run has a single Class III rapid (Rattlesnake Rapids) about midway through the run (1 mile downstream from the Dodge Bridge).

If you wanted to do a short run or extend the run from River's Edge Park (and avoid Rattlesnake Rapids), you could take out at Dodge Bridge, which is about 1.5 miles west of Ore. 62 on Ore. 234. Farther downstream, there is a very leisurely float that starts at the bridge in the town of Gold Hill and continues 8 miles down to Coyote Evans Park at the bridge in the town of Rogue River. Traffic noise from I-5 can be intrusive. The nicest stretch is the 2 miles along Valley of the Rogue State Park. The next easy run starts at Chinook Park and continues 8 miles downstream to Riverside Park on the edge of downtown Grants Pass. This run has a couple of riffles to add a bit of excitement. Expect to encounter large jet boats downriver from Gold Hill.

CLASS II

On the **North Umpqua,** the 6.5-mile run between the town of Winchester and River Forks Park (at the confluence of the Umpqua's north and south forks) has always been a local favorite, especially with tubers and novice rafters. The first 4.5 miles have plenty of fun little rapids, but then there is a mile of flat water before you hit several nice ledge drops. Put in at Amacher County Park in Winchester (right under the I-5 bridge) and take out at River Forks Park, which is reached by going west on Winchester Road, taking the left fork onto Wilbur–Garden Valley Road, and in 7 miles turning left on Garden Valley Road for 1 mile.

While the **Rogue River** is best known among paddlers for its 35-mile-long designated National Wild and Scenic River stretch, it is actually the 15-mile stretch from Hog Creek to Grave Creek Bridge that sees the most action. On a summer weekend, this run will be packed with people in all manner of rafts, canoes, and kayaks (enclosed, sit-on-tops, and inflatables), all of which will be trying to stay out of the way of the jet boats that roar up and down the river shuttling tourists between Grants Pass and Hellgate Canyon. If you think paddling Class II whitewater is exciting, wait until you look up to see one of these aircraft-carrier–sized river hogs bearing down on you at full throttle. Luckily, anyone holding a paddle has the right of way. Despite the jet boats, novice paddlers are magnetically drawn to the 10 Class II rapids and numerous other riffles on this run. One of the highlights is the easy section through Hellgate Canyon, which is strictly a scenic stretch with cliffs rising 250 feet above you as you drift through. Don't miss the take-out at Grave Creek Bridge or you'll be stuck on the 35-mile Wild and Scenic run.

Several companies in the Merlin and Galice areas rent inflatable and sit-on-top kayaks if you don't have your own boat but want to paddle this stretch of the Rogue. At **Sundance Kayak & River Supply,** 184 Merlin–Galice Rd. (tel. 541/476-8108), you can rent a sit-on-top for $25 a day. **Arrowhead River Adventures** (tel. 800/227-7741 or 541/830-3388) also rents sit-on-tops for $25 a day. **White Water Cowboys** (tel. 800/635-2925 or 541/479-5061) rents inflatable kayaks for $15 a day. If you need to arrange a car shuttle, try the **Galice Resort** (tel. 541/476-3818), which charges $55; **Sharon Miller McCall and Louise Miller** (tel. 541/479-1042); **Laverne Parry** (tel. 800/207-7886 or 541/247-6778); or **Rogue River Raft Trips** (tel. 800/826-1963 or 541/476-3825).

CLASS III

The **North Umpqua River** from just upstream of Boulder Flat Campground to the Swiftwater Recreation Site in the town of Idleyld Park is a designated National Wild and Scenic River. It is this 35-mile section that is the most popular with kayakers. Most of this stretch also happens to be the most popular fly-fishing water on the North Umpqua, a river fabled among anglers. Consequently, there are boating restrictions in some places during the peak summer and fall fishing season. At the time of writing, restrictions included a total closure to boaters between Gravel Bin and Bogus Campground between July 15 and October 31 (from July 1 to July 14, this stretch is closed to boating between 6pm and 10am). Between July 1 and October 31, the rest of this 35-mile stretch of river is also closed between 6pm and 10am. For an excellent map with information on rafting and kayaking on the North Umpqua, contact the North Umpqua Ranger Station (tel. 541/496-3532) in Glide and request the *North Umpqua River Recreation Guide*.

For wild nonstop action, the 14-mile run from Boulder Flat Campground to Gravel Bin, just above Steamboat, just can't be beat. This run has a dozen named Class III rapids, about half that many named Class II rapids, and one Class IV (Pinball). Midway through this run is Horseshoe Bend Campground, a favorite of paddlers and an alternate put-in/take-out. The 13-mile run from Bogus Creek Campground down to Cable Crossing Picnic Area (the last take-out before Deadline Falls) isn't as relentless as the upper run, but that doesn't mean this section isn't a challenge. Susan Creek Campground and Picnic Area is the midway point and is an alternate put-in/take-out.

The 21-mile stretch of the North Umpqua between Glide and Winchester lacks the wilderness feel of upstream runs but is still an enjoyable stretch of the river. This run is mostly Class II water, but there are several Class III drops along the way.

From the put-in below Colliding Rivers (where the North Umpqua meets the Little River head-on), it is 7 miles down to Whistlers Bend Campground on Horseshoe Bend, which makes a good take-out for a short run. From here it is another 15 miles down to the take-out at Amacher County Park under the I-5 bridge in Winchester. If you want to add a few more miles and run the churning waters of Colliding Rivers, put in at Lone Rock Park a mile east of Glide on Lone Rock Road. Just be sure to scout Colliding Rivers when you get to it.

The 35-mile-long National Wild and Scenic River section of the **Rogue River** is one of the most popular stretches in Oregon. People come from all over the country to run this river, and it didn't help things when scenes from the movie *The River Wild* were shot here. Because this is a two- to five-day trip, kayakers will need raft support, which adds considerably to the complexity of doing this run. Not surprisingly, this trip is more popular with rafters and drift boaters.

If you are planning to run the river any time between May 15 and October 15, just about the hardest part of the trip will be securing a permit. To restrict the number of people on the river at any given time, a limited number of permits is issued through a lottery system. For information on submitting your name for the lottery, contact **TRI,** P.O. Box 5149, Roseburg, OR 97470 (Internet address: http://www.umpcoos.com/rogue/index.html), or contact BLM's River Information (tel. 541/479-3735). The lottery is held in the early part of the year and applications are usually available late in the preceding year. Some permits are also available beginning the first business day of April at 8am. It is possible to get a permit on the day you plan to start your trip if there happens to be a no-show. First crack at no-show permits goes to anyone waiting at the **Rand Visitor Center,** 14335 Galice Rd., Merlin, OR 97532 (tel. 541/479-3735). For a mile-by-mile description of the river, contact this visitor center and ask for "The Wild and Scenic Rogue River" map.

You'll need to arrange a car shuttle to the take-out at Foster Bar if you're heading down this stretch of river. Several

> "Nothing is weaker than water, but when it attacks something hard or resistant, then nothing withstands it."
> —Lao Tzu

rafting companies and individuals in the area offer this service. Try **Rogue River Raft Trips** (tel. 800/826-1963 or 541/476-3825) or the **Galice Resort** (tel. 541/476-3818), both of which charge $55. **Sharon Miller McCall and Louise Miller** (tel. 541/479-1042) and **Laverne Parry** (tel. 800/207-7886 or 541/247-6778) also offer shuttle services.

CLASS IV & ABOVE

As fabulous as the North Umpqua and Rogue rivers are, they are still basically Class III rivers (which isn't to suggest that these are tame little trickles of water). For truly unforgettable thrills, advanced kayakers and psycho paddlers will want to check out a couple of other area rivers.

At first glance the **Illinois River** southwest of Grants Pass sounds a lot like the Rogue River. It's a designated National Wild and Scenic River. The run is 31 miles long and passes through a designated wilderness area. It takes three to four days to run the whole Wild and Scenic section. But that is where the similarities end. The Illinois, which can be run really only in the rainy season, is an unforgiving river that drills its way through the Klamath Mountains in the Kalmiopsis Wilderness. There are more than 150 rapids on this river (11 Class IV and one Class V). The Illinois has been described as one of the most remote runnable rivers in the contiguous 48 states and the most difficult river on the West Coast. Think long and hard before attempting this run, and don't do it without someone who has run it before. Once you start this trip, you are committed to completing it. There are no alternate take-outs, no cheat routes, not even a trail beside the river. Currently you need a permit to run the Illinois (available at Selma Market in the town of Selma on U.S. 199), but there is no quota system in effect. This could change in the future, so be sure to check

first with the **Illinois Valley Ranger Station** (tel. 541/592-2166) in Cave Junction. This ranger station also has a pamphlet titled *Floating the Wild Section of the Illinois River,* which makes a good introduction. However, no one should put a boat in this river without first acquiring a copy of *Handbook of the Illinois River Canyon* (Educational Adventures Inc., 1979) by Quinn, Quinn, and King.

If you aren't up to the Illinois, there is always the **Klamath River,** where the 17-mile Hell's Corner Gorge run, which starts in Oregon and ends in California, is a favorite of commercial rafting companies and expert kayakers. The highlight is nearly 7 miles of nonstop Class III through Class V whitewater that ends with Hell's Corner, the biggest and baddest rapid on this run. This outrageous Class V rapid is almost a quarter-mile long and sweeps around a big, wide curve. Because this is a dam-controlled river it is runnable year-round, which makes it one of the only summertime Class V runs in the Northwest. The biggest problem other than its extreme difficulty is the length of the shuttle, nearly 100 miles! The put-in is below the John C. Boyle Power Plant off Ore. 66 about 15 miles west of Klamath Falls, while the take-out is at the east end of Copco Lake in California (take Ore. 66 west to I-5 south to Hornbrook exit then east to the lake). There are several alternate take-outs upstream from Copco Lake.

WHITEWATER RAFTING

The **Rogue River,** which for 35 miles west of Galice is a designated National Wild and Scenic River, is legendary among rafters. The river was first brought to the attention of people around the country when writer Zane Grey wrote about it after living in a cabin on its banks and fishing its steelhead holes. The mail boats that brought the outside world to people living on remote ranches along the river further added to the allure of the Rogue. And then, of course, there is the name. What rafter could resist a river named Rogue? Along this stretch there are lots of Class III rapids (and a couple of Class IV–V rapids), plenty of campsites, and even several lodges that offer a bit of luxury in the wilderness. Rafting companies offering two- to four-day trips include **Noah's World of Water** (tel. 800/858-2811 or 541/488-2811), **River Adventure Float Trips** (tel. 541/476-6493), **River Trips Unlimited** (tel. 541/779-3798), **Rogue River Raft Trips** (tel. 800/826-1963 or 541/476-3825), **Rogue Wilderness, Inc.** (tel. 800/336-1647 or 541/479-9554), and **Sundance Kayak School & Expeditions** (tel. 541/479-8508). Rates start around $200 for a two-day camping trip and $300 for a two-day lodge trip. A three-day lodge trip will cost around $500, and a four-day camping trip will be around $450.

However, most people rafting on the Rogue have less time and money to spend and opt for an inexpensive half-day or full-day trip. Companies in the Grants Pass or Merlin/Galice areas specialize in the run from Hog Creek through Hellgate Canyon to Grave Creek. If you have only a day, this is where to spend it. Companies to try include **Ferron's Fun Trips** (tel. 800/404-2201 or 541/474-2201), **Galice Resort** (tel. 541/476-3818), **Orange Torpedo Trips** (tel. 800/635-2925 or 541/479-5061), **River Adventure Float Trips** (tel. 541/476-6493), **Rogue River Raft Trips** (tel. 800/826-1963 or 541/476-3825), and **Rogue Wilderness** (tel. 800/336-1647 or 541/479-9554). One other company to try is **Rough & Ready Guided Explorations** (tel. 541/471-3737), which does its trips in catarafts—a cross between a catamaran and a raft.

In the Ashland and Medford areas several companies offer trips both on the Rogue and on the **Upper Klamath River,** where there is a challenging 7-mile stretch of whitewater known as Hell's Corner. The section of the Rogue River run by Ashland companies is between the Gold Ray Dam and the town of Gold Hill, and has a very different character from the Hellgate run farther downriver. In Ashland, try **Noah's World of Water,** 53 N Main St. (tel. 800/858-2811 or 541/488-2811); **Siskiyou Adventures,** 358 Main St. (tel. 800/250-4602 or 541/488-1632); or **The Adventure Center,** 40 N Main St. (tel. 800/444-2819 or 541/766-4932). In the Medford area, try **Rogue Excursions Unlimited** (tel. 800/460-3865 or 541/826-6222), **Rogue/Klamath River Adventures** (tel. 800/231-0769 or 541/779-3708), or **River Trips Unlimited**

(tel. 541/779-3798). Rates start around $40 for a half day, $55 for a full day, and trips are offered between May and October.

In contrast to the Rogue River, which passes through a dry, low-elevation landscape, the **North Umpqua River** is solidly a Cascade Range river, with lush forests lining its banks. The waters of the North Umpqua are an astounding shade of blue-green, and all in all, this river gets my vote as most beautiful river in Oregon. Though more popular with fly anglers and kayakers, it is also a good rafting river. Trips of varying lengths on the North Umpqua are offered by **Noah's World of Water** (tel. 800/858-2811 or 541/488-2811), **North Umpqua Outfitters** (tel. 541/673-4599), **Orange Torpedo Trips** (tel. 800/635-2925 or 541/479-5061), and **Oregon Ridge & River Excursions** (tel. 541/496-3333).

The **Illinois River** is the wildest and most challenging river in southern Oregon. It can only be run for a short time in late spring and early summer, and its wilderness character and legendary whitewater keep all but the most experienced and die-hard whitewater enthusiasts away. There are, however, a couple of companies that offer three- and four-day trips down this remote river—**Ferron's Fun Trips** (tel. 800/404-2201 or 541/474-2201) and **Sundance Kayak School & Expeditions** (tel. 541/479-8508).

If you've had a little paddling experience already and feel like just renting a raft and exploring without a guide, that's also an option. Rental companies include **Bradbury's Gun-N-Tackle,** 1809 Rogue River Hwy., Grants Pass (tel. 541/474-1420 or 541/479-1531); **Ferron's Fun Trips,** 585 Rogue Rim Dr., Merlin (tel. 800/404-2201 or 541/474-2201); **Galice Resort Store,** 11744 Galice Rd., Merlin (tel. 541/476-3818); **Osprey Whitewater,** 330 Merlin–Galice Rd., Merlin (tel. 541/474-7656); and **Whitewater Cowboys,** 210 Merlin Rd., Merlin (tel. 800/635-2925 or 541/479-5061). If you want to paddle yourself on a different stretch of the Rogue, head up to Shady Cove 21 miles north of Medford where you can rent rafts from **62 Market & Deli** (tel. 800/797-RAFT or 541/878-3623), **Wet 'n' Wild** (tel. 541-878-2889), and **The Fishin Hole** (tel. 541/878-4000). Expect to pay between $50 and

$65 to rent a six- to eight-person raft for the day. Inflatable kayaks are between $15 and $20 per day.

WILDLIFE VIEWING

On the **North Umpqua River** at Deadline Falls, you can see **migrating salmon** and **steelhead** jumping the falls between June and October. Because the viewing area is 100 yards or so from the falls, you might want to bring binoculars. Deadline Falls are accessed from the North Umpqua trailhead across the river from Swiftwaters Park on Ore. 138. In September and October, at milepost 49 (28 miles east of Deadline Falls on Ore. 138), you can see spawning salmon downstream from Marster's Bridge at an area known as Weeping Rocks. Another 5 miles farther east and 1 mile up the Soda Springs Road off Ore. 138, you can also see spawning salmon at this same time of year. At Soda Springs, you can spot spawning steelhead in April, May, July, and August.

On the **Rogue River,** in the late summer and early fall, you can see **salmon** and **steelhead** in the fish ladders at Savage Rapids Dam east of Gold Hill. At Rainie Falls, 2 miles down the Rogue River Trail from Graves Creek Bridge (boat launch for people heading down the Wild and Scenic section of this river), you can see salmon jumping the falls in April, May, and August. To reach the Graves Creek Bridge, take exit 61 off I-5 north of Grants Pass and drive 24 miles west on the Merlin–Galice Road.

Campgrounds & Other Accommodations

CAMPING

Within **Crater Lake National Park,** there are only two campgrounds—one large and one small, both open each year from June to October. Neither of these campgrounds accepts reservations, which makes getting a campsite here quite difficult on summer weekends. **Mazama Village Campground** (198 campsites; seasonal) is a series of tightly packed paved loops that are usually filled with RVs. Tiny **Lost Creek Campground** (16 campsites; seasonal) on the park's east side has tent sites only, is quieter, and has a much more remote feel.

You'll find a greater range of campgrounds outside the national park. At **Diamond Lake,** 4 miles north of the park's north entrance, you'll find three U.S. Forest Service campgrounds—**Diamond Lake** (236 campsites; seasonal), **Broken Arrow** (148 campsites; seasonal), and **Thielsen View** (60 campsites; seasonal). The setting, amid spindly young pines, is none too attractive, but most campers are only here for the fishing or because the national park campgrounds were full. Here you'll also find the **Diamond Lake RV Park** (tel. 541/793-3318).

Lemolo Lake, roughly 12 miles north of Diamond Lake, is an amazing shade of green and has four campgrounds around its shores. These campgrounds are much more attractive than the campgrounds at Diamond Lake. Although this is a dammed lake, the word *lemolo* means wild or untamed in Chinook jargon (the old Native American trading language of the region). These campgrounds have attractive settings and good views. **Inlet Campground** (14 campsites; seasonal) is at the inlet of the North Umpqua River, among meadows along the banks of the shallow-flowing river. The lake's other campgrounds include **Bunker Hill** (5 campsites; seasonal), **East Lemolo** (15 campsites; seasonal), and **Poole Creek** (59 campsites; seasonal).

Southwest of the park on **Ore. 62,** the nearest campground is **Huckleberry Mountain Campground** (25 campsites; seasonal). However, this campground is set amid spindly young trees and is devoid of atmosphere. Farther west is **Farewell Bend Campground** (61 campsites; seasonal), which is set amid big trees on the Rogue River. The drawback here is that the campground is close to the highway. The next campgrounds are **Union Creek** (78 campsites; seasonal) and **Natural Bridge** (16 campsites; seasonal), both of which are also along the Rogue River. Northbound, off Ore. 62 on Ore. 230, you'll find the **Hamaker Campground** (10 campsites; seasonal), on a pretty bend in the Rogue River with big trees, new toilets, old stone stoves, and meadows across the river. This is a secluded, quiet, and very pretty campground that is a good choice for mountain bikers as well as people headed to the national park.

Southeast of Crater Lake and north of Chiloquin along **U.S. 97,** good camping choices include **Collier State Park Campground** (68 campsites, 50 with hookups; seasonal) on the Williamson River; the forest service's **Williamson River Campground** (10 campsites; seasonal); and the remote little **Spring Creek Campground** (26 campsites; seasonal) at the headwaters of Spring Creek, which is the most fascinating stretch of flat-water canoeing in the whole state. Another pretty spot in this area is **Jackson F. Kimball State Park** (10 campsites; seasonal), which is north of Fort Klamath off Ore. 232.

The **North Umpqua River,** which is paralleled by Ore. 138, is one of the most famous fishing rivers in Oregon and has numerous campgrounds along its banks between the town of Idleyld Park and Toketee Lake. The BLM's **Susan Creek Campground** (30 campsites; seasonal) is the most upscale public campground along the North Umpqua (it even has hot showers). The campsite pull-offs and campground road are all paved smooth enough for in-line skating, and consequently the campground is very popular with RVs.

To escape the sound of the highway, you can head up FS 38 (between mileposts 38 and 39) to **Canton Creek Campground** (5 campsites; seasonal), which is just off Steamboat Creek, or **Steamboat Falls Campground** (10 sites; year-round). Nearby but back on Ore. 138 is **Island Campground** (7 campsites; year-round). The larger **Horseshoe Bend Campground** (22 campsites; seasonal), near Steamboat, is popular with rafters and kayakers on weekends and has well-separated campsites, big views of surrounding cliffs, and access to North Umpqua Trail. Some of the campsites are right on the river. Continuing east, **Eagle Rock Campground** (25 campsites; seasonal) is in deep woods with campsites set back from the river (except site 23, which is right on the water). This campground is quite close to the highway. **Boulder Flat Campground** (11 campsites; seasonal), right on the highway east of

Eagle Rock, is the uppermost campground on the Wild and Scenic section of the river. **Toketee Lake Campground** (33 campsites; seasonal) at Toketee Lake is situated back from the lake but there are a few sites on the river. The lake is a pretty deep-green color and Umpqua Hot Springs are nearby. This is a good choice for mountain bikers and flat-water canoeists.

Along the **Rogue River,** you'll find the very busy **Valley of the Rogue State Park** (173 campsites, 152 with hookups) just off I-5 near the town of Rogue River. Farther downstream, there are several county park campgrounds west of Grants Pass. However, the nicest and most popular of these are **Indian Mary Park** (90 campsites; seasonal) and **Almeda Park** (25 campsites; seasonal), both of which are in the Hellgate Canyon area, are popular with rafters and anglers, and are close to the Grave Creek trailhead of the Rogue River Trail.

Although there are no campgrounds in **Oregon Caves National Monument,** there are plenty of national forest campgrounds nearby. On the road to the national monument, you'll find **Grayback Campground** (39 campsites, 1 with hookups; seasonal) and **Cave Creek Campground** (18 campsites, tents only; seasonal), both of which are in forest settings on creek banks. Farther from the national monument but still in the Cave Junction area is **Bolan Lake Campground** (12 campsites; seasonal), which is reached by taking County Road 5580 to FS 48 to FS 4812, and is set on a small lake with hiking and mountain-biking trails in the area.

The **Applegate Lake** area southwest of Jacksonville is popular with mountain bikers. Forest service campgrounds in the area include the walk-in **Watkins Campground** (14 campsites; seasonal) on a forested bluff at the south end of Applegate Lake. However, the **French Gulch Campground** at the north end (9 campsites; seasonal), also a walk-in campground, is more popular because it has waterfront campsites. There are also more walk-in campsites at **Squaw Lakes Campground** (17 campsites; year-round; reservations required, tel. 541/899-1812) on nearby Big Squaw Lake, which is on FS 1075, 8 miles east of Applegate Lake.

Along **Ore. 140** between Medford and Klamath Falls, there are several national forest campgrounds. On Fish Lake, **Fish Lake Campground** (27 campsites; seasonal) and **Doe Point Campground** (25 campsites; seasonal) are in nice locations but they both get a lot of traffic noise. Just west of Fish Lake on FS 37, the **North Fork Campground** (7 campsites; seasonal) provides a quieter setting at the west end of a scenic mountain-bike trail. This campground is set on the bank of Little Butte Creek, a good trout-fishing stream. **Sunset Campground** (67 campsites; seasonal) and **Aspen Point Campground** (60 campsites; seasonal) at Lake of the Woods are popular in summer with the boat fishing and water skiing crowd. The latter campground is near Great Meadow Recreation Area, has a swimming beach, and is right on the High Lakes mountain-bike trail. If you're searching for a campsite away from the rumble of the highway, drive north from Ore. 140 at Lake of the Woods to **Fourmile Lake Campground** (25 campsites; seasonal). Although the forest surrounding the lake is spindly and unattractive, there is a nice view of Mount McLoughlin and good hiking and mountain biking in the vicinity.

INNS & LODGES

Crater Lake Lodge

1211 Avenue C, White City, OR 97503. Tel. 541/830-8700. Fax 541/830-8514. 71 rms. $99–$185 double. MC, V. Closed mid-Oct to mid-May.

This lodge on the rim overlooking Crater Lake reopened in mid-1995 after a complete reconstruction. However, despite the loss of most of the original building, this lodge has the look and feel of a historic mountain lodge and now has modern conveniences as well. Slightly more than half the guest rooms overlook the lake, and although most of the rooms have modern bathrooms, there are eight rooms with claw-foot tubs.

Diamond Lake Resort

Diamond Lake, OR 97731. Tel. 800/733-7593. 40 rms, 10 studios, 43 cabins. $65 double in room; $69 double in studio; $95–$146 cabin. MC, V.

Located on the shores of Diamond Lake near the north entrance to the national park, this resort has long been a popular family vacation spot, and with mounts Thielsen and Bailey flanking the lake, this is one of the most picturesque settings in the Oregon Cascades. The variety of accommodations provides plenty of choices, but my favorites are the lakefront cabins. Rowboat, canoe, cross-country ski, and mountain-bike rentals are available, and there is a small sandy beach at the resort. In winter the resort is most popular with snowmobilers, but also sees a few cross-country skiers and downhillers snowcat skiing on Mount Bailey.

Union Creek Resort

56484 Hwy. 62, Prospect, OR 97536. Tel. 541/560-3339 or 541/560-3565. 9 rms, 15 cabins. $38–$48 double in room; $50–$85 double in cabin. MC, V.

Located almost across the road from the Rogue River Gorge, the resort has been catering to Crater Lake visitors since the early 1900s. Today there are both lodge rooms and cabins available, and most have been updated in recent years. Tall trees shade the grounds of the rustic resort, which is right on Ore. 62 about 23 miles from Rim Village.

Steamboat Inn

42705 N Umpqua Hwy., Steamboat, OR 97447-9703. Tel. 800/840-8825 or 541/498-2411. Fax 541/498-2411*2. 12 rms, 2 suites. $95–$150 double; $225 suite. MC, V. Closed Jan–Feb.

This inn on the bank of the North Umpqua River is one of the region's finest lodgings. The lodge appeals most to anglers but the gourmet meals served each evening have become legendary and now attract many gastronomes. If you aren't springing for one of the suites, which have their own soaking tubs overlooking the river, your best bet will be the streamside cabins. These rooms are beside the main lodge and feature a comfortably rustic styling and decks that overlook the river. There is a fly-fishing shop on the premises.

Oregon Caves Château

P.O. Box 128, Cave Junction, OR 97523. Tel. 541/592-3400. Fax 541/592-6654. 22 rms. $69–$99 double ($49–$69 in winter). MC, V.

This rustic six-story lodge was built in 1934. Huge fir beams support the lobby ceiling and two marble fireplaces beckon (it can be cool here any time of year). Because the lodge is in a canyon surrounded by tall trees, there are no views to speak of. Guest rooms have rather unattractive furnishings; if you spend your time exploring the caverns and hiking the forests, this shouldn't be too much of a drawback. A 1930s–style soda fountain serves burgers, shakes, and other simple meals, while in the main dining room dinners of steaks and seafood are available.

Morrison's Rogue River Lodge

8500 Galice Rd., Merlin, OR 97532. Tel. 800/ 826-1963 or 541/476-3825. Fax 541/476-4953. 4 rms, 9 cabins. $150–$240 double. Rates include all meals. MC, V. Closed Dec–Apr.

If you're in the area to do a bit of fishing or rafting, I can think of no better place to stay than at Morrison's Rogue River Lodge. Located on the banks of the Rogue, this fishing lodge epitomizes the Rogue River experience. The main lodge is a massive log building that is rustic yet comfortable, and has a wall of glass that looks across wide lawns to the river. There are bed-and-breakfast–style accommodations in this building, but I prefer the spacious cabins. Facilities include an outdoor pool, tennis courts, putting green, and private beach. Fishing guides and rafting trips are available through the lodge.

Mount Ashland Inn

550 Mount Ashland Rd., Ashland, OR 97520. Tel. 800/830-8707 or 541/482-8707. 6 rms. $95–$145 double. All rates include full breakfast. MC, V.

Located on 160 acres on the side of Mount Ashland, this massive log home commands distant panoramas from its forest setting. The Pacific Crest Trail passes through the front yard, and just a few miles up the road is the Mount Ashland ski area. There is also good cross-country skiing in winter, and the innkeepers are avid snowshoers (snowshoes are available to guests). In summer there is excellent mountain biking just up the road. The decor is straight out of an Eddie Bauer catalog with plenty of special touches such as handmade furniture and stained glass.

13

THE OREGON COAST & COAST RANGE

THERE ARE MANY REASONS TO BE THANKFUL FOR AUTOMOBILES (and as many reasons to curse their invention), but for me none is as powerful as the sight of undeveloped beaches stretching for hundreds of miles along the Oregon Coast. If not for the car, this amazing coastline would be a very different place. How can this be, you ask? How can cars be responsible for this natural jewel?

Well, way back in 1913, Governor Oswald West decided that beaches made good roadways, and therefore all beaches should be designated as public thoroughfares. Back in those days, the beach was indeed often the easiest route between two coastal points and the populace was thankful to have this public access. When eventually a paved highway replaced sand as the favored route for drivers, the beach was left to pedestrians (although a few beaches are still open to vehicles). To this day, if there's sand enough to drive a car, then you're on public beach.

However, forget about bringing your bathing suit. If you can get down to as little as shorts and a T-shirt, you can bet that people will be talking about the heat wave. The Oregon coast is not a place you go specifically for swimming. Never mind the killer beach logs and sneaker waves, the water here is just too cold. This is, for the most part, a take-in-the-scenery kind of coastline—but rest assured that the scenery more than makes up for the lack of good swimming or sunbathing opportunities. From the mouth of the Columbia River to the California state line, the Oregon coast dishes up rocky headlands, mist-shrouded mountains, long stretches of sandy beach, old-growth forests, monster sand dunes, and enough state parks to absorb the hordes that flee the Willamette Valley and other inland locales on hot summer weekends.

This coast, once considered remote and isolated, developed a reputation as a retirement haven decades ago, and there's a good reason for this. Not only is the climate exceedingly mild (if a bit too drizzly for some), but there just isn't much industry to speak of other than a few lumber mills and the log-exporting port at Coos Bay. This is not to say, however, that the coast is a wild, undeveloped land just waiting to be explored by the intrepid and adventurous. No, U.S. 101 hugs the coast for much of its length, and small towns dot this highway at regular intervals.

State parks, waysides, and other public beach accesses, however, far outnumber towns, and are strung out with enough regularity that you can hardly drive 10 miles without finding someplace to stop and take in the view, go for a hike, or do a little beachcombing or tide pooling. The beach might be a miles-long crescent of windswept sand, a craggy, wave-battered headland, or then again it might be a tiny rocky cove.

A longtime favorite way to do the Oregon coast is on a bicycle, and people come from around the country to do just this. The 350-mile-long coast lends itself well to a leisurely weeklong tour. However, cyclists with neither the time nor the stamina for such a trip will still find plenty of shorter routes to ride. Mountain bikers will even find a handful of good trails scattered along the length of this coast.

Many of the coast's headlands have been preserved as state parks and it is in these parks that you will find some of the best hikes. There is something magical about hiking several miles through old-growth Sitka spruce forest to arrive at a sunny clifftop where directly below you gray whales loll on the surface of the ocean.

The bird watching on the Oregon coast is also some of the best in the state. Migratory waterfowl and shorebirds gather at various locations in spring and fall. Other birds, such as tundra swans and Aleutian Canada geese, spend their winters here. In summer, seabirds such as tufted puffins, common murres, and three species of cormorants nest on rocky cliffs both on the mainland and on nearby islands.

Fish, too, follow the seasons on the Oregon coast and, consequently, so do anglers. Though virtually all the anadromous fish runs of coastal rivers are suffering from years of overfishing and habitat loss due to destructive logging practices, there are still enough fish in the water to attract large numbers of anglers each year. Outside Oregon, the Rogue River may be the best-known coastal river, but there are dozens more that support runs of spring and fall Chinook, summer and winter steelhead, as well as other less plentiful species.

Despite the frigid ocean temperatures along this coast, there are those hardy souls who find the temptations of wind and waves too great too resist. Surfers and boardsailors, zipped into thick wetsuits of course, have found numerous great spots along the Oregon coast. With knock-out settings and uncrowded waters, these spots more than compensate for the inconvenience of cold water.

The Lay of the Land

With the Coast Range sometimes rising straight from the ocean waves, the Oregon coast is a rugged and dramatic shoreline. Rocky capes and headlands that jut into the pounding surf seem to defy the power of the ocean to erode them. However, though it seems that this coast's rocky shores must be immutable, they are in fact constantly retreating from the relentless pounding of the Pacific's waves. The towering offshore rocks, known as **haystacks** or **seastacks,** are remnant reminders of where the Oregon coast once lay. The arch rocks, sea caves, and natural bridges that make this coastline so unique are all destined to one day give in to the power of the ocean and go crashing into the surf. Today's sea caves are tomorrow's arch rocks, and today's arch rocks are the sea stacks of tomorrow. Strange as it seems, many of the rocky headlands of the Oregon coast have their origins in vast basalt flows that originated hundreds of miles to the east some 15 million years ago. It is these basalt headlands that are the most erosion resistant and dramatic of the coast.

In other places along the coast, sandstone cliffs present a much more erodible face to the Pacific. Hug Point south of Cannon Beach, Cape Kiwanda west of Tillamook, the bluffs at Seal Rock south of Newport, and the shoreline between Sunset Bay and Cape Arago state parks west of Coos Bay are all sites where colorful, easily eroded sandstone can often be seen. In the latter area outside Coos Bay, the Cape Arago Lighthouse has twice been claimed by the Pacific as waves eroded the soft sandstone upon which it was built.

Both the erosion of sandstone shores and the sediment carried to the Pacific by the coast's many rivers provide the sand that forms the numerous beaches of this coast. This sand gathers between headlands and is shifted by ocean currents to form spits at the mouths of most bays. Most beaches are but a few miles long, but along the central coast, between Florence and Coos Bay, natural forces have conspired to create a landscape unlike that of the rest of the Oregon coast.

Beginning just south of Florence is the 47-mile-long **Oregon Dunes National Recreation Area,** which includes more than 14,000 acres of dunes. This is the largest area of sand dunes on the West Coast and contains dunes more than 500 feet tall. The first Oregon dunes were formed between 12 and 26 million years ago by the weathering of inland mountain ranges. Though the dunes are in constant flux, they reached their current size and shape about 7,000 years ago after the eruption of Mount Mazama formed Crater Lake. Water currents and winds are the factors that are responsible for the dunes. Currents move the sand particles north each winter and south each summer, while constant winds off the Pacific Ocean blow the sand eastward, piling it up into dunes that are slowly marching eastward. Over thousands of years, the dunes have swallowed up forests, leaving some groves of trees as remnant tree islands. Freshwater trapped behind the dunes has formed numerous freshwater lakes, many of which are now ringed by campgrounds and vacation homes.

However, these amazing dunes' days may be numbered. European beach grass, introduced in 1910 to stabilize sand near jetties, has aggressively colonized the dunes. By anchoring the sand closest to the beach, this grass has effectively cut off the supply of sand to the dunes farther east. However, winds continue to drive these inland dunes eastward. Eventually, as the eastward movement of the dunes slows, the sands will be colonized by surrounding forests, as the easternmost dunes have been for millions of years.

The **Coast Range,** which sometimes rises straight from the waves and sometimes retreats a few miles inland, is home to the wettest slopes in the state. It is here that giant Douglas firs, western red cedars, and Sitka spruce grow, watered annually by as much as 100 inches of rainfall. These trees, which grow straight and tall, have been the mainstay of the coast economy for more than a century. However, in the past decade, the "endless" supply of big trees has dwindled to almost nothing, and today the timber companies and environmentalists battle for the last stands of ancient forests. These trees are home to both the spotted owl and the marbled murrelet, two species of birds that depend on old-growth forests.

The casual visitor isn't likely to remark on the difference between the Coast Range and the **Siskiyou Mountains** of the southern Oregon coast, but these latter mountains are quite unique and have a decidedly different history from that of the Coast Range. While the Coast Range was formed by the uplifting of the seafloor, the Siskiyou Mountains are thought to have been a vast island drifting slowly across the Pacific Ocean on a tectonic plate that millions of years ago collided with the North American continent. It is this geologic heritage that is responsible both for the rugged character of the mountains and the amazing diversity of plants that exists here. More than 1,000 plant species grow within these mountains, making this one of the most botanically diverse regions in North America.

While there are no towns on the coast with more than 20,000 residents, these shores are hardly a wilderness. Dozens of small towns are scattered along **U.S. 101,** and seemingly any piece of oceanfront property that is not publicly owned now has a housing development or someone's retirement home on it. Luckily, there is plenty of green space and plenty of beach access in between the parcels of privately owned land.

With only one major port, at **Coos Bay,** and mountains stretching from the Columbia to California, the Oregon coast has always been somewhat isolated from the state's population centers in the Willamette Valley and along the I-5 corridor in southern Oregon. However, today there are a dozen highways that cross the Coast Range, as well as several less-traveled secondary roads that wind their way through often remote mountains.

With five highway connections to the Portland metropolitan area, the **north coast,** from Astoria to Lincoln City, is the most developed stretch of Oregon's shoreline. Favored by Portlanders for day trips and weekend getaways, the beaches here are less than a two-hour drive from the city. The towns of this stretch of the coast offer a little of everything: Victorian mansions in working-port **Astoria,** modern vacation homes in exclusive **Gearhart,** classic beach-resort atmosphere at **Seaside,** boutiques and flower gardens in **Cannon Beach** and **Manzanita,** spring break cheap beach houses at **Rockaway Beach,** endless souvenir shops at **Lincoln City,** and the coast's only genuine beach resort at Salishan in **Gleneden Beach.**

Farther south are **Newport** (home of Keiko the killer whale and the Oregon Coast Aquarium), **Waldport** (a popular fishing town), **Yachats** (one more quintessentially quaint coast getaway), **Florence** (gateway to the Oregon Dunes National Recreation Area and location of one of the coast's only truly historic downtowns), **Coos Bay** (the largest port between San Francisco and Seattle and supposedly the largest wood-products port in the world), **Bandon** (with galleries and cranberry bogs), **Gold Beach** (at the mouth of the Rogue River), and **Brookings** (in the coast's "Banana Belt" and a favorite retirement community).

Despite the growing human habitation of the Oregon coast, wildlife is still abundant, and sea lions and seals can often be seen sunning themselves on offshore rocks. Gray whales are also regular visitors to the Oregon coast. Twice a year, during their migrations between the arctic and the waters off Baja California, the whales pass close by the coast and can be easily spotted from coastal headlands. The best time to spot whales is in late winter and early spring. However, more than 200 whales now remain off the Oregon coast throughout the summer. At the Oregon Coast Aquarium in Newport, you can learn more about these and all the myriad other marine life of this coastline's diverse environments. Roosevelt elk are the most impressive of the coast's terrestrial mammals, and black-tailed deer are also often spotted.

Parks & Other Hot Spots

Fort Stevens State Park

Off U.S. 101, 10 miles west of Astoria. Tel. 503/861-1671. Camping, boardsailing, road biking, bird watching, wildlife watching.

This park is on the site of a fort that once guarded the mouth of the Columbia River. While the miles of beach are perhaps the main attraction, miles of paved bike paths, a lake with a swimming area, and a campground make this park a favorite with families and picnickers. However, bird watching and boardsailing are also popular.

Ecola State Park

Off U.S. 101, 2 miles north of Cannon Beach. Camping, hiking, surfing.

Located just north of Cannon Beach and encompassing Tillamook Head, this park has one of the best coastal viewpoints in the state. It also has a hiking trail along a route once followed by Lewis and Clark and a surfing beach.

Oswald West State Park

On U.S. 101, 10 miles south of Cannon Beach. Camping, hiking, surfing.

Both the campground and the beach in this park can only be reached by walking, which gives this park a decidedly different character from others along the coast. With headlands both north and south, the park's Short Sands Beach is an exquisite little crescent of sand backed by dense forest. This is also the site of the most popular surfing spot on the north Oregon coast.

Cape Lookout State Park

Off U.S. 101, 12 miles southwest of Tillamook on Three Capes Loop. Tel. 503/842-4981. Camping, hiking, bird watching, whale watching.

Cape Lookout, the longest point on the Oregon coast, juts out more than 2 miles into the Pacific Ocean. Its high cliffs are topped by a dense Sitka spruce forest, and around its base, gray whales can often be seen feeding as they migrate along the Oregon coast. The tip of the cape can only be reached by a hiking trail. The park also includes Netarts Spit, which forms Netarts Bay.

Cape Perpetua Scenic Area

On U.S. 101, 3 miles south of Yachats. Tel. 541/547-3289. Hiking, mountain biking, road biking, bird watching, whale watching.

With cliffs that rise more than 700 feet straight out of the water, Cape Perpetua claims to be the highest point right on the coast and is certainly one of the most dramatic. Located within Siuslaw National Forest, this scenic area has an informative visitor center perched on a hillside above the water (keep an eye out for whales). Several trails in the immediate area offer lots of options for short walks along the rocky coastline or long hikes through inland old-growth forests. One trail is even open to mountain bikes.

Oregon Dunes National Recreation Area

Along U.S. 101 between Florence and Coos Bay. Tel. 541/271-3611. Camping, hiking, mountain biking, canoeing, bird watching.

While most people associate the Oregon coast with rocky headlands and mist shrouded forests of giant fir trees, for 40 miles between Florence and Coos Bay, the highest points along the coast are huge sand dunes, some of which reach 500 feet.

Between Florence and Coos Bay, 40 miles of sand dunes have been preserved as the Oregon Dunes National Recreation Area. These dunes range from bare windswept expanses to old dunes that are now covered with forests. In the valleys between dunes are numerous lakes both large and small. While there are hiking trails through some of the dunes, recreation in the area is dominated by dune buggies and other ORVs. On the region's many lakes, ski boats and personal watercraft are the favored means of transportation. If you value peace and quiet, you might want to give this area a wide berth, although there are those areas that are off-limits to off-roaders.

Sunset Bay State Park

Off U.S. 101, 12 miles southwest of Coos Bay on the Cape Arago Hwy. Tel. 541/888-4902. Camping, hiking, swimming, scuba diving.

This state park west of Coos Bay is set on one of the prettiest little coves on the whole Oregon coast. Because it is shallow, sandy, and protected from winds, Sunset Bay is one of the only places on the coast where people go swimming with any frequency. A segment of the Oregon Coast Trail passes through the park and connects to both Shore Acres State Park and Cape Arago State Park.

Cape Arago State Park

Off U.S. 101, 14 miles southwest of Coos Bay off the Cape Arago Hwy. Hiking, bird watching, wildlife watching.

This third of the Coos Bay area state parks is best known for the seals and sea lions that haul out on the rocks of Simpson Reef just offshore. The sea lions keep up a constant cacophony of barking throughout the summer. Trails lead down to two beaches and out to the rugged blufftop pinniped viewing area.

Cape Blanco State Park

Off U.S. 101, 9 miles north of Port Orford. Tel. 541/332-6774. Camping, hiking, fishing, wildlife watching.

Cape Blanco, named in 1603 by a Spanish explorer for its white cliffs, is one of two points claiming to be the most westerly spot in the contiguous United States (the other is Cape Flattery, Washington). Popular with horse owners, the park has wide expanses of meadows and a maze of short trails. At the tip of the cape is the Cape Blanco Lighthouse, and inland a bit is a restored Victorian farmhouse. A boat ramp provides access to the Sixes River. Trails lead to beaches both on the north and south sides of the cape.

Samuel H. Boardman State Park

Along U.S. 101, 4–14 miles north of Brookings. Hiking, road biking.

This 10-mile-long stretch of cliff-edged shoreline is the most magnificent of the entire Oregon coast. Haystack rocks rise from the ocean and huge boulders are strewn on the beaches. Several short segments of the Oregon Coast Trail meander along the cliff edges here.

Loeb State Park

Off U.S. 101, 10 miles northeast of Brookings. Tel. 541/469-2021. Camping, hiking, swimming, canoeing, fishing.

This park is best known as the site of some of the northernmost coast redwood trees but was originally created to preserve a grove of myrtle trees. The beautiful turquoise waters of the Chetco River flow through the park, providing both great swimming and great Class I canoeing.

The North Coast (Astoria to Cape Perpetua) ◆ What to Do & Where to Do It

BEACHES

The beaches of the north coast vary widely in character. Here you'll find miles-long strands of sand, tiny pocket coves, cobble beaches, and rocky headlands sheltering fascinating tide pools. Also along these shores are numerous state parks, both large and small, as well as the most crowded beach towns on the coast.

From the mouth of the Columbia River south all the way to Tillamook Head are more than 16 miles of flat sand. **Fort Stevens State Park,** a former military reservation that guarded the mouth of the Columbia River, is the focus of beach activity here, with visits to the wreck of the *Peter Iredale* a favorite pastime. Also along this stretch of beach is the town of **Seaside,** one of Oregon's oldest beach resorts. Unlike other towns along the Oregon coast, Seaside has the flavor of a Jersey shore beach town. Beach biking, kite flying, strolling the Promenade, and surfing are popular.

Just over Tillamook Head from Seaside is the **Cannon Beach,** the coast's most upscale little village, a sort of Carmel of the Northwest. The setting is spectacular, with the huge Haystack Rock (one of two rocks bearing that name along this coast) and many other equally impressive rocks lying just offshore. Just north of Cannon

Outdoor Resources

Alsea Ranger District
18591 Alsea Hwy.
Alsea, OR 97324
Tel. 541/487-5811

Chetco Ranger District
555 Fifth St.
Brookings, OR 97415
Tel. 541/469-2196

Gold Beach Ranger District
1225 S Ellensburg Rd. (P.O. Box 7)
Gold Beach, OR 97444
Tel. 541/247-6651

Hebo Ranger District
Hebo, OR 97122
Tel. 503/392-3161

Mapleton Ranger District
P.O. Box 67
Mapleton, OR 97453
Tel. 541/268-4473

Waldport Ranger District
31049 SW Pacific Hwy.
(P.O. Box 400)
Waldport, OR 97394
Tel. 503/563-3211

Oregon Coastal Refuges
2030 S Marine Science Dr.
Newport, OR 97365-5296
Tel. 541/867-4550

Beach is **Ecola State Park,** site of **Indian Beach,** a little cove that is popular with surfers. South are the first of many state park waysides that dot the Oregon coast. **Arcadia Beach Wayside** provides quick access to one of my favorite stretches of beach. The beach is bounded by eroded sandstone rock wall at the base of which are numerous tide pools. Perhaps best of all, you can find spots that are sheltered from the wind. A little bit south, you'll find similar conditions at **Hug Point State Park,** named for the road that once hugged the rocks here. Hug Point—Humbug and Silver Points to the north—can all be rounded at low tide.

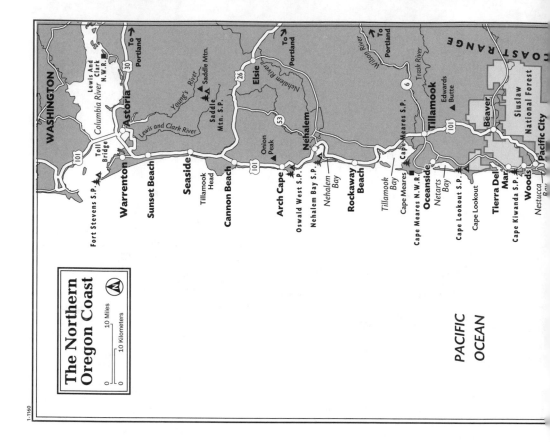

The Northern Oregon Coast

Continuing south, in **Oswald West State Park,** you'll find **Short Sands Beach** at the end of a 0.5-mile trail. Situated on Smuggler's Cove and backed by forested hillsides, this beach has the most remote feel of any along this coast. Personally, I think its the most beautiful beach on the whole north coast. South of Oswald West is the town of **Manzanita,** another upscale community. The winds and waves attract lots of surfers and boardsailors. To the south is **Nehalem Bay State Park,** with miles of good beach hiking along the Nehalem Spit.

Along the Three Capes Loop west of Tillamook, you can stroll miles of dunes-backed sand from the foot of Cape Meares north up the **Bayocean Spit,** passing the site of an old beach resort that washed into the sea after jetties were built at the mouth of Tillamook Bay. On the other side of Cape Meares is the community of **Oceanside,** which sprawls up a wooded hillside and has the feel of a town that time has passed by. The view from the beach here, of Three Arch Rocks, is one of the best around. Continuing south you come to **Cape Lookout State Park.** From the base of the cape, where there are tide pools to explore, the beach runs 6.0 miles north up the undeveloped Netarts Spit. If you want to get away from the crowds, hike up this spit. At the south end of the Three Capes Loop, you'll find **Cape Kiwanda State Park,** which has the biggest sand dunes on the north coast and is a popular hang-gliding and paragliding spot. Just south of Cape Kiwanda is **Robert W. Straub State Park,** on Nestucca Bay's North Spit.

At **Neskowin,** on the north side of Cascade Head, you'll find the forested Proposal Rock rising straight up from the beach and a village of old beach cottages and modern vacation homes. The beach stretches 4.0 miles north from here. On the south side of this headland lies **Lincoln City,** a miles-long strip of unsightly sprawl. Favored by families and college students, this beach has all the things you're likely looking to get away from—taffy stores, Go-Kart tracks, and souvenir shops by the

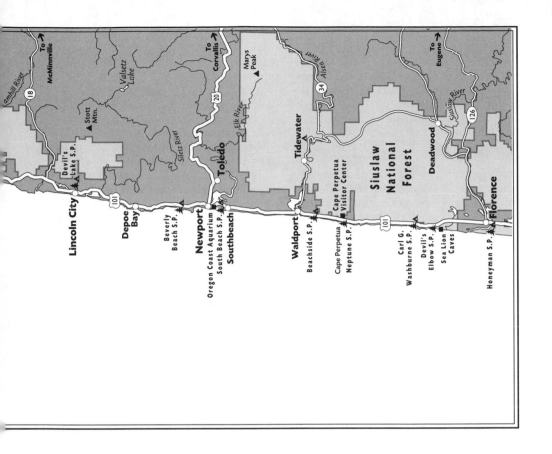

dozens. However, at the north end of town, in the area known as **Road's End,** you'll find the quietest and most scenic piece of Lincoln City sand.

South of the resort communities of Salishan and Gleneden Beach, the coast once again turns rocky. Along this stretch, you'll find **Fogarty Creek State Park** and **Boiler Bay State Wayside.** This latter has some of the most fascinating tide pools along the north coast. Continuing south, there is **Depoe Bay State Park** near the mouth of tiny Depoe Bay, the smallest natural harbor on the coast. The rocky coastline here, right along the highway, is famous for its spouting horns.

At **Devil's Punch Bowl State Park,** you'll find, on the north side of the Punch Bowl's churning waters, an extensive tide-pool area. Just south of here is **Beverly Beach State Park,** with a campground and good surfing. More tide pools can be explored a few miles farther south on the beach at **Yaquina Head,** which has been designated an outstanding natural area despite the fact that it was once used as a rock quarry. South of Yaquina Head is **Agate Beach State Wayside,** with a nice view of the headland, and **Nye Beach,** an old resort area where there are more tide pools to explore. Nye Beach is now part of Newport, which is home to the Oregon Coast Aquarium and the orca whale Keiko, star of the movie *Free Willy.* Two state park beaches flank the mouth of Yaquina Bay and stay crowded throughout the summer due to the popularity of the nearby aquarium. **Yaquina Bay State Park** is now surrounded by the town of Newport. **South Beach State Park** is a more natural setting.

Continuing south from Newport are several pretty state park beaches. At **Ona Beach** there is a long, wide beach at the mouth of tranquil Beaver Creek. The picnic area here is one of the prettiest around. At **Seal Rock State Park** you can explore more tide pools at the base of the impressive Seal Rock and usually observe the rock's namesake pinnipeds.

In the Yachats area, you can look for agates on the beaches at **Smelt Sands**

Wayside or at the mouth of the Yachats River at the **Yachats Ocean Road State Wayside.** Just south of this quaint little town is Cape Perpetua, at the base of which are tide pools and a spouting horn.

BIRD WATCHING

With its bays, marshes, headlands, and offshore rocks, the north Oregon coast is one of the best places in the state for a birdwatching foray. Call the birding hot line in Portland (tel. 503/292-0661) during the winter months and you're sure to learn about several unusual sightings on these bays.

At **Fort Stevens State Park,** you'll find several good birding spots, and there are even viewing blinds that will improve your chances. Fall through spring are the best times for birding here. You'll find the viewing blinds at Trestle Bay and Swash Lake. Between these areas you might see several species of ducks, American bitterns, Virginia rails, long-billed dowitchers, and several species of wrens. Trestle Bay is a good place to visit during spring and fall migratory seasons as well. At the South Jetty overlook, keep an eye out for rhinoceros auklets, western grebes, and brown pelicans.

The many bays of the north Oregon coast provide ample opportunities for birding throughout the year. During the fall shorebird migration (August through October), some of the best birding on the north coast is at **Bayocean Spit** on the west side of Tillamook Bay. Wide mudflats are covered with shorebirds for the hours before and after high tide. A small lake, forests, and sand dunes attract many other species of birds as well. On **Netarts Bay,** southwest of Tillamook, look for numerous species of shorebirds in spring and fall and Aleutian Canada geese and brants in winter. In the **Nestucca Bay** area south of Tillamook you might spot a few of the very small population of Aleutian Canada geese that winter here. On **Siletz Bay** on the south side of Lincoln City, look for loons and red-necked and horned grebes in winter and whimbrels in summer. The best birding spot on this bay is on the waterfront in the Cutler City neighborhood,

which is a third of the way down the bay from the north end.

The many rocky headlands along this coast also provide excellent birding. From April through August, many species of seabirds nest along these rocky cliffs and on offshore islands. Almost all of the offshore haystack rocks and islands along the northern Oregon coast are protected as the **Three Arch Rocks National Wildlife Refuge.** As such, the islands are off-limits to humans. Onshore there are also several other wildlife refuges. During the summer look for tufted puffins, auklets, storm-petrels, pigeon guillemots, common murres, marbled murrelets, gulls, and cormorants. Good places to check out include **Chapman Point** in Ecola State Park (nesting cormorants and common murres), **Haystack Rock** in Cannon Beach (nesting tufted puffins), **Cape Meares State Park** (a wide variety of seabirds), **Cape Lookout State Park** (if you don't mind a 5-mile round-trip hike to do your birding), **Yaquina Head** (one of the very best viewing spots on this coast; nesting western gulls, Brandt's cormorants, common murres, pigeon guillemots, and tufted puffins), and **Cape Perpetua** (look for marbled murrelets).

About 12 miles north of Yaquina Head (and just north of Depoe Bay), at **Boiler Bay State Wayside,** you stand a good chance of seeing federally threatened marbled murrelets in the spring and fall (also look for these birds at Cape Meares and at the north jetty on Tillamook Bay) and ancient murrelets in the winter months. This is also a surprisingly good place to pick up a few pelagic birds without having to get seasick. Over the years, Clark's grebes, horned puffins, jaegars, black-vented shearwaters, storm-petrels, and Laysan and black-footed albatrosses have all been spotted here.

Another unusual and productive birding spot is the mouth of the Yachats River in the town of Yachats. Here, from the **Yachats Ocean Road State Wayside** and adjacent beach, you can often see as many as five species of gulls (ring-billed, mew, California, western, and glaucous-winged). Wandering tattlers have also been spotted here.

If you're crazy about **tufted puffins,** there are several places along the coast where you stand a better than average chance of spotting these parrots of the sea. Tops on the list is Haystack Rock in Cannon Beach, a puffin nesting area. However, other good places to look for them are at Cape Meares, Cape Lookout, and Cape Kiwanda (all three of which are along the Three Capes Loop west of Tillamook), and at Yaquina Head north of Newport. Summer is the best time to spot puffins.

BOARDSAILING

One of the hottest boardsailing spots in this region is actually 30 miles inland from the coast up the Columbia River at Jones Beach, just west of Clatskanie. Here the summer winds blow with almost the same intensity that they do in the Columbia Gorge. To reach this beach, drive 6 miles west of Clatskanie on U.S. 30, turn north on Woodson Road, crossing the railroad tracks and Westport Slough, and continue 2.5 miles to the beach.

In the Astoria area, Young's Bay is a good spot for novice and intermediate sailors. There's a good launch area at the Warrenton end of the U.S. 101 bridge south of Astoria. For slightly stronger winds, head out to Fort Stevens State Park and launch on **Trestle Bay,** which is tucked into the curve of Clatsop Spit near the South Jetty. This bay gets good winds coming across the narrow spit, yet is protected from the thundering surf on the oceanside. If you're interested in some wave riding, check that surf on the other side of the spit. Sometimes it's just right for some good wave jumping.

The beach from **Manzanita** south to Nehalem Bay State Park is a popular spot for wave riding. Winds are often strong and the waves are frequently well shaped (which makes this a popular surfing spot as well). There is beach access both in Manzanita and in the state park. Intermediate and novice sailors can stick to the waters of **Nehalem Bay,** where they'll get the winds but not the waves. There's access from Nehalem Bay State Park.

Although quite narrow, **Devil's Lake** in Lincoln City is long enough that it gets

good winds that blow in off the ocean. Waves stay small but winds can be strong, which makes this a good intermediate sailing spot. Launch at Sand Point Park north of East Devil's Lake State Park on East Devil's Lake Road. If you're looking for some open-ocean wave riding, try **Road's End** at the north end of Lincoln City. **Siletz Bay,** at the south end of Lincoln City, is another spot that gets strong winds but that's protected from ocean waves. Launch from the beach at the north end of the bay. During the summer, there is often good novice-to-intermediate wave riding at the south jetty in Newport.

FISHING

The rivers of Oregon's north coast are some of the state's most heavily fished streams. These often narrow streams hold runs of salmon and steelhead, and the thrill of pulling a 50-pound Chinook out of a river barely 20 feet wide is unforgettable. However, most salmon and steelhead runs have been very low in the past few years and many restrictions have been imposed. Almost all coho fishing has been closed for several years now as the state wrangles with the Department of Fish and Wildlife over the possibility of listing all coho salmon as threatened under the Endangered Species Act. All rivers, with the exception of the Miami and Kilchis, have also been closed to fishing for chum salmon. All wild steelhead (non-fin–clipped) must be released. Check the current regulations.

Coastal sea-run cutthroat trout are severely depleted, and in 1996, the Umpqua River cutthroat trout run was listed as a threatened species under the Endangered Species Act. This listing had the effect of closing off virtually all coastal streams and rivers to fishing for wild sea-run cutthroats. However, many coastal rivers are stocked with cutthroat trout each year, and the opening day of trout fishing season on Memorial Day weekend always sees a frenzy of fishing.

While virtually all of the north coast's rivers have populations of salmon, steelhead, and cutthroat trout, each river has particular runs of fish for which it is best known. The following is a list of the region's rivers and the best fish to go after on each river:

◆ **Necanicum River** (hatchery winter steelhead);

◆ **Nehalem River** (winter steelhead, summer Chinook);

◆ **North Fork Nehalem River** (hatchery coho);

◆ **Salmonberry River** (winter steelhead);

◆ **Kilchis River** (winter steelhead, fall Chinook);

◆ **Miami River** (native cutthroat, catch-and-release chum salmon);

◆ **Wilson River** (winter steelhead, fall Chinook);

◆ **Trask River** (wild winter steelhead, fall Chinook, wild cutthroat);

◆ **Nestucca River** (sea-run cutthroat, spring Chinook, summer and winter steelhead);

◆ **Little Nestucca River** (wild cutthroat);

◆ **Salmon River** (fall Chinook, winter steelhead, sea-run cutthroat);

◆ **Siletz River** (fall Chinook, summer and winter steelhead, hatchery cutthroat);

◆ **Alsea River** (hatchery winter steelhead, fall Chinook).

While many of the above rivers are listed as salmon streams, much of the salmon fishing along the coast takes place in bays where the salmon gather before heading up the rivers. The best way to fish these bays is from a small boat, and marinas on these bays often have rentals. Good salmon-fishing bays include Nehalem Bay (fall Chinook), Tillamook Bay (spring and fall Chinook; bank fishing from north and south jetties, old coast guard pier in Garibaldi, along U.S. 101 between Bay City and Hobsonville Point, and along Bay Ocean Road on the west side of the bay), Nestucca Bay (fall Chinook; bank angling from end of North Spit in Bob Straub Park and at Fisher Landing on Brooten Road), Yaquina Bay (fall Chinook), and Alsea Bay (fall Chinook; bank angling on south side of bay). The Nehalem, Tillamook, and Yaquina are also good for bottomfish.

If you've got an urge to do some salmon or bottom fishing, you'll find charter boats operating out of several north coast ports. In Garibaldi try **Garibaldi/D&D Charters**

(tel. 800/900-HOOK or 503/322-0007), **Siggi-G Ocean Charters** (tel. 503/322-3285), or **Troller Charters** (tel. 800/546-3666 or 503/322-3666). In Depoe Bay, try **Tradewinds** (tel. 800/445-8730 or 541/765-2345), beside the bridge, or **Dockside Charters** (tel. 800/733-8915 or 541/765-2545), down by the marina. In Newport, try **Newport Sportfishing,** 1000 SE Bay Blvd. (tel. 800/828-8777 or 541/265-7558).

If you're looking for a guide to take you out on north coast rivers, try **Bob Brown's River Guide Service** (tel. 503/842-9696), **Clive's Fishing Guide Service** (tel. 503/397-6246), or **Rippling Brook Flies** (tel. 503/362-0624).

HIKING

Nehalem Spit

5 miles round-trip. Easy. No elevation gain. Access: In Nehalem Bay State Park, 15 miles south of Cannon Beach off U.S. 101. Map: Not necessary.

Guarding the mouth of almost every bay on the Oregon coast is a long sand spit. If you enjoy long walks on the beach, these spits are ideal. The bayside shores are usually good places for bird watching.

Nehalem Spit is one of my favorites. The length is just right, and not only are there birds to watch in the bay, but near the point of the spit, on the bay side, you can usually see harbor seals sleeping on the beach (that is, if they don't see you first). The middle of the spit is comprised of low sand dunes, through which runs a designated equestrian trail. It is just under 2.5 miles from the picnic area to the end of the spit, and you can return either the way you came, on the equestrian trail through the dunes, or along the shore of Nehalem Bay.

Saddle Mountain

6 miles round-trip. Moderate. 1,630-foot elevation gain. Access: 10 miles east of U.S. 101 on U.S. 26, turn north at the signed road for Saddle Mountain State Park, and continue 7 miles to the end of this one-laned paved road. Map: USGS Saddle Mountain.

This rocky peak has an unmistakable profile. It really does look like a saddle! It's also one of the best summit hikes in the entire Coast Range. The trail is a steady, often steep, uphill climb from the very start, and though it begins in an alder forest, it soon emerges into rocky terrain with constantly changing views. The exposed basalt of this peak offers plenty of fascinating rock formations to stop and admire as you climb. One of the most interesting sections of the trail is the crossing of the mountain's narrow saddle. Meadows cling to much of the upper elevations and put on spectacular wildflower displays in May and June. More than 300 species of plants have been recorded on this mountain, and some of the flowering plants in the meadows are quite rare. Any time of year (if it's a sunny day), the hike's real payoff is the view from the top, which includes the Coast Range, the Pacific Ocean, and Cascades peaks including Mount Rainier, Mount Adams, Mount St. Helens, and Mount Hood. Although Saddle Mountain is the highest peak in northwest Oregon, it is only 3,283 feet high and can be climbed throughout the year (I've climbed it on New Year's Eve).

Oswald West State Park Trails

3.4–8.8 miles. Easy–moderate. 400–800-foot elevation gain. Access: On U.S. 101, 10 miles south of Cannon Beach.

Within this state park is a 12-mile stretch of the Oregon Coast Trail that takes in some of the finest clifftop views on the north coast. Using the Oswald West State Park parking area as a starting point, you have a couple of options, both of which start with a hike of less than 0.5 miles down to Smuggler's Cove and Short Sands Beach. From this driftwood-lined cove you can hike north 2 miles to windswept Cape Falcon or south 1.3 miles to clifftop meadows that overlook the Devil's Cauldron, where the waters of the Pacific churn against rocks at the base of the cliffs (for an 8-mile hike, do both of these sections of trail). At Cape Falcon, you'll hike through incredibly dense thickets of salal as you approach the tip of the cape. On the southerly trail, which actually connects

to a trail up Neahkanie Mountain (another 2 miles to the summit), trees arch over the trail to form a natural tunnel just before you reach the meadows.

Cape Lookout

5 miles round-trip. Easy. 400-foot elevation gain. Access: On Three Capes Loop Dr., 16 miles south of Tillamook (follow signs to Cape Lookout State Park and continue past the campground entrance). Map: Trailhead maps.

This hike leads through dense forest to one of the best whale-watching vantage points on the Oregon coast. There are only a couple of views, one south and one north, as you hike out toward the tip of the cape. However, as you approach the end of the trail, you'll find yourself hiking along the edge of 400-foot-high cliffs. From these you can scan the waters below for whales, which are easily spotted if present.

Cascade Head

3.5 miles. Moderate. 1,200-foot elevation gain. Access: Off U.S. 101, 1.25 miles north of the U.S. 101/Ore. 18 junction. Take Three Rocks Rd. west 2.5 miles, and then fork right at the boat ramp and continue 0.5 miles to the trailhead. Map: Trailhead maps.

Cascade Head, which rises to the north of the Salmon River estuary between Lincoln City and Neskowin, is the site of one of the largest meadows on the north coast. These meadows, which are now a Nature Conservancy preserve, are home to threatened Oregon silverspot butterflies. For this reason, the Nature Conservancy requests that you hike only on the trail and that you not bring your dog with you. The trail up the headland has beautiful views down the coast to the south, with the Salmon River estuary in the immediate foreground. The view from the top of the meadows is as outstanding as any you'll find on the north coast. The trail climbs steadily through forest for 0.75 miles before reaching the lower end of the Cascade Head meadows. The trail then climbs steeply through the meadows and ever-changing views.

For an easier hike, start from the top of the headland 3.25 miles off U.S. 101 on FS 1861 and hike 1 mile through the woods to the upper end of the meadows. This trail involves only 150 feet of elevation gain. The trailhead is open only between July 16 and December 31.

Gwynn Creek-Cooks Ridge Loop Trail

5.5 miles. Moderate. 1,200-foot elevation gain. Access: At Cape Perpetua Visitor Center, 3 miles south of Yachats. Map: USGS Waldport.

Cape Perpetua, with its visitor center and breathtaking views, is a magnet for vacationers. However, most visitors are content to take in the ocean views, tide pools, and spouting horn. Few people realize that away from the shore this scenic area has a fascinating old-growth Sitka spruce forest that can be explored on an afternoon's hike. From the upper parking area of the visitor center, head up the Cooks Ridge Trail. In 0.5 miles, take either fork in the trail to continue. In another 0.2 miles, you enter a forest of majestic old Sitka spruce trees as you climb along Cooks Ridge. Beneath these trees grow sword ferns as tall as the average hiker. In a little less than 2.5 miles from the visitor center, go right on the Gwynn Creek Trail and drop down to the floor of this creek valley. Continue down the valley and in 2.5 miles go right on a stretch of the Oregon Coast Trail that used to be an old wagon road. It's 1 mile back along this road to the visitor center.

HORSEBACK RIDING

If you've always dreamed of riding a horse on the beach, there are several places along this coast where you can make that dream come true. **Faraway Farms,** on U.S. 101 south of Seaside (tel. 503/386-4236), offers rides both on their small ranch and on the beach. In Cannon Beach, guided rides are offered by the stables at the **Sea Ranch R.V. Park.** The rides head down Ecola Creek to the beach and then into Ecola State Park. In the tiny community of Neskowin, just north of Lincoln City, **Neskowin Stables,** 48490 Hawk Ave. (tel. 503/392-3277), also offers rides on the beach. Expect to pay around $20 per hour.

MOUNTAIN BIKING

In addition to the rides listed below, you'll find miles of challenging riding in the hills behind the **Astoria Column** in Astoria. Mountain bikes can be rented in Lincoln City at **David's Bicycle Rental,** 960 SE Hwy. 101 (tel. 541/996-6001) and at **Blue Heron Landing,** 4006 W Devil's Lake Rd. (tel. 541/994-4708).

Bayocean Spit

8 miles round-trip. Easy. No elevation gain. Access: On Bayocean Rd. west of Tillamook off the Three Capes Loop. Map: Not necessary.

Bring the binoculars and the bird book and turn a ride along this dirt road into a combination mountain-bike ride and bird-watching trip. The gated road, which follows the bay side of the spit for 4 miles, almost to the jetty at the entrance to the bay, has great views of mudflats that are particularly crowded with birds between August and October. As you pedal this dirt road, ponder the spit's history. During the first few decades of this century, there was a booming beach resort here. But when the jetty was built at the mouth of the bay, the spit began eroding, and within two more decades, the town was no more. Today nothing remains of the town of Bayocean.

Pioneer-Indian Trail

9 miles round-trip. Moderate–strenuous. 1,500-foot elevation gain. Access: From U.S. 101 at Hebo, go east on Ore. 22 and then immediately turn left onto FS 14. In 4.5 miles, park at the Hebo Lake Campground. Map: USFS Hebo Ranger District.

This loop climbs to the meadowed summit of Mount Hebo, which has a commanding view of the coast from Cape Kiwanda to Tillamook Bay. The meadows up here are also home to the endangered Oregon silverspot butterfly, so try to stay on the trail. Start by continuing another 4.5 miles up FS 14 from the Hebo Lake Campground. It's a slow, steady climb, but after about 3 miles you reach the meadows. Continue on to the primitive Mount Hebo Campground, and after a rest to take in the views, turn right to begin the descent on the Pioneer–Indian Trail, which was indeed once used by pioneers and Indians (a left turn will take you steeply downhill to South Lake if you want to make this a 2,300-foot elevation gain, 15-mile ride). From the campground, the trail rolls through the meadows for 2.5 miles before dropping quickly down through forest from the mountaintop to the Hebo Lake Campground.

Cummins Creek Trail

10 miles. Moderate. 1,200-foot elevation gain. Access: Start at the Cape Perpetua Visitor Center, 3 miles south of Yachats on U.S. 101. Map: USGS Waldport.

There aren't a lot of trails open to mountain bikes along the Oregon coast, which alone would make this a good choice. However, the trail segment of this route also passes through some outstanding groves of old-growth Sitka spruce trees, which makes this ride that much more enjoyable. The route begins just north of the Cape Perpetua Visitor Center on FS 55 (you could park near the Perpetua Campground, which is off this road) and immediately gets your heart pounding with 4 miles and 1,200 vertical feet of often steep uphill pedaling on the paved Cape Perpetua auto tour route.

After 4 miles, watch for the Cummins Creek/Gwynn Creek Trail on the right at the edge of a clear-cut. The trail continues to climb for a bit. In less than a half-mile down this trail, be sure to go left onto the Cummins Creek Trail (Gwynn Creek Trail is closed to bikes). Soon the trail begins its rocky 1-mile drop to the floor of the Cummins Creek Valley and an abandoned dirt road that is now somewhere between double-track and single-track. This valley-floor segment is through old Sitka spruce forest and is the smoothest, fastest, and funnest part of the ride, though you might want to slow down to appreciate some of these big trees. In a little more than 3 miles after hitting the old dirt road, the fun comes to an end as you reach U.S. 101. Go right and ride 1 mile up the highway to the visitor center entrance and the end of the ride.

If you just want to do a bit of easy riding, you can rent bikes in Seaside, Cannon Beach, Pacific City, and Lincoln City. Not only are there beach cruisers and mountain bikes for rent, but most shops also rent tandems, four-wheeled cycles known as surreys, and three-wheeled recumbent bikes for pedaling on the beach.

Fort Clatsop–Fort Stevens Loop

24 miles round-trip. Moderate. 50-foot elevation gain. Access: Start at the museum in Fort Stevens State Park, off U.S. 101 west of Astoria (follow signs).

This ride takes in two very different forts, one of which is now a state park and the other of which is a national monument. Fort Stevens, now a state park with 8.5 miles of paved bike paths, is a Civil War–era fort established to protect the mouth of the Columbia River from Confederate ships. Fort Clatsop, on the other hand, is a reconstruction of the fort that explorers Lewis and Clark built and lived in during the winter of 1805–06.

From the parking lot by the park's museum, follow paved bike paths or roads 3.0 miles out to the South Jetty overlook on Clatsop Spit. After having a look at the mouth of the Columbia River, known as the graveyard of the Pacific, head back the way you came, again following roads or bike paths, for 4 miles to Coffenbury Lake. This lake has a swimming beach, and at the end of the ride, you might want to go for a dip if it's a warm day. If you're interested, you could also ride 0.5 miles out to the beach to see the rusting remains of the wreck of the *Peter Iredale*. From Coffenbury Lake, ride 0.75 miles east and turn right on Ridge Road. Follow this road 2.75 miles south and go left on Oceanview Cemetery Road. At the end of this road, in 0.5 miles, turn left on Fort Stevens Highway and ride 0.25 miles north. Turn right on Fort Stevens Highway Spur and follow this road 1 mile to the intersection with U.S. 101. Go straight through the intersection onto Business U.S. 101 and follow this road 2.25 miles to Fort Clatsop Road. Turn right and follow this road 0.5 miles to Fort Clatsop

Bicycling the Oregon Coast

The Oregon coast is one of the nation's most fabled bicycle tour routes, ranking right up there with the back roads of Vermont, the Napa Valley, and the San Juan Islands. Its fame is in no way overrated. Cyclists will find not only breathtaking scenery, but interesting towns, parks and beaches to explore, wide shoulders, and well-spaced places to stay. Cyclists have the option of staying in campgrounds (all state park campgrounds have hiker/biker campsites) or hotels.

If you can afford it, an inn-to-inn pedal down this coast is the way to go (as you slowly grind your way up yet another seemingly endless hill, you'll appreciate the lack of camping gear weighing you down).

The entire route, from Astoria to California, covers between 368 and 378 miles (depending on your route) and includes a disheartening 16,000 total feet of climbing. While most of the route is on U.S. 101, which is a 55-mph highway for most of its length, the designated coast route leaves the highway for less crowded and more scenic roads whenever possible.

During the summer, when winds are generally out of the northwest, you'll have the wind at your back if you ride from north to south. In the winter (when you'll likely get very wet pedaling this coast), you're better off riding from south to north to take advantage of winds out of the southwest. However, planning a trip along this coast in winter is not advisable because, although there is less traffic, winter storms frequently blow in with winds of up to 100 mph.

For a map and guide to bicycling the Oregon coast, contact the **Oregon Bicycle/Pedestrian Program,** Oregon Department of Transportation, 210 Transportation Building, Salem, OR 97310 (tel. 503/986-3556). You might also want to get a copy of the *Umbrella Guide to Bicycling the Oregon Coast* (1990, Umbrella Books) by Robin Cody.

National Memorial. After touring the reconstructed log fort, head back the way you came and maybe go for that swim in Coffenbury Lake.

Cape Meares Loop

25 miles. Moderate. 1,200-foot elevation gain. Access: Start in downtown Tillamook.

This ride takes in an astounding variety of scenery, from cow pastures to mudflats to mountaintop views of the Pacific, and offers numerous opportunities for out-of-the-saddle diversions. There is great bird watching, so you might want to pack some binoculars. From downtown Tillamook, head west on the Netarts Highway, following signs for the Three Capes Loop. The road very quickly leaves town and strikes out across flat cow pastures through which flow both the Trask and Tillamook rivers.

In 1.75 miles from U.S. 101, turn right onto Bayocean Road and head north. In about a mile, the road reaches the shore of Tillamook Bay. For the next 3.5 miles, you are always within a few feet of the water. Keep an eye out for birds. On the opposite side of the road from the bay rise forested slopes. At Pitcher Point, the road jogs west. A roadside sign tells the history of the ghost resort town of Bayocean, which once stood on the spit to the north of this point. If you happen to be riding a mountain bike, you can ride more than 4 miles out to the end of this spit on a gravel road, most of which is closed to cars. If not, continue around the bend and follow signs into the little community of Cape Meares, where old beach cottages and modern vacation homes look out on the driftwood and waves at the base of the cape. You will soon be looking down on this same scene from high above.

Ride back out to the main road and go right. Very quickly the road begins climbing steeply, and within 1.5 miles you are 500 feet above the water. Partway up this grueling hill, there's a nice view of

Bayocean Spit and the houses of Cape Meares. Atop the cape, a side road leads steeply downhill into Cape Meares State Park, site of a historic lighthouse and a great place to bird and whale watch. Ride back up the hill and turn right on the main road to continue the loop around the cape. The road rolls along with occasional dramatic views of the ocean far below and then drops quickly to the turnoff for the community of Oceanside at about 2 miles from the state park. Turn right, ride into town, and have lunch at Roseanna's or a picnic on the beach. This is a great place to just kick back and relax for a while. The view of Three Arch Rocks just offshore is stupendous.

From here, ride south out of town. You'll face another steep climb in the 2 miles from here to Netarts. In this little town, you get a view of Netarts Bay, which is formed by a 5-mile–long sand spit. Here the road turns inland and climbs another long hill. In 1.25 miles, come to an intersection with the Netarts Highway and go left. In 3.5 miles you arrive back at the start of the loop portion of this ride. From here it is 1.5 miles back across the pastures to Tillamook.

Cape Perpetua–Yachats River Road Loop

22 miles. Strenuous. 1,600-foot elevation gain. Access: Start in downtown Yachats on U.S. 101.

Anyone with the stamina to climb 1,500 feet in 5 miles will surely enjoy this ride, which follows the designated Cape Perpetua auto tour route. Much of the ride is on a one-lane road that winds up into the hills behind Cape Perpetua. From downtown Yachats, ride south over the Yachats River Bridge. In 2.5 miles, turn left onto FS 55, which is signed for the Perpetua Campground, but when the road soon forks, go left to stay on FS 55 (the right fork goes to the campground). The road begins climbing immediately and continues with unrelenting steepness for the next 5.5 miles to FS 5590. Turn left onto this road and begin a steep 3.5-mile descent to Yachats River Road. Near this road junction you can stop at Keller Creek Picnic Area for water or a picnic. Turn left on Yachats River Road and head downriver

9.5 miles to return to Yachats, where you're sure to find someplace for a postride snack.

SCUBA DIVING

Due to difficult conditions, including low visibility, the Oregon coast is not an especially popular place to dive. However, there are those people who do dive here. It's a good idea to have an advanced open-water or rescue-diver certification in these often rough waters. Most dives are offshore. You might be able to join such a dive by contacting the **Eugene Dive Club** (tel. 541/998-8104). Popular destinations include Tacklebuster Reef off Depoe Bay and North Pinnacle and Arch Rock off Newport. If conditions are just right, jetty dives (try the jetties at the mouth of Yaquina Bay in Newport) are also possible.

For more information or for air, contact **Doug's Diving,** 609 Commercial Ave., Garibaldi (tel. 503/322-2200); **Garibaldi Aqua Sports,** 108 Seventh Ave., Garibaldi (tel. 503/322-0113); or **Newport Waters Sports,** South Jetty Road, Newport (tel. 541/867-3742).

SEA KAYAKING & FLAT-WATER CANOEING

If you haven't got your own boat, you can rent a kayak at a couple of places along the north coast. In the town of Wheeler on Nehalem Bay there's **Annie's Kayaks,** 487 Hwy. 101 (tel. 503/368-6055), and in Netarts on Netarts Bay there's **Days End Kayaks,** 2045 Netarts Bay Rd. (tel. 503/842-9978). Rates are $10 to $18 per hour or $25 to $45 per day. Both shops also offer guided tours.

Lewis & Clark National Wildlife Refuge

Up to 10 miles or more. Moderate. Access: 15 miles east of Astoria on U.S. 30, go north on Brownsmead Hill Rd. and then continue on Aldrich Point Rd. It's about 6 miles to the boat ramp.

This refuge near the mouth of the Columbia River is a maze of marshlands and islands and is one of the best bird-watching spots in northwest Oregon. It's also a great place to explore in a sea kayak or canoe. From the Aldrich Point boat ramp, paddle west in Prairie Channel along the shore of Tronson Island to Horsehoe Island. Between these two islands, you'll find hours of great exploring. Bring binoculars, a bird book, and a compass (in case you get disoriented in this maze). Winds and tides can both be a problem on this paddle. If you end up paddling against both the wind and the tide, you could be in for a long day.

Nehalem Bay

2–9 miles. Easy–moderate. Access: Put-in is in Nehalem or Wheeler on U.S. 101. For the Car Creek Park put-in, drive 1.3 miles east on Ore. 53 from between Nehalem and Wheeler and turn right. Go 1 mile more and turn left on Foss Rd. The park is just ahead on the right.

With six boat ramps around the bay, salt marshes to explore, Nehalem Bay State Park, and the flat waters of the North Fork Nehalem River leading miles inland, this is an excellent area to investigate in a sea kayak. Time your trip here with the tides or you'll end up struggling instead of enjoying the area. You can begin in the town of Wheeler and head straight into the marshes, or go to the town of Nehalem and ride the tide down the Nehalem River to the bay and its marshes. One other alternative is to start 6.5 miles upriver at Car Creek Park and, on an outgoing tide, paddle downriver to the bay. You should arrange a shuttle for this run.

Nestucca Bay

Up to 8–10 miles. Easy–moderate. Access: Boat ramps are in Pacific City on Brooten Rd. and on U.S. 101 where it crosses the Little Nestucca River.

Protected by the sand dunes of north Spit, Nestucca Bay is a good spot for a winter paddle and a bit of bird watching. This rather convoluted bay, which is fed by both the Nestucca and Little Nestucca rivers, is a wintering ground for the endangered Aleutian subspecies of Canada goose.

Beaver Creek

Up to 3–4 miles. Easy. Access: At Ona Beach State Park 8 miles south of Newport.

This pretty creek slices back into the hills and is bordered along its lower mile or so with marshes. The creek, which is actually quite wide near its mouth, meanders widely with the marshes on one side and forest on the other. This is a pretty spot for a leisurely paddle. Keep an eye out for river otters.

SURFING

While the Oregon coast certainly does not have a national reputation for its surf, it does have some very respectable breaks. The most popular are here on the north coast, where a few places can actually feel crowded on summer days when the surf is up. Summer swells range up to 9 or 10 feet, while in winter, storms can bring in much larger (though rarely ridden) waves. Coast surf shops that rent and sell boards include **Cleanline Surf Shop,** 719 First Ave., Seaside (tel. 503/738-7888); **Cleanline Surf Shop,** 171 Sunset Blvd., Cannon Beach (tel. 503/436-9726); **Oregon Surf Shop,** 4933 SW Hwy. 101, Lincoln City (tel. 541/996-3957); **Rock Reef Surf Shop,** 646 S Hwy. 101, Depoe Bay (tel. 541/765-2306); and **Ocean Pulse Surfboards,** 429 SW Coast Hwy., Newport (tel. 541/265-7745).

At the south end of the town of **Seaside** off Ocean Vista Drive, where the town bumps up against Tillamook Head, west waves come rolling in across the north shore of the headland and produce a good left break. Just north over the hill from Cannon Beach is one of the region's most popular surfing spots. **Indian Beach** in Ecola State Park lies at the end of the road on a small cove framed by headlands and rocky islets. Beginners might want to try the beach break in the Cannon Beach area in the summer.

By far the most popular surfing spot on the north coast is **Short Sands Beach** in Oswald West State Park. The fact that this beach is a half mile from the parking area only adds to its character. When waves are out of the southwest, they wrap around the headland on the south side of Smuggler's Cove, often forming a big clean left break. The beach at Manzanita, just south of Oswald West, is almost as popular as Short Sands Beach.

Gleneden Beach County Park, south of Lincoln City near the Salishan Resort, is one of the best places on the north Oregon coast to find a little tube action. Though the waves here are only rideable up to about 6 feet and the tubes are never very long, this is a fun spot. On the south side of Otter Rock and the Devil's Punch Bowl, and also down the beach a little ways at **Beverly Beach State Park,** there is often small but well-shaped beach break. In the Newport area, you'll often find excellent waves up to 8 feet just south of **Yaquina Head.** In summer, when the swell is moderate, there is often a good break at **Yaquina Bay's south jetty.** The low swells of summer also create a nice beach break at the Siuslaw River's south jetty near Florence.

SWIMMING & TUBING

While the waters of the Pacific are too cold for swimming, you can get the feel of being at the beach (sand in your toes and crashing surf nearby) at **Clatsop Spit** in Fort Stevens State Park. Ocean waters here are warmed by the waters of the Columbia River. In this same park is **Coffenbury Lake** with a designated swimming area that is popular with families. Another good place to get the feel of the ocean without having to subject yourself to the cold Pacific waters is at the south end of **Lincoln City on Siletz Bay,** where a narrow strip of sand attracts quite a few families.

For a more classically northwestern experience, head to one of the region's many little rivers. On the **Nehalem River,** check out Spruce Run County Park. You'll find this pleasant little swimming hole about 5 miles south of U.S. 26 on Nehalem River Road (20 miles east of U.S. 101). Continue downstream on this same road to find another swimming hole at Nehalem Falls. Just before the west end of the Nehalem river road, you'll find another good swimming hole at Roy Creek Park.

The **Wilson River,** which flows into Tillamook Bay at the town of Tillamook, abounds in good swimming holes. However, many of them get very crowded (and often rowdy), and the water is very cold. The popularity of this river is in part due to its easy access from Ore. 6, which parallels the river for most of its length. To find a good swimming hole, just pull over at any gravel turn-out or side road leading to the river. Parts of the Wilson River can be fun to tube on hot summer days.

South of the Wilson River is the **Trask River,** which also has quite a few good swimming holes. These start about 10 miles east of Tillamook up the Trask River Road, which can be reached either from Ore. 6 a few miles east of Tillamook or from Long Prairies Road a few miles south of Tillamook off U.S. 101. Sections of this river can be fun to tube in the summer when the water level is low.

On the **Siletz River** east of Newport, you'll find a very popular stretch of water at Moonshine Park (a county park and campground). This is a good place for doing a little tubing (you can follow the road upstream a bit to launch your tube). However, the park gets crowded and rowdy on some weekends (especially Memorial Day weekend, which is the start of trout fishing season and not a good weekend to try swimming). To reach this park, drive U.S. 20 east from Newport 10 miles, turn north to the town of Siletz, go right on Logsden Road, and continue almost 8 miles to a left turn onto Moonshine Park Road.

WALKS & NATURAL ROADSIDE ATTRACTIONS

Klootchy Creek County Park

Access: 2 miles east of U.S. 101 on U.S. 26.

In this little park you'll find the largest known Sitka spruce, which stands more than 200 feet tall and almost 20 feet across at its base.

Haystack Rock

Access: At the south end of Cannon Beach.

Supposedly the third largest monolith in the world, this huge rock just offshore from Cannon Beach rises 235 feet above the beach. The rock itself is off-limits because it is a bird nesting site. Its most famous residents are tufted puffins. Around the base, you can see starfish and other marine life.

Munson Creek Falls

0.5 miles round-trip. Easy. 100-foot elevation gain. Access: 8 miles south of Tillamook on U.S. 101, turn left onto the signed road to the falls and continue 1.5 miles. Map: Not necessary.

At 266 feet high, this is the tallest waterfall in Oregon's Coast Range. The falls are only partially visible, but the hike through an old-growth forest is as pleasant as the site of these multitiered falls.

Devil's Punch Bowl and Marine Gardens

Up to 1 mile (to Marine Gardens). Easy. 100-foot elevation gain. Access: Off Otter Crest Loop, 8 miles north of Newport on U.S. 101.

The rugged, rocky coast of Oregon is constantly being eroded by the action of the waves. Sometimes caves are carved out of these rocks, and sometimes these caves collapse. Devil's Punch Bowl is just such a collapsed cave, and seawaters still pour in through what were once the mouths of this cave. Just north of the Devil's Punch Bowl is a cove that has some of the finest tide pools on the coast. These Marine Gardens offer hours of fascinating exploring at low tide.

Cape Perpetua Trails

2–3 miles. Easy–moderate. 100–700-foot elevation gain. Access: 3 miles south of Yachats on U.S. 101. Map: Available at Cape Perpetua Visitor Center.

At Cape Perpetua Scenic Area just south of Yachats, there are several short trails worth walking. One trail leads to a rocky stretch of shore where there are tide pools and a spouting horn at Cook's Chasm. Another trail leads to the Devil's Churn, where seawater is whipped to a froth in a collapsed sea cave. Inland, a trail leads 1.0 mile to a giant Sitka spruce tree. The most demanding short hike here is the 1.5-mile St. Perpetua Trail, which climbs 700 feet in 1.5 miles to reach the Cape Perpetua overlook, which is also accessible by car.

WHALE WATCHING

Although gray whales can be seen year-round off the Oregon coast, the best times to look for them are during their annual migrations between the arctic and Baja California. Southbound whales begin showing up in December, and the last northbound whales usually pass by in May. During this migration, between 10,000 and 20,000 whales pass within 3 miles of shore. Consequently, it is very easy to spot whales from almost any elevated point on the Oregon coast. Occasionally, orca whales (killer whales) are spotted in Tillamook Bay.

From north to south, the best places to whale-watch from shore are the following: **Ecola State Park** (Tillamook Head), **Neahkanie Mountain** (turnout south of Oswald West State Park), **Cape Meares State Park, Cape Lookout State Park** (5-mile round-trip hike required), and the lobby of the **Inn at Spanish Head** in Lincoln City, **Boiler Bay State Park, Devil's Punch Bowl State Park, Yaquina Head Lighthouse, Yaquina Bay State Park, Cape Perpetua,** and **Sea Lion Caves Turnout.**

For a closer look at the coast's gray whales, take a whale-watching trip through one of the charter-boat companies operating out of Depoe Bay and Newport. These include **Tradewinds** (tel. 541/765-2345) and **Dockside Charters** (tel. 800/733-8915 or 541/765-2545) in Depoe Bay and **Marine Discovery Tours** (tel. 800/903-BOAT or 541/265-6200) in Newport.

WHITEWATER KAYAKING & CANOEING

CLASS I

The **Nehalem River,** which seems to spiral around the northwest corner of the state, has 28 miles of often bouncy and challenging Class I water beginning above the town of Vernonia and continuing down to the town of Mist. The uppermost put-in is at the second Timber Road bridge (2 miles south of Vernonia, go west on Timber Road for 5 miles). From here, it is a 9-mile run down to Anderson Park in Vernonia. From this park, it is 10 miles down to Big Eddy Park (8.5 miles north of Vernonia on Ore. 47). From Big Eddy Park, it is 9 miles downstream to Mist. Take out at the Burn Road bridge just west of town off Ore. 202. This last stretch of the river is the easiest to paddle. The upper runs, between Timber and Big Eddy Park, should be attempted only by experienced paddlers, and then only in winter or spring when the water is fairly high (though not at flood stage). To reach these runs, take Ore. 47 north from U.S. 26 west of Portland.

While the **Wilson River** is best known as a Class III and IV kayaking river (and as a salmon and steelhead stream), it also has an enjoyable Class I run. At only about 6 miles long, this is a short run, but there are a few riffles (the best are at the very start of the run), sand bars, rock outcroppings, and good salmon fishing in the fall. Put in at the Mills Bridge access area (across from the Little North Fork Wilson River) and take out at the Sollie Smith boat ramp on Wilson River Loop Road (turn right 3.5 miles west of the put-in and go 1.5 miles north). This river can usually be run right through the summer.

The **Nestucca River** is a pleasant little river that flows out of the mountains and across several miles of dairy pastures before emptying into Nestucca Bay at Pacific City. These 14 miles of river can be split into a couple of runs, with the upper 5 miles between Beaver (put in at the First Bridge boat ramp east of Beaver on Blaine Road or the Bixby boat ramp west of Beaver on U.S. 101) being a little swifter and more challenging. Below the Three Rivers boat ramp (just west of Hebo off U.S. 101), the river continues to have a strong current for another 2 miles or so before it reaches tidewater. If you're running this section, try for an outgoing tide. This is solidly dairy country from here on down to Pacific City. This is a rainy-season river.

The **Siletz River,** between the town of Siletz and Strome Park, offers 20 miles of good Class I paddling. The upper few miles of this run are pretty splashy, and it

helps to have some previous experience with fast water. You can break this 20 miles into shorter segments if you're so inlcined. Put in at Ojalla Bridge (on Ore. 229 north of Siletz) and you'll cut off the roughest 5 miles at the upper end of the run. The next put-in/take-out is at Morgan Park, 7 river miles from Ojalla Bridge (again on Ore. 229). The final take-out, Morgan Park, is another 8 miles downstream but only 4 miles by road (perfect for a bicycle shuttle). Take-outs, other than Ojalla Bridge, are hard to spot on this river, so pay attention when you park a car or bike for your return shuttle. This is a good spring run.

Paralleled by Ore. 34, the **Alsea River,** which flows into Alsea Bay at Waldport, has more than 30 miles of Class I water (sprinkled with a few Class II drops) between the community of Tidewater and Mill Creek Park.

CLASS II

The **Nestucca River,** between Blaine and Beaver, has a great stretch of water for anyone just working their way into Class II paddling. This 9-mile run is fast, with lots of riffles, but it also has a few ledge drops that will give novice boaters a taste for more difficult waters. Put in 0.25 miles west of Blaine and take out at the Bixby boat ramp on U.S. 101 just west of Beaver.

The **Siletz River,** between Moonshine Park and the Hee Hee Illahee boat ramp in the town of Siletz, provides a good introduction to Class II paddling. None of the Class II rapids are too difficult and they're widely spaced (with quick Class I water in between). This run can usually be done until late spring. To shorten the run to only 7 miles, take out at the Same Creek boat ramp.

The 17 miles of the **Siuslaw River** between Whittaker Creek Recreation Area and the community of Swisshome is primarily Class I water, but there are also several Class II rapids that make this run (or shorter sections of it) a good choice for paddlers just working their way into Class II water. Watch for rapids at the three railroad bridges around 11 miles into the run. In the first half of this run, there are three boat ramps below the Whittaker

Creek put-in, which is 1.5 miles south of Ore. 126 on Siuslaw River Road. To reach Swisshome, follow Stagecoach Road from Richardson or Ore. 36 from Mapleton.

CLASS III

The **Nehalem River,** which seems to wander all over the northwest corner of the state, has a good 15-mile-long Class III run between Spruce Run Recreation Site (off U.S. 26 near Elsie on Lower Nehalem Road south) and Nehalem Falls Recreation Site (up Foss River Road east of Wheeler). You can opt to take out above Nehalem Falls or below (at high flows, the falls push to Class IV). The many good drops and long rapids make it one of the north coast's best runs.

The **Wilson River,** which is paralleled by Ore. 6 for most of its length, is a beautiful river, popular with both kayakers and anglers from fall through spring. At low to medium flows, it has 15 miles of good Class III water between Jones Creek Forest Camp and the Siskeyville boat ramp at milepost 8. You can break these miles up into a couple of different runs.

The **Trask River,** which runs just south of and parallel to the Wilson River, also offers roughly 20 miles of Class III paddling on its various forks. Peninsula County Park is the lowermost take-out for these runs. This is a small stream and can be run only in the rainy season.

The **Siletz River** is a magnet for paddlers of all skill levels. Above Moonshine Park, you'll find a good 6.5-mile Class III run. The put-in is about a mile downstream from unrunnable Valsetz Falls at the Elk Creek bridge. Unless you really want to take on the Class IV Silache Rapids, be sure to take out at the steel bridge 2 miles below Buck Creek.

CLASS IV & ABOVE

At high flows during the winter months, the **Wilson River** east of Tillamook pushes into the Class IV range. Likewise the 11-mile run down the **Siletz River** from below Valsetz Falls to Moonshine Park bumps up from Class III to Class IV when the river level is up. Actually, the infamous Silache Rapids on this run are Class IV waters even at low water.

WILDLIFE VIEWING

Harbor seals and California and Steller sea lions are quite common along the north Oregon coast and can often be seen lounging on rocks just offshore or in remote spots on the mainland, such as the tips of jetties, sand spits not accessible by road, and the bases of sea cliffs. Harbor seals are much smaller than sea lions and can be distinguished by their lack of ears. Sea lions, on the other hand, have small, visible ears, but are best recognized by their distinctive bark, which was once likened to the roar of a lion (hence the name). Steller sea lions are the larger of the two sea-lion species that frequent these waters, with bulls sometimes weighing as much as a ton and reaching 12 feet in length. Aside from the resident colony of sea lions at Sea Lion Caves, Steller sea lions spend their summers along the Oregon coast, while California sea lions are here from fall through spring.

Some good places to look for seals and sea lions include **Clatsop Spit** in Fort Stevens State Park, rocks in **Ecola State Park** outside Cannon Beach, the tip of **Nehalem Spit** in Nehalem Bay State Park, **Bayocean Spit** at the mouth of Tillamook Bay, **Cape Meares State Park, Cape Lookout State Park, Yaquina Head** north of Newport, and **Seal Rock** south of Newport.

Inland 20 miles on U.S. 26 from the U.S. 26/U.S. 101 junction, a small sign directs travelers off the highway to **Jewell Meadows,** where you can see a large herd of Roosevelt elk grazing in pastures between September and March. At times there are as many as 200 elk here, and one of the most interesting times to visit is during the October rutting season when bull elk bugle and battle each other by locking antlers. During the winter months visitors may be able to go out with fish and wildlife workers to feed the elk. In the summer you may still see elk here early in the morning or in the evening, but they tend to stay in the cool of the forest at this time of year. The meadows are 9 miles off U.S. 26 (follow signs toward Jewell).

The South Coast (Cape Perpetua to the California Line) ◆ What to Do & Where to Do It

BEACHES

South of the cliffs of Cape Perpetua lies **Neptune State Park,** where three separate parking areas provide access to the beach, which is mostly rocky and covered with tide pools at low tide. Continuing south, there is a nice long beach at **Carl G. Washburne State Park.** This beach can be accessed from the north end near the park's campground, but the Hobbit Trail, at the south end of the park, is a more interesting route down to the waves. From this end, it is a short walk to the tide pools at the north base of Heceta Head. Over the headland to the south lies **Devils Elbow State Park,** where there is a striking little beach framed by the historic Heceta Head Lighthouse and an old arching bridge over Cape Creek, which flows across the beach.

South of Heceta Head, **Baker Beach,** accessed by wading across Sutton Creek from Holman Vista at the end of Sutton Beach Road, offers miles of leisurely strolling on a wide sand beach backed by dunes. It's about a 0.25-mile walk to the beach from Holman Vista. This rarely visited and secluded beach can also be accessed by a 0.5-mile trail from the end of gravel Baker Beach Road, which is 2 miles north of Sutton Beach Road off U.S. 101.

Within the 40 miles of Oregon Dunes National Recreation area south of Florence, there are miles and miles of secluded beaches backed by huge sand dunes. However, of the three beaches directly accessible by car, two are inundated with roaring dune buggies and other off-road vehicles. Therefore, the only car-accessible tranquil beach is the one along **Siuslaw Spit** just outside Florence on the south side of the Siuslaw River. Here you can walk the beach for miles. If you don't mind a bit of a hike to get to the beach, there is access at the **Siltcoos Recreation Area** (take the Waxmyrtle Trail), from **Carter Lake Campground,** from the **Oregon Dunes Overlook,** from **Tahkenitch Campground,** and from **Eel Creek Campground.** Stay away from Horsefall Beach and the Spinreel Campground area unless you enjoy dodging speeding ORVs.

Just outside the town of Coos Bay are three of the most popular state parks on the Oregon coast. **Sunset Bay State Park,** the first of these, is an idyllic little cove with a beach on one side and forest-topped sandstone cliffs on the other. Because the surf is gentle and the water just a touch warmer than that in the open ocean, people actually go swimming here. **Shore Acres State Park,** next down the road, is visited mostly for its beautiful gardens, but it also has an exquisite little beach on Simpson Cove. At the third state park, **Cape Arago,** sea lions on offshore rocks are the main attraction, but there are also two small beaches—North Cove and South Cove. North Cove is closed from March 1 to July 1 each year to protect seals and sea lions that give birth here. South Cove offers excellent tide pooling. North of these three beaches is **Bastendorff Beach County Park,** which is a long, wide beach popular with surfers. South of Coos Bay, off Seven Devil's Road, is the remote and little visited **Whiskey Run Beach** at Five Mile Point. Backed by bluffs, this windy beach is more than 2 miles long.

The beach at Bandon is one of the most dramatic in the state. High bluffs rise from the beach and offshore there are dozens of haystack rocks, including many that are named (Face Rock, Cat and Kittens). This beach is popular for sunset strolls. This area is part of **Bandon State Park,** which has several more access points south of here along Beach Loop Drive. Just north of Bandon is **Bullards Beach State Park,** where there are miles of flat-sand dune-backed beach.

South of Bandon, there are Wild and Scenic beaches at Floras Lake and Cape Blanco state parks. The remote beach at **Floras Lake State Park** is nearly 2 miles down a muddy trail from the Cape Blanco State Airport. Windswept **Cape Blanco** is the westernmost point in the contiguous United States, and there are trails to its

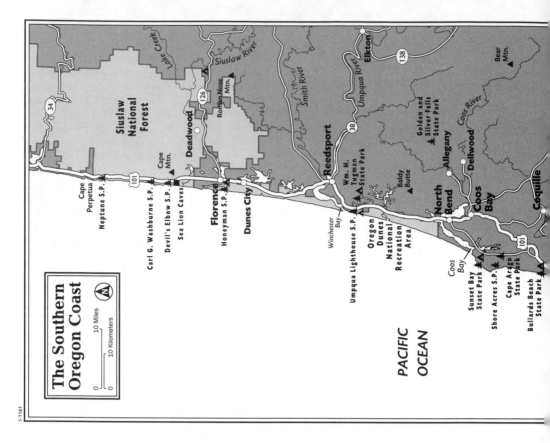

The Southern Oregon Coast

10 Miles

10 Kilometers

cliff-backed beaches both from the camp-ground and from the boat ramp on the Sixes River. At **Port Orford,** the beach on the edge of town is easily accessible from U.S. 101 and commands a striking view of Battle Rock and Port Orford Heads. Six miles south of Port Orford, a small beach with good tidepools lies at the north base of **Humbug Mountain** in the state park of the same name.

Just north of Gold Beach is the little-visited **Otter Point Wayside,** which pro-vides access to a forest-rimmed beach along an old section of the coast highway. South of Gold Beach, at **Pistol River State Park,** you'll come to one of the busiest and most visually compelling beaches on the south coast. It lies on the south side of Cape Sebastian. Here huge haystack rocks lie close to shore and boardsailors and surf-ers ride the waves. You can hike north along the beach beneath the cliffs of Cape Sebastian or south to the mouth of the Pis-tol River. There are a couple of beach ac-cess parking areas.

Just north of Brookings is the most spectacular stretch of the entire Oregon

coast. Preserved as **Samuel H. Boardman State Park,** this coastline has a couple of very pretty beaches. China Beach has a very secluded and remote feel due to the steep trail that leads down from the North Island Viewpoint high above. Whalehead Beach, though not quite as dramatic, is an easier walk from the parking area. Lone Ranch Beach has the feel of a northern California beach; it looks up at the grassy Cape Ferrelo. Just south of Boardman State Park is **Harris Beach State Park,** which has more big rocks scattered on its beach and just offshore.

BIRD WATCHING

Within the **Oregon Dunes National Rec-reation Area,** south of Florence, there are several good places to bird watch. The various river and creek estuaries (Siltcoos, Tahkenitch, Tenmile Creek), most of which are accessible only by trail or in a canoe, are particularly productive spots throughout most of the year (look for snowy plovers in summer). On the Siuslaw Spit near the south jetty just outside

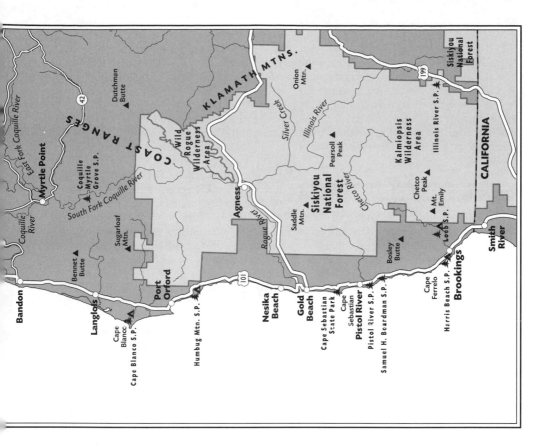

Florence, you can see thousands of tundra swans during the winter. In the summer look for American bitterns, and in the spring and fall you'll find large numbers of migrating waterfowl and shorebirds. Another good place to look for bitterns (and wood ducks and cinnamon teals) is along the Lagoon Trail at the Siltcoos Recreation Area between Florence and Reedsport. At Bluebill Lake, just north of Coos Bay, a trail leads through marshlands and forests that attract a wide variety of birds.

At **Heceta Head** in Devil's Elbow State Park and **near Sea Lion Caves,** look for tufted puffins and other seabirds. Heceta Head is also home to the largest nesting colony of Brandt's cormorants on the mainland.

One of the best winter birding spots on the south coast is at **Bandon Marsh National Wildlife Refuge** adjacent to Bullards Beach State Park on the Coquille River. Winters see lots of ducks and geese and a few tundra swans, but during spring and fall migration, a wide variety of birds can be sighted. Look for long-billed curlews,

whimbrels, spotted sandpipers, turnstones, red knots, scaups, buffleheads, teals, and black-shouldered kites. The marsh is also famed for its unusual sightings—Hudsonian and bar-tailed godwits, a great knot, Mongolian plovers, ruffs. You'll find marsh viewing areas off U.S. 101, 2 miles north of Bandon.

All the offshore rocks in the Bandon area are part of the **Oregon Islands National Wildlife Refuge** and many are nesting grounds for tufted puffins, fork-tailed and Leach's storm-petrels, Cassin's auklets, rhinoceros auklets, Common murres, pigeon guillemots, and Brandt's and pelagic cormorants. While all these nesting islands and rocks are off-limits, you can get good views of many of them (if you have good binoculars or a spotting scope) from Coquille Point on Beach Loop Road south of Bandon.

The **New River,** which flows north from Floras Lake and is accessible by hiking trail or small boat, is one of the staging areas for the rare Aleutian Canada goose. These geese can be seen here each year in March and April and again in

November. May through October are the best birding months, with various species of ducks, shorebirds, snowy plovers, peregrine falcons, and bald eagles all likely to be in residence. The New River can be reached form Croft Lake Road north of Langlois or Floras Lake Road south of Langlois.

BOARDSAILING

While the reputation of Oregon's south coast hasn't quite spread as far and wide as that of the Columbia Gorge, there are a couple of places in the area that attract more than just local boardsailors. Keep in mind that even though the southernmost stretch of coast is referred to as the Banana Belt, the waters here are still cold enough to require a full wetsuit even in summer. For boardsailing equipment and rentals, try **Big Air Windsurfing,** 48435 Hwy. 101, Langlois (tel. 541/348-2213), or **Tradewinds Sailboard Shop,** 28446 Hunter Creek Loop, Gold Beach (tel. 541/247-0835).

The very best place on this coast to venture into the surf for the first time is at the south jetty in Florence. Small, well-formed waves are perfect for beginners.

On Coos Bay just north of the town of North Bend, **Jordan Cove** and the waters between McCullough Bridge and the railroad bridge are a great beginner's spot. The water is shallow, the current usually isn't too strong, and there's little to obstruct ocean breezes. To reach this site, take the Transpacific Parkway west from U.S. 101 just north of the second bridge north of North Bend. Pony Point Park, at the north end of the airport in North Bend, is an alternative access for the same general area of Coos Bay.

Just south of **Bandon** there is sometimes good wave riding at a couple of beaches off Beach Loop Drive. Check in front of the Inn at Face Rock and at the southernmost Bandon day-use area along Beach Loop Road.

Floras Lake is perhaps the best known and most popular boardsailing spot on the south coast. Only a low strip of dunes separates this lake from the ocean. Consequently, sailors get unobstructed ocean winds without the crashing surf that's just over the dunes on the beach. The Floras

Lake B&B, 92870 Boice Cope Rd. (tel. 541/348-2573), caters to boardsailors, operates the Floras Lake Windsurfing School, and also rents equipment. You'll find Floras Lake west of U.S. 101 south of the community of Langlois.

If, on the other hand, strong winds *and* good waves are what you're looking for, you'll want to head south of Gold Beach 8 miles to **Pistol River State Park.** In the past few years, this spot has developed a reputation as one of the top wave-riding spots in the U.S. Summers bring strong winds and nearly perfect 4-foot waves that serve as launch ramps for skilled aerialists.

FISHING

The Rogue River is this region's premier river and is best known for its spring and fall Chinook and summer and winter steelhead. While the most popular fishing areas are much farther upstream, the lower road and boat-accessible 27 miles of the river are still very productive. There are numerous places for bank angling, though fishing from boats is more popular. Jet boats are used to reach the uppermost waters. The Rogue River is unusual in that it still supports a good wild winter steelhead run, and wild fish can still be kept for a short period each year.

The region's wild cutthroat trout fishery has not fared as well, and with the listing of the Umpqua River sea-run cutthroat as a federally threatened species, trout fishing has become even more limited. However, many south coast lakes are stocked with rainbows.

Rivers of the south coast and their best fisheries include the **Siuslaw** (fall Chinook, winter steelhead, hatchery cutthroat), the **Smith** (fall Chinook, wild and hatchery winter steelhead, striped bass, hatchery cutthroat trout, shad), the **Umpqua** (spring Chinook, summer and winter steelhead, shad, smallmouth bass), the **Coos** (fall **Chinook,** shad), the **Coquille** (fall Chinook, winter steelhead), the **Elk** (fall Chinook, winter steelhead), the **Sixes** (winter steelhead, wild cutthroat trout), the **Rogue** (spring and fall Chinook, summer and winter steelhead, hatchery coho), the **Pistol** (winter steelhead), and the **Chetco** (fall Chinook, hatchery winter steelhead).

While the steelhead and salmon of this region's rivers and streams offer the most excitement, there are also fish to be caught on the many lakes in and adjacent to the Oregon Dunes National Recreation Area. **Siltcoos Lake** is by far the most productive and yields largemouth bass, perch, and wild cutthroat. Other lakes worth trying include **Alder** (hatchery rainbows), **Dune** (hatchery rainbows), **Sutton** (panfish and hatchery rainbows), **Cleawox** (panfish and hatchery rainbows), **Carter** (hatchery rainbows), **Tahkenitch** (warm-water fish and hatchery rainbows), **Threemile** (cutthroat and perch), **Eel Lake** (hatchery rainbows, wild cutthroat, and largemouth bass), and **North and South Tenmile** (largemouth bass and hatchery rainbows). There's good fly-fishing on **Lake Marie** in Umpqua Lighthouse State Park and on **Saunders Lake** (in spring) near Lakeside.

If you'd like to hire a guide to take you to the best fishing holes, you've got plenty of options. Some guides to check out include **Rogue River Outfitters** (Denny Hughson), P.O. Box 1078, Gold Beach, OR 97444 (tel. 541/247-2684), and **Steve Beyerlin,** 94575 Chandler Rd., Gold Beach, OR 97444 (tel. 800/348-4138 or 541/247-4138). A half day of fishing will cost you around $100 and a full day will cost around $125.

If you want to go offshore for some bottom fishing or salmon fishing, you'll find charter boats at several marinas along the southern Oregon coast. In Winchester Bay, try **Todd Hannah Charters** (tel. 800/428-8585 or 541/584-2277). In the Coos Bay area (at the Charleston marina), try **Bob's Sport Fishing** (tel. 800/628-9633 or 541/888-4241) or **Betty Kay Charters** (tel. 800/752-6303 or 541/888-9021). In Gold Beach, try **Shamrock Charters** at Dot's Resort (tel. 541/247-6676) or **Briggs Charters** (tel. 541/247-7150).

HIKING

Oregon Dunes Overlook Loop

4.5 miles. Easy. 200-foot elevation gain. Access: Oregon Dunes Overlook 10 miles south of Florence. Map: USFS Oregon Dunes National Recreation Area.

The Oregon Dunes Overlook is as close as many people ever get to interacting with these shifting hills of sand. However, the view of forests and bare sand is so enticing, it is almost criminal to head off into the dunes at this point. The trail leads west then northwest 1 mile to the beach. From here, go left and follow the shore 1.5 miles south to a small sign that marks the return trail. Climb up and over the foredune (the dune nearest the beach), cross a wooden footbridge, and climb the first of three tree islands on this route. You'll glimpse Tahkenitch Creek just south. From the tree island, follow the trail, marked by posts, east then north to the second and third tree islands. At the junction with the outbound beach trail, turn right to return to the overlook parking lot.

Umpqua Dunes Trail

5 miles round-trip. Easy. 100-foot elevation gain. Access: Eel Creek Campground 11 miles south of Reedsport. Map: USFS Oregon Dunes National Recreation Area.

If you've ever thought of joining the French Foreign Legion, this trail will give you some idea of what you've been missing. The trail, which is actually more of a route, is the longest hikers' crossing of Oregon Dunes NRA. The trail starts out in the forest but soon leads onto the dunes and a 1-mile unmarked crossing of the shifting sands (as you cross the dunes, keep looking over your shoulder for landmarks to use on your return dune crossing). To reach the beach, just head for the tree island to the west. At the tree island, head west toward the trees, then north following blue posts along the deflation plain (zone where winds have stripped away dry sand and allowed plants to establish). The trail then cuts across the deflation plain, through a strip of shore pine, and over a marsh to reach the beach.

Humbug Mountain Trail

5.5 miles. Moderate. 1,730-foot elevation gain. Access: Humbug Mountain Trailhead 6 miles south of Port Orford. Map: Trailhead map.

The imposing bulk of Humbug Mountain rises 1,761 feet above the Pacific Ocean and provides the greatest elevation gain of any hike along U.S. 101. The trail starts out climbing steadily through old-growth forests where rhododendrons bloom in the spring. After 1 mile, there is a trail junction that marks the start of the loop portion of this hike. Go right and you'll soon have views north along the coast to Cape Blanco. In 1.5 miles from the trail junction, reach the summit and a view south to Cape Sebastian. Continue 2 miles around the mountain to return to the trail junction and the trail down to the parking lot.

Windy Valley

4 miles round-trip. Easy. 400-foot elevation gain. Access: From U.S. 101 in Brookings, take North Bank Chetco River Rd. 16 miles east, turn left onto gravel FS 1376, and continue 13 miles to the trailhead. Map: USGS Collier Butte.

A meadow filled with rare and unusual wildflowers and many other unique plants are the highlights of this easy hike just outside the Kalmiopsis Wilderness. June is the peak month for wildflowers and it is then that you'll see the area's wild azaleas in bloom. Along the trail you'll pass insectivorous *Darlingtonia* pitcher plants, groves of myrtle trees, Port Orford cedars, and old-growth Douglas firs. From the trailhead for this hike, you get a good view of the rugged Big Craggies, a series of peridotite peaks that support very few plants.

Vulcan Lake/Vulcan Peak Trails

3 miles round-trip to Vulcan Lake; 3 miles round-trip to Vulcan Peak. Easy. 500-foot elevation gain to Vulcan Lake; 900 feet to Vulcan Peak. Access: From U.S. 101 in Brookings, take North Bank Chetco River Rd. 16 miles east, turn right onto FS 1909, and in another 13 miles go right for 13 miles to the Vulcan Peak trailhead or 15 miles to the Vulcan Lake trailhead. Map: USGS Chetco Peak, USFS Kalmiopsis Wilderness.

These two short trails provide an excellent overview of the fascinating geology and botanical diversity of the Kalmiopsis Wilderness. The Vulcan Lake Trail climbs through sparse forest to a ridge top with views to the Pacific Ocean before dropping down to rock-rimmed Vulcan Lake. A side trail leads another 0.25 miles to Little Vulcan Lake, where tall, pitcherlike, insectivorous *Darlingtonia* plants can be seen. This is just one of the unusual types of plants to be seen along this trail and in the rest of this wilderness. Return the way you came.

The Vulcan Peak Trail climbs steeply and steadily up a ridge of reddish serpentine rock for a view that encompasses all of the Kalmiopsis Wilderness as well as the coast and Pacific Ocean.

HORSEBACK RIDING

There are several places along the south coast where you can ride a horse, either on the beach or inland. **C&M Stables,** 90241 Hwy. 101 N (tel. 541/997-7540), located 8 miles north of Florence, offers rides on either the beach or through the dunes. In Bandon, try **Bandon Beach Riding Stables** (tel. 541/347-3423), which is on Beach Loop Drive south of Face Rock. In the Gold Beach area, there is **Indian Creek Trail Rides** (tel. 541/247-7704), which is a half-mile up Jerry's Flat Road in Wedderburn. There are also stables at **Hawk's Rest Ranch** (tel. 541/247-6423) in Pistol River, 10 miles south of Gold Beach. Expect to pay between $20 and $30 for a 1- to 2- hour ride.

MOUNTAIN BIKING

Enchanted Valley Trail

6 miles round-trip. Easy. 200-foot elevation gain. Access: 5 miles north of Florence on U.S. 101, turn east on Mercer Lake Rd., drive 3.75 miles, and then go left on Twin Fawn Dr. for another 0.25 miles. Map: Not necessary.

This easy ride is through a delightful meadowed valley that was once the site of a dairy farm. Today it is elk (and occasionally deer and black bears) rather than cows that graze these fields. The chance of spotting a herd of elk is one of the best reasons to ride this area, which is really just

The Oregon Coast Trail

Stretching for 360 miles from the Columbia River's south jetty in Fort Stevens State Park to the California state line, the Oregon Coast Trail is more a concept than an actual trail. The trail, first envisioned in 1971 by Sam Dicken, a professor at the University of Oregon, follows beaches, trails over headlands, and roadways (including sections of U.S. 101) along its route.

Because the trail is not really a contiguous route, few people set out to hike it in a single go as they might on the Pacific Crest Trail (or the PCT through, say, all of Oregon or all of Washington). Instead, people choose to hike the more scenic stretches.

Some of the longer and more enjoyable segments include the trail over Tillamook Head from Seaside to Ecola State Park, the beach and trail segment from Cannon Beach over Arch Cape and Cape Falcon to Neahkanie Mountain, down Netarts Spit and over Cape Lookout to Sand Lake, the 47 miles through the Oregon Dunes National Recreation Area between Florence and Coos Bay (this is the most remote segment of the trail and is interrupted only by the Umpqua River, which could be ferried if you arranged for a boat to meet you), from Bandon to Port Orford, and along several short segments in Samuel H. Boardman State Park.

For a copy of the *Oregon Coast Trail Guide,* basically just a waterproof map, contact the Trails Coordinator, Oregon State Parks, 525 Trade St. SE, Salem, OR 97310 (tel. 503/378-5012).

an old farm road. Just remember to be quiet (and oil your chain before you start). Signs of the farm's old homesteads are still visible if you look closely. The first 1.5 miles or more of this trail is through an enchanting meadow. Bailey Creek, which is a spawning stream for spring Chinook, flows through the meadow. At 2 miles, watch for a clearing with an old apple orchard; look for a single-track trail on the left. It will add a bit of challenge to the ride if you're so inclined. When the trail ends, it's time to turn around.

Siltcoos Lake Trail

5 miles round-trip. Easy–moderate. 600-foot elevation gain. Access: 7 miles south of Florence on U.S. 101. Map: USFS Oregon Dunes National Recreation Area.

Although this trail is short, it's a whole lot of fun, and, if it happens to be a hot summer day, you can go for a swim in Siltcoos Lake. Unfortunately, the lake is at the bottom of the hill and not the top. From the trailhead, ride uphill for 0.5 miles on an old logging road. Over the top, the road becomes single-track and forks. Take the left fork and have a blast rolling down to the lake (keep an eye out for hikers). At the lake, follow the trail to the south for 0.5 miles to reach the return leg of this loop. Go left for 0.25 miles to visit the lake again, or just head uphill (and pay for that fun downhill). If you liked that, why not do it in reverse?

Lower Rogue River Trail

12 miles one way (with shuttle) or 24–35 miles round-trip. Strenuous. 2,000-foot elevation gain. Access: To reach the west trailhead, drive east up the Rogue River on Jerry's Flat Rd. for 9 miles, turn left over the Lobster Creek Bridge, and then take a right on FS 3533. In 5 miles, turn right onto FS 340, which ends at the trailhead. To reach the east trailhead, drive Jerry's Flat Rd. to Agness and continue through town to the combination library and school. Map: USFS Gold Beach Ranger District.

This trail should not be confused with the Upper Rogue River Trail, which is for hikers only. The Lower Rogue River Trail follows a slightly less scenic stretch of the river, and actually doesn't have all that many views of the river. However, it is an extremely challenging piece of single-track that passes through old-growth forests, along cliffs, and over numerous creeks as it winds upriver to the community of Agness (site of several lodges). You can ride one way if you can arrange a shuttle, as an out-and-back (for fans of rough riding), or as a long loop with two-thirds of the ride on paved and gravel roads. Beware of poison oak.

ROAD BIKING

Bandon Beach and Bog Loop

25 miles. Easy. 100-foot elevation gain. Access: Start in downtown Bandon.

Bandon is the south coast's most eclectic town and boasts a stunning coastline, a historic lighthouse, a cheese factory, art galleries, a couple of good restaurants, and lots of cranberry bogs. This ride takes it all in.

Start by heading west through town on First Street (you can shop now or shop later), which curves around to the south. Go right on Fourth Street, which becomes first Ocean Drive, then Seventh Street, and finally Beach Loop Drive, which parallels the beach and passes the famous haystack rocks of Bandon's beach. At 5.5 miles from downtown, this road ends at U.S. 101.

Turn right and ride 0.75 miles south and turn left on Twomile Road. In 0.7 miles, turn left onto Rosa Road and soon pass extensive cranberry bogs (the bogs are flooded and berries harvested in late September). In 2.75 miles, turn left to stay on Rosa Road and continue 1.75 miles back into Bandon and the end of Rosa Road at a T-intersection. Turn left and then immediately right onto Elmira Street and ride 0.4 miles to U.S. 101. Turn right, and in two blocks stop to visit the Bandon Cheese Factory (pick some up if you want to have a picnic on the beach).

From here, ride a block back the way you just came and turn right on Fillmore Street. In one block, go right onto River Road and follow this road north 1.5 miles to U.S. 101. Continue 1 mile north on the highway and turn left following signs to Bullards Beach State Park. From the highway it is 2.75 miles to the historic Coquille River Lighthouse. Along this road there are picnic areas and beach accesses.

Head back the way you came, but before reaching River Road, go left off U.S. 101, through more cranberry bogs. Follow this road for 2.4 miles (keeping right at all major road forks) to Ore. 42S (Coquille–Bandon Highway). Turn right on this road and in 1.75 miles return once again to U.S. 101. From here it is 0.5 miles back to downtown Bandon.

Carpenterville Road–Samuel H. Boardman State Park Loop

45 miles. Strenuous. 2,500-foot elevation gain. Access: Harris Beach State Park, 2 miles north of Brookings on U.S. 101.

This loop takes in both the most knock-out stretch of U.S. 101 in Oregon and a narrow, winding mountain road that climbs more than 1,500 feet into the coast range with dizzying views of the ocean far below. From Harris Beach State Park, where wave-sculpted rocks and cliffs give you a taste of what the second half of this ride has in store, ride north 1 mile and turn right onto Carpenterville Road. Before the opening in 1963 of the 345-foot–high Thomas Creek Bridge 7 miles north of here, this was the only road between Brookings and Pistol River. The road climbs steadily, though not too steeply, for the next 12 miles, topping out at 1,715 feet near the community of Carpenterville. Along the way there are lots of places to stop and soak up the views (and give your thighs a break).

Past Carpenterville, the road drops very quickly to U.S. 101. At the highway, stay on the old Carpenterville Road and continue north 2.5 miles to Pistol River, where you'll find an old general store. If you're interested, you could pedal another 2.5 miles north to Meyers Creek in Pistol River State Park and check out the boardsailors, surfers, and a gorgeous bit of coastline. Otherwise, head back south the way you came on Pistol River Loop Road to the bottom of Carpenterville Road, where you turn onto U.S. 101. Now begins the most scenic part of this ride, the 10-mile stretch through Samuel H. Boardman State Park. This wild coastline is scattered with offshore rocks and islands, and steep cliffs often drop down from the roadway to the water. As far as I'm concerned, this is the most beautiful piece of the entire Oregon coast. There are numerous viewpoints and picnic areas. Be sure to check them all out. There are also several short stretches of the Oregon Coast Trail if you feel like getting off your bike and going for a walk. From the end of the park, it is another 2.5 miles to Harris State Park.

Chetco River Redwood Ride

17 miles round-trip. Easy. 200-foot elevation gain. Access: Start at Azalea State Park, just off U.S. 101 on the south side of Brookings (follow signs from North Bank Rd.).

This ride follows the north bank of the beautiful Chetco River to Loeb State Park, where you can see both coast redwood trees and old-growth myrtles. The ride starts at Azalea State Park—26 acres of native azaleas that bloom around Memorial Day each year. From this park, ride downhill to North Bank Road and turn left. This road parallels the river, and you'll have plenty of time to enjoy the fascinating turquoise color. It is about 8 miles up this road to Loeb State Park, where you'll find 2.75 miles of hiking trails through the redwood and myrtle trees. You'll also find a fabulous swimming hole, which makes this an ideal ride for a hot summer day. If you want to add some miles, you can continue up North Bank Road for almost 6 more miles. Return the way you came.

SCUBA DIVING

As on the north Oregon coast, scuba diving is not as popular as one might expect. People do, however, do a bit of diving at Sunset Bay State Park and in Port Orford Harbor. For air, to find a buddy, or simply to learn a bit more about diving along this coast, check at **Central Coast Watersports,** 1560 Second St., Florence (tel. 800/ 789-3483).

SEA KAYAKING & FLAT-WATER CANOEING

Cleawox Lake

Up to 4 miles. Easy. Access: In Jesse M. Honeyman State Park 3 miles south of Florence on U.S. 101.

With tall evergreens on one shore and high sand dunes on the other, this lake is something of a natural bridge between the two wildly different habitats of this region. Cleawox Lake is also one of the most popular lakes in the state, and summer days see families happily splashing in the warm, tannin-brown waters. For a tranquil paddle, get on the water as soon after dawn as possible or wait until the off-season. The lake's narrow arms offer plenty of shoreline to explore.

Siltcoos Lake/Siltcoos River

6 miles round-trip. Easy–moderate. Access: 8 miles south of Florence on the east side of U.S. 101 at Tyee Campground.

If you want to do some canoe camping, head south from the Siltcoos River along the shore of the lake for about a mile where you'll find campsites on the mainland across from Booth Island. Unfortunately, the lake is noisy with powerboats and personal watercraft. For a quieter experience, paddle down the Siltcoos River from Tyee Campground, portaging a low dam to continue all the way to the river's estuary.

Tahkenitch Creek

4 miles round-trip. Easy–moderate. Access: From the Tahkenitch Trail, which has its trailhead 8 miles north of Reedsport on the west side of U.S. 101.

While the waters of Tahkenitch Lake are dominated by the roar of ski boats and personal watercraft, the waters of Tahkenitch Creek are blissfully tranquil. The only hard part of this paddle is that you have to carry your boat about 150 yards down a trail to the creek. The quiet waters here attract a good variety of birdlife, so bring the binoculars. This creek passes through some forests and marshes, but for much of its length it is bounded by sand dunes.

Eel Lake

Up to 8 miles. Easy. Access: In William M. Tugman State Park 8 miles south of Reedsport on U.S. 101.

Because there is a 10 mph speed limit on this lake, it stays quiet enough to make paddling enjoyable. The lake consists of two narrow arms, each about 2 miles long, that slice deep into the forest. Along these arms are many small coves that provide plenty of interesting shoreline to explore. The wildife viewing is often quite good, with otters keeping an eye on boats and elk grazing along the shoreline. The campground makes a great base for a weekend of paddling here and on other area waterways.

South Slough

Up to 6–8 miles. Easy–moderate. Access: To reach the Charleston bridge from Coos Bay, follow signs for the state parks. From the Charleston bridge (one possible launch sight), go east to Seven Devils Rd., turn left and follow this road south, turning left onto Hinch Rd. and following this road to the bridge over Winchester Creek.

South Slough, a long, convoluted finger of Coos Bay, is one of the largest and most pristine estuaries on the Oregon coast. From a boat launch at the south end of the estuary on Hinch Road (or from beside the bridge in Charleston), it is possible to explore many miles of remote marshlands. However, any explorations must be timed so that paddlers aren't stranded in mudflats at low tide. To learn more about canoeing in this area, pick up the *South Slough Reserve Canoe Guide* at the South Slough Interpretive Center (tel. 541/888-5558), 4 miles south of Charleston on Seven Devils Road.

Coquille River and Bandon Marsh

Up to 4–5 miles. Easy–moderate. Access: There is a boat ramp in Bullards Beach State Park

2 miles north of Bandon off U.S. 101 and one in downtown Bandon.

The Coquille River as it flows past the town of Bandon is an excellent place for a bit of exploring by sea kayak. Across from town is the Bandon Marsh National Wildlife Refuge, which is home to a wide variety of birdlife.

SURFING

If you're in the market for a board or just want to rent one, check out **Northwest Surf Shop,** 1946 Sherman Rd. (U.S. 101), North Bend (tel. 800/558-5792 or 541/756-5792); **Rocky Point Surf & Sport,** 831 S. Empire Blvd., Coos Bay (tel. 541/888-9370); **Sessions Surf Co.,** 605 Chetco Ave., Brookings (tel. 541/412-0810).

Bastendorff Beach, off the Cape Arago Highway just north of Sunset Bay, is tucked under the south jetty at the mouth of Coos Bay. Shoals formed by the jetty create a good break here, making this one of the most popular surfing beaches on the south coast. Another 1.5 miles down the beach, off a side road before you get to Sunset Bay State Park, is another good break at a spot known as **Lighthouse Beach.** To reach these beaches, follow signs from Coos Bay toward Sunset Bay, Shore Acres, and Cape Arago state parks.

The beach at the town of **Port Orford** produces some good summer beach break when the tide is low and the swells are between 4 and 6 feet. If you can catch these conditions early in the morning, so much the better; you'll have some glassy waves to shred.

Although the summer waves near the mouth of Meyers Creek in **Pistol River State Park,** 8 miles south of Gold Beach, never get very big (4–6 feet average), they tend to be very nicely shaped, which has turned this spot into a regional favorite. The setting, with huge haystack rocks rising all around, is outrageous. These waves are also favorites of boardsailors.

Farther south, in the town of Harbor at the mouth of the Chetco River, there is good surfing at the north end of **Sport Haven County Park,** where the Chetco River jetty creates a good break.

SWIMMING & TUBING

While the Pacific Ocean is much too cold for most people and rarely calm enough for leisurely swimming, there are plenty of lakes and rivers along the south Oregon coast that offer opportunities for swimming. There is, however, one place on this coast where people go swimming in the ocean with surprising regularity. This is **Sunset Bay State Bay** just outside the town of Coos Bay. Here a shallow bottom and wind-protected cove allow the waters to warm a few degrees above what it usually is on open beaches. It's a stunningly beautiful setting, with sandstone walls rising on one side of the bay, and even if you only wade around a bit, it's well worth a visit.

Between the towns of Florence and Coos Bay lie numerous lakes, both large and small. These lakes were formed long ago when shifting sand dunes dammed area streams. The waters are a tea-brown color due to the tannin (tannin is released by decaying leaves). Many of these lakes have designated swimming areas. Within Jesse Honeyman State Park, 3 miles south of Florence, there are two swimming areas that are very popular with families. The more scenic (in fact, one of the prettiest lakes on the coast) is on **Cleawox Lake,** which is on the west side of U.S. 101 and is bounded by sand dunes. East of the highway is **Woahink Lake,** which also has a roped-off swimming area, but which is noisy with speedboats and personal watercraft. About 5 miles south of these two lakes is **Carter Lake,** which is much smaller and a bit close to the highway, but not as crowded.

If you'd like to get away from both boats and traffic noise, hike out to **Threemile Lake,** which is in the middle of the Oregon Dunes National Recreation Area. The lake is at the end of a 1-mile trail that starts about 3 miles down Sparrow Park Road from U.S. 101 (don't leave any valuables in your car; this area is subject to car cloutings). South of Reedsport about 5 miles, there is a swimming beach at **Lake Marie** in Umpqua Light State Park. In William M. Tugman State Park, 10 miles south of Reedsport, there is swimming in **Eel Lake,** which is quieter than Woahink, though it does have fishing boats on it.

The **Elk River,** which flows into the Pacific north of Port Orford, is one of the prettiest streams on the south coast. Its waters are a beautiful green and flow clear and cool through the summer. Along this river are numerous great swimming holes. Beginning about 10 miles up the Elk River Road from U.S. 101, start checking roadside pull-offs and you'll begin to find glorious spots for a dip. The nicest is between mileposts 10 and 11. Tubing is popular on the **Rogue River** between Foster Bar and Agness.

Of all the rivers on the Oregon coast, the **Chetco River** is, in my opinion, the most beautiful. The river drains the Kalmiopsis Wilderness and is, at times, an incredible turquoise color. The Chetco flows into the Pacific Ocean between the towns of Brookings and Harbor. North Bank Chetco River Road follows the river upstream from U.S. 101. About 8 miles up this road is **Locb State Park,** which has an exquisite swimming hole. Farther upstream are several more excellent swimming holes. Just watch for roadside turnoffs and follow trails down to the river. You're sure to find the spot that's perfect for you.

WALKS & NATURAL ROADSIDE ATTRACTIONS

Darlingtonia Botanical Wayside

Access: On Mercer Lake Rd., 5 miles north of Florence.

This little bog just off U.S. 101 is just about the most convenient place to get a look at insectivorous *Darlingtonia californica* plants, which are also known as cobra lilies. In fact, these plants look very much like snakes that have reared up in the manner of a cobra. They even have what appears to be a forked tongue. The plants lure insects with a sweet fragrance. When the insects climb into the pitcher plant in search of nectar, they are trapped. The plant then slowly extracts nutrients from them. These plants grow only in southern Oregon and northern California.

Waxmyrtle Trail

3 miles. Easy. 50-foot elevation gain. Access: 8 miles south of Florence off U.S. 101 at the Siltcoos Recreation Area's Stagecoach Trailhead. Map: Not necessary.

This trail to the beach along the Siltcoos River is a popular trail with bird watchers, but it is a pleasant walk even if you don't own a pair of binoculars. From the parking lot, the trail crosses the Siltcoos River and then skirts the edge of a bluff with views of the river below. Dropping down from the bluff, the trail joins an old sand road and leads out to the beach. Go north to the river mouth for a good view of the small Siltcoos estuary. Keep an eye out for seals and beavers.

Tahkenitch Creek Trail

1.5–2.5 miles round-trip. Easy. 50–75-foot elevation gain. Access: 12 miles south of Florence on U.S. 101 at Tahkenitch Creek Trailhead. Map: Not necessary.

If you're short on time or energy but want to get out in the sand dunes of the Oregon Dunes National Recreation Area, this system of loop trails is a good choice. The trails start in the forest, but then cross over several patches of sand dunes. Along the way, there are several views of meandering Tahkenitch Creek. You can extend this hike on other connected trails if you want a longer hike.

Shore Acres State Park

Access: Off U.S. 101, 13 miles southwest of Coos Bay on the Cape Arago Hwy.

This park was once a private estate. All that remains today, however, are the extensive and beautiful gardens. While these gardens are the main reason most people visit the park, a breathtaking stretch of blufftop rocky coastline here is a great spot not only for simply gazing out to sea but for bird watching, whale watching, and storm watching. Easy trails, mostly paved, wander among the park's different gardens. For a longer hike, follow the Oregon Coast Trail to Sunset Bay State Park or Cape Arago State Park. This trail wanders along cliffs and bluffs overlooking the water.

Shrader Old-Growth Trail

1.5 miles. Easy. 100-foot elevation gain. Access: From U.S. 101 in Gold Beach, drive 11 miles east on Jerry's Flat Rd. to Lobster Creek and turn right on FS 090 for another 2 miles. Map: Trailhead maps.

This short loop trail is a good introduction to Oregon's majestic old-growth trees. On this loop you'll see the huge Laddie Gale Douglas fir, which stands more than 220 feet tall and is more than 10 feet in diameter at the base.

Samuel H. Boardman State Park

0.2–2.8 miles. Easy. 50–300-foot elevation gain. Access: 4–14 miles north of Brookings. Map: Not necessary.

This state park stretches for 10 miles along the coast just north of Brookings and preserves the most beautiful vistas on the entire Oregon coast. Steep cliffs fall away to narrow beaches strewn with boulders, and just offshore lie countless rocky islands, including Arch Rock. There are numerous viewpoints and picnic areas along U.S. 101 as it passes through the park, and many of these provide access to short segments of the Oregon Coast Trail. Some of the more enjoyable walks include the 0.2-mile Arch Rock Viewpoint trail; the 0.8-mile trails at Natural Bridges Cove Viewpoint, Whalehead Beach Picnic Area; the 1.5-mile round-trip hike down to China Beach from North Island Viewpoint; the 2.8-mile round-trip hike from Thomas Creek Bridge to Indian Sands; and the hike up meadow-covered Cape Ferrelo from Lone Ranch Wayside.

Redwood Nature Trail

2.75 miles. Easy. 400-foot elevation gain. Access: In Loeb State Park, 7 miles east of Brookings and U.S. 101 up North Bank Chetco River Rd. Map: Not necessary.

Just a few miles into Oregon, the coast redwood tree reaches its northernmost limit. While both the groves and trees are larger farther to the south in California, the trees in Loeb State Park are well worth seeing, especially if you aren't California bound. This park was actually created to preserve myrtle trees, not redwoods, and by starting this hike on the Riverview Trail, you'll walk through a forest of rare old-growth myrtles.

WHALE WATCHING

From north to south, the best places to whale watch are Sea Lion Caves Turnout, Umpqua Lighthouse State Park, Shore Acres State Park, Face Rock Wayside, Cape Blanco State Park (at the lighthouse), Battle Rock City Park (Port Orford), Cape Sebastian State Park, Cape Ferrelo (in Samuel H. Boardman State Park), and Harris Beach State Park.

WHITEWATER KAYAKING & CANOEING

CLASS I

While the **Rogue River** is the south coast's most famous river, it is the 35-mile, Class III stretch upstream from Foster Bar that is most popular with paddlers. However, as this river nears the coast, it widens considerably and becomes much tamer. Between the town of Agness and the Lobster Creek Campground (which marks the end of the river's Wild and Scenic designation), there are two enjoyable Class I runs. The 13-mile run from Agness, where there are two boat ramps, down to Quosatana Campground is the more scenic. It passes through rugged Copper Canyon and has constant views of the mountains rising on either side of the river. There are several big riffles along this stretch. For a shorter run, put in at Quosatana Campground and paddle 4 miles down to Lobster Creek Campground. The biggest drawback of these runs is the jet boats that roar up and down the river both with loads of sightseers and with anglers. Stay alert.

The **Chetco River,** which flows out of the Kalmiopsis Wilderness, is one of the most beautiful rivers in Oregon. Its clear waters take on an astounding turquoise hue when the sun shines, and a day spent paddling here will not soon be forgotten. From the put-in at the bridge on the South Chetco River (or another 1.5 miles down a side road to the main river), it is 8 miles downstream to Loeb State Park, which makes an excellent take-out and a good place to camp for the night.

CLASS II

Foster Bar on the **Rogue River** is the take-out point for paddlers who have just done the multiday trip down from Graves Creek Bridge. However, between Foster Bar and the town of Agness, there are 6 miles of river with several challenging rapids. These tend to get more difficult at lower water levels. Two Mile Rapid, 2 miles below Foster Bar, can become a Class IV rapid at low flows (when it should be portaged), but at higher flows it washes out somewhat. This run's other notable spot is Shasta Costa Riffle, 2 miles above Agness.

CLASS III

Although not a very long run, the Sawyer's Rapid on the **Umpqua River** is a very popular piece of water simply because it's a good place to develop Class III paddling skills. Best of all, because this run is on the big Umpqua River, it's runnable year-round. The take-out is off Ore. 38 between Scottsburg and Elkton at Scott Creek County Park, and the put-in is a couple of miles upstream at a pull-off near milepost 27.

CLASS IV & ABOVE

The **Elk River,** just north of Port Orford, is one of the most beautiful little streams on the Oregon coast. Its clear waters take on a turquoise hue when the sun shines. Above the river's fish hatchery are up to 15 miles of incredibly demanding Class IV paddling. However, it is the lower 6 miles or so, from Slate Creek down to the hatchery, that are the most popular.

WHITEWATER RAFTING

While most Rogue River rafting companies operate out of the Grants Pass area, you can also arrange a 7-mile, 4-hour Rouge River trip in Gold Beach. This excursion is offered by **Rogue White Water Rafting** (tel. 541/247-6022 or 541/247-6504) and includes several rapids upriver from the town of Agness. Trips cost $65 for adults and $30 for children, with a $250 minimum.

WILDLIFE VIEWING

Harbor seals and Steller and California sea lions can be seen all along the south Oregon coast, and it is here that the famous **Sea Lion Caves** are located. These caves, 11 miles north of Florence, are privately owned and something of a tourist trap (with a steep admission fee). However, the cave, which is more than 300 feet long and 120 feet high, is truly astounding. Hundreds of Steller sea lions reside in the cave and nearby rocks, and the cacophony of their constant barking echoes off the rock walls. While the summer sees the most human visitors, this is actually the worst time of year to see sea lions. Fall and winter are the best times to find the sea lions at home. This mainland colony of Steller sea lions is the largest in the country. The caves are open daily.

The south coast's other top pinniped viewing area is at **Cape Arago State Park** outside Coos Bay. Simpson Reef and Shell Island, just offshore from this park, are used by highly vocal California sea lions, whose barking resounds along this entire stretch of coast. Massive northern elephant seals also haul out on these rocks, as do much smaller harbor seals. Bring binoculars.

One other good pinniped viewing site is at **Strawberry Hill Wayside** in Neptune State Park a little ways north of Sea Lion Caves. Here you can often see as many as 100 harbor seals on offshore rocks. Also keep an eye out for whales.

Just a few miles east of Reedsport on Ore. 38, you can observe a herd of as many as 100 Roosevelt elk at the **Dean Creek Elk Viewing Area.** While the elk can be seen year-round here, they are more in evidence during the fall, winter, and spring. During the summer, when they prefer the cool of the forest, you can sometimes see them in the early morning and late afternoon.

Campgrounds & Other Accommodations

CAMPING

If you're heading down to the beach on a summer weekend, you're deluding yourself if you think you're going to get a campsite at a state park. These sites book up months in advance, and reservations are taken up to 11 months in advance. Friends of mine once tried a spur-of-the-moment beach camping trip and ended up camping somewhere in the Cascades east of Eugene more than 100 miles from the coast (that was the last time they ever tried camping at the beach). State park campground reservations can be made by calling **Reservations Northwest** (tel. 800/452-5687). The reservation fee is $6. To make a reservation you'll need to know the name of the campground you want to stay at and the dates you plan to visit. Have some alternatives, too. Of all the state park campgrounds along the coast, only Oswald West, Saddle Mountain, Carl G. Wash-burne, and Loeb do not take reservations.

All oceanfront parks have hiker/biker campsites if you happen to be hiking the Oregon Coast Trail or bicycling along U.S. 101. Many campgrounds now also have yurts (circular cabinlike tents) for rent. These are meant to encourage winter camping and are definitely a good way to keep yourself and your gear dry.

THE NORTH COAST
Fort Stevens State Park (594 campsites, 9 yurts; year-round) is the largest campground on the entire Oregon coast and is very popular with families who enjoy the paved bike trails, miles of beaches, and swimming area on Coffenbury Lake. However, the park's flat topography hardly reflects the rugged beauty that most people associate with the Oregon coast. A much smaller alternative in the Cannon Beach/

Seaside area is **Saddle Mountain State Park** (10 primitive campsites; seasonal), which is used mostly by people hiking to the top of Saddle Mountain.

Despite the fact that **Oswald West State Park** (37 walk-in campsites; seasonal) is a walk-in campground, the sites are closer together than those at most car campgrounds. Don't say I didn't warn you if the guy in the next campsite keeps you up all night with his snoring. Surfers and boardsailors will likely prefer **Nehalem Bay State Park** (284 campsites with hookups, 9 yurts; year-round), where they can keep a closer eye on their equipment. **Roy Creek County Park** (10 campsites; year-round) is a nearby, though inland, alternative to the area's state parks.

On the Three Capes Loop, west of Tillamook, there are several campgrounds. **Cape Lookout State Park** (146 campsites, 55 with hookups, 4 yurts; year-round) is the largest and nicest of these. A little farther south are the Forest Service's **Sand Beach Campground** (101 campsites; seasonal), which is an ORV staging area and very noisy, and **Whalen Island County Park** (27 campsites; year-round), which is right on Sand Lake. **Webb County Park** (30 campsites; year-round), just across the road from Cape Kiwanda, and **Woods County Park** (2 campsites; year-round), are both popular with hang-glider and paraglider pilots.

Inland alternatives in this area include **Kilchis River County Park** (40 campsites; year-round), north of Tillamook at the end of Kilchis River Road; six **Tillamook State Forest campgrounds** along the Wilson River; **Trask County Park** (60 campsites; year-round), 12 miles east of Tillamook on Trask River Road; **Rocky Bend Campground** (12 campsites; year-round), 15.5 miles east of Beaver up Blaine Road; **Hebo Lake Campground** (16 campsites; seasonal), 5 miles east of Hebo; and **Mount Hebo Campground** (3 primitive campsites; seasonal), 3 miles past Hebo Lake Campground.

In the Lincoln City area, you'll find **Devil's Lake State Park** (100 campsites; year-round), which is within the city limits but still has a very woodsy feel. This is the most expensive public campground on the Oregon coast, partly because Lincoln City charges a room tax on campsites.

In the Newport area, there is **Beverly Beach State Park** (265 campsites, 129 with hookups, 14 yurts; year-round) north of town and **South Beach State Park** (244 campsites with hookups, 10 yurts; seasonal) on the outskirts of town on the south side of Yaquina Bay. Both of these campgrounds are popular with families who have come to see Keiko the killer whale at the nearby Oregon Coast Aquarium. Beverly Beach is by far the nicer of the two with a much more rugged and natural setting.

Beachside State Park (82 campsites, 32 with hookups; year-round), on the beach just outside Waldport, is most popular with anglers heading out on the Alsea River for salmon and steelhead. **Canal Creek Campground** (17 campsites; year-round) is an inland option for anglers fishing the Alsea River (7 miles east of Walport on Ore. 34, then 3 miles south on FS 3462). For exploring the rugged Cape Perpetua area, the Forest Service's **Cape Perpetua Campground** (37 campsites; seasonal), in a wooded setting a little ways from the water, is your only option.

THE SOUTH COAST

Just south of Cape Perpetua, there are a couple of camprounds within Siuslaw National Forest. **Tillicum Beach Campground** (60 campsites; year-round) is right on the beach and is popular with RVs. **Rock Creek Campground** (9 campsites; seasonal) is tucked back in the woods along a pretty creek and is a good choice for tenters and anyone who dislikes crowds. The area's state park option is **Carl G. Washburne State Park** (66 campsites, 58 with hookups, 6 walk-in sites; year-round), which is the only coastal state park that does not take reservations. Campsites are across the highway from a pretty beach just north of Heceta Head.

South of this headland, the coast settles down for a long strand of uninterrupted sand dunes, most of which are within the Oregon Dunes National Recreation Area. North of Florence are the first of this region's many campgrounds—**Sutton** (80 campsites; year-round) and **Alder Dune**

(39 campsites; seasonal)—both of which are operated by the forest service. These campgrounds are linked by a hiking trail through the dunes. Just outside Florence at the Siuslaw River's north jetty is **Harbor Vista County Park** (27 campsites; year-round), an alternative to ever-crowded Honeyman State Park.

Jesse M. Honeyman State Park (388 campsites, 141 with hookups, 4 yurts; year-round), just a few miles south of Florence, is one of the most popular state parks in Oregon and stays full throughout the summer. With two lakes, swimming, canoeing, sand dunes, and shady forests, it's easy to understand its popularity. Just south of this state park you'll find the Siltcoos Recreation Area, which is favored by both the ORV and water-ski and personal watercraft crowds. If you value quiet, stay away from Tyee, Lodgepole, Lagoon, Waxmyrtle, and especially Driftwood II campgrounds. **Carter Lake Campground** (24 campsites; year-round), on a popular swimming and boating lake, is a much quieter choice in this area. However, the **Tahkenitch Campground** (35 campsites; seasonal) is probably the best choice in the area. It's set in the forest on the edge of the dunes. Nearby is lakefront **Tahkenitch Landing Campground** (15 campsites; seasonal), which is popular with anglers.

South of Reedsport, you'll find **William M. Tugman State Park** (115 campsites with hookups; year-round) at the south end of Eel Lake, and nearby **Eel Creek Campground** (52 campsites; seasonal), adjacent to the Umpqua Dunes, which are the quiet choices down at this end of the Oregon Dunes NRA. The southern end of the Oregon Dunes NRA has been given over to dune buggies and ORVs. Campgrounds catering to off-roaders include Spinreel, Horsfall, Horsfall Beach, Bluebill, and Umpqua Lighthouse State Park.

Between Coos Bay and Bandon, you'll find **Sunset Bay State Park** (135 campsites, 63 with hookups, 4 yurts; year-round), which has the only beach on this coast where people actually go in the water much. This park is on one of the prettiest stretches of coastline in the state.

However, it dosen't make a very good base for exploring due to its location well off U.S. 101. Just north of Bandon is **Bullards Beach State Park** (191 campsites with hookups, 6 yurts; year-round), which has miles of flat beach backed by low dunes. There's good bird watching here, but the setting can't compare with that of other south coast state parks.

Most people staying at **Boice Cope County Park** (26 campsites; year-round) are boardsailors lured by the strong winds that blow across Floras Lake, which is separated from the ocean by only a narrow strip of dunes. This campground is just south of Langlois. Also nearby (about 4 miles north of Port Orford and 5 miles off U.S. 101) is **Cape Blanco State Park** (58 campsites with hookups; year-round), where the campground is set in a Sitka spruce forest atop the most westerly point in the continental U.S. Six miles south of Port Orford is **Humbug Mountain State Park** (108 campsites, 30 with hookups; year-round), where the campground is too close to the highway, but which has good hiking and beach access.

Up the Rogue River between Gold Beach and Agness, you'll find two campgrounds—**Lobster Creek** (5 campsites; seasonal) and **Quosatana** (43 campsites; seasonal). A third, **Illahee** (23 campsites; seasonal), is another 6 miles past Agness, though not on the river. At Foster Bar, above Agness, there is an unofficial campground right on the river.

The best base for exploring the scenic wonders of Samuel H. Boardman State Park is **Harris Beach State Park** (152 campsites, 86 with hookups, 4 yurts; year-round), which is on the beach just a few miles to the south. Unfortunately, very few campsites have ocean views. Also nearby, up the North Bank Chetco River Road out of Brookings, is **Loeb State Park** (53 campsites with hookups; year-round), which is set amid redwood trees and old-growth myrtle trees along the bank of the beautiful Chetco River. A bit farther up the Chetco is the forest service's **Little Redwood Campground** (16 campsites; seasonal), which is the site of a very popular swimming hole. South of Brookings up the Winchuck River, you'll find the forest service's **Winchuck Campground** (12 campsites; seasonal).

INNS & LODGES

ON THE NORTH COAST

The Waves/Argonauta/White Heron

188 W Second St. (P.O. Box 3), Cannon Beach, OR 97110. Tel. 800/822-2468 or 503/436-2205. 52 rms and suites. $69–$275 double. DISC, MC, V.

This lodge, only a block from the heart of town, consists of four dozen rooms, suites, cottages, and beach houses at the Waves and two other jointly managed lodges—the Argonauta and the White Heron. If clean and new appeal to you, try one of the rooms in the Garden Court, but my favorites are the cottages of the Argonauta. Surrounded by beautiful flower gardens in the summer, these old cottages overlook the beach and capture the spirit of Cannon Beach. There are fireplaces in some rooms and a whirlpool spa overlooking the ocean.

Inn at Otter Crest

Otter Crest Loop Rd. (P.O. Box 50), Otter Rock, OR 97369. Tel. 800/452-2101 or 541/765-2111. Fax 541/765-2047. 110 rms and suites. $79–$249 double; $159–$249 suite. AE, DISC, MC, V.

The Inn at Otter Crest reflects the region in both its architecture and setting. The inn's numerous weathered-cedar buildings are surrounded by 35 acres of forests and beautifully landscaped gardens on a rocky crest above a secluded cove. If you want to get away from it all and enjoy a bit of forest seclusion on the beach, there is no better spot. My favorite rooms are the loft suites, which have fireplaces, kitchens, and high ceilings. Service here is rather casual, which is in keeping with Northwest attitudes. Facilities include a restaurant, outdoor swimming pool, hot tub, sauna, tennis court, and hiking trails.

Sylvia Beach Hotel

267 NW Cliff St., Newport, OR 97365. Tel. 541/265-5428. 20 rms. $60–$139 double. All rates include full breakfast. AE, MC, V.

This eclectic four-story green-shingled hotel is an homage to literature. Rooms are named for different authors, and in the rooms you'll find memorabilia, books, and decor that reflect these authors' lives, times, and works. The Agatha Christie room seems full of clues, while in the Edgar Allan Poe room, a pendulum hangs over the bed and a stuffed raven sits by the window. Among the writers represented are Tennessee Williams, Colette, Ernest Hemingway, Alice Walker, Jane Austen, F. Scott Fitzgerald, Emily Dickinson, and even Dr. Seuss.

ON THE SOUTH COAST

Tu Tu Tun Lodge

96550 N Bank Rogue, Gold Beach, OR 97444. Tel. 541/247-6664. Fax 541/247-0672. 16 rms, 2 suites. $135–$170 double; $180–$190 suite. Lower rates in winter. MC, V.

Tu Tu Tun is the most luxurious lodging on the south coast, and the main lodge building incorporates enough rock and natural wood to give it that rustic feel without sacrificing any modern comforts. Guest rooms are large and beautifully furnished with slate-topped tables and tile counters. Each room has a private patio or balcony, and some rooms also come with a fireplace or outdoor soaking tub. Facilities include an outdoor pool, four-hole pitch-and-putt golf course, horseshoe courts, game room with pool table, dock, and hiking trails. Fishing guide service and boat rentals can be arranged.

Sunset Motel

1755 Beach Loop Rd. (P.O. Box 373), Bandon, OR 97411. Tel. 800/842-2407 or 541/347-2453. Fax 541/347-3636. 58 rms, 14 cabins/condos. $35–$105 double; $70–$185 cabin/condo. AE, DISC, MC, V.

Nowhere in Oregon will you find a better ocean view than here at the Sunset Motel, where you'll also find everything from economy motel rooms to contemporary condos, rustic cabins, and classic cottages. Dozens of Bandon's famous rock spires, sea stacks, and monoliths rise from the beach or just offshore in front of the motel, making sunsets from the Sunset truly memorable.

Chetco River Inn

21202 High Prairie Rd., Brookings, OR 97415. Tel. 541/469-8128. 4 rms. $95 double; rate includes full breakfast. MC, V.

Set on 35 very secluded acres on the banks of the Chetco River, this contemporary B&B caters primarily to anglers but also makes a great weekend retreat for anyone looking to get away from it all. Before you can get away, you'll have to find the lodge, which is 16 miles from town up North Bank Road (the last 3 miles are on gravel). The lodge makes use of alternative energies and is connected to the outside world by a radio phone only.